A NORTON CRITICAL EDITION

Ford Madox Ford
THE GOOD SOLDIER

AUTHORITATIVE TEXT
TEXTUAL APPENDICES
CONTEMPORARY REVIEWS
LITERARY IMPRESSIONISM
BIOGRAPHICAL AND CRITICAL
COMMENTARY

Edited by

MARTIN STANNARD
UNIVERSITY OF LEICESTER

W • W • NORTON & COMPANY · *New York* • *London*

The text of this book is composed in Electra, with
the display set in Bernhard Modern. Composition by Maple-Vail Composition
Services.
Manufacturing by The Maple-Vail Book Manufacturing Group

Library of Congress Cataloging-in-Publication Data

Ford, Ford Madox, 1873–1939.
The good soldier : authoritative text, textual appendices, contemporary reviews,
literary impressionism, criticism / edited by Martin Stannard.
p.   cm.—(A Norton critical edition)
Includes bibliographical references (p. 399).
1. Ford, Ford Madox, 1873–1939.   Good soldier.   I. Stannard,
Martin, 1947–   .   II. Title.
PR6011.053G5   1995
823'.912—dc20   94-36708
ISBN 0-393-96634-8

W. W. Norton & Company, Inc., 500 Fifth Avenue, New York, N.Y. 10110
www.wwnorton.com

W. W. Norton & Company Ltd., Castle House, 75/76 Wells Street,
London W1T 3QT

7 8 9 0

Contents

Literary Impressionism

Biographical and Critical Commentary

Preface

When *The Good Soldier* appeared in March 1915, reviews were sparse and mixed. True, the *New York Times Book Review* described it as "a novel which extorts admiration," the *Observer* found it "absorbing," and Rebecca West lauded its "extreme beauty and wisdom." But others, while admiring its artistry, objected on the grounds that it failed the requirements of realism: "Captain Ashburnham . . . is described to us as a typical specimen of the best kind of Englishman. . . . It is therefore inconceivable that he should have behaved as . . . Mr. Hueffer[1] tells us he did behave." Many simply damned the "distorted, sex-morbid atmosphere" as the work of "an unpleasant imagination." It was seen as "long-winded and prosy" with a grossly misconceived title reflecting "the cant of anti-militarism," as of more use to the pathologist than to the decent British reader in search of an account of the "joys and sorrows of normal human life."[2]

Since then critical opinion has shifted radically to establish the book not only as Ford's masterpiece but also as a masterpiece of modernism. Graham Greene's 1962 compilation of selected Ford works was an act of homage to a genius overshadowed by his contemporaries—contemporaries Ford had often actively assisted: Conrad, Lawrence, Frost, Crane, Wyndham Lewis, Pound, H. D., Hemingway. *The Good Soldier*, Greene insisted, is "perhaps one of the finest novels of our century,"[3] and few would now disagree. This Norton Critical Edition is equally an act of homage. It should, I hope, provide everything necessary for careful study: the first properly edited text, detailed footnotes, a note on the text, and sections on manuscript development and textual variants, contemporary reviews, literary impressionism, and biographical and critical commentary.

Manuscript Development and Textual Variants allows the reader to trace each substantive variant through its modifications up to, and

---

1. Ford was then publishing under his original name: Ford Madox Hueffer.
2. All these reviews—NYTBR, *Observer*, *Daily News*, *Outlook*, *Boston Transcript*, *Independent*, *TLS*, *New Witness*, *Bookman*—and more appear in Contemporary Reviews, pp. 217–35 of this edition. *The Good Soldier* was sometimes reviewed alongside Woolf's *The Voyage Out*, which was received with similar bemusement.
3. "Introduction," *The Bodley Head Ford Madox Ford*, vol. 1 (London: The Bodley Head, 1962) 7.

including, the first English edition, which I take as copy-text. Readers are alerted to the points at which these variants occur by an asterisk inviting them to cross-refer to the MDATV section. The Note on the Text provides something of a detective story, still ultimately unresolved, about the history of the text and the mystery surrounding the time of the novel's completion. (Central to this is the date August 4, which Ford uses as a structural motif. He always claimed that he had finished the book before the start of World War I, and yet, by an apparently "amazing coincidence," he selects the very date of Germany's marching into Belgium as the spine of the novel's chronology.) Literary Impressionism provides a brief survey of that movement (now largely ignored as a literary category). The reader is first directed to the aesthetics of Literary Impressionism (Gundersteren), then to the Anglo-American movement in which Ford was active (Watt), then to an overview of Ford's impressionist technique (Meixner), then to Conrad's and James's classic statements about, respectively, making the reader "see" and the House of Fiction; finally to Ford's own statements on the subject. The last-named provide exercises in impressionist writing themselves. Ford always delighted in wrecking generic categories and writing criticism and memoirs as fiction. His "critical essays" nevertheless offer a magnificently straightforward explanation of the need to write abstractly. He can be seen, and indeed presents himself, as a cubist novelist, a Futurist, a Vorticist, yet the *dicta* of his "impressionism" are explained as common sense for the writer wishing to render life *as it is actually experienced* rather than as it is mythologized by conventional realism.

Contemporary Reviews and Biographical and Critical Commentary are, I trust, self-explanatory as contextualizing matter. Both are arranged chronologically and, ideally, should be read thus to reveal the development of the novel's reputation. Two essays, however, both by Americans, profoundly affected the history of this criticism. The first, by Mark Schorer (1948), later appeared strategically as the introduction to the third and fourth U.S. editions (1951, 1957). Its then revolutionary approach saw the book as a "comedy of humour," the "humour" being "phlegm." Dowell is seen as inept, passionless, and suffering from the "madness of moral inertia." He is thus regarded as an untrustworthy narrator. Samuel Hynes (1961), in partial reaction to this, addresses the problem directly: "What are we to make of the novel's narrator? Or, to put it more formally, what authority should we allow to the version of events which he narrates?" "In a novel which postulates such severe limits to human knowledge," he states, "—a novel of doubt, that is, in which the narrator's fallibility *is* the norm—the problem of authority cannot be settled directly, because the question which authority answers: 'How can we know what is true?' is itself what the novel is about." He therefore concludes that Schorer's reading is misdirected on two counts: first, that Dowell's failings are the failings of all the characters, and sec-

ond, that his honest doubt and capacity for love are positive moral qualities.

This division between Schorer and Hynes has laid the foundations for
most debate since. Is *The Good Soldier* a comedy (Schorer), a tragedy
(Meixner, Snitow), or a comi-tragedy (Eggenschwiler)? Is the collapse of
conventional categories (literary, psychological, moral, political, social,
etc.) precisely its subject? Is Dowell trustworthy (Armstrong) or untrustworthy (Smith)? Is he a hero (Lynn) or the Restoration Comedy cuckold
of Schorer's interpretation? Is it a book about epistemological questions
(Hynes) or does it go further? Several critics (Kermode, Jacobs) see it as
concerning the arbitrary nature of the word itself. Dowell's sign system,
the novel of his life, develops its range as it progresses; "knowing" and
the capacity for articulation are intimately related. He knows nothing
until it is written down and composition is not continuous. Can we
import external "information" to rationalize this: political circumstances
(Green), biographical "facts" (Mizener)? In 1986 Sondra Stang printed
a letter from Ford to his publisher describing *The Good Soldier* as a
"serious . . . analysis of the polygamous desires that underlie all men."[4]
How does this square with deconstructionist readings? The novel is meat
and drink to literary theorists precisely because it means so many things
to so many readers. What are we to make of Dowell's inconsistencies as
to matters of fact (Moser)? His chronology of events doesn't add up
(Cheng); he changes his mind about the meaning of events. Is this Fordian irony or simply carelessness about details?

All of which brings us back to the problems of editing this text. To
footnote it at all is in some respects to prostitute its spirit. Ford had no
respect for academics and less for facts. When arraigned for mistakes in
the articles which constituted his book of memoirs, *Ancient Lights*
(1911), his only response was to reprint them unchanged. "This book,"
he noted, ". . . is full of inaccuracies as to facts, but its accuracy as
to impressions is absolute." Editing his fiction thus creates a particular
difficulty. Are the factual inaccuracies deliberate or accidental? If deliberate, this places an ironical distance between Dowell and the reader.
Grover Smith points out what he considers to be one such "gap." Dowell
writes "Pennsylvania Duitsch" instead of "Pennsylvania Dutch" or
"Deutsch." Ford spoke fluent German. He must, Smith says, have
known the difference between "Dutch" and "German" here, and thus
Dowell is "marked as ignorant and pretentious."[5] It is possible, and as
such I have left the original spelling. But if Dowell spells "Frans Hals"
"Frantz," or "Cnossus" "Gnossus," or "Wouwerman" "Woovermans,"
are we also meant to condemn him as a fool? It seems unlikely—Ford

4. Sondra J. Stang, ed., *The Ford Madox Ford Reader* (Manchester: Carcanet, 1986) 477.
5. The correct term for the descendants of German immigrants, and for their (High German)
   language, is "Pennsylvania Dutch" or "*Deitsch*" (derived from "*Deutsche*"). It means "German," not "Dutch." "*Duits*" is Dutch for "German."

made similar errors throughout his criticism—and in such cases I have corrected matters of fact simply to make the text more comprehensible.

Having done this, should one footnote such items to explain to the reader less well-educated than Ford the identity of all the painters, historical figures, and so on? I hesitated over this. Ford would no doubt have roared with laughter at the idea. Dowell typically remarks "(I am not really interested in these facts but they have a bearing on my story)." It is Florence who is condemned for pretentiously trying to impress people with information. In Ford's ideology, information is the enemy of art. The "bearing" that the facts have on Dowell's story can be construed as the impression of Florence's trying to use them as a weapon of sexual warfare. Nevertheless, there is another way of reading his statement. Although Ford loathed allegory, there is more than a hint that the setting of the scene in which Dowell utters these words (the Marburg Schloss) is integral to the book's meaning.

Ford was a Catholic, albeit an eccentric one. His historical perspective, often reiterated in quiet corners of his journalism, is essentially religious. The Reformation, when "the Church, being split into fragments, gave up adorning the walls of its edifices with the arts and crafts of whole peoples,"[6] marked for him the beginning of the degraded modern world in which humanism overwhelmed feudalism. It is important, therefore, for the reader to realize the significance of the Marburg Colloquy, the relationship between Luther and Philip the Magnanimous, and so on in order to understand that this was a crucial doctrinal debate of the Reformation. As Carol Jacobs ingeniously points out, the debate hinged on the interpretation of the words "This is my body" while Flornce is effectively offering her body to Ashburnham. The apparently abstract issue of transubstantiation is, of course, nothing of the sort to the religious reader. It is the point at which the word becomes flesh. And for Ford, the Reformation was also the point at which religious idealism confronted physical passion in humankind's divided nature. The Protestants could countenance divorce. Luther granted Philip a special dispensation bigamously to marry a second wife. Thus Ford's sense of the theme of the book as an analysis of "the polygamous desires that underlie all men" is developed by our understanding of the historical backdrop.

I decided, then, that it was better to footnote in detail rather than not at all or half-heartedly, although I have not included much biographical information. Anyone who knew Ford at this time, however, would have found it difficult to dissociate the life from the fiction. The book grew out of a period of deep depression resulting in part from a scandal which had ruined his social reputation. In 1913 his estranged wife had successfully sued the *Throne* for describing his mistress, Violet Hunt, as "Mrs

6. TS of "Talk Delivered Over W.A.B.C., Saturday Dec. 19, 1936 . . . ," p. 7 (Cornell).

Hueffer." In court it was pretty well established that he had lied to every-one about having secured a divorce under German law. Much of the setting of the novel is in those places he and Hunt visited either when they were trying to pursue this crazy scheme (Marburg, Bad Nauheim), or after the case (Carcasonne, Provence) when they were effectively "on the run," having been spurned by "good people" (including James and Conrad). It was on their return, on his fortieth birthday, that Ford began the novel, and by that time he had already begun to tire of Hunt. The first part of the book was dictated to Brigit Patmore, with whom he was infatuated. Like Dante, he was entering a "dark wood,"[7] which in Ford's case was one of neurasthenia. All that he held dear—his honor as a gentleman, his two beloved daughters, even his art and his passion for life—seemed to have been taken from him by the absurd rituals of polite society.

Reading his journalism of the period, one catches echoes of his agony. Politically he described himself as "an obstinate, sentimental old-fashioned Tory"[8] but he was a defender of women's suffrage and of Home Rule for Ireland, and he found himself living with a new breed of Tory: materialistic, xenophobic, with a particular loathing for Germans. Culturally and intellectually he felt no sympathy for the English "nuv-vle." "For me," he wrote, ". . . the novel—broad stream of international culture that it is—began with Richardson and passed over the water to Diderot and the Encyclopaedists. They had for spiritual descendants Chateaubriand, Stendhal, Flaubert, Maupassant, Tourguenieff [sic]; and so that international stream comes back to these islands in the nine-ties . . . with Mr. Conrad and Mr. Henry James. It continues flowing in the veins of les jeunes."[9] As a Francophile with a German-born father, he found small sympathy for his internationalism in an England preparing for war—except among "les jeunes": Pound, H. D., Wynd-ham Lewis, toward whom he gravitated as an "uncle." Angry and frus-trated, he felt that "what we want most of all in the literature of today is religion, is intolerance, is persecution, and not the mawkish flapdoodle of culture, Fabianism, peace and good will. Real good religion, a vio-lent thing full of hatreds and exclusions . . . I must confess to rather inclining towards [the Futurists]—just because they want to smash things."[1] But that, of course, was not the kind of novel he was writing.

---

7. See Ford Madox Hueffer, "Literary Portraits—XIX. Gerhart Hauptmann and 'Atlantis,' " *Out-look*, 17 January 1914, 77–79: ". . . whereas England is the very worst place in which to suffer from any form of nervous complaint, Germany is the best of all asylums for the really neurasthenic. . . . And indeed *Atlantis* . . . is the story of adventure in a dark forest. The dark forest is the hero's neurasthenia."

8. "Didymus" [Ford Madox Hueffer], "A Declaration of Faith," *English Review* 4 (February 1910): 543–51, 544.

9. "Literary Portraits—VII. Professor Saintsbury and the English 'Nuvvle,' " *Outlook*, 1 Novem-ber 1913: 605.

1. "Literary Portraits—XVII. Nineteen-Thirteen and the Futurists," *Outlook*, 3 January 191 15.

His self-appointed task, as he had stated earlier while still working on
The Good Soldier, was "to record my own time, my own world, as I see
it," to aim at a style "so unobtrusive and so quiet . . . that the reader
shall not know he is reading, and be conscious only that he is living in
a book."[2] After war was declared, and probably around the time he
had put the finishing touches to his novel (September 1914), a note of
exhaustion creeps in: ". . . the present period . . . is too much for me.
I cannot get the hang of it. . . . I do not know whether I am a hero or
just a tired person."[3]

He was both, but it was a decade before he published his next major
fiction, *Some Do Not* (1924), the opening volume of the Tietjens tetralogy, which effectively rewrites Ashburnham's history. Sitting in Scotland with the rain pouring down in early August 1914, Ford read proofs
of the first and only installment of *The Good Soldier* in *Blast* while
Wyndham Lewis painted a Vorticist portrait of their hostess. It was the
end of an era. Four days after Germany had invaded Belgium an article
appeared which Ford probably wrote during his visit: "And what is the
good of writing about literature—the 'edler Beruf,' the noble calling?
There will not be a soul that will want to read about literature for years
and years. We go out. We writers go out. And, when the world again
has leisure to think about letters, the whole world will have changed.
. . . What is the good of it all? I don't know. . . . I like the French so
much; I like so much the South Germans and the Austrians. Whichever
side wins in the end—my own heart is certain to be mangled in either
case. . . . But what affects me . . . even more depressingly is the want
of chivalry in expressions of nationality."[4] Five months later he reviewed
the conduct of the war: ". . . we are fighting to answer the question
whether it is right to thank God for the deaths of a million fellow-beings.
Is it then right? Is it then wrong? I don't know. I know nothing any
more; nobody knows anything. We are down in the mud of the trenches
of right and wrong, grappling at each other's throats, gouging out each
other's eyes—and amazed, still, to think that we can be doing such
things."[5]

Here is the authentic voice of Dowell. And here, perhaps, we see a
reflection of *The Good Soldier*'s largest subject: the transference from a
culture of intellectual confidence to one of uncertainty. From the point
of view of Ford's art, the paradox centered on the earlier materialist base
of his impressionism: upon his technique being a heightened form of
realism in reaction against romance, and upon his growing, and contra-

XIII. Fydor Dostoievsky and 'The Idiot,' " *Outlook*, 14 February 1914:

II. 'Cedant Togae . . .' " *Outlook*, 5 September 1914: 303.
XLVIII. M. Charles-Louis Philippe and 'Le Père Perdrix,' " *Outlook*, 8

LXIX. Annus Mirabilis," *Outlook*, 2 January 1915: 15.

dictory, need for an art of visionary experience. "Cubists, Vorticists, and the rest of them are in fact visionaries," he wrote; "Post-Impressionists, Impressionists, Futurists, and the rest of us are materialists. I wish I could be a visionary myself, but I don't know how."[6]

6. "Literary Portraits—XLIV. Signor Marinetti, Mr. Lloyd George, St. Katharine, and Others," *Outlook*, 11 July 1914: 47.

Acknowledgments

My particular thanks go to the staff of the Karl A. Kroch Library (Cornell University), which holds all the MS material relating to the text of *The Good Soldier*, and much more besides, in their magnificent Ford and Violet Hunt collections. After my three weeks there examining the MS, they tirelessly photocopied this and four versions of the novel; also letters, diaries, notes, and articles. I could have done nothing without their serious scholarly engagement in the project. The staff of the University of Leicester Library have also been wonderfully supportive, as have Mary Arthur, Angie Kendall, and Pam Ross in the office of Leicester's Department of English. Thanks to University of Leicester Research Committee grants, I was able to visit not only Cornell but also Marburg and Bad Nauheim, where experts on local history and theology were generous with their time and knowledge. Dr. Martin Krautz, Dr. Lachmann, Dr. Hollenberg, and Heinrich Burk between them provided photographs and photocopies of documents and maps. I am especially indebted to Herr Burk for permission to reproduce two photographs from his book on Bad Nauheim. Others have helped through telephone inquiries: Michael Bott of Reading University Library; Cathy Henderson of the Harry Ransom Humanities Research Center, University of Texas at Austin; Derek Holder of Companies House; Dr. James Raven of Magdalen College, Cambridge; Dr. Alexis Weedon of the University of Luton. Professor Michael Freeman and Christopher Rolfe helped me with French references; John Gough with German; Duncan Cloud with Latin, Greek, and Roman Catholic ones. Dr. Alison Yarrington advised me on art history, and Dr. Stuart Ball on the history of the First World War. Sylvia Ouditt typed the MDATV section and helped with the proofs. I had many interesting discussions about *The Good Soldier* with Mark Rawlinson. Last, and far from least, I owe a huge debt to my partner, Dr. Sharon Ouditt, who, along with other friends (Duncan Cloud again, Professor Kelvin Everest, and Dr. Rick Rylance), suffered my inexhaustible enthusiasm for this novel and read long sections of the textual apparatus, offering corrections and suggestions.

Abbreviations

For more detailed explanation, see the list of abbreviations at the head of the Manuscript Development and Textual Variants section.

Texts (in chronological order)

MS: the manuscript of *The Good Soldier* [*The Saddest Story*]. 375 pp.

TSB: the ribbon-copy of the first section of **TS** (see below). Scholars have generally assumed that this was the section sent as copy to Wyndham Lewis for publication as the first part of *The Saddest Story* in his magazine *Blast*, 20 June 1914: 87–97. 42 pp.

B: Printed text of the first three-and-a-half chapters of *The Saddest Story* in *Blast* (see **TSB** above).

TS: a complete typescript of the novel, probably printer's copy. 305 pp.

UK: Ford Madox Hueffer, *The Good Soldier. A Tale of Passion* (London: John Lane, The Bodley Head, 1915). First UK edition.

US: Ford Madox Hueffer, *The Good Soldier. A Tale of Passion* (New York: John Lane Company, 1915). First US edition, probably published simultaneously with **UK.**

US2: Ford Madox Ford, *The Good Soldier. A Tale of Passion* (New York: Albert & Charles Boni, 1927), including "Dedicatory Letter to Stella Ford."

UK2: Ford Madox Ford, *The Good Soldier. A Tale of Passion* (London: John Lane, The Bodley Head Ltd., [1928]). Second UK, "Week-End Library," edition, published February 24, 1928, including "Dedicatory Letter" (see **US2** above).

General

AMS:	Autograph [holograph] manuscript
asp:	all subsequent printings in Ford's lifetime
BP:	Brigit Patmore: Ford's first amanuensis
COD:	*Concise Oxford Dictionary*
Cornell:	Department of Rare Books, Karl A. Kroch Library, Cornell University, Ithaca, New York
Del:	Deletion
ED:	Editorial decision, indicating the reading selected
FMF:	In Ford Madox Ford's hand
Harvey:	David Dow Harvey, *Ford Madox Ford 1873–1939. A Bibliography of Works and Criticism* (Princeton UP, 1962, and New York: Gordian Press, 1972)
HD:	H. D. [Hilda Doolittle], Ford's second amanuensis
[ink]:	Revision made by Ford in ink
MDATV:	Manuscript Development and Textual Variants section, pp. 194–216 below
Mizener:	Arthur Mizener, *The Saddest Story. A Biography of Ford Madox Ford* (London: The Bodley Head, 1971)

Moser:	Thomas C. Moser's edition of *The Good Soldier* (Oxford University Press, 1990) in The World's Classics series
[number; number]:	"External" page number of **MS** or **TS** followed by "internal" number of same. (See MDATV for definition of "external" and "internal.") Only one number appears in brackets for page reference to **TSB**, first section of **TS**, or any printed text
[pencil]:	Revision made by Ford in pencil
Perpetuated mistranscription:	Mistranscription by typist which continues through all printed states
RA:	Richard Aldington, Ford's third amanuensis
SOED:	*Shorter Oxford English Dictionary*
SPC:	Probably a substantive proof correction by Ford or editor
TccMS:	Typed carbon copy manuscript
TMS:	Typed manuscript, ribbon-copy
[TS]:	Revision made in type, usually indicating either composition on the typewriter or the contemporaneous correction of a misreading of the AMS
WL:	[Percy] Wyndham Lewis (editor of *Blast*)
*:	Signals a MS correction or textual variant. For details, see Manuscript Development and Textual Variants section, pp. 194–216 below
[ ]:	Page number lacking
[. . .]:	My ellipses, not author's
[*ital*]:	Section italicized and between square brackets deleted
\ /:	Section between slashes inserted from above line or superimposed on letters on line
/ \:	Section between slashes inserted from below line
|:	Word after vertical stroke on a lower line

Example:

MS [37;35]: "chinese"; **TSB** [24]: "chemise"; **B** [92]: "Chinese"; **TS** [24]: "[c]\C/h[*emi*]\ine/se": [ink]; **UK** [28] and asp: "Chinese" = In the holograph MS the amanuensis wrote "chinese," mistranscribed in the *Blast* typescript as "chemise"; the printed *Blast* text corrects this to "Chinese" and the typescript of the complete novel makes the same correction, in ink in Ford's hand, by canceling lower-case "c" and superimposing capital, and by canceling "emi" and inserting "ine" above it; the first British edition and all subsequent printings follow this correction.

The Text of
THE GOOD SOLDIER

Dedicatory Letter to Stella Ford [1]

MY DEAR STELLA,

I have always regarded this as my best book—at any rate as the best book of mine of a pre-war period; and between its writing and the appearance of my next novel nearly ten years must have elapsed, so that whatever I may have since written may be regarded as the work of a different man—as the work of *your* man. For it is certain that without the incentive to live that you offered me I should scarcely have survived the war-period and it is more certain still that without your spurring me again to write I should never have written again. And it happens that, by a queer chance, the *Good Soldier* is almost alone amongst my books in being dedicated to no one: Fate must have elected to let it wait the ten years that it waited—for this dedication.

What I am now I owe to you: what I was when I wrote the *Good Soldier* I owed to the concatenation of circumstances of a rather purposeless and wayward life. [2] Until I sat down to write this book—on the 17th December, 1913—I had never attempted to extend myself, to use a phrase of race-horse training. Partly because I had always entertained very fixedly the idea that—whatever may be the case with other writers—I at least should not be able to write a novel by which I should care to stand before reaching the age of forty; partly because I very definitely did not want to come into competition with other writers whose claim or whose need for recognition and what recognitions bring were greater than my own. I had never really tried to put into any novel of mine *all* that I knew about writing. I had written rather desultorily a number of books—a great number—but they had all been in the nature of *pastiches*, of pieces of rather precious writing, or of *tours de force*. But I have always been mad about writing—about the way writing should be done and partly alone, partly with the companionship of Conrad, [3] I had even at that date made exhaustive studies into how words should be handled and novels constructed.

So, on the day I was forty I sat down to show what I could do—and the *Good Soldier* resulted. I fully intended it to be my last book. I used to think—and I do not know that I do not think the same now—that one book was enough for any man to write, and, at the date when the

---

1. Australian-born painter (1893–1947) with whom Ford lived from 1919 to 1927 and with whom he had his third daughter, Julia; she always wrote and painted as "Stella Bowen" and, indeed, was never "Stella Ford" since she and Ford were not married.
2. Ford's separation from his wife (Elsie, née Martindale) and her subsequent refusal to allow Violet Hunt legal marriage to him or the adoption of his name (then Hueffer) produced a considerable scandal. He changed his surname to "Ford" in an attempt to prevent Elsie's (and Violet's) further interference when he set up home with Stella Bowen in June 1919.
3. Joseph Conrad (1857–1924), Polish-born English novelist; close friends for some years, Ford and Conrad collaborated on three novels—*The Inheritors* (1901), *Romance* (1903), *The Nature of a Crime* (1924)—and spent many hours discussing the theory of literary impressionism.

Good Soldier was finished, London at least and possibly the world appeared to be passing under the dominion of writers newer and much more vivid. Those were the passionate days of the literary Cubists, Vorticists, *Imagistes* [4] and the rest of the *tapageux* and riotous *Jeunes* [5] of that young decade. So I regarded myself as the Eel which, having reached the deep sea brings forth its young and dies—or as the Great Auk [6] I considered that, having reached my allotted I had laid my one egg and might as well die. So I took a formal farewell of Literature in the columns of a magazine called the *Thrush* [7]—which also, poor little auk that it was, died of the effort. Then I prepared to stand aside in favour of our good friends—yours and mine—Ezra, Eliot, Wyndham Lewis, H.D. [8] and the rest of the clamourous young writers who were then knocking at the door.

But greater clamours beset London and the world which till then had seemed to lie at the proud feet of those conquerors; Cubism, Vorticism, Imagism and the rest never had their fair chance amid the voices of the cannon and so I have come out of my hole again and beside your strong, delicate and beautiful works have taken heart to lay some work of my own.

The Good Soldier, however, remains my great auk's egg for me as being something of a race that will have no successors and as it was written so long ago I may not seem over-vain if I consider it for a moment or two. No author, I think, is deserving of much censure for vanity if, taking down one of his ten-year-old books, he exclaims: "Great Heavens, did I write as well as that then?" for the implication always is that one does not any longer write so well and few are so envious as to censure the complacencies of an extinct volcano.

Be that as it may, I was lately forced into the rather close examination

---

4. *"Imagistes"*: English and American poets (H. D. [Hilda Doolittle], Amy Lowell, James Joyce, Richard Aldington, Ezra Pound, and Ford himself) in revolt against romanticism. "Cubists": revolutionary abstract artists following work of Picasso and Braque in Paris (1907–14), abandoning conventions (e.g., perspective) of realist art as imitation of nature, often superimposing multiple perspectives of the subject, analyzed into geometrical planes. "Vorticists": pre-1914 British avant-garde artistic movement centering on Wyndham Lewis's Rebel Art Centre and the magazine *Blast*. Ford associated with Vorticism as benevolent, avuncular figure, and his patronage of young writers in *The English Review* was reciprocated by Lewis's publishing the opening of *The Good Soldier* in *Blast* (20 June 1914).
5. *Tapageux . . . Jeunes*: rowdy, boisterous Youth. "Young Things" might better translate Ford's affectionate description.
6. An extinct, flightless bird that, during the 19th century, was the rarest British species, inhabiting rocky islands bordering the North Atlantic.
7. Poetry magazine to which Ford did contribute an essay (Dec. 1909) but, as Mizener (563) points out, this was not Ford's "farewell." He seems to confuse this with statements made six years later in *Poetry and Drama*. See Literary Impressionism, p. 267 below.
8. H[ilda] D[oolittle] (1886–1961), poet, novelist, and playwright, co-founder of Imagist school (see n. 4 above); one of the amanuenses, along with Aldington and Brigit Patmore, of *The Good Soldier*. Ezra Pound (1885–1972), American expatriate poet, essayist, and translator, co-founder of Imagist school (see n. 4 above), close friend of both Ford and Eliot. [T. S.] Eliot (1885–1965), American expatriate poet, critic, and playwright. Wyndham Lewis (1884–1957), British painter, novelist, and critic, leader of Vorticist movement (see n. 4 above).

of this book, for I had to translate it into French,[9] that forcing me to give it much closer attention than would be the case in any reading however minute. And I will permit myself to say that I was astounded at the work I must have put into the construction of the book, at the intricate tangle of references and cross-references. Nor is that to be wondered at for, though I wrote it with comparative rapidity I had it hatching within myself for fully another decade. That was because the story is a true story and because I had it from Edward Ashburnham himself and I could not write it till all the others were dead.[1] So I carried it about with me all those years, thinking about it from time to time.

I had in those days an ambition: that was to do for the English novel what in *Fort Comme la Mort*, Maupassant[2] had done for the French. One day I had my reward, for I happened to be in a company where a fervent young admirer exclaimed: "By Jove, the *Good Soldier* is the finest novel in the English Language!" whereupon my friend Mr. John Rodker[3] who has always had a properly tempered admiration for my work remarked in his clear, slow drawl: "Ah yes. It is, but you have left out a word. It is the finest French novel in the English language!"

With that—which is my tribute to my masters and betters of France— I will leave the book to the reader. But I should like to say a word about the title. This book was originally called by me *The Saddest Story* but since it did not appear till the darkest days of the war were upon us, Mr. Lane[4] importuned me with letters and telegrams—I was by that time engaged in other pursuits![5]—to change the title which he said would at that date render the book unsaleable. One day, when I was on parade, I received a final wire of appeal from Mr. Lane, and the telegraph being reply-paid I seized the reply-form and wrote in hasty irony: "Dear Lane, Why not *The Good Soldier*?" . . . To my horror six months later the book appeared under that title.

9. A French translation in Ford's hand of the first part of the novel exists at Cornell, but it was never published. Moser (296) notes that Ford began this during the Battle of the Somme (1916) and apparently finished it in Paris during 1924. First published French translation: Jacques Papy (1953).
1. The provenance of Ford's story is uncertain, but he refers to it in *The Spirit of the People* (1907). Ford stayed with a married couple and their young ward; the husband and ward were in love; eventually, she was packed off on a world tour, Ford (like Dowell) accompanying the couple to the station in a dog-cart. The girl died at Brindisi; the man suffered nervous collapse and toured the Continent in search of a cure. The tale is told to illustrate the "superhuman" English repression of emotion. During their final journey, the man and girl exchange only dull pleasantries. Indeed, it is Ford's function as chaperon to prevent any expression of passion.
2. Guy de Maupassant (1850–1893), French naturalist novelist and short-story writer, pupil of Flaubert. *Fort Comme la Mort* (1889, *Strong as Death*) concerns a love triangle between Olivier Bertin (a painter), Mme. de Guilleroy, and her daughter, Anne. Bertin's love for Anne is, like Ashburnham's for Nancy, "as strong as death."
3. Writer, publisher, and translator from French (1894–1955).
4. John Lane (1854–1925), co-founder (with Elkin Mathews) of The Bodley Head (1887) and also publisher of the Nineties' poets (Davidson, Thompson, Dowson, Le Gallienne, etc.) and of *The Yellow Book* (1894–97).
5. Ford was by then working as a propaganda author for Charles Masterman, the Liberal cabinet minister (and friend) who marshaled a phalanx of British authors to draw America into the war.

I have never ceased to regret it but, since the War I have received so much evidence that the book has been read under that name that I hesitate to make a change for fear of causing confusion. Had the chance occurred during the War I should not have hesitated to make the change for I had only two evidences that any one had ever heard of it. On one occasion I met the adjutant of my regiment just come off leave and looking extremely sick. I said: "Great Heavens, man, what is the matter with you?" He replied: "Well, the day before yesterday I got engaged to be married and today I have been reading *The Good Soldier*."

On the other occasion I was on parade again, being examined in drill, on the Guards' Square at Chelsea. And, since I was petrified with nervousness, having to do it before a half dozen elderly gentlemen with red hatbands[6] I got my men about as hopelessly boxed as it is possible to do with the gentlemen privates of H.M. Coldstream Guards. Whilst I stood stiffly at attention one of the elderly red hatbands walked close behind my back and said distinctly in my ear, "Did you say *The Good Soldier*." So no doubt Mr. Lane was avenged. At any rate I have learned that irony may be a two-edged sword.

You, my dear Stella, will have heard me tell these stories a great many times. But the seas now divide us and I put them in this, your letter, which you will read before you see me in the hope that they may give you some pleasure with the illusion that you are hearing familiar— and very devoted—tones. And so I subscribe myself in all truth and in the hope that you will accept at once the particular dedication of this book and the general dedication of the edition.[7] Your

F. M. F.

NEW YORK, *January 9, 1927*.

---

6. Senior officers.
7. See Abbreviation, **UK2,** p. 176.

THE
GOOD SOLDIER
A TALE OF PASSION

BY

FORD MADOX HUEFFER

AUTHOR OF "THE FIFTH QUEEN," ETC.

"Beati Immaculati"[1]

LONDON : JOHN LANE, THE BODLEY HEAD
NEW YORK : JOHN LANE COMPANY
MCMXV

1. Psalm 119.1 (118.1 in the Vulgate): "Blessed are the undefiled. . . ."

The Good Soldier

PART I

I *

This is the saddest story I have ever heard. *

We had known the Ashburnhams for nine seasons of the town of
Nauheim with an extreme intimacy—or rather, with an acquaintanceship as loose and easy and yet as close as a good glove's with your hand.
My wife and I knew Captain and Mrs. Ashburnham as well as it was
possible to know anybody and yet, in another sense, we knew nothing
at all about them. This is, I believe, a state of things only possible with
English people of whom till today, when I sit down to puzzle out what
I know of this sad affair, I knew nothing whatever. Six months ago I had
never been to England and, certainly, I had never sounded the depths
of an English heart. I had known the shallows.

I don't mean to say that we were not acquainted with many English
people. Living, as we perforce lived, in Europe * and being, as we
perforce were, * leisured Americans, which is as much as to say
that we were un-American—we were thrown very much into the society
of the nicer English. Paris, you see, was our home. Somewhere between Nice and Bordighera [2] provided yearly winter quarters for us
and Nauheim [3] always received us from July to September. You will
gather from this statement that one of us had, as the saying is, a "heart",

---

* Asterisks indicate entries in Manuscript Development and Textual Variants, pp. 194–216
   below.
2. Mediterranean coastline (Côte d'Azur) running from southeast France to northeast Italy (the
   French and Italian Rivieras), colonized, particularly by the British upper class, in the late 19th
   century and 20th century as fashionable winter resort.
3. Bad Nauheim, German spa on the northeastern slopes of the Taunus Mountains near
   Frankfurt, a few miles north of Bad Homberg, c. 35 miles south of Marburg; Nauheim offered
   warm saline springs impregnated with carbonic acid gas; the water's curative properties, says
   Baedeker's Northern Germany of 1913, "especially in cardiac diseases, are of considerable re-
   pute" (344). Ford and Violet Hunt had visited the town (with Lita Crawfurd as chaperon)
   in 1910.

and, from the statement that my wife is dead, that she* was the sufferer.

Captain Ashburnham also* had a heart. But, whereas a yearly month or so at Nauheim tuned him up to exactly the right pitch for the rest of the twelvemonth, the two months or so were only just enough to keep poor Florence alive from year to year. The reason for his heart was approximately polo or too much hard sportsmanship in his youth. The reason for poor Florence's broken years was* a storm at sea upon our first crossing to Europe and the immediate reasons for our imprisonment in that continent were doctors' orders. They said that even the short Channel crossing might well kill the poor thing.

When we all first met, Captain Ashburnham, home on sick leave from an India to which he was never to return, was thirty-three; Mrs. Ashburnham—Leonora—was thirty-one. I was thirty-six and poor Florence thirty. Thus to-day Florence would have been thirty-nine and Captain Ashburnham forty-two; whereas I am forty-five and Leonora forty.[4]* You will perceive therefore that our friendship has been a young-middle-aged affair, since we were all of us of quite quiet dispositions, the Ashburnhams being more particularly what in England it is the custom to call "quite good people."

They were descended, as you will probably expect, from the Ashburnham who accompanied Charles I to the scaffold,[5] and, as you must also expect with this class of English people, you would never have noticed it. Mrs. Ashburnham was a Powys; Florence was a Hurlbird of Stamford, Connecticut, where, as you know, they are more old-fashioned than even* the inhabitants of Cranford,[6] England, could have been. I myself am a Dowell of Philadelphia, Pa. where, it is historically true, there are more old English families than you would find in any six English counties taken together. I carry about with me indeed—as if it were the only thing that invisibly anchored me to any spot upon the globe—the title deeds of my farm which once covered several blocks between Chestnut and Walnut Streets.[7]* These title deeds are of wampum,[8]* the grant of an Indian chief to the first Dowell, who left Farnham in Surrey in company with William Penn.[9] Florence's people, as is so often the case with the inhabitants of Connecticut, came from the

---

4. There is manifest confusion in **MS, TSB,** and **TS** about assigning specific ages to characters; see MDATV, p. 195, 10, 2nd entry below.
5. A royalist, loyal to Charles I, mentioned by Ford in *The Cinque Ports* (1900).
6. Alludes to Elizabeth Gaskell's *Cranford* (1853), a novel depicting a tranquil rural community and offering a mythologized image of essential "Englishness."
7. These streets are in fashionable downtown Philadelphia.
8. Cylindrical beads threaded on strings and used by North American Indians as currency and as a substitute for writing.
9. English Quaker (1644–1718), founding father of Pennsylvania.

neighbourhood of Fordingbridge,[1] where the Ashburnhams' place is. From there, at this moment, I am actually writing.*

You may well ask why I write. And yet my reasons are quite many. For it is not unusual in human beings who have witnessed the sack of a city or the falling to pieces of a people, to desire to set down what they have witnessed for the benefit of unknown heirs or of generations infinitely remote; or, if you please, just to get the sight out of their heads.* Someone has said that the death of a mouse from cancer is the whole sack of Rome by the Goths, and I swear to you that the breaking-up of our little four-square coterie was such another unthinkable event. Supposing that you should come upon us, sitting together at one of the little tables in front of the club house, let us say at Homburg,[2] taking tea of an afternoon and watching the miniature golf, you would have said that, as human affairs go we were an extraordinarily safe castle. We were, if you will, one of those tall ships with the white sails, upon a blue sea, one of those* things that seem the proudest and the safest of all the beautiful and safe things that God has permitted the mind of men to frame. Where better could one take refuge? Where better?

Permanence? Stability! I can't believe it's gone. I can't believe that that long tranquil life, which was just stepping a minuet, vanished in four crashing days at the end of nine years and six weeks. Upon my word, yes, our intimacy was like a minuet, simply because on every possible occasion and in every possible circumstance we knew where to go, where to sit,* which table we unanimously should choose; and we could rise and go, all four together, without a signal from any one of us, always to the music of the Kur orchestra,[3] always in the temperate sunshine, or if it rained, in discreet shelters. No indeed, it can't be gone. You can't kill a minuet de la cour.[4]* You may shut up the music-book; close the harpsichord; in the cupboard and presses the rats may destroy the white satin favours.[5]* The mob may sack Versailles; the Trianon[6] may fall, but surely the minuet—the minuet itself is dancing itself away into the furthest stars, even as our minuet of the Hessian bathing-places[7]

1. Small Hampshire market town near the southern coast of England, c. 14 miles south of Salisbury, on the Avon River bordering the western flank of the New Forest; literally: "bridge of the people of Ford."
2. Bad Homburg, German spa near Frankfurt and Bad Nauheim in the Taunus Mountains, c. 40 miles south of Marburg, favored by Edward VII.
3. Performed in kursaal (see p. 41, n. 5 below).
4. A slow, stately court dance, in pairs.
5. Something given as mark of favor—e.g., a knot of ribbons, a glove—especially in medieval or Renaissance texts by a young woman to her suitor.
6. The Palace (and the city) of Versailles, near Paris, principal residence of French kings for a century, was attacked by the mob in the early days of the Revolution. "Trianon": two small chateaux in the park at Versailles. The Petit Trianon (1762) was the favorite resort of Marie Antoinette.
7. Public (curative) baths or spa towns in the German grand duchy of Hessen.

must be stepping itself still. Isn't there any heaven where old beautiful dances, old beautiful intimacies prolong themselves? Isn't there any Nirvana [8] pervaded by the faint thrilling of instruments that have fallen into the dust of wormwood but that yet had frail, tremulous, and everlasting souls?

No, by God it is false! It wasn't a minuet that we stepped; it was a prison—a prison full of screaming hysterics,* tied down so that they might not outsound the rolling of our carriage wheels as we went along the shaded avenues of the Taunus Wald. [9]

And yet, I swear by the sacred name of my creator that it was true. It was true sunshine; the true music; the true plash of the fountains from the mouth of stone dolphins. For, if for me we were four people with the same tastes, with the same desires, acting—or no not acting—sitting here and there unanimously, isn't that the truth? If for nine years I have possessed a goodly apple that is rotten at the core and discover its rottenness only in nine years and six months less four days, isn't it true to say that for nine years I possessed a goodly apple? So it may well be with Edward Ashburnham, with Leonora his wife and with poor dear Florence. And, if you come to think of it, isn't it a little odd that the physical rottenness of at least two pillars of our four-square house never presented itself to my mind as a menace to its security? It doesn't so present itself now though the two of them are actually dead. I don't know. . . .

I know nothing—nothing in the world—of the hearts of men. I only know that I am alone—horribly alone. No hearthstone will ever again witness, for me, friendly intercourse. No smoking-room will ever be other than peopled with incalculable simulacra amidst smoke wreaths. Yet, in the name of God, what should I know if I don't know the life of the hearth and of the smoking-room, since my whole life has been passed in those places? The warm hearthside!—Well, there was Florence: I believe that for the twelve years her life lasted, after the storm that seemed irretrievably to have weakened her heart—I don't believe that for one minute she was out of my sight, except when she was safely tucked up in bed and I should be downstairs, talking to some good fellow or other in some lounge or smoking-room or taking my final turn with a cigar before going to bed. I don't, you understand, blame Florence. But how can she have known what she knew? How could she have got to know it? To know it so fully. Heavens! There doesn't seem to have been the actual time. It must have been when I was taking my baths, and my Swedish exercises,[1]* being manicured. Leading the life I did,

---

8. In Buddhist philosophy, the highest spiritual state, in which the ego and passions are extinguished and perfect beatitude is attained.
9. The Taunus Forest, a large stretch of woodland in the Taunus Mountains stretching north from Wiesbaden and Bad Homberg.
1. "Swedish drill" was "a system of muscular exercises as a form of hygienic or curative treatment" (SOED).

of the sedulous, strained nurse, I had to do something to keep myself fit. It must have been then! Yet even that can't have been enough time to get the tremendously long conversations [she must have had with Lenora—conversations]* full of worldly wisdom that Leonora has reported to me since their deaths. And is it possible to imagine that during our prescribed walks in Nauheim and the neighbourhood she found time to carry on the protracted negotiations which she did carry on between Edward Ashburnham and his wife? And isn't it incredible that during all that time Edward and Leonora never spoke a word to each other in private? What is one to think of humanity?

For I swear to you that they were the model couple. He was as devoted as it was possible to be without appearing fatuous. So well set up, with such honest blue eyes, such a touch of stupidity, such a warm goodheartedness! And she—so tall, so splendid in the saddle, so fair! Yes, Leonora was extraordinarily fair and so extraordinarily the real thing that she seemed too good to be true. You don't, I mean, as a rule, get it all so superlatively together. To be the county family,[2] to look the county family, to be so appropriately and perfectly wealthy; to be so perfect in manner—even just to the saving touch of insolence that seems to be necessary. To have all that and to be all that! No, it was too good to be true. And yet, only this afternoon, talking over the whole matter she said to me: "Once I tried to have a lover but I was so sick at the heart, so utterly worn out that I had to send him away." That struck me as the most amazing thing I had ever heard. She said "I was actually in a man's arms. Such a nice chap! Such a dear fellow! And I was saying to myself, fiercely, hissing it between my teeth, as they say in novels—and really clenching them together: I was saying to myself: 'Now, I'm in for it and I'll really have a good time for once in my life—for once in my life!' It was in the dark, in a carriage, coming back from a hunt ball. Eleven miles we had to drive! And then suddenly the bitterness of the endless poverty, of the endless acting—it fell on me like a blight, it spoilt everything. Yes, I had to realise that I had been spoilt even for the good time when it came. And I burst out crying and I cried and I cried for the whole eleven miles. Just imagine *me* crying! And just imagine me making a fool of the poor dear chap like that. It certainly wasn't playing the game, was it now?"

I don't know; I don't know; was that last remark of hers the remark of a harlot, or is it what every decent woman, county family or not county family, thinks at the bottom of her heart? Or thinks all the time for the matter of that? Who knows?

Yet, if one doesn't know that at this hour and day, at this pitch of civilisation to which we have attained, after all the preachings of all the moralists, and all the teachings of all the mothers to all the daughters *in*

2. Belonging to the upper or upper-middle class, usually having estates and a "seat" (large country house); prominent figures in county society.

saeculum saeculorum[3] . . . but perhaps that is what all mothers teach all daughters, not with lips but with the eyes, or with heart whispering to heart. And, if one doesn't know as much as that about the first thing in the world, what does one know and why is one here?

I asked Mrs. Ashburnham whether she had told Florence that and what Florence had said and she answered: "Florence didn't offer any comment at all. What could she say? There wasn't anything to be said. With the grinding poverty we had to put up with to keep up appearances, and the way the poverty came about—*you* know what I mean— any woman would have been justified in taking a lover and presents too. Florence once said about a very similar position—she was a little too well-bred, too American, to talk about mine—that it was a case of per- fectly open riding and the woman could just act on the spur of the moment. She said it in American of course, but that was the sense of it. I think her actual words were: "That it was up to her to take it or leave it". . . .

I don't want you to think that I am writing Teddy Ashburnham down a brute. I don't believe he was. God knows, perhaps all men are like that. For as I've said what do I know even of the smoking-room? Fellows come in and tell the most extraordinarily gross stories—so gross that they will positively give you a pain. And yet they'd be offended if you sug- gested that they weren't the sort of person you could trust your wife alone with. And very likely they'd be quite properly offended—that is if you can trust anybody alone with anybody. But that sort of fellow obvi- ously takes more delight in listening to or in telling gross stories—more delight than in anything else in the world. They'll hunt languidly and dress languidly and dine languidly and work without enthusiasm and find it a bore to carry on three minutes' conversation about anything whatever and yet, when the other sort of conversation begins they'll laugh and wake up and throw themselves about in their chairs. Then, if they so delight in the narration, how is it possible that they can be offended—and properly offended at the suggestion that they might make attempts upon your wife's honour? Or again: Edward Ashburnham was the cleanest looking sort of chap;—an excellent magistrate, a first rate soldier, one of the best landlords, so they said, in Hampshire, England. To the poor and to hopeless drunkards, as I myself have witnessed he was like a painstaking guardian.* And he never told a story that couldn't have gone into the columns of the *Field* more than once or twice in all the nine years of my knowing him. He didn't even like hearing them, he would fidget and get up and go out to buy a cigar or something of that sort. You would have said that he was just exactly the sort of chap that you could * have trusted your wife with. And I trusted mine—and it was madness.

3. "For ever and ever"; *in saecula saeculum* concludes most prayers (but not the Lord's Prayer) in the Tridentine Mass.

And yet again you have me. If poor Edward was dangerous because of the chastity of his expressions—and they say that that is always the hall-mark of a libertine—what about myself? For I solemnly avow that not only have I never so much as hinted at an impropriety in my conversation in the whole of my days; and more than that, I will vouch for the cleanness of my thoughts and the absolute chastity of my life. At what, then, does it all work out? Is the whole thing a folly and a mockery? Am I no better than a eunuch or is the proper man—the man with the right to existence—a raging stallion forever neighing after his neighbour's womenkind?

I don't know. And there is nothing to guide us. And if everything is so nebulous about a matter so elementary as the morals of sex, what is there to guide us in the more subtle morality of all other personal contacts, associations, and activities? Or are we meant to act on impulse* alone? It is all a darkness.

II *

I don't know how it is best to put this thing down—whether it would be better to try and tell the story from the beginning, as if it were a story; or whether to tell it from this distance of time, as it reached me from the lips of Leonora or from those of Edward himself.*

So I shall just imagine myself for a fortnight or so at one side of the fireplace of a country cottage, with a sympathetic soul opposite me. And I shall go on talking, in a low voice while the sea sounds in the distance and overhead the great black flood of wind polishes the bright stars. From time to time we shall get up and go to the door and look out at the great moon and say: "Why, it is nearly as bright as in Provence!" And then we shall come back to the fireside, with just the touch of a sigh because we are not in that Provence where even the saddest stories are gay. Consider the lamentable history of Peire Vidal.[1] Two years ago Florence and I motored from Biarritz to Las Tours,[2] which is in the Black Mountains. In the middle of a tortuous valley there rises up an immense* pinnacle and on the pinnacle are four castles—Las Tours, the Towers. And the immense mistral[3] blew down that valley which was the way from France into Provence so that the silver grey olive

1. Provençal troubadour, active from 1180 to 1206, one of whose patrons was Richard I; a high-spirited gallant whose love poetry is notable for strong personal feeling and simple style.
2. A few miles north of Carcassonne (see p. 16, n. 8 below), in the wilds of Montagne Noire, southwest France. "Biarritz": fashionable sea resort in southwest France, on the Bay of Biscay near the Spanish border. The journey, from France's Atlantic coast to near her Mediterranean one, is not the main route "from France into Provence"; that is Paris-Lyons-Marseilles, the railway journey mentioned below.
3. A cold northeast wind that blows down the Rhône valley into southern France and the Mediterranean.

leaves appeared like hair flying in the wind, and the tufts of rosemary crept into the iron rocks * that they might not be torn up by the roots.

It was of course poor dear Florence who wanted to go to Las Tours. You are to imagine that, however much her bright personality came from Stamford, Connecticut, she was yet a graduate of Poughkeepsie.[4] I never could imagine how she did it—the queer, chattery person that she was. With the faraway look in her eyes—which wasn't however in the least romantic—I mean that she didn't look as if she were seeing poetic dreams, or looking through you, for she hardly ever did look at you!—holding up one hand as if she wished to silence any objection— or any comment for the matter of that—she would talk. She would talk about William the Silent, about Gustave the Loquacious, about Paris frocks, about how the poor dressed in 1337, about Fantin Latour,[5] about the Paris-Lyons-Méditerranée train-de-luxe, about whether it would be worth while to get off at Tarascon and go across the windswept suspension-bridge, over the Rhône to take another look at Beaucaire.[6]

We never did take another look at Beaucaire of course—beautiful Beaucaire, with the high, triangular white tower, that looked as thin as a needle and as tall as the Flatiron,[7] between Fifth and Broadway— Beaucaire with the grey walls on the top of the pinnacle surrounding an acre and a half of blue irises, beneath the tallness of the stone pines. What a beautiful thing the stone pine is. . . .

No, we never did go back anywhere. Not to Heidelberg, not to Hamelin,* not to Verona, not to Mont Majour—not so much as to Carcassonne[8] itself. We talked of it of course, but I guess Florence got all she wanted out of one look at a place. She had the seeing eye.

---

4. Vassar College (Poughkeepsie, N.Y.), a leading institution for the higher education of women.
5. French painter, printmaker, and illustrator (1836–1904), noted for still-lifes with flowers and group portraits of French celebrities in the arts. "William the Silent": William I, prince of Orange (1533–1584); at first Catholic and ally of Philip II of Spain; later, a Calvinist opposing Spain; born near Wiesbaden; assassinated at Delft; four wives (the last a French princess and runaway nun); a figure of romance deeply implicated in the religious/cultural schism of the Reformation. "Gustave the Loquacious": probably Gustavus I, king of Sweden (1523–1560), founder of modern Swedish state and a prime mover in establishing national Protestant Church.
6. Tarascon and Beaucaire, near the mouth of the Rhône, c. 40 miles north of Marseilles, face each other across the river; both are on tourist schedules for their picturesque medieval buildings.
7. Triangular building (1902) at the junction of Fifth Avenue and Broadway, New York City.
8. Near Lastours, southern France; its ancient city (19th-century restoration) is a medieval fortress perched on a hilltop, one of the architectural marvels of Europe; towers (c. 6th century) built by Visigoths are still intact. "Heidelberg": city in the southwest of former West Germany, seat of an ancient university, bulwark of Reformation in the 16th century; romantic student life of the city much publicized in the 19th century; center for theological studies: the Heidelberg Catechism was a profession of faith of the German Reformed (Calvinistic) Church much adopted by Reformed Churches. "Hamelin" (Hameln): city in Lower Saxony in the north of former West Germany, on the Weser River, famous for the legend of the Pied Piper. "Verona": beautiful northeastern Italian city; important strategic position since Roman times, on the Brenner Road to central Europe; site of civil strife between Guelph and Ghibelline families as reflected in *Romeo and Juliet*; center for Renaissance artists (e.g., Veronese). "Montmajour": near Tarascon and Beaucaire in Provence; famous for medieval abbey and (like Carcassonne) its associations with Charlemagne.

I haven't, unfortunately, so that the world is full of p[...] want to return—towns with the blinding white sun up[on...] pines against the* blue of the sky; corners of gables, [...] painted with stags and scarlet flowers and crowstepped [...] little saint at the top; and grey and pink palazzi and walled towns a mile or so back from the sea, on the Mediterranean, between Leghorn[9] and Naples. Not one of them did we see more than once so that the whole world for me is like spots of colour on* an immense canvas. Perhaps if it weren't so I should have something to catch hold of now.*

Is all this digression or isn't it digression? Again I don't know. You, the listener, sit opposite me. But you are so silent. You don't tell me anything. I am at any rate trying to get you to see what sort of life it was I led with Florence and what Florence was like. Well she was bright; and she danced. She seemed to dance over the floors of castles and over seas and over and over the salons of modistes and over the *plages*[1] of the Riviera—like a gay tremulous beam, reflected from water upon a ceiling. And my function in life was to keep that bright thing in existence. And it was almost as difficult as trying to catch with your hand that dancing reflection. And the task lasted for years.

Florence's aunts used to say that I must be the laziest man in Philadelphia. They had never been to Philadelphia and they had the New England conscience. You see, the first thing they said to me when I called in on Florence in the little ancient, colonial, wooden house beneath the high, thin-leaved elms—the first question they asked me was not how I did but what did I do. And I did nothing. I suppose I ought to have done something but I didn't see any call to do it. Why does one do things? I just drifted in and wanted Florence. First I had drifted in on Florence at a Browning tea,[2] or something of the sort* in Fourteenth Street, which was then still residential. I don't know why I had gone to New York; I don't know why I had gone to the tea.* I don't see why Florence should have gone to that sort of spelling bee.[3] It wasn't the place at which, even then, you expected to find a Poughkeepsie graduate. I guess Florence wanted to raise the culture of the Stuyvesant crowd[4] and did it as she might have gone in slumming. Intellectual slumming, that was what it was. She always wanted to leave the world a little more elevated than she found it. Poor dear thing, I have heard her

9. Now Livorno, Italian town on the coast of Tuscany, south of Pisa. "Crowstepped": ("corbie-stepped"), steplike projections on sloping sides of gable. "Palazzi": palaces (Italian).
1. Beaches and/or seaside resorts (French). "Modistes": fashion designers and/or merchants, e.g., milliners, dressmakers (French).
2. Group of Robert Browning enthusiasts who would gather to discuss his work; sometimes associated with the intellectual pursuits of middle-class "blue-stocking" women at the turn of the century and possibly mocked here for its earnest domestication of art.
3. A spelling competition, another form of social gathering for women, more lowbrow than a Browning tea.
4. Possibly (see Moser 298) those who live near Stuyvesant Square in Manhattan; possibly also the name of imagined persons at the center of a rich and philistine social circle. See p. 57 below.

·cture Teddy Ashburnham by the hour on the difference between a Frans Hals and a Wouwerman and why the Pre-Mycenaic statues[5*] were cubical with knobs on the top. I wonder what he made of it? Perhaps he was thankful.

I know I was. For do you understand my whole attentions, my whole endeavours were to keep poor dear Florence on to topics like the finds at Cnossos and the mental spirituality of Walter Pater.[6*] I had to keep her at it, you understand, or she might die. For I was solemnly informed that if she became excited over anything or if her emotions were really stirred her little heart might cease to beat. For twelve years I had to watch every word that any person uttered in any conversation and I had to head it off what the English call "things"—off love, poverty, crime, religion and the rest of it.[*] Yes, the first doctor that we had when she was carried off the ship at Havre assured me that this must be done. Good God, are all these fellows monstrous idiots, or is there a freemasonry between all of them from end to end of the earth? . . . That is what makes me think of that fellow Peire Vidal.

Because of course his story is culture and I had to head her towards culture and at the same time it's so funny and she hadn't got to laugh, and it's so full of love and she wasn't to think of love. Do you know the story? Las Tours of the Four Castles had for chatelaine[7] Blanche Somebody-or-other who was called as a term of commendation, La Louve—the She-Wolf. And Peire Vidal the Troubadour[8] paid his court[*] to La Louve. And she wouldn't have anything to do with him. So, out of compliment to her—the things people do when they're in love!—he dressed himself up in wolfskins and went up into the Black Mountains. And the shepherds of the Montagne Noire and their dogs mistook him for a wolf and he was torn with the fangs and beaten with clubs. So they carried him back to Las Tours and La Louve wasn't at all impressed. They polished him up and her husband remonstrated seri-

5. Mycenae, a city of ancient Greece, excavated by Heinrich Schliemann and others after 1876; their findings thoroughly revised the early history of Greece. Mycenaeans were ancestors of the Greeks, although in 1915 thought to be Minoans. Frans Hals (c. 1580–1666), Dutch painter of portraits and genre scenes. Philips Wouwerman (1619–1668), Dutch painter of hilly country with horses, of battles, and of hunting scenes; appears to have been a pupil of Hals. Hals spent most of his life in poverty; Wouwerman made a fortune.
6. English essayist (1839–1894) and critic; his writings promoted "the beautiful" and "the profound"; author of *Studies in the History of the Renaissance* (1873) and *Marius the Epicurean* (1885); crucial influence on Oscar Wilde and on cultivated decadence of 1890s; seen here, surely, as outdated and "precious"; **MS** correction puts him in his place. Cf. Ford's "Literary Portraits-XL: Vernon Lee and 'Louis Norbert,' " *Outlook* (London) 33 (13 June 1914): 815–16, where he disparages the "sterilised atmosphere" of Pater's writings. "Cnossus" (Knossos): ancient city of Crete long before 3000 B.C.; center of Minoan culture; legendary home of King Minos and site of labyrinth.
7. Mistress of a chateau, or large country house generally. Historically, "chatelaine" also described an ornamental set of short chains attached to the belt of such a lady, for carrying keys and the like, an image which obliquely foreshadows Leonora's key (attached by a chain to her wrist) and associates her with the legendary medieval lady, La Louve.
8. Troubadours were medieval, aristocratic, Provençal poet-musicians, typically hymning courtly love, war, and nature.

ously with her. Vidal was, you see, a great poet and it was not proper to treat a great poet with indifference.

So Peire Vidal declared himself Emperor of Jerusalem or somewhere and the husband had to kneel down and kiss his feet though La Louve wouldn't. And Peire set sail in a rowing boat with four companions to redeem the Holy Sepulchre.[9] And they struck on a rock somewhere, and, at great expense, the husband had to fit out an expedition to fetch him back. And Peire Vidal fell all over the Lady's bed while the husband, who was a most ferocious warrior, remonstrated some more about the courtesy that is due to great poets. But I suppose La Louve was the more ferocious of the two. Anyhow, that is all that came of it. Isn't that a story?

You haven't an idea of the queer old fashionedness of Florence's aunts—the Misses Hurlbird, nor yet of her uncle. An extraordinarily lovable man, that Uncle John. Thin, gentle, and with a "heart" that made his life very much what Florence's afterwards became. He didn't reside at Stamford; his home was in Waterbury where the watches come from.[1] He had a factory there which, in our queer American way would change its functions almost from year to year. For nine months or so it would manufacture buttons out of bone. Then it would suddenly produce brass buttons for coachmen's liveries. Then it would take a turn at embossed tin lids for candy boxes. The fact is that the poor old gentleman, with his weak and fluttering heart didn't want his factory to manufacture anything at all. He wanted to retire. And he did retire when he was seventy. But he was so worried at having all the street boys in the town point after him and exclaim: "There goes the laziest man in Waterbury!" that he tried taking a tour round the world. And Florence and a young man called Jimmy went with him. It appears from what Florence told me that Jimmy's function with Mr. Hurlbird was to avoid exciting topics for him. He had to keep him, for instance, out of political discussions. For the poor old man was a violent Democrat in days when you might travel the world over without finding anything but a Republican.[2] Anyhow they went round the world.

I think an anecdote is about the best way to give you an idea of what the old gentleman was like. For it is perhaps important that you should know what the old gentleman was; he* had a great deal of influence in forming the character of my poor dear wife.

---

9. The purpose of the Crusades was to rescue the burial place of Christ from the Turks. The Church of the Holy Sepulchre was later erected on the site.
1. City in western Connecticut, then famous for manufacture of clocks, watches, tools, and instruments, and later also for plastics and electronic parts.
2. The Democratic Party developed from Republicans/Democratic Republicans led by Alexander Hamilton and Thomas Jefferson in the early 19th century. The Democrats were antifederalists suspicious of urban commercial interests who supported many ideals of the French Revolution and opposed close links with England. Republicanism in the 19th century was generally anti-slavery, Northern, and in favor of protective tariffs.

Just before they set out from San Francisco for the South Seas old Mr. Hurlbird said he must take something with him to make little presents to people he met on the voyage. And it struck him that the things to take for that purpose were oranges—because California is the orange country—and comfortable folding chairs. So he bought I don't know how many cases of oranges—the great cool California oranges; and half-a-dozen folding chairs in a special case that he always kept in his cabin. There must have been half a cargo of fruit.

For, to every person on board the several steamers that they employed—to every person with whom he had so much as a nodding acquaintance, he gave an orange every morning. And they lasted him right round the girdle of this mighty globe of ours. When they were at North Cape,[3] even, he saw on the horizon, poor dear thin man that he was, a lighthouse. "Hello," says he to himself, "these fellows must be very lonely. Let's take them some oranges." So he had a boatload of his fruit out and had himself rowed to the lighthouse on the horizon. The folding-chairs he lent to any lady that he came across and liked or who seemed tired and invalidish on the ship. And so, guarded against his heart and, having his niece with him, he went round the world. . . .

He wasn't obtrusive about his heart. You wouldn't have known he had one. He only left it to the physical laboratory at Waterbury for the benefit of science, since he considered it to be quite an extraordinary kind of heart. And the joke of the matter was that, when at the age of eighty-four, just five days before* poor Florence, he died of bronchitis there was found to be absolutely nothing the matter with that organ. It had certainly jumped or squeaked or something just sufficiently to take in the doctors but it appears that that was because of an odd formation of the lungs. I don't much understand about these matters.

I inherited his money because Florence died five days after* him. I wish I hadn't. It was a great worry. I had to go out to Waterbury just after Florence's death because the poor dear old fellow had left a good many charitable bequests and I had to appoint trustees. I didn't like the idea of their not being properly handled.

Yes, it was a great worry.* And just as I had got things roughly settled I received the extraordinary cable from Ashburnham begging me to come back and have a talk with him. And immediately afterwards came one from Leonora saying, "Yes please do come. You could be so helpful." It was as if he had sent the cable without consulting her and* [then] had afterwards told her. Indeed that was pretty much what had happened except that he had told the girl and the girl told the wife. I arrived however too late to be of any good if I could have been of any good. And then I had my first taste of English life. It was amazing. It was overwhelming. I never shall forget the polished cob that Edward,

---

3. A Norwegian promontory rising steeply from the Arctic Ocean, the northernmost point of Europe and a traditional stop for tourist steamers.

beside me, drove; the animal's action, its highstepping, its skin that was like satin. And the peace! And the red cheeks! And the beautiful, beautiful old house.

Just near Bramshaw Teleragh * it was and we descended on it from the high, clear, windswept waste of the New Forest.[4] I tell you it was amazing to arrive there from Waterbury. And it came into my head— for Teddy Ashburnham, you remember had cabled to me to "come and have a talk" with him—that it was unbelievable that anything essentially calamitous could happen to that place and those people. I tell you it was the very spirit of peace. And Leonora, beautiful and smiling, with her coils of yellow hair stood on the top doorstep, with a butler and footman and a maid or so behind her. And she just said: "So glad you've come", as if I'd run down to lunch from a town ten miles away, instead of having come half the world over at the call of two urgent telegrams.

The girl was out with the hounds, I think.

And that poor devil beside me was in an agony. Absolute, hopeless, dumb agony such as passes the mind of man to imagine. *

III *

It was a very hot summer, in August, 1904 *; and Florence had already been taking the baths for a month. I don't know how it feels to be a patient at one of those places. I never was a patient anywhere. I daresay the patients get a home feeling and some sort of anchorage in the spot. They seem to like the bath attendants, with their cheerful faces, their air of authority, their white linen. But, for myself, to be at Nauheim gave me a sense—what shall I say?—a sense almost of nakedness—the nakedness that one feels on the sea-shore or in any great open space. I had no attachments, no accumulations. In one's own home it is as if little, innate sympathies draw one to particular chairs that seem to enfold one in an embrace, or take one along particular streets that seem friendly when others may be hostile. And, believe me, that feeling is a very important part of life. I know it well, that have been for so long a wanderer upon the face of public resorts. And one is too polished up. Heaven knows I was never an untidy man. But the feeling that I had when, whilst poor Florence was taking her morning bath, I stood upon the carefully swept steps of the Englischer Hof,[1] looking at the carefully arranged trees in tubs upon the carefully arranged gravel whilst carefully arranged people walked past in carefully calculated gaiety, at the care-

4. Extensive area of woodland, heath, and rough pasture, bounded by the Avon and Solent rivers and by Southampton Water; organized as royal forest by William I; now parkland, one-quarter cultivated, famous for its ponies and as a nature reserve; wild country by English standards.

1. Probably Hotel d'Angleterre, now the Deutsches Hof, a substantial private hotel in a tree-lined street, 1 Kuchlerstrasse, one block from the Kurpark and baths. See illustration, p. 166 below.

fully calculated hour, the tall trees of the public gardens, going up to the right *; the reddish stone of the baths—or were they white half-timber châlets?[2] Upon my word I have forgotten, I who was there so often. That will give you the measure of how much I was in the landscape. I could find my way blindfolded to the hot rooms, to the douche rooms, to the fountain in the centre of the quadrangle where the rusty water gushes out. Yes I could find my way blindfolded. I know the exact distances. From the Hotel Regina[3] you took one hundred and eighty-seven paces, then, turning sharp, lefthanded, four hundred and twenty took you straight down to the fountain. From the Englischer Hof, starting on the sidewalk, it was ninety-seven paces and the same four hundred and twenty, but turning lefthanded this time. *

And now you understand that, having nothing in the world to do— but nothing whatever! I fell into the habit of counting my footsteps. I would walk with Florence to the baths. And of course she entertained me with her conversation. It was, as I have said, wonderful what she could make conversation out of. * She walked very lightly, and her hair was very nicely done, and she dressed beautifully and very expensively. * Of course she had money of her own, but I shouldn't have minded. And yet you know I can't remember a single one of her dresses. Or I can remember just one, a very simple one of blue figured silk—a Chinese * pattern—very full in the skirts and broadening out over the shoulders. And her hair was copper-coloured, and the heels of her shoes were exceedingly high, so that she tripped upon the points of her toes. And when she came to the door of the bathing place and, when it opened to receive her she would look back at me with a little coquettish smile, so that her cheek appeared to be caressing her shoulder.

I seem to remember that, with that dress, she wore an immensely broad Leghorn hat—like the Chapeau de Paille of Rubens,[4] only very white. The hat would be tied with a lightly knotted scarf of the same stuff as her dress. She knew how to give value to her blue eyes. And round her neck would be some simple pink, coral beads. And her complexion had a perfect clearness, a perfect smoothness. . . .

Yes, that is how I most exactly remember her, in that dress, in that hat, looking over her shoulder at me so that the eyes flashed very blue— dark pebble blue. . . . *

And, what the devil! For whose benefit did she do it? For that of the bath attendant? of the passers-by? I don't know. Anyhow, it can't have

2. Ford is struggling with documentary detail here because when he visited Bad Nauheim in 1910, the bathhouses around the central quadrangle had been completely rebuilt as an Art Nouveau complex; the original bathhouses *were* half-timbered (see illustrations, p. 167 below) and the atmosphere of the place was much more rural.

3. A few yards from the Englischer Hof and down the same street: 8 Kuchlerstrasse.

4. Peter Paul Rubens (1577–1640), foremost Flemish painter of the 17th century; his portrait of Susanna Fourment (1599–1643, sister of his second wife) is known as "The Straw Hat" and is in the National Gallery, London. See cover illustration. "Leghorn hat": hat made of bleached wheat-straw, from Leghorn (Livorno) in Tuscany, Italy.

been for me, for never, in all the years of her life, never on any possible occasion, or in any other place did she so smile to me, mockingly, invitingly. Ah, she was a riddle; but then, all other women are riddles. And it occurs to me that some way back I began a sentence that I have never finished . . . It was about the feeling that I had when I stood on the steps of my hotel every morning before starting out to fetch Florence back from the bath. Natty, precise, well-brushed, conscious of being rather small amongst the long English, the lank Americans, the rotund Germans, and the obese Russian Jewesses, I should stand there, tapping a cigarette on the outside of my case, surveying for a moment the world in the sunlight. But a day was to come when I was never to do it again alone. You can imagine, therefore, what the coming of the Ashburn-hams meant for me.

I have forgotten the aspect of many things but I shall never forget the aspect of the dining-room of the Hotel Excelsior[5] on that evening—and on so many other evenings.* Whole castles have vanished from my memory, whole cities that I have never visited again, but that white room, festooned with papier-maché fruits and flowers; the tall windows; the many tables; the black screen round the door with three golden cranes flying upward on each panel; the palm-tree in the centre of the room; the swish of the waiter's feet; the cold expensive elegance; the mien of the diners as they came in every evening—their air of earnest-ness as if they must go through a meal prescribed by the Kur authorities and their air of sobriety as if they must seek not by any means to enjoy their meals *—those things I shall not easily forget. And then, one eve-ning, in the twilight, I saw Edward Ashburnham lounge round the screen into the room. The head waiter, a man with a face all grey—in what subterranean nooks or corners do people cultivate those absolutely grey complexions?—went with the timorous patronage* of these crea-tures towards him and held out a grey ear to be whispered into. It was generally a* disagreeable ordeal for newcomers but Edward Ashburn-ham bore it like an Englishman and a gentleman. I could see his lips form a word of three syllables—remember I had nothing in the world to do but to notice these niceties—and immediately I knew that he must be Edward Ashburnham, Captain, Fourteenth Hussars,[6] of Bramshaw House, Bramshaw Teleragh.* I knew it because every evening just before dinner, whilst I waited in the hall I used, by the courtesy of Monsieur Schontz, the proprietor to inspect the little police reports that each guest was expected to sign upon taking a room.

5. Grander than the Englischer Hof and Hotel Regina, within easy walking distance of them, but still modest in comparison with Grand-Hotel Kaiserhof or Grand-Hotel Metropole and Monopole. Ford places characters in establishments exactly reflecting their social status rather than their wealth.
6. Light-cavalry regiment, employed for scouting, with dandyish braided uniform: busby and loose coat hanging from left shoulder. See p. 113, n. 8 below.

The head waiter piloted him immediately to a vacant table, three away from my own—the table that the Grenfalls* of Falls River, N. J. had just vacated. It struck me that that was not a very nice table for the newcomers, since the sunlight, low though it was, shone straight down upon it and the same idea seemed to come at the same moment into Captain Ashburnham's head. His face hitherto had, in the wonderful English fashion, expressed nothing whatever. Nothing. There was in it neither joy nor despair; neither hope nor fear; neither boredom nor satisfaction. He seemed to perceive no soul in that crowded room; he might have been walking in a jungle. I never came across such a perfect expression before and I never shall again. It was insolence and not insolence; it was modesty and not modesty. His hair was fair, extraordinarily, ordered in a wave, running from the left temple to the right; his face was a light brick-red, perfectly uniform in tint up to the roots of the hair itself;* his yellow moustache was as stiff as a toothbrush and I verily believe that he had his black smoking jacket thickened a little over the shoulder-blades so as to give himself the air of the slightest possible stoop. It would be like him to do that; that was the sort of thing he thought about. Martingales, Chiffney bits, [hunting]* boots; where you got the best soap, the best brandy, the name of the chap who rode a plater down the Khyber cliffs[7] ; the spreading power of number three shot before a charge of number four powder . . . by heavens, I hardly ever heard him talk of anything else. Not in all the years that I knew him did I hear him talk of anything but these subjects. Oh yes, once he told me that I could buy my special shade of blue ties cheaper from a firm in Burlington Arcade than from my own people in New York. And I have bought my ties from that firm ever since. Otherwise I should not remember the name of the Burlington Arcade.[8] I wonder what it looks like. I have never seen it. I imagine it to be two immense rows of pillars, like those of the Forum at Rome, with Edward Ashburnham striding down between them. But it probably isn't [in]* the least like that. Once also he advised me to buy Caledonian Deferred, since they were due to rise. And I did buy them and they did rise. But of how he got the knowledge I haven't the faintest idea. It seemed to drop out of the blue sky.

And that was absolutely all that I knew of him until a month ago—that and the profusion of his cases, all of pigskin and stamped with his initials E. F. A. There were guncases, and collar cases, and shirt cases, and letter cases [and cases each containing four bottles of scent]* and cases each containing four bottles of medicine; and hat cases and helmet

---

7. In Khyber Pass, then India, now Pakistan (see p. 41, n. 6 below). "Martingales": straps fixed between horses' chinstraps or reins and girths. "Chiffney bits": horses' bits, invented by the jockey Samuel Chiffney (1753?–1807). "Plater": a horse that chiefly competes in plate or prize races, thus an inferior racehorse.
8. Archetype of London's shopping arcades, with glass roof and delicately detailed shops, built on a narrow strip of Burlington House's garden after Waterloo, and copied from earlier continental models.

cases. It must have needed a whole herd of the Gadarene* swine[9] to make up his outfit. And, if I ever penetrated into his private room it would be to see him standing, with his coat and waistcoat off and the immensely long line of his perfectly elegant trousers from waist to boot heel. And he would have a slightly reflective air and he would be just opening one kind of case and just closing another.

Good God, what did they all see in him; for I swear that was all there was of him, * inside and out; though they said he was a good soldier. Yet Leonora adored him with a passion that was like an agony, and hated him with an agony that was as bitter as the sea. How could he rouse anything like a sentiment, in anybody? *

What did he even talk to them about—when they were under four eyes?—Ah, well, suddenly, as if by a flash of inspiration, I know. For all good soldiers are sentimentalists—all good soldiers of that type. Their profession, for one thing is full of the big words, courage, loyalty, honour, constancy. And I have given a wrong impression of Edward Ashburnham if I have made you think that literally never in the course of our nine years of intimacy did he discuss what he would have called "the graver things". Even before his final outburst to me, at times, very late at night, say, he has blurted out something that gave an insight into the sentimental view of the cosmos that was his. He would say how much the society of a good woman could do towards redeeming you, and he would say that constancy was the finest of the virtues. He said it very stiffly, * of course, but still as if the statement admitted of no doubt.

Constancy! Isn't that the queer thought? And yet, I must add that poor dear Edward was a great reader—he would pass hours lost in novels of a sentimental type—novels in which typewriter girls married Marquises and governesses, Earls. And in his books, as a rule, the course of true love ran as smooth as buttered honey. And he was fond of poetry, of a certain type—and he could even read a perfectly * sad love story. I have seen his eyes filled with tears at reading of a hopeless parting. And he loved, with a sentimental yearning, all children, puppies, and the feeble generally. . . .

So, you see, he would have plenty to gurgle about to a woman—with that and his sound common sense about martingales and his—still sentimental—experiences as a county magistrate; and with his intense, optimistic belief that the woman he was making love to at the moment was the one he was destined, at last, to be eternally constant to. . . . Well, I fancy he could put up a pretty good deal of talk when there was no man around to make him feel shy. And I was quite astonished, dur-

9. See Matthew 8.28–32, Mark 5.1–13, and Luke 8.26–33, where Jesus visits the land of the Gadarenes, encounters a violent, naked madman (two in Matthew), and casts out the devils into a herd of pigs that rush headlong into a lake and drown. The description of the possessed man echoes Dowell's "a prison full of screaming hysterics, tied down. . . ." "Gadarene" has come to mean "involving or engaged in suicidal rush or flight" (COD). See MDATV, p. 198, 25, 1st entry below.

ing his final burst out to me—at the very end of things, when the poor girl was on her way to that fatal Brindisi and he was trying to persuade himself and me that he had never really cared for her—I was quite astonished to observe how literary and how just his expressions were. He talked like quite a good book—a book not in the least cheaply sentimental. You see, I suppose he regarded me not so much as a man. I had to be regarded as a woman or a solicitor. Anyhow, it burst out of him on that horrible night. And then, next morning, he took me over to the Assizes[1] and I saw how, in a perfectly calm and business-like way he set to work to secure a verdict of not guilty for a poor girl, the daughter of one of his tenants who had been accused of murdering her baby. He spent two hundred pounds on her defence. . . . Well, that was Edward Ashburnham.

I had forgotten * about his eyes. They were as blue as the sides of a certain type of box of matches. When you looked at them carefully you saw that they were perfectly honest, perfectly straightforward, perfectly, perfectly stupid. But the brick pink of his complexion, running perfectly level to the brick pink of his inner eyelids, gave them a curious, sinister expression—like a mosaic of blue porcelain set in pink china. And that * chap, coming into a room snapped up the gaze of every woman in it, as dexterously as a conjurer pockets billiard balls. It was most amazing. You know the man on the stage who throws up sixteen balls at once and they all drop into pockets all over his person, on his shoulders, on his heels, on the inner side of his sleeves; and he stands perfectly still and does nothing. Well, it was like that. He had rather a rough, hoarse voice.

And, there he was, standing by the table. I was looking at him, with my back to the screen. And, suddenly, I saw two distinct expressions flicker across his immobile eyes. How the deuce did they do it, those unflinching blue eyes with the direct gaze? * For the eyes themselves never moved, gazing over my shoulder towards the screen. And the gaze was perfectly level and perfectly direct and perfectly unchanging. I suppose that the lids really must have rounded themselves a little and perhaps the lips moved a little too, as if he should be saying: "There you are my dear." At any rate the expression was that of pride, of * satisfaction, of the possessor. I saw him once afterwards, for a moment, gaze upon the sunny fields of Bramshaw * and say: "All this is my land!"

And then again, * the gaze was perhaps more direct, harder if possible—hardy too. It was a measuring look; a challenging look. Once when we were at Wiesbaden[2] watching him play in a polo match against the Bonner Hussaren I saw the same look come into his eyes, balancing

1. County court.
2. Elegant German spa town near Frankfurt, then in the Prussian province of Hesse-Nassau, c. 25 miles southwest of Bad Nauheim. The latter would have appeared provincial, much less obviously cosmopolitan, by comparison.

the possibilities, looking over the ground. The German Captain, Count Baron Idigon von Lelöffel,[3] was right up by their goal posts, coming with the ball in an easy canter in that tricky German fashion. The rest of the field were just anywhere. It was only a scratch sort of affair. Ashburnham was quite close to the rails not five yards from us and I heard him saying to himself: "Might just be done!" And he did it. Goodness! he swung that pony round with all its four legs spread out, like a cat dropping off a roof. . . .

Well, it was just that look that I noticed in his eyes: "It might", I seem even now to hear him muttering to himself, "just be done."

I looked round over my shoulder and saw, tall, smiling brilliantly and buoyant—Leonora. And, little and fair, and as radiant as the track of sunlight along the sea—my wife.

That poor wretch! to think that he was at that moment in a perfect devil of a fix, and there he was, saying at the back of his mind: "It might just be done." It was like a chap in the middle of the eruption of a volcano, saying that he might just manage to bolt into the tumult and set fire to a haystack. Madness? Predestination? Who the devil knows? *

Mrs. Ashburnham exhibited at that moment more gaiety than I have ever since known her to show. There are certain classes of English people—the nicer ones when they have been to many spas, who seem to make a point of becoming much more than usually animated when they are introduced to my compatriots. I have noticed this often. * Of course, they must first have accepted the Americans. But, that once done, they seem to say to themselves: "Hallo, these women are so bright. We aren't going to be outdone in brightness." And for the time being they certainly aren't. But it wears off. So it was with Leonora—at least until she noticed me. She began, Leonora did—and perhaps it was that that gave me the idea of a touch of insolence in her character, for she never afterwards did any one single thing like it—she began by saying in quite a loud voice and from quite a distance:

"Don't stop over by that stuffy old table, Teddy. Come and sit by these nice people!"

And that was an extraordinary thing to say. Quite extraordinary. I couldn't for the life of me refer to total strangers as nice people. But, of course, she was taking a line of her own in which I at any rate—and no one else in the room, for she too had taken the trouble to read through the list of guests—counted any more than so many clean, [well-behaved] * bull terriers. And she sat down rather brilliantly at a vacant table, beside ours—one that was reserved for the Guggenheimers. And she just sat absolutely deaf to the remonstrances of the head waiter with his face like a grey ram's. That poor chap was doing his steadfast duty

3. Ford and Violet Hunt knew a Count Lelöffel in Nauheim in 1910 (Moser 300).

too. He knew that the Guggenheimers of Chicago after they had stayed there a month and had worried the poor life out of him would give him two dollars fifty and grumble at the tipping system. And he knew that Teddy Ashburnham and his wife would give him no trouble whatever except what the smiles of Leonora might cause in his apparently unimpressionable bosom—though you never can tell what may go on behind even a not quite spotless plastron! [4]—And every week Edward Ashburnham would give him a solid, sound, golden English sovereign. Yet this stout fellow was intent on saving that table for the Guggenheimers of Chicago. It ended in Florence saying:

"Why shouldn't we all eat out of the same trough—that's a nasty New York saying. But I'm sure we're all nice quiet people and there can be four seats at our table. It's round."

Then came, as it were, an appreciative gurgle from the Captain and I was perfectly aware of a slight hesitation—a quick sharp motion in Mrs. Ashburnham, as if her horse had checked. But she put it at the fence all right, rising from the seat she had taken and sitting down opposite me, as it were, all in one motion.

I [*] never thought that Leonora looked her best in evening dress. She seemed to get it too clearly cut, there was no ruffling. She always affected black and her shoulders were too classical. She seemed to stand out of her corsage as a white marble bust might out of a black Wedgwood [5] vase. I don't know.

○ I loved Leonora always and, today, I would very cheerfully lay down my life, what is left of it, in her service. But I am sure I never had the beginnings of a trace of what is called the sex instinct towards her. And I suppose—no I am certain that she never had it towards me. As far as I am concerned I think it was those white shoulders that did it. I seemed to feel when I looked at them that, if ever I should press my lips upon them [*] they would be slightly cold—not icily, not without a touch of human heat, but, as they say of baths, with the chill off. I seemed to feel chilled at the end of my lips when I looked at her. . . .

No, Leonora always appeared to me at her best in a blue tailor-made. [6] Then her glorious hair wasn't deadened by her white shoulders. [*] Certain women's lines guide your eyes to their necks, their eyelashes, their lips, their breasts. But Leonora's seemed to conduct your gaze always to her wrist. And the wrist was at its best in a black or a dog-skin glove and there was always a gold circlet [round it—a gold circlet] [*] with a little chain supporting a very small golden key to a dispatch box. Perhaps it was that in which she locked up her heart and her feelings. ꙥ

4. A man's starched shirtfront but, historically, a steel breastplate.
5. Staffordshire pottery on which white bas-relief figures stand out sharply against a plain background of matt color, typically pale blue. Black would be unusual, suggesting funerary associations, perhaps to emphasize Leonora's coldness. "Corsage": bodice.
6. Plain, heavy, close-fitting woman's suit made by a tailor (rather than a dressmaker); hence here: rather severe, in accordance with strict propriety, the opposite of flirtatious.

Anyhow, she sat down opposite me and then, for the first time, she paid any attention to my existence. She gave me, suddenly yet deliberately, one long stare. Her eyes too were blue and dark and the eyelids were so arched that they gave you the whole round of the irises. And it was a most remarkable, a most moving glance, as if for a moment a lighthouse had looked at me. I seemed to perceive the swift questions chasing each other through the brain that was behind them. I seemed to hear the brain ask and the eyes answer with all the simpleness of a woman who was a good hand at taking in qualities of a horse—as indeed she was. "Stands well; has plenty of room for his oats behind the girth. Not so much in the way of shoulders", and so on. And so her eyes asked: "Is this man trustworthy in money matters; is he likely to try to play the lover; is he likely to let his women be troublesome? Is he, above all, likely to babble about my affairs?"

And suddenly, into those cold, slightly defiant, almost defensive china blue orbs, there came a warmth, a tenderness, a friendly recognition . . . oh, it was very charming and very touching—and quite mortifying. It was the look of a mother to her son, of a sister to her brother. It implied trust; it implied the want of any necessity for barriers. By God, she looked at me as if I were an invalid—as any kind woman may look at a poor chap in a bath chair. And, yes, from that day forward she always treated me and not Florence as if I were the invalid. Why, she would run after me with a rug upon chilly days. I suppose therefore that her eyes had made a favourable answer. Or perhaps it wasn't a favourable answer. And then Florence said: "And so the whole round table is begun." [7] Again Edward Ashburnham gurgled slightly in his throat; but Leonora shivered a little, as if a goose had walked over her grave. And I was passing her the nickel-silver basket of rolls. Avanti! . . . *

IV *

So began those nine years of uninterrupted tranquillity. They were characterised by an extraordinary want of any communicativeness on the part of the Ashburnhams to which, we on our part replied by leaving out quite as extraordinarily, and nearly as completely, the personal note. Indeed you may take it that what characterised our relationship * was an atmosphere of taking everything for granted. The given proposition was,

7. Echoes Dante Gabriel Rossetti's "So the whole round table is dissolved," describing the disintegration of the Pre-Raphaelite Brotherhood. Through Rossetti's words, Ford refers us ironically to the chivalric tradition of King Arthur and the Knights of the Round Table while simultaneously suggesting the bohemianism of the P.R.B. Dowell's group reflects neither the strict moral code of the feudal tradition nor the Brotherhood's intellectual rigor and disregard for polite convention. The high ideals of both groups were compromised by adultery within their circle. Ford's first serious book (1896) was a biography of his grandfather, the P.R.B. painter Ford Madox Brown, a formative influence on the young Ford.

that we were all "good people". We took for granted that we all liked
beef underdone but not too underdone; that both men preferred a good
liqueur brandy after lunch; that both women drank a very light Rhine
wine qualified with Fachingen water[1]—that sort of thing. It was also
taken for granted that we were both sufficiently well off to afford anything that we could reasonably want in the way of amusements fitting to
our station—that we could take motor cars and carriages by the day; that
we could give each other dinners and dine our friends and we could
indulge if we liked in economy. Thus, Florence was in the habit of
having the *Daily Telegraph* sent to her every day from London. She was
always an Anglo-maniac, was Florence; the Paris edition of the *New
York Herald* was always good enough for me. But when we discovered
that the Ashburnham's copy of the London paper * followed them from
England, Leonora and Florence decided between them to suppress one
subscription one year and the other the next. Similarly it was the habit
of the Grand Duke of Nassau Schwerin, who came yearly to the baths,
to dine once with about eighteen families of regular Kur guests. In
return he would give a dinner to all the eighteen at once. And, since
these dinners were rather expensive (you had to take the Grand Duke
and a good many of his suite and any members of the diplomatic bodies
that might be there)—Florence and Leonora, putting their heads
together, didn't see why we shouldn't give the Grand Duke his dinner
together. And so we did. I don't suppose the Serenity minded that economy, or even noticed it. At any rate, our joint dinner to the Royal
Personage gradually assumed the aspect of a yearly function. Indeed it
grew larger and larger, until it became a sort of closing function for the
season, at any rate as far as we were concerned.

   I don't in the least mean to say that we were the sort of persons who
aspired to mix "with royalty". We didn't; we hadn't any claims; we were
just "good people". But the Grand Duke was a pleasant, affable sort of
royalty, like the late King Edward VII, and it was pleasant to hear him
talk about the races and, very occasionally, as a bonne bouche,[2] about
his nephew the Emperor; or to have him pause for a moment in his
walk to ask after the progress of our cures or to be benignantly interested
in the amount of money we had put on Lelöffel's hunter for the Frankfurt Welter Stakes.

   But upon my word, I don't know how we put in our time. How does
one put in one's time? How is it possible to have achieved nine years
and to have nothing whatever to show for it? Nothing whatever you
understand. Not so much as a bone penholder, carved to resemble a
chessman and with a hole in the top through which you could see four
views of Nauheim. And, as for experience, as for knowledge of one's

---

1. A popular German mineral water with supposedly curative and digestive properties.
2. A treat; literally "a pleasant taste in the mouth" (French).

fellow beings—nothing either. Upon my word, I couldn't tell you off-hand whether the lady who sold the so expensive violets at the bottom of the road that leads to the station, was cheating me or no; I can't say whether the porter who carried our traps[3]* across the station at Leghorn was a thief or no when he said that the regular tariff was a lira* a parcel. The instances of honesty that one comes across in this world are just as amazing as the instances of dishonesty. After* forty-five years of mixing with one's kind, one ought to have acquired the habit of being able to know something about one's fellow beings. But one doesn't.

I think the modern civilised habit—the modern English habit of taking everyone for granted is a good deal to blame for this. I have observed this matter long enough to know the queer, subtle thing that it is; to know how the faculty, for what it is worth, never lets you down.*

Mind, I am not saying that this is not the most desirable type of life in the world; that it is not an almost unreasonably high standard. For it is really nauseating, when you detest it, to have to eat every day several slices of thin, tepid, pink india rubber,* and it is disagreeable to have to drink brandy when you would prefer to be cheered up by warm, sweet Kümmel.[4] And it is nasty to have to take a cold bath in the morning when what you want is really a hot one at night. And it stirs a little of the faith of your fathers that is deep down within you to have to have it taken for granted that you are an Episcopalian when really you are an old-fashioned Philadelphia Quaker.

But these things have to be done; it is the cock that the whole of this society owes to Æsculapius.[5]*

And the odd, queer thing is that the whole collection of rules applies to anybody—to the anybodies that you meet in hotels, in railway trains, to a less degree perhaps in steamers, but even, in the end, upon steamers. You meet a man or a woman and,* from tiny and intimate sounds, from the slightest of movements, you know at once whether you are concerned with good people or with those who won't do. You know that is to say, whether they will go rigidly through with the whole programme from the underdone beef to the Anglicanism. It won't matter whether they be short or tall; whether the voice squeak like a marionette or rumble like a town bull's; it won't* matter whether they are Germans, Austrians, French, Spanish, or even Brazilians—they will be the Germans or Brazilians who take a cold bath every morning and who move, roughly speaking, in diplomatic circles.

3. Baggage.
4. Sweet north German liqueur, flavored with cumin.
5. Greek, and later Roman, god of healing whose widespread cult was characterized by sacred snakes, baths, and a gymnasium for therapeutic treatment. Dowell is citing the last words of Socrates as imagined by Plato in the *Phaedo*: that he owed a cock, the traditional sacrifice for a cure, to Asclepius. According to a widely held view, Plato/Socrates meant that death was the supreme cure for life.

But the inconvenient—well hang it all I will say it—the damnable nuisance of the whole thing is, that with all the taking for granted, you never really get an inch deeper than the things I have catalogued.

I can give you a rather extraordinary instance of this. I can't remember whether it was in our first year—the first year of us four at Nauheim, because of course, it would have been the fourth year of Florence and myself—but it must have been in the first or second year. And that gives the measure at once of the extraordinariness of our discussion and of the swiftness with which intimacy had grown up between us. On the one hand we seemed to start out on the expedition so naturally and with so little preparation, that it was as if we must have made many such excursions before; and our intimacy seemed so deep. . . .

Yet the place to which we went was obviously one to which Florence at least would have wanted to take us quite early. So * you would almost think we should have gone there together at the beginning of our intimacy. Florence was singularly expert as a guide to archæological exceptions and there was nothing she liked so much as taking * people round ruins and showing you the window from which someone looked down upon the murder of someone else. She only did it once; but she did it quite magnificently. She could find her way, with the sole help of Baedeker,[6] as easily about any old monument as she could about any American city where the blocks are all square and the streets all numbered, so that you can go perfectly easily from Twenty-fourth to Thirtieth.

Now it happens that fifty minutes away from Nauheim, by a good train is the ancient city of M——,[7] upon a great pinnacle of basalt, girt with a triple road running sideways up its shoulder like a scarf. And at the top there is a castle—not a square castle like Windsor—but a castle all slate gables and high peaks with gilt weathercocks flashing bravely— the castle of St. Elizabeth of Hungary.[8] It has the disadvantage of being in Prussia; and it is always disagreeable to go into that country;[9] but it is

6. The most popular tourist guidebook, still in use in the 20th century.
7. Marburg: Prussian university city, original capital of Hessen, and ancient seat of learning where in 1529 Luther and Zwingli debated transubstantiation in the Schloss (Castle) under the patronage of the Landgrave, Philip the Magnanimous. Nauheim is c. 35 miles north. Ford and Violet Hunt stayed at Marburg in 1910 while he was trying to secure a German divorce from Elsie.
8. Hungarian saint (1207–1231); she built a hospital in Marburg; canonized (1235) for her care of the poor and sick. Above the site of her grave the Teutonic Knights erected the earliest purely Gothic building on German soil, Elisabethkirche. This and the Schloss towering above it are the two outstanding architectural features of the city, symbolizing the religious rift of the Reformation. The "castle of St. Elizabeth" is a misnomer: the present castle was not built in her time. Married to Ludwig IV, Landgrave of Thuringia (most of the territory of Hessen) in 1221, she first lived unhappily as an aristocrat in the Wartburg above Eisenach, then after Ludwig's death, came to Marburg (1228), where she became a Franciscan nun and turned her back on courtly splendor. It was her cult, formerly the chief attraction of the city as a major pilgrimage center, which Philip the Magnanimous abolished in 1527 by establishing the University, the first in the world to be subject to the Protestant faith.
9. Before World War I, Germany stretched from Alsace-Lorraine to part of modern Poland and included as two-thirds of its land-mass the kingdom of Prussia. Dowell's remarks (like Ford's until 1915) are pro-German and anti-Prussian; Germany is associated with the arts, Prussia

very old and there are many double-spired churches and it stands up like a pyramid out of the green valley of the Lahn. I don't suppose the Ashburnhams wanted especially to go there and I didn't especially want to go there myself. But, you understand, there was no objection. * It was part of the cure to make an excursion three or four times a week. So that we were all quite unanimous in being grateful to Florence for providing the motive power. Florence, of course, had a motive of her own. She was at that time engaged in educating Captain Ashburnham—oh, of course, quite pour le bon motif![1] She used to say to Leonora: "I simply can't understand how you can let him live by your side and be so ignorant!" Leonora herself always struck me as being remarkably well educated. At any rate she knew beforehand all that Florence had to tell her. Perhaps she got it up out of Baedeker before Florence was up in the morning. I don't mean to say that you would ever have known that Leonora knew anything, but if Florence started to tell us how Ludwig the Courageous[2] wanted to have three wives at once—in which he differed from Henry VIII who wanted them one after the other, and this caused a good deal of trouble—if Florence started to tell us this, Leonora would just nod her head in a way that quite pleasantly rattled my poor wife.

She used to exclaim: "Well if you knew it, why haven't you told it all already to Captain Ashburnham? I'm sure he finds it interesting!" And Leonora would look reflectively at her husband and say: "I have an idea that it might injure his hand—the hand, you know, used in connection with horses' mouths. . . ." And poor Ashburnham would blush and mutter and would say: "That's all right. Don't you bother about me." *

I fancy his wife's irony did quite alarm poor Teddy; because one evening he asked me seriously in the smoking-room if I thought that having too much in one's head would really interfere with one's quickness in polo. It struck him, he said, that brainy Johnnies generally were rather muffs[3] when they got on to four legs. I reassured him as best I could. I told him that he wasn't likely to take in enough to upset his balance. At that time the Captain was quite evidently enjoying being educated by Florence. She used to do it about three or four times a week under the approving eyes of Leonora and myself. It wasn't, you understand, systematic. It came in bursts. It was Florence clearing up one of the dark

---

with totalitarian militarism. In the **MS**, Dowell expresses equal loathing of Belgium, in keeping with Conrad's attack on its rapacious imperialism in *Heart of Darkness* (1899, 1902). These asides were cut, presumably when the Kaiser's unprovoked invasion of Belgium sparked off the war. See pp. 34, n. 4 and 38, n. 1 below.

1. With the best intentions (French).
2. Presumably Ludwig IV (see p. 32, n. 8 above), who died of plague on his way to fight the Sixth Crusade. Dowell is in fact referring to Landgrave Philip the Magnanimous (see p. 32, n. 8 above), a pious man who reputedly had three testicles and an insatiable sexual appetite. His study in the Schloss had two doors: one leading to the chapel and the other to the bedroom. Luther allowed him a dispensation bigamously to marry a second (not a third) wife.
3. Those awkward or clumsy at sports; generally: duffers, failures, or bunglers.

places of the earth,[4] leaving the world a little lighter than she had found
it. She would tell him the story of Hamlet; explain the form of a sym-
phony, humming the first and second subjects to him, and so on; she
would explain to him the difference between Armenians and Erastians;[5]
or she would give him a short lecture on the early history of the United
States. And it was done in a way well calculated to arrest a young attention. Did you ever read Mrs. Markham?[6] Well, it was like that. . . .

But our excursion to M—— was a much larger, a much more full
dress affair. You see, in the archives of the Schloss[7] in that city there
was a document which Florence thought would finally give her the
chance to educate the whole lot of us together. It really worried poor
Florence that she couldn't, in matters of culture, ever get the better of
Leonora. I don't know what Leonora knew or what she didn't know
but certainly she was always there whenever Florence brought out any
information. And she gave somehow, the impression of really knowing
what poor Florence gave the impression of having only picked up. I
can't exactly define it. It was almost something physical. Have you ever
seen a retriever dashing in play after a greyhound? You see the two
running over a green field, almost side by side, and suddenly the
retriever makes a friendly snap at the other. And the greyhound simply
isn't there. You haven't observed it quicken its speed or strain a limb;
but there it is, just two yards in front of the retriever's outstretched muzzle. So it was with Florence and Leonora in matters of culture.

But on this occasion I knew that something was up. I found Florence
some days before, reading books like Ranke's *History of the Popes*,
Symonds' *Renaissance*, Motley's *Rise of the Dutch Republic*, and
Luther's *Table Talk*.[8]

I must say that, until the astonishment came, I got nothing but pleasure out of the little expedition. I like catching the two-forty; I like the
slow, smooth roll of the great big trains—and they are the best trains in
the world! I like being drawn through the green country and looking at

---

4. Cf. p. 32, n. 9 above. Dowell's words contain a buried quotation from *Heart of Darkness*:
    " 'And this also,' said Marlow suddenly, 'has been one of the dark places of the earth.' "
    Marlow refers to Britain before the Roman conquest.
5. Developers of the teachings of Thomas Erastus (Liebler) (1524–1583), Swiss physician and
    theologian who maintained the theory of the supremacy of the State in ecclesiastical affairs.
    "Arminians": followers of the teachings of James Arminius of Harmensen (1560–1609), Dutch
    Protestant theologian who opposed Calvin, especially regarding predestination, which the Ar-
    minians believed to be conditional, the Calvinists absolute.
6. Pseudonym of Mrs. Elizabeth Penrose (1730–1837), writer of superficial history books for
    children. Dowell continually denigrates Florence's intellectual powers. See p. 17, nn. 2 and
    3 above.
7. German castle.
8. Leopold von Ranke, *The Ecclesiastical and Political History of the Popes of Rome During the
    Sixteenth and Seventeenth Centuries* (tr. from German text of vol. 2–4 of *Fursten und Volker
    von Sud-Europa* by S. Austin, 3 vol., 1840); John Addington Symonds, *The Renaissance in
    Italy* (7 vol., 1875–76)]; John Lothrop Motley, *The Rise of the Dutch Republic* (3 vol., 1856);
    Martin Luther, *The Table Talk Or Familiar Discourses of Martin Luther* (1566; tr. W. Hazlitt,
    1848). All classic works, they would provide Florence with a survey of views on the art and
    theology of Marburg.

it through the clear glass of the great windows. Though of course the country isn't really green. The sun shines, the earth is blood red and purple and red and green and red. And the oxen in the ploughlands are bright varnished brown and black and blackish purple; and the peasants are dressed in the black and white of magpies; and there are great flocks of magpies too. Or the peasants' dresses in another field where there are little mounds of hay that will be grey-green on the sunny side and purple in the shadows—the peasants' dresses are vermilion with emerald green ribbons and purple skirts and white shirts and black velvet stomachers.[9] Still, the impression is that you are drawn through brilliant green meadows that run away on each side to the dark purple fir-woods; the basalt pinnacles; the immense forests. And there is meadow-sweet[1] at the edge of the streams and cattle. Why, I remember on that afternoon I saw a brown cow hitch its horns under the stomach of a black and white animal and the black and white one was thrown right into the middle of a narrow stream. I burst out laughing. But Florence was imparting information so hard and Leonora was listening so intently that no one noticed me. As* for me, I was pleased to be off duty; I was pleased to think that Florence for the moment was indubitably out of mischief— because she was talking about Ludwig the Courageous (I think it was Ludwig the Courageous but I am not an historian) about Ludwig the Courageous of Hessen who wanted to have three wives at once and patronised Luther—something like that!—I was so relieved to be off duty, because she couldn't possibly be doing anything to excite herself or set her poor heart a-fluttering—that the incident of the cow was a real joy to me. I chuckled over it from time to time for the whole rest of the day. Because it does look very funny you know to see a black and white cow land on its back in the middle of a stream. It is so just exactly what one doesn't expect of a cow.

I suppose I ought to have pitied the poor animal; but I just didn't. I was out for enjoyment. And I just enjoyed myself. It is so pleasant to be drawn along in front of the spectacular town* with the peaked castle and the many double spires. In the sunlight gleams come from the city—gleams from the glass of windows; from the gilt signs of apothecaries; from the ensigns of the student corps[2] high up in the mountains; from the helmets of the funny little soldiers moving their stiff little legs in white linen trousers. And it was pleasant to get out in the great big spectacular Prussian station with the hammered bronze ornaments and the paintings of peasants and flowers and cows[3]; and to hear Florence

9. Either a man's waistcoat or a woman's ornamental chest covering. Dowell could be describing the female (dresses, ribbons) and the male (shirts, stomachers) peasants' clothes here.
1. Wild flower with dense, creamy-white, highly fragrant blossoms.
2. Fraternity houses, usually for the richer students.
3. Ford/Dowell appears to be confusing Marburg's station (a modest building erected in the year he visited the city, 1910) with that of Wiesbaden.

bargain energetically with the driver of an ancient droschka[4] drawn by two lean horses. Of course I spoke German much more correctly than Florence though I never could rid myself quite of the accent of the Pennsylvania Duitsch[5] of my childhood. Anyhow we were drawn in a sort of triumph, for five marks without any trinkgeld,[6] right up to the castle. And we were taken through the museum and saw the firebacks,[7] the old glass, the old swords and the antique contraptions. And we went up winding corkscrew staircases and through the Rittersaal, the great painted hall where the Reformer[8] and his friends met for the first time under the protection of the gentleman that had three wives at once and formed an alliance with the gentleman that had six wives one after the other (I'm not really interested in these facts but they have a bearing on my story). And we went through chapels, and music rooms, right up immensely high in the air to a large old chamber, full of presses,[9] with heavily-shuttered windows all round. And Florence became positively electric. She told the tired, bored custodian what shutters to open; so that the bright sunlight streamed in palpable shafts into the dim old chamber. She explained that this was Luther's bedroom[1] and that just where the sunlight fell had stood his bed. As a matter of fact I believe that she was wrong and that Luther only stopped, as it were, for lunch, in order to evade pursuit. But no doubt it would have been his bedroom if he could have been persuaded to stop the night. And then, in spite of the protest of the custodian, she threw open another shutter and came tripping back to a large glass case.

"And there," she exclaimed with an accent of gaiety, of triumph and of audacity. She was pointing at a piece of paper, like the half-sheet of a letter with some faint pencil scrawls that might have been a jotting of the amounts we were spending during the day. And I was extremely happy at her gaiety, in her triumph, in her audacity. Captain Ashburnham had his hands * upon the glass case. "There it is—the Protest."[2]

---

4. Small four-wheeled carriage for hire as taxi.
5. Descendants of 18th-century German immigrants who maintain the Calvinist tradition. As Grover Smith points out (Biographical and Critical Commentary, pp. 326–27 below), Ford uses the wrong word (it should be "Dutch").
6. Tip, gratuity; literally: "drink money."
7. Ornamental metal plates forming the back surface of a fireplace, usually in cast iron.
8. Martin Luther (1483–1546), in early manhood an Augustinian monk, the biblical scholar and translator responsible for the initial Protestant revolt from the Roman Catholic Church when he nailed his ninety-five theses to the Schlosskirche doors at Wittenberg on October 31, 1517, attacking the corrupt sale of papal indulgences. Myth inaccurately suggested that he and the other clerics (see n. 2 below) held their Colloquy in the Rittersaal (see p. 37, n. 4 below). The murals Ford saw there in 1910 were Shafer's late 19th-century fakes, now removed.
9. Recessed, shelved cupboards for storing clothes, books, and the like.
1. Luther stayed one night in the town and three in the Schloss as guest of Philip the Magnanimous (see p. 33, n. 2 above). No one knows (or knew in Ford's time) in which room he slept.
2. This formal declaration of dissent from the decision of the Diet of Spires (1529, which forebade further religious innovation and affirmed the edict of the Diet of Worms [1521], excommunicating Luther) was made by a group of German princes and free cities. The document which Ford took Violet Hunt to see in 1910, and to which Dowell/Florence presumably refer, was

And then, as we all properly stage-managed our bewilderment, she continued: "Don't you know that is why we were all called Protestants? That is the pencil draft of the Protest they drew up. You can see the signatures of Martin Luther, and Martin Bucer, and Zwingli,[3] and Ludwig the Courageous. . . ."

I may have got some of the names wrong, but I know that Luther and Bucer were there.•And her animation continued and I was glad. She was better and she was out of mischief. She continued looking up into Captain Ashburnham's eyes: "It's because of that piece of paper that you're honest, sober, industrious, provident, and clean-lived. If it weren't for that piece of paper you'd be like the Irish or the Italians or the Poles, but particularly the Irish. . . ."

And she laid one finger upon Captain Ashburnham's wrist.

I* was aware of something treacherous, something frightful, something evil in the day. I can't define it and can't find a simile for it. It wasn't as if a snake had looked out of a hole. No, it was as if my heart had missed a beat. It was as if we were going to run and cry out; all four of us in separate directions, averting our heads. In Ashburnham's face I know that there was absolute panic. I was horribly frightened and then I discovered that the pain in my left wrist was caused by Leonora's clutching it:

"I can't stand this," she said with a most extraordinary passion; "I must get out of this."

I was horribly frightened.•It came to me for a moment, though I hadn't time to think it, that she must be a madly jealous woman—jealous of Florence and Captain Ashburnham, of all people in the world! And it was a panic in which we fled! We went right down the winding stairs, across the immense Rittersaal[4] to a little terrace that overlooks the Lahn, the broad valley and the immense plain into which it opens out.

"Don't you see?" she said, "don't you see what's going on?" The panic again stopped my heart. I muttered, I stuttered—I don't know how I got the words out:

---

not the Protest but the fifteen-point doctrinal statement (the "protocol") drawn up at the Marburg Colloquy (1529). This represents agreement on all points but the last: the interpretation of the Eucharist (see n. 3 below). It is not the "half-sheet of a letter with some faint pencil scrawls" but a large, clearly copied document in ink (see illustrations, pp. 170–71), signed by Luther, Bucer, and Zwingli, among others, but not by Ludwig the Courageous, who had been dead for three hundred years.

3. Huldreich Zwingli (1484–1531), Swiss Protestant leader, more liberal than Luther, who opposed Luther's literalist interpretation of the Eucharist as the actual body and blood of Christ, preferring to see the bread and wine as sign or metaphor. Luther supposedly prepared for the confrontation by chalking "This is" (Words of Institution in Eucharistic prayers: "This is my body . . .") in Greek on the tabletop beneath the cloth. At the crucial moment he pulled back the cloth and pointed to the words, a scene depicted inaccurately in a 19th-century painting. Martin Bucer (1491–1551), German Protestant who negotiated differences of opinion between the followers of Luther and of Zwingli.

4. State room; literally, "knights' room," although it never had a military function.

"No! What's the matter? Whatever's the matter?"

She looked me straight in the eyes; and for a moment I had the feeling that those two blue discs were immense, were overwhelming, were like a wall of blue that shut me off from the rest of the world. I know it sounds absurd; but that is what it did feel like.

"Don't you see," she said, with a really horrible bitterness, with a really horrible lamentation in her voice.* "Don't you see that that's the cause of the whole miserable affair; of the whole sorrow of the world? * And of the eternal damnation of you and me and them. . . ."

I don't remember how she went on; I was too frightened; I was too amazed. I think I was thinking of running to fetch assistance—a doctor perhaps, or Captain Ashburnham. Or possibly she needed Florence's tender care, though of course it would have been very bad for Florence's heart. But I know that when I came out of it she was saying: "Oh where are all the bright, happy, innocent beings in the world? Where's happiness? One reads of it in books!"

She ran her hand with a singular clawing motion upwards over her forehead. Her eyes were enormously distended; her face was exactly that of a person looking into the pit of hell and seeing horrors there. And then suddenly she stopped. She was most amazingly, just Mrs. Ashburnham again. Her face was perfectly clear, sharp and defined; her hair was glorious in its golden coils. Her nostrils twitched with a sort of contempt. She appeared to look with interest at a gypsy caravan that was coming over a little bridge far below us.

"Don't you know," she said, in her clear hard voice, "don't you know that I'm an Irish Catholic?" *

V *

Those words gave me the greatest relief that I have ever had in my life. They told me, I think, almost more than I have ever gathered at any one moment—about myself. I don't think that before that day I had ever wanted anything very much except Florence. I have of course had appetites, impatiences . . . Why, sometimes at a table d'hôte when there would be, say, caviare handed round, I have been absolutely full of impatience for fear that when the dish came to me there should not be a satisfying portion left over by the other guests. I have been exceedingly impatient at missing trains. The Belgian State Railway has a trick of letting the French trains miss their connections at Brussels. That has [1] * always infuriated me. I have written about it letters to *The Times* that

---

1. **MS** [83; [80]] and **TS** [5[2]\3/]: [pencil]: "Brussels. The Belgian Government does this on purpose so as to force passengers to travel by way of Ostend rather than by Calais. It is a mean, dirty trick, typical of the Belgians; and it has"; **SPC** excision removes Dowell's prejudice against Belgians. See p. 32, n. 9 above.

The Times never printed; those that I wrote to the Paris edition of the *New York Herald* * were always printed, but they never seemed to satisfy me when I saw them. Well, that was a sort of frenzy with me. . . . *

It was a frenzy that now I can hardly realise. I can understand it intellectually. You see, in those days I was interested in people with "hearts". There was Florence, there was Edward Ashburnham—or perhaps it was Leonora that I was more interested in. I don't mean in the way of love. But, you see, we were both of the same profession—at any rate as I saw it. And the profession was that of keeping heart patients alive.

You have no idea how engrossing such a profession may become. Just as the blacksmith says: "By hammer and hand all Art doth stand"; just as the baker thinks that all the solar system revolves around his morning delivery of rolls; as the postmaster general believes that he alone is the preserver of society—and surely, surely, these delusions are necessary to keep us going—so did I and, as I believed, Leonora, imagine that the whole world ought to be arranged so as to ensure the keeping alive of heart patients. You have no idea how engrossing such a profession may become—how imbecile, in view of that engrossment, appear the ways of princes, of republics, of municipalities. A rough bit of road beneath the motor tyres, a couple of succeeding "thank'ee-marms"[2] with their quick jolts would be enough to set me grumbling to Leonora against the Prince or the Grand Duke or the Free City[3] through whose territory we might be passing. I would grumble like * a stockbroker whose conversations over the telephone are incommoded by the ringing of bells from a city church. I would talk about mediæval survivals, about the taxes being surely high enough. The point, by the way, about the missing of the connections of the Calais boat trains at Brussels was that the shortest possible sea journey is frequently of great importance to sufferers from the heart. Now, on the Continent, there are two special heart cure places, Nauheim and Spa,[4] and to reach both of these baths from England * if in order to ensure a short sea passage, you come by Calais— you have to make the connection at Brussels. And the Belgian train never waits by so much of * the shade of a second for the one coming from Calais or from Paris. And even if the French trains are just on time, you have to run—imagine a heart patient running!—along the unfamiliar * ways of the Brussels station and to scramble up the high steps of the moving train. Or, if you miss the connection, you have to wait five or six hours. . . . * I used to keep awake whole nights cursing that abuse. *

---

2. Potholes or bumps in road.
3. Bremen, Hamburg, or Lubeck: sovereign states within Germany. The princes of the Free Cities were leading Reformation figures. See p. 36, n. 2 above.
4. The original "spa" town, in southeast Belgium, c. twenty miles southwest of Liège, famous for its curative mineral springs.

My wife used to run—she never, in whatever else she may have misled me, tried* to give me the impression that she was not a gallant soul. But once in the German Express she would lean back, with one hand to her side and her eyes closed. Well, she was a good actress. And I would be in hell. In hell, I tell you. For in Florence I had at once a wife and an unattained mistress—that is what it comes to—and in the retaining of her in this world I had my occupation, my career, my ambition. It is not often that these things are united in one body.* Leonora was a good actress too. By Jove she was good! I tell you, she would listen to me by the hour, evolving my plans for a shock-proof world. It is true that, at times I used to notice about her face an air of inattention as if she were listening, a mother, to the child at her knee, or as if, precisely, I were myself the patient.

You understand that there was nothing the matter with Edward Ashburnham's heart—that he had thrown up his commission and had left India and come half the world over in order to follow a woman who had really had a "heart" to Nauheim. That was the sort of sentimental ass he was. For, you understand too that they really needed to live in India, to economise, to let the house at Bramshaw* Teleragh.

Of course, at that date, I had never heard of the Kilsyte case. Ashburnham had, you know, kissed a servant girl in a railway train and it was only the grace of God, the prompt functioning of the communication cord and the ready sympathy of what I believe you call the Hampshire bench, that kept the poor devil out of Winchester Gaol for years and years. I never heard of that case until the final stages of Leonora's revelations. . . .

But just think of that poor wretch. . . . I who have surely the right, beg you to think of that poor wretch. Is it possible that such a luckless devil should be so tormented by blind and inscrutable destiny? For there is no other way to think of it. None. I have the right to say it, since for years he was my wife's lover, since he killed her, since he broke up all the pleasantnesses that there were in my life. There is no priest that has the right to tell me that I must not ask pity for him, from you, silent listener beyond the hearthstone, from the world, or from the God who created in him those desires, those madnesses. . . .

Of course I should not hear of the Kilsyte case. I knew none of their friends; they were for me just good people—fortunate people with broad and sunny acres in a southern county. Just good people. By Heavens, I sometimes think that it would have been better for him, poor dear, if the case had been such a one that I must needs have heard of it—such a one as maids and couriers and other Kur guests whisper about for years after until gradually it dies away in the pity that there is knocking about here and there in the world. Supposing he had spent his seven years in Winchester Gaol or whatever it is that inscrutable and blind justice allots to you for following your natural but ill-timed inclinations—there would have arrived a stage when nodding gossips on the Kursaal[5] terrace would have said "Poor fellow", thinking of his * ruined career. He would have been the fine soldier with his back now bent. . . . Better for him, poor devil, if his back had been prematurely bent.

Why, it would have been a thousand times better.* . . . For of course the Kilsyte case, which came at the very beginning of his finding Leonora cold and unsympathetic gave him a nasty jar. He left servants alone after that.

It turned him, naturally, all the more loose amongst women of his own class. Why, Leonora told me that Mrs. Maidan—the woman he followed from Burma to Nauheim—assured her he awakened her attention by swearing that when he kissed the servant in the train he was driven to it. I daresay he was driven to it, by the mad passion to find an ultimately satisfying woman. I daresay he was sincere enough. Heaven help me. I daresay he was sincere enough in his love for Mrs. Maidan. She was a nice * little thing, a dear little dark woman with long lashes, of whom Florence grew quite fond. She had a lisp and a happy smile. We saw plenty of her for the first month of our acquaintance, then she died, quite quietly—of heart trouble.*

But you know, poor little Mrs. Maidan. She was so gentle, so young. She cannot have been more than twenty-three and she had a boy husband out in Chitral[6] not more than twenty-four, I believe. Such young things ought to have been left alone. Of course Ashburnham could not leave her alone. I do not believe that he could. Why even I, at this distance of time am aware that I am a little in love with her memory. I can't help smiling when I think suddenly of her—as you might at the thought of something wrapped carefully away in lavender, in some drawer, in some old house that you have long left. She was so—so submissive. Why, even to me she had the air of being submissive—to me that not the youngest child will ever pay heed to. Yes, this is the saddest story. . . .

No, I cannot help wishing that Florence had left her alone—with her playing with adultery * I suppose it was; though she was such a child that one has the impression that she would hardly have known how to spell such a word. No, it was just submissiveness—to the importunities, to the tempestuous forces that pushed that miserable fellow on to ruin. And I do not suppose that Florence really made much difference. If it had not been for her that Ashburnham left his allegiance for Mrs. Maidan, then it would have been some other woman. But still, I do not

5. Literally "cure hall," the visitors' grand public building at German health resorts and the focus of social life of the Kurpark. See p. 11, n. 3 above.
6. Remote outpost in mountainous country on the northwest frontier of what was then British India and is now Pakistan, close to the Afghanistan border, c. 120 miles north of the Khyber Pass.

know. Perhaps the poor young thing would have died—she was bound to die anyhow quite soon—but she would have died without having to soak her noonday pillow with tears whilst Florence, below the window talked to Captain Ashburnham about the Constitution of the United States. . . . Yes, it would have left a better taste in the mouth if Florence had let her die in peace. . . .

Leonora behaved better in a sense. She just boxed Mrs. Maidan's ears—yes, she hit her, in an uncontrollable access of rage, a hard blow on the side of the cheek, in the corridor of the hotel, outside Edward's room. It was that, you know, that accounted for the sudden, odd intimacy that sprang up between Florence and Mrs. Ashburnham.

Because it was, of course, an odd intimacy. If you look at it from the outside nothing could have been more unlikely than that Leonora, who is the proudest creature on God's earth, would have struck up an acquaintanceship with two casual Yankees whom she could not really have regarded as being much more than a carpet beneath her feet. You may ask what she had to be proud of. Well she was a Powys married to an Ashburnham—I suppose that gave her the right to despise casual Americans as long as she did it unostentatiously. I don't know what anyone has to be proud of. She might have taken pride in her patience, in her keeping her husband out of* the bankruptcy court. Perhaps she did.

At any rate that was how Florence got to know her. She came round a screen at the corner of the hotel corridor and found Leonora with the gold key that hung from her wrist caught in Mrs. Maidan's hair just before dinner. There was not a single word spoken. Little Mrs. Maidan was very pale, with a red mark* down her left cheek and the key would not come out of her black hair. It was Florence who had to disentangle it, for Leonora was in such a state that she could not have brought herself to touch Mrs. Maidan without growing sick.

And there was not a word spoken. You see, under those four eyes— her own and Mrs. Maidan's—Leonora could just let herself go as far as to box Mrs. Maidan's ears. But the moment a stranger came along she pulled herself wonderfully up. She was at first silent and then, the moment the key was disengaged by Florence she was in a state to say: "So awkward of me. . . . I was just trying to put the comb straight in Mrs. Maidan's hair. . . ."

Mrs. Maidan however was not a Powys married to an Ashburnham; she was a poor little O'Flaherty whose husband was a boy of country parsonage origin. So there was no mistaking the sob that she let go as she went desolately away along the corridor. But Leonora was still going to play up. She opened the door of Ashburnham's room quite ostentatiously so that Florence should hear her address Edward in terms of intimacy and liking. "Edward," she called [in].* But there was no Edward there.

You understand that there was no Edward there. It was then, for the only time of her career that Leonora really compromised herself—She exclaimed: "How frightful! . . . Poor little Maisie! . . . ." *

She caught herself up at that, but of course it was too late. It was a queer sort of affair. . . .

I want to do Leonora every justice. I love her very dearly for one thing and in this matter, which was certainly the ruin of my small household cockleshell, she certainly tripped up. I do not believe—and Leonora herself does not believe that poor [dear] * little Maisie Maidan was ever Edward's mistress. Her * heart was really so bad that she would have succumbed to anything like an impassioned embrace. That is the plain English of it, and I suppose plain English is best. She was really what the other two, for reasons of their own just pretended to be. Queer, isn't it? Like one of those sinister jokes that Providence plays upon one. Add to this that I do not suppose that Leonora would much have minded, at any other moment, if Mrs. Maidan had been her husband's mistress. It might have been a relief from Edward's sentimental gurglings over the lady and from the lady's submissive acceptance of those sounds. No, she would not have minded.

But, in boxing Mrs. Maidan's ears Leonora was just striking the face of an intolerable universe. For, that afternoon she had had a frightfully painful scene with Edward.

As far as his letters went she claimed the right to open them when she chose. She arrogated to herself that right because Edward's affairs were in such a frightful state and he lied so about them that she claimed the privilege of having his secrets at her disposal. There was not, indeed, any other way, for the poor fool was too ashamed of his lapses ever to make a clean breast of anything. She had to drag these things out of him.

It must have been a pretty elevating job for her. But that afternoon, Edward being on his bed for the hour and a half prescribed by the Kur authorities, she had opened a letter that she took to come from a Colonel Hervey. They were going to stay with him in Linlithgowshire[7] for the month of September and she did not know whether the date fixed would be the eleventh or the eighteenth. The address on this letter was, in handwriting, as like Colonel Hervey's as one blade of corn is like another. So she had at the moment no idea of spying on him.

But she certainly was. For she discovered that Edward Ashburnham was paying a blackmailer of whom she had never heard something like three hundred pounds a year. . . . It was a devil of a blow; it was like death; for she imagined that by that time she had really got to the bottom of her husband's liabilities. You see, they were pretty heavy. What had really smashed them up had been a perfectly commonplace affair at

7. Scottish county, former name of West Lothian.

Monte Carlo—an affair with a cosmopolitan harpy who passed for the mistress of a Russian Grand Duke. She exacted a twenty[*] thousand pound pearl tiara from him as the price of her favours for a week or so. It would have pipped[8] him a good deal to have found so much, and he was not in the ordinary way a gambler. He might indeed just have found the twenty thousand and the not slight charges of a week at an hotel with the fair creature. He must have been worth at that date five hundred thousand dollars[9] and a little over.

Well, he must needs go to the tables and lose forty thousand pounds[1]. . . . Forty thousand solid pounds, borrowed from sharks! And even after that he must—it was an imperative passion—enjoy the favours of the lady. He got them, of course, when it was a matter of solid bargaining, for far less than twenty thousand, as he might no doubt have done from the first. I daresay ten thousand dollars covered the bill.

Anyhow, there was a pretty solid hole in a fortune of a hundred thousand pounds or so. And Leonora had to fix things up; he would have run from money-lender to money-lender. And that was quite in the early days of her discovery of his infidelities—if you like to call them infidelities. And she discovered that one from public sources. God knows what would have happened if she had not discovered it from public sources. I suppose he would have concealed it from her until they were penniless. But she was able, by the grace of God, to get hold of the actual lenders of the money, to learn the exact sums that were needed. And she went off to England.

Yes, she went right off to England to her attorney and his while he was still in the arms of his Circe—at Antibes,[2] to which place they had retired. He got sick of the lady quite quickly, but not before Leonora had had such lessons in the art of business from her attorney that she had her plan as clearly drawn up as was ever that of General Trochu[3] for keeping the Prussians out of Paris in 1870.[*] It was about as effectual at first, or it seemed so.

That would have been, you know, in 1895,[*] about nine years before the date of which I am talking—the date of Florence's getting her hold over Leonora; for that was what it amounted to. . . . Well, Mrs. Ashburnham had simply forced Edward to settle all his property upon her. She could force him to do anything; in his clumsy, good-natured, inarticulate way he was as frightened of her as of the devil. And he admired her enormously, and he was as fond of her as any man could be of any

---

8. Financially embarrassed, hurt.
9. About £100,000 then, c. $7,500,000 or £5,000,000 now.
1. About $200,000 then, c. $3,000,000 or £2,000,000 now.
2. Fashionable French resort on the Côte d'Azur between Nice and Cannes. "Circe": goddess and sorceress in Homer's *Odyssey* who changes Odysseus's men into pigs. Unlike Ashburnham, Odysseus resists her spells and lives with her for a year, after which she advises him on his visit to the Underworld and his return home to Penelope.
3. Governor of Paris during the Franco-Prussian War when Prussians took the city.

woman. She took advantage of it to treat him as if he had been* a person whose estates are being managed by the court of bankruptcy. I suppose it was the best thing for him.

Anyhow she had no end of a job for the first three years or so. Unexpected liabilities kept on cropping up*—and that afflicted fool did not make it any easier. You see, along with the passion of the chase went a frame of mind that made him be extraordinarily ashamed of himself. You may not believe it, but he really had such a sort of respect for the chastity of Leonora's imagination that he hated—he was positively revolted at the thought that she should know that the sort of thing that he did existed in the world. So he would stick out in an agitated way against the accusation of ever having done anything. He wanted to preserve the virginity of his wife's thoughts. He told me that himself during the long talks we had at the last—while the girl was on the way to Brindisi.[4]

So of course, for those three years or so, Leonora had many agitations. And it was then that they really quarrelled.

Yes,[5]* they quarrelled bitterly. That seems rather extravagant. You might have thought that Leonora would be just calmly loathing and he lachrymosely contrite. But that was not it a bit. . . . Along with Edward's passions and his shame for them went the violent conviction of the duties of his station—a conviction that was quite unreasonably expensive. I trust I have not, in talking of his liabilities, given the impression that poor Edward was a promiscuous libertine. He was not; he was a sentimentalist. The servant girl in the Kilsyte case had been pretty, but mournful of appearance. I think that, when he had kissed her, he had desired rather to comfort her. And, if she had succumbed to his blandishments I daresay he would have set her up in a little house in Portsmouth or Winchester and would have been faithful to her for four or five years. He was quite capable of that.

No, the only two of his affairs of the heart that cost him money were that of the Grand Duke's mistress and that which was the subject of the blackmailing letter that Leonora opened. That had been a quite passionate affair with quite a nice woman. It had succeeded the one with the Grand Ducal Lady. The lady was the wife of a brother officer and Leonora had known all about the passion, which had been quite a real passion and had lasted for several years. You see, poor Edward's passions were quite logical in their progression upwards. They began with a servant, went on to a courtesan and then to a quite nice woman, very unsuitably mated. For she had a quite nasty husband who, by means of letters and things went on blackmailing poor Edward to the tune of three or four hundred a year—with threats of the divorce court. And, after

4. Italian port on the Adriatic coast of Italy.
5. Beginning of TS insertion reducing Ashburnham's libertinage. See MDATV, p. 201, 45, 3rd entry below.

this lady came Maisie Maidan, and after poor Maisie only one more affair and then—the real passion of his life. His marriage with Leonora had been arranged by his parents and, though he always admired her immensely, he had hardly ever pretended* to be much more than tender to her, though he desperately needed her moral support, too. . . .

But his really trying liabilities were mostly in the nature of generosities proper to his station. He was, according to Leonora,* always remitting his tenants' rents and giving the tenants to understand that the reductions would be permanent; he was always redeeming drunkards who came before his magisterial bench; he was always trying to put prostitutes into respectable places—and he was a perfect maniac about children. I don't know how many [little]* ill-used people he did not pick up and provide with careers—Leonora has told me, but I daresay she exaggerated and* the figure seems so preposterous that I will not put it down. All these things, and the continuance of them seemed to him to be his duty—along with impossible subscriptions to hospitals and boy scouts and to provide prizes at cattle shows* and anti-vivisection societies. . . .

Well, Leonora saw to it that most of these things were not continued. They could not possibly keep up Bramshaw Manor at that rate after the money had gone to the Grand Duke's mistress.* She put* the rents back at their old figures; discharged the drunkards from their Homes, and sent all the Societies* notice that they were to expect no more subscriptions. To* the children she was more tender; nearly all of them she supported till the age of apprenticeship or domestic service. You see, she was childless herself.[6]*

She was childless herself and she considered herself to be to blame. She had come of a penniless branch of the Powys family and they had forced her upon poor dear Edward without making the stipulation that the children should be brought up as Catholics. And that, of course was spiritual death to Leonora. I have given you a wrong impression if I have not made you see that Leonora was a woman of a strong, cold conscience, like all English Catholics. (I cannot, myself, help disliking this religion; there is always, at the bottom of my mind, in spite of Leonora, the feeling of shuddering at the Scarlet Woman,[7] that filtered in upon me in the tranquillity of the little old Friends' Meeting House in Arch* Street,[8] Philadelphia.) So I do set down a good deal of Leonora's mismanagement of poor dear Edward's case to the peculiarly English form of her religion. Because of course, the only thing to have done for

---

6. **MS** [93; 88b]: end of TS (ribbon-copy) insertion, followed by long deletion [94; 88c] removing references to Ashburnham's various illegitimate children and their mothers whom "he ruined" See p. 45, n. 5 above. See MDATV, p. 201, 46, 10th entry below.

7. Abusive epithet for the Roman Catholic Church taken from Revelation 17.1–18, which describes the great whore of Babylon as "clothed in purple and scarlet."

8. The Meeting House in Arch Street, the largest in the world, is the oldest one still in use in Philadelphia (Moser 302).

Edward would have been to let him sink down until he became a tramp
of gentlemanly address, having, maybe, chance love-affairs[9]* upon the
highways. He would have done so much less harm, he would have been
much less agonised too. At any rate, he would have had fewer chances
of ruining and of remorse. For Edward was great at remorse.

But Leonora's English Catholic conscience, her rigid principles, her
coldness, even her very patience, were, I cannot help thinking, all
wrong in this special case. She quite seriously and naïvely imagined that
the Church of Rome disapproves of divorce; she quite seriously and
naïvely believed that her church could be such a monstrous and imbecile institution as to expect her to take on the impossible job of making
Edward Ashburnham a faithful husband.* She had, as the English
would say, the Nonconformist[1] temperament. In the United States of
North America we call it the New England conscience. For of course
that frame of mind has been driven in on the* English Catholics. The
centuries that they have gone through—centuries of blind and malig-
nant oppression, of ostracism from public employment, of being as it
were a small beleaguered garrison in a hostile country and therefore
having to act with great formality—all these things have combined to
perform that conjuring trick. And I suppose that Papists in England are
even technically Nonconformists.

Continental Papists are a dirty, jovial and unscrupulous crew. But
that, at least, lets them be opportunists.* They would have fixed poor
dear Edward up all right. (Forgive my writing of these monstrous things
in this frivolous manner. If I did not I should break down and cry.) In
Milan, say, or in Paris Leonora would have had her marriage dissolved
in six months for two hundred dollars* paid in the right quarter. And
Edward would have drifted about until he became a tramp of the kind I
have suggested. Or* he would have married a barmaid who would have
made him such frightful scenes in public places and would so have torn
out his moustache and left visible signs upon his face that he would have
been faithful to her for the rest of his days. That was what he wanted to
redeem him. . . .

For,* along with his passions and his shames there went the dread of
scenes in public places, of outcry, of excited physical violence; of publicity, in short. Yes, the barmaid would have cured him. And it would
have been all the better if she drank; he would have been kept busy
looking after her.

I know that I am right in this. I know it because of the Kilsyte case.
You see the servant girl that he then kissed was nurse in the family of
the Nonconformist head of the county—whatever that post may be

9. **MS** [94; 88c]: "address, *[committing rapes]*\having, maybe, chance love-affairs/upon the high-
    ways": [ink]. Another correction which shifts the image of Ashburnham from that of libertine to
    that of hopeless sentimentalist.
1. Literally, Protestant dissenter from Anglican Church, but OED suggests that at the turn of the
    century Nonconformist conscience was chiefly concerned with correction in social behavior.

called. And that gentleman was so determined to ruin Edward, who was the chairman of the Tory caucus, or whatever it is—that the poor dear sufferer had the very devil of a time. They asked questions about it in the House of Commons; they tried to get the Hampshire magistrates degraded;[2] they suggested to the War Ministry that Edward was not the proper person to hold the King's commission. Yes, he got it hot and strong.

The result you have heard. He was completely cured of[3*] philandering amongst the lower classes. And that seemed a real blessing to Leonora. It[4*] did not revolt her so much to be connected—it is a sort of connection—with people like Mrs. Maidan, instead of with a little kitchenmaid.[5*]

In a dim sort of way, Leonora was almost contented when she arrived at Nauheim, that evening. . . .

She had got things nearly straight by the long years of scraping in little stations in Chitral and Burma[6]—stations where living is cheap in comparison with the life of a county magnate, and where, moreover, liaisons of one sort or another are normal and inexpensive too. So that when Mrs. Maidan came along—and the Maidan affair might have caused trouble out there because of the youth of the husband—Leonora had just resigned herself to coming home. With pushing and scraping and with letting Bramshaw Teleragh, and with selling a picture and a relic of Charles I or so, she had got—and, poor dear, she had never had a really decent dress to her back in all those years and years—she had got, as she imagined, her poor dear husband back into much the same financial position as had been his before the mistress of the Grand Duke had happened along. And of course Edward himself had helped her a little on the financial side. He was a fellow that many men liked. He was so presentable and quite ready to lend you his cigar puncher. That[*] sort of thing. So, every now and then some financier whom he met about would give him a good, sound, profitable tip. And Leonora was never afraid of a bit of a gamble—English Papists seldom are, I do not know why.

So nearly all her investments turned up trumps, and Edward was really in fit case to reopen Bramshaw Manor and once more to assume his position in the county. Thus Leonora had accepted Maisie Maidan almost with resignation—almost with a sigh of relief. She really liked

2. Lowered in rank or status.
3. **MS** [96; 90]: "cured of *[the trick of doing his]*: [ink]. Again, correction heightens Ashburnham's moral status.
4. **MS** [96; 90–97; 91]: "*[It certainly meant the end of expenditures on bastards and blackmailers. The upper classes manage these things more efficiently. Moreover i]* \I/t": [ink]. More deletion of Ashburnham's moral turpitude.
5. **MS** [97; 91]: "with *[dirty]* \a/ little kitchen maid*[s]*": [ink]. Again, reduces scope and depravity of Ashburnham's casual liaisons.
6. A country then a province of British India in southeast Asia, now a republic between Thailand and Bangladesh.

the poor child—she had to like somebody. And, at any rate, she felt she could trust Maisie—she could trust her not to rook[7] Edward for several thousands a week, for Maisie had refused to accept so much as a trinket ring from him. It is true that Edward gurgled and raved about the girl in a way that she had never yet experienced. But that, too, was almost a relief. I think she would really have welcomed it if he could have come across the love of his life. It would have given her a rest.

And there could not have been anyone better than poor little Mrs. Maidan; she was so ill she could not want to be taken on expensive jaunts. . . . It was Leonora herself who paid Maisie's expenses to Nauheim. She handed over the money to the boy husband, for Maisie would never have allowed it; but the husband was in agonies of fear. Poor devil.

I fancy that, on the voyage from India, Leonora was as happy as ever she had been in her life. Edward was wrapped up, completely, in his girl—he was almost like a father with a child, trotting about with rugs and physic and things from deck to deck. He behaved however with great circumspection, so that nothing leaked through to the other passengers. And Leonora had almost attained to the attitude of a mother towards Mrs. Maidan. So it had looked very well—the benevolent, wealthy couple of good people, acting as saviours to the poor, dark-eyed, dying young thing. And that attitude of Leonara's towards Mrs. Maidan no doubt partly accounted for the smack in the face. She was hitting a naughty child who had been stealing chocolates at an inopportune moment.

It was certainly an inopportune moment. For, with the opening of that blackmailing letter from that injured brother officer, all the old terrors had re-descended upon Leonora. Her road had again seemed to stretch out endless; she imagined that there might be hundreds and hundreds of such things that Edward was concealing from her—that they might necessitate more mortgagings, more pawnings of bracelets, more and always more horrors. She had spent an excruciating afternoon. The matter was one of a divorce-case, of course, and she wanted to avoid publicity as much as Edward did,[8*] so that she saw the necessity of continuing the payments. And she did not so much mind that. They could find three hundred a year. But it was the horror of there being more such obligations.

She had had no conversation with Edward for many years—none that went beyond the mere arrangements for taking trains or engaging servants. But that afternoon she had to let him have it. And he had been just the same as ever. It was like opening a book after a decade to find

7. Swindle.
8. **MS** [99; 93]: "The matter was one [of what in France it is customary to call détournement de mineure; it was, in consequence a criminal offence] \of a divorce-case, of course & she wanted to avoid publicity as much as Edward did,/": [ink]. More toning down of Ashburnham's sexual offences.

the words the same. He had the same motives. He had not wished to
tell her about the case because he had not wished her to sully her mind
with the idea that there was such a thing as a brother officer who could
be a blackmailer—and he had wanted to protect the credit of his old
light of love. That lady was certainly not concerned with her husband.[9]*
And he swore, and swore, and swore, that there was nothing else in the
world against him. She did not believe him.

He had done it once too often—and she was wrong for the first time,
so that he acted a rather creditable part in the matter. For he went
right straight out to the post office and spent several hours in coding a
telegram to his solicitor bidding that hard-headed man to threaten to *
take out at once a warrant against the fellow who was on his track. He
said afterwards that it was a bit too thick on poor old Leonora to be
ballyragged[1] any more. That was really the last of his outstanding
accounts and he was ready to take his personal chance of the divorce
court* if the blackmailer turned nasty. He would face it out—the publicity, the papers, the whole bally show. Those were his simple
words. . . .

He had made however the mistake of not telling Leonora where he
was going, so that, having seen him go to his room to fetch the code for
the telegram, and seeing, two hours later, Maisie Maidan come out of
his room, Leonora imagined that the two hours she had spent * in silent
agony Edward had spent[2] with Maisie Maidan in his arms. That seemed
to her to be too much.

As a matter of fact Maisie's being in Edward's room had been the
result partly of poverty, partly of pride, partly of sheer innocence. She
could not in the first place afford a maid; she refrained as much as
possible from sending the hotel servants on errands, since every penny
was of importance to her, and she feared to have to pay high tips at the
end of her stay. Edward had lent her one of his fascinating cases containing fifteen different sizes of scissors and, having seen, from her window, his departure for the post office she had taken the opportunity of
returning the case. She could not see why she should not, though she
felt a certain remorse at the thought that she had kissed the pillows of
his bed. That was the way it took her.

But Leonora could see that, without the shadow of a doubt, the incident gave Florence a hold over her. It let Florence into things and Florence was the only created being who had any idea that the * Ashburn-

9. **MS** [99; 93]: "such a thing as a [detournement de mineure] \brother officer who could be a
   blackmailer—& he had/ wanted // to protect the credit of his old light of love. That lady was
   certainly not concerned with her husband\": [ink]. See p. 49, n. 8 above.
1. Played tricks on, harassed, messed about.
2. **MS** [100; 96]: "spent [in agony (for she really imagined that Ashburnham was going to let her
   in again for all sorts of past misdeeds, she really thought that once more they would have to let
   Bramshaw Teleragh; pawn the plate; sell another picture by Gainsborough and scrape on for
   another ten years at the ends of the earth) so she imagined that the two hours she had spent]":
   [ink]. Deletion reduces the sense of financial havoc wreaked by Ashburnham's wantonness.

hams were not just good people with nothing to their tails. She determined at once, not so much to give Florence the privilege of her intimacy—which would have been the payment of a kind of blackmail—as to keep Florence under observation until she could have demonstrated to Florence that she was not in the least jealous of poor Maisie. So that was why she had entered the dining room arm in arm with my wife, and why she had so markedly planted herself at our table. She never left us, indeed, for a minute that night except just to run up to Mrs. Maidan's room to beg her pardon and to beg her also to let Edward take her very markedly out into the gardens that night. She said herself, when Mrs. Maidan came rather wistfully down into the lounge where we were all sitting: "Now Edward, get up and take Maisie to the Casino. I want Mrs. Dowell to tell me all about the families in Connecticut who came from Fordingbridge." For it had been discovered that Florence came of a line that had actually owned Bramshaw Teleragh for two centuries before the Ashburnhams came there. And there she sat with me in that hall long after Florence had gone to bed, so that I might witness her gay reception of that pair. She could play up.

And that enables me to fix exactly the day of our going to the town of M——. For it was the very day poor Mrs. Maidan died. We * found her dead when we got back—pretty awful, that, when you come to figure out what it all means. . . .

At any rate the measure of my relief when Leonora said that she was an Irish Catholic gives you the measure of my affection * for that couple. It was an affection so intense that even to this day I cannot think of Edward without sighing. I do not believe that I could have gone on any more without them. I was getting too tired. And I verily believe too, that if my suspicion that Leonora was jealous of Florence had been the reason she gave for her outburst I should have turned upon Florence with the maddest kind of rage. Jealousy * would have been incurable. But Florence's mere silly gibes at the Irish and at the Catholics could be apologised out of existence. And that I appeared to fix up in two minutes or so.

She looked at me, for a long time rather fixedly and queerly while I was doing it. And at last I worked myself up to saying:

"Do accept the situation. I confess * that I do not like your religion. But I like you so intensely. I don't mind saying that I have never had anyone to be really fond of and I do not believe that anyone has ever been fond of me, as I believe you really to be."

"Oh,* I'm fond enough of you," she said. "Fond enough to say that I wish every man was like you. But there are others to be considered." She was thinking, as a matter of fact of poor Maisie. She picked a little piece of pellitory [3]* out of the breast-high wall in front of us. She chafed

---

3. A wall plant, "the root of which has a pungent flavour, and is used as a local irritant and salivant, and as a remedy for toothache" (SOED).

it for a long minute between her finger and thumb, then she threw it over the coping.

"Oh, I accept the situation," she said at last, "if you can."

VI *

I remember laughing at the phrase "accept the situation" which she seemed to repeat with a gravity too intense. I said to her something like:

"It's hardly as much as that. I mean, that I must claim the liberty of a free American citizen to think what I please about your co-religionists. And I suppose that Florence must have liberty to think what she pleases and to say what politeness allows her to say."

"She had better," Leonora answered, "not say one single word against my people or my faith."

It struck me, at the time, that there was an unusual, an almost threatening hardness in her voice. It was almost as if she were trying to convey to Florence, through me, that she would seriously harm my wife if Florence went to something that was an extreme. Yes, I remember thinking at the time that it was almost as if Leonora were saying, through me to Florence:

"You may outrage me as you will, you may take all that I personally possess, but do not you dare to say one single thing in view of the situation that that will set up—against the faith that makes me become the doormat for your feet."

But obviously, as I saw it, that could not be her meaning. Good people, be they ever * so diverse in creed, do not threaten each other. So that I read Leonora's words to mean just no more than:

"It would be better if Florence said nothing at all against my co-religionists, because it is a point that I am touchy about."

That was the hint that, accordingly I conveyed to Florence when, shortly afterwards, she and Edward came down from the tower. And I want you to understand that, from that moment, until after Edward and the girl and Florence were all dead together I had never the remotest glimpse, not the shadow of a suspicion, that there was anything wrong, as the saying is. For five minutes, then, I entertained the possibility that Leonora might be jealous; but there was never another flicker in that flame-like personality. How in the world should I get it?

For all that time, I was just a male sick nurse. And what chance had I against those three hardened gamblers who were all in league to conceal their hands from me? What earthly chance? They were three to one—and they made me happy. Oh God, they made me so happy that I doubt if even paradise, that shall smooth out all temporal wrongs, shall ever give me the like. And what could they have done better, or what could they have done that could have been worse? I don't know. . . .

I suppose that, during all that time I was a deceived husband and that
Leonora was pimping for Edward. That was the cross that she had to
take up during her long Calvary of a life. . . .

You ask how it feels to be a deceived husband. Just Heavens, I do not
know. It feels just nothing at all. It is not Hell, certainly [; certainly] it
is not* necessarily Heaven. So I suppose it is the intermediate stage.
What do they call it? Limbo. No, I feel nothing at all about that. They
are dead, they have gone before their Judge who,* I hope, will open to
them the springs of His compassion. It is not my business to think about
it. It is simply my business to say, as Leonora's people say: "*Requiem
aeternam dona eis, domine, et lux perpetua luceat per eis. In memoriam
aeternam erit. . . .*"[1] But what were they? The just? The unjust? God
knows! I think that the pair of them were only* poor wretches, creeping
over this earth in the shadow of an eternal wrath. It is very terrible. . . .

It is almost too terrible, the picture of that Judgment, as it appears to
me sometimes, at nights. It is probably the suggestion of some picture
that I have seen somewhere. Upon* an immense plain, suspended in
mid air, I seem to see three figures,* two of them clasped close in an
intense embrace, and one intolerably solitary. It is in black and white,
my picture of that Judgment,* an etching, perhaps; only I cannot tell
an etching from a photographic reproduction. And the immense plain
is the hand of God, stretching out for miles and miles, with great spaces
above it and below it. And they are* in the sight of God, and it is
Florence that is alone. . . .

And, do you know, at the thought of that intense solitude I feel an
overwhelming desire to rush forward and comfort her. You cannot, you
see, have acted as nurse to a person for twelve years without wishing to
go on nursing them, even though you hate them with the hatred of the
adder, and even in the palm of God. But, in the nights, with that vision
of Judgment* before me, I know that I hold myself back. For I hate
Florence. I hate Florence with such a hatred that I would not spare her
an eternity of loneliness. She need not have done what she did. She was
an American, a New Englander. She had not the hot passions of these
Europeans. She cut out* that poor imbecile of an Edward—and I pray
God that he is really at peace, clasped close in the arms of that poor,
poor girl. And no doubt Maisie Maidan will find her young husband
again, and Leonora will burn, clear and serene, a Northern light* and
one of the Archangels* of God. And me. . . . Well, perhaps, they will
find me* an elevator to run. . . . But Florence. . . .

She should not have done it. She should not have done it. It was
playing it too low down. She cut out poor dear Edward from sheer van-

---

1. Mass for the dead from the Gradual of the Tridentine; the complete text of Dowell's excerpt
translates as, "Eternal rest give to them, O Lord; and let perpetual light shine upon them. The
just shall be in everlasting remembrance." Dowell's Latin is faulty; the text is *in memoria
aeterna*. As Moser points out (303), Dowell adds *per* and stops before uttering the last word:
justus ("the just").

ity; she meddled between him and Leonora from a sheer, imbecile spirit of district visiting.[2] Do you understand that, whilst she was Edward's mistress, she was perpetually trying to reunite him to his wife? She would gabble on to Leonora about forgiveness—treating the subject from the bright, American point of view. And Leonora would treat her like the whore* she was. Once she said to Florence in the early morning:

"You come to me straight out of his bed to tell me that that is my proper place. I know it, thank you."

But even that could not stop Florence. She went on saying that it was her ambition to leave this world a little brighter by the passage of her brief life, and how thankfully she would leave Edward, whom she thought she had brought to a right frame of mind, if Leonora would only give him a chance. He needed, she said, tenderness beyond anything.

And Leonora would answer—for she put up with this outrage for years—Leonora, as I understand would answer something like:

"Yes, you would give him up. And you would go on writing to each other in secret, and committing adultery in hired rooms. I know the pair of you, you know. No. I prefer the situation as it is."

Half the time Florence would ignore Leonora's remarks. She would think they were not quite ladylike.* The other half of the time she would try to persuade Leonora that her love for Edward was quite spiritual— on account of her heart. Once she said:

"If you can believe that of Maisie Maidan, as you say you do, why cannot you believe it of me?"

Leonora was, I understand, doing her hair at that time, in front of the mirror in her bedroom. And she looked round at Florence to whom she did not usually vouchsafe a glance—she looked round coolly and calmly, and said:

"Never do you dare to mention Mrs. Maidan's name again. You murdered her. You and I murdered her between us. I am as much a scoundrel as you. I don't like to be reminded of it." *

Florence went off at once into a babble of how could she have hurt a person whom she hardly knew, a person whom, with the best intentions, in pursuance of her efforts to leave the world a little brighter, she had tried to save from Edward. That was how she figured it out to herself. She really thought that. . . . So Leonora said, patiently:

"Very well, just put it that I killed her and that it's a painful subject. One does not like to think that one had killed * someone. Naturally not. I ought never to have brought her from India."

And that, indeed, is exactly how Leonora looked at it. It is stated a little baldly, but Leonora was always a great one for bald statements.

2. Literally: voluntary assistance to the poor; the term "district visiting" was often used pejoratively to suggest a patronizing and interfering philanthropy.

What had happened on the day of our jaunt to* the ancient city of M——had been this:

Leonora, who had been even then filled with pity and contrition for the poor child, on returning to our hotel, had gone straight to Mrs. Maidan's room. She had wanted just to pet* her. And she had perceived at first only, on the clear, round table covered with red velvet, a letter addressed to her. It ran something like:

"Oh, Mrs. Ashburnham, how could you have done it? I trusted you so. You never talked to me about me and Edward but I trusted you. How could you buy me from my husband? I have just heard how you have—in the hall they were talking about it, Edward and the American lady. You paid the money for me to come here.* Oh, how could you? How could you? I am going straight back to Bunny. . . ."

Bunny was Mrs. Maidan's husband.

And Leonora said that, as she went on reading the letter, she had, without looking round her, a sense that that hotel room was cleared, that there were no papers on the table, that there were no clothes on the hooks, and that there was a strained silence—a silence, she said, as if there were something in the room that drank up such sounds as there were. She had to fight against that feeling, whilst she read the postscript of the letter.

"I did not know you wanted me for an adulteress," the postscript began. The poor child was hardly literate.[3] "It was surely not right of you and I never wanted to be one. And I heard Edward call me a poor little rat to the American lady. He always called me little rat* in private, and I did not mind. But if he called me it to her, I think he does not love me any more. Oh, Mrs. Ashburnham, you knew the world and I knew nothing. I thought it would be all right if you thought it could, and I thought you would not have brought me if you did not too. You should not have done it, and we out of the same convent. . . ."

Leonora said that she screamed when she read that.

And then she saw that Maisie's boxes were all packed, and she began a search for Mrs. Maidan herself—all over the hotel. The manager said that Mrs. Maidan [had] paid* her bill, and had gone up to the station to ask the Reiseverkehrsbureau[4] to make her out a plan for her immediate return to Chitral. He imagined that he had seen her come back, but he was not quite certain. No one in the large hotel had bothered his head about the child. And she, wandering solitarily in the hall had no doubt sat down beside a screen that had Edward and Florence on the other side. I never heard then or after what had passed between that precious couple. I fancy Florence was just about beginning her cutting out of poor dear Edward by addressing to him some words of friendly warning as to the ravages he might be making in the girl's heart. That

3. Maisie's grammatical error is presumably to use "for" rather than "as" or "to be."
4. Travel agency.

would be the sort of way she would begin. And Edward would have sentimentally assured her that there was nothing in it; that Maisie was just a poor little rat whose passage to Nauheim his wife had paid out of her own pocket. That would have been enough to do the trick.

For the trick was pretty efficiently done. Leonora, with panic growing and with contrition very large in her heart, visited every one of the public rooms of the hotel—the dining-room, the lounge, the schreibzim-mer, the winter garden.[5] God knows what they wanted with a winter garden in a hotel that is only open from May till October. But there it was. And then Leonora ran—yes, she ran up the stairs to see if Maisie had not returned to her rooms. She had determined to take that child right away from that hideous place. It seemed to her to be all unspeakable. I do not mean to say that she was not quite cool about it. Leonora was always Leonora. But[*] the cold justice of the thing demanded that she should play the part of mother to this child who had come from the same convent. She figured it out to amount to that. She would leave Edward to Florence—and to me—and she would devote all her time to providing that child with an atmosphere of love until she could be returned to her poor young husband. It was naturally too late.

She had not cared to look round Maisie's rooms at first. Now, as soon as she came in she perceived, sticking out beyond the bed, a small pair of feet in high-heeled shoes. Maisie had died in the effort to strap up a great portmanteau. She had died so grotesquely that her little body had fallen forward into the trunk and it had closed upon her, like the jaws of a gigantic alligator. The key was in her hand. Her dark hair, like the hair of a Japanese had come down and covered her body and her face.

Leonora lifted her up—she was the merest feather-weight—and laid her on the bed with her hair about her. She was smiling as if she had just scored a goal in a hockey match. You understand, she had not committed suicide. Her heart had just stopped.[*] I saw her, with the long lashes on the cheeks, with the smile about the lips, with the flowers all about her. The stem of a[*] white lily rested in her hand so that the spike of flowers was upon her shoulder. She looked like a bride in the sunlight of the mortuary candles that were all about her, and the white coifs of the two nuns that knelt at her feet with the faces hidden might have been two swans that were to bear her away to kissing-kindness land or wherever it is. Leonora showed her to me. She would not let either of the others see her. She wanted, you know, to spare poor dear Edward's feelings. He never could bear the sight of a corpse. And, since she never gave him an idea that Maisie had written to her, he imagined that the death had been the most natural thing in the world. He soon got over it. Indeed, it was the one affair of his about which he never felt much remorse.[*]

---

5. Conservatory where plants can flourish during winter. "Schreibzimmer": writing room.

PART II

I *

The death of Mrs. Maidan occurred on the 4th of August 1904. * And then nothing happened until the 4th of August 1913. There is the curious coincidence of dates, but I do not know whether that is one of those sinister, as if half-jocular and altogether merciless proceedings on the part of a cruel Providence that we call a coincidence. Because it may just as well have been the superstitious mind of Florence that forced her to certain acts, as if she had been hypnotised. It is however certain that the fourth of August always proved a significant date for her. To begin with she was born on the fourth of August. Then, on that date in the year 1899 * she set out with her uncle for the tour round the world in company with a * young man called Jimmy. But that was not merely a coincidence. Her kindly old uncle with the supposedly damaged heart was, in his delicate way, offering her, in this trip, a birthday present to celebrate her coming of age. Then, on the fourth of August 1900, she yielded to an action that certainly coloured her whole life—as well as mine. She had no luck. She was probably offering herself a birthday present, that morning. . . . *

On the fourth * of August 1901 she married me and set sail for Europe in a great gale of wind—the gale that affected her heart. And no doubt there, again, she was offering herself a birthday gift—the birthday gift of my miserable life. It occurs to me that I have never told you anything about my marriage. That was like this. I have told you, as I think, that I first met Florence at the Stuyvesants in Fourteenth Street. And, from that moment, I determined with all the obstinacy of a possibly weak nature, if not to make her mine, at least to marry her. I had no occupation, I had no business affairs. I simply camped down there in Stamford, in a vile hotel and just passed my days in the house, or on the verandah of the Misses Hurlbird. The Misses Hurlbird, in an odd, obstinate way, did not like my presence. But they were hampered by the national manners of these occasions. Florence had her own sitting-room. She could ask to it whom she liked and I simply walked into that apartment. I was as timid as you will, but in that matter I was like a chicken that is determined to get across the road in front of an automobile. I would * walk into Florence's pretty little, old-fashioned room, take off my hat, and sit down.

Florence had, of course, several other fellows too—strapping young New Englanders who worked during the day in New York and spent only the evenings in the village of their birth. * And, in the evenings, they would march in on Florence with almost as much determination as I myself showed. * And I am bound to say that they were

received with as much disfavour as was my portion—from the Misses
Hurlbird. . . .

They were curious old creatures, those two. It was almost as if they
were members of an ancient family under some curse—they were so
gentlewomanly, so proper, and they sighed so. Sometimes I would see
tears in their eyes. I do not know that my courtship of Florence made
much progress at first. Perhaps that was because it took place almost
entirely during the day-time, on hot afternoons, when the clouds of dust
hung like fog, right up as high as the tops of the thin-leaved elms. The
night, I believe, is the proper season, for the gentle feats of love, not a
Connecticut July afternoon when any sort of proximity is an almost
appalling thought. But, if I never so much as kissed Florence, she let
me discover very easily, in the course of a fortnight, her simple wants.
And I could supply those wants. . . .

She wanted to marry a gentleman of leisure; she wanted a European
establishment. She wanted her husband to have an English accent, an
income of fifty thousand dollars[1] a year from real estate and no ambitions to increase that income. And—she faintly hinted—she did not
want much physical passion in the affair. Americans, you know, can
envisage such unions without blinking.

She gave out this information in floods of bright talk—she would pop
a little bit of it into comments over a view of the Rialto,[2] Venice, and
whilst she was brightly describing Balmoral Castle[3] she would say that
her ideal husband would be one who could get her received at the British Court. She had spent, it seemed, two months in Great Britain—
seven weeks in touring from Stratford to Strathpeffer[4] and one as paying
guest in an old English Family near Ledbury— *an impoverished, but
still stately family called Bagshawe.* They were to have spent two
months more in that tranquil bosom, but inopportune events, apparently in her uncle's business, had caused their rather hurried return to
Stamford. The young man called Jimmy had remained in Europe to
perfect his knowledge of that continent. He certainly did: he was most
useful to us afterwards.

But the point that came out—that there was no mistaking—was that
Florence was coldly and calmly determined to take no look at any man
who could not give her a European settlement. Her glimpse of English
home life had effected this. She meant, on her marriage, to have a
year in Paris and then to have her husband buy some real estate in the
neighbourhood of Fordingbridge, from which place the Hurlbirds had

1. About £10,000 then, c. $750,000 or £500,000 now.
2. The Rialto Bridge, a great tourist attraction on the Grand Canal.
3. Scottish country seat of the British royal family.
4. A remote Scottish village (with mineral springs) in Ross and Cromerty. "Stratford": presumably
   Stratford-upon-Avon, Warwickshire.

come in the year 1688.[5] On the strength of that she was going to take her place in the ranks of English county society. That was fixed.

I used to feel mightily elevated when I considered these details, for I could not figure out that, amongst her acquaintance in Stamford there was any fellow that would fill the bill. The most of them were not as wealthy as I, and those that were, were not the type to give up the fascinations of Wall Street even for the protracted companionship of Florence. But nothing really happened during the month of July. On the first of August Florence apparently told her aunts that she intended to marry me.

She had not told me so, but there was no doubt about the aunts, for, on that afternoon, Miss Florence Hurlbird, Senior,* stopped me on my way to Florence's sitting room and took me, agitatedly, into the parlour. It was a singular interview, in that old-fashioned colonial room, with the spindle-legged* furniture, the silhouettes, the miniatures, the portrait of General Braddock[6] and the smell of lavender. You see, the two poor maiden ladies were in agonies—and they could not say one single thing direct. They would almost wring their hands and ask if I had considered such a thing as different* temperaments. I assure you they were almost affectionate, concerned for me even. As* if Florence were too bright for my solid and serious virtues.

. For they had discovered in me solid and serious virtues. That might have been because I had once dropped the remark that I preferred General Braddock to General Washington.[7] For the Hurlbirds had backed the losing side in the War of Independence, and had been seriously impoverished and quite efficiently oppressed for that reason. The Misses Hurlbird could never forget it.

Nevertheless they shuddered at the thought of a European career for myself and Florence. Each of them really wailed when they heard that that was what I hoped to give their niece. That may have been partly because they regarded Europe as a sink of iniquity where strange laxities prevailed. They thought the Mother Country as Erastian[8] as any other. And they carried their protests to extraordinary lengths, for them. . . .

They even, almost, said that marriage was a sacrament; but neither Miss Florence nor Miss Emily could quite bring herself to utter the

---

5. The "Glorious Revolution" (1688–89) deposed the Catholic James II and facilitated the accession to the English throne of William III and Mary II of Orange. The subsequent Bill of Rights (1689) barred any future Catholic succession.

6. British general (1695–1755) in the French and Indian Wars; when commander in chief of British forces in North America against the French, with George Washington (see n. 7 below) as one of his *aides de camp*, he led his troops into massacre trying to attack Fort Dusquesne. Braddock had four horses shot from under him before being mortally wounded.

7. First president of the United States, commander in chief of the Continental army in the American Revolution. Washington (1732–1799) served honorably in Braddock's fiasco (see n. 6 above) but was not so dramatic a military hero as his former commander.

8. See p. 34, n. 5 above.

word. And they almost brought themselves to say that Florence's early life had been characterised by flirtations. Something* of that sort.

I know I ended the interview by saying:

"I don't care. If Florence has robbed a bank I am going to marry her and take her to Europe."

And at that Miss Emily wailed and fainted. But Miss Florence, in spite of the state of her sister, threw herself on my neck and cried out:

"Don't do it, John. Don't do it. You're a good young man," and she added whilst I was getting out of the room to send Florence to her aunt's rescue:

"We ought to tell you more. But she's our dear sister's child."

Florence, I remember, received me with a chalk-pale face and the exclamation:

"Have those old cats been saying anything against me?" But I assured her that they had not and hurried her into the room of her strangely afflicted relatives. I had really forgotten all about that exclamation of Florence's until this moment. She treated me so very well—with such tact—that, if I ever thought of it afterwards, I put it down to her deep affection for me.

And that evening, when I went to fetch her for a buggy-ride she had disappeared. I did not lose any time. I went into New York and engaged berths on the "Pocahontas" [9] that was to sail on the evening of the fourth of the month and then, returning to Stamford, I tracked out,[1] in the course of the day, that Florence had been driven to Rye Station. And there I found that she had taken the cars [2] to Waterbury. She had of course gone to her uncle's. The old man received me with a stony, husky face. I was not to see Florence; she was ill; she was keeping her room. And, from something that he let drop—an odd biblical phrase that I have forgotten, I gathered that all that family simply did not intend her to marry ever in her life.

I procured at once the name of the nearest minister and a rope ladder—you have no idea how primitively these matters were arranged in those days in the United States. I daresay that* may be so still. And, at one o'clock in the morning of the fourth of August I was standing in Florence's bedroom. I was so one-minded in my purpose that it never struck me there was anything improper in being, at one o'clock in the morning, in Florence's bedroom. I just wanted to wake her up. She was not, however, asleep. She expected me, and her relatives had only just

9. Ford names the ship after the American Indian woman, daughter of Chief Powhatan, who was imprisoned, brought from Virginia to England in the 17th century, baptized and married to an English gentleman; a symbolic historical and "literary" figure, perhaps suggesting an early example of the Jamesian scenario (inverted by Florence) of American "innocence" transposed into the corrupt "experience" of Europe.
1. Worked out by examining their "tracks."
2. Rye, a suburb of New York City, had a trolley car (tram) station for commuters. But Waterbury, Conn., is c. forty miles from the New York suburbs, so the reference is probably to a railway train.

left her. She received me with an embrace of a warmth. . . . Well, it was the first time I had ever been embraced by a woman—and it was the last when a woman's embrace has had in it any warmth for me. . . .

I suppose it was my own fault, what followed. At any rate I was in such a hurry to get the wedding over and was so afraid of her relatives'* finding me there that I must have received her advances with a certain amount of absence of mind. I* was out of that room and down the ladder in under half a minute. She kept me waiting at the foot an unconscionable time—it was certainly three in the morning before we knocked up that minister. And I think that that wait was the only sign Florence ever shewed of having a conscience as far as I was concerned—unless her lying for some moments in my arms was also a sign of conscience. I fancy that if I had shown warmth then she would have acted the proper wife to me—or would have put me back again. But, because I acted like a Philadelphia* gentleman she made me, I suppose, go through with the part of a male nurse. Perhaps she thought that I should not mind.

After that, as I gather, she had not any more remorse. She was only anxious to carry out her plans. For, just before she came down the ladder, she called me* to the top of that grotesque implement that I went up and down like a tranquil jumping-jack. I* was perfectly collected. She said to me with a certain fierceness:

"It is determined that we sail at four this afternoon? You are not lying about having taken berths?"

I understood that she would naturally be anxious to get away from the neighbourhood of her apparently insane relatives, so that I readily excused her for thinking that I should be capable of lying about such a thing. I made it therefore plain to her that it was my fixed determination to sail by the "Pocahontas". She said then—it was a moonlit morning and she was whispering in my ear whilst I stood on the ladder. The hills that surround Waterbury showed, extraordinarily tranquil, around the villa—she* said, almost coldly:

"I wanted to know, so as to pack my trunks," and* she added: "I may be ill, you know. I guess my heart is a little like Uncle Hurlbird's. It runs in families."

I whispered that the "Pocahontas" was an extraordinarily steady boat. . . .

Now I wonder what had passed through Florence's mind during the two hours that she had kept me waiting at the foot of the ladder. I would give not a little to know. Till then, I fancy she had had no settled plan in her mind. She certainly never mentioned her heart till that time. Perhaps the renewed sight of her Uncle Hurlbird had given her the idea. Certainly her Aunt Emily who had come over with her to Waterbury would have rubbed into her, for hours and hours, the idea that any accentuated discussions would kill the old gentleman. That would recall to her mind all the safeguards against excitement with which the poor silly old gentleman had been hedged in during their trip round the world. That, perhaps, put it into her head. Still, I believe there was some remorse on my account too. Leonora told me that Florence said there was—for Leonora knew all about it, and once went so far as to ask her how she could do a thing so infamous. She excused herself on the score of an overmastering passion. Well, I always say that an overmastering passion is a good excuse for feelings. You cannot help them. And it is a good excuse for straight actions—she might have bolted with the fellow, before or after she married me. And, if they had not enough money to get along with they might have cut their throats or sponged on her family, though of course Florence wanted such a lot that it would have suited her very badly to have for a husband a clerk in a dry-goods store, which was what old Hurlbird would have made of that fellow. He hated him. No, I do not think that there is much excuse for Florence.

God knows. She was a frightened fool, and she was fantastic, and I suppose that, at that time, she really cared for that imbecile. He certainly didn't care for her. Poor thing.* . . . At any rate,* after I had assured her that the "Pocahontas" was a steady ship, she just said:

"You'll have to look after me in certain ways—like Uncle Hurlbird is looked after. I will tell you how to do it." And then she stepped over the sill as if she were stepping on board a boat. I suppose she had burnt hers!

I had no doubt eye-openers enough. When we reentered the Hurlbird mansion at eight o'clock the Hurlbirds were just exhausted. Florence had a hard triumphant air. We had got married about four in the morning and had sat about in the woods above the town till then, listening to a mocking-bird imitate an old tom-cat. So I guess Florence had not found getting married to me a very stimulating process. I had not found anything much more inspiring to say than how glad I was, with variations. I think I was too dazed. Well, the Hurlbirds were too dazed to say much. We had breakfast together, and then Florence went to pack her grips and things. Old Hurlbird took the opportunity to read me a full-blooded lecture, in the style of an American oration, as to the perils for young American girlhood lurking in the European jungle. He said that Paris was full of snakes in the grass of which he had had bitter experience. He concluded as they always do, poor, dear old things, with the aspiration that all American women should one day be sexless—though that is not the way they put it. . . .

Well, we made the ship all right by one-thirty—and there was a tempest blowing. That helped Florence a good deal. For we were not ten minutes out from Sandy Hook[3] before Florence went down into her cabin and her heart took her. An agitated stewardess came running up to me, and I went running down. I got my directions how to behave to

3. Sandy peninsula in New Jersey, just north of Long Branch; last American landmark passed by ships leaving New York before entering the open Atlantic.

my wife. Most of them came from her, though it was the ship's* doctor who discreetly suggested to me that I had better refrain from manifestations of affection. I was ready enough.

I was, of course, full of remorse. It occurred to me that her heart was the reason for the Hurlbirds'* mysterious desire to keep their youngest and dearest unmarried. Of course they would be too refined to put the motive into words. They were old stock New Englanders. They would not want to have to suggest that a husband must not* kiss the back of his wife's neck. They would not like to suggest that he might, for the matter of that. I wonder, though, how Florence got the doctor to enter the conspiracy—the several doctors.

Of course her heart squeaked a bit—she had the same configuration of the lungs as her Uncle Hurlbird. And, in his company, she must have heard a great deal of heart talk from specialists. Anyhow, she and they tied me pretty well down—and Jimmy, of course. That* dreary boy—what in the world did she see in him? He was lugubrious, silent, morose. He had no talent as a painter, he* was very sallow and dark and he never shaved sufficiently. He met us at Havre and he proceeded to make himself useful for the next two years, during which he lived in our flat in Paris whether we were there or not. He studied painting at Julian's,[4]* or some such place. . . .

That fellow had his hands always in the pockets of his odious, square-shouldered, broad-hipped, American coats and his dark eyes were always full of ominous appearances. He was besides, too fat.* Why, I was much the better man. . . .

And I daresay Florence would have given me the better. She showed signs of it. I think perhaps the enigmatic smile with which she used to look back at me over her shoulder when she went into the bathing place was a sort of invitation. I have mentioned that. It was as if she were saying: "I am going in here. I am going to stand so stripped and white and straight—and you are a man. . . ." Perhaps it was that. . . .

No, she cannot have liked that fellow long. He looked like sallow putty. I understand that he had been slim and dark and very graceful at the time of her first disgrace. But, loafing about in Paris, on her pocket money and on the allowance that old Hurlbird made him to keep out of the United States, had given him a stomach like a man of forty, and dyspeptic irritation on top of it.

God, how they worked me. It was those two between them who really elaborated the rules. I have told you something about them—how I had to head conversations, for all those eleven years off such topics as love, poverty, crime, and so on. But, looking over what I have written, I see that I have unintentionally misled you when I said that Florence was

---

4. Académie Julian, founded by Rudolphe Julian in 1873; in the early 20th century, it was a flourishing commercial concern with numerous studios in Paris; noncompetitive entry, popular with English and Americans looking for sound training in drawing and painting.

never out of my sight. Yet that was the impression that I really had until just now. When I come to think of it she was out of my sight most of the time.

You see, that fellow impressed upon me that what Florence needed most of all were * sleep and privacy. I must never enter her room without knocking, or her poor little heart might flutter away to its doom. He said these things with his lugubrious croak, and his black eyes like a crow's, so that I seemed to see poor Florence die ten times a day—a little, pale, frail corpse. Why, I would as soon have thought of entering her room without her permission as of burgling * a church. I would sooner have committed that crime. I would certainly have done it if I had thought the state of her heart demanded the sacrilege. So at ten o'clock at night the door closed upon Florence, who had gently and as if reluctantly backed * up that fellow's recommendations; and she would wish me good night as if she were a *cinque cento*[5] Italian lady saying good-bye to her lover. And at ten o'clock of the next morning there she would come out the door of her room as fresh as Venus rising from any of the couches that are mentioned in Greek legends.[6]

Her room door was locked because she was nervous about thieves; but an electric contrivance * on a cord was understood to be attached to her little wrist. She had only to press a bulb to raise the house. And I was provided with an axe—an axe!—great * gods, with which to break down her door in case she ever failed to answer my knock, after I knocked really loud * several times. . . . It was pretty well thought out, you see.

What wasn't so well thought out were the ultimate consequences— our being tied to Europe. For that young man rubbed it so well into me that Florence would die if she crossed the Channel—he impressed it so fully on my mind that, when later, Florence wanted to go to Fordingbridge I cut the proposal short. Absolutely * short, with a curt no. It fixed her and it frightened her. I was even backed up by all the doctors. I seemed to have had endless interviews with doctor after doctor, cool, quiet men, who would ask, in reasonable tones whether there was any reason for our going to England—any special reason. And since I could not see any special reason, they would give the verdict: "Better not, then." I daresay they were honest enough, as things go. They probably imagined that the mere associations of the steamer might have effects on Florence's nerves. That would be enough, that and a conscientious desire to keep our money on the Continent.

It must have rattled poor Florence pretty considerably. For * you see, the main idea—the only mad * idea of her heart that was otherwise cold—was to get to Fordingbridge and be a county lady in the home of her ancestors. But Jimmy got her, there: he shut on her the door of the Channel; even on the fairest day of blue sky, with the cliffs of England

5. Sixteenth-century.
6. Roman goddess of beauty (in Greek myth, Aphrodite), later symbolic of love and sensuality.

shining like mother of pearl in full view of Calais, I would not have let her cross the steamer gangway to save her life. I tell you it fixed her.

It fixed her beautifully because she could not announce herself as cured, since that would have put an end to the locked bedroom arrangements.* And, by the time she was sick of Jimmy—which happened in the year 1903—she had taken on Edward Ashburnham. Yes, it was a bad fix for her, because Edward could have taken her to Fordingbridge and, though he could not give her Bramshaw Manor, that home of her ancestors being settled on his wife, she could at least have pretty considerably queened it there or thereabouts, what with our money and the support of the Asburnhams.* Her uncle, as soon as he considered that she had really settled down with me—and I sent him only the most glowing accounts of her virtue and constancy—made over to her a very considerable part of his fortune for which he had no use. I suppose that we had, between us, fifteen thousand a year in English money, though I never quite knew how much of hers went to Jimmy. At any rate we could have shone in Fordingbridge.

I never quite knew, either, how she and Edward got rid of Jimmy. I fancy that fat and disreputable raven must have had his six golden front teeth knocked down his throat by Edward one morning whilst I had gone out to buy some flowers in the Rue de la Paix, leaving Florence and the flat in charge of those two. And serve him very right, is all that I can say. He was a bad sort of blackmailer; I hope Florence does not have his company in the next world.

As God is my Judge, I do not believe that I would have separated those two if I had known that they really and passionately loved each other. I do not know where the public morality of the case comes in, and of course no man really knows what he would have done in any given case. But I truly believe that I would have united them, observing ways and means as decent as I could.* I believe that I should have given them money to live upon and that I should have consoled myself somehow. At that date I might have found some young thing, like Maisie Maidan, or the poor girl, and I might have had some peace. For peace I never had with Florence, and I hardly believe that I cared for her in the way of love after a year or two of it. She became for me a rare and fragile object, something burdensome but very frail. Why, it was as if I had been given a thin-shelled pullet's egg to carry on my palm from Equatorial Africa to Hoboken.[7] Yes, she became for me, as it were, the subject of a bet—the trophy of an athlete's achievement, a parsley crown[8] that is the symbol of his chastity, his soberness, his abstentions, and of his inflexible will. Of intrinsic value as a wife, I think she had none at all for me. I fancy I was not even proud of the way she dressed.

---

7. Town in northeast New Jersey, just across the Hudson River from New York.
8. In ancient times parsley was twined into a chaplet to honor such virtues and also used as a funerary decoration.

But her passion for Jimmy was not even a passion—and, mad as the suggestion may appear, she was frightened for her life. Yes, she was afraid of me. I will tell you how that happened.

I had, in the old days a darky servant, called Julius who valeted me, and waited on me and loved me, like the crown of his head. Now, when we left Waterbury to go to the "Pocahontas," Florence intrusted to me one very special and very precious leather grip. She told me that her life might depend on that grip which contained her drugs against heart attacks. And, since I was never much of a hand at carrying things, I intrusted this, in turn, to Julius who was a grey-haired chap of sixty or so, and very picturesque at that. He made so much impression on Florence that she regarded him as a sort of father and absolutely refused to let me take him to Paris. He would have inconvenienced her.

Well, Julius was so overcome with grief at being left behind that he must needs go and drop the precious grip. I saw red, I saw purple. I flew at Julius. On the ferry, it was, I filled up one of his eyes; I threatened to strangle him. And, since an unresisting negro can make a deplorable noise and a deplorable spectacle and since that was Florence's first adventure in the married state she got a pretty idea of my character. It affirmed in her the desperate resolve to conceal from me the fact that she was not what she would have called "a pure woman".[9] For that was really the mainspring of her fantastic actions. She was afraid that I should murder her. . . .

So she got up the heart attack, at the earliest possible opportunity on board the liner. Perhaps she was not so very much to be blamed. You must remember that she was a New Englander, and that New England had not yet come to loathe darkies as it does now. Whereas, if she had come from even so little south as Philadelphia and had been of an oldish family she would have seen that for me to kick Julius was not so outrageous an act as for her cousin, Reggie* Hurlbird, to say—as I have heard him say to his English butler—that for two cents he would bat him on the pants. Besides, the medicine-grip did not bulk as largely in her eyes as it did in mine where it was the symbol of the existence of an adored wife of a day. To her it was just a useful * lie. . . .

Well, there you have the position, as clear as I can make it—the husband an ignorant fool, the wife a cold sensualist with imbecile fears—for I was such a fool that I should never have known what she was or was not—and the blackmailing lover. And then the other lover came along. . . .

Well, Edward Ashburnham was worth having. Have I conveyed to you the splendid fellow that he was—the fine soldier, the excellent landlord, the extraordinarily kind, careful and industrious magistrate, the upright, honest, fair-dealing, fair-thinking, public character? I suppose

---

9. Subtitle of Thomas Hardy's novel *Tess of the D'Urbervilles* (1891).

I have not conveyed it to you. The truth is that I never knew it until the poor girl came along—the poor girl who was just as straight, as splendid and as upright as he. I swear she was. I suppose I ought to have known. I suppose that was, really, why I liked him so much—so infinitely much. Come to think of it, I can remember a thousand little acts of kindliness, of thoughtfulness for his inferiors, even on the Continent. Look here, I know of two * families of dirty, unpicturesque, Hessian [1] paupers that that fellow, with an infinite patience, rooted up, got their police reports, set on their feet or exported to my patient land. And he would do it quite inarticulately, set in motion by seeing a child crying in the street. He would wrestle with dictionaries, in that unfamiliar tongue. . . . Well, he could not bear to see a child cry. Perhaps he could not bear to see a woman and not give her the comfort of his physical attractions.

But although I liked him so intensely, I was rather apt to take these things for granted. They made me feel comfortable with him, good towards him; they made me trust him. But I guess I thought it was part of the character of any English gentleman. Why, one day he got it into his head that the head waiter at the Excelsior had been crying—the fellow with the grey face and grey whiskers. And then he spent the best part of a week, in correspondence and up at the British consul's, in getting the fellow's wife to come back from London and bring back his girl baby. She had bolted with a Swiss scullion. [2] If she had not come inside the week, he would have gone to London himself to fetch her. He was like that.

Edward Ashburnham was like that and I thought it was only the duty of his rank and station. Perhaps that was all that it was—but I pray God to make me discharge mine as well. And, but for the poor girl, I daresay that I should never have seen it, however much the feeling might have been over me. She had for him such enthusiasm that although even now I do not understand the technicalities of English life, I can gather enough. She was with them during the whole * of our last stay at Nauheim.

Nancy Rufford was her name; she was Leonora's only friend's only child, and Leonora was her guardian, if that is the correct term. She had lived with the Ashburnhams ever since she had been of the age of thirteen * when her mother was said to have committed suicide * owing to the brutalities of her father. Yes, it is a cheerful story. . . .

Edward always called her "the girl" and it was very pretty, the evident affection he had for her and she for him. And Leonora's feet she would have kissed; those two were for her the best man and the best woman on earth—and in * heaven. I think that she had not a thought of evil in her head. The poor girl. . . .

1. Inhabitants of Hessen, a grand duchy of Germany of which Marburg was the original capital.
2. Lowest order of servant.

Well, anyhow, she chanted Edward's praises to me for the hour together, but, as I have said, I could not make much of it. It appeared that he had the D.S.O.[3] and that his troop loved him beyond the love of men. You never saw such a troop as his. And he had the Royal Humane Society's Medal with a clasp. That meant, apparently, that he had twice* jumped off the deck of a troopship to rescue what the girl called "Tommies" who had fallen overboard in the Red Sea and such places. He had been twice recommended for the V. C.[4] whatever that might mean and although * owing to some technicalities he had never received that apparently coveted order, he had some special place* about his sovereign at the coronation. Or perhaps it was some post in the Beefeaters'.[5] She made him out like a cross between Lohengrin and the Chevalier Bayard.[6] Perhaps he was. . . . But he was too silent a fellow to make that side of him really decorative. I remember going to him, at about that time and asking him what the D. S. O. was and he grunted out:

"It's a sort of a thing they give grocers who've honourably supplied the troops with adulterated coffee in war-time"—something of that sort. He did not quite carry conviction to me, so, in the end I put it directly to Leonora. I asked her fully and squarely—prefacing the question with some remarks, such as those that I have already given you, as to the difficulty one has in really getting to know people when one's intimacy is conducted as an English acquaintanceship—I asked her whether her husband was not really a splendid fellow—along at least the lines of his public functions. She looked at me with a slightly awakened air—with an air that would have been almost startled if Leonora could ever have been startled.

"Didn't you know?" she asked. "If I come to think of it there * is not a more splendid fellow in any three counties, pick them where you will—along those lines." And she added, after she had looked at me reflectively for what seemed a long time:

"To do my husband justice there could not be a better man on the earth. There would not be room for it—along those lines."

"Well," I said, "then he must really be Lohengrin and the Cid[7] in one body. For there are not any other lines that count."

3. Companion of the Distinguished Service Order; a "modern" order (1886) rather than a "true" feudal one.
4. Victoria Cross, the highest British military and naval decoration: for conspicuous bravery in battle.
5. The Yeomen of the Guard; also refers to Warders of the Tower of London, but it is unlikely that Dowell is alluding to them.
6. Two heroes of mythical courage, honorable and knightly in their dealings with women. Lohengrin belongs to German legend; Chevalier Bayard (Pierre Terrail, 1473–1524) to French history.
7. Rodrigo, Dias de Vivar (1043–1099), Spanish general and free lord in a feudal society, mythologized for his courage, who fought against Moors and Christians alike and in 1094 conquered the kingdom of Valencia, which he ruled until his death. Corneille based a tragedy on his life, Le Cid (1637); Massenet's opera (1885) popularized the story.

Again she looked at me for a long time.

"It's your opinion that there are no other lines that count?" she asked slowly.

"Well," I answered gaily,* "you're not going to accuse him of not being a good husband? Or* of not being a good guardian to your ward?"

She spoke then slowly, like a person who is listening to the sounds in a sea-shell held to her ear—and, would you believe it?—she told me afterwards that, at that speech of mine, for the first time she had a vague inkling of the tragedy that was to follow so soon—although the girl had lived with them for eight years or so:

"Oh, I'm not thinking of saying that he is not the best of husbands or that he is not very fond of the girl."

And then I said something like:

"Well, Leonora, a man sees more of these things than even a wife. And let me tell you that, in all the years I've known Edward he has never, in your absence, paid a moment's attention to any other woman—not by the quivering of an eyelash. I should have noticed. And he talks of you as if you were one of the angels of God."

"Oh," she came up to the scratch, as you could be sure Leonora would always come up to the scratch, "I am perfectly sure that he always speaks nicely of me."

I daresay she had practice in that sort of scene;* people must have been always complimenting her on her husband's fidelity and adoration. For half the world—the whole of the world that knew Edward and Leonora believed that his conviction in the Kilsyte affair had been a miscarriage of justice—a conspiracy of false evidence, got together by Nonconformist adversaries*. But think of the fool that I was. . . .

II *

Let me think where we were.* Oh, yes . . . that conversation took place on the fourth of August, 1913. I remember saying to her that on that day, exactly nine years before, I had made their acquaintance, so that it had seemed quite appropriate and like a birthday speech to utter my little testimonial to my friend Edward. I could quite confidently say that, though we four had been about together in all sorts of places, for all that length of time, I had not, for my part one single complaint to make of either of them. And I added, that that was an unusual record for people who had been so much together. You are not to imagine that it was only at Nauheim that we met. That would not have suited Florence.

I find, on looking at my diaries that on September the fourth, 1904, Edward accompanied Florence and myself to Paris, where we put him up till the twenty-first of that month. He made another short visit to us in December of that year—the first year of our acquaintance. It must have been during this visit that he knocked Mr. Jimmy's teeth down his throat. I daresay Florence had asked him to come over for that purpose.* In 1905 he was in Paris three times—once with Leonora who wanted some frocks. In 1906 we spent the best part of six weeks together at Mentone and Edward stayed with us in Paris on his way back to London. That was how it went.

The fact was that in Florence the poor wretch had got hold of a Tartar[1] compared with whom Leonora was a sucking kid. He must have had a hell of a time. Leonora wanted to keep him for—what shall I say—for the good of her Church, as it were; to show that Catholic women do not lose their men. Let it go at that, for the moment; I will write more about her motives later, perhaps. But Florence was sticking on to the proprietor of the home of her ancestors. No doubt he was also a very passionate lover. But I am convinced that he was sick of Florence within three years of even interrupted companionship. And* the life that she led him. . . .

If ever Leonora so much as mentioned in a letter that they had had a woman staying with them—or if she so much as mentioned a woman's name in a letter to me—off would go a desperate cable in cipher to that poor wretch at Bramshaw, commanding him on pain of an instant and horrible disclosure to come over and assure her of his fidelity. I daresay he would have faced it out; I daresay he would have thrown over Florence and taken the risk of exposure. But there he had Leonora to deal with. And Leonora assured him that if the minutest fragment of the real situation ever got through to my senses, she would wreak upon him the most terrible vengeance that she* could think of. And he did not have a very easy job. Florence called for more and more attentions from him as the time went on. She would make him kiss her at any moment of the day; and it was only by his making it plain* that a divorced lady could never assume a position in the county of Hampshire that he could prevent her from making a bolt of it with him in her train. Oh, yes, it was a difficult job for him.

For Florence, if you please, gaining in time a more composed view of [my] nature* and overcome by her habits of garrulity, arrived at a frame of mind in which she found it almost necessary* to tell me all about it. Nothing* less than that. She said that her situation was too unbearable, with regard to me.

She proposed to tell me all; secure a divorce from me and go with Edward and settle in California. . . . I do not suppose that she was really serious in this. It would have meant the extinction of all hopes of Bramshaw Manor for her. Besides she had got it into her head that Leonora, who was as sound as a roach, was consumptive. She was always begging

1. A vixen, shrew.

Leonora, before me, to go and see a doctor. But none the less, poor Edward seems to have believed in her determination to carry him off. He would not have gone; he cared for his wife too much. But, if Florence had put him at it,[2] that would have meant my getting to know of it, and his incurring Leonora's vengeance. And she could have made it pretty hot for him in ten or a dozen different ways. And she assured me that she would have used every one of them. She was determined to spare my feelings. And she was quite aware that, at that date,* the hottest she could have made it for him would have been to refuse, herself, ever to see him again. . . .

Well, I think I have made it pretty clear. Let me come to the fourth of August 1913, the last day of my absolute ignorance—and, I assure you, of my perfect happiness. For the coming of that dear girl only added to it all.

On that fourth of August I was sitting in the lounge with a rather odious Englishman called Bagshawe who had arrived that night, too late for dinner. Leonora had just gone to bed and I was waiting for Florence and Edward and the girl to come back from a concert at the Casino. They had not gone there all together. Florence, I remember, had said at first that she would remain with Leonora and me and Edward and the girl had gone off alone. And then Leonora had said to Florence with perfect calmness:

"I wish you would go with those two. I think the girl ought to have the appearance of being chaperoned with Edward in these places. I think the time has come." So Florence, with her light step had slipped out after them. She was all in black for some cousin or other. Americans are particular in those matters.

We had gone on sitting in the lounge till towards ten, when Leonora had gone up to bed. It had been a very hot day, but there it was cool. The man called Bagshawe had been reading *The Times* on the other side of the room, but then he moved over to me with some trifling question as a prelude to suggesting an acquaintance. I fancy he asked me something about the poll-tax on Kur-guests, and whether it could not be sneaked out of. He was that sort of person.

Well, he was an unmistakable man, with a military figure, rather exaggerated, with bulbous eyes that avoided your own, and a pallid complexion that suggested vices practised in secret, along with an uneasy desire for making acquaintance at whatever cost. . . . The filthy toad. . . .

He began by telling me that he came from Ludlow Manor, near Ledbury. The name had a slightly familiar sound, though I could not fix it in my mind. Then he began to talk about a duty on hops, about Califor-

---

2. As one might put a horse at a fence—i.e., she forced the issue, imposed her will on him. Dowell's narrative is full of colloquial hunting and equestrian metaphors.

nian hops, about Los Angeles where he had been. He was fencing for a topic with which he might gain my affection.

And then, quite suddenly, in the bright light of the street, I saw Florence running. It was like that—Florence running with a face whiter than paper and her hand on the black stuff over her heart. I tell you, my own heart stood still; I tell you I could not move. She rushed in at the swing doors. She looked round that place of rush chairs, cane tables and newspapers. She saw me and opened her lips. She saw the man who was talking to me. She stuck her hands over her face as if she wished to push her eyes out. And she was not there any more.

I could not move; I could not stir a finger. And then that man said:

"By Jove: Florry Hurlbird." He turned upon me with an oily and uneasy sound meant for a laugh. He was really going to ingratiate himself with me.

"Do you know who that is?" he asked. "The last time I saw that girl she was coming out of the bedroom of a young man called Jimmy at five o'clock in the morning. In my house at Ledbury. You saw her recognise me." He was standing on his feet, looking down at me. I don't know what I looked like. At any rate he gave a sort of gurgle and then stuttered:

"Oh I say. . . ." Those were the last words I ever heard of Mr. Bagshawe's. A long time afterwards I pulled myself out of the lounge and went up to Florence's room. She had not locked the door—for the first night of our married life!* She was lying, quite respectably arranged, unlike Mrs. Maidan, on her bed. She had a little phial that rightly should have contained nitrate of amyl,[3] in her right hand. That was on the fourth of August, 1913.

PART III*

I*

*The odd thing is that what sticks out in my recollection of the rest of that evening was Leonora's saying:

"Of course you might marry her," and, when I asked whom, she answered:

"The girl."

Now that is to me a very amazing thing—amazing for the light of possibilities that it casts into the human heart. For I had never had the

---

3. A flammable, clear, yellowish liquid with a peculiar, ethereal, fruity odor; it is inhaled to dilate blood vessels and to relieve pain from angina pectoris (see p. 74, n. 2 below); also, ironically, it is used to relieve symptoms of cyanide poisoning (see p. 75, n. 3 below).

slightest conscious* idea of marrying the girl; I never had the slightest idea even of caring for her. I must have talked in an odd way, as people do who are* recovering from an anaesthetic. It is as if one had a dual personality, the one I being entirely unconscious of the other. I had thought nothing; I had said such an extraordinary thing.

I don't know that analysis of my own psychology matters at all to this story. I should say that it didn't or, at any rate, that I had given enough of it. But that odd remark of mine had a strong influence upon* what came after. I mean, that Leonora would probably never have spoken to me at all about Florence's relations with Edward if I hadn't said, two hours after my wife's death:

"Now I can marry the girl."◦

She had then, taken it for granted that I had been suffering all that she had been suffering, or at least that I had permitted all that she had permitted. So that, a month ago—about a week after the funeral of poor Edward she could say to me in the most natural way in the world—I had been talking about the duration of my stay at Bramshaw—she said with her clear, reflective intonation:

"O stop here for ever and ever if you can." And then she added, "You couldn't be more of a brother to me, or more of a counsellor, or more of a support. You are all the consolation I have in the world. And isn't it odd to think that, if your wife hadn't been my husband's mistress, you would probably never have been here at all?"

That was how I got the news—full in the face, like that. I didn't say anything and I don't suppose I felt anything, unless maybe it was with that mysterious and unconscious self that underlies most people.* Perhaps one day when I am unconscious or walking in my sleep I may go and spit upon poor Edward's grave. It seems about the most unlikely thing I could do; but there it is.

No, I remember no emotion of any sort, but just the clear feeling that one has from time to time when one hears that some Mrs. So-and-So is *au mieux*[1] with a certain gentleman. It made things plainer, suddenly, to my curiosity. It was as if I thought, at that moment of a windy November evening, that, when I came to think it over afterwards, a dozen unexplained things would fit themselves into place. But I wasn't thinking things over then. I remember that distinctly. I was just sitting back, rather stiffly, in a deep armchair. That is what I remember. It was twilight.*

Bramshaw Manor lies in a little hollow with lawns across it and pine-woods on the fringe of the dip. The immense wind, coming from across the forest, roared overhead. But the view from the window was perfectly quiet and grey. Not a thing stirred, except a couple of rabbits on the extreme edge of the lawn. It was Leonora's own little study that we were

1. Familiar, intimate (French).

in and we were waiting for the tea to be brought. I, as I have said, was sitting in the deep chair, Leonora was standing in the window twirling the wooden acorn at the end of the window-blind cord desultorily round and round. She looked across the lawn and said, as far as I can remember:

"Edward has been dead only ten days and yet there are rabbits on the lawn."

I understand that rabbits do a great deal of harm to the short grass in England. And then she turned round to me and said without any adornment at all, for I remember her exact words:

"I think it was stupid of Florence to commit suicide."

I cannot tell you the extraordinary sense of leisure that we two seemed to have at that moment.* It wasn't as if we were waiting for a train, it wasn't as if we were waiting for a meal—it was just that there was nothing to wait for. Nothing.

There was an extreme stillness with the remote and intermittent sound of the wind. There was the grey light in that brown, small room. And there appeared to be nothing else in the world.

I knew then that Leonora was about to let me into her full confidence. It was as if—or no, it was the actual fact that—Leonora with an odd English sense of decency had determined to wait until Edward had been in his grave for a full week before she spoke. And with some vague motive of giving her an idea of the extent to which she must permit herself to make confidences, I said slowly—and these words too I remember with exactitude—

"Did Florence commit suicide? I didn't know."

I was just, you understand, trying to let her know that, if she were going to speak she would have to talk about a much wider range of things than she had before thought necessary.

So that that was the first knowledge I had that Florence had committed suicide. It had never entered my head. You may think that I had been singularly lacking in suspiciousness; you may consider me even to have been an imbecile. But consider exactly the position.

In such circumstances of clamour, of outcry, of the crash of many people running together, of the professional reticence of such people as hotel-keepers, the traditional reticence of such "good people" as the Ashburnhams—in such circumstances it is some little material object, always, that catches the eye and that appeals to the imagination. I had no possible guide to the idea of suicide and the sight of the little flask of nitrate of amyl in Florence's hand suggested instantly to my mind the idea of the failure of her heart. Nitrate of amyl, you understand, is the drug that is given to relieve sufferers from angina pectoris.*2

2. Full name of angina, "a dangerous disease marked by sudden and severe pain in the lower part of the chest, with a feeling of suffocation" (SOED).

Seeing Florence, as I had seen her, running with a white face and with one hand held over her heart, and seeing her, as I immediately afterwards saw her, lying upon her bed with the so familiar little brown flask clenched in her fingers, it was natural enough for my mind to frame the idea. As happened now and again, I thought, she had gone out without her remedy and, having felt an attack coming on whilst she was in the gardens, she had * run in to get the nitrate in order, as quickly as possible, to obtain relief. And it was equally inevitable my mind should frame the thought that her heart, unable to stand the strain of the running, should have broken in her side. * How could I have known that, during all the years of our married life, that little brown flask had contained, not nitrate of amyl, but prussic acid? [3] It was inconceivable.

Why, not even Edward Ashburnham, who was after all more intimate with her than I was, had an inkling of the truth. He just thought that she had dropped dead of heart disease. Indeed, I fancy that the only people who ever knew that Florence had committed suicide were Leonora, the grand-duke, the head of the police and the hotel-keeper. I mention these last three because, my recollection of that night is only the sort of pinkish effulgence from the electric lamps in the hotel lounge. There seemed to bob into my consciousness, like floating globes the faces of those three. Now it would be the bearded, monarchical, benevolent head of the grand-duke; then the sharp-featured, brown, cavalry-moustached features of the chief of police; then the globular, polished and high-collared vacuousness that represented Monsieur Schontz, the proprietor of the hotel. At times one head would be there alone, at another the spiked helmet of the official would be close to the healthy baldness of the prince; then M. Schontz's oiled locks would push in between the two. The sovereign's soft, exquisitely trained voice would say "Ja, ja, ja!", each word dropping out like so many soft pellets of suet; the subdued rasp * of the official would come: "Zum Befehl Durchlaucht," [4] like five revolver-shots; the voice of Mr. Schontz would go on and on under its breath like that of an unclean priest reciting from his breviary in the corner of a railway-carriage. That was how it presented itself to me.

They seemed to take no notice of me; I don't suppose that I was even addressed by one of them. But, as long as one or the other, or all three of them were there, they stood between me as if, I being the titular possessor of the corpse, had a right to be present at their conferences. Then they all went away and I was left alone for a long time.

And I thought nothing; absolutely nothing. I had no ideas; I had no strength. I felt no sorrow, no desire for action, no inclination to go

3. Hydrogen cyanide: colorless, volatile, and extremely poisonous compound whose vapors have a bitter, almond odor. Florence supposedly replaced something administered for cyanide poisoning with cyanide itself.
4. "Very good, Serene Highness" (German).

upstairs and fall upon the body of my wife. I just saw the pink effulgence, the cane tables, the palms, the globular match-holders, the
indented ash-trays. And then Leonora came to me and it appears that I
addressed to her that singular remark:

"Now I can marry the girl."

But I have given you absolutely the whole of my recollection of that
evening, as it is the whole of my recollection of the succeeding three or
four days. I was in a state just simply cataleptic. They put me to bed and
I stayed there; they brought me my clothes and I dressed; they led me to
an open grave and I stood beside it. If they had taken me to the edge of
a river, or if they had flung me beneath a railway train I should have
been drowned or mangled in the same spirit. I was the walking dead.

Well, those are my impressions. . . .[*]

What had actually happened had been this. I pieced it together afterwards. You will remember I said that Edward Ashburnham and the girl
had gone off, that night, to a concert at the Casino[5] and that Leonora
had asked Florence, almost immediately after their departure, to follow
them and to perform the office of chaperone. Florence, you may also
remember, was all in black, being the mourning that she wore for a
deceased cousin, Jean Hurlbird. It was a very black night and the girl
was dressed in cream-coloured muslin. That[*] must have glimmered
under the tall trees of the dark park like a phosphorescent fish in a cupboard. You couldn't have had a better beacon.

And it appears that Edward Ashburnham led the girl not up the
straight allée that leads to the Casino but in under the dark trees of the
park. Edward Ashburnham told me all this in his final outburst. I have
told you that, upon that occasion, he became deucedly vocal. I didn't
pump him. I hadn't any motive. At that time I didn't in the least connect him with my wife. But the fellow talked like a cheap novelist. Or
like a very good novelist for the matter of that, if it's the business of a
novelist to make you see things clearly.[6] And I tell you I see that thing
as clearly as if it were a dream that never left me. It appears that, not
very far from the Casino, he and the girl sat down in the darkness upon
a public bench. The lights from that place of entertainment must have
reached them through the tree-trunks since, Edward said, he could
quite plainly see the girl's face—that beloved face with the high forehead, the queer mouth, the tortured eye-brows and the direct eyes. And
to Florence, creeping up behind them, they must have presented the
appearance of silhouettes. For I take it that Florence came creeping up
behind them over the short grass to a tree that, as I quite well remember,
was immediately behind that public seat. It was a not very difficult feat

5. The casino in Bad Nauheim's Kurhaus closed in 1872, but its mirrored room was possibly still
   known by this name in the early 20th century.
6. Cf. Conrad's "Preface" to *The Nigger of the* "*Narcissus*" (1897): "My task . . . is, by the power
   of the written word . . . to make you *see!*" See p. 255 below.

for a woman instinct with jealousy. The Casino orchestra was, as Edward remembered to tell me, playing the Rakocsy march[7] and although it was not loud enough, at that distance, to drown the voice of Edward Ashburnham it was certainly sufficiently audible to efface, amongst the noises of the night, the slight brushings and rustlings that might have been made by the feet of Florence or by her gown in coming over the short grass. And that miserable woman must have got it in the face, good and strong. It must have been horrible for her. Horrible! Well, I suppose she deserved all that she got.

Anyhow, there you have the picture, the immensely tall trees, elms most of them, towering and feathering away up into the black mistiness that trees seem to gather about them at night; the silhouettes of those two upon the seat; the beams of light coming from the Casino, the woman all in black peeping with fear * behind the tree-trunk. It is melodrama; but I can't help it.

And then, it appears, something happened to Edward Ashburnham.[8]* He assured me—and I see no reason for disbelieving him—that until that moment he had had no idea whatever of caring for the girl. He said that he had regarded her exactly as he would have regarded a daughter. He certainly loved her, but with a very deep, very tender and very tranquil love. He had missed her when she went away to her convent-school; he had been glad when she had returned. But of more than that, he had been totally unconscious. Had he been conscious of it, he assured me, he would have fled from it as from a thing accursed. He realized that it was the last outrage upon Leonora.* But the real point was his entire unconsciousness. He had gone with her into that dark park with no quickening of the pulse, with no desire for the intimacy of solitude. He had gone, intending to talk about polo-ponies and tennis-racquets; about the temperament of the Reverend Mother at the convent she had left and about whether her frock for a party when they got home should be white or blue. It hadn't come into his head that they would talk about a single thing that they hadn't always talked about; it had not even come into his head that the tabu which extended around her was not inviolable. And then, suddenly, that———

He was very careful to assure me that at that time there was no physical motive about his declaration. It did not appear to him to be a matter of a dark night and a propinquity and so on. No, it was simply of her effect on the moral side of his life that he appears to have talked. He said that he never had the slightest notion to enfold her in his arms or so much as to touch her hand. He swore that he did not touch her hand. He said that they sat, she at one end of the bench, he at the other; he

7. Rákóezi March, composed on traditional tunes by János Bihari (1809); probably Berlioz's arrangement (1846, for orchestra) rather than Liszt's (for piano).
8. Large pencil deletion: Ashburnham's "dual personality." See MDATV, p. 205, 77, 2nd entry below.

leaning slightly towards her and she looking straight towards the light of the Casino, her face illuminated by the lamps. The expression upon her face he could only describe as "queer".

At another time indeed he made it appear that he thought she was glad. It is easy to imagine that she was glad, since at that time she could have had no idea of what was really happening. Frankly, she adored Edward Ashburnham. He was for her, in everything that she said at that time the model of humanity, the hero, the athlete, the father of his county, the law-giver. So that for her, to be suddenly, intimately and overwhelmingly praised must have been a matter for mere gladness, however overwhelming it were.* It must have been as if a god had approved her handiwork* or a king, her loyalty. She just sat still and listened, smiling.

And it seemed to her that all the bitterness of her childhood, the terrors of her tempestuous father, the bewailings of her cruel-tongued* mother were suddenly atoned for. She had her recompense at last. Because of course if you come to figure it out, a sudden pouring forth of passion by a man whom you regard as a cross between a pastor and a father might,* to a woman, have the aspect of mere praise for good conduct. It wouldn't, I mean, appear at all in the light of an attempt to gain possession. The girl at least regarded him as firmly anchored to his Leonora. She had not the slightest inkling of any infidelities. He had always spoken to her of his wife in terms of reverence and deep affection. He had given her the idea that he regarded Leonora as absolutely impeccable[9] and as absolutely satisfying. Their union had appeared to her to be one of those blessed things that are spoken of and contemplated with reverence by her Church.

So that, when he spoke of her as being the person he cared most for in the world, she naturally thought that he meant to except Leonora and she was just glad. It was like a father saying that he approved of a marriageable daughter. . . . And Edward, when he realised what he was doing, curbed his tongue at once.[1]* She was just glad and she went on being just glad.

I suppose that that was the most monstrously wicked thing that Edward Ashburnham ever did in his life. And yet I am so near to all these people that I cannot think any of them wicked. It is impossible for* me to think of Edward Ashburnham as anything but straight, upright and honourable. That, I mean, is in spite of everything my permanent view of him. I try at times by dwelling on some of the things that he did to push that image of him away, as you might try to push aside a large pendulum. But it always comes back—the memory of his

---

9. Incapable of sin.
1. Large MS deletion in ink: revision of whole paragraph reducing Ashburnham's rash protesta-
   tions of love to Nancy. See MDATV, p. 205, 78, 5th entry below.

innumerable acts of kindness, of his efficiency, of his unspiteful tongue. He was such a fine fellow.

So I feel myself forced to attempt to excuse him in this as in so many other things. It is, I have no doubt, a most monstrous thing to attempt to corrupt a young girl just out of a convent. But I think Edward had no idea at all of corrupting her. I believe that he simply loved her. He said that that was the way of it and I at least believe him and I believe too that she was the only woman he ever really loved. He said that that was so; and he did enough to prove it. And Leonora said that it was so and Leonora knew him to the bottom of his heart.

I have come to be very much of a cynic in these matters; I mean that it is impossible to believe in the permanence of man's or woman's love. Or at any rate it is impossible to believe in the permanence of any early passion. As I see it, at least with regard to men, a love affair—a love * for any definite woman—is something in the nature of a widening of the experience. With each new woman that a man is attracted to there appears to come a broadening of the outlook, or, if you like, an acquiring of new territory. A turn of the eye-brow, a tone of the voice, a queer characteristic gesture—all these things, and it is these things that cause to arise the passion of love, all these things are like so many objects on the horizon of the landscape that tempt a man to walk beyond the horizon, to explore. He wants to get as it were behind those eye-brows with the peculiar turn, as if he desired to see the world with the eyes that they overshadow. He wants to hear that voice applying itself to every possible proposition, to every possible topic; he wants to see those characteristic gestures against every possible background. Of the question of the sex-instinct I know very little and I do not think that it counts for very much in a really great passion. It can be aroused by such nothings—by an untied shoe-lace, by a glance of the eye in passing that I think it might be left out of the calculation. I don't mean to say that any great passion can exist without a desire for consummation. That seems to me to be a commonplace and to be therefore a matter needing no comment at all. It is a thing, with all its accidents, that must be taken for granted, as, in a novel, or a biography you take it for granted that the characters have their meals with some regularity. But the real fierceness of desire, the real heat of a passion long continued and withering up the soul of a man is the craving for * identity with the woman that he loves. He desires to see with the same eyes, to touch with the same sense of touch, to hear with the same ears, to lose his identity, to be enveloped, to be supported. For, whatever may be said of the relation of the sexes, there is no man who loves a woman that does not desire * to come to her for the renewal of his courage, for the cutting asunder of his difficulties. And that will be the mainspring of his desire for her. We are all so afraid, we are all so alone, we all so need from the outside the assurance of our own worthiness to exist.[2]

So, for a time, if such a passion come to fruition, the man will get what he wants. He will get the moral support, the encouragement, the relief from the sense of loneliness, the assurance of his own worth. But these things pass away; inevitably they pass away as the shadows pass across sun-dials. It is sad, but it is so. The pages of the book will become familiar; the beautiful corner of the road will have been turned too many times. Well, this is the saddest story.

And yet I do believe that for every man there comes at last a woman— or no, that is the wrong way of formulating it. For every man there comes at last a time of life when the woman who then sets her seal upon his imagination has set her seal for good. He will travel over no more horizons; he will never again set the knapsack over his shoulders; he will retire from those scenes. He will have gone out of the business.

That at any rate was the case with Edward and the poor girl. It was quite literally the case. It was quite literally the case that his passions— for the mistress of the grand-duke, for Mrs. Basil, for little Mrs. Maidan, for Florence, for whom you will—these passions were merely preliminary canters compared to his final race with death for her. I am certain of that. I am not going to be so American as to say that all true love demands some sacrifice. It doesn't. But I think that love will be truer and more permanent in which self-sacrifice has been exacted. And, in the case of the other women, Edward just cut in and cut them out as he did with the polo-ball from under the nose of Count Baron von Lelöffel.* I don't mean to say that he didn't wear himself as thin as a lath in the endeavour to capture the other women; but over her he wore himself to rags and tatters and death—in the effort to leave her alone.

And, in speaking to her on that night he wasn't, I am convinced, committing a baseness. It was as if his passion for her hadn't existed; as if the very words that he spoke, without knowing that he spoke them, created the passion as they went along. Before he spoke, there was nothing; afterwards, it was the integral fact of his life. Well, I must get back to my story.

And my story was concerning itself with Florence—with Florence who heard those words from behind the tree. That of course is only conjecture, but I think the conjecture is pretty well justified. You have the fact that those two went out, that she followed them almost immediately afterwards through the darkness and, a little later, she came running back to the hotel with that pallid face and the hand clutching her

---

2. Ford presumably saw the passage "The real fierceness of desire . . . worthiness to exist" as an important statement on heterosexual love since he once transcribed it as dedication of a copy of the novel. See Catalogue 5 (1992), Ulysses Bookshop, Charing Cross Road, London, Item 226, p. 19.

dress over her heart. It can't have been only Bagshawe. Her face was
contorted with agony before ever her eyes fell upon me or upon him
beside me. But I dare say Bagshawe* may have been the determining
influence in her suicide. Leonora says that she had that flask, apparently
of nitrate of amyl but actually of prussic acid for many years and that
she was determined to use it if ever I discovered the nature of her relationship with that fellow Jimmy. You see, the mainspring of her nature
must have been vanity. There is no reason why it shouldn't have been;
I guess it is vanity that makes most of us keep straight, if we do keep
straight, in this world.

If it had been merely a matter of Edward's relations with the girl I
dare say Florence* would have faced it out. She would no doubt have
made him scenes,* have threatened him, have appealed to his sense of
honour, to his promises. But Mr. Bagshawe and the fact that the date
was the 4th of August must have been too much for her superstitious
mind. You see, she had two things that she wanted. She wanted to be a
great lady, installed in Bramshaw Teleragh. She wanted also to retain
my respect.

She wanted, that is to say, to retain my respect for as long as she lived
with me. I suppose, if she had persuaded Edward Ashburnham to bolt
with her she would have let the whole thing go with a run.[3] Or perhaps
she would have tried to exact from me a new respect for the greatness of
her passion on the lines of all for love and the world well lost. That
would be just like Florence.

In all matrimonial associations there is, I believe, one constant fac-
tor—a desire to deceive the person with whom one lives as to some weak
spot in one's character or in one's career. For it is intolerable to live
constantly with one human being who perceives one's small mean-
nesses. It is really death to do so—that is why so many marriages turn
out unhappily.

I, for instance, am a rather greedy man; I have a taste for good cookery
and a watering tooth at the mere sound of the names of certain comesti-
bles. If Florence had discovered this secret of mine I should have found
her knowledge of it so unbearable that I never could have supported all
the other privations of the régime that she extracted from me. I am
bound to say that Florence never discovered this secret.* Certainly she
never alluded to it; I dare say she never took sufficient interest in me.*

And the secret weakness of Florence—the weakness that she could
not bear to have me discover was just that early escapade with the fellow
called Jimmy. Let me, as this is in all probability the last time I shall
mention Florence's name, dwell a little upon* the change that had

3. Another colloquial hunting metaphor, developing the notion of Ashburnham's "bolting" with
her—i.e., she would have given the impetus of the elopement its head, let it run away with
her. Women who eloped were perjoratively known as "bolters."

taken place in her psychology. She would not, I mean, have minded if I had discovered that she was the mistress of Edward Ashburnham. She would rather have liked it. Indeed, the chief trouble of poor Leonora in those days was to keep Florence from making, before me, theatrical displays, on one line or another of that very fact. She wanted, in one mood, to come rushing to me, to cast herself on her knees at my feet and to declaim a carefully arranged, frightfully emotional, outpouring as to her passion. That was to show that she was like one of the great erotic women of whom history tells us. In another mood she would desire to come to me disdainfully and to tell me that I was considerably less than a man and that what had happened was what must happen when a real male came along. She wanted to say that in cool, balanced and sarcastic sentences. That was when she wished to appear like the heroine of a French comedy. Because of course she was always play-acting.

But what she didn't want me to know was the fact of her first escapade with the fellow called Jimmy. She had arrived at figuring out the sort of low-down Bowery tough[4] that that fellow was. Do you know what it is to shudder, in later life, for some small, stupid action—usually for some small, quite genuine piece of emotionalism—of your early life? Well, it was that sort of shuddering that came over Florence at the thought that she had surrendered to such a low fellow. I don't know that she need have shuddered. It was her footling old uncle's work; he ought never to have taken those two round the world together and shut himself up in his cabin for the greater part of the time. Anyhow, I am convinced that the sight of Mr. Bagshawe and the thought that Mr. Bagshawe—for she knew that unpleasant and toad-like personality—the thought that Mr. Bagshawe would almost certainly reveal to me that he had caught her coming out of Jimmy's bedroom at five* o'clock in the morning on the 4th of August, 1900[5]*—that was the determining influence in her suicide. And no doubt the effect of the date was too much for her superstitious personality. She had been born on the 4th of August: she had started to go round the world on the 4th of August; she had become a low fellow's mistress on the 4th of August. On the same day of the year she had married me;* on that 4th she had lost Edward's love and Bagshawe had appeared like a sinister omen—like a grin on the face of Fate.[6]* It was the last straw. She ran upstairs, arranged herself decoratively upon her bed—she was a sweetly pretty woman with smooth pink

4. Thuggish character from rough neighborhood in lower Manhattan, New York City.
5. MS [180; 40]: "4th of August, 1900", i.e., uncorrected date in early holograph appears to provide evidence for "amazing coincidence" theory of Ford's selecting precise date of outbreak of World War I before the event (see A Note on the Text, p. 187 below). However, see n. 6 below.
6. MS [180; 40]: "She had been born [. . .] on the face of Fate" is large AMS insertion in ink from l.h. margin, establishing the date 4th August as spine of novel's diffuse chronology. Although the date appears unchanged on MS [180; 40] (see n. 5 above), this addition developing its significance could have been made after the outbreak of war.

and white cheeks, long hair, the eyelashes falling like a tiny curtain on her cheeks. She drank the little phial of prussic acid and there she lay— O,* extremely charming and clearcut—looking with a puzzled expression at the electric-light bulb that hung from the ceiling, or perhaps through it, to the stars above. Who knows? Anyhow there was an end of Florence.

You have no idea how quite extraordinarily for me that was the end of Florence. From that day to this I have never given her another thought; I have not bestowed upon her so much as a sigh. Of course, when it has been necessary to talk about her to Leonora or when, for the purpose of these writings I have tried to figure her out I have thought about her as I might do about a problem in Algebra.[7]* But it has always been as a matter for study, not for remembrance. She just went completely out of existence, like yesterday's paper.

I was so deadly tired. And I dare say that my week or ten days of affaissement[8]—of what was practically catalepsy—was just the repose that my exhausted nature claimed after twelve years of the repression of my instincts, after twelve years of playing the trained poodle. For that was all that I had been. I suppose that it was the shock that did it—the several shocks. But I am unwilling to attribute my feelings at that time to anything so concrete as a shock. It was a feeling so tranquil. It was as if an immensely heavy—an unbearably heavy knapsack, supported upon my shoulders by straps, had fallen off and had left my shoulders themselves that the straps had cut into, numb and without sensation of life. I tell you, I had no regret. What had I to regret? I suppose that my inner soul—my dual personality—had realized long before that Florence was a personality of paper—that she represented a real human being with a heart, with feelings, with sympathies and with emotions only as a bank note represents a certain quantity of gold. I know that that sort of feeling came to the surface in me the moment the man Bagshawe told me that he had seen her coming out of that fellow's bedroom. I thought suddenly that she wasn't real; she was just a mass of talk out of guide-books, of drawings out of fashion-plates. It is even possible that, if that feeling had not possessed me, I should have run up sooner to her room and might have prevented her drinking the prussic acid. But I just couldn't do it; it would have been like chasing a scrap of paper—an occupation ignoble for a grown man.

And, as it began, so that matter has remained. I didn't care whether she had come out of that bedroom or whether she hadn't. It simply didn't interest me. Florence didn't matter.

I suppose you will retort that I was in love with Nancy Rufford and

---

7. **MS** [181;41]: "Algebra, *[or about the solution of a date in [?] this [?] story [?]]*": [ink, HD?]. Cancellation suggests that Ford did not wish to present Dowell as confused about the narrative's chronology.
8. Depression, mental breakdown.

that my indifference was therefore discreditable. Well, I am not seeking to avoid discredit. I was in love with Nancy Rufford as I am in love with the poor child's memory, quietly and quite tenderly in my American sort of way. I had never thought about it until I heard Leonora state that I might now marry her. But, from that moment until her worse than * death, I do not suppose that I much thought about anything else. I don't mean to say that I sighed about her or groaned; I just wanted to marry her as some people want to go to Carcassonne. *

Do you understand the feeling—the sort of feeling that you must get certain matters out of the way,* smooth out certain fairly negligible complications before you can go to a place that has, during all your life, been a sort of dream city? I didn't attach much importance to my superior years. I was forty-five and she, poor thing, was only just rising twenty-two. * But she was older than her years and quieter. She seemed to have an odd quality of sainthood, as if she must inevitably end in a convent with a white coif framing her face. But she had frequently told me that she had no vocation; it just simply wasn't there—the desire to become a nun. Well, I guess that I was a sort of convent myself; it seemed fairly proper that she should make her vows to me.

No, I didn't see any impediment on the score of age. I dare say no man does, and I was pretty confident that, with a little preparation, I could make a young girl happy. I could spoil her as few young girls have ever been spoiled; and I couldn't regard myself as personally repulsive. No man can, or, if he ever comes to do so, that is the end of him. But, as soon as I came out of my catalepsy I seemed to perceive that my problem—that what I had to do to prepare myself for getting into contact with her, was just to get back into contact with life. I had been kept for twelve years in a rarefied atmosphere; what I then had to do was a little fighting with real life, some wrestling with men of business, some travelling amongst larger cities, something harsh, something masculine. I didn't want to present myself to Nancy Rufford as a sort of an old maid. That was why, just a fortnight after Florence's suicide I set off for the United States.

II *

Immediately after Florence's death Leonora began to put the leash upon Nancy Rufford and Edward. She had guessed what had happened under the trees near the Casino. They stayed at Nauheim some three weeks after I went and Leonora has told me that that was the most deadly time of her existence. It seemed like a long, silent duel with invisible weapons, so she said. And it was rendered all the more difficult by the girl's entire innocence. For Nancy was always trying to go off alone with

Edward—as she had been doing all her life, whenever she was home for holidays. She just wanted him to say nice things to her again.

You see, the position was extremely complicated. It was as complicated as it well could be, along delicate lines. There was the complication caused by the fact that Edward and Leonora never spoke to each other except when other people were present. Then, as I have said, their demeanours were quite perfect. There was the complication caused by the girl's entire innocence; there was the further complication that both Edward and Leonora really regarded the girl as their daughter. Or it might be more precise to say that they regarded her as being Leonora's daughter. And Nancy was a queer girl; it is very difficult to describe her to you.

She was tall and strikingly thin; she had a tortured mouth, agonised eyes, and a quite extraordinary sense of fun. You might put it that at times she was exceedingly * grotesque and at times extraordinarily beautiful. Why, she had the heaviest head of black hair that I have ever come across; I used to wonder how she could bear the weight of it. She was just over twenty-one and at times she seemed as old as the hills, at times not much more than sixteen. At one moment she would be talking of the lives of the saints and at the next she would be tumbling all over the lawn with the St. Bernard puppy. She could ride to hounds like a Mænad [1]* and she could sit for hours perfectly still, steeping handkerchief after handkerchief in vinegar when Leonora had one of her headaches. She was, in short, a miracle of patience who could be almost miraculously impatient. It was no doubt the convent training that effected that. I remember that one of her letters to me, when she was about sixteen, ran something like:

"On Corpus Christi" [2]—or it may have been some other saint's day, I cannot keep these things in my head—"our school played Roehampton [3] at hockey. And, seeing that our side was losing, being three goals to one against us at half-time, we retired into the chapel and prayed for victory. We won by five goals to three." And I remember that she seemed to describe afterwards a sort of saturnalia. [4] Apparently, when the victorious fifteen, or eleven, came into the refectory for supper, the whole school jumped upon the tables and cheered and broke the chairs on the floor and smashed the crockery—for a given time, until the Reverend Mother rang a hand-bell. That is of course the Catholic tradition—saturnalia that can end in a moment, like the crack of a whip. I don't of course

1. In Greek legend, female follower of Dionysus (in Roman, of Bacchus); cult known for its orgiastic release of powerful, irrational impulses through controlled ritual. See n. 4 below. See also MDATV, p. 206, 85, 2nd entry below.
2. Thursday of the week after Whitsun; Catholic festival honoring the Eucharist.
3. Probably the Convent of the Sacred Heart of Jesus, Roehampton Lane, London, an élite boarding school for girls.
4. Scene of unrestrained license and revelry.

like the tradition but I am bound to say that it gave Nancy—or at any rate Nancy had, a sense of rectitude that I have never seen surpassed. It was a thing like a knife that looked out of her eyes and that spoke with her voice, just now and then. It positively frightened me. I suppose that I was almost afraid to be in a world where there could be so fine a standard. I remember when she was about fifteen or sixteen on going back to the convent I once gave her a couple of English sovereigns as a tip. She thanked me in a peculiarly heartfelt way saying that it would come in extremely handy. I asked her why and she explained. There was a rule at the school that the pupils were not to speak when they walked through the garden from the chapel to the refectory. And, since this rule appeared [to Nancy's inscrutable mind] * to be idiotic and arbitrary she broke it on purpose day after day. In the evening the children were all asked if they had committed any faults during the day and every evening Nancy confessed that she had broken this particular rule. It cost her sixpence a time, that being the fine attached to the offence. Just for the information I asked her why she always confessed and she answered in these exact words: *

"Oh well, the girls of the Holy Child have always been noted for their truthfulness. It's a beastly bore, but I've got to do it."

I dare say that the miserable nature of her childhood, coming before the mixture of saturnalia and discipline that was her convent life, added something to her queerness. Her father was a violent madman of a fellow, a major in one of what I believe are called the Highland regiments. He didn't drink but he had an ungovernable temper and the first thing that Nancy could remember was seeing her father strike her mother with his clenched fist so that her mother fell over sideways from the breakfast table and lay motionless. The mother was no doubt an irritating woman and the privates of that regiment appear to have been irritating too so that the house was a place of outcries and perpetual disturbance. Mrs. Rufford was Leonora's dearest friend and Leonora could be cutting enough at times. But I fancy [that] * she was as nothing to Mrs. Rufford. The Major would come in to lunch harassed and already spitting out oaths after an unsatisfactory morning's drilling of his stubborn men beneath a hot sun. And then Mrs. Rufford would make some * cutting remark and pandemonium would break loose. Once, when she had been about twelve, Nancy had tried to intervene between the pair of them. Her father had struck her full upon the forehead a blow so terrible that she had lain unconscious for three days. Nevertheless Nancy seemed to prefer her father to her mother. She remembered rough kindnesses from him. Once or twice when she had been quite small he had dressed her in a clumsy, impatient but very tender * way. It was nearly always impossible to get a servant to stay in the * family and, for days at a time, apparently, Mrs. Rufford would be incapable. I fancy she drank. At any rate she had so cutting a tongue that even Nancy was afraid of her—she so made fun of any tenderness, she so sneered at all emotional displays. Nancy must have been a very emotional child. . . .

Then one day, quite suddenly, on her return from a ride, at Fort William,[5] Nancy had been sent, with her governess, who had a white face, right down South to that convent school. She had been expecting to go there in two months' time. Her mother disappeared from her life at that time. A fortnight later Leonora came to the convent and told her that her mother was dead. Perhaps she was. At any rate I never heard until the very end* what became of Mrs. Rufford. Leonora never spoke of her.

And then Major Rufford went to India from which he returned very seldom and only for very short visits; and Nancy lived herself gradually into the life at Bramshaw Teleragh. I think that, from that time onwards, she led a very happy life, till the end. There were dogs and horses and old servants and the Forest.[6] And there were Edward and Leonora, who loved her.

I had known her all the time—I mean that she always came to the Ashburnhams* at Nauheim for the last fortnight of their stay, and I watched her gradually growing. She was* very cheerful with me. She always even kissed me, night and morning, until she was about eighteen. And she would skip about and fetch me things and laugh at my tales of life in Philadelphia. But, beneath her gaiety I fancy that there lurked some terrors. I remember one day, when she was just eighteen, during one of her father's rare visits to Europe we were sitting in the gardens, near the iron-stained fountain. Leonora had one of her headaches and we were waiting for Florence and Edward to come from their baths. You have no idea how beautiful Nancy looked that morning.

We were talking about the desirability of taking tickets in lotteries—of the moral side of it, I mean. She was all in white, and so tall and fragile; and she had only just put her hair up, so that the carriage of her neck had that charming touch of youth and of unfamiliarity. Over her throat there played the reflection from a little pool of water, left by a thunderstorm of the night before, and all the rest of her features were in the diffused and luminous shade of her white parasol. Her dark hair just showed beneath her broad, white hat of pierced, chip straw; her throat was very long and leaned forward, and her eyebrows, arching a little as she laughed at some old-fashionedness in my phraseology, had abandoned their tense line. And there was a little colour in her cheeks and light in her deep blue eyes. And to* think that that vivid white thing, that saintly and swanlike being—to think that. . . . Why, she was like the sail of a ship, so white and so definite in her movements. And to

---

5. Town in western Scotland (Inverness-shire), in remote and beautiful countryside north of Glasgow; for western Scotland, very Catholic (famous Benedictine monastery there).
6. New Forest. See p. 21, n. 4 above.

think that she will never. . . . Why she will never do anything again. I can't believe it. . . .

Anyhow we were chattering away about the morality of lotteries. And then, suddenly, there came from the arcades behind us the overtones of her father's unmistakable voice; it was as if a modified foghorn had boomed* with a reed inside it. I looked round to catch sight of him. A tall, fair, stiffly upright man of fifty he was walking away with an Italian baron who had had much to do with the Belgian Congo. They must have been talking about the proper treatment of natives, for I heard him say:

"Oh, hang humanity!"

When I looked again at Nancy her eyes were closed and her face was more pallid than her dress which had at least some pinkish reflections from the gravel. It was dreadful to see her with her eyes closed like that.

"Oh," she exclaimed, and her hand that had appeared to be groping, settled for a moment on my arm. "Never speak of it. Promise never to tell my father of it. It brings back those dreadful dreams. . . ." And, when she opened her eyes she looked straight into mine. "The blessed saints," she said, "you would think they would spare you such things. I don't believe* all the sinning in the world could make one deserve them."

They say the poor thing was always allowed a light at night, even in her bedroom. . . .* And yet, no young girl could* more archly and lovingly have played with an adored father. She was always holding him by both coat lapels; cross-questioning him as to how he spent his time; kissing the top of his head. Ah, she was well-bred, if ever anyone was.

The poor, wretched man cringed before her—but she could not have done more to put him at his ease. Perhaps she had had lessons in it at her convent. It was only that peculiar note of his voice, used when he was overbearing or dogmatic, that could unman her—and that was only visible when it came unexpectedly. That was because the bad dreams that the blessed saints allowed her to have for her sins always seemed to her to herald themselves by the booming sound of her father's voice. It was that sound that had always preceded his entrance for the terrible lunches of her childhood. . . .*

I have reported, earlier in this chapter that Leonora said, during that remainder of their stay at Nauheim, after I had left, it had seemed to her that she was fighting a long duel with unseen weapons against silent adversaries. Nancy, as I have also said, was always trying to go off with Edward alone. That had been her habit for years. And Leonora found it to be her duty to stop that. It was very difficult. Nancy was used to having her own way, and* for years she had been used to going off with Edward, ratting, rabbiting, catching salmon down at Fordingbridge, district-visiting of the sort that Edward indulged in, or calling on the tenants. And, at Nauheim she and Edward had always gone up to the Casino alone in the evenings—at any rate whenever Florence did not call for his attendance. It shows the obviously innocent nature of the regard of those two that even Florence had never had any idea of jealousy. Leonora had cultivated the habit of going to bed at ten o'clock.

I don't know how she managed it, but, for all the time they were at Nauheim she contrived never to let those two be alone together, except in broad daylight, in very crowded places. If a Protestant had done that it would no doubt have awakened a self-consciousness in the girl. But Catholics, who have always reservations and queer spots of secrecy, can manage these things better. And I daresay that two things made this easier—the death of Florence and the fact that Edward was obviously sickening. He appeared, indeed, to be very ill; his shoulders began to be bowed; there were pockets under his eyes; he had extraordinary moments of inattention.

And Leonora describes herself as watching him as a fierce cat watches an unconscious pigeon in a roadway. In that silent watching, again, I think she was a Catholic—of a people that can think thoughts alien to ours and keep them to themselves. And the thoughts passed through her mind; some of them even got through to Edward with never a word spoken. At first she thought that it might be remorse, or grief, for the death of Florence that was oppressing him. But she watched and watched, and uttered apparently random sentences about Florence before the girl, and she perceived that he had no grief and no remorse. He had not any idea that Florence could have committed suicide without writing at least a tirade to him. The absence of that made him certain that it had been heart disease. For Florence had never undeceived him on that point. She thought it made her seem more romantic.

No, Edward had no remorse. He was able to say to himself that he had treated Florence with gallant attentiveness of the kind that she desired until two hours before her death. Leonora gathered that from the look in his eyes, and from the way he straightened his shoulders over her as she lay in her coffin—from that and a thousand other little things. She would speak suddenly about Florence to the girl and he would not start in the least; he would not even pay attention, but would sit with bloodshot eyes gazing at the tablecloth. He drank a good deal, at that time—a steady soaking of drink every evening till long after they had gone to bed.

For Florence made the girl go to bed at ten, unreasonable though that seemed to Nancy. She could * understand that, whilst they were in a sort of half mourning for Florence she ought not to be seen at public places, like the Casino; but she could not see why she should not accompany her uncle upon his evening strolls through the park. I don't know what Leonora put up as an excuse—something, I fancy, in the nature of a nightly orison[7] that she made the girl and herself perform for the soul of Florence. And then, one evening, about a fortnight later, when the girl, growing restive at even devotional exercises, clamoured once more to be allowed to go for a walk with Edward and when Leonora was really at her wits' end Edward himself gave himself into her hands. He was just standing up from dinner and had his face averted.

But he turned his heavy head and his bloodshot eyes upon his wife and looked full at her.

"Doctor von Hauptmann," he said, "has ordered me to go to bed immediately after dinner. My heart's much worse."

He continued to look at Leonora for a long minute—with a sort of heavy contempt. And Leonora * understood that, with his speech, he was giving her the excuse that she needed for separating him from the girl and with his eyes he was reproaching her for thinking that he would try to corrupt Nancy.

He went silently up to his room and sat there for a long time—until the girl was well in bed—reading in the Anglican prayer book. And about half past ten she heard his footsteps pass her door, going outwards. Two and a half hours later they * came back, stumbling heavily.

She remained, reflecting upon this position until the last night of their stay at Nauheim. Then, she suddenly acted. For, just in the same way, suddenly after dinner, she looked at him and said:

"Teddy, don't you think you could take a night off from your doctor's orders and go with Nancy to the Casino. The poor child has had her visit so spoiled."

He looked at her, in turn, for a long, balancing minute.

"Why, yes," he said at last. Nancy jumped out of her chair and kissed him.

Those two words, Leonora said, gave her the greatest relief of any two syllables she had ever heard in her life. For she realised that Edward was breaking up, not under the desire for possession, but from the dogged determination to hold his hand. She could relax some of her vigilance.

Nevertheless she sat in the darkness behind her half-closed jalousies[8] looking over the street and the night and the trees until, very late, she could hear Nancy's clear voice coming closer and saying:

"You did look an old guy[9] with that false nose."

There had been some sort of celebration of a local holiday up in the Kursaal. And Edward replied with his sort of sulky good nature:

"As for you, you looked like old Mother Sideacher."[1]

7. Prayer.
8. Blinds or shutters with sloping slats to exclude sun and rain but admit air.
9. Person of comically grotesque looks or dress.
1. Possibly a derogatory reference to Nancy's headmistress (Reverend Mother), or "a joke about an old beggar woman who always amused them at Bramshaw" (see p. 91 below).

The girl came swinging* along, a silhouette beneath a gas-lamp; Edward, another, slouched at her side. They were talking just as they had talked any time since the girl had been seventeen; with the same tones, the same joke about an old beggar woman who always amused them at Bramshaw. The girl, a little later, opened Leonora's door whilst she was still kissing Edward on the forehead as she had done every night.

"We've had a most glorious time," she said. "He's ever so much better. He raced me for twenty yards home. Why are you all in the dark?"

Leonora could hear Edward going about in his room but, owing to the girl's chatter, she could not tell whether he went out again or not. And then, very much later, because she thought that if he were drinking again something must be done to stop it, she opened for the first time, and very softly, the never-opened door between their rooms. She wanted to see if he had gone out again. Edward was kneeling beside his bed with his head hidden in the counterpane. His arms, outstretched, held out before him a little image of the blessed virgin—a tawdry, scarlet and Prussian blue affair that the girl had given him on her first return from the convent. His shoulders heaved convulsively three times and heavy sobs came from him before she* could close the door. He was not a Catholic; but that was the way it took him.

Leonora slept for the first time that night* with a sleep from which she never once started.*

III*

And then Leonora completely broke down—on the day that they returned to Bramshaw Teleragh. It is the infliction* of our miserable minds—it is the scourge of atrocious but probably just destiny that no grief comes by itself. No, any great grief, though the grief itself may have gone, leaves in its place a train of horrors,* of misery, and despair. For Leonora was, in herself, relieved. She felt that she could trust Edward with the girl and she knew that Nancy could be absolutely trusted. And then, with the slackening of her vigilance, came the slackening of her entire mind. This is perhaps the most miserable part of the entire story. For it is miserable to see a clear intelligence waver; and Leonora wavered.

You are to understand that Leonora loved Edward with a passion that was yet like an agony of hatred. And she had lived with him for years and years without addressing to him one word of tenderness. I don't know how she could do it. At the beginning of that* relationship she had been just married off to him. She had been one of seven daughters in a bare, untidy Irish manor-house to which she had returned from the convent I have so often spoken of.* She had left it just a year and she was just nineteen. It is impossible to imagine such inexperience as was hers. You might almost say that she had never spoken to a man except a priest. Coming straight from the convent, she had gone in, behind the high walls of the manor-house that was almost more cloistral than any convent could have been. There were the seven girls, there was the strained mother, there was the worried father at whom, three times, in the course of that year the tenants took pot-shots from behind a hedge. The women-folk, upon the whole, the tenants respected. Once a week each of the girls, since there were seven of them, took a drive with the mother in the old basketwork chaise[1] drawn by a very fat, very lumbering pony. They paid occasionally a call, but even these were so rare that, Leonora has assured me, only three times in the year that succeeded her coming home from the convent did she enter another person's house. For the rest of the time the seven sisters[2] ran about in the neglected gardens between the unpruned espaliers. Or they played lawn-tennis or fives[3] in an angle of a great wall that surrounded the garden—an angle from which the fruit trees had long died away. They painted in water-colour; they embroidered; they copied verses into albums. Once a week they went to mass; once a week to the confessional accompanied by an old nurse. They were happy since they had known no other life.

It appeared to them a singular extravagance when, one day, a photographer was brought over from the county town and photographed them standing, all seven, in the shadow of an old apple-tree with the grey lichen on the raddled trunk.

But it wasn't an extravagance.

Three weeks before Colonel Powys had written to Colonel Ashburnham:

"I say, Harry, couldn't your Edward marry one of my girls? It would be a god-send to me, for I'm at the end of my tether and, once one girl begins to go off the rest of them will follow."

He went on to say that all his daughters were tall, upstanding, clean-limbed and absolutely pure, and he reminded Colonel Ashburnham that, they having been married on the same day, though in different churches, since the one was a Catholic and the other an Anglican—they had said to each other the night before, that, when the time came, one of their sons should marry one of their daughters. Mrs. Ashburnham had been a Powys and remained Mrs. Powys' dearest friend. They had drifted about the world as English soldiers do, seldom meeting, but their women always in correspondence one with another. They wrote about minute things such as the teething of Edward and of the earlier daughters or the best way to repair a Jacob's ladder in a [silk] * stocking.

1. A one-horse, light, open carriage, usually for two people.
2. Possibly an oblique reference to the Seven Sisters, a striking chain of white cliffs overlooking the English Channel to the west of Beachy Head, West Sussex: an image of stark purity.
3. A public-school game, similar to squash and usually played by boys, in which a ball is struck by the hand against the wall of a prepared court. "Espaliers": fruit trees trained to grow around a framework of stakes.

And, if they met seldom, yet it was often enough to keep each other's personalities fresh in their minds, gradually growing greyer, gradually growing a little stiff in the joints but always with enough to talk about and with a store of reminiscences. Then, as his girls began to come of an age when they must leave the convent in which they were regularly interned during his years of active service, Colonel Powys retired from the army with the necessity of making a home for them. It happened that the Ashburnhams had never seen any of the Powys girls, though, whenever the four parents met in London Edward Ashburnham was always of the party. He was at that time twenty-two and, I believe, almost as pure in mind as Leonora herself. It is odd how a boy can have his virgin intelligence untouched in this world.

● That was partly due to the careful handling of his mother, partly to the fact that the house to which he went at Winchester had a particularly pure tone and partly to Edward's own peculiar aversion from anything like coarse language or gross stories. At Sandhurst [4] he had just kept out of the way of that sort of thing. He was keen on soldiering, keen on mathematics, on land-surveying, on politics and,* by a queer warp of his mind, on literature. Even when he was twenty-two he would pass hours reading one of Scott's novels or the Chronicles of Froissart. [5]*

Mrs. Ashburnham considered that she was to be congratulated and almost every week she wrote to Mrs. Powys, dilating upon her satisfaction.

Then, one day, taking a walk down Bond Street with her son, after having been at Lord's, [6] she noticed Edward suddenly turn his head round to take a second look at a well-dressed girl who had passed them. She wrote about that, too, to Mrs. Powys and expressed some alarm. It had been, on Edward's part the merest reflex-action. He was so very abstracted at that time owing to the pressure his crammer [7] was putting upon him that he certainly hadn't known what he was doing. ●

It was this letter of Mrs. Ashburnham's to Mrs. Powys that had caused the letter from Colonel Powys to Colonel Ashburnham—a letter that was half humorous, half longing. Mrs. Ashburnham caused her husband to reply, with a letter a little more jocular—something to the effect that Colonel Powys ought to give them some idea of the goods that he was marketing. That was the cause of the photograph. I have seen it, the seven girls, all in white dresses, all very much alike in feature—all,

---

4. The Royal Military Academy, Berkshire: the premier officer-training college, then confined almost exclusively to public school (meaning in American terms "private school") entrants. "Winchester": Winchester College, elite English public school then famous for its rigorous intellectual and moral standards.
5. Jean Froissart (1333[?]–1400), author of a feudal history of Britain, France, and Spain from 1325 to 1400. See MDATV, p. 207, 93, 2nd entry below. Sir Walter Scott (1771–1832), author of historical romances such as *Ivanhoe* (1819), often set in feudal times.
6. Lord's Cricket Ground, St. John's Wood, London, home of the MCC (governing body of British cricket), and then center of cricket as a society function.
7. Tutor who rapidly "crams" information into students to prepare them for examinations.

except Leonora, a little heavy about the chins and a little stupid about the eyes. I dare say it would have made Leonora too look a little heavy and a little stupid for it was not a good photograph. But the black shadow from one of the branches of the apple-tree cuts* right across her face which is all but invisible.

There followed an extremely harassing time for Colonel and Mrs. Powys. Mrs. Ashburnham had written to say that, quite sincerely, nothing would give greater ease to her maternal anxieties than to have her son marry one of Mrs. Powys' daughters if only he showed some inclination to do so. For, she added, nothing but a love-match was to be thought of in her Edward's case. But the poor Powys couple had to run things so very fine[8] that even the bringing together of the young people was a desperate hazard.

The mere expenditure upon sending one of the girls over from Ireland to Bramshaw was terrifying to them; and whichever girl they selected might not be the one to ring Edward's bell. On the other hand the expenditure upon mere food and extra sheets for a visit from the Ashburnhams to them was terrifying too. It would mean, mathematically, going short in so many meals themselves, afterwards. Nevertheless they chanced it and all the three Ashburnhams came on a visit to the lonely manor-house. They could give Edward some rough shooting, some rough fishing and a whirl of femininity; but I should say the girls made really more impression upon Mrs. Ashburnham than upon Edward himself. They appeared to her to be so clean run and so safe. They were indeed so clean run that, in a faint sort of way Edward seems to have regarded them rather as boys than as girls. And then, one evening, Mrs. Ashburnham had with her boy one of those conversations that English mothers have with English sons. It seems to have been a criminal sort of proceeding though I don't know what took place at it. Anyhow, next morning Colonel Ashburnham asked on behalf of his son for the hand of Leonora. This caused some consternation to the Powys couple since Leonora was the third daughter and Edward ought to have married the eldest. Mrs. Powys, with her rigid sense of the proprieties, almost wished to reject the proposal. But the Colonel, her husband, pointed out that the visit would have cost them sixty pounds, what with the hire of an extra servant, of a horse and car, and with the purchase of beds and bedding and extra tablecloths. There was nothing else for it but the* marriage.* In that way Edward and Leonora became man and wife.

I don't know that a very minute study of their progress towards complete disunion is necessary. Perhaps it is. But there are many things that I cannot well make out, about which I cannot well question Leonora, or about which Edward did not tell me. I do not know that there was

8. Economize so carefully.

ever any question of love from Edward to her. He regarded her, certainly, as desirable amongst her sisters. He was obstinate to the extent of saying that if he could not have her he would not have any of them. And no doubt, before the marriage he made her pretty speeches out of books that he had read. But, as far as he could describe his feelings at all, later, it seems that calmly and without any quickening of the pulse, he just carried* the girl off, there being no opposition. It had, however, been all so long ago that it seemed to him, at the end of his poor life, a dim and misty affair. He had the greatest admiration for Leonora.

He had the very greatest admiration. He admired her for her truthfulness, for her cleanness of mind, and the clean-run-ness of her limbs, for her efficiency, for the fairness of her skin, for the gold of her hair, for her religion, for her sense of duty. It was a satisfaction to take her about with him.

But she had not for him a touch of magnetism.* I suppose, really, he did not love her because she was never mournful; what really made him feel good in life was to comfort somebody who would be darkly and mysteriously mournful. That he had never had* to do for Leonora. Perhaps, also, she was at first too obedient. I do not mean to say that she was submissive—that she deferred, in her judgments, to his. She did not. But she had been handed over to him, like some patient mediæval virgin; she had been taught all her life that the first duty of a woman is to obey. And there she was.

In her, at least, admiration for his qualities very soon became love of the deepest description. If his pulses never quickened* she, so I have been told, became what is called an altered being when he approached her from the other side of a dancing floor. Her eyes followed him about full of trustfulness, of admiration, of gratitude, and of love. He was also, in a great sense, her pastor and guide—and he guided her into what, for a girl straight out of a convent, was almost heaven.* I have not the least idea of what an English officer's wife's existence may be like. At any rate there were feasts, and chatterings, and nice men who gave her* the right sort of admiration, and nice women who treated her as if she had been a baby. And her confessor approved of her life and Edward let her give little treats to the girls of the convent she had left, and the Reverend Mother approved of him. There could not have been a happier girl for five or six years.

For it was only at the end of that time that clouds began, as the saying is, to arise. She was then about twenty-three, and her purposeful efficiency made her perhaps have a desire for mastery.* She began to perceive that Edward was extravagant in his largesses.[9] His parents died just about that time and Edward, though they both decided that he should continue his soldiering, gave a great deal of attention to the man-

9. Bountiful gifts, freely bestowed.

agement of Bramshaw through a steward. Aldershot[1] was not [so] very far away, and* they spent all his leaves there.

And, suddenly, she seemed to begin to perceive that his generosities were almost fantastic. He subscribed much too much to things connected with his mess, he pensioned off his father's servants, old or new, much too generously. They had a large income, but every now and then they would find themselves hard up. He began to talk of mortgaging a farm or two, though it never actually came to that.

She made tentative efforts at remonstrating with him. Her father, whom she saw now and then, said that Edward was much too generous to his tenants,* the wives of his brother officers remonstrated with her in private; his large subscriptions made it difficult for their husbands to keep up with them. Ironically enough, the first real trouble between them came from his desire to build a Roman Catholic chapel at Bramshaw. He wanted to do it to honour Leonora and he proposed to do it very expensively. Leonora did not want it; she could perfectly well drive from Bramshaw to the nearest Catholic Church as often as she liked. There were no Roman Catholic tenants and no Roman Catholic servants except her old nurse who could always drive with her. She had as many priests to stay with her as could be needed—and even the priests did not want a gorgeous chapel in that place where it would have merely seemed an invidious instance of ostentation. They were perfectly ready to celebrate mass for Leonora and her nurse, when they stayed at Bramshaw, in a cleaned-up outhouse. But Edward was as obstinate as a hog about it.

He was truly grieved at his wife's want of sentiment—at her refusal to receive that amount of public homage from him. She appeared to him to be wanting in imagination—to be cold and hard. I don't exactly know what part her priests played in the tragedy that it all became; I daresay they behaved quite creditably but mistakenly. But then, who would not have been mistaken with Edward? I believe he was even hurt that Leonora's confessor did not make [more]* strenuous efforts to convert him. There was a period when he was quite ready to become an emotional Catholic.

I don't know why they did not take him on the hop; but they have queer sorts of wisdoms, those people, and queer sorts of tact. Perhaps they thought that Edward's too early conversion would frighten off other Protestant desirables from marrying Catholic girls. Perhaps they saw deeper into Edward than he saw himself and thought that he would make a not very creditable convert. At any rate they—and Leonora—left him very much alone. It mortified him very considerably. He has

1. Hampshire town, another center of military training, a few miles south of Sandhurst. See MDATV, p. 207, 96, 1st entry below.

told me that if Leonora had then taken his aspirations seriously everything would have been different. But I daresay that was nonsense.

At any rate it was over the question of the chapel that they had their first and really disastrous quarrel. Edward at that time was not well; he supposed himself to be overworked with his regimental affairs—he was managing the mess at the time. And Leonora was not well—she was beginning to fear that their union might be sterile. And then her father came over from Glasmoyle to stay with them.

Those were troublesome times in Ireland, I understand. At any rate Colonel Powys had tenants on the brain—his own tenants having shot at him with shot-guns. And, in conversations with [Edward—and in much longer conversations with] Edward's land-steward [—]* he got it into his head that Edward managed his estates with a mad generosity towards his tenants. I understand also that those years—the nineties— were very bad for farming. Wheat was fetching only a few shillings the hundred; the price of meat was so low that cattle hardly paid for raising; whole English counties were ruined. And Edward allowed his tenants very high rebates.

To do [them]* both justice Leonora has since acknowledged that she was in the wrong at that time and that Edward was following out a more far-seeing policy in nursing his really very good tenants over a bad period. It was not as if the whole of his money came from the land; a good deal of it was in rails. But old Colonel Powys had that bee in his bonnet and, if he never directly approached Edward himself on the subject, he preached unceasingly, whenever he had the opportunity, to Leonora. His pet idea was that Edward ought to sack all his own tenants and import a set of farmers from Scotland. That was what they were doing in Essex. He was of opinion that Edward was riding hot-foot to ruin.

That worried Leonora very much—it worried her dreadfully; she lay awake nights; she had an anxious line round her mouth. And that, again, worried Edward. I do not mean to say that Leonora actually spoke to Edward about his tenants—but he got to know that someone, probably her father, had been talking to her about the matter. He got to know it because it was the habit of his steward to look in on them every morning about breakfast time to report any little happenings. And there was a farmer called Mudford* who had only paid half his rent for the last three years. One morning the land-steward reported* that Mudford* would be unable to pay his rent at all that year. Edward reflected for a moment and then he said something like:*

"O well, he's an old fellow and his family have been our tenants for over two hundred years. Let him off altogether."

And then Leonora—you must remember that she had reason for being very nervous and unhappy at that time—let out a sound that was very like a groan. It startled Edward, who more than suspected what was passing in her mind—it startled him into a state of anger. He said sharply:

"You wouldn't have me turn out people who've been earning money for us for centuries—people to whom we have responsibilities—and let in a pack of Scotch farmers?"

He looked at her, Leonora said, with what was practically a glance of hatred and then, precipitately, he left the breakfast-table. Leonora knew that it probably made it all the worse that he had been betrayed into a manifestation of anger before a third party. It was the first and last time that he ever was betrayed into such a manifestation of anger. The land-steward, a moderate and well-balanced man whose family also had been with the Ashburnhams for over a century, took it upon himself to explain that he considered Edward was pursuing a perfectly proper course with his tenants. He erred perhaps a little on the side of generos-ity, but hard times were hard times and everyone had to feel the pinch, landlord as well as tenants. The great thing was not to let the land get into a poor state of * cultivation. Scotch farmers just skinned your fields and let them go down and down. But Edward had a very good set of tenants who did their best for him and for themselves. These arguments at that time carried very little conviction to Leonora. She was neverthe-less much concerned by Edward's outburst * of anger.

The fact is that Leonora had been practising economies in her depart-ment. Two of the under-housemaids had gone and she had not replaced them; she had spent much less that year upon dress. The fare she had provided at the dinners they gave had been much less bountiful and not nearly so costly as had been the case in preceding years, and Edward began to perceive a hardness and determination in his wife's character. He seemed to see a net closing round him—a net in which they would be forced to live like one of the comparatively poor county families of the neighbourhood. And, in the mysterious way in which two people, living together, get to know each other's thoughts without a word spo-ken, he had known, even before his outbreak, that Leonora was wor-rying about his managing of the estates. This appeared to him to be intolerable. He had, too, a great feeling of self-contempt because he had been betrayed into speaking harshly to Leonora before that land-steward. He imagined that his nerve must be deserting him and there can have been few men more miserable than Edward was at that period.

You see, he was really a very simple soul—very simple. He imagined that no man can satisfactorily accomplish his life's work without loyal and wholehearted coöperation of the woman he lives with. And he was beginning to perceive dimly that, whereas his own traditions were entirely collective, his wife was a sheer individualist. His own ideal *— the feudal theory of an over-lord doing his best by his dependents, the dependents meanwhile doing their best for the over-lord—this theory was entirely foreign to Leonora's nature. She came of a family of small

Irish landlords—that hostile garrison in a plundered country. And she was thinking unceasingly of the children she wished to have.

I don't know why they never had any children—not that I really believe that children would have made any difference. The dissimilarity of Edward and Leonora was too profound. It will give you some idea of the extraordinary naïveté of Edward Ashburnham that, at the time of his marriage and for perhaps a couple of years after, he did not really know how children are produced. Neither did Leonora. I don't mean to say that this state of things continued but there it was. I dare say it had a good deal of influence on their mentalities. At any rate they never had a child. It was the Will of God.

It certainly presented itself to Leonora as being the Will of God—as being a mysterious and awful chastisement of the Almighty. For she had discovered shortly before this period that her parents had not exacted from Edward's family the promise that any children she should bear should be brought up as Catholics. She herself had never talked of the matter with either her father, her mother, or her husband. When at last her father had let drop some words leading her to believe that that was the fact she tried desperately to extort the promise from Edward. She encountered an unexpected obstinacy. Edward was perfectly willing that the girls should be Catholic; the boys must be Anglican. I don't understand the bearings of these things in English society. Indeed, Englishmen seem to me to be a little mad in matters of politics or of religion. In Edward it was particularly queer because he himself was perfectly ready to become a Romanist.[2] He seemed however to contemplate going over to Rome himself and yet letting his boys be educated in the religion of their immediate ancestors. This may appear illogical, but I dare say it is not so illogical as it looks. Edward, that is to say, regarded himself as having his own body and soul at his own disposal. But his loyalty to the traditions of his family would not permit him to bind any future inheritors of his name or beneficiaries by the deeds * of his ancestors. About the girls it did not so much matter. They would know other homes and other circumstances. Besides, it was the usual thing. But the boys must be given the opportunity of choosing—and they must have first of all the Anglican teaching. He was perfectly unshakable about this.

Leonora was in an agony during all this time. You will have to remember * she seriously believed that children who might be born to her went in danger, if not absolutely of damnation at any rate of receiving false doctrine. It was an agony more terrible than she could describe. She didn't indeed attempt to describe it but I could tell from her voice when she said, almost negligently, "I used to lie awake whole nights. It was no good my spiritual advisers trying to console me." I knew from

2. Roman Catholic.

her voice how terrible and how long those nights must have seemed and of how little avail were the consolations of her spiritual advisers. Her spiritual advisers seemed to have taken the matter a little more calmly. They certainly told her that she must not consider herself in any way to have sinned. Nay, they seem even to have exhorted, to have threatened her, with a view to getting her out of what they considered to be a morbid frame of mind. She would just have to make the best of things, to influence the children when they came, not by propaganda but by personality. And they warned her that she would be committing a sin if she continued to think that she had sinned. Nevertheless, she continued to think that she had sinned.

Leonora could not but be aware that the man whom she loved passionately* and whom, nevertheless, she was beginning to try to rule with a rod of iron—that this man was becoming more and more estranged from her. He seemed to regard her as being not only physically and mentally cold but even as being actually wicked and mean. There were times when he would almost shudder if she spoke to him. And she could not understand how he could consider her wicked or mean. It only seemed to her a sort of madness in him that he should try to take upon his own shoulders the burden of his troop, of his regiment, of his estate and of half of his county. She could not see that in trying to curb what she regarded as megalomania she was doing anything wicked. She was just trying to keep* things together for the sake of the children who did not come. And, little by little the whole of their intercourse became simply one of agonised discussion as to whether Edward should subscribe to this or that institution or should try to reclaim this or that drunkard. She simply could not see it.

Into this really terrible position of strain, from which there appeared to be no issue, the Kilsyte case came almost as a relief. It is part of the peculiar irony of things that Edward would certainly never have kissed that nurse-maid if he had not been trying to please Leonora. Nursemaids do not travel first-class and, that day, Edward travelled in a third-class carriage in order to prove to Leonora that he was capable of economies. I have said that the Kilsyte* case came almost as a relief to the strained situation that then existed between them. It gave Leonora an opportunity of backing him up in a whole-hearted and absolutely loyal manner. It gave her the opportunity of behaving to him as he considered a wife should behave to her husband.

You see, Edward found himself in a railway carriage with a quite pretty girl of about nineteen. And the quite pretty girl of about nineteen, with dark hair and red cheeks and blue eyes was quietly weeping. Edward had been sitting in his corner thinking about nothing at all. He had chanced to look at the nurse-maid; two large, pretty tears came out of her eyes and dropped into her lap. He immediately felt that he had got to do something to comfort her. That was his job in life. He was desperately unhappy himself and it seemed to him the most natural thing in the world that they should pool their sorrows. He was quite democratic; the idea of the difference in their station never seems to have occurred to him. He began to talk to her. He discovered that her young man had been seen walking out with Annie of Number 54. He moved over to her side of the carriage. He told her that the report probably wasn't true; that after all a young man might take a walk with Annie from Number 54 without its denoting anything very serious. And he assured me that he felt at least quite half-fatherly when he put his arm around her waist and kissed her. The girl, however, had not forgotten the difference of her station.

All her life, by her mother, by other girls, by school-teachers, by the whole tradition of her class she had been warned against gentlemen. She was being kissed by a gentleman. She screamed, tore herself away; sprang up and pulled a communication cord.

Edward came fairly well out of the affair in the public estimation; but it did him, mentally, a good deal of harm.

IV *

It is very difficult to give an all-round impression of any man. I wonder how far I have succeeded with Edward Ashburnham. I dare say I haven't succeeded at all. It is even very difficult to see how such * things matter. Was it the important point about poor Edward that he was very well built, carried himself well, was moderate at the * table and led a regular life—that he had in fact all the virtues that are usually accounted English? Or have I in the least succeeded in conveying that he was all those things and had all those virtues? He certainly was them and had them up to the last months of his life. They were the things that one would set upon his tombstone. They will indeed be set upon his tombstone by his widow.

And have I, I wonder, given * the due impression of how his life was portioned and his time laid out? Because, until the very last, the amount of time taken up by his various passions was relatively small. I have * been forced to write very much about his passions * but you have to consider—I should like to be able to make you consider—that he rose every morning at seven, took a cold bath, breakfasted at eight, was occupied with his regiment from nine until one; played polo, * or cricket with the men when it was the season for cricket, till tea-time. Afterwards he would occupy himself with the letters from his land-steward or with the affairs of his mess, till dinner time. He would dine and pass the evening playing cards, or playing billiards with Leonora or at social functions of one kind or another. And the greater part of his life was taken up by that—by far the greater part of his life. His love-affairs, until the very end, were sandwiched in at odd moments or took place during the social evenings, the dances and dinners. But I guess I have made it hard for you, O silent listener, to get that impression. Anyhow, I hope I have not given you the idea that Edward Ashburnham was a pathological case. He wasn't. He was just a normal man and very much of a sentimentalist. I dare say the quality of his youth, the nature of his mother's influence, his ignorances, the crammings that he received at the hands of army coaches—I dare say that all these excellent influences upon his adolescence were very bad for him. But we all have to put up with that sort of thing and no doubt it is very bad for all of us. Nevertheless the outline of Edward's life was an outline perfectly normal of the life of a hard-working, sentimental and efficient professional man.

That question of first impressions has always bothered me a good deal—but quite academically. I mean that, from time to time I have wondered whether it were or were not best to trust to one's first impressions in dealing with people. But I never had anybody to deal with except waiters and chambermaids and the Ashburnhams with whom I didn't know that I was having any dealings. And, as far as waiters and chambermaids were concerned I have generally found that my first impressions were correct enough. If my first idea of a man was that he was civil, obliging, and attentive, he generally seemed to go on being all those things. Once, however, at our Paris flat we had a maid who appeared to be charming and transparently honest. She stole, nevertheless, one of Florence's diamond rings. She did it, however, to save her young man from going to prison. So here, as somebody says somewhere, was a special case.

And, even in my short incursion into American business life—an incursion that lasted during part of August and nearly the whole of September—I found that to rely upon first impressions was the best thing I could do. I found myself automatically docketing and labelling each man as he was introduced to me, by the run of his features and by the first words that he spoke. I can't, however, be regarded as really doing business during the time that I spent in the United States. I was just winding things up. If it hadn't been for my idea of marrying the girl I might possibly have looked for something to do in my own country. For my experiences there were vivid and amusing. It was exactly as if I had come out of a museum into a riotous fancy-dress ball. During my life with Florence I had almost come to forget that there were such things as fashions or occupations or the greed of gain. I had in fact forgotten that there was such a thing as a dollar and that a dollar can be extremely desirable if you don't happen to possess one. And I had forgotten too that there was such a thing as gossip that mattered. In that particular, Philadelphia was the most amazing place I have ever been in my life. I was not in that city for more than a week or ten days and I didn't there transact anything much in the way of business, nevertheless the number of times that I was warned by everybody against everybody else was simply amazing. A man I didn't know would come up behind my lounge chair in the hotel, and, whispering cautiously beside my ear, would warn me against some other man that I equally didn't know but who would be standing by the bar. I don't know what they thought I was there to do—perhaps to buy out the city's debt or get a controlling hold of some railway interest. Or perhaps they imagined that I wanted to buy a newspaper, for they * were either politicians or reporters, which of course comes to the same thing. As a matter of fact my property in Philadelphia was mostly real estate in the old-fashioned part of the city and all I wanted to do there was just to satisfy myself that the houses were in good repair and the doors kept properly painted. I wanted * also to see my relations of whom I had a few. These were mostly professional people and they were mostly rather hard up because of the big bank failure in 1907 [3*] or thereabouts. Still, they were very nice. They would have been nicer still if they hadn't, all of them, had what appeared to me to be the mania that what they called influences were working against them. At any rate the impression of that city was one of old-fashioned rooms, rather English than American in type in which handsome but care-worn ladies, cousins of my own, talked principally about mysterious movements that were going on against them. I never got to know what it was all about; perhaps they thought I knew or perhaps there weren't any movements at all. It was all very secret and subtle and subterranean. But there was a nice young fellow called Carter who was a sort of second-nephew of mine, twice removed. He was handsome and dark and gentle and tall and modest. I understand also that he was a good cricketer. He was employed by the real-estate agents who collected my rents. It was he therefore who took me over my own property and I saw a good deal of him and of a nice girl called Mary to whom he was engaged. At that time I did, what I certainly shouldn't do now,—I made some careful inquiries as to his character. I discovered from his employers that he was just all that he appeared, honest, industrious, high-spirited, friendly and ready to do anyone a good turn. His relatives, however,—* they were mine too—seemed to have something darkly mysterious against him. I imagined that he must have been mixed up in some case of graft or that he had at least betrayed several innocent and trusting maidens. I pushed, however, that particular mystery home and discovered it was only that he was a Democrat. My own people were mostly Republicans. It seemed to make it worse and more darkly mysterious to them that young Carter was what they called a sort

---

3. The banking crisis, panic selling of shares in October 1907, foreshadowed the stock market crash of 1929.

of a Vermont Democrat* which was the whole ticket[4] and no mistake. But I don't know what it means. Anyhow I suppose that my money* will go to him when I die—I like the recollection of his friendly image and of the nice girl he was engaged to. May Fate deal very kindly with them.

I have said just now that, in my present frame of mind, nothing would ever make me make inquiries as to the character of any man that I liked at first sight. (The little digression as to my Philadelphia* experiences was really meant to lead around to this.) For who in this world can give anyone a character? Who in this world knows anything of any other heart—or of his own? I don't mean to say that one cannot form an average estimate of the way a person will behave. But one cannot be certain of the way any man will behave in every case—and until one can do that a "character" is of no use to anyone. That, for instance,* was the way with Florence's maid in Paris. We used to trust that girl with blank cheques for the payment of the tradesmen. For quite a time she was so trusted by us. Then, suddenly, she stole a ring. We should not have believed her capable of it; she would not have believed herself capable of it. It was nothing in her character. So perhaps it was with Edward Ashburnham.

Or perhaps it wasn't. No, I rather think it wasn't. It is difficult to figure out. I have said that the Kilsyte case eased the immediate tension for him and Leonora. It let him see that she was capable of loyalty to him; it gave her her chance to show* that she believed in him. She accepted without question his statement that, in kissing the girl he wasn't trying to do more than administer fatherly comfort to a weeping child. And indeed his own world—including the magistrates—took that view of the case. Whatever people say, one's world can be perfectly charitable at times. . . . But, again, as I have said it did Edward a great deal of harm.

That, at least, was his view of it. He assured me that, before that case came on and was wrangled about by counsel with all the sorts of dirty-mindedness* that counsel in that sort of case can impute, he had not had the least idea that he was capable of being unfaithful to Leonora. But, in the midst of that tumult—he says that it came suddenly into his head whilst he was in the witness box—in the midst of those august ceremonies of the law there came suddenly into his mind the recollection of the softness of the girl's body as he had pressed her to him. And, from that moment that girl appeared desirable to him—and Leonora completely unattractive.

He* began to indulge in day-dreams in which he approached the nurse-maid more tactfully and carried the matter much further. Occa-

---

4. Political expression: the straight, or whole, ticket is the regular nomination of a voter's party, as opposed to a "split ticket" representing divisions in the party; i.e., here: an extreme Democrat, on the far left of liberal American politics.

sionally he thought of other women in terms of wary courtship—or perhaps it would be more exact to say that he thought of them in terms of tactful comforting, ending in absorption. That was his own view of the case. He saw himself as the victim of the law. I don't mean to say that he saw himself as a kind of Dreyfus.[5] The law, practically, was quite kind to him. It stated that in its view Captain Ashburnham had been misled by an ill-placed desire to comfort a member of the opposite sex and it fined him five shillings for his want of tact, or of knowledge of the world. But Edward maintained that it had put ideas into his head.

I don't believe it, though he certainly did. He was twenty-seven then, and his wife was out of sympathy with him—some crash was inevitable. There was between them a momentary rapprochement; but it could not last. It made it, probably, all the worse that, in that particular matter Leonora had come so very well up to the scratch.[6] For whilst Edward respected her more and was grateful to her it made her seem by so much the more cold in other matters that were near his heart—his responsibilities, his career, his tradition. It brought his despair of her up to a point of exasperation—and it rivetted on him the idea that he might find some other woman who would give him the moral support that he needed. He wanted to be looked upon as a sort of Lohengrin.[7]

At that time, he says, he went about deliberately looking for some woman who could help him. He found several—for there were quite a number of ladies in his set who were capable of agreeing with this handsome and fine fellow that the duties of a feudal gentleman were feudal. He would have liked to pass his days talking to one or other of these ladies. But there was always an obstacle—if the lady were married there would be a husband who claimed the greater part of her time and attention. If on the other hand it were an unmarried girl he could not see very much of her for fear of compromising her. At that date, you understand, he had not the least idea of seducing any one * of these ladies. He wanted only moral support at the hands of some female, because he found men difficult to talk to about ideals. Indeed, I do not believe that he had, at any time, any idea of making any one his mistress. That sounds queer; but I believe it is quite true as a statement of character.

It was I believe one of Leonora's priests—a man of the world—who suggested that she should take him to Monte Carlo. He had the idea that what Edward needed, in order to fit him for the society of Leonora was a touch of irresponsibility. For Edward, at that date, had much the

5. A man misjudged and betrayed like Alfred Dreyfus (1859–1935), French Jewish officer, victim of anti-Semitism; in 1894, he was wrongly convicted of treason and deported for life to Devil's Island; Dreyfus was released in 1906 after the revelation of forged evidence; the case was the focus of French political life for a decade, the right-wing periodicals and mainly Catholic high command refusing to admit error.
6. Another equestrian expression; the "scratch" is the starting point of a race; hence here: responded so well to the challenge.
7. See p. 68, n. 6 above.

aspect of a prig. I mean that, if he played polo and was an excellent dancer he did the one for the sake of keeping himself fit and the other because it was a social duty to show himself at dances, and, when there, to dance well. He did nothing for fun except what he considered to be his work in life. As the priest saw it this must for ever estrange him from Leonora—not because Leonora set much store by the joy of life, but because she was out of sympathy with Edward's work. On the other hand, Leonora did like to have a good time, now and then, and, as the priest saw it, if Edward could be got to like having a good time now and then too, there would be a bond of sympathy between them. It was a good idea, but it worked out wrongly.

It worked out, in fact, in the mistress of the Grand Duke. In anyone less sentimental than Edward that would not have mattered. With Edward it was fatal. For, such was his honourable* nature, that for him, to enjoy a woman's favours, made him feel that she had a bond on him for life. That was the way it worked out in practice. Psychologically it meant that he could not have a mistress without falling violently in love with her. He was a serious person—and in this particular case it was very expensive. The mistress of the Grand Duke—a Spanish dancer of passionate appearance—singled out Edward for her glances at a ball that was held in their common hotel. Edward was tall, handsome, blond and very wealthy as she understood—and Leonora went up to bed early. She did not care for public dances, but she was relieved to see that Edward appeared to be having a good time with several amiable girls. And that was the end of Edward—for the Spanish dancer of passionate appearance wanted one night of him for his beaux yeux. He took her into the dark gardens and, remembering suddenly the girl of the Kilsyte case, he kissed her. He kissed her passionately, violently with a sudden explosion of the passion that had been bridled all his life—for Leonora was cold, or, at any rate well behaved. La Dolciquita liked this reversion, and he passed the night in her bed.

When the palpitating creature was at last asleep in his arms he discovered that he was madly, was passionately, was overwhelmingly in love with her. It was a passion that had arisen like fire in dry corn. He could think of nothing else; he could live for nothing else. But La Dolciquita was a reasonable creature without an ounce of passion in her. She wanted a certain satisfaction of her appetites and Edward had appealed to her the night before. Now that was done with and, quite coldly, she said that she wanted money if he was to have any more of her. It was a perfectly reasonable commercial transaction. She did not care two buttons for Edward or for any man and he was asking her to risk a very good situation with a Grand Duke. If Edward could put up sufficient money to serve as a kind of insurance against accident she was ready to like Edward for a time that would be covered, as it were, by the policy. She was getting fifty thousand dollars a year from her Grand

Duke; Edward would have to pay a premium of two years' hire for a month of her society. There would not be much risk of the Grand Duke's finding it out and it was not certain that he would give her the keys of the street[8] if he did find out. But there was the risk—a twenty per cent risk, as she figured it out. She talked to Edward as if she had been a solicitor with an estate to sell—perfectly quietly and perfectly coldly without any inflections in her voice. She did not want to be unkind to him; but she could see no reason for being kind to him. She was a virtuous business woman with a mother and two sisters and her own old age to be provided comfortably for. She did not expect more than a five years' further run. She was twenty-four and, as she said: "We Spanish women are horrors at thirty." Edward swore that he would provide for her for life if she would come to him and leave off talking so horribly; but she only shrugged one shoulder slowly and contemptuously. He tried to convince this woman, who as he saw it, had surrendered to him her virtue, that he regarded it as in any case his duty to provide for her, and to cherish her and even to love her—for life. In return for her sacrifice he would do that. In return, again, for his honourable love she would listen for ever to the accounts of his estate. That was how he figured it out.

She shrugged the same shoulder with the same gesture and held out her left hand with the elbow at her side:

"Enfin, mon ami," she said, "put in this hand the price of that tiara at Forli's[9] or. . . ." And she turned her back on him.

Edward went mad; his world stood on its head; the palms in front of the blue sea danced grotesque dances. You see, he believed in the virtue, tenderness and moral support of women. He wanted more than anything to argue with La Dolciquita; to retire with her to an island and point out to her the damnation of her point of view and how salvation can only be found in true love and the feudal system. She had once been his mistress, he reflected, and, by all the moral laws she ought to have gone on being his mistress or at the very least his sympathetic confidante. But her rooms were closed to him; she did not appear in the hotel. Nothing: blank silence. To break that down he had to have twenty thousand pounds. You have heard what happened.

He spent a week of madness; he hungered; his eyes sank in; he shuddered at Leonora's touch. I daresay that nine tenths of what he took to be his passion for La Dolciquita was really discomfort at the thought that he had been unfaithful to Leonora. He felt uncommonly bad, that is to say—oh, unbearably bad, and he took it all to be love. Poor devil, he was incredibly naif. He drank like a fish after Leonora was in bed and he spread himself over the tables, and this went on for about a fort-

8. Throw her out.
9. Possibly a mistake for "Florie's," a jewelery shop in Monte Carlo in 1910; no "Forli's" is listed.

night.* Heaven knows what would have happened; he would have thrown away every penny that he possessed.

On the night after he had lost about* forty thousand pounds and whilst the whole hotel was whispering about it La Dolciquita walked composedly into his bedroom. He was too drunk to recognise her, and she sat in his armchair, knitting and holding smelling salts to his* nose—for he was pretty far gone with alcoholic poisoning—and, as soon as he was able to understand her, she said:

"Look here, mon ami, do not go to the tables again. Take a good sleep now and come and see me this afternoon."

He slept till the lunch hour.* By that time Leonora had heard the news. A Mrs. Colonel Whelen had told her. Mrs. Colonel Whelen seems to have been the only sensible person who was ever connected with the Ashburnhams. She had argued it out that there must be a woman of the harpy variety connected with Edward's incredible behaviour and mien; and she advised Leonora to go straight off to Town [1]— which might have the effect of bringing Edward to his senses—and to consult her solicitor and her spiritual adviser. She had better go that very morning; it was no good arguing with a man in Edward's condition.

Edward, indeed, did not know that she had gone. As soon as he woke he went straight to La Dolciquita's room and she stood him his lunch in her own apartments. He fell on her neck and wept, and she put up with it for a time. She was quite a good-natured* woman. And, when she had calmed him down with Eau de Melisse,[2]* she said:

"Look here, my friend, how much money have you left? Five thousand dollars? Ten?" For the rumour went that Edward had lost two kings' ransoms a night for fourteen* nights and she imagined that he must be near the end of his resources.

The Eau de Melisse had calmed Edward to such an extent that, for the moment, he really had a head on his shoulders. He did nothing more than grunt:

"And then?"

"Why," she answered, "I may just as well have the ten* thousand dollars[3] as the tables. I will go with you to Antibes for a week for that sum."

Edward grunted: "Five." She tried to get seven thousand five hundred; but he stuck to his five thousand and the hotel expenses at Antibes. The sedative carried him just as far as that and then he collapsed again. He had to leave for Antibes at three; he could not do without it. He left a note for Leonora saying that he had gone off for a week with the Clinton Morleys, yachting.

He did not enjoy himself very much at Antibes. La Dolciquita could

1. London.
2. Melissa cordial (melissa is a herb, a balm).
3. Then $10,000 was c. £2,000 or c. $150,000, £100,000 now.

talk of nothing with any enthusiasm except money, and she tired him unceasingly, during every waking hour for presents of the most expensive description. And, at the end of a week, she just quietly kicked him out. He hung about in Antibes for three days. He was cured of the idea that he had any duties towards La Dolciquita—feudal or otherwise. But his sentimentalism required of him an attitude of Byronic gloom—as if his court had gone into half-mourning. Then his appetite suddenly returned, and he remembered Leonora. He found at his hotel at Monte Carlo a telegram from Leonora, despatched from London, saying: "Please return as soon as convenient." He could not understand why Leonora should have abandoned him so precipitately when she only thought that he had gone yachting with the Clinton Morleys. Then he discovered that she had left the hotel before he had written the note. He had a pretty rocky journey back to town; he was frightened out of his life—and Leonora had never seemed so desirable to him.

V *

I call this the Saddest Story, rather than "The Ashburnham Tragedy", just because it is so sad, just because there was no current to draw things along to a swift and inevitable end. There is about it none of the elevation that accompanies tragedy; there is about it no nemesis, no destiny. Here were two noble people—for I am convinced that both Edward and Leonora had noble natures—here then, were two noble natures, drifting down life, like fire-ships[1] afloat on a lagoon and causing miseries, heartaches, agony of the mind and death. And they themselves steadily deteriorated? And why? For what purpose? To point what lesson? It is all a darkness.

There is not even any villain in the story—for even Major Basil, the husband of the lady who next—and really—comforted the unfortunate Edward—even Major Basil was not a villain in this piece. He was a slack, loose, shiftless sort of fellow—but he did not *do* * anything to Edward. Whilst they were in the same station in Burma he borrowed a good deal of money—though really, since Major Basil had no particular vices, it was difficult to know why he wanted it. * He collected—different types of horses' bits from the earliest times to the present day—but, since he did not prosecute even this occupation with any vigour, he cannot have needed much money for the acquirement say of the bit of Genghis Khan's charger—if Genghis Khan had a charger. And when I say that he borrowed a good deal of money from Edward I do not mean to say

---

1. Literally, a ship filled with combustibles, set adrift among enemy ships to destroy them; also archaic slang for one suffering from venereal disease.

that he had more than a thousand pounds[2] from him during the five years that the connection lasted. Edward, of course, did not have a great deal of money; Leonora was seeing to that. Still he may have had five hundred pounds a year English, for his menus plaisirs[3]—for his regimental subscriptions and for keeping his men smart. Leonora hated that; she would have preferred to buy dresses for herself or to have devoted the money to paying off a mortgage. Still, with her sense of justice, she saw that, since she was managing a property bringing in three thousand a year with a view to re-establishing it as a property of five thousand a year, and since the property really, if not legally, belonged to Edward, it was reasonable and just that Edward should get a slice of his own. Of course she had the devil of a job.

I don't know that I have got the financial details exactly right. I am a pretty good head at figures, but my mind, still, sometimes mixes up pounds with dollars and I get a figure wrong. Anyhow, the proposition was something like this: properly* worked and without rebates to the tenants and keeping up schools and things the Bramshaw estate should have brought in about five thousand a year when Edward had it. It brought in actually about four. (I am talking in pounds not dollars.) Edward's excesses with the Spanish Lady had reduced its value to about three—as the maximum figure, without reductions. Leonora wanted to get it back to five.

She was, of course, very young to be faced with such a proposition—twenty-four is not a very advanced age. So she did things with a youthful vigour that she would, very likely,* have made more merciful, if she had known more about life. She got Edward remarkably on the hop. He had to face her in a London hotel,* when he crept back from Monte Carlo with his poor tail between his poor legs. As far as I can make out she cut short his first mumblings and his first attempts at affectionate speech with words something like:

"We're on the verge of ruin. Do you intend to let me pull things together? If not I shall retire to Hendon on my jointure."[4] (Hendon represented a convent to which she occasionally went for what is called a "retreat" in Catholic circles.)

And poor dear Edward knew nothing—absolutely nothing. He did not know how much money he had, as he put it, "blued"[5] at the tables. It might have been a quarter of a million for all he remembered. He did not know whether she knew about La Dolciquita or whether she imagined that he had gone off yachting or had* stayed at Monte Carlo. He was just dumb and he just wanted to get into a hole and not [to] have* to talk. Leonora did not make him talk and she said nothing herself.

2. About $5,000 then, c. $75,000 or £50,000 now.
3. Abbreviation of *argent pour menus plaisirs*: pocket money (French).
4. Part of the estate which is exclusively the wife's property.
5. Squandered.

I do not know much about English legal procedure—I cannot, I mean, give technical details of how they tied him up. But I know that, two days later, without her having said more than I have reported to you, Leonora and her attorney had become the trustees, as I believe it is called, of all Edward's property and there was an end of Edward as the good landlord and father of his people. He went out.

Leonora then had three thousand a year at her disposal. She occupied Edward with getting himself transferred to a part of his regiment that was in Burma—if that is the right way to put it. She herself had an interview, lasting a week or so—with Edward's land-steward. She made him understand that the estate would have to yield up to its last penny. Before they left for India she had let Bramshaw * for seven years at a thousand a year. She sold two Vandykes and a little silver for eleven thousand pounds and she raised, on mortgage, twenty-nine thousand. That went to Edward's money-lending friends in Monte Carlo. So she had to get the twenty-nine thousand back, for she did not regard the Vandykes and the silver as things she would have to replace. They were just frills to the Ashburnham vanity. Edward cried for two days over the disappearance of his ancestors and then she wished she had not done it; but it did not teach her anything and it lessened such esteem as she had for him. She did not also understand that to let Bramshaw affected him with a feeling of physical soiling—that it was almost as bad for him as if a woman belonging to him had become a prostitute. That was how it did affect him; but I daresay she felt just as bad about the Spanish dancer.

So she went at it. They were eight years in India and during the whole of that time she insisted that they must be self-supporting—they had to live on his Captain's pay plus the extra allowance for being at the front. She gave him [however] * the five hundred a year for Ashburnham frills as she called it to herself—and she considered she was doing him very well.

Indeed, in a way, she did him very well—but it was not his way. She was always buying him expensive things which, as it were, she took off her own back. I have for instance spoken of Edward's leather cases. Well, they were not Edward * at all; they were Leonora's manifestations. He liked to be clean, but he preferred, as it were, to be threadbare. She never understood that and all that pigskin was her idea of a reward to him for putting her up to a little speculation by which she made eleven hundred pounds. She did, herself, the threadbare business. When they went up to a place called Simla,[6] where, as I understand, it is cool in the summer and very social—when they went up to Simla for their healths it was she who had him prancing around, as we should say in

6. Now Shimla, in Punjab, northeastern India, in the foothills of the Himalayas, c.180 miles north of Delhi; then a summer retreat for the Viceroy and his entourage, a fashionable center for British colonials.

the United States, on a thousand dollar horse with the gladdest of glad rags all over him. She herself used to go into "retreat". I believe that was very good for her health and it was also very inexpensive.

It was probably also very good for Edward's health, because he pranced about mostly with Mrs. Basil who was a nice woman and very, very kind to him. I suppose she was his mistress, but I never heard it from Edward, of course. I seem to gather that they carried it on in a high romantic fashion, very proper to both of them—or at any rate for Edward; she * seems to have been a tender and gentle soul who did what * he wanted. I do not mean to say that she was without character; that was her job, to do what Edward wanted. So I figured it out that, for those five years, Edward wanted long passages of deep affection kept up in long, long talks and that every now and then they "fell", which would give Edward an opportunity for remorse and an excuse to lend the Major another fifty. I don't think that Mrs. Basil considered it to be "falling"; she just pitied him and loved him.

You see Leonora and Edward had to talk about something during all those years. You cannot be absolutely dumb when you live with a person unless you are an inhabitant of the North of England or the State of Maine. So Leonora imagined the cheerful device of letting him see the accounts of his estate and discussing them with him. He did not discuss them much; he was trying to behave prettily. But it was old Mr. Mudford—the farmer who did not pay his rent—that threw Edward into Mrs. Basil's arms. Mrs. Basil * came upon Edward in the dusk, in the Burmese garden, with all sorts of flowers and things. And he was cutting up that crop—with his sword, not a walking stick. He was also carrying on and cursing in a way you would not believe.

She ascertained that an old gentleman called Mudford had been ejected from his farm and had been given a little cottage rent-free where he lived on ten shillings a week from a farmers' benevolent society, supplemented by seven that was being allowed him by the Ashburnham trustees. Edward had just discovered that fact from the estate accounts. Leonora had left them in his dressing room and he had begun to read them before taking off his marching kit. That was how he came to have a sword. Leonora considered that she had been unusually generous to old Mr. Mudford in allowing him to inhabit a cottage rent-free and in giving him seven shillings a week. Anyhow, Mrs. Basil * had never seen a man in such a state as Edward was. She had been passionately in love with him for quite a time, and he had been longing for her sympathy and admiration with a passion as deep. That was how they came to speak about it, in the Burmese garden, under the pale sky, with sheaves of severed vegetation, misty and odorous in the night around their feet. I think they behaved themselves with decorum for quite a time after that, though Mrs. Basil * spent so many hours over the accounts of the Ashburnham estate that she got the name of every field by heart. Edward had a huge map of his lands in his harness room and Major Basil did not seem to mind. I believe that people do not mind much in lonely stations.

It might have lasted for ever if the Major had not been made what is called a brevet-colonel during the shuffling of troops that went on just before the South African War.[7] He was sent off somewhere else and of course Mrs. Basil could not stay with Edward. Edward ought, I suppose, to have gone to the Transvaal. It would have done him a great deal of good to get killed. But Leonora would not let him; she had heard awful stories of the extravagance of the hussar regiment [8*] in war-time—how they left hundred-bottle * cases of champagne at five guineas a bottle, on the veldt[9] and so on. Besides, she preferred to see how Edward was spending his five hundred a year. I don't mean to say that Edward had any grievance in that. He was never a man of the deeds of heroism sort and it was just as good for him to be sniped at up in the hills on the North Western Frontier,[1] as to be shot at by an old gentleman in a top hat at the bottom of some spruit.[2] Those are more or less his words about it. I believe he quite distinguished himself over there. At any rate he had his D. S. O. and was made a brevet-major.

Leonora, however, was not in the least keen on his soldiering. She hated also his deeds of heroism. One of their bitterest quarrels came after he had, for the second time, in the Red Sea, jumped overboard from the troopship and rescued a private soldier. She stood it the first time and even complimented him. But the Red Sea was awful, that trip, and the private soldiers seemed to develop a suicidal craze. It got on Leonora's nerves; she figured Edward, for the rest of that trip, jumping overboard every ten minutes. And the mere cry of "Man overboard" is a disagreeable, alarming and disturbing thing. The ship gets stopped and there are all sorts of shouts. And Edward would not promise not to do it again, though, fortunately they struck a streak of cooler weather when they were in the Persian Gulf. Leonora had got it into her head that Edward was trying to commit suicide, so I guess it was pretty awful for her when he would not give the promise. Leonora ought never to have been on that troop-ship; but she got there somehow as an economy.

Major Basil * discovered his wife's relation with Edward just before he was sent to his other station. I don't know whether that was a blackmailer's adroitness or just a trick of destiny. He may have known of it all the time or he may not. At any rate he got hold of, just about then, some

7. A "brevet" confers nominally higher rank on an officer without entitlement to extra pay. The South African War, or Boer War (1899–1902), was between Great Britain and the two Boer republics, the Orange Free State and the Transvaal, both of which became British colonies.
8. Light cavalry, one of the "smart" regiments. See p. 23, n. 6 above. See also MDATV, p. 209, 113, 2nd entry below.
9. Open pasture land in South Africa.
1. Then a province of British India on its northwest border with Afghanistan; now a province of Pakistan. See p. 41, n. 6 above.
2. Small stream in South Africa, almost dry except in wet season.

letters and things. It cost Edward three hundred pounds immediately. I
do not know how it was arranged; I cannot imagine how even a blackmailer can make * his demands. I suppose there is some sort of way of
saving your face. I figure the Major as disclosing the letters to Edward
with furious oaths, then accepting his explanations that the letters were
perfectly innocent if the wrong construction were not put upon them.
Then the Major would say: "I say, old chap, I'm deuced hard up.
Couldn't you lend me three hundred or so?" I fancy that was how it was.
And, year by year, after that there would come a letter from the Major,
saying that he was deuced hard up and couldn't Edward lend him three
hundred or so.

Edward was pretty hard hit when Mrs. Basil had to go away. He really
had been very fond of her, and he remained faithful to her memory for
quite a long time. And Mrs. Basil had loved him very much and continued to cherish a hope of reunion with him. Three days ago there came
a quite proper, but very lamentable letter from her to Leonora, asking
to be given particulars as to Edward's death. She had read the advertisement of it in an Indian paper. I think she must have been a very nice
woman. . . .

And then the Ashburnhams were moved somewhere up towards a
place or a district called Chitral. I am no good at geography of the Indian
Empire. * By that time they had settled down into a model couple and
they never spoke in private to each other. Leonora had given up even
showing the accounts of the Ashburnham estate to Edward. He thought
that that was because she had piled up such a lot of money that she did
not want him to know how she was getting on any more. But, as a
matter of fact, after five or six years it had penetrated to her mind that it
was painful to Edward to have to look on at the accounts of his estate
and have no hand in the management of it. She was trying to do him a
kindness. And, up in Chitral, poor dear little Maisie Maidan came
along. . . .

That was the most unsettling to Edward of all his affairs. It made him
suspect that he was inconstant. The affair with the Dolciquita he had
sized up as a short attack of madness like hydrophobia. His relations
with Mrs. Basil had not seemed to him to imply moral turpitude of a
gross kind. The husband had been complaisant; they had really loved
each other; his wife was very cruel * to him and had long ceased to be a
wife to him. He thought that Mrs. Basil had been his soul-mate, separated from him by an unkind fate—something sentimental of that sort.

But he discovered that, whilst he was still writing long weekly letters
to Mrs. Basil, he was beginning to be furiously impatient if he missed
seeing Maisie Maidan during the course of the day. He discovered himself watching the doorways with impatience; he discovered that he disliked her boy husband very much for hours at a time. He discovered
that he was getting up at unearthly hours in order to have time, later in

the morning, to go for a walk with Maisie Maidan. He discovered himself using little slang words that she used and attaching a sentimental value to those words. These, you understand, were discoveries that came so late that he could do nothing but drift. He was losing weight; his eyes were beginning to fall in; he had touches of bad fever. He was, as he described it, pipped. [3]

And, one ghastly hot day, he suddenly heard himself say to Leonora:

"I say, couldn't we take little Mrs. Maidan with us to Europe and drop her at Nauheim."

He hadn't had the least idea of saying that to Leonora. He had merely been standing, looking at an illustrated paper, waiting for dinner. Dinner was twenty minutes late or the Ashburnhams would not have been alone together. No, he hadn't had the least idea of framing that speech. He had just been standing in a silent agony of fear, of longing, of heat, of fever. He was thinking that they were going back to Bramshaw* in a month and that Maisie Maidan was going to remain behind and die. And then, that had come out.

The punkah swished in the darkened room; Leonora lay exhausted and motionless in her cane-lounge; [4] neither of them stirred. They were both at that time very ill in indefinite ways.

And then Leonora said:

"Yes. I promised it to Charlie Maidan this afternoon. I have offered to pay her ex's [5] myself."

Edward just saved himself from saying: "Good God!"* You see, he had not the least idea of what Leonora knew—about Maisie, about Mrs. Basil, or even about La Dolciquita. It was a pretty enigmatic situation for him. It struck him that Leonora must be intending to manage his loves as she managed his money affairs and it made her more hateful to him—and more worthy of respect.

Leonora, at any rate, had managed his money to some purpose. She had spoken to him, a week before, for the first time in several years *— about money. She had made twenty-two thousand pounds out of the Bramshaw land and seven by the letting of Bramshaw furnished. By fortunate investments—in which Edward had helped her—she had made another six or seven thousand that might well become more. The mortgages were all paid off so that, except for the departure of the two Vandykes and the silver they were as well off as they had been before the Dolciquita had acted the locust. It was Leonora's great achievement. She laid the figures before Edward who maintained an unbroken silence.

"I propose," she said, "that you should resign from the army and that

3. Depressed, exhausted.
4. Day-bed made of cane. "Punkah": large swinging fan made of cloth stretched on rectangular frame suspended from ceiling and operated by a string pulled by a "punkah-wallah."
5. Expenses.

we should go back to Bramshaw. We are both too ill to stay here any longer."

Edward said nothing at all.

"This," Leonora continued passionlessly, "is the great day of my life."

Edward said:

"You have managed the job amazingly. You are a wonderful woman." He was thinking that if they went back to Bramshaw they would leave Maisie Maidan behind. That thought occupied him exclusively. They must undoubtedly return to Bramshaw; there could be no doubt that Leonora was too ill to stay in that place. She said:

"You understand that the management of the whole of the expenditure of the income will be in your hands. There will be five thousand a year."

She thought that he cared very much about the expenditure of an income of five thousand a year and that the fact that she had done so much for him would rouse in him some affection for her. But he was thinking exclusively of Maisie Maidan—of Maisie thousands of miles away from him. He was seeing the mountains between them—blue mountains and the sea and sunlit plains.* He said:

"That is very generous of you." And she did not know whether that were praise or a sneer. That had been a week before. And all that week he had passed in an increasing agony at the thought that those mountains, that sea and those sunlit plains would be between him and Maisie Maidan. That thought shook him in the burning nights: the sweat poured from him and he trembled with cold, in the burning noons—at that thought. He had no minute's rest; his bowels turned round and round within him: his tongue was perpetually dry;* and it seemed to him that the breath between his teeth was like air from a pest-house.[6]

He gave no thought to Leonora at all; he had sent in his papers.[7] They were to leave in a month. It seemed to him to be his duty to leave that place and to go away, to support Leonora. He did his duty.

It was horrible, in their relationship at that time, that whatever she did caused him to hate her. He hated her when he found that she proposed to set him up as the lord of Bramshaw* again—as a sort of dummy lord, in swaddling clothes. He imagined that she had done this in order to separate him from Maisie Maidan. Hatred hung in all the heavy nights and filled the shadowy corners of the room. So when he heard that she had offered to the Maidan boy to take his wife to Europe with him, automatically he hated her since he hated all that she did. It seemed to him, at that time that she could never be other than cruel even if, by accident, an act of hers* were kind. . . . Yes, it was a horrible situation.

6. Hospital for those infected by plague.
7. Made formal application to resign his military commission.

But the cool breezes of the ocean seemed to clear up that hatred as if it had been a curtain. They seemed to give him back admiration for her, and respect. The agreeableness of having money lavishly at command, the fact that it had bought for him the companionship of Maisie Maidan—these things began to make him see that his wife might have been right in the starving and scraping upon which she had insisted. He was at ease; he was even radiantly happy when he carried cups of bouillon[8] for Maisie Maidan along the deck.* One night, when he was leaning, beside Leonora, over the ship's side he said suddenly:

"By Jove, you're the finest woman in the world. I wish we could be better friends."

She just turned away, without a word and went to her cabin. Still, she was very much better in health.*

And,* now, I suppose I must give you Leonora's side of the case. . . .

That is very difficult. For Leonora, if she preserved an unchanged front, changed very frequently her point of view. She had been drilled—in her tradition, in her upbringing—to keep her mouth shut. But there were times, she said, when she was so near yielding to the temptation of speaking that afterwards she shuddered to think of those times. You must postulate that what she desired above all things was to keep a shut mouth to the world, to Edward and to the women that he loved. If she spoke she would despise herself.

From the moment of his unfaithfulness with La Dolciquita she never acted the part of wife to Edward. It was not that she intended to keep herself from him as a principle, for ever. Her spiritual advisers, I believe, forbade that. But she stipulated that he must, in some way, perhaps symbolical, come back to her. She was not very clear as to what she meant; probably she did not know herself. Or perhaps she did.

There were moments when he seemed to be coming back to her; there were moments when she was within a hair of yielding to her physical passion for him. In just the same way, at moments, she almost yielded to the temptation to denounce Mrs. Basil* to her husband or Maisie Maidan to hers. She desired then to cause the horrors and pains of public scandals. For, watching Edward more intently and with more straining of ears than that which a cat bestows upon a bird overhead, she was aware of the progress of his passion for each of these ladies. She was aware of it from the way in which his eyes returned to doors and gateways; she knew from his tranquillities when he had received satisfactions.

At times she imagined herself to see more than was warranted. She imagined that Edward was carrying on intrigues with other women—with two at once; with three. For whole periods she imagined him to be

8. Broth, soup.

a monster of libertinage and she could not see that he could have anything against her. She left him his liberty; she was starving herself to
build up his fortunes; she allowed herself none of the joys of femininity—no dresses, no jewels—hardly even any friendships, for fear they
should cost money.

And yet, oddly, she could not but be aware that both Mrs. Basil and
Maisie Maidan were nice women. The curious, discounting eye which
one woman can turn on another did not prevent her seeing that Mrs.
Basil was very good to Edward and Mrs. Maidan * very good for him.
That seemed to her to be a monstrous and incomprehensible working of
Fate's. * Incomprehensible! Why, she asked herself again and again, did
none of the good deeds that she did for her husband ever come through
to him, or appear to him as good deeds? By what trick of mania could
not he let her be as good to him as Mrs. Basil was? * Mrs. Basil was not
so extraordinarily dissimilar to herself. She was, it was true, tall, dark,
with a soft mournful voice and a great kindness of manner for every
created thing, from punkah men [9] to flowers on the trees. But she was
not so well-read as Leonora, at any rate in learned books. Leonora could
not stand novels. But, even with all her differences Mrs. Basil did not
appear to Leonora to differ so very much from herself. She was truthful,
honest and, for the rest, just a woman. And Leonora had a vague sort of
idea that, to a man, all women are the same after three weeks of close
intercourse. She thought that the kindness should no longer appeal, the
soft and mournful voice no longer thrill, the tall darkness no longer give
a man the illusion that he was going into the depths of an unexplored
wood. She could not understand how Edward could go on and on
maundering [1] over Mrs. Basil. She could not see why he should continue to write her long letters after their separation. After that, indeed,
she had a very bad time.

She had at that period what I will call the "monstrous" theory of
Edward. She was always imagining him ogling at every woman that he
came across. She did not, that year, go into "retreat" at Simla because
she was afraid that he would corrupt her maid in her absence. She imagined him carrying on intrigues with native women or Eurasians. At
dances she was in a fever of watchfulness. . . .

She persuaded herself that this was because she had a dread of scandals. Edward might get himself mixed up with a marriageable daughter
of some man who would make a row or some husband who would matter. But really, she acknowledged afterwards to herself, she was hoping
that, Mrs. Basil being out of the way, the time might have come when
Edward should return to her. All that period she passed in an agony of
jealousy and fear—the fear that Edward might really become promiscuous in his habits.

9. See p. 115, n. 4 above.
1. Talking incoherently and/or dreamily.

So that, in an odd way, she was glad when Maisie Maidan* came along—and she realised that she had not, before, been afraid of husbands and of scandals, since, then, she did her best to keep Maisie's husband unsuspicious. She wished to appear so trustful of Edward that Maidan could not possibly have any suspicions. It was an evil position for her. But Edward was very ill and she wanted to see him smile again. She thought that if he could smile again through her agency he might return, through gratitude and satisfied love—to her. At that time she thought that Edward was a person of light and fleeting passions. And she could understand Edward's passion for Maisie, since Maisie was one of those women to whom other women will allow magnetism.

She was very pretty; she was very young; in spite of her heart she was very gay and light on her feet. And Leonora was really very fond of Maisie who was fond enough of Leonora. Leonora indeed imagined* that she could manage this affair all right. She had no thought of Maisie's being led into adultery; she imagined that if she could take Maisie and Edward to Nauheim, Edward would see enough of her to get tired of her pretty little chatterings, and of the pretty little motions of her hands and feet. And she thought she could trust Edward. For there was not any doubt of Maisie's* passion for Edward. She raved about him to Leonora as Leonora had heard girls rave about drawing masters in schools. She was perpetually asking her boy husband why he could not dress, ride, shoot, play polo, or even recite sentimental poems, like their major. And young Maidan had the greatest admiration for Edward and he adored, was bewildered by and entirely trusted his wife. It appeared to him* that Edward was devoted to Leonora. And Leonora imagined that when poor Maisie was cured of her heart and Edward had seen enough of her, he would return to her. She had the vague, passionate idea that, when Edward had exhausted a number of other types of women he must turn to her. Why should not her type have its turn in his heart? She imagined that, by now, she understood him better, that she understood better his vanities and that, by making him happier, she could arouse his love.

Florence knocked all that on the head. . . .

PART IV*

I*

I have, I am aware, told this story in a very rambling way so that it may be difficult for anyone to find their path through what may be a sort of maze. I cannot help it. I have stuck to my idea of being in a country cottage with a silent listener, hearing between the gusts of the wind and amidst the noises of the distant sea, the story as it comes. And, when one discusses an affair—a long, sad affair—one goes back, one goes forward. One remembers points that one has forgotten and one explains them all the more minutely since one recognises that one has forgotten to mention them in their proper places and that one may have given, by omitting them, a false impression. I console myself with thinking that this is a real story and that, after all, real stories are probably told best in the way a person telling a story would tell them. They will then seem most real.

At any rate I think I have brought my story up to the date of Maisie Maidan's death. I mean that I have explained everything that went before it from the several points of view that were necessary—from Leonora's,* from Edward's and to some extent, from my own. You have the facts for the trouble of finding them; you have the points of view as far as I could ascertain or put them. Let me imagine myself back, then, at the day of Maisie's death—or rather at the moment of Florence's dissertation on the Protest, up in the old Castle of the town of M——. Let us consider Leonora's point of view with regard to Florence; Edward's, of course, I cannot give you for Edward naturally never spoke of his affair with my wife. (I may, in what follows be a little hard on Florence; but you must remember that I have been writing away at this story now for six months and reflecting longer and longer upon these affairs.)

And the longer I think about them the more certain I become that Florence was a contaminating influence—she depressed and deteriorated poor Edward; she deteriorated, hopelessly, the miserable Leonora. There is no doubt that she caused Leonora's character to deteriorate. If there was a fine point about Leonora it was that she was proud and that she was silent. But that pride and that silence broke when she made that extraordinary outburst, in the shadowy room that contained the Protest, and in the little terrace looking over the river. I don't mean to say that she was doing a wrong thing. She was certainly doing right in trying to warn me that Florence was making eyes at her husband. But, if she did the right thing, she was doing it in the wrong way. Perhaps* she should have reflected longer; she should have spoken, if she wanted to speak, only after reflection. Or it would have been better if she had acted—if for instance she had so chaperoned Florence that private communication between her and Edward became impossible. She should have gone eaves-dropping; she should have watched* outside bedroom doors. It is odious; but that is the way the job is done. She should have taken Edward away the moment Maisie was dead. No, she acted wrongly. . . .

And yet, poor thing, is it for me to condemn her—and what did it matter in the end? If it had not been Florence, it would have been some other. . . . Still, it might have been a better woman than my wife. For Florence was vulgar; Florence was a common flirt who would not, at the last, *lâcher prise*;[1] and Florence was an unstoppable talker. You could not stop her; nothing would stop her. Edward and Leonora were at least proud and reserved people. Pride and reserve are not the only things in life; perhaps they are not even the best things. But, if they happen to be your particular virtues you will go all to pieces if you let them go. And Leonora* let them go. She let them go before poor Edward did even. Consider her position when she burst out over the Luther-Protest. . . . Consider her agonies. . . .

You are to remember that the main passion of her life was to get Edward back*; she had never, till that moment, despaired of getting him back. That may seem ignoble; but you have also to remember that her getting him back represented to* her not only a victory for herself. It would, as it appeared to her, have been a victory for all wives and a victory for her Church. That was how it presented itself to her. These things are a little inscrutable. I don't know why the getting back of Edward should have represented to her a victory for all wives, for Society and for her Church. Or maybe I have a glimmering of it.

She saw life as a perpetual sex-battle between husbands who desire to be unfaithful to their wives, and wives who desire to re-capture their husbands in the end. That was her sad and modest view of matrimony. Man, for her, was a sort of brute who must have his divagations, his moments of excess, his nights out, his, let us say, rutting seasons. She had read few novels, so that the idea of a pure and constant love, succeeding the sound of wedding bells had never been very much presented to her. She* went, numbed and terrified to the Mother Superior of her childhood's convent with the tale of Edward's infidelities with the Spanish dancer and all that the old nun, who appeared to her to be infinitely wise, mystic and reverend,* had done had been to shake her head sadly and to say:

"Men are like that. By the blessing of God it will all come right in the end."

That was what was put before her by her spiritual advisers as her programme in life. Or at any rate that was how their teachings came through to her—that was the lesson she told me she had learned of them. I don't know exactly what they taught her. The lot of women was patience and patience and again patience—*ad majorem Dei gloriam*[2]—until upon the appointed day, if God saw fit, she should have her reward. If then, in the end, she should have succeeded in getting Edward back she would have kept her man within the limits that are all that wife-hood has to expect. She was even taught that such excesses in men are natural, excusable—as if they had been children.*

1. Let go (French).
2. For the greater glory of God (Latin): Jesuits' motto.

And the great thing was that there should be no scandal before the congregation. So she had clung to the idea of getting Edward back with a fierce passion that was like an agony. She had looked the other way; she had occupied herself solely with one idea. That was the idea of having Edward appear, when she did get him back, wealthy, glorious as it were on account of his lands and upright. She would show, in fact, that in an unfaithful world one Catholic woman had succeeded in retaining the fidelity of her husband. And she thought she had * come near her desires.

Her plan with regard to Maisie had appeared to be working admirably. * Edward had seemed to be cooling off towards the girl. He did not hunger to pass every minute of the time at Nauheim beside the child's recumbent form; he went out to polo matches; he played auction bridge in the evenings; he was cheerful and bright. She was certain that he was not trying to seduce that poor child; she was beginning to think that he had never tried to do so. He seemed in fact to be dropping back into what he had been for Maisie in the beginning—a kind, attentive, superior officer in the regiment, paying gallant attentions to a bride. They were as open in their little flirtations as the dayspring from on high.[3] And Maisie had not appeared to fret when he went off on excursions with us; she had to lie down for so many hours on her bed every afternoon, and she had not appeared to crave for the attentions of Edward at those times.

And Edward was beginning to make little advances to Leonora. Once or twice, in private—for he often did it before people—he had said: "How nice you look," or "What a pretty dress." * She had gone with Florence to Frankfurt where they dress as well as in Paris, and had got herself a gown or two. She could afford it and Florence was an excellent adviser as to dress. She seemed to have got hold of the clue to the riddle.

Yes, Leonora * seemed to have got hold of the clue to the riddle. She imagined herself to have been in the wrong to some extent in the past. She should not have kept Edward on such a tight rein with regard to money. She thought she was on the right tack in letting him—as she had done only with fear and irresolution *—have again the control of his income. He came even a step towards her and acknowledged, spontaneously, that she had been right in husbanding, for all those years, their resources. He said to her one day:

"You've done right, old * girl. There's nothing I like so much as to have a little to chuck away. And I can do it, thanks to you."

That was really, she said, the happiest moment of her life. And he,

3. Literally, "dayspring" means "daybreak" but cf. Zacharias's [Zechariah's] prophecy in Luke 1.76–79 about his son John's future role as "prophet of the Highest: | For thou shalt go before the face of the Lord | To prepare his ways . . . | Whereby the dayspring from on high hath visited us, | To give light to them that sit in darkness. . . ." Here the "dayspring" is a metaphor both for the Grace of God and for the Messiah as its (future) terrestrial manifestation.

seeming to realise it, had ventured to pat her on the shoulder. He had, ostensibly, come in to borrow a safety pin of her.

And the occasion of her boxing Maisie's ears, had, after it was over, rivetted in her mind the idea that there was no intrigue between Edward and Mrs. Maidan. She imagined that, from henceforward, all that she had to do was to keep him well-supplied with money and his mind amused with pretty girls. She was convinced that he was coming back to her. For that month she no longer repelled his timid advances that never went very far. For he certainly made timid advances. He patted her on the shoulder; he whispered into her ear little jokes about the odd figures that they saw up at the Casino. It was not much to make a little joke— but the whispering of it was a precious intimacy. . . .

And then—smash—it all went. It went to pieces at the moment when Florence laid her hand upon Edward's wrist, as it lay on the glass sheltering the manuscript of the Protest, up in the high tower with the shutters where the sunlight here and there streamed in. Or rather, it went when she noticed the look in Edward's eyes as he gazed back into Florence's. She knew that look.

She had known—since the first moment of their meeting, since the moment of our all sitting down to dinner together—that Florence was making eyes at Edward. But she had seen so many women make eyes at Edward—hundreds and hundreds of women, in railway trains, in hotels, aboard liners, at street corners. And she had arrived at thinking that Edward took little stock in women that made eyes at him. She had formed what was, at that time, a fairly correct estimate of the methods of, the reasons for, Edward's loves. She was certain that hitherto they had consisted of the short passion for the Dolciquita, the real sort of love for Mrs. Basil, and what she deemed the pretty courtship of Maisie Maidan. Besides she despised Florence so haughtily that she could not imagine Edward's being attracted by her. And she and Maisie were a sort of bulwark round him.

She wanted, besides, to keep her eyes on Florence—for Florence knew that she had boxed Maisie's ears. And Leonora so desperately desired that her union with Edward should appear to be flawless. But all that went. . . .

With the answering gaze of Edward into Florence's blue and up-lifted eyes, she knew that it had all gone. She knew that that gaze meant that those two had had long conversations of an intimate kind—about their likes and dislikes, about their natures, about their views of marriage. She knew what it meant that she, when we all four walked out together, had always been with me * ten yards ahead of Florence and Edward. She did not imagine that it had gone further than talks about their likes and dislikes, about their natures or about marriage as an institution. But, having watched Edward all her life, she knew that that laying on of hands, that answering of gaze with gaze, meant that the thing was unavoidable. Edward was such a serious person.

She knew that any attempt on her part to separate those two would be to rivet on Edward an irrevocable passion; that, as I have before told you, it was a trick of Edward's nature to believe that the seducing of a woman gave her an irrevocable hold over him for life. And that touching of hands, she knew, would give that woman an irrevocable claim—to be seduced. And she so despised Florence that she would have preferred it to be a parlour-maid. There are very decent parlour-maids.

And suddenly there came into her mind the conviction that Maisie Maidan had a real passion for Edward; that this would break her heart—and that, she, Leonora,* would be responsible for that. She went, for the moment, mad. She clutched me by the wrist; she dragged me down those stairs and across that whispering Rittersaal with the high painted pillars, the high painted chimney piece. I guess she did not go mad enough.

She ought to have said:

"Your wife is a harlot who is going to be my husband's mistress. . . ." That might have done the trick. But, even in her madness she was afraid to go as far as that. She was afraid that, if she did, Edward and Florence would make a bolt of it and that, if they did that she would lose for ever all chance of getting him back in the end. She acted very badly to me.

Well, she was a tortured soul who put her Church before the interests of a Philadelphia Quaker. That is all right—I daresay the Church of Rome is the more important of the two.

A week after Maisie Maidan's death she was aware that Florence had become Edward's mistress. She waited outside Florence's door and met Edward as he came away. She said nothing and he only grunted. But I guess he had a bad time.*

Yes, the mental deterioration that Florence worked in Leonora was extraordinary; it smashed up her whole life and all her chances. It made her, in the first place, hopeless—for she could not see how, after that Edward could return to her—after a vulgar intrigue with a vulgar woman. His affair with Mrs. Basil, which was now all that she had to bring, in her heart, against him, she could not find it in her to call an intrigue. It was a love affair—a pure enough thing in its way. But this seemed to her to be a horror—a wantonness, all the more detestable to her, because she so detested Florence. And Florence talked. . . .

That was what was terrible because Florence forced Leonora herself to abandon her high reserve—Florence and the situation. It appears that Florence was in two minds whether to confess to me or to Leonora. Confess she had to. And she pitched at last on Leonora, because if it had been me she would have had to confess a great deal more. Or, at least, I might have guessed a great deal more,* about her "heart", and about Jimmy. So she went* to Leonora one day and began hinting and hinting. And she enraged Leonora to such an extent that at last Leonora said:

"You want to tell me that you are Edward's mistress. You can be. I have no use for him."

That was really a calamity for Leonora, because, once started, there was no stopping the talking. She tried to stop—but it was not to be done. She found it necessary to send Edward messages through Florence; for she would not speak to him. She had to give him, for instance, to understand that if I ever came to know of his intrigue she would ruin him beyond repair. And it complicated matters a good deal that Edward, at about this time, was really a little in love with her. He thought that he had treated her so badly; that she was so fine. She was so mournful that he longed to comfort her, and he thought himself such a blackguard that there was nothing he would not have done to make amends. And Florence communicated these items of information to Leonora.

I don't in the least blame Leonora for her coarseness to Florence; it must have done Florence a world of good. But I do blame her for giving way to what was in the end a desire for communicativeness. You see that business cut her off from her Church.* She did not want to confess what she was doing because she was afraid that her spiritual advisers would blame her for deceiving me. I rather imagine that she would have preferred damnation to breaking my heart. That is what it works out at. She need not have troubled.

But, having no priests to talk to she had to talk to someone and, as Florence insisted on talking to her, she talked back, in short, explosive sentences, like one of the damned. Precisely like one of the damned. Well, if a pretty period in hell on this earth can spare her any period of pain in Eternity—where there are not any periods—I guess Leonora will escape Hell fire.

Her conversations with Florence would be like this. Florence would happen in on her, whilst she was doing her wonderful hair, with a proposition from Edward, who seems about that time to have conceived the naïve idea that he might become a polygamist. I daresay it was Florence who put it into his head. Anyhow, I am not responsible for the oddities of the human psychology. But it certainly appears that, at about that date Edward cared more for Leonora than he had ever done before—or at any rate, for a long time. And, if Leonora had been a person to play cards and if she had played her cards well, and if she had had no sense of shame and so on, she might then have shared Edward with Florence until the time came for jerking that poor cuckoo out of the nest.

Well, Florence would come to Leonora with some such proposition. I do not mean to say that she put it baldly, like that. She stood out that she was not Edward's mistress until Leonora said that she had seen

Edward coming out of her room at an advanced hour of the night. That checked Florence a bit; but she fell back upon her "heart" and stuck out that she had merely been conversing with Edward in order to bring him to a better frame of mind. Florence had, of course, to stick to that story; for even Florence would not have had the face to implore Leonora to grant her favours to Edward if she had admitted that she was Edward's mistress. That could not be done. At the same time Florence had such a pressing desire to talk about something. There would have been nothing else to talk about but a rapprochement between that estranged pair. So Florence would go on babbling and Leonora would go on brushing her hair. And then Leonora would say suddenly something like:

"I should think myself defiled if Edward touched me now that he has touched you."

That would discourage Florence a bit; but after a week or so, on another morning she would have another try.

And, even in other things Leonora deteriorated. She had promised Edward to leave the spending of his own income in his own hands. And she had fully meant to do that. I daresay she would have done it too; though, no doubt she would have spied upon his banking account in secret. She was not a Roman Catholic for nothing. But she took so serious a view of Edward's unfaithfulness* to the memory of poor little Maisie that she could not trust him any more at all.

So, when she got back to Bramshaw she started, after less than a month, to worry him about the minutest items of his expenditure. She allowed him to draw his own cheques, but there was hardly a cheque [of his]* that she did not scrutinise—except for a private account of about five hundred a year which, tacitly, she allowed him to keep for expenditure on his mistress or mistresses. He had to have his jaunts to Paris; he had to send expensive cables in cipher* to Florence about twice a week. But she worried him about his expenditure on wines, on fruit trees, on harness, on gates, on the account at his blacksmith's for work done to a new patent army stirrup that he was trying to invent. She could not see why he should bother to invent a new army stirrup and she was really enraged when, after the invention was mature, he made a present to the War Office of the designs and the patent rights. It was a remarkably good stirrup.

I have told you, I think, that Edward spent a great deal of time, and about two hundred pounds for law-fees on getting a poor girl, the daughter of one of his gardeners, acquitted of a charge of murdering her baby. That was positively the last act of Edward's life. It came at a time when Nancy Rufford was on her way to India; when the most horrible gloom was over the household; when Edward, himself, was in an agony and behaving as prettily as he knew how. Yet even then Leonora made him a terrible scene about this expenditure of time and trouble. She sort of had the vague idea that what had passed with the girl and the rest of it ought to have taught Edward a lesson—the lesson of economy. She threatened to take his banking account away from him again.* I guess that made him cut his throat. He might have stuck it out otherwise—but the thought that he had lost his Nancy and that, in addition there was nothing left for him but a dreary, dreary succession of days in which he could be of no public service. . . . Well, it finished him.

It was during those years* that Leonora tried to get up a love affair of her own with a fellow called Bayham—a decent sort of fellow. A really nice man. But the affair was no sort of success. I have told you about it already. . . .

II *

Well, that about brings me up to the date of my receiving, in Waterbury, the laconic cable from Edward to the effect that he wanted me to go to Bramshaw and have a chat. I was pretty busy at the time and I was half minded to send him a reply cable to the effect that I would start in a fortnight. But I was having a long interview with old Mr. Hurlbird's attorneys and immediately afterwards I had to have a long interview with the Misses Hurlbird so I delayed cabling.

I had expected to find the Misses Hurlbird excessively old—in the nineties or thereabouts. The time had passed so slowly that I had the impression that it must have been thirty years since I had been in the United States. It was only twelve years.* Actually Miss Hurlbird was just sixty-one and Miss Florence Hurlbird fifty-nine and they were both, mentally and physically, as vigorous as could be desired. They were, indeed, more vigorous, mentally, than suited my purpose which was to get away from the United States as quickly as I could. The Hurlbirds were an exceedingly united family—exceedingly united except on one set of points. Each of the three of them had a separate doctor whom they trusted implicitly—and each had a separate attorney. And each of them distrusted the other's doctor and the other's attorney. And naturally the doctors and the attorneys warned one all the time—against each other. You cannot imagine how complicated it all became for me. Of course I had an attorney of my own—recommended to me by young Carter, my Philadelphia* nephew.

I do not mean to say that there was any unpleasantness of a grasping kind. The problem was quite another one—a moral dilemma. You see, old Mr. Hurlbird had left all his property to Florence with the mere request that she would have erected to him in the city of Waterbury, Conn.,* a memorial that should take the form of some sort of institution for the relief of sufferers from the heart. Florence's money had all come to me—and with it old Mr. Hurlbird's. He had died just five days before* Florence.

Well, I was quite ready to spend a round million dollars on the relief of sufferers from the heart. The old gentleman had left about a million and a half; Florence had been worth about eight hundred thousand—and as I figured it out, I should cut up at about a million myself. Anyhow, there was ample money. But, I naturally wanted to consult the wishes of his surviving relatives and then the trouble really began. You see it had been discovered that Mr. Hurlbird had had nothing whatever the matter with his heart. His lungs had been a little affected all through his life and he had died of bronchitis.

It struck Miss Florence Hurlbird that, since her brother had died of lungs and not of heart, his money ought to go to lung-patients. That, she considered, was what her brother would have wished. On the other hand, by a kink, that I could not at the time understand, Miss Hurlbird insisted that I ought to keep the money all to myself. She said that she did not wish for any monuments to the Hurlbird family.

At the time I thought that that was because of a New England dislike for necrological ostentation. But I can figure out now, when I remember certain insistent and continued questions that she put to me, about Edward Ashburnham, that there was another idea in her mind. And Leonora has told me that, on Florence's dressing-table, beside her dead body there had lain a letter to Miss Hurlbird—a letter which Leonora posted without telling me.* I don't know how Florence had time to write to her aunt; but I can quite understand that she would not like to go out of the world without making some comments.* So I guess Florence had told Miss Hurlbird a good bit about Edward Ashburnham in a few scrawled words—and that that was why the old lady did not wish the name of Hurlbird perpetuated. Perhaps also she thought that I had earned the Hurlbird money.

It meant a pretty tidy lot of discussing, what with the doctors warning* each other about the bad effects of discussions, on the health of the old ladies, and warning me covertly against each other, and saying that old Mr. Hurlbird might have died of heart after all, in spite of the diagnosis of *his* doctor. And the solicitors all had separate methods of arranging about how the money should be invested and entrusted and bound.

Personally, I wanted to invest the money so that the interest could be used for the relief of sufferers from the heart. If old Mr. Hurlbird had not died of any defects in that organ he had considered that it was defective. Moreover, Florence had certainly died of her heart, as I saw it. And when Miss Florence Hurlbird stood out that the money ought to go to chest sufferers I was brought to thinking that there ought to be a chest institution too, and I advanced the sum that I was ready to provide to a million and a half of dollars. That would have given seven hundred and fifty thousand to each class of invalid.* I did not want money at all badly. All I wanted it for was to be able to give Nancy Rufford a good time. I did not know much about house-keeping expenses in England where, I presumed, she would wish to live. I knew that her needs at that time were limited to good chocolates, and a good horse or two and simple pretty frocks. Probably she would want more than that later on. But even if I gave a million and a half dollars to these institutions I should still have the equivalent of about twenty thousand a year English, and I considered that Nancy could have a pretty good time on that or less.

Anyhow, we had a stiff* set of arguments up at the Hurlbird mansion, which stands on a bluff over the town. It may strike you, silent listener, as being funny if you happen to be European. But moral problems of that description and the giving of millions to institutions are immensely serious matters in my country. Indeed, they are the staple topics for consideration amongst the wealthy classes. We haven't got peerages and social climbing to occupy us much, and decent people do not take interest in politics or elderly people in sport. So that there were real tears shed by both Miss Hurlbird and Miss Florence before I left that city.

I left it quite abruptly. Four hours after Edward's telegram came another from Leonora saying: "Yes, do come. You could be so helpful."* I simply told my attorney that there was the million and a half; that he could invest it as he liked, and that the purposes must be decided by the Misses Hurlbird. I was anyhow, pretty well worn out by all the discussions. And, as I have never heard yet* from the Misses Hurlbird, I rather think that Miss Hurlbird, either by revelations or by moral force, has persuaded Miss Florence that no memorial to their names* shall be erected in the city of Waterbury, Conn.* Miss Hurlbird wept dreadfully when she heard that I was going to stay with the Ashburnhams, but she did not make any comments. I was aware, at that date, that her niece had been seduced by that fellow Jimmy before I had married her—but I contrived to produce on her the impression that I thought* Florence had been a model wife. Why, at that date I still believed that Florence had been perfectly virtuous after her marriage to me. I had not figured it out that she could have played it so low down as to continue her intrigue with that fellow under my roof. Well, I was a fool. But I did not think much about Florence at that date. My mind was occupied with what was happening at Bramshaw.

I had got it into my head that the telegrams had something to do with Nancy. It struck me that she might have shown signs of forming an attachment for some undesirable fellow and that Leonora wanted me to come back and marry her out of harm's way. That was what was pretty firmly in my mind. And it remained in my mind for nearly ten days after my arrival at that beautiful old place. Neither Edward nor Leonora made any motion to talk to me about anything other than the weather and the crops. Yet, although there were several young fellows about I could not see that any one in particular was distinguished by the girl's preference. She certainly appeared illish and nervous except when she woke up to talk gay nonsense to me. Oh, the pretty thing that she was. . . .

I imagined that what must have happened was that the undesirable young man had been forbidden the place and that Nancy was fretting a little.

What had happened was just Hell. Leonora had spoken to Nancy; Nancy had spoken to Edward; Edward had spoken to Leonora—and they had talked and talked. And talked. You have to imagine horrible pictures of gloom and half light, * and emotions running through silent nights—through whole nights. You have to imagine my beautiful Nancy appearing suddenly to Edward, rising up at the foot of his bed, with her long hair falling, like a split cone of shadow, in the glimmer of a night-light that burned beside him. You have to imagine her, a silent, a no doubt agonised figure, like a spectre, suddenly offering herself to him—to save his reason! And you have to imagine his frantic refusal—and talk. And talk! My God!

And yet, to me, living in the house, enveloped with the charm of the quiet and ordered living, with the silent, skilled servants whose mere laying out of my dress clothes was like a caress—to me who was hourly with them they appeared like tender, * ordered and devoted people, smiling, absenting themselves at the proper intervals; driving me to meets— just good people! * How the devil—how the devil do they do it?

At dinner one evening Leonora said—she had just opened a telegram: "Nancy will be going to India, to-morrow, to be with her father."

No one spoke. Nancy looked at her plate; Edward went on eating his pheasant. I felt very bad; I imagined that it would be up to me to propose to Nancy that evening. It appeared to me to be queer that they had not given me any warning of Nancy's departure. But I thought that that was only English manners—some sort of delicacy that I had not got the hang of. You must remember that at that moment I trusted in Edward and Leonora and in Nancy Rufford, and in the tranquillity of ancient haunts of peace, as I had trusted in my mother's love. And that evening Edward spoke to me.

What in the interval had happened had been this:

Upon her return from Nauheim Leonora had completely broken down—because she knew [that] * she could trust Edward. That seems odd but, if you know anything about breakdowns, you will know that, by the ingenious torments that fate prepares for us, these things come as soon as, a strain having relaxed, there is nothing more to be done. It is after a husband's long illness and death that a widow goes to pieces; it is at the end of a long rowing contest that a crew collapses and lies forward upon its oars. And that was what happened to Leonora.

From certain tones in Edward's voice; from the long, steady stare that

he had given her from his bloodshot eyes on rising from the dinner table
in the Nauheim hotel, she knew that, in the affair of the poor girl, this
was a case in which Edward's moral scruples, or his social code, or his
idea that it would be playing it *too* low down, rendered Nancy perfectly
safe. The girl, she felt sure, was in no danger at all from Edward. And,
in that she was perfectly right. The smash was to come from herself.

She relaxed; she broke; she drifted, at first quickly, then with an
increasing momentum, down the stream of destiny. You may put it
that, having been cut off from the restraints [1] of her religion, for the first
time in her life, she acted along the lines of her instinctive desires. I do
not know whether to think that, in that * she was no longer herself; or
that, having let loose the bonds of her standards, her conventions and
her traditions, she was being, for the first time, her own natural self.
She was torn between her intense, maternal love for the girl and an
intense jealousy of the woman who realises that the man she loves has
met what appears to be * the final passion of his life. She was divided
between an intense disgust for Edward's weakness in conceiving this
passion, an intense pity for the miseries that he was enduring, and a
feeling equally intense, but one that she hid from herself—a feeling of
respect for Edward's determination to keep himself, in this particular
affair, unspotted.

And the human heart is a very mysterious thing. It is impossible to
say that Leonora, in acting as she then did, was not filled with a sort of
hatred of Edward's final virtue. She wanted, I think, to despise him. He
was, she realised, gone from her for good. Then let him suffer, let him
agonise; let him, if possible break and go to that Hell that is the abode
of broken resolves. She might have taken a different line. It would have
been so easy to send the girl away to stay with friends; * to have taken
her away herself upon some pretext or other. That would not have cured
things but it would have been the decent line. . . . But, at that date,
poor Leonora was incapable of taking any line whatever.

She pitied Edward frightfully at one time—and then she acted along
the lines of pity; she loathed him at another and then she acted as her
loathing dictated. She gasped, as a person dying of tuberculosis gasps for
air. She craved madly for communication with some other human soul.
And the human soul that she selected was that of the girl.

Perhaps Nancy was the only person that she could have talked to.
With her necessity for reticences, with her coldness of manner, Leonora
had singularly few intimates. She had none at all with the exception of
the Mrs. Colonel Whelen who had advised her about the affair with La
Dolciquita and the one or two religious, who had guided her through
life. The Colonel's wife was at that time in Madeira *; the religious she
now avoided. Her visitors' * book had seven hundred names in it; there

---

1. Possibly another echo of *Heart of Darkness:* "He [the native helmsman] had no restraint, no
restraint—just like Kurtz—a tree swayed by the wind."

was not a soul that she could speak to. She was Mrs. Ashburnham of Bramshaw Teleragh.

She was the great Mrs. Ashburnham of Bramshaw and she lay all day upon her bed in her marvellous, light, airy bedroom with the chintzes and the Chippendale and the portraits of deceased Ashburnhams by Zoffany and Zucchero.[2] When there was a meet she would struggle up—supposing it were within driving distance—and let Edward drive her* and the girl to the cross-roads or the country house. She would drive herself back alone; Edward would ride off with the girl. Ride Leonora could not, that season—her head was too bad. Each pace of her mare was an anguish.

But she drove with efficiency and precision; she smiled at the Gimmers and ffoulkes* and the Hedley Seatons. She threw with exactitude pennies to the boys who opened gates for her; she sat upright* on the seat of the high dog-cart;[3] she waved her hands to Edward and Nancy as they rode off with the hounds and everyone could hear her clear, high voice, in the chilly weather, saying:

"Have a good time!"

Poor forlorn woman. . . .

There was however one spark of consolation. It came from the fact that Rodney Bayham of Bayham followed her always with his eyes. It had been three years since she had tried her abortive love-affair with him. Yet still, on the winter mornings he would ride up to her shafts and just say: "Good day,"* and look at her with eyes that were not imploring, but that seemed to say: "You see, I am still, as the Germans say, A. D.—at disposition."

It was a great consolation, not because she proposed ever to take him up again but because it showed her that there was in the world one faithful soul in riding breeches. And it showed her that she was not losing her looks.

And indeed she was not losing her looks. She was forty, but she was as clean run as on the day she had left the convent—as clear in outline, as clear coloured in the hair, as dark blue in the eyes. She thought that her looking-glass told her this; but there are always the doubts. . . . Rodney Bayham's eyes took them away.

It is very singular that Leonora should not have aged at all. I suppose that there are some types of beauty and even of youth* made for the embellishments that come with enduring sorrow. That is too elaborately put. I mean that Leonora, if everything had prospered might have become too hard and maybe, overbearing. As it was she was tuned down to appearing efficient—and yet sympathetic. That is the rarest of all

2. Federigo Zuccaro (1543–1609); known also as "Zuccari" or "Zuchero," Renaissance Italian painter who traveled to England where he painted portraits of Queen Elizabeth and Mary Stuart. Johann Zoffany (1735–1810), portraitist and painter of conversation pieces.
3. One-horse, two-wheeled light carriage.

blends. And yet I swear that Leonora, in her restrained way gave the impression of being intensely sympathetic. When she listened to you she appeared also to be listening to some sound that was going on in the distance. But still, she listened to you and took in what you said, which, since the record of humanity is a record of sorrows, was as a rule something sad.

I think that she must have taken Nancy through many terrors of the night and many bad places of the day. And that would account for the girl's passionate love for the elder woman. For Nancy's love for Leonora was an admiration that is awakened in Catholics by their feeling for the Virgin Mary and for various of the saints. It is too little to say that the girl would have laid her life at Leonora's feet. Well, she laid there the offer of her virtue—* and her reason. Those were sufficient instalments of her life. It would today be much better for Nancy Rufford if she were dead.

Perhaps all these reflections are a nuisance; but they crowd on me. I will try to tell the story.

You see—when she came back from Nauheim Leonora began to have her headaches—headaches lasting through whole days, during which she could speak no word and could bear to hear no sound. And, day after day Nancy would sit with her, silent and motionless for hours, steeping handkerchiefs in vinegar and water, and thinking her own thoughts. It must have been very bad for her—and her meals alone with Edward must have been bad for her too—and beastly bad for Edward. Edward, of course, wavered in his demeanour. What else could he do? At times he would sit silent and dejected over his untouched food. He would utter nothing but monosyllables when Nancy spoke to him. Then he was simply afraid of the girl falling in love with him. At other times he would take a little wine; pull himself together; attempt to chaff Nancy about a stake and binder hedge[4] that her mare had checked at or talk about the habits of the Chitralis. That was when he was thinking that it was rough on the poor girl that he should have become a dull companion. He realised that his talking to her in the park at Nauheim had done her no harm.

But all that was doing a great deal of harm to Nancy. It gradually opened her eyes to the fact that Edward was a man with his ups and downs and not an invariably gay uncle like a nice dog, a trustworthy horse or a girl friend. She would find him in attitudes of frightful dejection, sunk into his armchair in the study that was half a gun-room. She would notice through the open door that his face was the face of an old, dead man, when he had no one to talk to. Gradually it forced itself upon her attention that there were profound differences between the

4. A fence with branches woven between stakes.

pair that she regarded as her uncle and her aunt. It was a conviction that came very slowly.

It began with Edward's giving an oldish horse to a young fellow called Selmes. Selmes' father had been ruined by a fraudulent solicitor and the Selmes family had had to sell their hunters. It was a case that had excited a good deal of sympathy in that part of the county. And Edward, meeting the young man one day, unmounted, and * seeing him to be very unhappy had offered to give him an old Irish cob upon which he was riding. It was a silly sort of thing to do, really. The horse was worth from thirty to forty pounds and Edward might have known that the gift would upset his wife. But Edward just had to comfort that unhappy young man whose father he had known all his life. And what made it all the worse was that young Selmes could not afford to keep the horse even. Edward recollected this, immediately after he had made the offer and said quickly:

"Of course I mean that you should stable the horse at Bramshaw until you have time to turn round or want to sell him and get a better."

Nancy went straight home and told all this to Leonora who was lying down. She regarded it as a splendid instance of Edward's quick consideration for the feelings and the circumstances of the distressed. She thought it would cheer Leonora up—because it ought to cheer any woman up to know that she had such a splendid husband. That was the last girlish thought she ever had. For Leonora whose headache had left her collected but miserably weak, turned upon her bed and uttered words that were amazing to the girl:

"I wish to God," she said, "that he was your husband, and not mine. We shall be ruined. We shall be ruined. Am I *never* to have a chance?" * And suddenly Leonora burst into a passion of tears. She pushed herself up from the pillows with one elbow and sat there—crying, crying, crying, with her face hidden in her hands and the tears falling through her fingers.

The girl flushed, stammered and whimpered as if she had been personally insulted.

"But if Uncle Edward . . . ," she began.

"That man," said Leonora, * with an extraordinary bitterness, "would give the shirt off his back and off mine—and off yours to any. . . ." She could not finish the sentence.

At that moment she had been feeling an extraordinary hatred and contempt for her husband. All the morning and all the afternoon she had been lying there thinking that Edward and the girl were together— in the field and hacking it home at dusk. She had been digging her sharp nails into her palms.

The house had been very silent in the drooping winter weather. And then, after an eternity of torture there had invaded it the sound of opening doors, of the girl's gay voice saying:

"Well, it was only under the mistletoe." . . . And there was Edward's gruff undertone. Then Nancy had come in, with feet that had hastened up the stairs and that tiptoed as they approached the open door of Leonora's room. Bramshaw had a great big hall with oak floors and tiger skins. Round this hall there ran a gallery upon which Leonora's doorway gave. And even when she had the worst of her headaches she liked to have her door open—I suppose so that she might hear the approaching footsteps of ruin and disaster. At any rate she hated to be in a room with a shut door.

At that moment Leonora hated Edward with a hatred that was like hell and she would have liked to bring her riding whip down across the girl's face. What right had Nancy to be young, and slender and dark and gay at times, at times mournful? What right had she to be exactly the woman to make Leonora's husband happy? For Leonora knew that Nancy would have made Edward happy.

Yes, Leonora wished to bring her riding whip down on Nancy's young face. She imagined the pleasure she would feel when the lash fell across those queer features; the pleasure she would feel at drawing the handle at the same moment toward her so as to cut deep into the flesh and to leave a lasting weal.

Well, she left a lasting weal,* and her words cut deeply into the* girl's mind. . . .

They neither of them spoke about that again. A fortnight went by—a fortnight of deep rains, of heavy fields, of bad scent.[5] Leonora's headaches seemed to have gone for good. She hunted once or twice, letting herself be piloted by Bayham whilst Edward looked after the girl. Then one evening when those three were dining alone Edward said, in the queer, deliberate heavy tones that came out of him in those days (he was looking at the table):*

"I have been thinking that Nancy ought to do more for her father. He is getting an old man. I have written to Colonel Rufford suggesting that she should go to him."

Leonora called out:

"How dare you? How dare you?"*

The girl put her hand over her heart and cried out: "Oh, my sweet Saviour, help me!"* That was the queer way she thought within her mind, and the words forced themselves to her lips. Edward said nothing.

And that night, by a merciless trick of the devil that pays attention to this sweltering hell of ours, Nancy Rufford had a letter from her mother. It came whilst Leonora was talking to Edward or Leonora would have intercepted it as she had intercepted others. It was an amazing and a horrible letter. . . .

5. A "bad scent" is a false trail when hunting.

I don't* know what it contained. I just average out from its effect[s] *
on Nancy that her mother, having eloped with some worthless sort of
fellow had done what is called "sinking lower and lower". Whether she
was actually on the streets I do not know, but I rather think that she
eked out a small allowance that she had from her husband by that means
of livelihood. And I think that she stated as much in her letter to Nancy
and upbraided the girl with living in luxury whilst her mother starved.
And it must have been horrible in tone, for Mrs. Rufford was a cruel
sort of woman at the best of times—it* must have seemed to that poor
girl, opening her letter, for distraction from another grief, up in her
bedroom, like the laughter of a devil.

I just cannot bear to think of my poor dear girl at that moment. . . .

And, at the same time, Leonora was lashing, like a cold fiend, into
the unfortunate Edward. Or perhaps he was not so unfortunate; [per-
haps] because* he had done what he knew to be the right thing, he may
be deemed happy. I leave it to you. At any rate he was sitting in his deep
chair and Leonora came into his room—for the first time in nine years.
She said:

"This is the most atrocious thing you have done in your atrocious
life." He never moved and he never looked at her. God knows what was
in Leonora's mind exactly.

I like to think that, uppermost in it were* concern and horror at the
thought of the poor girl's going back to a father whose voice* made her
shriek in the night. And indeed that motive was very strong with Leonora. But I think there was also present the thought that she wanted to
go on torturing Edward with the girl's presence. She was, at that time,
capable of that.

Edward was sunk in his chair; there were in the room two candles
hidden by green glass shades. The green shades were reflected in the
glasses of the bookcases that contained not books but guns with gleaming
brown barrels and fishing rods in green baize over-covers. There was
dimly to be seen, above a mantel-piece encumbered with spurs, hooves
and bronze models of horses, a dark brown picture of a white horse.

"If you think," Leonora said, "that I do not know that you are in love
with the girl. . . ." She began spiritedly but she could not find any ending for the sentence. Edward did not stir; he never spoke. And then
Leonora said:

"If you want me to divorce you, I will. You can marry her then. She's
in love with you."

He groaned at that, a little, Leonora said. Then she went away.

Heaven knows what happened in Leonora after that. She certainly
does not herself know. She probably said a good deal more to Edward
than I have been able to report; but that is all that she has told me and I
am not going to make up speeches. To follow her psychological development of that moment I think we must allow that she upbraided him for

a * great deal of their past life whilst Edward sat absolutely silent. And, indeed, in speaking of it afterwards, she has said several times: "I said a great deal more to him than I wanted to. Just * because he was so silent." She talked, * in fact, in the endeavour to sting him into speech.

She must have said so much that, with the expression of her grievance her mood changed. She went back to her own room in the gallery and sat there for a long time thinking. And she thought herself into a mood of absolute unselfishness, of absolute self-contempt too. She said to her-self that she was no good; that she had failed in all her efforts—in her efforts to get Edward back as in her efforts to make him curb his expendi-ture. She imagined herself to be exhausted; she imagined herself to be done. Then a great fear came over her.

She thought * that Edward, after what she had said to him, must have committed suicide. She went out onto the gallery and listened; there was no sound in all the house except the regular beat of the great clock in the hall. But, even in her debased condition, she was not the person to hang about. She acted. She went straight to Edward's room; opened the door, and looked in.

He was oiling the breech * action of a gun. It was an unusual thing for him to do, at that time of night, in his evening clothes. It never occurred to her, nevertheless, that he was going to shoot himself with that implement. She knew that he was doing it just for occupation—to keep himself from thinking. He looked up when she opened the door, his face illuminated by the light cast upwards from the round orifices in the * green candle shades.

She said:

"I didn't imagine that I should find Nancy here." She thought that she owed that to him. He answered then:

"I don't imagine that you did imagine it." Those were the only words he spoke that night. She went, like a lame duck, back through the long corridors, she stumbled over the familiar tiger-skins in the dark hall. She could hardly drag one limb after the other. In the gallery she perceived that Nancy's door was half open and that there was a light in the girl's room. A sudden madness possessed her, a desire for action, a thirst for self-explanation. *

Their rooms all gave on to the * gallery; Leonora's to the east, the girl's next, then Edward's. The sight of those three open doors, side by side, gaping to receive whom the chances of the black night might bring made Leonora shudder all over her body. She went into Nancy's room.

The girl was sitting perfectly still in an armchair, very upright, as she had been taught to sit at the convent. She appeared to be as calm as a church; her hair fell, black and like a pall, down over both her shoul-ders. The fire beside her was burning brightly; she must have just put coals on. She was in a white silk kimono that covered her to the feet. The clothes that she had taken off were exactly folded upon the proper seats. Her long hands were one upon each arm of the * chair that had a pink and white chintz back.

Leonora told me these things. She seemed to think it extraordinary that the girl could have done such orderly things as fold up the clothes she had taken off upon such a night—when Edward had announced that he was going to send her to her father and when from her mother, she had received that letter. The letter, in its envelope was in her right hand.

Leonora did not at first perceive it. She said:

"What are you doing so late?" The girl answered:

"Just thinking." They seemed to think in whispers and to speak below their breaths. Then Leonora's eyes fell on the envelope and she recognised Mrs. Rufford's handwriting.

It was one of those moments when thinking was impossible, Leonora said. It was as if stones were being thrown at her from every direction and she could only run. She heard herself exclaim:

"Edward's dying—because of you. He's dying. He's worth more than either of us. . . ."

The girl looked past her at the panels of the half-closed door.

"My poor father," she said, "my poor father."

"You must stay here," Leonora answered fiercely. "You must stay here. I tell you you must stay here."

"I am going to Glasgow," Nancy answered. "I shall go to Glasgow to-morrow morning. My mother is in Glasgow."

It appears that it was in Glasgow that Mrs. Rufford pursued her disorderly life. She had selected that city, not because it was most profitable, but because it was the natal home of her husband to whom she desired to cause as much pain as possible.

"You must stay here," Leonora began. "To * save Edward. He's dying for love of you."

The girl turned her calm eyes upon Leonora.

"I know it," she said. "And I am dying for love of him." *

Leonora uttered an "Ah," that, in spite of herself was an "Ah" of horror and of grief.

"That is why," the girl continued, "I am going to Glasgow—to take my mother away from there." She added: "To the ends of the earth," for, if the last months had made her nature that of a woman, her phrases were still * romantically those of a school-girl. It was as if she had grown up so quickly that there had not been time to put her hair up. But she added: "We're no good—my mother and I." *

Leonora said, with her fierce calmness:

"No. No. You're not no good. It's I that am no good. You can't let that man go on to ruin for want of you. You must belong to him."

The girl, she said, smiled at her with a queer, far-away smile—as if she were a thousand years old, as if Leonora were a tiny child.

"I knew you would come to that," she said, very slowly. "But we are not worth it—Edward and I."

III *

Nancy had in fact been thinking ever since Leonora had made that comment over the giving of the horse to young Selmes. She had been thinking and thinking because she had had to sit for many days silent beside her aunt's bed. (She had always thought of Leonora as her aunt.) And she had had to sit thinking during many silent meals with Edward. And then, at times, with his bloodshot eyes and creased, heavy mouth, he would smile at her. And gradually the knowledge had come to her that Edward did not love Leonora and that Leonora hated Edward. Several * things contributed to form and to harden this conviction.

She was allowed to read the papers in those days—or rather since Leonora was always on her bed and Edward breakfasted alone and went out early, over the estate, she was left alone with the papers. One day, in the paper, she saw the portrait of a woman she knew very well. Beneath it she read the words: "The Hon. Mrs. Brand, plaintiff in the remarkable divorce case reported on p. 8." Nancy hardly knew * what a divorce case was. She had been so remarkably well brought up, [so carefully] and Roman Catholics do not practise divorce. * I don't know how Leonora had done it exactly. I suppose she had always impressed it on Nancy's mind that nice women did not read these things, and that would have been enough to make Nancy skip those pages.

She read, at any rate, the account of the Brand divorce case—principally because she wanted to tell Leonora about it. She imagined that Leonora, when her headache left her, would like to know what was happening to Mrs. Brand who lived at Christchurch[1] and whom they both liked very well. The case occupied three days and the report that Nancy first came upon was that of the third day. Edward however kept the papers of the week, after his methodical fashion, in a rack in his gun-room and when she had finished her breakfast Nancy went to that quiet apartment and had what she would have called a good read. It seemed to her to be a queer affair. She could not understand why one counsel should be so anxious to know all about the movements of Mr. Brand upon a certain day; she could not understand why a chart of the bedroom accommodation at Christchurch Old Hall should be produced in court. She did not even see why they should want to know that, upon a certain occasion the drawing-room door * was locked. It made her laugh; it appeared to be all so senseless that grown people should occupy themselves with such matters. It struck her, nevertheless, * as odd that

1. South coast Hampshire town, near Bournemouth, c. twenty miles south of Fordingbridge.

one of the counsel should cross-question Mr. Brand so insistently and
so impertinently as to his feelings for Miss Lupton. Nancy knew Miss
Lupton of Ringwood[2] very well—a jolly girl who rode a horse with two
white fetlocks. Mr. Brand persisted that he did not love Miss Lupton.
. . . Well, of course he did not love Miss Lupton; he was a married
man. You might as well think of Uncle Edward loving . . . loving anybody but Leonora. When people were married there was an end of loving. There were, no doubt, people who misbehaved—but they were
poor people—or people not like those she knew.*

So these matters presented themselves to Nancy's mind.

But later on in the case she found that Mr. Brand had to confess to a
"guilty intimacy" with someone or other. Nancy imagined that he must
have been telling someone* his wife's secrets; she could not understand
why that was a serious offence. Of course it was not very gentlemanly; it
lessened her opinion of Mr. Brand. But, since she found that Mrs.
Brand had condoned that offence she imagined that they* could not
have been very serious secrets that Mr. Brand had told. And then, suddenly, it was forced on her conviction that Mr. Brand—the mild Mr.
Brand that she had seen a month or two before their departure to
Nauheim, playing Blind Man's Buff with his children and kissing his
wife when he caught her—Mr. Brand and Mrs. Brand had been on the
worst possible terms. That was incredible.

Yet there it was—in black and white. Mr. Brand drank; Mr. Brand
had struck Mrs. Brand to the ground when he was drunk. Mr. Brand
was adjudged, in two or three abrupt words, at the end of columns and
columns of paper to have been guilty of cruelty to his wife and to have
committed adultery with Miss Lupton. The last words conveyed nothing
to Nancy—nothing real, that is to say. She knew that one was com-
manded not to commit adultery—but why, she thought, should one? It
was probably something like catching salmon out of season—a thing
one did not do. She gathered it had something to do with kissing, or
holding someone in your arms. . . .

And yet the whole effect of that reading upon Nancy was mysterious,
terrifying and evil. She felt a sickness—a sickness that grew as she read.
Her heart beat painfully; she began to cry. She asked God how He*
could permit such things to be. And she was more certain that Edward
did not love Leonora and that Leonora hated Edward. Perhaps then
Edward loved someone else. It was unthinkable.

If he could love someone else than Leonora, her fierce, unknown
heart suddenly spoke in her side, why could it not be herself? And he
did not love her. . . .* This had occurred about a month before she got
the letter from her mother.

2. Hampshire town on the road between Fordingbridge and Christchurch, bordering on New
Forest.

She * let the matter rest until the sick feeling went off; it did that in a day or two. Then, finding that Leonora's headaches had gone she suddenly told Leonora that Mrs. Brand had divorced her husband. She asked what, exactly, it all meant. *

Leonora was lying on the sofa in the hall; she was feeling so weak that she could hardly find any words. She answered just:

"It means that Mr. Brand will be able to marry again."

Nancy said:

"But. . . . But, . . ." and then: "He will be able to marry Miss Lupton." Leonora just moved a hand in assent. Her eyes were shut.

"Then . . . ," Nancy began. Her blue eyes were full of horror; her brows were tight above them; the lines of pain about her mouth were very distinct. In her eyes the whole of that familiar, great hall had a changed aspect. The andirons[3] with the brass flowers at the ends appeared unreal; the burning logs were just logs that were burning and not the comfortable symbols of an indestructible mode of life. The flame[s] * fluttered before the high fireback; the St. Bernard sighed in his sleep. Outside the winter rain fell and fell. And suddenly she thought that Edward might marry someone else; and she nearly screamed. *

Leonora opened her eyes, lying sideways, with her face upon the black and gold pillow of the sofa that was drawn half across the great fireplace.

"I thought," Nancy said, "I never imagined. . . . Aren't marriages sacraments? Aren't they indissoluble? I thought you were married and. . . . And. . . ," she was sobbing. "I thought you were married or not married as you are alive or dead."

"That," Leonora said, "is the law of the Church. It is not the law of the land. . . ."

"Oh yes," Nancy said, "the Brands are Protestants. . . ." *

She felt a sudden safeness descend upon her and for an hour or so her mind was at rest. It seemed to her idiotic not to have remembered Henry VIII and the basis upon which Protestantism rests.[4] She almost laughed at herself.

The long afternoon wore on; the flames still fluttered when the maid made up the fire; the St. Bernard awoke and lolloped away towards the kitchen. And then Leonora opened her eyes and said almost coldly:

"And you? Don't you think you will get married?"

It was so unlike Leonora that, for the moment the girl was frightened in the dusk. But then again, it seemed a perfectly reasonable question.

"I don't know," she answered. "I don't know that anyone wants to marry me."

3. Pair of horizontal bars on short feet, one placed on each side of hearth to support burning wood.
4. Henry VIII broke from the Roman Catholic Church, establishing the Church of England with himself (and all future English monarchs) at its head, in order to facilitate his divorce from Catherine of Aragon and his marriage to Anne Boleyn.

"Several people want to marry you," Leonora said.

"But I don't want to marry," Nancy answered. "I should like to go on living with you and Edward. I don't think I am in the way or that I am really an expense. If I went you would have to have a companion. Or perhaps I ought to earn my living. . . ."

"I wasn't thinking of that," Leonora answered in the same dull tone. "You will have money enough from your father. But most people want to be married."

I believe that she then asked the girl if she would not like to marry me and that Nancy answered that she would marry me if she were told to; but that she wanted to go on living there. She added:

"If I married anyone I should want him to be like Edward."

She was frightened out of her life. Leonora writhed on her couch and called out: "Oh, God. . . ."*

Nancy ran for the maid; for tablets of aspirin; for wet handkerchiefs. It never occurred to her that Leonora's expression of agony was for anything else than physical pain.

You are to remember that all this happened a month before Leonora went into the girl's room at night. I have been casting back again; but I cannot help it. It is so difficult to keep all these people going. I tell you about Leonora and bring her up to date; then about Edward who has fallen behind. And then the girl gets hopelessly left behind. I wish I could put it down in diary form. Thus: On the 1st of September they returned from Nauheim. Leonora at once took to her bed. By the 1st of October* they were all going to meets together. Nancy had already observed very fully that Edward was strange in his manner. About the 6th of that month Edward gave the horse to young Selmes and Nancy had cause to believe that her aunt did not love her uncle. On the 20th she read the account of the divorce case which is reported in the papers of the 18th and the two following days. On the 23rd she had the conversation with her aunt in the hall—about marriage in general and about her own possible marriage. Her aunt's coming to her bedroom did not occur until the 12th of November. . . .

Thus she had three weeks for introspection—for introspection beneath gloomy skies, in that old house, rendered darker by the fact that it lay in a hollow crowned by fir trees with their black shadows.* It was not a good situation for a girl. She began thinking about love, she who had never before considered it as anything other than a rather humorous, rather nonsensical matter. She remembered chance passages in chance books—things that had not really affected her at all at the time. She remembered someone's love for the Princess Badrulbadour[5]; she remembered to have heard that love was a flame; a thirst; a withering up of the vitals—though she did not know what the vitals were. She had a

5. Heroine of an *Arabian Nights* story about Aladdin.

vague recollection that love was said to render a hopeless lover's eyes hopeless; she remembered a character in a book who was said to have taken to drink through love; she remembered that lovers' existences were said to be punctuated with heavy sighs. Once she went to the little cottage piano that was in a corner of the hall and began to play. It was a tinkly, reedy instrument, for none of that household had any turn for music. Nancy herself could play a few simple songs and she found herself playing. She had been sitting on the window seat, looking out on the fading day. Leonora had gone to pay some calls; Edward was looking after some planting up in the new spinney.[6] Thus * she found herself playing on the old piano. She did not know how she came to be doing it. A silly, lilting, wavering tune came from before her in the dusk—a tune in which major notes with their cheerful insistence wavered and melted into minor sounds as, beneath a bridge the highlights on dark waters melt and waver and disappear into black depths. Well, it was a silly old tune. . . .

It goes with the words—they are about a willow tree, I think:

> Thou art to all lost loves the best,
> The only true plant found[7]*

—That sort of thing. It is Herrick I believe, and the music was the reedy, irregular, lilting sound that goes with Herrick. And it was dusk; the heavy, hewn, dark pillars that supported the gallery were like mourning presences; the fire had sunk to nothing—a mere glow amongst white ashes. . . . It was a sentimental sort of place and light and hour. . . .

And suddenly Nancy found that she was crying. She was crying quietly; she went on to cry with long convulsive sobs. It seemed to her that everything gay, everything charming, all light, all sweetness had gone out of life. Unhappiness; unhappiness; unhappiness * was all around her. She seemed to know no happy being and she herself was agonising. . . .

She remembered that Edward's eyes were hopeless; she was certain that he was drinking too much; at times he sighed deeply. He appeared as a man who was burning with inward flame; drying up in the soul with thirst; withering up in the vitals. Then, the torturing conviction came to her—the conviction that had visited her again and again—that Edward must love someone other than Leonora. With her little, pedagogic sec-

---

6. A small wood planted or preserved to protect game birds.
7. Lines by Robert Herrick (1591–1674), English Cavalier poet and ordained clergyman famous for his controlled but passionate love lyrics, often dealing with sexual frustration. The quotation is from the opening lines of his "To The Willow Tree." **MS** [329; 322] deletes the rest of the opening quatrain and the whole of the last. See MDATV, p. 213, 143, 2nd entry below. As it stands, the allusion is obscure; Herrick personifies willow as "plant" of neglected lovers because a willow crown was worn by "Maids" "When once the Lovers Rose is dead, / Or laid aside forlorne." Perhaps also an oblique reference to Desdemona's song about "False Love," *Othello* 4.3.

tarianism she remembered that Catholics do not do this thing. But Edward was a Protestant. Then Edward loved somebody. . . .

And after that thought her eyes grew hopeless; she sighed as the old St. Bernard beside her did. At meals she would feel an intolerable desire to drink a glass of wine, and then another and then a third. Then she would find herself grow gay. . . . But in half an hour the gaiety went; she felt like a person who is burning up with an inward flame; desiccating at the soul with thirst; withering up in the vitals. One evening she went into Edward's gun-room—he had gone to a meeting of the National Reserve Committee.[8]* On the table beside his chair was a decanter of whiskey. She poured out a wine-glassful and drank it off.

Flame then really seemed to fill her body; her legs swelled; her face grew feverish. She dragged her tall height up to her room and lay in the dark. The bed reeled beneath her; she gave way to the thought that she was in Edward's arms; that he was kissing her on her face that burned; on her shoulders that burned and on her neck that was on fire.

She never* touched alcohol again. Not once after that did she have such thoughts. They died out of her mind; they left only a feeling of shame so insupportable that her brain could not take it in and they vanished. She imagined that her anguish at the thought of Edward's love for another person was solely sympathy for Leonora; she determined that the rest of her life must be spent in acting as Leonora's hand-maiden—sweeping, tending, embroidering, like some Deborah,[9] some mediaeval saint—I am not unfortunately up in the Catholic hagiology[1] —but* I know that she pictured herself as some personage with a depressed earnest face and tightly closed lips, in a clear white room, watering flowers or tending an embroidery frame. Or, she desired to go with Edward to* Africa and to throw herself in the path of a charging lion so that Edward might be saved for Leonora at the cost of her life. Well, along with her sad thoughts she had her childish ones.

She knew nothing—nothing of life except that one must live sadly. That she now knew. What happened to her on the night when she received at once the blow that Edward wished her to go to her father in India and the blow of the letter from her mother was this. She called first upon her sweet Saviour—and she thought of Our Lord as her sweet Saviour!—that He might make it impossible that she should go to India. Then she realised from Edward's demeanour that he was determined that she should go to India. It must then be right that she should go. Edward was always right in his determinations. He was the Cid; he was Lohengrin; he was the Chevalier Bayard.[2]

Nevertheless her mind mutinied and revolted. She could not leave

---

8. No such committee seems to have existed. See MDATV, p. 201, 46, 5th entry below.
9. An invented saint, and clearly not the Old Testament prophetess (Judges 4 and 5), a powerful, warlike female.
1. Literature describing lives of the saints.
2. See p. 68, n. 6 above.

that house. She imagined that he wished her gone that she might not witness his amours with another girl. Well, she was prepared to tell him that she was ready to witness his amours with another young girl. She would stay there—to comfort Leonora.

Then came the desperate shock of the letter from her mother. Her mother said, I believe, something like: "You have no right to go on living your life of prosperity and respect. You ought to be on the streets with me. How do you know that you are even Colonel Rufford's daughter? . . ."* She did not know what these words meant. She thought of her mother as sleeping beneath the arches whilst the snow fell. That was the impression conveyed to her mind by the words "on the streets". A Platonic[3] sense of duty gave her the idea that she ought to go to comfort her mother—the mother that bore her, though she hardly knew what the words meant. At the same time she knew that her mother had left her father with another man—therefore she pitied her father and thought it terrible in herself that she trembled at the sound of her father's voice. If her mother was that sort of woman it was natural that her father should have had accesses[4] of madness in which he had struck herself to the ground. And the voice of her conscience said to her that her first duty was to her parents. It was in accord with this awakened sense of duty that she undressed with great care and meticulously folded the clothes that she took off. Sometimes,* but not very often, she threw them helter-skelter about the room.

And that sense of duty was her prevailing mood when Leonora, tall, clean-run, golden-haired, all in black, appeared in her doorway, and told her* that Edward was dying of love for her. She knew then with her conscious mind what she had known within herself for months— that Edward* was dying—actually and physically dying—of love for her. It seemed to her that for one short moment her spirit could say: "*Domine, nunc dimittis.* . . . Lord, now lettest thou thy servant depart in peace."[5] She imagined that she could cheerfully go away to Glasgow and rescue her fallen mother.

IV *

And it seemed to her to be in tune with the mood, with the hour and with the woman in front of her to say: that she knew Edward was dying of love for her and that she was dying of love for Edward. For that fact had suddenly slipped into place and become real for her as the niched

3. No literal meaning but Dowell is presumably using the word in a loose modern sense deriving from the notion of Platonic love: purely spiritual, unimpassioned.
4. Fits.
5. First words of the Song of Simeon (Luke 2.29), which is sung or said at Compline, at the end of the day, as a form of night prayer. To sing one's *nunc dimittis* is "to declare oneself contented to depart from life or from some occupation" (SOED).

marker on a whist tablet slips round with the pressure of your thumb. That rubber[1] at least was made.

And suddenly Leonora seemed to have become different and she seemed to have become different in her attitude towards Leonora. It was as if she, in her frail, white, silken kimono, sat, beside her fire, but upon a throne. It was as if Leonora, in her close dress of black lace with the gleaming white shoulders and the coiled yellow hair that the girl had always considered the most beautiful thing in the world—it was as if Leonora had become pinched, shrivelled, blue with cold, shivering, suppliant. Yet Leonora was commanding her. It was no good commanding her. She was going on the morrow to her mother who was in Glasgow.

Leonora went on saying that she must stay there to save Edward who was dying of love for her. And, proud and happy in the thought that Edward loved her and that she loved him, she did not even listen to what Leonora said. It appeared to her that it was Leonora's business to save her husband's body; she, Nancy, possessed his soul—a precious thing that she would shield and bear away up in her arms—as if Leonora were a hungry dog trying to spring up at a lamb that she was carrying. Yes, she felt as if Edward's love were a precious lamb that she were bearing away from a cruel and predatory beast. For, at[*] that time, Leonora appeared to her as a cruel and predatory beast. Leonora, Leonora with her hunger, with her cruelty, had driven Edward to madness. He must be sheltered by his love for her and by her love—her love from a great distance and unspoken, enveloping him, surrounding him, upholding him; by her voice speaking from Glasgow, saying that she loved, that she adored, that she passed no moment without longing, loving, quivering at the thought of him.

Leonora said loudly,[*] insistently, with a bitterly imperative tone:

"You must stay here; you must belong to Edward. I will divorce him."

The girl answered:

"The Church does not allow of divorce. I cannot belong to your husband. I am going to Glasgow to rescue my mother."

The half-opened door opened noiselessly to the full.[*] Edward was there. His devouring doomed eyes were fixed on the girl's face; his shoulders slouched forward; he was undoubtedly half-drunk and he had the whiskey decanter in one hand, a slanting candlestick in the other. He said with a heavy ferocity to Nancy:

"I forbid you to talk about these things. You are to stay here until I hear from your father. Then you will go to your father."

The two women, looking at each other, like beasts about to spring, hardly gave a glance to him. He leaned against the door-post. He said again:

1. A winning set of games.

"Nancy, I forbid you to talk about these things. I am the master of this house." And, at the sound of his voice, heavy, male, coming from a deep chest, in the night, with the blackness behind him, Nancy felt as if her spirit bowed before him, with folded hands. She felt that she would go to India and that she desired never again to talk of these things.

Leonora said:

"You see that it is your duty to belong to him. He must not be allowed to go on drinking."

Nancy did not answer. Edward was gone; they heard him slipping and shambling on the polished black oak of the stairs. Nancy screamed when there came the sound of a heavy fall. Leonora said again:

"You see!"

The sounds went on from the hall below; the light of the candle Edward held flickered up between the hand rails of the gallery. Then they heard his voice:

"Give me Glasgow . . . Glasgow in Scotland . . . I want the number* of a man called White of Simrock Park, Glasgow . . . Edward White, Simrock Park, Glasgow. . . . Ten minutes. . . . At* this time of night. . . ." His voice was quite level, normal and patient. Alcohol took him in the legs, not the speech. "I can wait," his voice came again. "Yes, I know they have a number. I have been in communication with them before."

"He is going to telephone to your mother," Leonora said. "He will make it all right for her." She got up and closed the door. She came back to the fire and added bitterly: "He can always make it all right for everybody. Except me. Excepting me!"*

The girl said nothing. She sat there in a blissful dream. She seemed to see her lover, sitting as he always sat, in a round-backed chair, in the dark hall—sitting low, with the receiver at his ear, talking in a gentle, slow* voice, that he reserved for the telephone—and saving the world and her, in the black darkness.* She moved her hand over the bareness of the base of her throat, to have the warmth of flesh upon it and upon her bosom.

She said nothing; Leonora went on talking. . . .

God knows what Leonora said. She repeated that the girl must belong to her husband. She said that she used that phrase because, though she might have a divorce, or even a dissolution of the marriage by the Church, it would still be adultery that the girl and Edward would be committing. But she said that that was necessary; it was the price the girl must pay for the sin of having made Edward love her, for the sin of loving her husband. She talked on and on, beside the fire. The girl must become an adulteress; she had wronged Edward by being so beautiful, so gracious, so good. It was sinful to be so good. She must pay the price so as to save the man she had wronged.

In between her pauses the girl could hear the voice of Edward droning on, indistinguishably, with jerky pauses for replies. It made her glow with pride; the man she loved was working for her. He at least was resolved; was malely determined; knew the right thing. Leonora talked on with her eyes boring into Nancy's. The girl hardly looked at her and hardly heard her. After a long time Nancy said—after hours and hours:

"I shall go to India as soon as Edward hears from my father. I cannot talk about these things because Edward does not wish it."*

At that Leonora screamed out and wavered swiftly towards the closed door. And Nancy found that she was springing out of her chair with her white arms stretched wide. She was clasping the other woman to her breast; she was saying:

"Oh, my poor dear, oh, my poor dear." And they sat, crouching together in each other's arms, and crying and crying; and they lay down in the same bed, talking and talking, all through the night. And all through the night Edward could hear their voices through the wall. That was how it went. . . .

Next* morning they were all three as if nothing had happened. Towards eleven Edward came to Nancy who was arranging some Christmas roses in a silver bowl. He put a telegram beside her on the table. "You can uncode it for yourself," he said. Then, as he went out of the door, he said:

"You can tell your aunt I have cabled to Mr. Dowell to come over. He will make things easier till you leave."

The telegram, when it was uncoded, read as far as I can remember:

"Will take Mrs. Rufford to Italy. Undertake to do this for certain. Am devotedly attached to Mrs. Rufford. Have no need of financial assistance. Did not know there was a daughter and am much obliged to you for pointing out my duty. White." It was something like that.

Then that household resumed its wonted course of days until my arrival.

V *

It is this part of the story that makes me saddest of all. For I ask myself unceasingly, my mind going round and round in a weary, baffled space of pain—what should these people have done? What, in the name of God, should they have done?

The end was perfectly plain to each of them—it was perfectly manifest at this stage that, if the girl did not, in Leonora's phrase "belong to Edward", Edward must die, the girl must lose her reason because Edward died—and, that after a time, Leonora who was the coldest and the strongest of the three would console herself by marrying Rodney Bayham and have a quiet, comfortable, good time. That end, on that night whilst Leonora sat in the girl's bedroom and Edward telephoned down below—that end was plainly manifest. The girl, plainly, was half mad already; Edward was half dead; only Leonora, active, persistent, instinct with her cold passion of energy was "doing things". What then, should they have done? It worked out in the extinction of two very splendid personalities—for Edward and the girl *were* splendid personalities, in order that a third personality, more normal, should have after a long period of trouble, a quiet, comfortable, good time.

I am writing this now, I should say, a full eighteen months after the words that end my last chapter. Since writing the words "until my arrival", which I see end that paragraph, I have seen again, for a glimpse, from a swift train, Beaucaire with the beautiful white tower, Tarascon with the square castles, the great Rhone, the immense stretches of the Crau.[1] I have rushed through all Provence—and all Provence no longer matters. It is no longer in the olive hills that I shall find my heaven; because there is only Hell. . . .*

Edward is dead; the girl is gone—oh utterly gone; Leonora is having her good time with Rodney Bayham, and I sit alone in Bramshaw Teleragh. I have been through Provence; I have seen Africa; I have visited Asia to see, in Ceylon, in a darkened room, my poor girl, sitting motionless, with her wonderful hair about her, looking at me with eyes that did not see me and saying distinctly:* *"Credo in unum Deum Omnipotentem. . . . Credo in unum Deum Omnipotentem."*[2] Those are the only reasonable words she uttered; those are the only words, it appears, that she ever will utter. I suppose that they are reasonable words; it must be extraordinarily reasonable for her, if she can say that she believes in an omnipotent deity.* Well, there it is. I am very tired of it all. . . .

For I daresay all this may sound romantic—but it is tiring, tiring, tiring to have been in the midst of it; to have taken the tickets; to have caught the trains; to have chosen the cabins; to have consulted the nurse* and the stewards as to diet for* the quiescent patient who did nothing but announce her belief in an omnipotent deity. That may sound romantic—but it is just a record of fatigue.

I don't know why I should always be selected to be serviceable. I don't resent it—but I have never been* the least good. Florence selected me for her own purposes, and I was no good to her; Edward called me to come and have a chat with him and I couldn't stop him cutting his throat.

1. La Crau is an extensive dry plain of the Rhône between Tarascon and Marseilles, a notoriously depressing and featureless landscape. Dowell repeats the journey described near the beginning of the novel on the Paris-Lyons-Mediterranée Express (see p. 16 above), presumably to take ship from Marseilles to Ceylon via the Suez Canal.
2. "I believe in one omnipotent God . . . ," from the Nicene Creed. As Moser (306) points out, Nancy omits the word *Patrem* ("the father") after *Deum*.

And then, one day eighteen months ago, I was quietly writing in my room at Bramshaw when Leonora came to me with a letter. It was a very pathetic letter from Colonel Rufford—about Nancy. Colonel Rufford had left the Army * and had taken up the management of a tea-planting estate in Ceylon. His letter was pathetic because it was so brief, so inarticulate and so business-like. He had gone down to the boat to meet his daughter and had found his daughter quite mad. It appears that at Aden Nancy had seen in a local paper * the news of Edward's suicide. In the Red Sea she had gone mad. She had remarked to Mrs. Colonel Luton, who was chaperoning her, that she believed in an omnipotent deity. She hadn't made any fuss; her eyes were quite dry and glassy. Even when she was mad Nancy could behave herself. [She was well trained.]*

Colonel Rufford said the doctor[s] * did not anticipate that there was any chance of his child's recovery. It was nevertheless possible that if she could see someone from Bramshaw it might soothe her and it might have a good effect. And he just simply wrote to Leonora: "Please come and see if you can do it."

I seem to have lost all sense of the pathetic; but still, that simple, enormous request of the old Colonel * strikes me as pathetic. He was cursed by his atrocious temper; he had been cursed by a half-mad wife who drank and went on the streets. His daughter was totally mad—and yet he believed in the goodness of human nature. He believed that Leonora would take the trouble to go all the way to Ceylon in order to soothe his daughter. Leonora wouldn't. Leonora didn't ever want to see Nancy again. I daresay that that, in the circumstances, was natural enough. At the same time she agreed, as it were on public grounds, that someone soothing ought to go from Bramshaw to Ceylon. She sent me and her old nurse who had looked after Nancy from the time when the girl, a child of thirteen, had first come to Bramshaw. So off I go, rushing through Provence to catch the steamer at Marseilles. And I wasn't the least good when I got to Ceylon; and the nurse wasn't the least good. Nothing has been the least good.

The doctors said, at Kandy,[3] that if Nancy could be brought to England the sea air, the change of climate, the voyage and all the usual sort of things might restore her reason. Of course they haven't restored her reason. She is, I am aware, sitting in the hall, forty paces from where I am now writing. I don't want to be in the least romantic about it. She is very well-dressed; she is quite quiet; she is very beautiful. The old nurse looks after her very efficiently.

Of course you have the makings of a situation here, but it is all very humdrum, as far as I am concerned. I should marry Nancy if her reason

3. Former capital city of Ceylon (now Sri Lanka), off the southeast tip of India.

were ever sufficiently restored to let her appreciate the meaning of the Anglican marriage service. But it is probable that her reason will never be sufficiently restored to let her appreciate the meaning of the Anglican marriage service. Therefore I cannot marry her, according to the law of the land.

So here I am very much where I started thirteen years ago. I am the attendant, not the husband, of a beautiful girl who pays no attention to me. I am estranged from Leonora, who married Rodney Bayham in my absence and went* to live at Bayham. Leonora rather dislikes me because she has got it into her head that I disapprove of her marriage with Rodney Bayham. Well, I disapprove of her marriage. Possibly I am jealous.

Yes, no doubt I am jealous. In my fainter sort of way I seem to perceive myself following the lines of Edward Ashburnham. I suppose that I should really like to be a polygamist; with Nancy, and with Leonora and with Maisie Maidan and possibly even with Florence. I am no doubt like every other man; only, probably because of my American origin I am fainter. At the same time I am able to assure you that I am a strictly respectable person. I have never done anything that the most anxious mother of a daughter or the most careful dean of a cathedral would object to. I have only followed, faintly, and in my unconscious desires—Edward Ashburnham. Well, it is all over. Not one of us has got what he really wanted. Leonora wanted Edward and she has got Rodney Bayham, a pleasant enough sort of sheep. Florence wanted Bramshaw and it is I who have bought it from Leonora. I didn't really want it; what I wanted mostly was to cease being a nurse-attendant. Well, I am a nurse-attendant. Edward wanted Nancy Rufford and I have got her. Only she is mad. It is a queer and fantastic world. Why can't people have what they want? The things were all there to content everybody; yet everybody has the wrong thing. Perhaps you can make head or tail of it; it is beyond me.

Is there then any terrestrial paradise where, amidst the whispering of the olive-leaves, people can be with whom they like and have what they like and take their ease in shadows and in coolness? Or are all men's lives like the lives of us good people—like the lives of the Ashburnhams, of the Dowells, of the Ruffords—broken, tumultuous, agonised, and unromantic lives, periods punctuated by screams, by imbecilities, by deaths, by agonies? Who the devil knows?

For there was a great deal of imbecility about the closing scenes of the Ashburnham tragedy. Neither of those two women knew what they wanted. It was only Edward who took a perfectly clear line and he was drunk most of the time. But, drunk or sober, he stuck to what was demanded by convention and by the traditions of his house. Nancy Rufford had to be exported to India and Nancy Rufford hadn't to hear a word of love from him. She was exported to India and she never heard a word from Edward Ashburnham.

It was the conventional line; it was in tune with the tradition of Edward's house. I daresay it worked out for the greatest good of the body politic. Conventions and traditions I suppose work blindly but surely for the preservation of the normal type; for the extinction of proud, resolute and unusual individuals.

Edward was the normal man, but there was too much of the sentimentalist about him and society does not need too many sentimentalists. Nancy was a splendid creature but she had about her a touch of madness. Society does not need individuals with touches of madness about them. So Edward and Nancy found themselves steam-roll[er]ed * out and Leonora survives, the perfectly normal type, married to a man who is rather like a rabbit. For Rodney Bayham is rather like a rabbit and I hear that Leonora is expected to have a baby in three months' time.

So those splendid and tumultuous creatures with their magnetism and their passions—those two that I really loved—have gone from this earth. It is no doubt best for them. What would Nancy have made of Edward if she had succeeded in living with him; what would Edward have made of her? For there was about Nancy a touch of cruelty—a touch of definite actual cruelty that made her desire to see people suffer. Yes, she desired to see Edward suffer. And, by God, she gave him hell.

She gave him an unimaginable hell. Those two women pursued that poor devil and flayed the skin off him as if they had done it with whips. I tell you his mind bled almost visibly. I seem to see him stand, naked to the waist, his forearms shielding his eyes, and flesh hanging from him in rags. I tell you that is no exaggeration of what I feel. It was as if Leonora and Nancy banded themselves together to do execution, for the sake of humanity, upon the body of a man who was at their disposal. They were like a couple of Sioux who had got hold of an Apache and had him well tied to a stake. I tell you there was no end to the tortures they inflicted upon him.

Night after night he would hear them [talking,] talking; talking; * maddened, sweating, seeking oblivion in drink, he would lie there and hear the voices going on and on. And day after day Leonora would come to him and would announce the results of their deliberations.

They were like judges debating over the sentence upon a criminal; they were like ghouls with an immobile corpse in a tomb beside them.

I don't think that Leonora was any more to blame than the girl—though Leonora was the more active of the two. Leonora, as I have said, was the perfectly normal woman. I mean to say that in normal circumstances her desires were those of the woman who is needed by society. She desired children, decorum, an establishment; she desired to avoid waste, she desired to keep up appearances. She was utterly and

entirely normal even in her utterly undeniable beauty. But I don't mean
to say that she acted perfectly normally in this perfectly abnormal situation. All the world was mad around her and she herself, agonised, took
on the complexion of a mad woman; of a woman very wicked; of the
villain of the piece. What would you have? Steel is a normal, hard,
polished substance. But, if you put it in a hot fire it will become red,
soft, and not to be handled. If you put it in a fire still more hot it will
drip away. It was like that with Leonora. She was made for normal
circumstances—for Mr. Rodney Bayham, who will keep a separate
establishment, secretly, in Portsmouth, and make occasional trips to
Paris and to Buda-Pesth.[4]

In the case of Edward and the girl Leonora broke and simply went all
over the place. She adopted unfamiliar and therefore extraordinary and
ungraceful attitudes of mind. At one moment she was all for [self-sacri-
fice; at the next she was all for] revenge.* After haranguing the girl for
hours through the night she harangued for hours of the day the silent
Edward. And Edward just once tripped up and that was his undoing.
Perhaps he had had too much whiskey that afternoon.

She asked him perpetually what he wanted. What did he want? What
did he want? And all he ever answered was: "I have told you." He meant
that he wanted the girl to go to her father in India as soon as her father
should cable that he was ready to receive her. But just once he tripped
up. To Leonora's eternal question he answered that all he desired in life
was that—that he could pick himself together again and go on with his
daily occupations if—the girl being five thousand miles away, would
continue to love him. He wanted nothing more. He prayed his God for
nothing more. Well, he was a sentimentalist.

And the moment that she heard that, Leonora* determined that the
girl should not go five thousand miles away and that she should not
continue to love Edward. The way she worked it was this:

She continued to tell the girl that she* must belong to Edward; she
was going to get a divorce; she was going to get a dissolution of marriage
from Rome. But she considered it to be her duty to warn the girl of the
sort of monster that Edward was. She told the girl of La Dolciquita, of
Mrs. Basil, of Maisie Maidan, of Florence. She spoke of the agonies
that she had endured during her life with the man, who was violent,
overbearing, vain, drunken, arrogant, and monstrously* a prey to his
sexual necessities. And, at hearing of the miseries her aunt had suffered—for Leonora once more had the aspect of an aunt to the girl—
with the swift cruelty of youth and, with the swift solidarity that attaches
woman to woman, the girl made her resolves. Her aunt said incessantly:
"You must save Edward's life; you must save his life. All that he needs

4. Now Budapest, capital city of Hungary on the Danube River, formerly the twin cities of old
   Buda, once the site of the castle of Hungarian kings, and Pesth, the sprawling residential and
   industrial suburb, then a regular haunt of wealthy Europeans in search of "low-life."

is a little period of satisfaction from you. Then he will tire of you as he has of the others. But you must save his life."

And, all the while, that wretched fellow knew, by a curious instinct that runs between human beings living together—exactly what was going on. And he remained dumb; he stretched out no finger to help himself. All that he required to keep himself a decent member of society was, that the girl, five thousand miles away, should continue to love him. They were putting a stopper upon that.

I have told you that the girl came one night to his room. And that was the real hell for him. That was the picture that never left his imagination—the girl, in the dim light, rising up at the foot of his bed. He said that it seemed to have a greenish sort of effect as if there were a greenish tinge in the shadows of the tall bedposts that framed her body. And she looked at him with her straight eyes of an unflinching cruelty and she said: "I am ready to belong to you—to save your life."

He answered: "I don't want it; I don't want it; I don't want it."

And he says that he didn't want it; that he would have hated himself; that it was unthinkable. And all the while he had the immense temptation to do the unthinkable thing, not from the physical desire but because of a mental certitude. He was certain that if she had once submitted to him she would remain his for ever. He knew that.

She was thinking that her aunt had said he had desired her to love him from a distance of five thousand miles. She said: "I can never love you now I know the kind of man you are. I will belong to you to save your life. But I can never love you."

It was a fantastic display of cruelty. She didn't in the least know what it meant—to belong to a man. But, at that, Edward pulled himself together. He spoke in his normal tones; gruff, husky, overbearing, as he would have done to a servant or to a horse.

"Go back to your room," he said. "Go* back to your room and go to sleep. This is all nonsense."

They were baffled, those two women.*
And then I came on the scene.

VI *

My coming on the scene certainly calmed things down—for the whole fortnight that intervened between my arrival and the girl's departure. I don't mean to say that the endless talking did not go on at night or that Leonora did not send me out with the girl and, in the interval, give Edward a hell of a time. Having discovered what he wanted—that the girl should go five thousand miles away and love him steadfastly as people do in sentimental novels, she was determined to smash that aspiration. And she repeated to Edward in every possible tone that the girl did not love him; that the girl detested him for his brutality, his overbearingness, his drinking habits. [She pointed out more than a dozen good reasons why the girl should not love him.]* She pointed out that Edward, in the girl's eyes, was already pledged three or four deep. He was pledged to Leonora herself, to Mrs. Basil and to the memories of Maisie Maidan and of Florence.* Edward never said anything.

Did the girl love Edward, or didn't she? I don't know. At that time I daresay she didn't, though she certainly had done so before Leonora had got to work upon his reputation. She certainly had loved him for what I will call the public side of his record—for his good soldiering, for his saving lives at sea, for the excellent landlord that he was and the good sportsman. But it is quite possible that all those things came to appear as nothing in her eyes when she discovered that he wasn't a good husband. For, though women, as I see them, have little or no feeling of responsibility towards a county or a country or a career—although they may be entirely lacking in any kind of communal solidarity—they have an immense and automatically working instinct* that attaches them to the interest[s]* of womanhood. It is of course possible for any woman to cut out and to carry off any other woman's husband or lover. But I rather think that a woman will only do this if she has reason to believe that the other woman has given her husband a bad time. I am certain that if she thinks* the man has been a brute to his wife she will, with her instinctive feeling for suffering femininity, "put him back", as the saying is. I don't attach any particular importance to these generalisations of mine. They may be right, they may be wrong; I am only an ageing American with very little knowledge of life. You may take my generalisations or leave them. But I am pretty certain that I am right in the case of Nancy Rufford—that she had loved Edward Ashburnham very deeply and tenderly.

It is nothing to the point that she let him have it good and strong as soon as she discovered that he had been unfaithful to Leonora and that his public services had cost more than Leonora thought they ought to have cost. Nancy would be bound to let him have it good and strong then. She would owe that to feminine public opinion; she would be driven to it by the instinct for self-preservation, since she might well imagine that if Edward had been unfaithful to Leonora, to Mrs. Basil and to the memories of the other two he might be unfaithful to herself. And, no doubt she had her share of the sex instinct that makes women be intolerably cruel to the beloved person. Anyhow, I don't know whether, at this point, Nancy Rufford loved Edward Ashburnham. I don't know whether she even loved him when, on getting, at Aden, the news of his suicide she went mad. Because that may just as well have been for the sake of Leonora as for the sake of Edward. Or it may have

been for the sake of both of them. I don't know. I know nothing. I am
very tired.

Leonora held passionately the doctrine that the girl didn't love
Edward. She wanted desperately to believe that. It was a doctrine as
necessary to her existence as a belief in the personal immortality of the
soul. She said that it was impossible that Nancy could have loved
Edward after she had given the girl her view of Edward's career and
character. Edward on the other hand believed maunderingly that some
essential attractiveness in himself must have made the girl continue to
go on loving him—to go on loving him, as it were, in underneath her
official aspect of hatred. He thought [that] * she only pretended to hate
him in order to save her face and he thought that her quite atrocious
telegram from Brindisi was only another attempt to do that—to prove
that she had feelings creditable to a member of the feminine common-
weal. I don't know. I leave it to you.

There is another point that worries me a good deal in the aspects of
this sad affair. Leonora says that, in desiring that the girl should go five
thousand miles away and yet continue to love him, Edward was a monster of selfishness. He was desiring the ruin of a young life. Edward on
the other hand put it to me that, supposing that the girl's love was a
necessity to his existence, and, if he did nothing by word or by action to
keep Nancy's love alive, he couldn't be called selfish. Leonora replied
that showed he had an abominably selfish nature even though his
actions might be perfectly correct. I can't make out which of them was
right. I leave it to you.

It is at any rate certain that Edward's actions were perfectly—were
monstrously, were cruelly—correct. He sat still and let Leonora take
away his character, and let Leonora damn him to deepest hell, without
stirring a finger. I daresay he was a fool; I don't see what object there
was in letting the girl think worse of him than was necessary. Still there
it is. And there it is also that all those three presented to the world the
spectacle of being the best of good people. I assure you that during my
stay for that fortnight in that fine old house, I never so much as noticed
a single thing that could have affected that good opinion. And even
when I look back, knowing the circumstances, I can't remember a single
thing any of them said that could have betrayed them. I can't remember,
right up to the dinner, when Leonora read out that telegram—not the
tremor of an eyelash, not the shaking of a hand. It was just a pleasant
country house-party. *

And Leonora kept it up jolly well, for even longer than that—she kept
it up as far as I was concerned until eight days after Edward's funeral.
Immediately after that particular dinner—the dinner at which I received
the announcement that Nancy was going to leave for India on the following day—I asked Leonora to let me have a word with her. She took

me into her little sitting-room and I then said—I spare you the record of my emotions—that she was aware that I wished to marry Nancy; that she had seemed to favour my suit and that it appeared to be rather a waste of money upon tickets and rather a waste of time upon travel to let the girl go to India if Leonora thought that there was any chance of her marrying me.

And Leonora, I assure you, was the absolutely perfect British matron. She said that she quite favoured my suit; that she could not desire for the girl a better husband; but that she considered that the girl ought to see a little more of life before taking such an important step. Yes, Leonora used the words "taking such an important step". She was perfect. Actually, I think she would have liked the girl to marry me well enough but my programme included the buying of the Kershaws' house, about a mile and a half away upon the Fordingbridge road, and settling down there with the girl. That didn't at all suit Leonora. She didn't want to have the girl within a mile and a half of Edward for the rest of their lives. Still, I think she might have managed to let me know, in some periphrasis or other, that I might have the girl if I would take her to Philadelphia or Timbuktu.* I loved Nancy very much—and Leonora knew it.

However, I left it at that. I left it with the understanding that Nancy was going away to India on probation. It seemed to me a perfectly reasonable arrangement and I am a reasonable sort of man. I simply said that I should follow Nancy out to India after six months' time or so. Or perhaps after a year. Well, you see, I did follow Nancy out to India after a year. . . .

I must confess to having felt a little angry* with Leonora for not having warned me earlier that the girl would be going. I took it as one of the queer, not very straight methods that Roman Catholics seem to adopt in dealing with matters of this world. I took it that Leonora had been afraid I should propose to the girl or at any rate have made considerably greater advances to her than I did, if I had known earlier that she was going away so soon. Perhaps Leonora was right; perhaps Roman Catholics, with their queer, shifty ways, are always right. They are dealing with the queer, shifty thing that is human nature. For it is quite possible that, if I had known Nancy was going away so soon, I should have tried making love to her.[1] And that would have produced another complication. It may have been just as well.

It is queer the fantastic things that quite good people will do in order to keep up their appearance of calm poco-curantism.[2] For Edward Ashburnham and his wife called me half the world over in order to sit on the back seat of a dog-cart whilst Edward drove the girl to the railway

---

1. Courting, paying amorous attention to.
2. Nonchalance, indifference.

station from which she was to take her departure to India. They wanted, I suppose, to have a witness of the calmness of that function. The girl's luggage had been already packed and sent off before. Her berth on the steamer had been taken. They had timed it all so exactly that it went like clockwork. They had known the date upon which Colonel Rufford would get Edward's letter and they had known almost exactly the hour at which they would receive his telegram asking his daughter to come to him. It had all been quite beautifully and quite mercilessly arranged, by Edward himself. They gave Colonel Rufford as a reason for telegraphing the fact that Mrs. Colonel Somebody or Other* would be traveling by that ship and that she would serve as an efficient chaperon for the girl. It was a most amazing business, and I think that it would have been better in the eyes of God if they had all attempted to gouge out each other's eyes with carving knives. But they were "good people".

After my interview with Leonora I went desultorily into Edward's gun-room. I didn't know where the girl was and I thought I might find her there. I suppose I had a vague idea of proposing to her in spite of Leonora. So, I presume, I don't come of quite such good people as the Ashburnhams. Edward was lounging in his chair smoking a cigar and he said nothing for quite five minutes. The candles glowed in the green shades; the reflections were green in the glasses of the book-cases that held guns and fishing-rods. Over the mantel-piece was the brownish picture of the white horse. Those were the quietest moments that I have ever known. Then suddenly Edward looked me straight in the eyes and said:

"Look here, old man, I wish you would drive with Nancy and me to the station to-morrow."

I said that of course I would drive with him and Nancy to the station on the morrow. He lay there for a long time, looking along the line of his knees at the fluttering fire and then suddenly, in a perfectly calm voice, and without lifting his eyes, he said:

"I am so desperately in love with Nancy Rufford that I am dying of it."

Poor devil—he hadn't meant to speak of it. But I guess he just had to speak to somebody and I appeared to be like a woman or a solicitor. He talked all night.

Well, he carried out the programme to the last breath.

It was a very clear winter morning, with a good deal of frost in it. The sun was quite bright, the winding road between the heather and the bracken was very hard. I sat on the back seat of the dog-cart; Nancy was beside Edward. They talked about the way the cob went; Edward pointed out with the whip a cluster of deer upon a coomb[3] three-quarters of a mile away. We passed the hounds in the level bit of road beside

3. The flank of a hill.

the high trees going into Fordingbridge and Edward pulled up the dog-cart so that Nancy might say good-bye to the huntsman and cap[4] him a last sovereign. She had ridden with those hounds ever since she had been thirteen.

The train was five minutes late and they imagined that that was because it was market-day at Swindon or wherever the train came from. That was the sort of thing they talked about. The train came in; Edward found her a first-class carriage with an elderly woman in it. The girl entered the carriage, Edward closed the door and then she put out her hand to shake mine. There was upon those people's faces no expression of any kind whatever. The signal for the train's departure was a very bright red; that is about as passionate a statement as I can get into that scene.* She was not looking her best; she had on a cap of brown fur that did not very well match her hair. She said:

"So long," to Edward.

Edward answered: "So long."

He swung round on his heel and, large, slouching, and walking with a heavy deliberate pace, he went out of the station. I followed him and got up beside him in the high dog-cart. It was the most horrible performance I have ever seen.

And, after that, a holy peace, like the peace of God which passes all understanding,[5] descended upon Bramshaw Teleragh. Leonora went about her daily duties with a sort of triumphant smile—a very faint smile, but quite triumphant. I guess she had so long since given up any idea of getting her man back that it was enough for her to have got the girl out of the house and well cured of her infatuation. Once, in the hall, when Leonora was going out, Edward said, beneath his breath—but I just caught the words:

"Thou hast conquered, O pale Galilean."

It was like his sentimentality to quote Swinburne.[6]*

But he was perfectly quiet and he had given up drinking. The only thing that he ever said to me after that drive to the station was:

"It's very odd. I think I ought to tell you, Dowell, that I haven't any feelings at all about the girl now it's all over. Don't you worry about me. I'm all right." A long time afterwards he said: "I guess it was only a flash in the pan." He began to look after the estates again; he took all that trouble over getting off the gardener's daughter* who had murdered her baby. He shook hands smilingly with every farmer in the market-place. He addressed two political meetings; he hunted twice. Leonora made him a frightful scene about spending the two hundred pounds on getting

4. "Cap-money" is that collected for the huntsman; hence here: "tip."
5. See the Epistle to the Philippians 4.7: "And the peace of God, which passeth all understanding, shall keep your hearts and minds through Christ Jesus."
6. Algernon Charles Swinburne (1837–1909); "Hymn to Proserpine," in which the "pale Galilean" is, of course, Christ.

the gardener's daughter acquitted. Everything went on as if the girl had
never existed. It was very still weather.*

Well, that is the end of the story. And, when I come to look at it I
see that it is a happy* ending with wedding bells and all. The villains—
for obviously Edward and the girl were villains—have been punished by
suicide and madness. The heroine—the perfectly normal, virtuous and
slightly deceitful heroine—has become the happy wife of a perfectly
normal, virtuous and slightly-deceitful husband. She will shortly
become a mother of a perfectly normal, virtuous, slightly-deceitful son
or daughter. A happy ending, that is what it works out at.

I cannot conceal from myself the fact that I now dislike Leonora.
Without doubt I am jealous of Rodney Bayham. But I don't know
whether it is merely a jealousy arising from the fact that I desired myself
to possess Leonora or whether it is because to her were sacrificed the
only two persons that I have ever really loved—Edward Ashburnham
and Nancy Rufford. In order to set her up in a modern mansion, replete
with every convenience and dominated by a quite respectable and emi-
nently economical master of the house, it was necessary that Edward
and Nancy Rufford should become, for me at least, no more than
tragic shades.

I seem to see poor Edward, naked and reclining amidst darkness,
upon cold rocks, like one of the ancient Greek damned, in Tartarus[7] or
wherever it was.

And as for Nancy. . . . Well, yesterday at lunch she said suddenly:
"Shuttlecocks!"[8]

And she repeated the word "shuttlecocks"* three times. I know what
was passing in her mind, if she can be said to have a mind, for Leonora
has told me that, once, the poor girl said she felt like a shuttlecock
being tossed backwards and forwards between the violent personalities of
Edward and his wife. Leonora, she said, was always trying to deliver her
over to Edward, and Edward tacitly and silently forced her back again.
And the odd thing was that Edward himself considered that those two
women used *him* like a shuttlecock. Or rather he said that they sent him
backwards and forwards like a blooming parcel that someone didn't want
to pay the postage on. And Leonora also imagined that Edward and
Nancy picked her up and threw her down as suited their purely vagrant
moods. So there you have the pretty picture.*

Mind, I am not preaching anything contrary to accepted morality. I
am not advocating free love in this or any other case. Society must go
on, I suppose, and society can only exist if the normal, if the virtuous,

---

7. Some in Tartarus (Hell) were punished for sexual misdemeanors; the accounts of Tartarus's
   tortures in *Aeneid* 6 greatly influenced Dante and Christian concepts of Hell; *Aeneid* 6 specifically mentions adulterers (612) and those who lust after their daughters (623).
8. Feathered objects hit back and forth in the game of battledore, or badminton—i.e., here:
   people knocked arbitrarily about by Fate.

and the slightly-deceitful flourish, and if the passionate, the headstrong, and the too-truthful are condemned to suicide and to madness. But I guess that I myself, in my fainter way, come into the category of the passionate, of the headstrong, and the too-truthful. For I can't conceal from myself the fact that I loved Edward Ashburnham—and that I love him because he was just myself. If I had had the courage and the virility and possibly also the physique of Edward Ashburnham I should, I fancy, have done much what he did. He seems to me like a large elder brother who took me out on several excursions and did many dashing things whilst I just watched him robbing the orchards, from a distance. And, you see, I am just as much of a sentimentalist as he was. . . .

Yes, society must go on; it must breed, like rabbits. That is what we are here for. But then, I don't like society—much. I am that absurd figure, an American millionaire, who has bought one of the ancient haunts of English peace. I sit here, in Edward's gun-room, all day and all day in a house that is absolutely quiet. No one visits me, for I visit no one. No one is interested in me, for I have no interests. In twenty minutes or so I shall walk down to the village, beneath my own oaks, alongside my own clumps of gorse, to get the American mail. My tenants, the village boys and the tradesmen will touch their hats to me. So life peters out. I shall return to dine and Nancy will sit opposite me with the old nurse standing behind her. Enigmatic, silent, utterly well-behaved as far as her knife and fork go, Nancy will stare in front of her with the blue eyes that have over them strained, stretched brows. Once, or perhaps twice, during the meal her knife and fork will be suspended in mid-air as if she were trying to think of something that she had forgotten. Then she will say that she believes in an omnipotent deity or she will utter the one word "shuttlecocks",* perhaps. It is very extraordinary to see the perfect flush of health on her cheeks, to see the lustre of her coiled black hair, the poise of the head upon the neck, the grace of the white hands—and to think that it all means nothing—that it is a picture without a meaning. Yes, it is queer.°

But at any rate there is always Leonora to cheer you up; I * don't want to sadden you. Her husband is quite an economical person of so normal a figure that he can get quite a large proportion of his clothes ready-made. That is the great desideratum[9] of life, and that is the end of my story. The child is to be brought up as a Romanist.*

―――――――――

It suddenly occurs to me that I have forgotten to say how Edward met his death. You remember that peace had descended upon the house; that Leonora was quietly triumphant and that Edward said his love for the girl had been merely a passing phase. Well, one afternoon we were

9. Thing desired.

in the stables together, looking at a new kind of flooring that Edward was trying in a loose-box.[1] Edward was talking with a good deal of animation about the necessity of getting the numbers[*] of the Hampshire territorials[2] up to the proper standard. He was quite sober, quite quiet, his skin was clear-coloured; his hair was golden and perfectly brushed; the level brick-dust red of his complexion went clean up to the rims of his eyelids; his eyes were porcelain blue and they regarded me frankly and directly. His face was perfectly expressionless; his voice was deep and rough. He stood well back upon his legs and said:

"We ought to get them up to two thousand three hundred and fifty."

A stable-boy brought him a telegram and went away. He opened it negligently, regarded it without emotion, and, in complete silence, handed it to me. On the pinkish paper in a sprawled handwriting I read: "Safe Brindisi. Having rattling good time. Nancy."

Well, Edward was the English gentleman; but he was also, to the last, a sentimentalist, whose mind was compounded of indifferent poems and novels. He just looked up to the roof of the stable, as if he were looking to Heaven, and whispered something that I did not catch.[3][*]

Then he put two fingers into the waistcoat pocket of his grey, frieze[4] suit; they came out with a little neat pen-knife—quite a small pen-knife. He said to me:

"You might just take that wire to Leonora." And he looked at me with a direct, challenging, brow-beating glare. I guess he could see in my eyes that I didn't intend to hinder him. Why should I hinder him?[*] I didn't think he was wanted in the world, let his confounded tenants, his rifle-associations, his drunkards, reclaimed and unreclaimed, get on as they liked. Not all the hundreds and hundreds of them deserved that that poor devil should go on suffering for their sakes.

When he saw that I did not intend to interfere with him his eyes became soft and almost affectionate. He remarked:

"So long, old man, I must have a bit of a rest, you know."

I didn't know what to say. I wanted to say, "God bless you", for I also am a sentimentalist. But[*] I thought that perhaps that would not be quite English good form, so I trotted off with the telegram to Leonora. She was quite pleased with it.

---

1. Stable in which a horse may move freely.
2. The Territorial Army or Force (British Army of Home Defence) was instituted on a local basis in 1908. The threat of German invasion was already in the air.
3. **MS** [374; 367] and **TS** [304; 90–305; 91]: "Heaven and he remarked: | 'Girl, I will wait for you there.' "; **SPC**.
4. Coarse woollen cloth.

Map of Bad Nauheim, c. 1916.

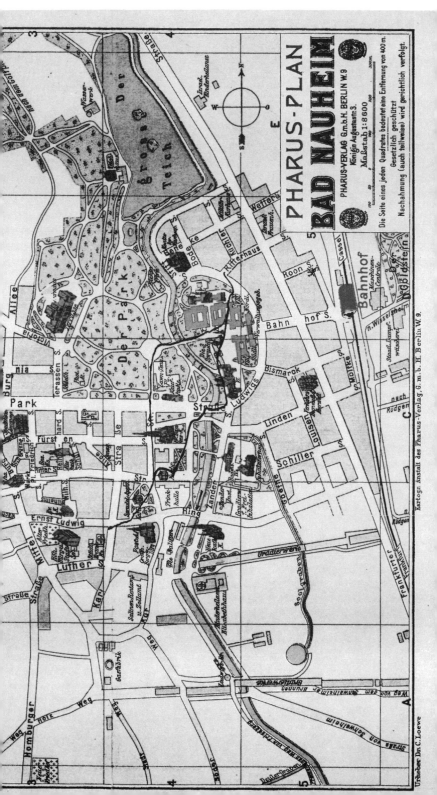

PHARUS-PLAN
BAD NAUHEIM

PHARUS-VERLAG G.m.b.H. BERLIN W.9
Königin Augustastr.3.
Maßstab 1:8600

Die Seite eines jeden Quadrates bedeutet eine Entfernung von 400 m.

Gesetzlich geschützt
Nachahmung (auch teilweise) wird gerichtlich verfolgt.

Kartogr. Anstalt des Pharus-Verlags, G. m. b. H. Berlin W. 9.

Urheber: Dr. C. Loewe.

Deutsches Hof today, formerly the Englischer Hof, where Ford sets Dowell and Florence's stay in Bad Nauheim.

The former Hotel Excelsior today, where Ford sets the first meeting between Dowell, Florence, Edward, and Leonora amid "cold, expensive elegance."

Victorian and Edwardian Bad Nauheim, confused in Dowell's recollection. The half-timbered bathhouses he half-remembers were demolished and replaced by an Art Nouveau complex. Even the fountains were rebuilt. *Reproduced by permission of Heinrich Burk.*

The old Kurhaus, seen from the Kurpark. The Spielbank (casino) was to the right. *Reproduced by permission of Heinrich Burk.*

The Marburg Schloss and the "ancient droschkas" used to take visitors up to it. *Foto Marburg/Art Resource, NY.*

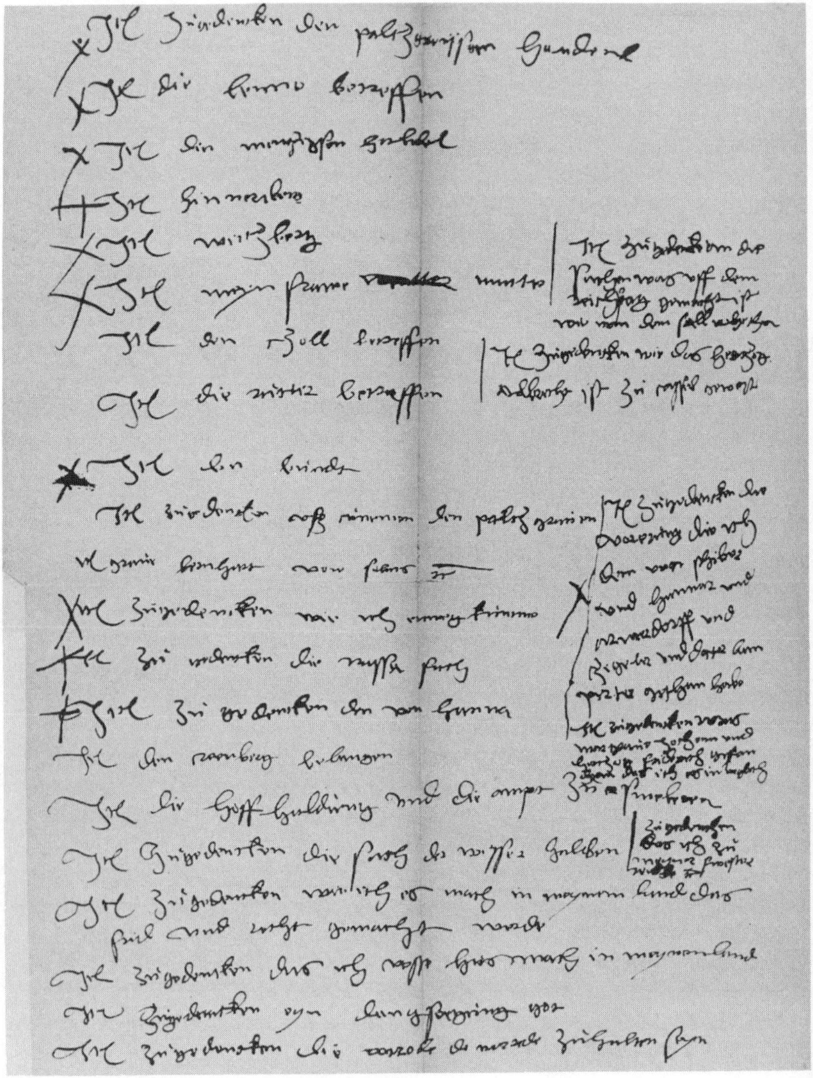

Memorandum of Philip of Hesse, April 1521.

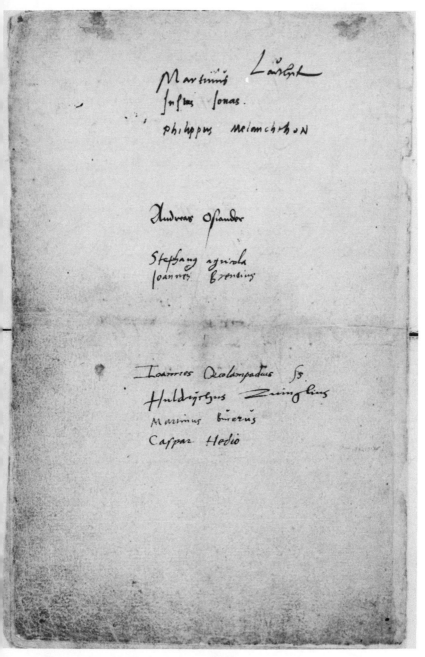

Signatures of the Reformers on the Transcript of the Marburg Religious Colloquies, 1529.

TEXTUAL APPENDICES

Abbreviations

Texts (in chronological order)

MS: the manuscript of *The Good Soldier* [*The Saddest Story*] (Harvey, C i, 9 (a), p. 108; see A Note on the Text, p. 179 below). "Manuscript" here refers to the earliest known draft of the novel (Cornell University Library), a collation of holograph and typescript. The holograph sections are in the three hands of Ford's amanuenses: Brigit Patmore, H. D., and Richard Aldington; the typed sections were usually executed by Ford but sometimes by a third party. The whole is corrected both by the amanuenses in the process of composition and later by Ford in ink and in pencil. 375 pp.

TSB: the ribbon-copy of the first section of **TS** (see below) (Harvey, C i, 9 (b), p. 108; also held at Cornell; see A Note on the Text, p. 179 below). Probably the section sent as copy to Wyndham Lewis for publication as the first part of *The Saddest Story* in his magazine *Blast*, 20 June 1914: 87–97. 42pp.

B: Printed text of the first three-and-a-half chapters of *The Saddest Story* in *Blast* (see **TSB**), erroneously citing the author as "Ford Maddox [sic] Hueffer."

TS: a complete typescript of the novel (Harvey, C i, 9 (c), p. 108; also held at Cornell; see A Note on the Text, p. 179 below). Harvey cites an "enclosing folder" (now lacking) inscribed: "Printer's Copy." The text is marked up for division into galley proofs and, although superficially "clean" in that it has only sparse pencil corrections, it contains numerous small corrections made by erasure and re-typing. "Typescript" here refers to a collation of TMS and TccMS (see below). 305 pp.

UK: Ford Madox Hueffer, *The Good Soldier. A Tale of Passion* (London: John Lane, The Bodley Head, 1915). First UK edition, and copy-text for this Norton edition, published 17 March 1915. 294 pp. + 16 pp. of advertisements, among which the novel is cited as *The Saddest Story*. Second impression (identical) printed during 1915.

US: Ford Madox Hueffer, *The Good Soldier. A Tale of Passion* (New York: John Lane Company, 1915). First US edition, probably published simultaneously with UK: 17 March 1915 (Harvey, A 46, (a), p. 44). 294 pp. (+ 16 pp. of advertisements as above).

US2: Ford Madox Ford, *The Good Soldier. A Tale of Passion* (New York: Albert & Charles Boni, 1927). Second US edition, probably published in April (Harvey, A 46, (b), p. 45). Probably printed simultaneously with signed, limited edition of 300 copies, printed on rag laid deckle edge paper, of which 25 copies were for presentation. Both 260 pp. + i–x including "Dedicatory Letter to Stella Ford" (v–ix).

UK2: Ford Madox Ford, *The Good Soldier. A Tale of Passion* (London: John Lane, The Bodley Head Ltd., [1928]). Second UK, "Week-End Library," edition, published 24 February 1928, including "Dedicatory Letter" (see **US2** above) and, as Harvey points out, an "erroneous footnote": "This letter was written as a special introduction to *The Good Soldier* in the collection of the author's works published in America." "No collected edition of Ford's works," Harvey states, "had been published by that date" (A 46, (c), p. 45), but one was certainly advertised by Boni, with *The Good Soldier* as the first in the series.

General

AMS:	Autograph [holograph] manuscript
asp:	all subsequent printings in Ford's lifetime (see above)
BP:	Brigit Patmore: Ford's first amanuensis
COD:	*Concise Oxford Dictionary*
Cornell:	Department of Rare Books, Karl A. Kroch Library, Cornell University, Ithaca, New York
Del:	Deletion
ED:	Editorial decision, indicating the reading selected
FMF:	In Ford Madox Ford's hand
Harvey:	David Dow Harvey, *Ford Madox Ford 1873–1939. A Bibliography of Works and Criticism* (Princeton UP, 1962; New York: Gordian Press, 1972)
HD:	H. D. [Hilda Doolittle], Ford's second amanuensis
[ink]:	Revision made by Ford in ink
MDATV:	Manuscript and Textual Variants section, pp. 194–216 below
Mizener:	Arthur Mizener, *The Saddest Story. A Biography of Ford Madox Ford* (London: The Bodley Head, 1971)
Moser:	Thomas C. Moser's edition of *The Good Soldier* (Oxford University Press, 1990) in The World's Classics series
[number; number]:	"External" page number of **MS** or **TS** followed by "internal" number of same. Only one number appears in brackets for page reference to **TSB,** first section of **TS,** or any printed text
*:	Signals a **MS** correction or textual variant. For details, see Manuscript Development and Textual Variants section, pp. 194–216 below
[ ]:	Page number lacking
[pencil]:	Revision made by Ford in pencil
Perpetuated mistranscription:	Mistranscription by typist which continued through all printed states

RA:	Richard Aldington, Ford's third amanuensis
SOED:	*Shorter Oxford English Dictionary*
SPC:	Probably a substantive proof correction by Ford or editor
TccMS:	Typed carbon copy manuscript
TMS:	Typed manuscript, ribbon-copy
[TS]:	Revision made in type, usually indicating either composition on the typewriter or the contemporaneous correction of a misreading of the AMS
WL:	[Percy] Wyndham Lewis (editor of *Blast*)
[...]:	My ellipses, not author's
[ital]:	Section italicized and between square brackets deleted
\ /:	Section between slashes inserted from above line or superimposed on letters on line
/ \:	Section between slashes inserted from below line
|:	Word after vertical stroke on a lower line

Example

MS [37; 35]: "chinese"; **TSB** [24]: "chemise"; **B** [92]: "Chinese"; **TS** [24]: "[*c*]\C/h*[emi]*\ine/se": [ink]; **UK** [28] and asp: "Chinese" = In the holograph MS the amanuensis wrote "chinese," mistranscribed in the *Blast* typescript as "chemise"; the printed *Blast* text corrects this to "Chinese" and the typescript of the complete novel makes the same correction, in ink in Ford's hand, by canceling lower-case "c" and superimposing capital, and by canceling "emi" and inserting "ine" above it; the first British edition and all subsequent printings follow this correction.

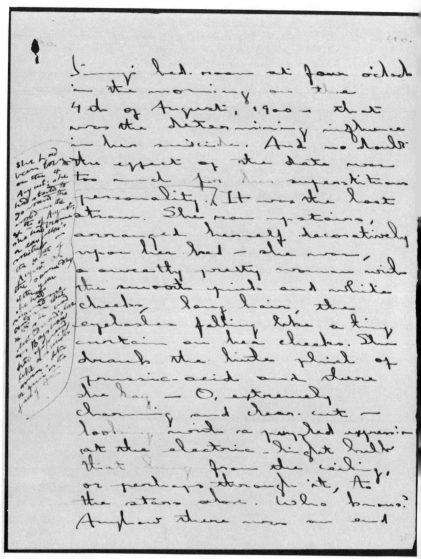

Manuscript page 180, in H. D.'s hand with Ford's insertion in left margin. Courtesy of the Division of Rare and Manuscript Collections, Cornell University Library.

A Note on the Text

[Abbreviations repeatedly used throughout annotation are cited in parentheses. For a full list, see Abbreviations, pp. 175–77 above.]

There are four MSS relating to *The Good Soldier*, the first three of which are entitled *The Saddest Story*. The first is the manuscript (**MS**), corrected in Ford's hand, consisting of a complex patchwork of autograph manuscripts that are probably the work of three amanuenses (Brigit Patmore, H[ilda] D[oolittle], and Richard Aldington), spliced with TccMS and TMS typed by Ford. The second (**TSB**) is a TMS (almost certainly not typed by Ford), uncorrected, being the top-copy of pp. 1–42 of the TMS cited next in my list, and probably the version used for the first printing of a section of the novel in Wyndham Lewis's magazine *Blast* (20 June 1914: 87–97); the third (**TS**) is the "printer's copy" (according to its original folder, now lacking), a full text (TccMS, pp. 5–42, and TMS, pp. 1–4 and 43–end) typed (not by Ford) from the earliest MS and corrected in his and another (his editor's?) hand. The fourth, and last, is an AMS French translation in Ford's hand of the first few chapters of the novel, never published.

The first printing of any part of the novel was, then, the first three and a half chapters, which appeared in *Blast* (**B**) as "The Saddest Story by Ford Maddox [sic] Hueffer." (Ford did not change his name until after the war [see p. 3, n. 2 above].) The first English edition (**UK**) appeared on March 17, 1915, probably simultaneously with the first American edition (**US**) and bound from the same sheets (with the exception of the title page). A second impression of **UK** (identical) was printed during 1915. Other editions to appear in Ford's lifetime were the second American edition (**US2**, February 24, 1927, which probably appeared simultaneously with the textually identical signed, limited edition), both printings including the "Dedicatory Letter to Stella Ford"; and the second English edition (**UK2**, probably April 1928, also including the "Dedicatory Letter"). For more detailed descriptions of these various states, see Abbreviations, pp. 175–77 above.

This edition collates all states up to and including **UK**. **US** is identical with **UK**, and there is no proof of Ford's having overseen either **US2** or **UK2**. Some small changes were made to **US2**, which seem to have appeared in order to clarify English usage for American readers. Arthur Mizener cites one of these (568, n. 36) adding that it "may well have been Ford's revision" but offers no evidence to suggest that this was anything more than guesswork. Indeed, his own account of Ford's life immediately prior to the publication of **US2** provides a not untypical picture of Ford frantic with work and social engagements and involved in complex, fractious negotiations with publishers to get his books reprinted, and new ones out, as quickly as possible. It seems unlikely (and against his normal practice) that he would have taken the time to revise for reprinting. Thomas C. Moser's more detailed examples of **US2** variants [1] only serve to confirm this. With the exception of his silent correction of "the relatively few and obvious errors" (xxxiii), his edition (see below) reprints **UK**.

MDATV provides a detailed catalog of Ford's major **MS** revisions and variants between **MS, TSB, B, TS,** and **UK,** which I take to be the chronological order of their production (although the chronological relationship of **TSB** and **TS,** as explained later, is complicated). Two other editions of the novel are in print: Thomas C. Moser's for Oxford University Press (World's Classics Series, 1990) and Alan Judd's and Max Saunders's for Everyman's Library (1991). This is the first to collate variant states to produce a new text. The theoretical problems which beset any editor seeking a single, authoritative text are, however, manifold. MDATV is my attempt, as explained in the last two sections of this note, to confront these difficulties and to explain why I have chosen **UK** as copy-text but have followed **TS** for punctuation.

History of Composition

Ford always said (see "Dedicatory Letter") that he began writing *The Good Soldier* on his fortieth birthday (December 17, 1913) and finished the book before the war began (August 4, 1914). Mizener (245) revises the first date by suggesting that Ford probably began immediately after finishing *Henry James* in the summer of 1913. It was then that Violet Hunt invited Brigit Patmore to her cottage in Selsey. Ford and Hunt were living together between Selsey and her London house, South Lodge, Campden Hill, and the latter is the address which appears on the cover-sheet of **MS**. He had a habit of asking any guest to act as an amanuensis, and it seems that Patmore was the first to occupy this role for *The Good Soldier*. [2] If not debilitated by neurasthenia, his routine was to write every day, playing long, silent games of Patience in the mornings while he worked out what he wanted to say over (approximately) the next thousand words of dictation. "When I did begin on it," he noted in 1928, "I had almost every word of it in my head, and I dictated it very quickly." [3]

---

1. Moser notes US2's changes to "American grammatical convention," the alteration of a few English expressions ("cut out" becomes "annex," "knocked up" becomes "woke up"), some use of American spelling ("cheques" becomes "checks"), the translation of "fifteen thousand a year in English money" to "seventy-five thousand dollars," and the attempt to remove racially offensive descriptions of Dowell's black servant, Julius ("darky servant" becomes "dark servant"; "New England had not yet come to loathe the darkies as it does now" becomes "that New England no longer idealizes darkies as it did formerly"). He adds: "Although these revisions may well be Ford's, they could easily be the work of an American copy-editor" (xxxii). My view is that they are so inconsistent (many American spellings are *not* used, many sums *not* translated) and clumsily "correct" that they are almost certainly not Ford's work.
2. Violet Hunt, *The Flurried Years* (London: Hurst & Blachett, 1926) 216, and her diaries (Cornell) February 3, 1914.
3. Publicity release, Boni & Liveright, April 6, 1928 [Janice Biala collection]; Mizener 565, n. 22.

The history of the rest of the dictation is even more uncertain. It seems clear from the handwriting in **MS** that the imagist poets H. D. and her husband, Richard Aldington, were the other two amanuenses. But there is no mention of H. D.'s doing this in Barbara Guest's biography of her,[4] and Aldington's account of his period as Ford's secretary after the declaration of war[5] has often been thought by Ford scholars to be vitiated by inconsistencies. Firstly, we cannot be sure that Aldington's memory is accurate when he says that this took place *post-bellum* (his account was written many years later). Secondly, he says that he took dictation not only of *The Good Soldier* but also of *Between St. Dennis and St. George* (1915), i.e., not the propaganda book that Ford would have been writing at the time (*When Blood Is Their Argument* [1915; see Mizener 251]). Mizener suggests that Aldington may have been thinking of dealing with the proofs of the novel rather than taking dictation of the first draft of its last two chapters, i.e., conflating an earlier action with a later one.

The balance of the evidence, however, would seem to suggest that Aldington was not mistaken, at least about when he was Ford's amanuensis. Even Mizener admits that there is a strong possibility that this was in the autumn of 1914 and, although he tucks the information away in a footnote, that the confusion about the war books is perfectly understandable. Aldington was, after all, also taking dictation for Ford's weekly articles in *Outlook*, the material from many of which he used in *When Blood Is Their Argument*. The text for the latter would thus have been familiar to Aldington, and it would not have been unreasonable for him to think of it collectively under the title of the published book. It is also interesting to note here that the articles used dated from October 3, 1914 to December 12, 1914, and from February 6 to 27, 1915. Even allowing for conflation in Aldington's memory and excluding the later pieces, this offers the tantalizing suggestion of Ford's still being at work on the novel in October 1914.

Recent research might encourage this speculation. Moser suggests that "some of the wording of the last two chapters echoes poems Ford wrote and published just after the outbreak of hostilities" (xxxiv). He also cites Ford's article in *Outlook* (5 September 1914: 303–4), which states that he had written "twenty poems and two chapters of a novel" since the war began. Harvey, Ford's bibliographer, comments on those last five words: "most probably *The Good Soldier*" (200), and Moser agrees with him. Alan Judd, reviewing this debate about when the novel was completed, remains cautious. "The truth is," he says, "we do not know . . ." (xii).

To add to this confusion we have Violet Hunt's assertion, recorded by Douglas Goldring in *The Last Pre-Raphaelite* (1948), that: "in a fit of neurasthenic depression [Ford] consigned the MS [of *The Good Soldier*] to the dustbin. . . . She rescued it, had it re-typed and was responsible for getting John Lane to issue it" (170). Her own version of this (which Goldring must have consulted) had been published over twenty years earlier in *The Flurried Years:* "I found the sheets that she [presumably Patmore] had written at his dictation in the dustbin at the bottom of the orchard [at the Selsey cottage] in a hundred pieces, and it took me a week to mend each one separately and

4. *Herself Defined. The Poet H. D. and Her World* (London: Collins, 1984).
5. "Ford Madox Ford," *New Directions*, no. 7, 457; see pp. 303–4 below.

send it to a publisher" (244). Mizener's view is that the story "is not literally true: the printer's copy for *The Good Soldier* . . . is an unmended typescript; however pp. 113–40 are scorched" (566). This might be seen as a confused response to both versions. Hunt is surely not talking of the typescript here. Even Goldring speaks of the "manuscript," which Hunt then has typed. Nevertheless, Mizener's suspicion of untruth might also be borne out by **MS**: Hunt speaks of only one amanuensis when there were clearly three, and **MS**, although comprising many different sections and often rather ragged, has *not* been torn up and pasted together.

Violet Hunt has generally received a bad press from Ford's (predominantly male) commentators. Mizener is impatient with her. The general implication is that she is neurotic and vain, overestimating her own talents and her influence on Ford. Her *Good Soldier* story is often seen as an attempt to cash in on Ford's greater talent. In fact, she was a leading figure among her generation of women writers, admired by and close friends with Rebecca West. It is true that she was the rejected lover when she wrote her account and that there is a tinge of revenge in it. But it is generally sympathetic to Ford, and it is surely unlikely that she would have lied so baldly when he was still alive to contradict her (he never did). If we allow that, although details might have become confused by failing memory or the writerly instinct to recount a vivid story, she might have been telling the truth about finding a discarded version and restoring it for publication, two alternative interpretations present themselves. Firstly, that **MS** is not the version she found but a later one. This seems improbable. Secondly, her phrase "in a hundred pieces" does not necessarily mean "torn into a hundred pieces." It might simply signify a huge confusion of papers dumped into the dustbin, which she then spent a week re-ordering to send for typing. This scenario is perfectly credible. Even Mizener admits that "Ford certainly left most of his dealings with [John] Lane to Violet" and quotes a letter from Ford to his agent (J. B. Pinker): "I did not make the agreement for the 'Good Soldier'; was told what it purported to contain and signed it in a great hurry without looking it through" (566).[6]

This returns us to the much-debated date of completion. In a letter dated August 1915, Ford asked Lane for "the fifty pounds that became due to me on the delivery of the ms. of the 'Saddest Story.' "[7] Mizener's revision of this date to August 1914 might seem to settle the matter. Ford, however, goes on to say, "I have had to give up literature and offer myself for service to George Five," and, as Mizener points out: "Ford did not offer his services to George V until Aug., 1915." In Mizener's view, "it is hardly conceivable this letter was written then and misdated by a year, and it is reasonable to suppose he did consider enlisting before Masterman offered him the job at Wellington House" (565). Masterman secured Ford's services as a propaganda author in September 1914; Ford got his Army commission in August 1915. True, he might have considered his propaganda work to be tantamount to giving up literature, but if the letter is to be re-dated, then that

6. Ford to Pinker, July 28, 1920 [Princeton]. Ford's contract (University of Reading) is dated July 30, 1914.

7. Mizener (565) cites this letter as belonging to the Naumberg collection and adds: "the exact day appears to be the 10th, but the second digit is not unquestionably clear." Ludwig's *Letters of Ford Madox Ford* (1965) dates the letter as 12 August 1915 (61).

takes us back to a point before he began work for Masterman. Ford is not "considering" war work in the letter: it is a *fait accompli*, and the fact remains that, while he was not writing a new novel in the year following August 1914, he was as deeply embroiled in literary life as ever, producing in addition to his propaganda, poems, short stories, and weekly "Literary Portraits" articles for *Outlook*. It is surely more likely that the letter refers to his military commission and that Lane had simply not paid him in full.[8] There was a long-running dispute between author and publisher about who had profited from the contract, and, as we shall see, Lane may well have deferred publication pending certain revisions which he felt to be necessary in a book appearing in wartime.

One crucial piece of evidence concerning the book's completion date remains obscure. The last page of **TS** has a date stamp. It is very faint but reads:

RECEIVED

J. LITTLE & IVES CO.

OCT 3 1[?]1[?] 19 AM 191[?]4[?]

The final date is indecipherable, even with ultraviolet light, but "Oct 3" is clear enough, the third digit of the year date must be a "1" and the fourth a "4." It can't possibly have read "1915" since the book was published on March 17, 1915. Again, that might seem to settle the matter. Mizener assumes that "J. Little & Ives Co." was the printer: "Oct. 3, 1914, would be just about the time the printer would be likely to receive the ms. if the novel had been completed when Ford said it was" (565).[9] But *was* this company the printer? The preliminary matter of **US** and **UK** cites no printer. No London printer under the name of "J. Little & Ives Co." is listed for 1914. **TS** was almost certainly not typed by Ford. Supposing this firm to be not a printer but a typing agency, and supposing that Ford would have sent off **MS** soon after completion, this would firmly suggest that the latter was not complete until September 1914.

Ultimately, I must agree with Judd that we do not, and probably never shall, *know* when the novel was completed. On re-reading the evidence from Ford, Hunt, Goldring, Mizener, and Moser, however, one begins to sense the strong possibility that Ford was "mistaken" in asserting that he had finished before the war. He had a habit of reconstructing his personal history in order to present himself as either phenomenally perspicacious or as a figure at the epicenter of an historical moment.[1] And the date August 4 is, of course, the lynchpin of the novel's chronology. Is it possible, as both Mizener and Moser suggest, that Ford's choice of that date was simply "an amazing coincidence" (Moser xxiv). And can the collation of prepublication material help us to resolve this mystery?

---

8. Lane's account book (Harry Ransom Humanities Research Center, University of Texas at Austin) contains the following entry: "Feb. 16 [1915]: . . . To Royalty Account: *The Good Soldier* proportion of advance made to Author (£50) on account of Royalty, as per Author's Agreement 30.7.14 (⅓): £16.3.4." Ford was presumably due one-third on signature, one-third on submission of MS, and one-third on publication. This is the first payment.

9. Ford gave two dates: June 28, 1914 (*Return to Yesterday* 417), and July 1914 (*Time*, December 19, 1927).

1. See Mizener 564, n. 15.

Analysis of MS, TSB, B, and TS

Close analysis of paper, type, and handwriting reveals not a continuous composition, as Ford suggested, but a complex amalgam representing several early stages of composition. It is indeed likely that Ford dictated a great deal, if not all, of the novel and then used the holograph as a "rough draft," some of which he kept, revising it only with autograph corrections, but much of which he clearly re-wrote and scrapped as he progressed, typing in new sections before starting dictation again. The evidence of the disruption of composition reveals over thirty such "joints" in the total structure and at least six different batches of paper. Another possibility as to the dating of the novel's completion thus emerges: that he had dictated most of the novel before the war but that this was far from being the end of the process of composition. Evidence from the change in paper for both MS and TS pages suggests a distinct disruption after **MS** p. 339. This concludes Chapter IV, Part IV with the words "And then I came on the scene" (154). Was this the end of the novel in Ford's original conception? The first two MS pages which follow are typed by Ford, presumably as a rewrite of the beginning of the section for which Aldington acted as amanuensis because the TS is dovetailed into Aldington's holograph. It is quite possible, then, that this last part, including Nancy's telegram and Ashburnham's suicide, was written after the war began, possibly as an afterthought in the light of the historical circumstances. Ford, then, need not have been "lying." He may well have finished the first draft before the war; and to it he may have added some thirty-five MS pages (probably five or six days' work) to pull it into shape. Equally, as Moser suggests, he may have written the final two chapters (i.e., the whole of Aldington's dictation) after August 4.

Ford was, however, disingenuous to suggest that he held the entire novel in his head and that it simply poured out complete. There were constant and substantial revisions during the process of dictation. His whole concept of Ashburnham altered from that of rake and wastrel to that of tragic sentimentalist.[2] Ford also seems to have toyed with the idea of making the novel more a study of Edward's schizophrenia—his "nervous affection [. . .] [which] can be cured by a counter dread,"[3] his "dual personality"[4]—but subdued the theme. Leonora was originally more chilly and sardonic, with good reason to fear her husband's excesses,[5] Nancy more self-aware in her craving for Edward,[6] Dowell more passionate,[7] Florence even less innocent,[8] and Jimmie more sympathetic.[9] As the revisions progress, one senses Ford's concern to etherealize his characters, to befog any clear-cut motiva-

2. See MDATV, pp. 196, (p. 14, 1st entry), 198 (p. 25, 3rd entry) and 201 (p. 45, 3rd entry) for three major insertions modifying Ashburnham's character. In particular, note p. 46, n. 6, which speaks of "the girls he ruined," p. 47, n. 9, where the draft of the passage about the danger of his becoming a tramp deletes phrase "committing rapes," p. 48, n. 4, which mentions "expenditure on bastards and blackmailers," and pp. 49, n. 8 and 50, n. 9, canceling notion of "*détournement de mineur*".
3. See MDATV, p. 201 (p. 47, 7th entry).
4. See MDATV, p. 205 (p. 73, 4th entry).
5. See MDATV, p. 200 (p. 35, 1st entry) and 202 (p. 50, 4th entry).
6. See MDATV, p. 214 (p. 145, 4th entry) and 210 (p.119, 3rd entry).
7. See MDATV, p. 202 (p. 51, 2nd entry).
8. See MDATV, p. 195 (p. 10, 3rd entry).
9. See MDATV, p. 203 (p. 62, 1st entry).

tion, to displace authority for information from the narrator to his characters. Much of this, of course, is purely technical, Ford's sitting down "to show what [he] could do" as an impressionist writer. It also allows the focus of the novel to shift from what is known to what is unknown and to suggest those epic, abstract patterns of coherence which appear only in parodic form in the savage narrative present: chivalry, courtly love, the just war, the Universal (Catholic) Church—all the values of feudal society which the Reformation unstitched. But whatever the motivation for these revisions, the fact remains that they are copious, involve frequent patches of heavy rewriting, and that they did not stop with the correction of **MS**. On the penultimate page there is a major SPC. In **MS** and **TS** Ashburnham looks up to heaven and remarks, " 'Girl, I will wait for you there.' " In **UK** he whispers, "something that I did not catch."[1] There is even evidence to suggest that some corrections to **MS** were made *after* the corrections to **TS**.[2]

As mentioned earlier, the chronological relationship between **TSB** and **TS** is complicated. The first is uncorrected (save for Ford's "To be continued" scribbled at the end of p. 42), the second corrected by Ford and another (his editor?). **TS** pp. 5–42 is the carbon copy of the same pages in **TSB**; **TS** pp. 1–4 is ribbon-copy, an exact transcription of **TSB** pp. 1–4 (or, more probably, of the original first four pages of **TS**'s carbon copy, now lacking). Both **TSB** and **TS** reveal a break point at p. 42. In **TSB**, this is simply the end of the **TS** and of the text printed in **B**. When we move on to the next page in **TS**, however, we find something odd. The text at the top of p. 43 repeats that at the bottom of p. 42, and the redundancy is deleted. At first sight this appears to evidence a different **TS** of pp. 1–42, now lost, which was scrapped and replaced by the section sent to *Blast*. But checking back to **MS**, we discover that the typing of p. 43 has begun with the first word of the **MS** page [66; 63] on which the *Blast* section breaks off rather than with the first word after the break. This prompts a more credible theory. The fact of the typist's returning to the first word suggests that s/he did not have **TS** p. 42 from which to work. Two things appear to emerge from this: first, that **TSB** and **TS** pp. 1–42 (also probably the rest of Part I, Chapter IV, which would form a discrete unit as the whole of Patmore's dictation) were typed separately from the bulk of **TS**; and second, that the chronological gap between the two provides more evidence for the theory that the whole **TS** was not completed until after the declaration of war. Ford, then, did not simply cream off the first 42 pp. of the *completed* **TS** to send to Wyndham Lewis. Had he done so, the odd deletion at the top of p. 43 would not have occurred and the typing would have been continuous.

What seems to have happened is this. Ribbon-copy of pp. 1–42 was sent to *Blast*. The carbon of those pages Ford kept, later having the first five retyped (without changes), probably to smarten up the appearance of a battered TS for the publisher, and adding the rest in four stages: pp. 43–87, 88–118, 119–214, and 215–305. (The inception of each of these stages is evidenced by the internal pagination recommencing at "1.") The *Blast* issue is dated June 20, 1914, a month and a half before general mobilization on August 4, 1914, but we cannot be certain that it appeared on its publication

1. See MDATV, p. 216 (p. 162, 2nd entry).
2. See MDATV, pp. 195–96, n. 3.

date. It is true that Lewis threw a party on that night to celebrate the launch, but it is also true that Ford recalls paying a visit to Scotland with Lewis in late July and that "[Lewis] had brought the proofs from London of my one novel [*The Good Soldier*]."[3] Collation suggests that Ford *did* correct proofs for *Blast*, although hastily and with astonishing inaccuracy (on the first page "Dowell" appears as "Lowell" and "Hurlbird" as "Hurlbirl"). He always retained a vivid memory of that holiday as "a last, magical Edwardian pause before the crash of the war" (Mizener 248). If his memory is accurate and Lewis did arrive with proofs (rather than published copies), then this pushes the real date of publication closer to the brink of the war. Ford printed an article on *Blast* in early July[4] but this could have been an advertisement for something forthcoming.

All this, then, raises substantial doubts about Mizener's notion that the novel was finished before the war. It seems likely that Lewis received a copy of work in progress, and that Ford would have hoped for the return of his ribbon-copy to complete his final text. It was presumably returned too late because Ford had to use the carbon copy for most of the section. This is perfectly credible. The original agreement was that Lewis should serialize the whole novel. The second number of *Blast*, however, was so long delayed that it appeared after **UK**. Lewis would have retained the typescript of the first installment (he may well have been sent carbons of later ones) in the hope of continuing the project. After this was rendered redundant, he would have returned his copy. **B** might thus more accurately be described as a foretaste than as a fragment of finished work. It was quite usual practice then for a writer to issue work-in-progress like this (Joyce did it), and the copy date for the magazine might well have been more pressing than the deadline for the novel, given that it was Lewis's first issue. This might also explain why Lewis's version was uncorrected.

It is impossible at this distance to disentangle Lewis's editorial interference from Ford's corrections. **B** makes several cuts and obliterates the break between chapters III and IV. These emendations were probably Lewis's, the substantive ones Ford's at proof stage. But we cannot be sure, and collation raises the interesting notion that some of Lewis's corrections might have found their way into the final text. There is no question that **TSB** and not **TS** was the printer's copy, yet variants appear between **TSB** and **B**, the corrections for which appear only in **TS**. This suggests either that Ford had corrected **TS** before seeing proofs and then transferred these corrections to the proofs or that **TS** acted as Ford's record of decisions he was making while correcting proofs. As we shall see, I believe the latter to be more likely, in which case it is possible that some of Lewis's suggestions were also transferred. This does not, however, present an editorial problem in the absence of corrected proofs given that (a) disentanglement is impossible, and (b) Ford must tacitly have approved any such suggestions or he would not have recorded them. **B**, then, is regarded for the purposes of this edition, as simply a "bad" text hurriedly produced, full of misprints (and one sentence of

3. *Return to Yesterday*, 416–17; Mizener 248 and 564.
4. "Literary Portraits—XLIII: Mr. Wyndham Lewis and 'Blast,' " *Outlook* (London) XXXIV (4 July 1914): 15–16: "I who am, relatively speaking, about to die, prophesy that these young men will smash up several elderly persons—and amuse a great many others."

gibberish), probably repunctuated and restructured by Lewis, which has less authority than **TS** where the substantive changes are noted in Ford's hand.

Unfortunately, as Moser points out, **B** stops short of the first mention of the date August 4. Had it appeared there, this would have clinched the "amazing coincidence" theory. Nevertheless, the theory is persistent. All discussions of the novel's composition (including my own) agree that the three sections in H. D.'s handwriting[5] were almost certainly written before the war. Moser tells us, quite accurately, that, "Although the 4 August date generally appears in the typescript rather than in the holograph portions of the first manuscript, it does appear in the holograph section assigned to H. D. On only one occasion does Ford later insert in the margin a perhaps later reference to 4 August." The crucial page here is **MS** p. 180, pp. [82–83] (see illustration, p. 178), where both of Moser's examples appear. It seems clear that the second is a detailed elaboration of the first. Moser's conclusion is that ". . . Ford did not finish the novel until after the war started. On the other hand, I also believe that he wrote then only the last two chapters and that, therefore, Mizener is right about the 4 August date being an amazing coincidence" (xxxiv). If correction were contemporaneous with dictation, then the "amazing coincidence" theory would hold up. But, as Moser admits ("perhaps later"), the extensive marginal note might have been an afterthought. In fact, much of the novel's dating has been revised in Ford's hand. The question is: "When?"

Given the unlikelihood of the "amazing coincidence" theory being true, another scenario suggests itself: that while Ford made many corrections as he composed (and immediately afterward), at least one series of corrections was made to the novel *as a whole* after August 4, 1914, to determine its final shape and tone. An aspect of this revision was his attempt to juggle with the dates. True, there is one instance of coincidence in his choosing the date randomly while dictating, but it is the correction which elaborates it as a structural motif. And the first date, of course, might only have been random in the sense that it later corresponded with that of the outbreak of hostilities. As Judd points out, "it may have been chance, or it may have had significance in his own history, or perhaps in that of the mysterious P——" (x).[6]

Collation of pre-publication material with **UK** produces one last piece of evidence in this debate. There are several substantive variants between **TS** and **UK**, among which are three abusive remarks about Belgium. Talking of Belgian railway timetabling, Dowell says in **MS** and **TS**: "It is a mean, dirty trick, typical of the Belgians."[7] He speaks of Brussels as "hideous" and "that most hideous of all metropolises."[8] All are canceled, presumably at proof stage. Belgium, often criticized for her rapacious imperialism, suddenly became on August 4, 1914, the focus of British sympathies. Posters read: "Remember Belgium. Enlist To-Day." Dowell's views would surely have seemed outrageous to English readers after that date.

---

5. MS pp. 141–96, 206–18, and 225–53.
6. The "mysterious P——" is the man mentioned by Ford in *The Spirit of the People* (1907) as the "original" of Ashburnham. See p. 5, n. 1 of text.
7. MDATV, p. 200 (p. 38, last entry).
8. MDATV, p. 200 (p. 39, 6th and 7th entries). See also p. 32, n. 9 of text.

It might be that Ford made these changes himself in proof. This would seem to support the notion that **TS** was complete and corrected before the war because he would otherwise have altered his typescript in the light of recent events. But this does not necessarily follow: **TS** might have been out of his hands. Even Mizener believes that **TS** was not sent to the printer until October 3, 1914, in which case Ford would presumably have been correcting it during September. Why didn't he make his corrections then? The answer could well be that the original text was unprintable during wartime and that Lane insisted upon changes. By the publishing standards of the day (a book could move from typescript to print in six weeks), and even allowing for the crisis, there was an astonishing delay in *The Good Soldier*'s appearance.[9]

Again, in the absence of a corrected proof, it is impossible to disentangle Ford's interventions from his editor's (see Methodology below) but it is clear that Lane *did* intervene. "This book," Ford states in his "Dedicatory Letter," "was originally called by me *The Saddest Story* but since it did not appear till the darkest days of the war . . . , Mr. Lane importuned me with letters and telegrams . . . to change the title which he said would at that date render the book unsaleable. One day, when I was on parade, I received a final wire of appeal from Mr. Lane, and the telegraph being reply-paid I seized the reply-form and wrote in hasty irony: 'Dear Lane, Why not *The Good Soldier?*' . . . To my horror six months later the book appeared under that title."[1] There is a certain amount of confusion here, perhaps for dramatic effect. (What was he doing on parade six months before March 17, 1915, if he wasn't commissioned in the Army until August 1915?) But the general memory of Lane's bombarding him with messages seems valid enough, and it is probable that these did not solely concern the title.

There appears to have been something of a dispute about the text, which adds force to the argument against redating Ford's letter requesting payment. Lane might have been withholding payment first until the dispute was settled, and then until he was sure that the book would not have to be withdrawn. The novel was plainly "dangerous" for all sorts of reasons, not least because of its frank discussion of adultery. When it appeared, it was often dealt with only cursorily and reviewers were quick to condemn its depravity. Lane had good reason to be cautious. He stood to make very little money and, if he is to be believed, made a loss.

It is, however, unlikely that the "moral" corrections to **MS** (playing down Asburnham's libertinage, etc.) were made at Lane's request given that he would probably not have read **MS** before it was typed. He certainly required the change of title and possibly a couple of other alterations.[2] But readers who look through all those entries in MDATV marked "SPC" will see that

9. Lane's account book for March 4, 1915, states: "Davis, Turner & Co. [international carriers] . . . for excess charge made by Midland Ry. Co. for redelivery of Cases [book covers] (The Good Soldier) to Leighton, Son & Hodge [London bookbinders]: nil." This could refer to the American edition to be shipped from Liverpool. It might also suggest that the cases were first printed as "The Saddest Story" and had to be reprinted.
1. Stang's *The Ford Madox Ford Reader* (1986) prints the original letter (17 December 1814): ". . . Why not call the book 'The Roaring Joke'? Or call it anything you like, or perhaps it would be better to call it 'A Good Soldier'—that might do. At any rate it is all I can think of . . ." (477).
2. See MDATV, p. 201 (p. 47, 5th entry) and p. 202 (p. 50, 3rd entry).

nearly all of them represent "technical" proof corrections of a mundane variety which merely serve to clarify meaning or to remove repetition. As such, Ford is probably responsible for most of them and was liable under his contract to pay for the majority. This might explain Lane's reluctance to hand more money over to Ford. If there was a dispute over the text, then it was over the whole text rather than over details. Lane possibly got cold feet in the autumn of 1914 but ultimately decided to publish and hope not to be damned.

Theoretical Problems

This is not the place for a disquisition on textual criticism. Suffice it to say that textual scholarship has undergone some dramatic changes over the last decade and that the theory of copy-text is at the center of the debate. For many years, the theory of textual editing concerned only printed texts. Prepublication material (MSS, letters, contextualizing biographical/historical information) were of little interest to the textual editor. In retrospect, as D. F. McKenzie has pointed out,[3] this approach bears a striking resemblance to the ideology of Practical and New Criticism, which in its turn share some concepts with Russian Formalism. All are forms of formalism: one is entitled, indeed required, to isolate the text from its historical context in order to decipher transhistorical codes of meaning. In textual work this transhistoricism centers on the notion of the "ideal" text which may be deduced scientifically from a study of various printed states and which most faithfully represents the author's intentions. Two major changes, however, have occurred to alter the premises upon which such work might now be performed. Both concern the implicit object of investigation.

First, textual criticism up to Fredson Bowers tended to concentrate on Renaissance and earlier texts, often poetry, and "contextualizing information" was sparse. It often only had the printed texts on which to work with the help of the *Stationers' Register*. The complex investigation of typographical patterns, for instance, attempted to isolate which compositors set up which sections of type, whether the author attended the press, and so on. The object of this, as with all other early textual strategies, was to remove the "impurities" introduced by third parties and, effectively, to reconstruct the MS that went to the printer, adding to this (in W. W. Greg's theory[4]) any later authorial emendations. During the nineteenth and twentieth centuries, the raw material available for the detection of third-party corruption has hugely increased, not least because of the invention of the typewriter. Any prominent writer these days can make a regular income from selling early drafts. Until recently, however, there has been no textual theory which could easily accommodate this material into the process of textual editing because in the search for the ideal text, MS material necessarily appeared as a preliminary (and thus superseded) stage in the creation of that sacrosanct item, the latest edition overseen by the author.

3. See *The Panizzi Lectures 1985. Bibliography and the Sociology of Texts* (The British Library, 1986).
4. "The Rationale of Copy-Text" (1950), in Ronald Gottesman and Scott Bennett, eds., *Art and Error: Modern Textual Editing* (Methuen, 1970; reprinted as University Paperback, 1973).

Second, literary theory has done a great deal to demolish our assumptions about intention and the ideal text. In the poststructuralist world, it seems nonsense to suppose that an author's intentions could either be transposed unmolested into the weave of textual signifiers or that those intentions could ever have been "known" to the author in any but the vaguest form in the first place. And once the text is printed, of course, we are asked to believe that it simply floats free of its author to be "completed" variously by whoever decodes it in an indeterminate future. Formalist, structuralist, and post-structuralist literary theory, then, has continuously attempted to break that link between author and text on which textual criticism has so long relied.

All that may be changing. A new breed of theoretically informed textual critic has begun to emerge and new debates have begun about, for instance, "textual primitivism" and hypertext. At the center of these arguments often lies the problem of authorial intention, of "authority," of the demonstrable arbitrariness of editorial decisions, and this leads us back to the origins of the text. Textual critics these days are often intent on restoring what has been "corrupted" not only by third parties (editors, censors, printers, "pirates,") but also by the author himself. And it is this interest in the history of the text's production which has extended the range of examinable materials for textual criticism to include any pre-publication material. It is now frequently suggested that there is a serious problem in the conventional theory of copy-text which allows the editor to meld various states.

One response to this has been the Cornell Wordsworth, which prints the earliest complete version of the poems (with massive textual apparatus to describe variants). It was in partial opposition to this that Jack Stillinger coined the phrase "textual primitivism"[5] because the poems often appear in unrecognizable form. If I had adopted this approach to *The Good Soldier*, I would probably have printed **MS**.

Another response is hypertext. We are, perhaps, presiding over the death of the book as a medium of cultural exchange, and hypertext might appear to be the answer to all our textual and theoretical problems. What has bedeviled us is the need to produce a single text. Hypertext can sidestep the problems of intention and textual corruption by simply giving us everything—all states, all contextualizing material—within which readers may weave to their heart's content. But there is also a difficulty here. One of the aspects of the historical production of our text is the fact that it was produced *as a book*, to be read as a book. The reading of a book is a quite different experience from the plunging in and out of windows on a computer screen. The text, in short, is in danger of losing its impact as an intimate emotional experience and of becoming merely another gobbit of information in an information culture. Is there a happy medium?

I have tried to find one in this edition. It is a single text. It does meld various states. I work on the principle that it is no more arbitrary to follow the author's declared intention (in the sense of those states overseen in corrected form) than to alter it with something I might prefer, but that there are instances where alternative readings might take precedence on logical grounds (see Methodology below). I accept that any single text, and particu-

---

5. "Textual Primitivism and the Editing of Wordsworth," *Studies in Romanticism* 28.1 (Spring 1989): 3–28.

larly one which melds various states, is ultimately an arbitrary construct which has unavoidably involved the editor's aesthetic decisions. But I have tried to keep the latter to an absolute minimum, and I hope to have tempered the paradoxes of conventional editing practice with the textual apparatus. MDATV allows the reader at any point to see how a "variable" reading came into being, what editorial decision was made and, in difficult cases, why. The reader is thus not constrained by my decisions but can reconstruct the text in whichever way seems preferable.

With the support structure of MDATV, then, I have felt able to take **UK** as my copy-text. The first edition seemed to be a reasonable point of equilibrium between pre-publication material and later editions, a midpoint, as it were, in the turmoil of a text's multiple forms. But I immediately struck a problem. Ford corrected both **MS** and **TS**, making precise, if hurried, emendations to punctuation. However, when the punctuation of **TS** is collated with that of **UK** a huge number of variants appears. It seemed extremely unlikely that he would have overpunctuated his text to this extent at proof stage. The **TS** version is much looser and in keeping with Dowell's easy conversational flow. **UK** appears to have imposed a house style which causes the text to halt unnecessarily, or to lose Ford's idiosyncratic sentence structure. (He had a habit of writing in short, verbless statements, many of which **UK** flattens into conventional usage by tacking them on to the preceding or following sentence.[6]) I have therefore followed the punctuation of **TS** wherever possible and noted any exceptions in MDATV.

Methodology

The new freedom to use pre-publication material presents its own difficulties. There is not, I believe, a standard procedure for the sifting of MS and TS variants in the editing of a single text. We can find them easily enough but what do we do with them? Charles G. Hoffmann's "Ford's Manuscript Revisions of *The Good Soldier*" is a skillful essay but one which seems to take as its basis for analysis a belief in the unerring aesthetic rectitude of the blessed FMF. If Ford adds or cancels a passage, Hoffmann implies that this is obviously the right thing to do because it results in the perfect end product: the classic modernist text we know. It is not offered as a matter for debate that, when a long section is deleted, "In revision Ford recognized the obtrusiveness of overstressing Dowell's diffidence as a narrator and of overexplaining the 'occasion' for the narration."[7] Such remarks are common in work on twentieth-century MSS. The result is a sort of inventive practical criticism which tries to re-imagine the creative process. This can be stimulating, but there is always the danger that critics will plunder MSS randomly in search of confirmation for their own critical bias. And, ultimately, this sort of work does not help the textual critic: it is not comprehensive and it is not objective.

I therefore felt it necessary to develop a methodology which, whatever its shortcomings, aspires to the virtue of logical consistency. The object of this

---

6. See MDATV, p. 203 (p. 59, 4th entry).
7. Charles G. Hoffmann, "Ford's Manuscript Revisions of *The Good Soldier*," *English Literature in Transition* 9.4 (1966): 145–51; 147.

was to try to produce a system of analysing pre-publication material for the purposes of textual editing which would remove most of the editor's subjectivity in choosing between variants. Like all systems, of course, it is far from foolproof. At certain points aesthetic choice remains the only option. But at least the methodology can explain to the reader *why* this is so, and as such, render the choice not wholly arbitrary.

RULES OF ENGAGEMENT

1. If **MS** and **TS** agree but **UK** is variant, I rarely restore the earlier reading but print **UK** on the grounds that Ford was probably responsible for the proof correction (see pp. 188–89 above). In MDATV all states are recorded and an "SPC" (probable substantive proof correction) noted. Exceptions to this are the names "Branshaw" and "Mumford." These appear predominantly in **MS** and **TS** as "Bramshaw" and "Mudford." I restore them as such because early mistranscriptions in **TS** have caused the compositor to start setting up the names wrongly, and, having begun in one form, he continues with it. One might argue that the corrupt forms received Ford's tacit approval at proof stage, but it would have been wearisome (and costly) to go through the whole text altering the names. Perhaps he did not care, in which case I hope still to be on safe ground because either reading will do. But there is a strong argument for removing textual corruption here as the product of external agency (the typist) and economic factors.

2. If **TS** and **UK** agree and **MS** is variant, there might be a case for restoration of the **MS** reading on the grounds of perpetuated mistranscription, but it is a case which is usually vitiated by Ford's tacit approval of the altered state in failing to correct it in both **TS** and proof. In most instances, therefore, this will be noted as a perpetuated mistranscription in MDATV but **UK** will be printed (e.g., MDATV, p. 197 [p. 17, 3rd entry]). On rare occasions a clearer reading in **MS** is restored but only if a case can be made for it in MDATV (e.g., MDATV, p. 204 [p.64, last entry]). Readings are only automatically restored in these circumstances when eye-slip has caused the typist to lose part of **MS**. The lost words are restored in square brackets, i.e., the editor is drawing attention to them as something which formed part of the original conception but he is not validating them (e.g., MDATV, p. 196 [p. 13]).

3. If **MS** and **UK** agree but **TS** is variant I follow **UK** on the grounds that this is probably Ford's proof correction of a **TS** mistranscription; all states are recorded in MDATV and SPC noted (e.g., MDATV, p. 204, [p. 64, 2nd entry]).

4. If **MS**, **TS**, and **UK** are all variant, I usually follow **UK** on the grounds that there might have been an SPC to produce the **UK** reading (e.g., MDATV, p. 208, [p.98, 2nd entry]) but also feel free to follow **MS** or **TS** for a clearer reading (e.g., MDATV, p. 206 [p. 79, 1st entry]); all states are noted in MDATV.

5. Punctuation variants from **TS** are only noted in MDATV when I print the variant or when following the punctuation of **TS** alters the sentence structure of **UK**. Whenever possible, I follow the punctuation of **TS**, but on rare occasions I might draw on that of **UK** or even **MS** for a clearer reading.

Only as a last resort would I introduce my own punctuation to clarify a reading. "Punctuation" here is understood to include paragraph and line breaks (e.g., MDATV, p. 196 [p. 11, 2nd entry and p. 11, 1st entry]).

6. I usually correct inaccuracies in matters of fact in spelling and nomenclature and record the original readings in MDATV (e.g., p. 196 [p. 12, last entry]).

7. I standardize presentation. (**MS**, **TS**, and **UK** sometimes use "Church" and sometimes "church" for the Catholic Church; I standardize to "Church." **MS**, **TS**, and **UK** sometimes use the forms: "to-day"; "bed-room"; "arm-chair", and "up-right" and sometimes use the modern, unhyphenated, forms; I modernize throughout. I also modernize "shew" to "show." **MS**, **TS**, and **UK** are erratic in the number of ellipses dots used; I standardize to four if concluding a sentence, three if in mid-sentence.)

8. Critical comments are sometimes made in MDATV but only to offer an interpretation of the technical effect of revisions rather than to suggest the author's putative intentions (e.g., MDATV, p. 200 [p. 41, last entry]).

9. Major **MS** and **TS** deletions are recorded even when they are not replaced by alternative text so that the reader may see "the writer at work."

10. Obscure substantive readings must remain obscure if there is no textual authority for change, i.e., if **MS**, **TS**, and **UK** agree (e.g., MDATV, p. 200 [p. 39, 5th entry]), or if variant readings produce equal obscurity.

Manuscript Development and
Textual Variants

This section allows the reader to follow the chronological development of the text from **MS** to **UK**. I have included only substantive **MS** corrections which seem to alter the sense of a reading and have concentrated on those made by Ford himself. Sometimes **MS** deletions are recorded which are not replaced by alternative readings. There seemed little point in noting many contemporaneous corrections made by his amanuenses since most of these will have resulted from secretarial error: a mishearing altered after verbal clarification, slips of the pen rapidly adjusted, and so on. **MS** notations are far, then, from a complete register of corrections, but are comprehensive enough for us to see "the writer at work." The entries are organized on a page-by-page basis, the last-mentioned state in each entry being its final form. Thus each entry will not contain all states but only as many as are necessary to catalog the progression to final form.

"Final form," however, is inevitably an unhappy phrase in an edition like this which takes **UK** as its copy-text and restores (most of) the punctuation of **TS** (see A Note on the Text above). This list, for instance, does not include hundreds of punctuation variants, but only those where I have (rarely) intervened to "correct" something or to make an exception and to follow the punctuation of **UK** or **MS**. In addition, the text produced here does not include variants in **UK2** or **US2**, since there is no evidence that Ford oversaw those changes (see A Note on the Text). **US** is identical with **UK** (presumably bound from the same batch of sheets) with the exception of the reversal of two lines on the title page.

In a tiny minority of cases, therefore, the "final form" in the sense of the latest chronological state, does not correspond to the text printed here. The major exception to this is the Dedicatory Letter to Stella Bowen, which appeared first in **US2** and then in all subsequent (British and American) editions. The letter is printed here as it appeared in **US2** with only small adjustments to the punctuation of the TS (Cornell), which is corrected in Ford's hand and almost certainly typed by Ford.

The more important entries from this list have been repeated in the footnotes, and an example is given above (p. 177) of how the system of annotation operates. **MS**, housed at Cornell, has two sets of numeration: a continuous series in pencil, presumably inserted by institutional or commercial collaters, and a disrupted series which regularly recommences according to the various stages of composition or typing. Similarly, Ford has added continuous pagination to **TS**, whose numeration was disrupted by the different batches of its production. I shall distinguish the first as "external" pagination, and the second as "internal" pagination. When referring to the numeration of **MS** and **TS**, both figures are cited in square brackets but, for the sake of clarity, the external pagination is always cited first.

Textual Notes

DEDICATORY LETTER

Minor textual changes have silently been made to the Dedicatory Letter: italicizing Ford's use of three French words ("Imagistes," "tapageur," "Jeunes"—also pluralizing "tapageur" to "tapageux") and adding hyphens to "ten year old" and "two edged."

CHAPTER I, PART I

Page

9   **MS**[1]: cover sheet: "S.S." [misplaced; see p. 72, 1st entry below]; 2nd cover sheet: "The Saddest Story. | [*M.S. the property of* | *W. L. Farley*[2] | *16 rue de la Paix* | *Paris*]\M.S. the property of | Ford Madox Hueffer| South Lodge | Camden Hill | W./" [pencil]; **TS**: no cover sheet; **UK** and **US** title pages identical save for reversal of 'LONDON' and 'NEW YORK' lines (see facsimile of **UK** version p. 7); **US2**: "THE GOOD | SOLDIER | A TALE OF PASSION | BY FORD MADOX FORD | '*Beati Immaculati*' | ALBERT & CHARLES BONI | NEW YORK MCMXXVII".

9   **MS** [3; 1]: "The Saddest Story | 1"; **TSB** and **TS** [1]: "THE SADDEST STORY | PART I | [L]'; **B** [87]: "THE SADDEST STORY | BY | FORD MADDOX [sic] HUEFFER | '*Beati Immaculati*'"; **UK** and **US** [7]: "THE GOOD SOLDIER | I"; **US2** [3]: "I".

9   **MS** [3;1], **TSB and TS** [1]: white line after "This is the saddest story I have ever heard" lacking asp; **B** [87]: whole sentence omitted; **ED**: restore white line.

9   **MS** [4; 2], **TSB and TS** [1]: "perforce were"; **UK** [7] and asp: "perforce were,"; **ED**: follow **UK** punctuation.

10   **MS** [4; 2] and **TSB** [2] and **B** [87]: "that she, poor thing, was the sufferer"; **TS** [2]: "that she *[poor thing]*, was the sufferer": [ink]; **UK** [8] and **UK** [8] and asp follow **TS** but canceling comma; **ED**: follow **UK**.

10   **MS** [4; 2], **TSB and TS** [2]: "Captain Ashburnham also,"; comma deleted **UK** [8] and asp; **ED**: follow **UK** punctuation.

10   **MS** [4; 2], **TSB** [2], and **B** [87]: "Florence's broken years may have been in the first instance congenital, but the immediate occasion was"; **TS** [2]: "Florence's broken years *[may have been in the first instance congenital, but the immediate occasion]* was": [ink]; **UK** [8] and asp, except **B**, follow **TS**. Ford's deletion removes any hint of Florence's original innocence.

10   **MS** [5; 3]: "to which he was never to return, was thirty-*[three]* \five/; Mrs. Ashburnham—Leonora—was *[twenty-eight]* \thirty/. [. . .] Florence would have been thirty-nine & Captain Ashburnham forty-*[two]* \forty four/; whereas I am *[thirty]* forty-five & Leonora *[thirty-seven]* \forty/: [ink][3]; **TSB** [2]: "to which he was never to return, was thirty-three; Mrs. Ashburnham—Leonora—was twenty-eight. [. . .] Florence would have been

---

1.   First section of **AMS** begins here [1; 1–44; 42] and [47; 43–82; 79], with 2pp. of TS insertion (Ford's typing, [45; 42(a)–46; 42(b)]) spliced into an otherwise continuous script. The **AMS** is probably in the hand of Brigit Patmore. The hand which wrote "M.S. the property of W. L. Farley . . .", however, appears to be that of the amanuensis for the main text. Harvey presumed from this (C i, 9 [a], p. 108) that Farley was the amanuensis, but this does not necessarily follow.

2.   Presumably the husband of Agnes Farley, an old friend of Violet Hunt.

3.   It is difficult to tell whether these corrections are in the hand of Ford or of his amanuensis. Either way, Ford was responsible for them, and the corrections to Ashburnham's age ("thirty-*[three]* \five/", and "forty-*[two]* \forty four/") are ignored, nowhere finding their way through to

thirty-nine and Captain Ashburnham forty-two; whereas I am forty-five and Leonora thirty-seven"; **TS** [2]: "to which he was never to return, was thirty-three; Mrs. Ashburnham—Leonora—was *[twenty-eight]* \ thirty one/. [. . .] Florence would have been *[thirty-nine]* and Captain Ashburnham forty-two; whereas I am forty-five and Leonora *[thirty-seven]* \forty/: [ink]; **UK** and asp except **B** (which follows **TSB**): "to which he was never to return, was thirty-three; Mrs. Ashburnham—Leonora—was thirty-one. [. . .] Florence would have been thirty-nine and Captain Ashburnham forty-two; whereas I am forty-five and Leonora forty."

10   **MS** [6; 4], **TSB** [2], **B** [87], and **TS** [2]: "ever"; **UK** and asp: "even"; **SPC**.

10   **MS** (6; 4), **TSB** [3], **TS** [3], **and B** [87]: "the blocks between Chestnut and Walnut Streets and Sixteen to Twenty-sixth"; **UK** [9] and asp: "several blocks between Chestnut and Walnut Streets"; **SPC**.

10   **MS** [6; 4], **TSB** [3], **B** [87], and **TS** [3]: "upon wampum"; **UK** [9] and asp: "of wampum"; **SPC**.

11   **MS** [7; 5]: after "I am actually writing": "Drop one line"; **TSB**, **TS** [3], and asp: instruction ignored; **ED**: restore white line break.

11   **MS** [7; 5], **TSB, and TS** [4]: no new paragraph after "out of their heads"; **UK** [9] and asp: para. break inserted, probably because typist (not Ford) has habit of finishing last line of page short and starting new sentence on new page; **B** consistently inserts extra para. breaks at these points. **ED**: cancel para. break.

11   **B** [88] cuts "tall ships [. . .] one of those".

11   **B** [88] cuts "where to sit,".

11   **MS** [8; 6]: "cour"; **TSB** and **TS** [4]: "coeur," **B** [88], **UK** [10], and asp: "cour"; **ED**: follow **B** and **UK** since word surely means "court" rather than "heart."

11   **TS** [4]: "white satin favours" concludes 4pp. of clean, top-copy paper; **TS** [5]: "The mob may sack Versailles "begins long section of smudgy TccMS in black and purple carbon [5–42], a copy of **TSB** [5–42]. **TSB** concludes with p. 42.

12   **MS** [9; 7], **TSB** [5], **B** [88], **UK** [11], and asp: "screaming hysterics"; **TS** [5]: "screaming hysteri\a/cs": [ink]; **ED**: follow **UK**.

12   **MS** [11; 9]: "Swedish"; **TS** [5], **TSB** [5], **B** [88], and **UK** [12]: "Sweedish"; **ED**: correct.

13   **MS** [11; 9]: "conversations she must have had with Leonora the conversations full"; typist (**TSB and TS** [7]) loses "she [. . .] conversations" (eye-slip); **ED**: restore.

14   **MS** [16; 14]: "—an excellent magistrate [. . .] painstaking guardian" is later TccMS insertion by Ford in l.h. margin.

14   **MS** [16; 14]: "would"; **TSB** [10], **B** [89], **TS** [10], **UK** [16], and asp: "could"; **SPC**.

15   **MS** [17; 15]: "impulses"; **TSB** [11], **B** [89], **TS** [11], **UK** [16], and asp: "impulse".

CHAPTER II, PART I

15   **MS** [18; 16]: "The Saddest Story | II"; **TSB** [12]: "THE SADDEST STORY | PART II"; **B** [89]: "II"; **TS** [12]: "[*THE SADDEST STORY | PART]* II": [ink]; **UK** [17] and asp: "II".

15   **MS** [18; 16]: "*[I have asked novelists about these things, but they don't seem able to tell you much. They say it comes. // I don't know that I particularly want to write a novel; but I do know that I want what I write to be read by at least one sympathetic soul, or by all souls that are in sympathy throughout the world. How many are they? A million? A hundred million? Or isn't there one? // Here again one has just no means of knowing—none! But, I suppose, if I want to write something that will be read by one sympathetic soul I must want to write a novel—I don't see how to get away from that.]*": *[pencil]*.

15   **B** [90] cuts "immense" after "a" (rather than "an")

16   **MS** [20; 18], **TSB** [13]: "rocks so"; **TS** [13]: "rocks *[so]*": [ink]; **B** [90], **UK** [18] and asp: "rocks".

---

typed or printed form. **TSB** and **TS** are near-identical TSS (see A Note on the Text, p. 185 above), the former uncorrected, the latter corrected. The uncorrected readings in both should therefore correspond with the corrected **MS**. The fact that **TSB** and **TS** reproduce the *canceled* **MS** reading of Leonora's age ("*[twenty-eight]*") strongly suggests that some corrections to the **MS** (notably those concerning dates and ages) were not contemporaneous but made *after* the text was typed. This, in its turn, suggests that the corrections are probably in Ford's hand and that he was struggling to adjust the relative ages of his characters at a late stage of composition. Another anomaly appears to support this: Florence's age ("*[thirty-nine]*") is canceled in **TS** but not replaced by anything. Beneath the canceled words Ford has inserted a row of dots, as though to mark her age as requiring further consideration. In the event, however, **UK** and asp reproduce the canceled **TS** reading.

16   **MS** [21; 19], **TSB** [14], **B** [90], and **TS** [14]: "Hamblin"; **UK** [18] and asp: "Hamelin"; **SPC**.

17   **MS** [21; 19–22; 20]: "the blinding white sun [. . .] the *[blinding]*": [pencil]; **TSB** [14]: "the blinking white sun [. . .] the blinking"; **B** [90]: "the white sun [. . .] the blinking"; **TS** [14]: "the blin*[k]*\d/ing white sun [. . .] the *[blin[k]\d/ing]*": [ink]; **UK** [19] and asp: "the blinding white sun [. . .] the."

17   **MS** [22; 20]: "on"; **TSB** [14] and all other states: "in"; perpetuated mistranscription; **ED**: restore "on" as clearer reading.

17   **MS** [22; 20]: "now . . ."; **TSB** [14] and all other states: "now."; perpetuated mistranscription but follow **TSB** and **UK** [19].

17   **MS** [23; 21]: "at a *[spelling bee]* \Browning tea, or something of the sort/": [pencil].

17   **MS** [23; 21] and **TSB** [15]: "spelling bee"; **B** [90]: "tea"; **TS** [15]: "*[spelling bee]* \tea/": [ink]; **UK** [20] and asp: "tea."

18   **MS** [24; 22]: "Franz Hals & a *[Philip?]* Wouvermans & why the Pre-*[m]*\M/ycenaic statues": [ink, BP]; **TSB** [16]: "Frantz Hals and a Wóovermans and why the Pre-Mycenaie statues"; **B** [90]: "Franz Hals and a Wouvermans, and why the Pre-Mycenaie statues"; **TS** [16]: Frantz Hals and a Woovermans and why the Pre-Mycenai*[e]*\c/ statues": [ink]; **UK** [20] and asp: "Frantz Hals and a Woovermans and why the Pre-Mycenaic statues"; **ED**: correct names to "Frans Hals" and "Wouwerman." Although Dowell can be seen as an unreliable narrator, the various attempts in various states suggest that Ford would have spelled the names correctly had he noticed the errors.

18   **MS** [24; 22]: "Gnossos and the *[mind]*\ mental spirituality/ of Walter Pater": [pencil]; **TSB** and **TS** [16], **B** [90], **UK** [20], and asp: "Gnossos [. . .] Pater"; **ED**: correct to "Cnossos."

18   **MS** [25; 23]: "crime, *[horse-racing, billiards]*\religion & the rest of it/": [pencil].

18   **MS** [26; 24]: "suit"; **TSB** [17]: "visit"; **B** [91]: "court"; **TS** [17]: "*[visit]*\court/"; **UK** [21] and asp: "court."

19   **MS** [28; 26]: "what the old gentleman was *[like]* since of course he"; **TS** [18]: "what the old gentleman was since of course he"; **UK** [23]: "what the old gentleman was; he"; **SPC**.

20   **MS** [30; 28], **TSB** [19], **B** [92], and **TS** [19]: "after"; **SPC** to concur with correction in next entry, and to make legal sense.

20   **MS** [31; 29], **TSB** [20], and **B** [92]: "before"; **TS** [20]: "*[before]* \after/": [ink]. Clear evidence that **TS** not printer's copy for **B**.

20   **MS** [31; 29]: "worry [. . .] worry"; **TSB** [20]: "wrong [. . .] wrong"; **B** [92]: "wrong [. . .] wrong"; **TS** [20]: "*[wrong]*\worry/ [. . .]*[wrong]*\worry/"; **UK** [24–25] and asp: "worry [. . .] worry".

20   **MS** [31; 29]: "her & then"; **TS** [20] and asp: "her and"; **ED**: restore.

21   **MS** [32; 30]: "Bramshaw Tellragh"; **TS** [20]: "Branshaw Tellragh"; **B** [92], **UK** [25], and asp: "Branshaw Teleragh". Although later consistently corrected in **MS** and **TS** to "Bramshaw Teleragh," the compositor takes the typist's first mistranscription as the standard and prints "Branshaw" throughout; **ED**: restore "Bramshaw" throughout.

21   **MS** [33; 31]: "*[But all this is rather wandering round sort of stuff. Only its the way it comes into my head [.] I must try to be more direct. I will put down very shortly the essential facts about Florence & myself & then we can get on to the first meeting of all us four at Nauheim. // Or no, I will go straight on to Nauheim. I don't know how to tell this story [.]]*": [pencil].

CHAPTER III, PART I

21   **MS** [34; 32]: "III"; **TSB** [22]: "THE SADDEST STORY | PART III"; **B** [92]: "III"; **TS** [22]: "*[THE SADDEST STORY | PART]* III": [pencil]; **UK** and asp: "III".

21   **MS** [34; 32]: "in *[July]*\August//190*[6]*\4/": [ink (**BP**) and pencil]. The insertion of "July" before "1906" is in ink in the hand of the amanuensis. The correction to "August 1904" is a later revision, in pencil, by Ford.

22   **B** [92] cuts: ", the tall trees [. . .] up to the right".

22   **MS** [36; 34]: "*[From the end of the tennis courts to Florence's seat after she had been at Nauheim a week was exactly five hundred steps; from the same place to a seat higher up the hill—she was allowed so much to extend her walk during the second week—was just seven hundred & fifty. From the same place to the steps of the Casino, by the path Dr Bittelmann told us to take during the fourth week was exactly seven hundred & fifty.]* \And so on . . ./": [pencil]. "And so on" mistranscribed in **TSB** and **TS** [23] as "And now" at the beginning of following new paragraph, and remains thus in asp; **ED**: follow **UK**.

22   **MS** [37; 35]: *"[-the husband of the lady who sold the so very expensive violets in the kiosk at the bottom of the street that comes from the station; the expression on the face of the wife of the Czar of Russia as she drove in from Friedberg where her girlhood had been spent; the quality of the rubber on the tyres of a cab we took a drive in. Anything in the world she could talk about. So I would walk with her as far as the bath . . .]"*: [pencil].

22   **MS** [37; 35] and **TSB** [24]: "costlily"; **B** [92]: "costily" [sic]; **TS** [24]: "costlily"; **UK** and asp: "expensively"; **SPC**.

22   **MS** [37; 35]: "chinese"; **TSB** [24]: "chemise"; **B** [92]: "Chinese"; **TS** [24]: "[c]\C/h[emi]\ine/se": [ink]; **UK** [28] and asp: "Chinese". The mistranscription of "chinese" as "chemise", corrected by Ford in **TS**, strongly suggests that he was not the typist. The fact that **B** gets it right offers more evidence for Ford's proof correction of **B**.

22   **B** [93] cuts whole para.: "Yes, [. . .] blue. . . ."

23   **MS** [39; 37–40; 38] and **TSB** [25]: "on that morning [. . .] many other mornings"; **B** [93]: "on that evening [. . .] many other evenings"; **TS** [25]: "on that [mor]\eve/ning [. . .] many other [mor]\eve/nings"; **UK** [30] and asp follow **B**. See p. 22 re. "chinese" etc. above.

23   **MS** [40; 38]: "viands"; mistranscribed as "meals" in **TSB** and **TS** [25] and replicated asp; **ED**: follow **UK**.

23   **MS** [40; 38], **TSB** [26], and **B** [93]: "deference"; **TS** [26]: "[deference]\patronage/": [ink]; **UK** [30] and asp: "patronage."

23   **MS** [41; 39]: "[always]\generally/ a [most]".

23   **MS** [41; 39]: "Bramshaw House, Bramshaw Teleraigh"; **TSB** [26]: "Branshaw House, Branshaw Tellragh"; **B** [93]: "Branshaw House, Branshaw Teleragh"; **TS** [26]: "Branshaw House, Branshaw Tel[ll]\e/rah": [ink]; **UK** [31] and asp follow **B**.See p. 21, 1st entry above

24   **MS** [41; 39]: "Grenfells"; **TSB** and **TS** [26]: "Grenfalls"; mistranscription replicated asp; **ED**: follow **UK**.

24   **B** [93] cuts "up to [. . .] hair itself;".

24   **MS** [42; 40]: "bits, hunting boots"; **TSB** and **TS** [27]: "bits, boots"; mistranscription replicated asp; **ED**: restore "hunting".

24   **MS** [43; 41]: "in"; **TSB** [27]: "—"; **B** [93]: "in"; **TS** [27], **UK** [32], and asp: "—" **ED**: follow **NS** and **B** for clearer sense. See p. 22 re. "chinese" etc. above.

24   **MS** [44; 42]: "& cases each containing four bottles of scent"; **TSB** [28], **B** [94], **TS** [28], **UK** [32], and asp: phrase omitted (eye-slip), **ED**: restore.

25   **MS** [44; 42]: "Gaderine"; **TSB** [28] and **B** [94]: "Gaderene"; **TS** [28]: "Gad\a/rine": [ink]; **UK** [33] and asp: "Gadarine". Corrections suggest clear evidence that corrected **TS** was not copy-text for **B**,which follows **TSB** misspelling; perpetuated mistranscription not picked up in **B** proofs, and only corrected at **TS** stage.

25   **MS** [44; 42], **TSB**[28], and **TS** [28]: "for I swear that was all there was of him"; **B** [94] "for what there was of him". **B** reading clearly nonsense, suggesting that if Ford did correct **B** proofs, he did so very hurriedly. See p. 22 re. "chinese" etc. above.

25   **MS** [44; 42]: *"[I had forgotten]"*: [pencil]. Del. of last words of AMS page to make way for (later) insertion of 2pp. of TccMS [42a, 42b], rectifying the balance of Ashburnham's characterization towards that of a tragic sentimentalist, and emphasizing the phrase "good soldier." Probably typed (by Ford) at the same time as insertion on **MS** [16; 14]. See p. 14, 1st entry above.

25   **MS** [45; 42a], **TSB** [29], and **B** [94]: "shily"; **TS** [29]: "[shily] \stiffly/": [ink]; **UK** [34] and asp: "stiffly". See p. 22 re "chinese" etc. above.

25   **MS** [45; 42a], **TSB** [29], **B** [94]: "hopelessly"; **TS** [29]: "[hopelessly] \perfectly/": [ink]; **UK** and asp: "perfectly".

26   **MS** [47; 43]: "\I had forgotten/": [pencil]. Insertion replaces deletion of same before 2 pp. of TccMS; see p. 25, 3rd entry, above. BP's holograph recommences here.

26   **MS** [47; 43]: *"[white] \pink/ china. And that [was all there was to him. I tell you that]"*: [pencil].

26   **MS** [48; 44]: *"[It must have been by some minute movement of the lids]"*: [pencil].

26   **MS** [48; 44]: "of pride, \the/": [pencil]; **TSB** [31], **B** [94], and **TS** [31]: "of pride, the"; **UK** [36] and asp: "of pride, of"; **SPC**.

26   **MS** [48; 44]: "Bramshaw"; **TSB** [31], **B** [94], **TS** [31], **UK** [36], and asp: "Branshaw".

26   **MS** [48; 44]: *"[with actually what appeared to be a flicker, the upper lid became perhaps straighter;]"*: [pencil].

27   **MS** [50; 46]: canceled opening to new para: *"[I can't for the life of me make up my mind how to tell this part.]"*: [pencil], followed by "Drop a line" [pencil]. **ED**: restore white line break lacking in **TSB** and **TS** [32], **UK** [37] and asp.

27   **MS** [50; 46]: "often"; **TSB** [33] and **B** [95]: "after"; **TS** [33]: "[a]\o/fte[r]\n/": [ink]; **UK** and asp: "often".

27   **MS** [51; 47]: "clean, well-behaved"; **TSB** [33], **B** [95], **TS** [33], **UK** [38], and all printings: "clean,"; **ED**: perpetuated mistranscription: restore "well-behaved".

28   **MS** [53; 49], **TSB**, and **TS** [34]:"—I"; **B** [95] and **UK** [39] and asp:"I"; **ED**: follow **UK**.

28   **MS** [53; 49], and **TSB**, [35]: "them that"; **B** [95]: "them"; **TS** [35], **UK** [39], and asp: "them that; **ED**: follow **B** as textual authority for cutting redundant repeated "that."

28   **MS** [54; 50], **TSB** [35], and **B** [95]: "deadened by anything in the world"; **TS** [35]: "deadened by *[anything in the world]* \her white shoulders/": [ink]; **UK** [39] and asp: "deadened by her white shoulders".

28   **MS** [54; 50]: "gold circlet round it—a gold circlet with"; **TSB** [35], **B** [95], **TS** [35], **UK** [39], and asp: "gold circlet with"; perpetuated mistranscription (eye-slip); **ED**: restore lost phrase.

29   **MS** [56; 52]: "Avanti! . . ."; **TSB** [36]: "Avati! . . ."; **B** [96]: "Avanti! . . ."; **TS** [36], **UK** [41], and asp: "Avati! . . .". Clearly "Avanti" is correct (Italian for "Forward!"). **ED**: follow **B**.

CHAPTER IV, PART I

29   **MS** [57; 53]: "\Part I/IV": [pencil]; **TSB** [37]: "THE SADDEST STROY [sic] | PART I | IV"; **B** [96]: no break: text runs straight on with new para.; **TS** [37]: "*[THE SADDEST STROY [sic] | PART I]*: [pencil] | IV"; **UK** [42] and asp: "IV".

29   **MS** [57; 53], **TSB** [37], and **B** [96]: "relationships more than anything else"; **TS**: [37]: "relationship *[s more than anything else]*": [ink]; **UK** [42] and asp: "relationship".

30   **MS** [58; 54] and **TSB** [38]: "that paper"; **B** [96]: "that London paper"; **TS** [38]: "[that] \the London/ paper"; **UK** [42] and asp: "the London paper".

31   **MS** [60; 56], **TSB** [39]: "trap"; **B** [96]: "traps"; **TS** [39]: "traps"; **UK** [44] and asp: "traps". See p. 22 re "chinese" etc.

31   **MS** [60; 56], **TSB** [39], **B** [96], **TS** [39], and asp: "lire"; **ED**: correct to "lira" ("lire" is plural).

31   **MS** [60; 56]: "But one ought after"; **B** [96]: "One ought to have acquired the habit [. . .]"; **TS** [40]: *[But one ought a]*\A/fter": [ink]; **UK** [44] and asp: "After".

31   **MS**: [61; 5*[6]*\7/–62; 59]: " *[Of course there is the regular introduction with a character— as it were the sort of character you get with a cook or a housemaid. You are introduced to Mr & Mrs So-&-So of Clopton [?] Hough. And it is suggested to you that these are quite good Lancashire people. It may be cotton; or it may be land. But you may be quite certain that if your friend Mrs Fuller introduces you to the So-& sos that in that case the cotton will be the very best Bolton sheeting—meaning I suppose that the factory is in a second or third generation; for I do not really understand these things I only know that in the case of Mrs Fuller her tact is so certain that the So-& sos must be all right & that Clopton [?] Hough is the sort of place to which it is a privilege to be invited for a week. That is the introduction with a character. And then the taking for granted begins at once. You will all four take it for granted that you like your beef [p. 62;59 begins here] also take for granted that you change your shirt three times a day . . .]*"

31   **MS** [62; 59]: "pink indiarubber"; **TSB** [40]: "fish indiarubber"; **B** [96–97]: "pink Indiarubber"; **TS** [40]: "*[fish]* \pink/indiarubber": [ink]; **UK** [44] and asp: "pink india rubber"; **ED**: follow **UK**. See p. 22 re. "chinese" etc. above.

31   **MS** [62; 59]: "Aesculapius"; **TSB** [40], **B** [97], and **TS** [40]: "Aesulapius"; **UK** [45] and asp: "Æsculapius"; **ED**: follow **UK**.

31   **MS** [63; 60]: "*[from the look in his eyes, from the part of the throat from which his voice comes; from her method of sitting down in a deck-chair; from the fact that she offers you a certain type of novel which she has done reading when you are sitting with nothing in your lap after lunch—]*": [pencil].

31   **MS** [63; 60], **TSB** [41], and **B** [97]: "won't for the matter of that"; **TS** [41]: "won't *[for the matter of that]*"; **UK** [45] and asp: "won't".

32   **MS** [65; 62]: "early \./ *[that]* \So/": [ink]; **TSB** [42], **B** [97], **TS** [42], **UK** [46], and asp: "early, so that"; perpetuated mistranscription; **ED**: restore "early. So".

32   **MS** [65; 62]: "toting"; **TS** [42] and asp: "taking"; perpetuated mistranscription; **ED**: follow **UK**.

33   **TSB** [42] and **B** [97] end here with "To be continued" [penciled on **TSB**]. **B** followed the **TS** breaks for Chapters I–III but runs over the break opening Chapter IV. **TS** [43] begins with canceled repeated passage "[the disadvantage of [. . .] there was no objection]", suggesting that typing of pp. 1–42 and 43–end was not continuous but performed at different times. Cancelled section corresponds with opening of **MS** [66; 63]. Typist has clearly begun second section from **MS** without checking back to earlier **TS** [42].

33   **MS** [67; 64]: " 'That's all right, *[old girl]*. Don't you bother about me. *[But it is awfully interesting you know, Mr Dowell.']*": [ink].

35   **MS** [72; 69]: "*[Leonora had a way of listening so intently that it was almost a cruelty. But a]\A/s*": [ink].

35   **MS** [74; 71]: "town"; **TS** [47] and asp: "towns"; **ED**: restore **MS** reading since Dowell seems to be referring to his approach to Marburg.

36   **MS** [77; 74]: "hand"; **TS** [49] and asp: "hands"; **ED**: follow **UK**, although "hand" makes better dramatic sense since this would visually locate the wrist upon which Florence lays her finger.

37   **MS** [78; 75]: "*[And for a moment]* I"; [ink, BP].

38   **MS** [80; 77]: "in her voice. 'Don't"; **TS** [51] and asp: "in her voice, 'Don't"; **ED**: correct comma after "voice" to full-stop.

38   **MS** [80; 77]: "world? *[Of grief, of all agonies,—]* \And/": [ink].

38   End of first section of **MS** in BP's holograph.

                                    CHAPTER V, PART I

38   Beginning of second section of **MS**: TccMs, typed by Ford. **MS** [83; [ ]]: "THE SAD-DEST STORY/ \Part I/ | V": [pencil]. Mauve carbon, typed by Ford, and corrected by him in ink and pencil; **TS**: [5[2]\3/]: [pencil]: \"V"/: [ink]; **UK** [56] and asp: "V".

38   **MS** [83; [ ]] and **TS** [5[2] \3/]: [pencil]: "Brussels. The Belgian Government does this on purpose so as to force passengers to travel by way of Ostend rather than by Calais. It is a mean, dirty trick, typical of the Belgians; and it has"; **SPC**; excision removes Dowell's prejudice against Belgians.

39   **MS** [83;]]: "the *Times*" (twice, ink underlining) and "*New York Herald*" (ink underlining); **TS** [5[2]\3/]: [pencil]: follows corrections but **UK** and asp read: "the *Times*" and "*New York Herald*"; **ED**: correct to "*The Times*" and "*New York Herald*".

39   **MS** [83; [ ]]: "with me. . . ."; **TS** [5[2]\3/]: [pencil], **UK**, and asp: "with me."; **ED**: restore ellipses dots.

39   **MS** [84; 81]: "like *[an artist whose view has been spoiled by the erection of a factory chimney, like]*": [ink].

39   **MS** [84; 81] and **TS** [55]: "England you have,"; **UK** [58] and asp: "England"; **SPC**.

39   **MS** [84; 81], **TS** [55], **UK** and **US** [58]: "of"; **US2** [48]: "as", which is surely correct.

39   **MS** [84; 81] and **TS** [55]: "unfamiliar, hideous"; **UK** [58] and asp: "unfamiliar"; **SPC**. See p. 38, last entry, above.

39   **MS** [84; 81] and **TS** [55]: "hours in that most hideous of all metropolises"; **UK** [58] and asp: "hours . . ."; **SPC**. See p. 38, last entry, and p. 39, 6th entry.

39   **MS** [84; 81]: "abuse *[with my lips]*": [ink].

40   **MS** [84; 81] and **TS** [55]: "ever tried"; **UK** [58] and asp: "tried"; **SPC**.

40   **MS** [84; 81]: "body \./, *[and in such a pretty body]* . . .": [ink].

40   **MS** [85; 82] and **TS** [56]: "Bramshaw". All subsequent references in **MS** and **TS** read thus except when Ford not typing MS.

41   **MS** [86; 83]: "his *[case and of his]*": [ink].

41   **MS** [86; 83]: large deletion and insertion from l.h. margin: "*[He could have put his fingers to his nose to the scoundrels that blackmailed him till the end of his days.]* For of course the Kilsyte case, *[if it were the only one that came to light, that 'got into the papers', as they say \,/ wasn't the only occurrence of his life. I am bound however to say that it was the last, it gave him too]* \which came at the very beginning of his finding Leonora cold & unsympathetic gave him a/": [ink]. Correction reduces Ashburnham's profligacy.

41   **MS**: [86; 83]: "nice *[enough]*": [ink].

41   **MS** [86; 83]: "trouble. *[Well there are tragedies. . . .]*": [ink].

41   **MS** [87; 84]: "left her alone with her—with her \playing with/ adultery,": [ink]. **TS** [59] follows but **UK** [61] and asp read: "left her alone—with her playing with adultery,"; **SPC** which, in cutting repetition of "with her", loses sense of Dowell's exasperated search for the right phrase.

42   **MS** [87; 84]: "out of *[jail or]*": [ink].

42   **MS** [87; 84]: "red *[weal]* \mark/": [ink].

42   **MS** [88; 85]: "called in"; **TS** [61] and asp: "called"; **ED**: restore "in".

43   **MS** [88; 85]: "—She exclaimed *['Good God]* . . .\/ How frightful \!/ Poor little \Maisie!/ . .':" [ink]; **TS** [61]: "—She exclaimed . . 'How frightful! . . . Poor little mouse! . . ' "; **UK** and all printings: "—She exclaimed . . . 'How frightful! . . . Poor little Maisie! . . . ' ". Ford has restored "Maisie" for "mouse" but leaves redundant suspension stops after canceled "Good God!"; **ED**: cancel redundancy and replace with colon.

43   **MS** [88; 85]: "poor dear"; **TS** [61] and asp: "poor"; **ED**: restore.

43   **MS** [88; 85] and **TS** [61]: "Her little"; **SPC.**
44   **MS** [89; 86]: "*[fifty]* \twenty/": [ink].
44   **MS** [90; 87], **TS** [64], and asp: "in 1870" lacking; **SPC.**
44   **MS** [90; 87]: "you know, \in 1895,/": [ink]. Ford still juggling with dating of his narrative.
45   **MS** [90; 87]: "been *[a sick monkey or]*": [ink]
45   **MS** [90; 87]: "cropping up—*[always, always connected with the same sort of thing. Yes, she had the devil of a fight for it]*": [ink].
45   Beginning of TS (ribbon-copy) insertion into **MS**'s TccMS [91; 88], [92; 88a], [93; 88b]; **TS** [65–67]; **UK** [68–70]). When carbon recommences (**MS** [94; 88c]) half the page is canceled. It seems that **MS** [94; 88c] was written first, then composition halted for revised version of opening para. (both versions begin and end with the same words ("Yes, they quarrelled bitterly [. . .] You see, she was childless herself"), which was then written to dovetail into remainder of **MS** p. 94; 88c. Insertion possibly added contemporaneously with similar insertion earlier (see p. 25, 3rd entry) to play down Ashburnham's libertinage and to clarify the history of his "conquests".
46   **MS** [92; 88a] and **TS** [64]: "hardly ever pretended ever"; **SPC.**
46   **MS** [92; 88a] and **TS** [67] lack: ", according to Leonora,"; **SPC.**
46   **MS** [92; 88a]: "many little"; **TS** [67] and asp: "many"; **ED:** restore "little".
46   **MS** [92; 88a] and **TS** [67] lack: "I daresay she exaggerated and"; **SPC.**
46   **MS** [92; 82a]: "boy scouts and *[National Reserve Movements]* \to provide prizes at cattle shows/": [ink].
46   **MS** [92; 88a]: "rate \after the money had gone to the Grand Duke's mistress/": [ink]; **TS** [67] reads "supply" for "money"; **SPC.**
46   **MS** [92; 88a] and **TS** [67]: "put"; asp: "puts"; "put" agrees with tense of the following past participles; **ED:** restore "put".
46   **MS** [93; 88b] and **TS** [67]: "Homes [. . .] Societies"; asp: "homes [. . .] societies"; **ED:** restore upper case.
46   **MS** [93; 88b] and **TS** [67]: "But, as to"; asp: "To"; **SPC.**
46   **MS** [94; 88c]: "*[Yes, they quarrelled bitterly. That seems rather extravagant; you might have thought that Leonora would be just calmly loathing and he lachrimosely contrite. But that was not it a bit. For along with Edward's passions and his shame for them went the violent conviction that he must behave like a gentleman. Yes, every one of the girls that he ruined must be provided for as if she were at least the wife, say, of a bank manager; and every one of his illegitimate offspring must be sent to Eton or to the convent at Roehampton. It could not be done of course. // And Leonora saw to it that it was not done. Her idea was that about fifty pounds a piece [sic] was enough for the minxes and the children she put generally under the guardianship of her solicitor, providing about fifty pounds a year for each of them, or a little more in special cases. Yes, to the children she was quite generous. You see, she was childless herself.]*"
46   **MS** [94; 88c] and **TS** [68]: "Walnut"; asp: "Arch"; **SPC.**
47   **MS** [94; 88c]: "address, *[committing rapes]* \having, maybe, chance love-affairs/ upon the highways": [ink]. Another correction which shifts the image of Ashburnham from that of libertine to that of hopeless sentimentalist. See p. 25 (3rd entry) and 45 (3rd entry) above.
47   **MS** [95; 89]: "job of *[reclaiming]* \making/ Edward Ashburnham \a faithful husband/": [ink].
47   **MS** [95; 89] and **TS** [69]: "the poor"; **UK** [71] and asp: "the"; **SPC.**
47   **MS** [95; 89] and **TS** [69]: "opportunist"; **UK** [71] and asp: "opportunists"; **SPC.**
47   **MS** [95; 89] and **TS** [69]: "twopence halfpenny"; **UK** [72] and asp: "two hundred dollars"; **SPC.**
47   **MS** [95; 89] and **TS** [69]: "suggested; or"; **UK** [72] and asp: "Suggested. Or"; **SPC; ED:** follow **UK.**
47   **MS** [96; 90]: "*[For thvugh [sic] I am not a scientist in any way, I believe—for the matter of that I am certain—that the disease from which Edward suffered is simply a nervous affection—such a nervous [sic] affection as can be cured for good by a counter dread. And]*": [ink].
48   **MS** [96; 90]: "cured of *[the trick of doing his]*": [ink]. Again, correction heightens Ashburnham's moral status.
48   **MS** [96; 90–97; 91]: "*[It certainly meant the end of expenditures on bastards and blackmailers. The upper classes manage these things more efficiently. Moreover i]* \I/ t": [ink]. More deletion of Ashburnham's moral turpitude. See pp. 25 (3rd entry), 45 (3rd entry), and 48 (1st entry) above.
48   **MS** [97; 91]: "with *[dirty]* \a/little kitchen maid*[s]*": [ink]. Again, reduces scope and depravity of Ashburnham's casual liaisons. See pp. 25 (3rd entry), 45 (3rd entry), 47 (1st entry), and 48 (first two entries).

48   **MS** [97; 91] and **TS** [71]: "puncher. That"; asp: "puncher—that": **ED**: restore **MS** and **TS** punctuation.

49   **MS** [99; 93]: "The matter was one *[of what in France it is customary to call détournement de mineure; it was, in consequence a criminal offence]* \of a divorce-case, of course & she wanted to avoid publicity as much as Edward did,/": [ink]. More toning down of Ashburnham's sexual offences. See pp. 25 (3rd entry), 45 (3rd entry), 47 (1st entry), and 48 (first three entries).

50   **MS** [99; 93]: "such a thing as a *[detournement de mineure]* \brother officer who could be a blackmailer—& he had wanted // to protect the credit of his old light of love. That lady was certainly not concerned with her husband\": [ink]. See p. 49 above.

50   **MS** [100; 96]: "solicitor *[begging]* \bidding/ that hard-headed man \to threaten to/": [ink].

50   **MS** [100; 96] and **TS** [74]: "chance of gaol"; **UK** and asp: "chance of the divorce court"; **SPC**.

50   **MS** [100; 96]: "spent *[io [sic] agony (for she really imagined that Ashburnham was going to let her in again for all sorts of past misdeeds, she really thought that once more they would have to let Bramshaw Teleragb [sic]; pawn the plateb [sic]; sell another picture by Gainsborough and scrape on for another ten years at the ends of the earth) so she imagined that the two hours she had spent]*": [ink].

50   **MS** [101; 97] and **TS** [75]: "being that had any idea the"; **UK** [77] and asp: "being who had any idea that the"; **SPC**.

51   **MS** [102; 98]: "We"; **TS** [76]: "He"; **UK** and asp [78]: "We". Correction back to **MS** reading surely clear evidence of Ford's having corrected proofs.

51   **MS** [102; 98]: "my *[intense]* relief [. . .] my *[intense]* affection": [ink].

51   **MS** [102; 98]: "*[That]* \Jealousy/": [ink].

51   **MS** [102; 98]: "*[can't help saying]* \confess/": [ink].

51   **MS** [103; [ ]], last page of **MS** of Chapter V opens here (" 'Oh, I'm fond [. . .]") with no internal pagination. Also no internal pagination for next section of **MS** (Part I, Chapter VI, **MS** [104]; [ ]–113; [ ]), suggesting that last page of Part I, Chapter V was revised when composition of Chapter VI began.

51   **MS** [103; [ ]]: "*[agrimony]* \pellitory/": [ink and TS].

CHAPTER VII, PART I

51   **MS** [104; [ ]]: "THE SADDEST STORY | VI"; **TS** [78]: "VI"; **UK** [80] and asp: "VI".

52   **MS** [104; [ ]] and **TS** [78]: "never"; **UK** [80] and asp: "ever"; **SPC**.

53   **MS** [105; [ ]]: "It is not Hell, certainly; certainly it is not"; **TS** [80], **UK** [81] and asp: "It is not Hell, certainly it is not". Typist loses "certainly", probably through eye-slip; **ED**: restore.

53   **MS** [105; [ ]] and **TS** [80]: "Who"; **UK** [82] and asp: "who"; **ED**: follow **UK**.

53   **MS** [106; [ ]] and **TS** [80]: "were just"; **UK** and asp: "were only"; **SPC**, presumably to avoid repetition of "just".

53   **MS** [106; [ ]]: "*[but u]*\U/pon": [ink]; **TS**: "But Upon"; **UK** [82] and asp: "But upon". Typist ignores deletion; **ED**: follow **MS** (typed and corrected by Ford).

53   **MS** [106; [ ]]: "three *[naked]* figures."

53   **MS** [106; [ ]] and **TS** [80]: "Judgment [. . .] Judgment"; **UK** [82] and asp: "judgment"; **ED**: restore capitalization.

53   **MS** [106; [ ]]: "they are *[naked]*".

53   **MS** [106; [ ]] and **TS** [81]: "Judgment"; **UK** [83] and asp: "judgment"; **ED**: restore capitalization.

53   **MS** [106; [ ]] and **TS** [81]: "she cut"; **UK** [83] and asp: "she cut out"; **SPC**.

53   **MS** [107; [ ]] and **TS** [81]: "Northern light"; **UK** and asp: "northern light"; **ED**: restore capitalization.

53   **MS** [107; [ ]] and **TS** [81]: "Archangels"; **UK** [83] and asp: "archangels"; **ED**: restore capitalization.

53   **MS** [107; [ ]]: "find me *[a crossing to sweep or]*": [ink].

54   **MS** [107; [ ]] and **TS** [82]: "like the whore that"; **UK** and asp: "like the whore"; **SPC**.

54   **MS** [108; [ ]]: "ladylike*[,]* \./*[not really worthy of Mrs Ashburnham of Bramshaw Teleragh]*": [ink].

54   **MS** [108; [ ]]: "of it \/*[Remember that if you please\/]*": [ink].

54   **MS** [108; [ ]]: "put it that I *[murdered]* \killed/ her [. . .] think that one had *[murdered]* \killed/someone": [ink].

55   **MS** [109; [ ]]: "*[return from]* \jaunt to/": [TS].

55   **MS** [109; [ ]]: "just to be *[kind to]* \pet/": [ink]; "be" redundant in **MS**.

55   **MS** [109; [ ]]: "\You paid the money to me to come here./": [ink]; **TS** [84] reads "live" for "come"; **UK** [85] and asp: "come"; more evidence of Ford's proof-correction?

55   **MS** [109; [ ]]: "called me little rat"; **TS** [84], **UK** [86], and asp: "called me a little rat";

perpetuated mistranscription, in adding "a" to **MS**'s "little rat", changes sense of Ash-burnham's phrase from affectionate derogation to harsh dismissal. Flaubert's sister, Caroline, in her letters to him, signs herself "little rat." **ED:** cancel "a".

55   **MS** [110; [ ]]: "had paid"; **TS** [85] and asp: "paid"; perpetuated mistranscription; **ED:** restore "had".
56   **MS** [111; [ ]]; "But [\,/*it seemed to her, that*]": [ink].
56   **MS** [111; [ ]]: "hockey match. [*My God, My God, may the earth rest very lightly on her.*] \You understand she had not committed suicide. Her heart just stopped./": [ink].
56   **MS** [111; [ ]]: "[*A single*] \The stem of a/": [ink].
56   **MS** [112; [ ]] and **TS** [87]: "his that he never felt remorse about"; **UK** and asp: "his about which he never felt much remorse"; **SPC.**

CHAPTER I, PART II

57   **MS** [no cover sheet]; **TS** [88], **UK** [89], and asp: "THE SADDEST STORY | PART II."
57   **MS** [113; [ ]]: "THE SADDEST STORY | PART II. | I."; **TS** [89; 1]: "PART II. | I."; **UK** [91] and asp except US2: "I"; US2 [79]: "PART II | I".
57   **MS** [113; [ ]]: "190/3\4/": [ink].
57   **MS** [113; [ ]]: "[*1900*] \1899/": [TS].
57   **MS** [113; [ ]] and **TS** [89; 1]: "with the"; **UK** [91] and asp: "with a"; **SPC.**
57   **MS:** [113; [ ]]: "no luck\./[*on that occasion.*] \She was probably offering herself a birthday present, that morning......./": [TS]
57   **MS** [113; [ ]] and **TS** [89; 1]: "Then on the 4th [. . .] On the 4th [. . .]"; **UK** [91] and asp: "Then on the fourth [. . .] On the fourth"; **SPC.**
57   **MS** [114; 110]: "Florence *[simply]* had [. . .] ask to it *[simply]* whom [. . .] I would *[simply]*": [ink].
57   **MS** [114; 110] and **TS** [92; 2]: "births"; **UK** [92] and asp: "birth"; **SPC.**
57   **MS** [114; 110] and **TS** [90; 2]: "shewed"; **UK** [92] and asp: "showed"; **ED:** follow **UK** modernization throughout for spelling of "shew/show".
58   **MS** [115; 111] and **TS** [92; 4]: "paying guest*[s]* in an old English Family near Ledbury—"; **UK** [93] and asp: "paying guest in an old English family near Ledbury"; **ED:** restore cap. "F" and concluding hyphen.
58   **MS** [115; 111]: "family \called Bagshawe/": [ink].
59   **MS** [116; 112] and **TS** [93; 5]: "Sen."; **UK** [95] and asp: "Senior"; **SPC.**
59   **MS** [116; 112]: "*[colonial]* \spindle-legged/": [TS].
59   **MS** [116; 112]: "differ*[e]*\i/ng": [ink]; **TS** [93; 5]: "differing"; **UK** [95] and asp: "different"; **SPC.**
59   **MS** [116; 112] and **TS** [93; 5]: "even. As"; **UK** [95] and asp: "even, as"; **ED:** restore **MS** and **TS** punctuation.
59   **MS** [117; 115] and **TS** [94; 6]: "flirtations. Something"; **UK** [96] and asp: "flirtations—something"; **ED:** restore **MS** and **TS** punctuation.
60   **MS** [118; 114]: "they"; **TS** [95; 7]; **UK** [97] and asp: "that"; perpetuated mistranscription but follow **UK** as equally clear reading.
61   **MS** [119; 115] and **TS** [96; 8]: "relatives' "; **UK** [97] and asp: "relatives"; **ED:** restore apos-trophe.
61   **MS** [119; 115]: "I *[suppose I]* \must have/ [. . .] *[I suppose]* I": [ink].
61   **MS** [119; 115] and **TS** [96; 8]: "Philadelphian"; **UK** [98] and asp: "Philadelphia"; **SPC.**
61   **MS** [119; 115] and **TS** [96; 8]: "called me up"; **UK** [98] and asp: "called me"; **SPC.**
61   **MS** [119; 115] and **TS** [97; 9]: "jumping-jack—for I"; **UK** [98] and asp: "jumping-jack. I"; **SPC,** cutting repetition of "for".
61   **MS** [120; 117] and **TS** [97; 9]: "villa—She said"; **UK** [98] and all printings: "villa. She said"; **ED:** restore hyphen and alter upper-case "S" to lower case.
61   **MS** [120; 117]: "trunks', and"; **TS** [97; 9]: "trunks,' and"; **UK** [97] and asp: "trunks.' And"; **ED:** restore **TS** punctuation.
62   **MS** [121; 118]: "He certainly \didn't/ care*[d]* for her. Poor thing*[s]*": [ink]. Correction alters conception of Jimmy from object of sympathy to that of contempt.
62   **MS** [121; 118–122; 119]: "*[Well, anyhow, I daresay she did feel remorse whilst she kept me waiting. I do not see how else she can have put in her time. [I regard it not that s]\S/he had been lying in her bed practically dressed; and she did not do any packing until late that forenoon. So, as I figure it out still, from the moment I came into her room until the time when she came to me at the top of the ladder she was wrestling with herself. Because]* \at any rate/": [ink]; **TS** [99; 11]: "At any rate". In **MS**, "[I regard it not that s]\S/" is TS correction and "\at any rate/" ink correction before whole passage was canceled. Strong evidence of Ford's spontaneous composition on typewriter.
63   **MS** [123; 120]: "ship's"; **TS** [100; 12], **UK** [101], and asp: "ship"; **ED:** restore **MS** apostro-phe "s".

63   **MS** [123; 120]: "that *[this]* \her heart/ was the reason for the Hurlbirds' ": [ink]; **TS** [100; 12], **UK** [101], and asp: "that her heart [. . .] Hurlbird's"; **ED**: restore **MS** punctuation.
63   **MS** [123; 120]: "not *[want to]*": [ink].
63   **MS** [123; 120] and **TS** [100; 12]: "of course. That"; **UK** [102] and asp: "of course, that"; **ED**: restore **MS** and **TS** punctuation.
63   **MS** [123; 120] and **TS** [100; 12]: "painter, he"; **UK** [102] and asp: "painter. He"; **ED**: restore **MS** and **TS** punctuation.
63   **MS** [123; 120], **TS** [101; 13], **UK** [102], and asp: "Julien's"; **ED**: correct to "Julian's".
63   **MS** [124; 121]: "*[much]* too fat": [ink].
64   **MS** [124; 121] and **TS** [102; 14]: "was"; **UK** [103] and asp: "were"; **SPC.**
64   **MS** [125; 122]: "burgling"; **TS** [102; 14]: "burning"; **UK** [103] and asp: "burgling"; **SPC**; **ED**: follow **MS** and **UK.**
64   **MS** [125; 122]: "backed ["b" indistinct] up that fellow's recommendations *[.]*\/\& she would wish me goodnight/"; **TS**: "packed up [. . .] good-night"; **UK** [103] and asp: "backed up [. . .] good night"; **ED**: follow **MS** and **UK.**
64   **MS** [125; 122]: "*[bell]* \contrivance/": [ink].
64   **MS** [125; 122] and **TS** [103; 15]: "an axe . . . An axe! great"; **UK** [104] and asp: "an axe—an axe!—great"; **ED**: follow **UK.**
64   **MS** [125; 122] and **TS** [103; 15]: "loudly"; **UK** [104] and asp: "loud"; **SPC.**
64   **MS** [125; 122] and **TS** [103; 15]: "short. Absolutely"; **UK** [104] and asp: "short—absolutely"; **ED**: restore **MS** and **TS** punctuation.
64   **MS** [126; 123] and **TS** [103; 15]: "considerably. For"; **UK** [104] and asp: "considerably, for"; **ED**: restore **MS** and **TS** punctuation.
64   **MS** [126; 123]: "mad"; **TS** [103; 15], **UK** [104], and asp: "main"; perpetuated mistranscription; **ED**: restore as better sense in opposition to "that was otherwise cold."
65   **MS** [126; 123]: "*[—and she could not possibly get to her Promised Land without announcing herself as cured]*": [ink].
65   **MS** [126; 123]: "thereabouts.\what with our money & the support of the Ashburnhams/ ": [ink].
65   **MS** [127; 124]: "could, *[for the sake of the public good]*": [ink].
66   **MS** [129; [ ]]: "her *[uncle]* \cousin, Reggie/": [TS].
66   **MS** [129; [ ]]: "useful *[symbol of a]*": [ink].
67   **MS** [130; 127]: "*[four]* \two/": [ink].
67   **MS** [131; 128]: "during the *[last month]* \whole/": [ink].
67   **MS** [131; 128]: "age of *[eighteen]* thirteen": [TS].
67   **MS** [131; 128]: "had committed suicide *[after* [?]]": [ink]. Evidence of Ford's making ink corrections while typewriting.
67   **MS** [131; 128]: "kissed; [. . .] woman on *[God's]* earth—and in *[God's]* heaven": [ink]; **TS** [109; 21]: as **MS** but "kissed,"; **UK** [110] and asp: as **MS** and **TS** but "kissed—"; **ED**: follow **MS** punctuation.
68   **MS** [131; 128]: "Medal with *[two]* \a/ clasp*[s]*. That meant, apparently, that he had *[three times]* \twice/": [ink]; **TS** [109; 21] follows **MS**; **UK** [110] and asp: "medal"; **ED**: restore cap. "M".
68   **MS** [131; 128] and **TS** [110; 22]: "although,"; **UK** [111] and asp: "although"; **ED**: follow **UK** punctuation.
68   **MS** [132; 129]: "coveted *[decoration]* \order/, he had some special *[station]* \place/": [ink].
68   **MS** [132; 129]: "\If I come to think of it,/*[T]*\t/here": [ink].
69   **MS** [133; 130] and **TS** [111; 23]: "gaily"; **UK** [112] and asp: "gayly"; **ED**: restore **MS** and **TS** spelling.
69   **MS** [133; 130] and **TS** [111; 23]: "husband? Or"; **UK** [112] and asp: "husband, or"; **ED**: restore **MS** and **TS** punctuation.
69   **MS** [133; 130]: "scene;"; **TS** [112; 24]: "scene,"; **UK** [113] and asp: "scene—"; **ED**: restore **MS** punctuation.
69   **MS** [134; 131] and **TS** [112; 24]: "adversaries of a political character"; **UK** and asp: "adversaries"; **SPC.**

CHAPTER .II, PART II

69   **MS** [135; 132] and **TS** [113; 25]: "THE SADDEST STORY | PART II | II"; **UK** [114] and asp: "II".
69   **MS** [135; 132] and **TS** [113; 25]: "where I was"; **UK** [114]: "where we were"; **SPC.**
70   **MS** [135; 132]: "(It must have been [. . .] for that purpose.)"; **TS** [113; 25], **UK** [114] and asp: parentheses lacking; **SPC.**
70   **MS** [136; 133] and **TS** [114; 26]: "companionship. And"; **UK** [115] and asp: "companionship and"; **ED**: restore **MS** and **TS** punctuation.

70   MS [136; 133] and TS [114; 26]: "he"; UK and asp: "she"; SPC.

70   MS [136; 133] and TS [115; 27]: "plain to her"; UK and asp: "plain"; SPC.

70   MS [136; 133]: "of my nature"; TS [115; 27], UK [116], and asp: "of nature"; perpetuated mistranscription; ED: restore "my".

70   MS [137; 134]: "almost a necessity"; TS [115; 27], UK [116], and asp: "almost necessary"; ED: follow TS and UK.

70   MS [137; 134] and TS [115; 27]: "about it. Nothing"; UK [116] and asp: "about it— nothing"; ED: follow MS and TS punctuation.

71   MS [137; 134] and TS [116; 28]: ", at that date" lacking; SPC.

72   MS [139; 137]: "life \!/": [ink]; TS [118; 30], UK [119], and asp: "life."; ED: restore MS punctuation.

CHAPTER I, PART III

72   MS: "S.S." (cover sheet misplaced from front of whole MS); TS [119; [ ]]: "THE SADDEST STORY | PART III"; UK [121]: "THE GOOD SOLDIER | PART III".

72   MS [141; 1]: "The Saddest Story. | Part III | I."; TS [120; [ ]]: "THE SADDEST STORY. | PART III. | I."; UK [123] and asp except US2: "I"; US2 [105]: "PART III | I".

73   MS [141; 1]: "slightest \conscious/": [ink].

73   MS [141; 1]: "[like a person] \as people do who are/: [ink].

73   MS [142; 2]: "upon [the development of]": [ink].

73   MS [143; 3]: "[dual personality] \self that underlies most people/": [ink].

73   MS [144; 4]: no new para.; TS [122; 3]: introduces new para., followed in UK [125] and asp; ED: follow UK.

74   MS [145; 5] and TS [123; 4]: "I can not [TS: "cannot"] tell you the extraordinary sense of leisure that we seemed to have at that moment, we two"; UK [125] and asp: "I cannot tell you the extraordinary sense of leisure that we two seemed to have at that moment"; SPC.

74   MS [148; 8]: "relieve [the pressure of blood upon the valves of the heart] \sufferers from angina pectoris/": [ink].

75   MS [149; 9] and TS [125; 6]: "should"; UK [127] and asp: "had"; SPC.

75   MS [149; 9]: "side. [before the remedy, when she had got to it could take effect]": [ink].

75   MS [151; 11]: "harp"[?]; TS [126; 7], UK [128], and asp: "rasp".

76   MS [154; 14]: "impressions . . ."; TS [127; 8]: "impressions"; ED: restore MS punctuation.

76   MS [154; 14]: "muslin. That"; TS [127; 8], UK [129], and asp: "muslin, that"; ED: restore MS reading since comma in UK is awkward.

77   MS [158; 18]: "peeping out from"; TS [129; 29], UK [132], and asp: "peeping with fear"; ED: perpetuated mistranscription but no textual authority for restoration.

77   MS [158; 18]: "[—something very similar to what happened to me [?] a [?] little [?] later [?] in the same evening. As far as I can make [it] it out the other half of his dual personality spoke—to the girl.]": [pencil].

77   MS [159; 19] and TS [130; 11]: "Leonora; that it was the accursed thing."; UK [137] and asp: final clause lacking; SPC.

78   MS [161; 21]: "were; [however blinding]": [ink, possibly HD].

78   MS [161; 21] and TS [131; 12]: "handiworks"; UK [133] and asp: "handiwork"; ED: follow UK.

78   MS [162; 22]: "her [intemperate] \tempestuous/ father, the bewailing of her [sad] \cruel-tongued/": [ink].

78   MS [162; 22] and TS [131; 12]: "must"; UK [133] and asp: "might"; SPC.

78   MS [163; 23]: "So that, when he spoke of her as being the [most beautiful woman] \person he most cared for/in the world, \she [mentally] thought that he meant to except Leonora and /she was just glad. It was like a father [approving the looks [?]] \saying that he approves of/of [redundant] [a marriageable daughter . . . And when he spoke of her as the only woman he had ever loved—and, upon my soul, I believe that she was the only woman that he had ever loved!—she simply took it, making allowances for the odd phraseology, as the kindliness of a father loving his young daughter. She was just glad and she went on being just glad!] \And Edward, when he realised what he was doing, curbed his tongue at once/": [ink]; TS [132; 13], UK [133], and all printings follow corrections with exception of "she [mentally] thought" which becomes "she naturally thought"; perpetuated mistranscription or SPC.

78   MS [164; 24]: "for"; TS [132; 13], UK [134], and asp: "of"; ED: perpetuated mistranscription; restore "for" here to clarify sense and avoid repetition of "of."

79   MS [166; 26]: "regard to men, a love affair—a love"; TS [133; 14]: "regard to man, a love

affair is a love"; **UK** [134] and asp: "regard to man, a love affair, a love"; perpetuated mistranscription; **ED**: restore **MS** reading as clearer.

79   **MS** [168; 28] and **TS** [134; 15]: "the craving—the craving for"; **UK** [135] and asp cut "—the craving"; **SPC**.

79   **MS** [169; 29]: "does not *[believe that he will be able]* \desire/": [ink, HD].

80   **MS** [171; 31] and **TS** [136; 17]: "Count-baron von Lollöfel"; **UK** [137] and asp: "Count Baron von Lelöffel"; **ED**: follow **UK**.

81   **MS** [173; 33] and **TS** [137; 18]: "Bagshaw"; **UK** [137] and asp: "Bagshawe"; possibly perpetuated mistranscription but equally possibly **SPC**; **ED**: follow **UK** throughout.

81   **MS** [174; 34] and **TS** [137; 18]: "she"; **UK** [138] and asp: "Florence"; **SPC**.

81   **MS** [174; 34]: [illegible]; **TS** [137; 18]: "nervous"; **UK** [138] and asp: "scenes"; **ED**: follow **UK**.

81   **MS** [176; 36]: no new para. after "secret"; **TS** [139; 19]: mistranscription adds new para.; **UK** [139] and asp perpetuate mistranscription; **ED**: cancel new para.

81   **MS** [176; 36]: "in me *[to bother her head about my peculiarities]*": [ink, HD].

81   **MS** [177; 37]: "name, *[differentiate]* \dwell/ a little *[as]* \upon/ to [redundant]".

82   **MS** [180; 40]: "four"; **TS** [140; 21]: "*[four]* \five/": [pencil, not Ford]; **UK** [140] and asp: "five".

82   **MS** [180; 40]: "4th of August, 1900", i.e., uncorrected date in early holograph appears to provide evidence for "amazing coincidence" theory of Ford's selecting precise date of outbreak of World War I before the event. However, see p. 82, 4th entry below.

82   **MS** [180; 40] and **TS** [140; 21]: "married me and"; **UK** [141] and asp: "married me;"; **SPC**.

82   **MS** [180; 40]: "She had been born [. . .] on the face of Fate" is large AMS insertion in ink from l.h. margin, establishing the date August 4 as spine of novel's diffuse chronology. Although the date appears unchanged on **MS** [180; 140] (see n. 8 above), this addition developing its significance could have been made after the outbreak of war.

83   **MS** [180; 40]: "lay—O."; **TS** [141; 22]: "lay. O."; **UK** [142] and asp: "lay,—O,"; **ED**: follow **MS**.

83   **MS**: [181; 41]: "Algebra, *[or about the solution of a date in* [?] *this* [?] *story* [?]]": [ink, HD?].

84   **MS** [185; 45] and **TS** [143; 24]: "worse than" lacking; **SPC**.

84   **MS** [185; 45]: no new para.; **TS** [143; 24], **UK** [142], and asp: new para. added; **ED**: follow **TS** and **UK**.

84   **MS** [185; 45] and **TS** [143; 24]: "way, to"; **UK** [142], and asp: "way,"; **SPC**.

84   **MS** [185; 45]: "twenty-*[one]* \two/": [ink].

CHAPTER II, PART III

84   **MS** [188; 48]: "Part III | II"; **TS** [145; 26]: "*[PART III]*: [pencil] | II."; **UK** [145] and asp: "II".

85   **MS** [190; 50]: "extraordinarily"; **TS** [146; 27], **UK** [146], and asp: "exceedingly"; mistranscription avoids "extraordinary [. . .] extraordinarily [. . .] extraordinarily" repetition; **ED**: follow **UK**.

85   **MS** [190; 50]: "hounds screaming like a Maenead"; **TS** [146; 27]: "hounds screaming like a Maenad"; **UK** [146] and asp: "hounds like a Maenad"; **SPC**.

86   **MS** [193; 53]: "appeared to Nancy's inscrutable mind"; **TS** [147; 28], **UK** [147], and asp: "appeared"; whole line of **MS** lacking **TS** (eye-slip); **ED**: restore.

86   **MS** [194; 54]: "words:"; **TS** [148; 29], **UK** [147], and asp: "words."; **ED**: restore **MS** punctuation.

86   **MS** [195; 55]: "fancy that"; **TS** [149; 30], **UK** [148], and asp: "fancy"; perpetuated mistranscription; **ED**: restore "that."

86   **MS** [196; 56]: "some *[violently]* cutting": [ink, HD?].

86   HD's AMS breaks off at "tender" and runs seamlessly into next TS section, typed by Ford. There was, surely, more of HD's holograph, which Ford scrapped, continuing revision/composition on typewriter. As internal pagination is consecutive, this also suggests break in dictation, taken up again after his revision of TS section, at **MS** [206; 66].

86   **MS** [197; 57]: "their"; **TS** [149; 30], **UK** [149], and asp: "the"; **ED**: perpetuated mistranscription but follow **UK**.

87   **MS** [197; 57]: "heard \until the very end/": [ink].

87   **MS** [197; 57] and **TS** [150; 31]: "Ashburnham's"; **UK** [149] and asp: "Ashburnhams"; **ED**: surely a simple plural so follow **UK**.

87   **MS** [197; 57] and **TS** [150; 31]: "was always"; **UK** [49] and asp: "was"; **SPC**.

87   **MS** [198; 5] and **TS** [151; 32]: "Oh, to"; **UK** [150] and asp: "And to"; **SPC**.

88   **MS** [199; 59] and **TS** [151; 32]: "fog-horn boomed"; **UK** [151] and asp: "foghorn had boomed"; **SPC**.

88   **MS** [199; 59] and **TS** [152; 33]: "don't think"; **UK** [151] and asp: "don't believe"; **SPC**.

88   **MS** [199; 59] and **TS** [152; 33]: "bedroom . ."; **UK** [151] and asp: "bedroom. . . ."; **ED:** follow **UK** punctuation.

88   **MS** [199; 59] and **TS** [152; 32]: "could have"; **UK** [151]: "could"; **SPC**.

88   **MS** [200; 60]: white line break after "childhood. . . ."; **TS** [152; 33]: "childhood. . . ." is last word on page and white line break gets lost; **UK** [152] and asp: no white line break; **ED:** restore.

88   **MS** [200; 60] and **TS** [153; 34]: "way and,"; **UK** [152] and asp: "way, and"; **ED:** follow **UK** punctuation.

89   **MS** [202; 62]: "could"; **TS** [154; 35], **UK** [154], and asp: "would"; perpetuated mistranscription; **ED:** restore "could" for plainer reading.

90   **MS** [203; 63]: "look at Florence [. . .] And Florence"; **TS** [155; 36], **UK** [155], and asp: "look at Leonora [. . .] And Leonora". "Leonora" in **TS** has been erased and typed over, suggesting authorial correction.

90   **MS** [203; 63] and **TS** [155; 36–156; 37]: "footstep [. . .] later it"; **UK** [155] and asp: "footsteps [. . .] later they"; **SPC**.

91   **MS** [204; 64] and **TS** [157; 38]: "swinging and dancing"; **UK** [156] and asp: "swinging"; **SPC**.

91   **MS** [205; 65]: "before \s/he": [ink].

91   **MS** [205; 65] and **TS** [157; 38]: "night,"; **UK** [157] and asp: "night"; **ED:** follow **UK** punctuation.

91   **MS:** end of ribbon-copy TS (Ford's typing), **MS** [197; 57–205; 65].

CHAPTER III, PART III

91   HD's second holograph section begins here. **MS** [206; 66]: "Part III | 3.-"; **TS** [158; 39]: "[PART III.] | III": [pencil]; **UK** [158] and asp: "III".

91   **MS** [206; 66]: "affliction"; **TS** [158; 39], **UK** [158], and asp: "infliction"; perpetuated mistranscription; **ED:** follow **UK** since no change in sense.

91   **MS** [206; 66]: "horror"; **TS** [158; 39], **UK** [158], and asp: "horrors"; perpetuated mistranscription; **ED:** follow **UK**.

91   **MS** [207; 67]: "of [our] \their/; **TS** [158; 39], **UK** [158], and asp: "of that"; perpetuated mistranscription; **ED:** follow **UK**.

91   **MS** [207; 57]: "convent [about \of/ which] I have so often spoken \of/": [ink].

92   **MS** [211; 71]: "silk stocking "; **TS** [161; 42], **UK** [160], and asp: "stocking"; perpetuated mistranscription; **ED:** restore "silk".

93   **MS** [213; 73] and **TS** [161; 42]: "keen even on mathematics [. . .] politics and even,"; **UK** [161] and asp: "keen on mathematics [. . .] politics and,"; **SPC**.

93   **MS** [213; 73] and **TS** [161; 42]: "Froissart"; **UK** and **US** [161]: "Froisart"; **US2**: "Froissart"; **ED:** follow **MS** and **US2** as correct spelling.

94   **MS** [215; 75]: "cuts"; **TS** [162; 43], **UK** [162], and asp: "cut"; **ED:** restore "s".

94   HD's second holograph section in **MS** [206; 66–218; 78] ends with "but the". Subsequent **TS** (Ford's typing) continues seamlessly with consecutive pagination.

94   Ribbon-copy TS (Ford's typing) recommences with "marriage", pp. [219; 79–224; 84].

95   **MS** [219; 79] and **TS** [164; 45]: "that he just calmly [. . .] pulse, carried"; **UK** [164] and asp: "that, calmly [. . .] pulse, he just carried"; **SPC** transposition of "he just".

95   **MS** [219; 79]: "magnetism; [all that was not love]": [ink].

95   **MS** [220; 80]: "he never had"; **TS** [165; 46], **UK** [164], and asp: "he had never had"; perpetuated mistranscription; **ED:** follow **UK**.

95   **MS** [220; 80] "his [splendid] qualities" [ink] [. . .] quickened [when she entered the room]": [TS]. Latter correction evidence of Ford's spontaneous composition on typewriter.

95   **MS** [220; 80] and **TS** [166; 47]: "heaven. There were regimental festivities, and outings—"; **UK** [165] and asp: "There [. . .] outings—" cut; **SPC**.

95   **MS** [220; 80]: "who [treated] \gave/ her [to]": [ink].

95   **MS** [221; 81]: "master[fulness]\y/": [ink].

96   **MS** [221; 81]: "\Aldershot was not so very far away and/": [ink]. **TS**: [166; 47], **UK** [166], and asp: "so" lacking; perpetuated mistranscription; **ED:** restore.

96   **MS** [221; 81]: "Edward [gave himself too much side] \was much too generous to his tenants/": [ink].

96   **MS** [222; 82]: "make more"; **TS** [169; 49], **UK** [167], and asp: "make"; perpetuated mistranscription; **ED:** restore "more".

97   **MS** [223; 83]: "conversation with Edward—and in much longer conversations with Edward's land-steward—"; **TS** [169; 49]: "conversation with Edward's land-steward—"; **UK** [168] and asp: "conversation with Edward's land-steward,"; perpetuated mistranscription (eye-slip); **ED:** restore **MS** reading.

97   **MS** [223; 83]: "do them"; **TS** [169; 50], **UK** [168], and asp: "do"; **ED:** restore "them."

97   **MS** [224; 84] and **TS** [169; 50]: "Mudford"; **UK** [169] and asp: "Mumford"; **ED:** restore **MS** and **TS** reading since consistently "Mudford" in Ford's TMS in **MS** and in **TS** (both corrected by him).

97   **MS** [224; 84]: Ford's TS insertion [219; 79–224; 84] concludes, leaving one-third of sheet blank, with words: "One morning the land-steward reported". These appear again at head of HD's subsequent third section of holograph. Pagination is consecutive, suggesting that she began to take dictation again after Ford had finished his TS revision.

97   **MS** [225; 84 [sic]]: "Mudford"; **TS** [170; 51], **UK** [169], and asp: "Mumford"; perpetuated mistranscription begins here and continues throughout; **ED:** restore "Mudford" throughout. See p. 208, 97, 3rd entry above.

97   **MS** [225; 84[sic]] and **TS** [170; 51]: "like,"; **UK** [169] and asp: "like:"; **ED:** follow **UK** punctuation since standard practice elsewhere.

98   **MS** [227; 86] and **TS** [171; 52]: "state of poor"; **UK** [170] and asp: "poor state of"; **SPC** transposition.

98   **MS** [227; 86]: "very much concerned by Edward's outbreak"; **TS** [171; 52]: "very much concerned by Edward's outburst"; **UK** [170] and asp: "much concerned by Edward's outburst"; perpetuated mistranscription and **SPC; ED:** follow **UK.**

98   **MS** [229; 88]: "ideal"; **TS** [172; 53]: "indeed"; **UK** [171] and asp: "theory"; **TS** reading, seemingly nonsense, has been replaced by Ford or editor with repeated "theory"—which makes sense but is less precise than "ideal"; **ED:** restore **MS** reading.

99   **MS** [233; 92]: "deeds"; **TS** [173; 54], **UK** [172], and asp: "death." Sentence reads awkwardly, and a little more so with "death" than with "deeds". The "his" before "ancestors" is ambiguous but sentence is clearer if "his" is seen to refer to the inheritor's (or beneficiary's) ancestors (i.e., Ashburnham in this case). Had he become a Catholic, he would not have bound his male children, by that decision, to become Catholics themselves. By raising them as Anglicans, he believed, as he says four sentences later, that he would leave them freedom of choice. **ED:** restore "deeds" since more precise and also a pun (title deeds).

99   **MS** [233; 92] and **TS** [174; 55]: "remember that"; **UK** [173] and asp: "remember"; **SPC.**

100   **MS** [235; 94] and **TS** [174; 55]: "passionately loved"; **UK** [173] and asp: "loved passionately"; **SPC** transposition.

100   **MS** [237; 96] and **TS** [175; 56]: "put"; **UK** [174] and asp: "keep"; **SPC.**

100   **MS** [237; 96–238; 97]: "no issue, the Kilsight [. . .] said that the Killsight"; **TS** [175; 56]: "[. . .] Kilsyte [. . .] Kilsyte" after **TS** erasure and correction. Clear signs of Ford's *not* typing **TS.**

CHAPTER IV, PART III

101   **MS** [242; 101]: "Part III | III"; **TS** [178; 59]: PART III | I \V/": [pencil]; **UK** [177] and asp: "IV".

101   **MS** [242; 101]: "much"; **TS** [178; 59], **UK** [177], and asp: "such"; possibly perpetuated mistranscription but **TS** "s" might be erasure and retyping.

101   **MS** [242; 101]: "at *[the]* table": [ink]; **TS** [178; 59], **UK** [177] and asp: "at the table"; typist restores Ford's cancellation; perpetuated mistranscription; **ED:** follow **UK.**

101   **MS** [243; 101A] and **TS** [178; 59]: "wonder given"; **UK** [177] and asp: "wonder, given"; **ED:** follow **UK** punctuation.

101   **MS** [243; 101A] and **TS** [178; 59]: "have, however,"; **UK** [177] and asp: "have"; **SPC.**

101   **MS** [243; 101A] and **TS** [178; 59]: "about him"; **UK** [177] and asp: "about his passions"; **SPC.**

101   **MS** [243; 101A], **TS** [179; 60], **UK** [177], and asp: "polo or"; **ED:** correct to "polo, or" to clarify difference between polo and cricket seasons.

103   **MS** [250; 108]: "for the people who mostly warned me"; **TS** [181; 62]: "for the people"; **UK** [180] and asp: "for they"; perpetuated mistranscription and **SPC; ED:** follow **UK.**

103   **MS** [250; 108]: "wanted"; **TS** [181; 62]: "waited"; **UK** [180] and asp: "wanted"; **SPC.**

103   **MS** [251; 109] and **TS** [182; 63]: "1906"; **UK** [180] and asp: "1907"; **SPC.**

103   **MS** [253; 111]: "however,—"; **TS** [182; 63], **UK** [181], and asp: "however, as"; perpetuated mistranscription; **ED:** restore **MS** reading.

104   **MS** [253; 111] and **TS** [183; 64]: "democrat" and "republican", and throughout; **UK** [181] and asp: "Democrat" and "Republican", and throughout; **SPC.**

104   **MS** [253; 111]: "my money" concludes HD's third section of holograph (225; 84–253; 111). Subsequent TS (typed by Ford) follows seamlessly with consecutive pagination, suggesting that there was more of HD's holograph, scrapped in Ford's TS revision.

104   **MS** [254; 112] and **TS** [183; 64]: "Philadelphian"; **UK** [182] and asp: "Philadelphia"; **SPC.**

104   **MS** [254; 112] and **TS** [183; 64]: "That, for instance"; **UK** [182] and asp: "That, for instance,"; **ED:** follow **UK** punctuation.

104   **MS** [254; 112] and **TS** [184; 65]: "shew"; **UK** [182] and asp: "show"; **SPC** consistent throughout; see p. 57, 1st entry above.

104   **MS** [255; 113]: "dirtimindedness"; **TS** [184; 65], **UK** [183], and asp: "dirty-mindedness"; **ED**: follow **TS** and **UK**.

104   **MS** [255; 113] and **TS** [185; 66]: "From that time on he"; **UK** [183] and asp: "He"; **SPC**.

105   **MS** [257; 115], **TS** [186; 67], **UK** [185], and asp: "anyone"; **ED**: correct to "any one" for clearer reading.

106   **MS** [258; 116]: "*[sentimental]* \honourable/": [TS].

108   **MS** [261; 199] and **TS** [190; 71]: "the tables"; **UK** [189] and asp: "the tables, and this went on for about a fortnight"; **SPC**.

108   **MS** [261; 119] and **TS** [191; 72]: "the"; **UK** [189] and asp: "about"; **SPC**.

108   **MS** [261; 119]: "his"; **TS** [191; 72], **UK** [189] and asp: "her"; perpetuated mistranscription; **ED**: restore **MS** reading.

108   **MS** [261; 119] and **TS** [191; 72]: "till lunch time"; **UK** [189] and asp: "till the lunch hour"; **SPC**.

108   **MS** [262; 120] and **TS** [191; 72]: "good natured"; **UK** [190] and asp: "good-natured"; **ED**: follow **UK** punctuation.

108   **MS** [262; 120] and **TS** [192; 73]: "Melisses"; **UK** [190] and asp: "Melisse"; **ED**: follow **UK** as correct spelling.

108   **MS** [262; 120] and **TS** [192; 73]: "seven"; **UK** [190] and asp: "fourteen"; **SPC**.

108   **MS** [262; 120]: "*[five]*t ten": [TS]; Ford's spontaneous composition on typewriter accentuates Ashburnham's recklessness.

CHAPTER V, PART III

109   **MS** [264; [ ]]: "THE SADDEST STORY | Part iii | *[L]*\I/V."; **TS** [194; 75]: "THE SADDEST STORY | Part III | v."; **UK** [192] and asp: "V". Ford probably did not type Part V [264; [ ]–273; 131] (see p. 112, 4th entry) but recommenced typing on [273; 131] with "And then the Ashburnhams were moved" (p. 114), breaking off again on [276; 134] to leave last two pages to be typed by third party.

109   **MS** [264; [ ]]: "<u>do</u>"; **TS** [194; 75], **UK** [192], and asp: "do"; perpetuated mistranscription; **ED**: restore italics.

109   **MS** [264; [ ]] and **TS** [194; 75]: "wanted the money"; **UK** [192] and asp: "wanted it"; **SPC**.

110   **MS** [265; 123], **TS** [195; 76], **UK** [193], and asp: "this: Properly"; **ED**: correct to "properly".

110   **MS** [266; 124] and **TS** [197; 77]: "likely"; **UK** [194] and asp: "likely,"; **ED**: follow **UK**.

110   **MS** [266; 124] and **TS** [197; 77]: "Hotel"; **UK** [194] and asp: "hotel"; **ED**: follow **UK**.

110   **MS** [266; 124] and **TS** [197; 77]: "that he had"; **UK** [194] and asp: "or had"; **SPC**.

110   **MS** [266; 124]: "not to have"; **TS** [197; 77], **UK** [194], and asp: "not have"; **ED**: restore "to".

111   **MS** [267; 125]: "Branshaw". First example of this spelling in TS parts of **MS** but Ford probably not typing this section (see p. 112, 4th entry below).

111   **MS** [268; 126]: "front \./*[or whatever it is called.]* She *[allowed]* \gave/ him however"; **TS** [198; 79], **UK** [196], and asp: "front. She gave him"; perpetuated mistranscription; **ED**: restore "however".

111   **MS** [268; 126] and **TS** [198; 79]: "Edward"; **UK** [196] and asp: "Edward's"; possible **SPC** but restore **MS** and **TS** reading since it makes better sense. The cases *are* Edward's (i.e., they belong to him) but they are not "Edward" (i.e., a reflection of his character).

112   **MS** [269; 127] and **TS** [199; 80]: "Edward; for she"; **UK** [196] and asp: "Edward; she"; **SPC**.

112   **MS** [269; 127] and **TS** [199; 80]: "did mostly what"; **UK** [196] and asp: "did what"; **SPC**.

112   **MS** [269; 127] and **TS** [199; 80]: "She"; **UK** [196] and asp: "Mrs. Basil"; **SPC**.

112   **MS** [270; 128]: "Brail"; **TS** [200; 81]: "Basil"; strong evidence that Ford did *not* type this section of **MS** (see p. 109, 1st entry above), which would explain how "Bramshaw" becomes "Branshaw" (see p. 111, 1st entry above).

112   **MS** [270; 128]: "B*[ra]*\as/il": [ink]. See n. 3 above. Ford seems to correct third party's error here but misses earlier "Brail".

113   **MS** [270; 128] and **TS** [200; 81] "brevet colonel"; **UK** [198] and asp: "brevet-colonel"; **ED**: follow **UK** punctuation since "brevet-major" appears all states at end of paragraph.

113   **MS** [271; 129] and **TS** [201; 82]: "regiments"; **UK** [199] and asp: "regiment"; **SPC**.

113   **MS** [271; 129] and **TS** [201; 82]: "hundred bottle"; **UK** [199] and asp: "hundred-bottle"; **ED**: follow **UK** punctuation.

113   **MS** [272; 130]: "Major \Basil/": [ink]. More evidence of Ford's not typing this section: word seems to have been omitted as illegible in AMS draft (now lost) and to have been later replaced by Ford.

114   **MS** [272; 130]: "can *[have the face to]* make": [ink].
114   **MS** [273; 131]: "\I am no good at geography of the Indian Empire/": [TS]. Evidence of spontaneous composition on typewriter? Ford possibly recommences typing from beginning of the para., or typist was taking dictation.
114   **MS** [273; 131]: "cruel \ *[and cold]*/": [TS]. See entry immediately above.
115   **MS** [274; 132] and **TS** [204; 85]: "Bramshaw"; **UK** [202] and asp: "Branshaw". More evidence of Ford's typing **MS**.
115   **MS** [275; 133]: ' "Good God'."; **TS** [205; 86]: ' "Good God.' "; **UK** [203] and asp: " 'Good God!' "; **ED**: follow **UK** punctuation.
115   **MS** [275; 133] and **TS** [205; 86]: "years and years"; **UK** [203] and asp: "several years"; **SPC**.
116   **MS** [276; 134] and **TS** [206; 87]: "huge plains all sunlit"; **UK** [204] and asp: "sunlit plains"; **SPC**.
116   **MS** [277; 135]: "perpetually \dry/": [ink]. Evidence of Ford's not typing last two sheets of section, which probably explains recurrence of "Branshaw" below, after three "Bramshaws" on previous **MS** page. Last two sheets have three ink insertions/corrections by Ford, possibly suggesting third party could not read AMS draft, now lost.
116   **MS** [277; 135]: "lord of Branshaw"; **TS** [207; 88]: "Lord of Bramshaw"; **UK** [205] and asp: "Lord of Branshaw"; **ED**: restore "lord" to correct perpetuated mistranscription; follow **TS** "Bramshaw" as consistently this when written by Ford, and "m" in **TS** superimposed over correction erasure.
116   **MS** [277; 135]: "act \of hers/": [ink]. See p. 116, 2nd entry above.
117   **MS** [278; 136]: "Maidan \along the deck/": [ink]. See p. 116, 2nd and 4th entries above.
117   **MS** [278; 136]: half page left blank. Below "health": "<u>Drop one line</u>"; **TS** [208; 89], **UK** [206], and asp insert row of asterisks which seems arbitrary and is not in keeping with white-line breaks elsewhere; **ED**: delete asterisks as perpetuated mistranscription.
117   **MS** [279; [ ]]: "*[THE SADDEST STORY | PART IV [I]*": [ink]; **TS** [208; 89], **UK** [206], and asp: text continues under line of asterisks. **MS** probably not typed by Ford. See next two entries, pp. 117, 118.
117   **MS** [280; 138] and **TS** [209; 90]: "Brail"; **UK** [207] and asp: "Basil"; suggests Ford not typing this section of **MS**.
118   **MS** [280; 138]: "to Edward and Mrs. Maisie"; **TS** [210; 91]: "for Edward and Mrs. Maisie"; **UK** [207] and asp: "to Edward and Mrs. Maiden"; **SPC**.
118   **MS** [280; 138] and **TS** [210; 91]: "fate's"; **UK** [208] and asp: "Fate's"; **SPC**.
118   **MS** [280; 138–28; 139] and **TS** [210; 91]: "deeds. [. . . .] was"; **UK** [208] and asp: "deeds. [. . . .] was?"; **ED**: follow **UK** punctuation but also correct stop after "deeds" to question mark.
119   **MS** [282; 140]: "Maifan"; **TS** [211; 92], **UK** [209], and asp: "Maidan." See pp. 116 (2nd and 4th entries), 117 (last entry), and 118 (1st entry).
119   **MS** [282; 140] and **TS** [212; 93]: "thought"; **UK** [210] and asp: "imagined"; **SPC**, presumably to remove repetition of "thought" in next sentence.
119   **MS** [283; 141] and **TS** [212; 93]: "trust Maisie [. . .] doubt of her"; **UK** [210] and asp: "trust Edward [. . .] doubt of Maisie's"; **SPC** shifting betrayal from Maisie to Edward.
119   **MS** [283; 141] and **TS** [213; 94]: "appeared also"; **UK** [210] and asp: "appeared to him".

CHAPTER I, PART IV

119   **MS** [284; [ ]] and **TS** [215; [ ]]: "THE SADDEST STORY | PART IV"; **UK** [211] and asp except US2 (no title sheet): "THE GOOD SOLDIER | PART IV". Ford probably typed this section of **MS**: [284; [ ]–317; 310].
119   **MS** [285; [ ]] and **TS** [216; [ ]]: "THE SADDEST STORY | PART IV | I"; **UK** [213] and asp except US2: "I"; US2 [187]: "PART IV | I".
120   **MS** [28; [ ]] and **TS** [216; [ ]]: "Leonora's;"; **UK** [213] and asp: "Leonora's,"; **ED**: follow **UK** punctuation.
120   **MS** [286; 280] and **TS** [217; 2]: "Rightly,"; **UK** [214] and asp: "Perhaps"; **SPC**.
120   **MS** [287; 281]: "*[listened]* \watched/"; [TS]: evidence of Ford's typing.
121   **MS** [287; 281] and **TS** [218; 3]: "Florence"; **UK** [215] and all printings: "Leonora"; **SPC**. In **TS** someone has circled "Florence" in pencil and put "?" by it.
121   **MS** [287; 281] and **TS** [218; 3]: "get Edward"; **UK** [215] and asp: "get Edward back"; **SPC** possibly altering motivation from possessiveness to desire for reconciliation.
121   **MS** [287; 281] and **TS** [219; 4]: "represented, for"; **UK** [215] and asp: "represented to"; **SPC**.
121   **MS** [288; 282] and **TS** [219; 4]: "And when she"; **UK** [216] and asp: "She"; **SPC**.
121   **MS** [288; 282]: "old, *[wise]* nun \who appeared to her to be infinitely wise, mystic and reverend/"; [TS]: correction specifying source of impression and removing it from status of omniscient authorial commentary. See p. 119, last entry.

121   **MS** [289; 283]: "*[pardonable]* \children/": [ink].
122   **MS** [289; 283]: "she *[had appeared]* \thought she had/": [ink].
122   **MS** [289; 283] and **TS** [220; 5]: "come so near her desires [. . .] working so admirably";
        UK [217] and asp: "come near her desires [. . .] working admirably"; **SPC**.
122   **MS** [290; 284]: "look'." [. . .] dress.' "; **TS** [221; 6]: "look,' [. . .] dress' "; **UK** [218] and
        asp: "look!' [. . .] dress!' "; **ED**: restore **TS** readings, as more effective for *not* being
        exclamations.
122   **MS** [290; 284] and **TS** [221; 6]: "she"; **UK** [218] and asp: "Leonora"; **SPC**.
122   **MS** [290; 284]: "done \only with fear and irresolution/": [TS]. More evidence of Ford's
        typing (and spontaneous composition).
122   **MS** [290; 284] and **TS** [222; 7]: "right old"; **UK** [218] and asp: "right, old"; **ED**: follow
        UK punctuation.
123   **MS** [292; 286]: "been \with me/": [ink].
124   **MS** [293; 287] and **TS** [224; 9]: "she, Leonora"; **UK** [221] and asp: "she, Leonora,"; **ED**:
        follow **UK** punctuation.
124   **MS** [293; 287] and **TS** [225; 10]: white line break after "time"; **UK** [221] and asp: white
        line lacking, probably because it appears at the bottom of **TS** page; **ED**: restore.
125   **MS** [294; 288]: "more, or at Least I might *[ab]* \have guessed/ great deal more"; **TS** [226;
        11]: "more or at least I might have guessed a great deal more"; **UK** [222] and asp:
        "more. Or, at least, I might have guessed a great deal more"; **SPC** to sentence division;
        ED: follow **UK**.
125   **MS** [294; 288]: "went"; **TS** [226; 11]: "sent"; **UK** [222] and asp: "went"; **SPC**.
125   **MS** [295; 289] and **TS** [227; 12]: "church"; **UK** [223] and asp: "Church"; **ED**: follow **UK**
        and standardize throughout when referring to Roman Catholic Church.
126   **MS** [297; 291]: "faithlessness"; **TS** [229; 14], **UK** [225], and asp: "unfaithfulness"; perpetu-
        ated mistranscription; **ED**: follow **UK** for clearer sense.
126   **MS** [297; 291]: "cheque of his"; **TS** [229; 14], **UK** [225], and asp: "cheque"; perpetuated
        mistranscription; **ED**: restore "of his".
126   **MS** [297; 291] and **TS** [230; 15]: "cypher"; **UK** [225] and asp: "cipher"; **SPC**.
127   **MS** [298; 292]: "\She threatened to take his banking account away from him again/": [TS].
        More evidence of Ford's typing, or dictating to typist.
127   **MS** [298; 292]: "*[at about that time]* \during those years/": [ink].

CHAPTER II, PART IV

127   **MS** [299; 293] and **TS** [232; 17]: "THE SADDEST STORY | PART IV | II."; **UK** [227]:
        and asp: "II".
127   **MS** [299; 293]: "\It was only twelve years./": [ink]; possibly evidence for theory that Ford
        tinkered with dates during correction of whole **MS**.
127   **MS** [300; 294] and **TS** [233; 18]: "Philadelphian"; **UK** [228] and asp: "Philadelphia"; **SPC**.
127   **MS** [300; 294], **TS** [233; 18], **UK** [228], and asp: "Waterbury, Ill."; perpetuated error (this
        Waterbury is in Connecticut—see p. 129, 5th entry below); **ED**: correct to "Conn.".
127   **MS** [300; 294]: "*[after]* \before/": [ink]. See p. 127, 4th entry above.
128   **MS** [301; 295] and **TS** [234; 19]: "without any comments"; **UK** [229] and asp: "without
        telling me"; **SPC**.
128   **MS** [301; 295]: "comments *[to somebody on the matter of her sudden retirement]*":
        [pencil].
128   **MS** [301; 295]: "doctors *[discussing]* warning"; evidence of spontaneous composition and
        thus of Ford's typing, or dictating to typist.
128   **MS** [302; 296]: "of invalid"; **TS** [235; 20]: "individual"; **UK** [230] and asp: "of invalid";
        SPC.
129   **MS** [302; 296] and **TS** [236; 21]: "pretty good"; **UK** [230] and asp: "stiff"; **SPC**, presumably
        to avoid repetition of "pretty".
129   **MS** [303; 297]: "*[of use]* \so helpful/": [pencil].
129   **MS** [303; 297] and **TS** [236; 21]: "yet,"; **UK** [231] and asp: "yet"; **ED**: follow **UK** punctu-
        ation.
129   **MS** [303; 297]: "name"; **TS** [237; 22], **UK** [231] and asp: "names"; perpetuated mistran-
        scription; **ED**: follow **UK** since reading makes equal sense.
129   **MS** [303; 297] and **TS** [237; 22]: "Waterbury, Ill."; **UK** [231] and asp: "Waterbury,
        Conn."; **SPC** but Ford (or editor) forgot to alter reference on p. 127, 6th entry above.
129   **MS**: [303; 297]: "impression that \I thought/"; **TS** [237; 22], **UK** [231], and asp: "impres-
        sions that I thought"; perpetuated mistranscription; **ED**: follow **MS** for clearer sense.
130   **MS** [304; 296]: "half light"; **TS** [238; 23], **UK** [232], and asp: "half lights"; perpetuated
        mistranscription; **ED**: follow **MS** for clearer sense.

130   **MS** [305; 299] and **TS** [238; 23]: "tender"; **UK** [233] and asp: "tender,"; **ED**: follow **UK** punctuation.

130   **MS** [305; 299]: "driving *[me—to meet good people]* \me to meets—just good people/": [TS].

130   **MS** [306; 300]: "knew that"; **TS** [239; 24], **UK** [233], and asp: "knew"; perpetuated mistranscription; **ED**: restore "that".

131   **MS** [306; 300] and **TS** [240; 25]: "whether to put it that, in what"; **UK** [234] and asp: "whether to think that, in that"; **SPC**.

131   **MS** [307; 301]: "met \what appears to be/": [pencil].

131   **MS** [307; 301]: "with friends"; **TS** [241; 26], **UK** [235], and asp: "with some friends"; perpetuated mistranscription; **ED**: delete "some" since creates repetition with "some pretext".

131   **MS** [308; 302]: "religious *[whom she now avoided.]* who [. . .] at that time in *[India]* Madeira"; appears to be Ford's spontaneous composition on typewriter, re-structuring sentence and changing his mind about location of Colonel's wife.

131   **MS** [308; 302], **TS** [242; 27], **UK** [236], and asp: "visitor's"; **ED**: correct to "visitors' ".

132   **MS** [308; 302] and **TS** [242; 27]: "herself"; **UK** [236] and asp: "her"; **SPC**.

132   **MS** [308; 302]: "ffoulkes"; **TS** [242; 27], **UK** [236], and asp: "Ffoulkes"; perpetuated mistranscription (double "f" = capital letter); **ED**: restore **MS** reading.

132   **MS** [308; 302] and **TS** [242; 27]: "exactitude, pennies [. . .] sat up-right"; **UK** [236] and asp: "exactitude pennies [. . .] sat upright"; **ED**: follow **UK** punctuation.

132   **MS** [309; 303]: " 'Good morning',"; **TS** [243; 29]: " 'Good-morning,' "; **UK** [237] and asp: " 'Good day,' "; **SPC**.

132   **MS** [309; 303]: "some types *[to which sorrow, enduring and never holding up, gives a touch of]* \of beauty and even of *[youth]* *[made for youth]/* of beauty and even of youth": [TS]; surely Ford composing on typewriter; opening words of insertion "of beauty and even of" should also have been canceled.

133   **MS** [310; 304]: "laid there \the offer of/ her virtue \—/": [pencil].

134   **MS** [311; 305], **TS** [246; 31]. **UK** [240], and asp: "unmounted and"; **ED**: insert comma after "unmounted" to clarify fact that it was the young man, not Edward, who was "unmounted".

134   **MS** [312; 306]: "chance'."; **TS** [247; 32], **UK** [240], and asp: "chance.' "; **ED**: replace stop with question mark.

134   **MS** [313; 307]: "Leonora said"; **TS** [247; 32], **UK** [241], and asp: "said Leonora"; perpetuated mistranscription; **ED**: follow **UK**.

135   **MS** [314; 308] and **TS** [248; 33–249; 34]: "towards her [. . .] leave a lasting wheal" [. . .] left a lasting wheal"; **UK** [242] and asp: "toward her [. . .] left a lasting wheal"; **SPC** and ambivalent spelling (a wheal is more a sore than an injury); **ED**: correct "wheal" to "weal".

135   **MS** [314; 308] and **TS** [249; 34]: "the features of the"; **UK** [242] and asp: "the"; **SPC**.

135   **MS** [314; 308] and **TS** [249; 34]: "days. He was looking at the table:"; **UK** [242] and asp: "days (he was looking at the table):"; **ED**: follow **UK** punctuation.

135   **MS** [314; 308] and **TS** [249; 34]: no new para. after "dare you?' "; **UK** [242] and asp insert new para; **ED**: follow **UK**.

135   **MS** [314; 308]: "Saviour \help me!/": [pencil].

136   **MS** [315; 307 [sic]]: "*[But]* I don't just": [pencil]; **TS** [250; 35], **UK** [243], and asp: "I don't"; Perpetuated mistranscription; **ED**: follow **UK** since "just" is redundant.

136   **MS** [315; 307 [sic]]: "effects"; **TS** [250; 35], **UK** [243], and asp: "effect"; perpetuated mistranscription; **ED**: restore "s".

136   **MS** [315; 307 [sic]]: "times—it"; **UK** [243] and asp: "times. It"; **ED**: follow **MS** and **TS** punctuation.

136   **MS** [315; 307 [sic]]: "*[fort]* unfortunate; perhaps because": [TS]; **TS** [250; 35]: "unfortunate because"; **UK** [243] and asp: "unfortunate; because"; perpetuated mistranscription; **ED**: restore **MS** reading since repetition of "perhaps" concords better with "I leave it to you".

136   **MS** [316; 309]: "*[was]* \were/": [pencil]; **TS** [251; 36], **UK** [244], and asp: "was"; perpetuated mistranscription; **ED**: restore **MS** reading as grammatically accurate.

136   **MS** [316; 309]: "voice, *[when she remembered it,]*": [ink].

137   **MS** [317; 310]: "she *[went over a]* \upbraided him for/": [ink]. **TS** [252; 37] restores inadvertently canceled "a" after "over".

137   **MS** [317; 310] and **TS** [252; 37]: "wanted to. Just"; **UK** [245] and asp: "wanted to, just"; **ED**: restore **MS** and **TS** punctuation.

137   **MS** [317; 310] and **TS** [252; 37]: "said so much"; **UK** [245] and asp: "talked"; **SPC**.

137   **MS** [317; 310] and **TS** [252; 37]: "imagined"; **UK** [245] and asp: "thought"; **SPC**, presumably to avoid repetition.

137   **MS** [317; 310]: "breech"; **TS** [253; 38], **UK** [246], and asp: "breach"; **ED**: restore **MS** spelling as correct.

137   **MS** [318; 311] and **TS** [253; 38]: "his"; **UK** [246] and asp: "the"; **SPC.**
137   **MS** [318; 311]: "self-explanation. *[She went into Nancy's room.]*": [TS]; evidence of Ford's spontaneous composition, anticipating last sentence of next paragraph but inserting more detail of domestic topography first? Or eye-slip mistranscription of **MS** now lost?
137   **MS** [318; 311]: "onto that"; **TS** [253; 38], **UK** [246], and asp: "on to the"; perpetuated mistranscription; **ED:** follow **UK.**
138   **MS** [319; 302]: "her"; **TS** [254; 39], **UK** [247], and asp: "the"; perpetuated mistranscription; **ED:** follow **UK.**
138   **MS** [320; 303] and **TS** [255; 40]: "began again. 'To"; **UK** [248] and asp: "began, 'to"; **ED:** follow **MS** and **TS** punctuation. These short, "ungrammatical" sentences ("To save Edward") are consistently removed, indicating imposition of house style. See p. 137, 2nd entry above.
138   **MS** [320; 303]: "him.' *[That is why]*": [TS].
138   **MS** [320; 303]: "her *[ideas were those]* *[phrases were still]*/": [TS]; spontaneous composition again?
138   **MS** [320; 303]: "no good *[.]* \—my mother and I./' ": [pencil]; another correction shifting blame from Ashburnham?

CHAPTER III, PART IV

139   **MS** [322; 315] and **TS** [257; 42]: "THE SADDEST STORY | Part IV | III."; **UK** [250] and asp: "III".
139   **MS** [322; 315] and **TS** [257; 42]: "And several"; **UK** [250] and asp: "Several"; **SPC.**
139   **MS** [322; 315]: "Nancy *[did not even]* \hardly/ know": [pencil]; example of Ford's hasty correction of **MS**, leaving typist to alter "know" to "knew".
139   **MS** [322; 315]: "brought up, so carefully \and Roman Catholics do not practise divorce/": [pencil]; **TS** [257; 42]: "brought up, and Roman Catholics do not practice divorce"; **UK** [250] and asp: "brought up, and Roman Catholics do not practise divorce"; **UK** corrects "practice" but follows perpetuated mistranscription, losing "so carefully"; **ED:** restore lost phrase.
139   **MS** [323; 316] and **TS** [258; 43]: "drawing door"; **UK** [251] and asp: "drawing-room door"; **SPC:** example of Ford's hasty correction of **MS** and **TS**.
139   **MS** [323; 316] and **TS** [258; 43]: "her, nevertheless"; **UK** [251] and asp: "her, nevertheless,"; **ED:** follow **UK.**
140   **MS** [324; 317]: "\They were, no doubt [. . .] she knew./": [pencil, from top margin].
140   **MS** [324; 317]: "telling \someone/": [pencil].
140   **MS** [324; 317] and **TS** [259; 44]: "it"; **UK** [252] and asp: "they"; **SPC.**
140   **MS** [325; 318] and **TS** [260; 46 [sic]]: "God, in her heart, how he"; **UK** [253] and asp: "God how He"; **SPC.**
140   **MS** [325; 318]: "\If he could love someone else [. . .] did not love her. . . ./": [TS]. Clear evidence of Ford's spontaneous composition on typewriter or dictation to typist. He seems first to have typed: "This had occurred [. . .] mother.", continuing with next para.: "She let the matter rest [. . .]" etc., then stopped to introduce above insertion, developing end of previous para., then transposed initial sentence (probably later) with pencil correction, to follow insertion.
141   **MS** [325; 318]: "She" opens new para.; **TS** [260; 46 [sic]], **UK** [253], and asp: para. break lacking; perpetuated mistranscription; **ED:** restore para. break.
141   **MS** [325; 318]: "what, exactly, *[did divorce]* \it all/ mean\t/": [pencil].
141   **MS** [326; 319]: "flames"; **TS** [261; 47], **UK** [254], and asp: "flame"; perpetuated mistranscription; **ED:** restore "s".
141   **MS** [326; 319]: "screamed. *[And suddenly again she felt that someone else might love Edward. . . .]*": [pencil].
141   **MS** [326: 319]: "Protestants. . . .' "; **TS** [262; 48]: "Protestants . .' "; **UK** [254] and asp: "Protestants.' "; **ED:** restore **MS** suspension points.
142   **MS** [327; 320]: " 'Oh, God. . . .' *[Edwrad [sic] is the only man I like]*/": [TS].
142   **MS** [328; 321] and **TS** [263; 49]: "Ist September [. . .] 1st. October"; **UK** [256] and asp: "Ist of September [. . .] Ist of October"; **SPC.**
142   **MS** [328; 321]: "black *[hollows of]* shadow\s/": [pencil].
143   **MS** [329; 322] and **TS** [265; 51]: "Then"; **UK** [257] and asp: "Thus"; **SPC.**
143   **MS** [329; 322]:

> *[Wherewith young men and maids distressed*
> *And left of love are crowned*
> *And underneath thy cooling shade*
> *When weary of the light*

> *The love-lorn youth and [young] love-sick maid*
> *Come to weep out the night. . . .]:* [pencil].

With the exception of punctuation details and "love-lorn" for "love-spent", Ford's memory was accurate.

143   **MS** [330; 323] and **TS** [265; 51]: "unhappiness;"; **UK** [258] and asp: "unhappiness"; **ED:** follow **UK** punctuation.

144   **MS** [331; 324] and **TS** [266; 52]: "Committee—."; **UK** [259] and asp: "Committee."; **ED:** follow **UK** punctuation.

144   **MS** [331; 324]: "She never *[took wine again; she never]*": [pencil].

144   **MS** [331; 324] and **TS** [267; 53]: "hagiology—but"; **UK** [259] and asp: "hagiology. But"; **ED:** follow **MS** and **TS** punctuation.

144   **MS** [332; 325]: "\with Edward/": [TS]; "\to/": [pencil].

145   **MS** [332; 325] and **TS** [268; 54]: "daughter?'. . . ."; **UK** [260] and asp: "daughter?' "; **ED:** given that, when typing, Ford almost invariably places punctuation outside closing quotation marks, restore ellipses dots inside inverted comma.

145   **MS** [333; 326] and **TS** [269; 55]: "Sometimes—"; **UK** [261] and asp: "Sometimes,"; **ED:** follow **UK** punctuation.

145   **MS** [333; 326] and **TS** [269; 55]: "her—"; **UK** [261] and asp: "her,"; **ED:** follow **UK** punctuation.

145   **MS** [333; 326] and **TS** [269; 55]: "knew then that [sic] she had known for months—that for months she had longed, craved and prayed within herself—that Edward"; **UK** [261] and asp: "knew then with her conscious mind what she had known within herself for months—that Edward"; **SPC** removes Nancy's craving for Edward's love.

CHAPTER IV, PART IV

145   **MS** [334; [ ]] and **TS** [270; 56]: "THE SADDEST STORY | PART IV | IV."; **UK** [262] and asp: "IV".

146   **MS** [335; 328] and **TS** [271; 57]: "for"; **UK** [262] and asp: "at"; **SPC,** presumably to avoid repetition: "For, for".

146   **MS** [335; 328] and **TS** [271; 57]: "loudly:"; **UK** [262] and asp: "loudly,"; **ED:** follow **UK** punctuation.

146   **MS** [335; 328]: "The \half opened/ door opened noiselessly \to the full/": [pencil].

147   **MS** [336; 329]: "the *[address]* number": [TS]; evidence of Ford's spontaneous composition on typewriter, or dictation to typist.

147   **MS** [336; 329]: "Glasgow . . . Ten minutes . . At"; **TS** [273; 59]: "Glasgow. . . . Ten minutes . . . At"; **UK** [264] and asp: "Glasgow . . . ten minutes . . . at"; **ED:** restore **MS** and **TS** "Ten" and "At" and adjust ellipses dots to standard four at end of sentences.

147   **MS** [337; 330] and **TS** [273; 59]: "everybody. Except me. Excepting me!' "; **UK** [265] and asp: "everybody except me—excepting me!' "; **ED:** restore **MS** and **TS** punctuation.

147   **MS** [337; 330]: "gentle *[low]* \slow/": [pencil].

147   **MS** [337; 330] and **TS** [273; 59]: "dark"; **UK** [265] and asp: "darkness"; **SPC.**

148   **MS** [337; 330]: the two sentences of speech ending "[. . .] wish it" were typed (by Ford or amanuensis) in reverse order; pencil transposition.

148   **MS** [338; 331] and **TS** [275; 61]: "And next"; **UK** [266]: "Next"; **SPC.**

CHAPTER V, PART IV

148   **MS** [340; [ ]] and **TS** [276; 62]: "THE SADDEST STORY | PART IV | V."; **UK** and asp: "V".

149   **MS** [341; 334] and **TS** [277; 63]: "my heaven; because there is only Hell. . . ."; **UK** [269] and asp: "my Heaven; because there is only Hell"; **ED:** restore "heaven" since **MS** and **TS** distinguish between a temporal "heaven" and a metaphysical "Hell".

149   **MS** [341; 334] and **TS** [277; 63]: "distinctly '*Credo*"; **UK** [269] and asp: "distinctly: '*Credo*"; **ED:** follow **UK** punctuation.

149   **MS** [341; 334] and **TS** [277; 63]: "omnipotent deity"; **UK** [269] and asp: "Omnipotent Deity"; **ED:** restore **MS** and **TS** reading as it is always thus hereafter in **MS** (corrected by Ford), and standardize.

149   **MS** [341; 334]: "nurse"; **TS** [278; 64]: "purse"; **UK** [269] and asp: "purser"; perpetuated mistranscription; **ED:** restore "nurse" as only state authenticated by Ford (his typing).

149   **MS** [342; 335–75; 368]: "for the quiescent patient" opens final holograph section, in RA's hand. Top margin contains cancellations: "*[This is the]* p. *[336]* | *[This is the]* 335". AMS continues seamlessly from Ford's TS in **MS,** and pagination is consecutive, suggesting that there was more of RA's AMS, now lost, probably revised by Ford from beginning of Part IV, Chapter V. The canceled words might have been the original opening of Chapter V, now "It is this".

149   **MS** [342; 335] and **TS** [278; 64]: "been in"; **UK** [270] and asp: "been"; **SPC**.

150   **MS** [342; 335] and **TS** [278; 64]: "Army"; **UK** [270] and asp: "army"; **ED**: restore "Army".

150   **MS** [342; 335] and **TS** [278; 64]: "paper,"; **UK** [270] and asp: "paper"; **ED**: follow **UK** punctuation.

150   **MS** [343; 336]: "herself. She was well trained."; **TS** [279; 65], **UK** [270], and asp: "herself."; perpetuated mistranscription (eye-slip); **ED**: restore "She [. . .] trained."

150   **MS** [343; 336]: "doctors"; **TS** [279; 65], **UK** [270], and asp: "doctor"; perpetuated mistranscription; **ED** restore 's'.

150   **MS** [343; 336] and **TS** [279; 65]: "Colonel"; **UK** [271] and asp: "colonel"; **ED**: restore "Colonel".

151   **MS** [345; 338] and **TS** [280; 66]: "who had married Rodney [. . .] and had gone"; **UK** [272] and asp: "who married Rodney [. . .] and went"; **SPC**.

152   **MS** [348; 341] and **TS** [283; 69]: "steam-rollered"; **UK** [274] and asp: "steam-rolled"; **ED**: possible **SPC** but restore **MS** and **TS** reading as more forceful and precise.

152   **MS** [350; 343]: "talking, talking; talking;"; **TS** [284; 70], **UK** [275], and asp: "talking; talking"; perpetuated mistranscription (eye-slip); **ED**: restore "talking,".

153   **MS** [351; 344]: "all for self-sacrifice; at the next she was all for revenge."; **TS** [285; 71], **UK** [276], and asp: "all for revenge"; perpetuated mistranscription (eye-slip); **ED**: restore lost phrase.

153   **MS** [352; 345], **TS** [285; 71], **UK** [277], and asp: "heard that Leonora"; **ED**: insert comma after "that" to clarify sense.

153   **MS** [352; 345]: "continued to *[say]* \tell the girl/ that *[the girl]* \she/": [pencil].

153   **MS** [353; 348]: "monstrously"; **TS** [286; 72]: "monstrous,"; **UK** [277] and asp: "monstrously".

154   **MS** [355; 348]: "he said. *[I have never asked you to love me.]* Go": [pencil].

154   **MS** [355; 348]: "those two \women/": [pencil].

CHAPTER VI, PART IV

154   **MS** [356; 349]: "*[Chapter 5]* | V [sic]": [ink, RA]; **TS** [289; 75]: "THE SADDEST STORY | PART IV | V [sic]"; **UK** [280] and asp: "VI".

155   **MS** [356; 349]: "habits. She pointed out *[over]* more than a dozen good reasons why the girl should not love him.": [ink, RA]; **TS** [289; 75], **UK** [280], and asp: "habits."; perpetuated mistranscription (eye-slip); **ED**: restore lost sentence.

155   **MS** [356; 349]: "Maidan \& of Florence/.": [pencil].

155   **MS** [357; 281]: "*[solidarity]* \instinct/": [pencil].

155   **MS** [357; 350]: "interests"; **TS** [290; 76], **UK** [281], and asp: "interest"; perpetuated mistranscription; **ED**: restore "s".

155   **MS** [357; 350]: "time. \But I am certain that/ *[I]*\i/f she thinks'": [pencil]; **TS** [290; 76]: "time. But I am certain that if she thinks"; **UK** [281] and asp: "time. I am certain that if she thinks"; **SPC**.

156   **MS** [359; 352]: "thought that"; **TS** [292; 78], **UK** [282], and asp: "thought"; perpetuated mistranscription; **ED**: restore "that".

156   **MS** [361; 354]: "(drop a line)" after "house-party" [ink, RA]; **TS** [293; 79] obeys instruction but **UK** [283] and asp lose white line break at bottom of page; **ED**: restore white line break.

157   **MS** [362; 355]: "Philadelphia \or Timbuctoo/": [pencil]; **ED**: modernize spelling.

157   **MS** [363; 356]: "*[nervous]* \angry/": [pencil]; correction allows Dowell a little more courage.

158   **MS** [364; 357]: "Other"; **TS** [296; 82], **UK** [286], and asp: "other"; perpetuated mistranscription; **ED**: follow **MS**.

159   **MS** [367; 360]: "scene. *[The girl put her hand out of the [hand] \window/ to shake mine.]*": [pencil].

159   **MS** [368; 361]: "\It was like his sentimentality to quote Swinburne./": [pencil].

159   **MS** [368; 361]: "getting off the *[girl]* \gardener's daughter/": [pencil].

160   **MS** [368; 361]: "(drop one line)" after "weather"; **TS**: white line lost at bottom of page; **UK** [289] and asp: no white line; **ED**; restore white line break.

160   **MS** [369; 362]: "*[heavy]* [?]] \happy/": [pencil].

160   **MS** [370; 363]: " 'Shuttlecock\s/.' [. . .] the word 'shuttlecock \s/' ": [pencil].

160   **MS** [370; 363] and **TS** [301; 87]: para. break after "picture"; **UK** [291] and asp: para. break lacking; **ED**: restore.

161   **MS** [372; 365]: " 'shuttlecock\s/' ": [pencil]; see p. 160, 3rd entry above.

161   **MS** [373; 366]: "I" underlined pencil; **TS** [303; 89], **UK** [293], and asp: no italics; perpetuated mistranscription; **ED**: restore italic "I".

161   **MS** [373; 366] "/The child is to be brought up as a Romanist\": [pencil]. Beneath this a

short line is added in pencil, appears in **TS** [303; 89] but is lacking in **UK** [292] and asp; **ED**: restore.

162   **MS** [373; 366]: "numbers"; **TS** [304; 90]: "members"; **UK** [293] and asp: "numbers"; **SPC**.

162   **MS** [374; 367] and **TS** [304; 90–305; 91]: "Heaven and he remarked: | 'Girl, I will wait for you there.' "; **UK** [293] and asp: "Heaven, and whispered something that I did not catch."; **SPC**.

162   **MS** [374; 367]: no para. break after "hinder him?"; **TS** [305; 91] introduces one probably because "I didn't think" begins new **MS** page [375; 368]; **UK** [294] and asp replicate **TS** mistranscription; **ED**: cancel para. break.

162   **MS** [375; 368]: "you, ⁀for I also am a sentimentalist. *[,b]* \B/ut": [pencil].

CONTEMPORARY
REVIEWS

The New York Times Book Review [U.S.] †

They were presumably "good people," the five who are the important characters in this book. Well-born and well-bred, they all of them presented to the world the appearance of living perfectly tranquil, conventional lives. Yet in reality those lives were "broken, tumultuous, agonized, and unromantic"—all save one—and out of the five two committed suicide and another went insane. No wonder that John Dowell, who is himself one of the five and the narrator, calls this "the saddest story I have ever heard." For it was all so futile, so unnecessary. Only Florence was really evil, and she was vulgar and vain and silly, "a personality of paper," whose inherent falseness ought to have been far from difficult to discern. And on the surface everything went quite smoothly during the nine years' friendship of the Dowells and Ashburnhams. So smoothly, indeed, that John Dowell suspected nothing until the coming of "the girl," Nancy Rufford, proved a match put to powder.

It all began, however, some years before the first meeting of the quartet, with the marriage of Leonora Powys and Edward Ashburnham—"two noble people" who had the worst possible effect on each other. They had scarcely a taste or a point of view in common; Edward was a Protestant, his wife a Roman Catholic; his ideas were collective, hers entirely individualistic; he had the feudal theory of doing his best for his tenants while they did their best for him, and to Leonora the result seemed mere wanton extravagance. The duties, the generosities he believed in she regarded as just so much folly. And meanwhile she did her very best from her own standpoint, was patient and loyal and long-suffering, efficient, practical, economical, entirely virtuous. Then when the natural result of such mismating came, bringing financial disaster in its train, she ruled him with a rod of iron and wholly admirable intentions.

It was he who committed the overt acts of wrong-doing, and her greatest wish was that he should return to her: "She saw life as a perpetual sex-battle between husbands who desire to be unfaithful to their wives, and wives who desire to recapture their husbands in the end . . . the idea of a pure and constant love succeeding the sound of wedding bells had never been much presented to her." Moreover, she was in love with her husband, and he had never at any time been really in love with her. But they had the reputation of being a model couple, when Dowell first met them at Nauhreim, and a model couple he believed them to be during the nine years' intimacy which ensued—until the girl came and the long silence was broken.

The story is related in an odd, rambling sort of way, going forward, then back again almost to the starting point in order that the events

† 7 March 1915: 86.

already told may be recounted from another point of view. For the author's main concern is with the psychology of his characters, "the passionate, the headstrong, and the too truthful" pair who were outside the normal, the eternally play-acting Florence, and the "perfectly normal, virtuous, and slightly deceitful heroine," Leonora, and he certainly succeeds in presenting them well and vividly. The reader's sympathies, like the narrator's, fluctuate more or less throughout, for these are real people, and so no one of them, save perhaps Florence, is ever wholly in the wrong or wholly in the right. And when the final tragedy is in plain view, with its inevitable extinction of the man who was too much of a sentimentalist and the girl who had a "touch of madness," no more than the narrator can the reader answer the question: "What should these people have done?" What they did do resulted in horror for two of them, and for the third, after an interval, "a quiet, comfortable, good time."

In spite of the repetitions which are unavoidable in a novel constructed as Mr. Hueffer has chosen to construct this one, the interest is well sustained. From the very beginning one knows that there is darkness and terror, but only little by little are the full depths of the tragedy revealed. The book has artistry, force, and truthfulness; it carries conviction, and it shows an unusual power of psychological analysis. One gets, too, the effect of an almost unendurable strain, of a tension which must break, sooner or later, while the nightmare quality of those final scenes stamps them deep in one's imagination. *The Good Soldier* is a novel which extorts admiration.

Boston Transcript [U.S.] †

This novel tells the story of one Mr. McDowell [sic], an American * * * He tells his story of aggrieved perplexity, not once, but many times, starting now from the ending, now from the beginning, now from the middle of events. He says thoughts crowd upon him. He certainly produces the effect of distracted chaos, and he maintains consistently the attitude of the stupid man, mild and small-minded, but with too little spirit for ill-will. He gives, too, an air of truth to his story, and the novel may be correctly called "realistic"—with all the limitations of the term.

This realism and consistency are the sole virtues of the story. The portrayal of marital infidelity is dangerous enough even when delicately handled, and for the written page to linger upon the indecencies of intrigue—details to be expected from the reeking tongue of an alley-gossip—there is no excuse whatever. For all the author's clever manipu-

† 17 March 1915: 24.

lation of words, he has given his story nothing to compensate for its artistic feebleness or to clear its distorted, sex-morbid atmosphere.

Independent [U.S.] †

An unpleasant imagination and not much thought are the prerequisites of such stuff as Ford Madox Hueffer's new book contains. If his conception of *The Good Soldier* be a true one, open-faced, honest evil is a much less dangerous companion. The semblance of a plot carelessly flung together is swamped by tawdry detail that finds a ready, frank narrator in an American millionaire of exaggerated density.

Times Literary Supplement [U.K.] ‡

The story of two unsuccessful marriages related by one of the husbands. One of them closes through the suicide of the wife, a shallow flirt; the other by the suicide of the husband and the madness of the girl he had made love to. Mr. Hueffer—or rather Dowell, the husband who did not commit suicide—describes the whole as "the saddest story I have ever heard." It is sad enough, certainly, so far as its facts go; but the sadness is not conveyed by Mr. Hueffer. His avowed method is to tell it all as if he were on one side of the fireplace of a country cottage and a listener opposite him. He allows for the process "a fortnight or so." But frankly Mr. Hueffer is so terribly long-winded and prosy that it is impossible to conceive the listener lasting out a fortnight or anything like it. The longing to go and do something else would be too strong for him long before the tale was well afoot; and we are afraid most readers will share his feeling.

Observer [U.K.] *

Easy writing, according to Byron, "makes d——d hard reading." Yet the illusion of consummately easy writing, in this discursive book, *The Good Soldier*, makes reading so absorbing that one has the puerile itch to look at the end. The infinitely artistic development of events, their slow growth and inevitability, the turning inside out of character to show amazing linings, have no hint of tediousness for those who can rejoice in every pen-touch of our artist's work, while the sheer interest of the

† 81 (22 March 1915): 432.
‡ 25 March 1915: 103.
* 28 March 1915: 5.

drama should hold him or her who reads to be amused in the crudest sense. There is a subtle but profound immorality, to the bigoted mind, in the sympathetic treatment of the (married) man of many loves. That he should be distinguished in the title as *par excellence* the good soldier is perhaps a pity. It looks like a desire to catch that public that does not want to hear of any other kind of excellence but military excellence. Edward is a good soldier, a good landlord, and many other decent things. In this study of him it is not these that matter, though they help enormously to keep him in right proportion before those who judge him. He is the sentimental amorist, a disastrous mixture of sheer innocence and utter want of self-control. Such a man wreaks far more tragedy than the cold-blooded libertine. His Catholic wife, the girl (poor child!), and the other couple, one of whom narrates the story, all are marvellous figures; but Edward is the gem. It is "the saddest story" (the title originally given to it) just because of the utter futility of it all, the tragic waste; and there are not three people in England who could have told it, or two who could have told it just that way.

REBECCA WEST

Daily News and Leader [U.K.] †

Mr. Ford Madox Hueffer is the Scholar Gipsy of English letters: he is the author who is recognised only as he disappears round the corner. It is impossible for anybody with any kind of sense about writing to miss some sort of distant apprehension of the magnificence of his work: but unfortunately this apprehension usually takes the form of enthusiastic but belated discoveries of work that he left on the doorstep ten years ago.

The Good Soldier will put an end to any such sequestration of Mr. Hueffer's wealth. For it is as impossible to miss the light of its extreme beauty and wisdom as it would be to miss the full moon on a clear night. Its first claim on the attention is the obvious loveliness of the colour and cadence of its language: and it is also clever as the novels of Mr. Henry James are clever, with all sorts of acute discoveries about human nature, and at times it is radiantly witty. And behind these things there is the delight of a noble and ambitious design, and behind that, again, there is the thing we call inspiration—a force of passion which so sustains the story in its flight that never once does it appear as the work of a man's invention. It is because of that union of inspiration and the finest technique that this story, this close and relentless recital of how the good

† Rebecca West, "Mr. Hueffer's New Novel," *Daily News and Leader*, 2 April 1915: 6. Reprinted with the permission of the Peters, Fraser & Dunlop Group, Ltd. West (1892–1983) was a feminist novelist, biographer, travel writer, critic, and friend of Ford and Violet Hunt.

soldier struggled from the mere clean innocence which was the most his class could expect of him to the knowledge of love, can bear up under the vastness of its subject. For the subject is, one realises when one has come to the end of this saddest story, much vaster than one had imagined that any story about well-bred people, who live in sunny houses, with deer in the park, and play polo, and go to Nauheim for the cure, could possibly contain.

It is the record of the spiritual life of Edward Ashburnham, who was a large, fair person of the governing class, with an entirely deceptive appearance of being just the kind of person he looked. It was his misfortune that he had brought to the business of landowning a fatal touch of imagination which made him believe it his duty to be "an overlord doing his best by his dependents, the dependents meanwhile doing their best by the overlord"; to make life splendid and noble and easier for everybody by his government. And since this ideal meant that he became in his way a creative artist, he began to feel the desire to go to some woman for "moral support, the encouragement, the relief from the sense of loneliness, the assurance of his own worth." And although Leonora, his wife, was fine and proud, a Northern light among women, she simply could not understand that marriage meant anything but an appearance of loyalty before the world and the efficient management of one's husband's estate. She "had a vague sort of idea that, to a man, all women are the same after three weeks of close intercourse. She thought that the kindness should no longer appeal, the soft and mournful voice no longer thrill, the tall darkness no longer give a man the illusion that he was going into the depths of an unexplored wood." And so poor Edward walked the world starved.

His starvation leads him into any number of gentle, innocent, sentimental passions: it delivers him over as the prey of a terrible and wholly credible American, a cold and controlled egoist who reads like the real truth about an Anne Douglas Sedgwick or Edith Wharton heroine.[1] And meanwhile his wife becomes so embittered by what she considers as an insane, and possibly rather nasty, obsession, that she loses her pride and her nobility and becomes, in that last hour when Edward has found a real passion, so darkly, subtly treacherous that he and the quite innocent young girl whom he loves are precipitated down into the blackest tragedy. All three are lost: and perhaps Leonora, robbed of her fineness, is most lost of all.

And when one has come to the end of this beautiful and moving story it is worth while reading the book over again simply to observe the won-

1. Edith Wharton (1862–1937), American novelist, short-story writer, and poet whose novels criticize old New York society (*The House of Mirth* [1905]) and the institution of marriage (*Ethan Frome* [1911]). Anne Douglas Sedgwick (1873–1935), American novelist and short-story writer best known for *The Little French Girl* (1924); her work often explores disastrous marriages.

ders of its technique. Mr. Hueffer has used the device, invented and used successfully by Mr. Henry James, and used not nearly so credibly by Mr. Conrad, of presenting the story not as it appeared to a divine and omnipresent intelligence, but as it was observed by some intervener not too intimately concerned in the plot. It is a device that always breaks down at the great moment, when the revelatory detail must be given; but it has the great advantage of setting the tone of the prose from the beginning to the end. And out of the leisured colloquialism of the gentle American who tells the story Mr. Hueffer has made a prose that falls on the page like sunlight. It has the supreme triumph of art, that effect of effortlessness and inevitableness, which Mengs[2] described when he said that one of Velazquez's pictures seemed to be painted not by the hand but by pure thought. Indeed, this is a much, much better book than any of us deserve.

Morning Post [U.K.] †

Mr. Hueffer's story is a challenge, like his way of telling it. Edward Ashburnham, the "good soldier" of the provocative title, is one of a quartette of people with sufficient money and leisure to cultivate mischief, and if need be a "heart." The * * * only characters besides these four who effectively intervene in their story are victims or accomplices of Captain Ashburnham's infidelities; for this good soldier and exemplary landowner is a sentimentalist, impelled to make a mistress of every woman he, so to say, "mothers." The exceptions are Mr. Bagshawe, who makes a single dramatic entry, a young man called Jimmy, who never appears at all, and "the girl" Nancy Rufford, whose role, on reflection, may be either accomplice or victim.

It is the American Mr. Dowell who tells their story, and he does so, as he explains more than once, after the manner of one in a country cottage with a silent and sympathetic soul for listener, days of time on his hands, and no reason to brush aside the distractions of the wind and the sea. He lingers over it with immense satisfaction, hops on to its close (about 1913), toddles back to its beginning (*circa* 1904), and, despite a profession of being tired, is still on the last page with the greatest gusto picking and fingering at the threads of the intervening years. And the story, when all is said and done, is just this: that for many of these years, during which these people have been meeting and living together in apparently the most easy yet correct amity at Continental resorts, Florrie Dowell—despite her "heart"—has been Edward Ashburnham's mistress, and previously to that and to her marriage was the mistress of the young

2. Anton Raffael Mengs (1728–1779), German painter and leading exponent of European Neo-Classicism; he formulated a treatise on "Beauty" in 1762.
† 5 April 1915: 2.

man Jimmy, as revealed at last in Mr. Bagshawe's one dramatic appearance to the unsuspecting, sedulous, strained nurse of a husband, who here relates her shame. "A tale of passion" Mr. Hueffer calls it, but there is no more passion in it than in an entomologist's enthusiasm over his drawer of pinned and varnished beetles. The characters are specimens, their story is a "case," before ever Mr. Dowell gets settled down in his chair, to his leisurely analysis of them and it. Our exposition of Mr. Hueffer's novel is quite fair in respect of the readers to whom, in essence and manner, it will be simply detestable. It will have no indifferent readers. To the residue, let us add, the comic situation it imagines, and the slight mockery with which the narrator hedges on the solemn seriousness of his analysis of it, will afford immense entertainment. That is why we say that *The Good Soldier* is a challenge, in matter and method alike.

Athenæum [U.K.] †

Mr. Hueffer's book is unpleasant—about that there cannot be two opinions. For the two men he describes we can feel neither sympathy nor admiration. The one is that worst kind of hypocrite, a rake impregnated with lachrymose sensibility; the other would be the worst type of "complacent" husband, were it not for short-sightedness that even George Dandin[1] would scorn to plead. His wife is even worse—dissolute with open eyes, yet assuming conscientious motives for her worst acts. The wife of the rake is, to a certain degree, tolerable; she is at least upright, led astray by a conception of her religion which persuades her to condone her husband's ill-doing with the idea, so far as one can make out, that his possible redemption to fidelity is better than the publicity and punishment he really merited. Of her the author says:

> Perhaps Leonora was right; perhaps Roman Catholics, with their queer, shifty ways, are always right. They are dealing with that queer, shifty thing that is human nature.

At any rate, Mr. Hueffer exculpates no one; he presents his case impartially as a "real story," pleading, moreover, this reality as the reason for his discursive way of telling it. Here—from an academic point of view—he has some justification; he does achieve a certain sinister realism, at least in his characterization; the people and the scenes in which they move are thoroughly lifelike. But then Mr. Hueffer has the professional touch; he can express himself effectively, in description or epigram; also he can see certain things clearly. His book would have had distinct claims to great value had he only chosen a less sordid theme.

† 10 April 1915: 334.
1. The eponymous hero of Molière's *George Dandin ou le Mari Complaisant* (1668): a cuckold.

Outlook [U.K.] †

This novel, despite its faults, and they are many and glaring, is amazingly well written. Its plot is most unsavoury, and consequently the mere fact that, in spite of constant annoyance and even disgust, one is able to enjoy the rich humour of its unravelling, and the fine flavour of its author's style demonstrates the cunning[1] of its intricate workmanship. The method which Mr. Hueffer has here employed is akin to, though very different from, the method which Mr. Henry James employs in his analytic studies of poor humanity. But whereas Mr. James concerns himself with the minds and motives of his characters, Mr. Hueffer is concerned with their actions, deducing their psychology from what they do rather than from what they think. Necessarily the result is cruder, for situations which, dealt with in the former method, would merely astonish, dealt with in the latter are apt to revolt us. It has been said that the plot is unsavoury, and that is to put it mildly, but Mr. Hueffer has the artist's right to choose his subject, and so long as he deals with it sincerely, much as his choice may be regretted, it is capable of justification. It is essential, however, no matter how great an artist a novelist may be, that he should assure himself and be able to convince his readers that he has got his characters right, and that their behaviour, no matter how objectionable, should be natural to them in the circumstances in which they are placed. The more objectionably they behave the more necessary is it to know that their conduct is the inevitable result of their environment reacting on their character. Here Mr. Hueffer has failed, and failed badly, with the result that he has libelled at least three, and perhaps four, very distinct types of humanity. * * * It is not a nice story, but, worse still, it is not a true story. It might be true of a quintette of déclassées cosmopolitans, but it is not true of the persons whom Mr. Hueffer has chosen for the protagonists of his drama. Captain Ashburnham, for instance, is described to us as a typical specimen of the best kind of Englishman, an officer and a gentleman, a good landlord, a staunch friend. It is therefore inconceivable that he should have behaved as in close on three hundred pages of brilliant writing Mr. Hueffer tells us he did behave. The American girl and wife is also typically American, semi-cultured, illusively charming, and obviously sexless. And she behaves like a drab![2] Leonora Ashburnham, the Irish Catholic, is more difficult to place, but that the vile complaisance with

---

† 17 April 1915: 507–8.

1. Use of this word is possibly sly racism. On the same page a book attacking Germany's "cunning subterranean methods" of controlling the Belgian economy in preparation for invasion was favorably reviewed. The "Catholic party in the Belgian Parliament" is seen to be largely responsible for allowing this. Readers who knew Ford (a Catholic of German extraction who had already fallen under suspicion of being a spy) would surely have made the connection, which implies under the guise of praise that Ford's style was of a piece with other German trickery.

2. Slattern, whore.

which Mr. Hueffer credits her is anything but a libel on her class and her religion there can be little doubt. As for the American husband, Mr. Hueffer may have him, though such guileless innocence, even in a native of Philadelphia, Pa., takes some assimilating. The girl Nancy is just a girl, and her madness is at any rate more sane than the sanity of her companions. It must not be supposed that the characters ring falsely as one reads the book—Mr. Hueffer is too great a master of words for that—it is only on reflection that their essential incongruity becomes apparent. Nevertheless the novel may be enjoyed as an essay in style, even after it is recognised that as an essay in characterisation it is one long blunder.

C. E. LAWRENCE

Daily Chronicle [U.K.]†

If the fortune of a novel were commensurate with its art, then would Mr. Hueffer's *The Good Soldier* march away with bags of shekels, whereas its very cleverness and subtlety will probably undo it, and cause it to be less popular than Sir Gilbert Parker's easier effort.[1]

Both the books tell tales of marriage tangles, and Mr. Hueffer's tangle is so involved that many readers will probably think it not worth the unravelling. Any such decision would, however, be an unfairness and unwise, for, with all its unpleasantness, it is as cleverly told a story as has been printed for months. The effectiveness of the book is in the telling, with its suggestions, its implications, and the light and airy, cold and passionless manner in which a deadly story is unfolded. The design of the book is bold. Two couples stay regularly year after year at a Swiss[2] sanatorium, and the husband of the one happy pair makes free with the wife of the other. It is the cuckold—to use an old, expressive word which false shamefacedness should not be permitted to suppress—who tells the so-called sad story in a cold-blooded manner reminiscent of the ways and works of the Borgias, the Medici,[3] and other such magnificent wrong-doers, who could kiss and slay, smile and at the same time poison. Put down into plain print, the results are preposterous. Of the five persons most concerned, two commit suicide and one goes incurably

† C. E. Lawrence, "Passion and People: The Old Story in New Settings," *Daily Chronicle*, 28 April 1915: 4.
1. Parker's *You Never Know Your Luck: Being the Story of a Matrimonial Deserter* (London: Hodder, 1915) was reviewed alongside *The Good Soldier*.
2. Not Swiss but German.
3. Medieval and Renaissance dynasty, dukes of Forence and, later, Tuscany; under Cosimo III, the government of Tuscany degenerated into corruption and despotism. "Borgias": Lucrezia Borgia (1480–1519), mythologized (probably unfairly) as leading figure in family of prisoners and plotters by Victor Hugo and Donizetti.

mad. As horrible as a pre-Shakespearean Elizabethan tragedy; and yet
so deftly and artfully is the tale narrated that we read of these deaths and
misadventures as if they were the misfortunes of mice and rabbits. *The
Good Soldier* is an ill-named, clever book, but we should have admired
it more had Mr. Hueffer put a little more force and energy into its
smooth passages.

Nation [U.S.] †

Not a war-story, but a tale of modern loves, told with skill and ingenu-
ity and, on the whole, unreality. Mr. Hueffer has collaborated, more
than once, with Joseph Conrad,[1] and would seem to have absorbed
something of his method if not of his manner. Here is a story told in
disjointed, cumulative fashion, by a participant in the action who has
been even more an observer of it. The action, with episodes of physical
intensity, is chiefly mental or "psychical." The episodes themselves,
after being worked up with care, are not exploited for their own sake,
but disposed of with a kind of negligence; they are simply visible phases
of the volcanic forces always at work beneath the smooth and landscaped
surface of a half-dozen lives. The story-teller is an American million-
aire-absentee. He has married a pretty girl of loose morals who has for
years reduced him to the rôle of nurse by pretending to be an invalid,
and is easily able to deceive him in other ways. At the baths of Nauheim
they meet an English pair named Ashburnham. The man is a captain,
in his thirties, home on sick-leave from India. As with Florence, the
American's wife, his illness is a fraud; he has really left India in pursuit
of a woman. His own wife, Leonora, is beautiful and loves him, but she
has no physical attraction for him, and he has had a series of mistresses
before the story proper begins. Florence is to be his last "affair," as he is
to be hers, though by his will rather than by his inclination. She poisons
herself when she finds that she has lost him; he cuts his throat because
he cannot allow himself to take her successor, a young girl to whom he
has been in a relation almost fatherly. It is here, at this forlorn last ditch,
that he proves himself "the good soldier." Leonora marries again. The
young girl for whom Ashburnham has died goes mad and becomes a
new patient for the nursing millionaire, whom we leave maundering
rather piteously about the whole matter, "the saddest story he has ever
heard." To feel it that, one must take the people seriously, find them
real and breathing. And here is the prime distinction between Mr. Hueffer and Mr. Conrad. The dream-like, musing atmosphere of this story

---

† 100 (29 April 1915): 470–71.
1. On *The Inheritors* (1901) and *Romance* (1903). Later, they co-wrote *The Nature of a Crime*
(1924). Ford may also have been responsible for part of *Nostromo* (1904) and of Conrad's
unsuccessful play *One Day More* (first produced 1905; published 1917). See Judd, *Ford Madox
Ford* 79.

is not unlike that of *Chance*,[2] for example. Its undercurrent of fierce emotional experience is a characteristic of Conrad's narratives. But somehow the whole thing fails to focus. We do not quite believe in these people and their affairs—or our belief in them seems a matter of scant importance. It is a book to be read with curiosity and with appreciation of its skilfulness as a "stunt," rather than as a true human document or a sound piece of fiction.

THOMAS SECCOMBE

New Witness [U.K.] †

This is a novel remarkable alike for its misappropriation of such a title as *The Good Soldier*, its style and its subject-matter or fable. Its style is its most outstanding feature. The story goes along like the wild Whitsun dance of Vianden, four steps forwards and then three back. It is projected along by means of the most curiously colloquial nudges, puffs, shuffles and short rushes. The peculiarity of the style is a studied *negligé*.[1] The author commences rather more consecutive sentences with "and" than has ever been known before. His sentences are dwarfish in length, and sometimes in malignity. He commences again and again with the colloquial "yes" or "well" and ends them with "and all that." Mr. Wells, the George Moore of *Vale* and *Salve*,[2] Henry James, have gone before. Mr. Hueffer combines their manner of hinting and winking with a prodigious nonchalance of his own. But he exaggerates the physical side of life out of all proportion. People have waves of it, but good soldiers soon escape the fumes and do not descend so readily to the inferno of caddishness. Florence is cleverly drawn, very. Laura [presumably, Leonora] is a precious fiend. The diablerie might have occurred once, but people could hardly have gone on like that. People in ordinary life manage to forget their disqualifications for a sane existence. To be always harping on them admits a false quantity into a book otherwise penetrating, in many respects original and excessively clever. The dot and dash system justifies itself. Each paragraph ending with a demonstrative. "Well—it was a silly old tune." "She did not believe him." "Those were his simple words. . . ." "That was the way it took her." "Poor devil." "I don't know why." "No, she wouldn't have minded." "Of course." "Perhaps she did." "Well, that was a sort of frenzy with

---

2. *Chance* (1913) was Conrad's first popular success.

† Thomas Seccombe, "The Good Soldier," *New Witness*, 3 June 1915: 113–14. Seccombe was Professor of History, Royal Military Academy, Sandhurst, during World War I; popular London man of letters.

1. Casualness, but also suggesting slovenliness.

2. Moore's autobiography *Hail and Farewell: A Trilogy* (3 vols.: *Ave, Salve, Vale*, 1911–14).

me." "Anyhow, Leonora shivered a little as if a goose had walked over her grave. And I was passing her the nickel-silver basket of rolls. Avati! . . . .'[3] "And what the devil!" "What a beautiful thing the stone pine is!" "And then. . . ." "No, we never did go back anywhere. Not to Heidelberg, not to Hamelin, not to Verona, not to Mont Majour—not so much as to Carcassonne itself. We talked of it, of course, but I guess Florence got all she wanted out of one look at a place. She had the seeing eye." *Léger de main;*[4] Oscar Wilde! But the protagonist of all these eyelash quivers and *demi-sourires*[5] is, of course, Lawrence [sic] Sterne—creator, too, of *the* good soldier. Perhaps the best ever projected in print. "My Uncle."[6] True, he could not accept the necessity of the Treaty of Utrecht.[7] But a tenderer heart never beat under a British Warm.[8] "When we read over the siege of Troy, brother, which lasted ten years and eight months—though with such a train of artillery as we had at Namur the town might have been carried in a week—was I not as much concerned for the destruction of the Greeks and Trojans as any boy in the school?"; and "What is war? What is it, Yorick, when fought as ours has been, upon principles of *liberty* and upon principles of *honour*—what is it but the getting together of quiet and harmless people, with their swords in their hands, to keep the ambitious and the turbulent within bounds?" " 'And, for my part,' said my uncle, 'I could have done no more at Namur had my name been Alexander; I could have done no more than my duty.' 'Bless your honour!' cried Trim, advancing three steps as he spoke; 'does a man think of his Christian name when he goes to the attack?'—'Or when he's standing in the trench, Trim?' cried my uncle Toby, looking firm.—'Or when he enters a breach?' said Trim, pushing in between two chairs.—'Or forces the lines?' cried my uncle, rising up and pushing his crutch like a pike.—'Or facing a platoon?' cried Trim, presenting his stick like a firelock.—'Or when he marches up the glacis?' cried my uncle Toby, looking warm and setting his foot upon his stool. . . ." Here we have the good soldier. Surely the finest that lives in Fiction, and the usurpation of such a title by Mr. Hueffer's hero is nothing short of profanation. Had we known how to appreciate our soldiers as our best novelists have, Sterne, Scott, Meredith and Hardy, to wit, the cant of anti-militarism would never have caught us as it has.

---

3. Seccombe's patronizing air of easy learning is somewhat punctured by his following UK's error in Italian here. See MDATV, p. 199, 29, 1st entry above.
4. Sleight of hand (French).
5. Half-smiles (French).
6. Laurence Sterne (1713–1768), English clergyman and novelist whose Uncle Toby in *Tristram Shandy* (1760–67) is an old soldier, a loveable eccentric constantly reliving the battles of his youth.
7. A series of treaties (1713–15) that concluded the War of the Spanish Succession in which England had become embroiled after the accession of William of Orange; ended French expansion and signaled the rise of the British Empire.
8. British Warm Overcoat: soldier's coat.

THEODORE DREISER

New Republic [U.S.] †

* * * "I have, I am aware, told this story in a very rambling way, so that it may be difficult for any one to find their path through what may be a sort of maze. I cannot help it. I have stuck to my idea of being in a country cottage with a silent listener, hearing between the gust of the wind and amidst the noises of the distant sea, the story as it comes. And, when one discusses an affair—a long, sad affair—one goes back, one goes forward. One remembers points that one has forgotten, and one explains them all the more minutely since one recognizes that one has forgotten to mention them in their proper places, and that one may have given, by omitting them, a false impression. I console myself with thinking that this is a real story, and that, after all, real stories are best told in the way that a person telling a story would tell them. They will then seem most real."

Thus Mr. Hueffer in explanation of his style; a good explanation of a bad method.

In this story * * * the author makes Dowell, Florence's husband, the narrator, and it is he who dubs it the "saddest one." This is rather a large order when one thinks of all the sad stories that have been told of this mad old world. Nevertheless it is a sad story, and a splendid one from a psychological point of view; but Mr. Hueffer, in spite of the care he has bestowed upon it, has not made it splendid in the telling. In the main he has only suggested its splendor, quite as the paragraph above suggests, and for the reasons it suggests. One half suspects that since Mr. Hueffer shared with Mr. Conrad in the writing of *Romance*, the intricate weavings to and fro of that literary colorist have, to a certain extent, influenced him in the spoiling of this story. For it is spoiled to the extent that you are compelled to say, "Well, this is too bad. This is quite a wonderful thing, but it is not well done." Personally I would have suggested to Mr. Hueffer, if I might have, that he begin at the beginning, which is where Colonel Powys wishes to marry off his daughters—not at the beginning as some tertiary or quadrutiary character in the book sees it, since it really concerns Ashburnham and his wife. This is neither here nor there, however, a mere suggestion. A story may begin in many ways.

Of far more importance is it that, once begun, it should go forward in a more or less direct line, or at least that it should retain one's uninterrupted interest. This is not the case in this book. The interlacings, the

† Theodore Dreiser, "The Saddest Story," *New Republic* 3 (12 June 1915): 155–56. Reprinted with the permission of the *New Republic*. Dreiser (1871–1945) was an American novelist and short-story writer; author of *Sister Carrie* (1900), *Jennie Gerhardt* (1911), and *An American Tragedy* (1925), among others. Dreiser's socialist sympathies and predilection for naturalism are plain to see in his irritation with Ford's style and subject matter.

cross references, the re-re-references to all sorts of things which subsequently are told somewhere in full, irritate one to the point of one's laying down the book. As a matter of fact, except for the perception that will come to any man, that here is a real statement of fact picked up from somewhere and related by the author as best he could, I doubt whether even the lover of naturalism—entirely free of conventional prejudice—would go on.

As for those dreary minds who find life morally ordered and the universe murmurous of divine law—they would run from it as from the plague. For, with all its faults of telling, it is an honest story, and there is no blinking of the commonplaces of our existence which so many find immoral and make such a valiant effort to conceal. One of the most irritating difficulties of the tale is that Dowell, the American husband who tells the story, is described as, first, that amazingly tame thing, an Englishman's conception of an American husband; second, as a profound psychologist able to follow out to the last detail the morbid minutiae of this tragedy, and to philosophize on them as only a deeply thinking and observing man could; and lastly as one who is as blind as a bat, as dull as a mallet, and as weak as any sentimentalist ever. The combination proves a little trying before one is done with it.

This story has been called immoral. One can predict such a charge to-day in the case of any book, play, or picture which refuses to concern itself with the high-school ideal of what life should be. It is immoral apparently to do anything except dress well and talk platitudes. But it is interesting to find this English author (German by extraction, I believe) and presumably, from all accounts, in revolt against these sickening strictures, dotting his book with apologies for this, that, and another condition not in line with this high-school standard (albeit it is the wretched American who speaks) and actually smacking his lips over the stated order that damns his book. And worse yet, Dowell is no American. He is that literary pack-horse or scapegoat on whom the native Englishman loads all his contempt for Americans. And Captain and Mrs. Ashburnham, whom he so soulfully lauds for their love of English pretence and order, are two who would have promptly pitched his book out of doors, I can tell him. Yet he babbles of the fineness of their point of view. As a matter of fact their point of view is that same accursed thing which has been handed on to America as "good form," and which we are now asked to sustain by force of arms as representing civilization.

After all, I have no real quarrel with the English as such. It is against smug conventionalism wherever found, too dull to perceive the import of anything except money and social precedence, that I uncap my fountain pen. It is this condition which makes difficult—one might almost fear impossible at times—the production of any great work of art, be it picture, play, philosophy, or novel. It is the Leonoras, the Dowells, and the Nancys that make life safe, stale, and impossible. They represent that thickness of wit which prospers impossible religions, and moral codes, and causes the mob to look askance at those finer flowers of fancy which are all the world has to show for its power to think in the drift of circumstance. All the rest is formalism and parade, and "go thou and do likewise." We all, to such a horrible extent, go and do likewise.

But you may well suspect that there is a good story here and that it is well worth your reading. Both suppositions are true. In the hands of a better writer this jointure of events might well have articulated into one of the finest pictures in any language. Its facts are true, in the main. Its theme beautiful. It is tragic in the best sense that the Greeks knew tragedy, that tragedy for which there is no solution. But to achieve a high result in any book its component characters must of necessity stand forth unmistakeable in their moods and characteristics. In this one they do not. Every scene of any importance has been blinked or passed over with a few words or cross references. I am not now referring to any moral fact. Every conversation which should have appeared, every storm which should have contained revealing flashes, making clear the minds, the hearts, and the agonies of those concerned, has been avoided. There are no paragraphs or pages of which you can say "This is a truly moving description," or "This is a brilliant vital interpretation." You are never really stirred. You are never hurt. You are merely told and referred. It is all cold narrative, never truly poignant.

This is a pity. This book had the making of a fine story. I half suspect that its failure is due to the author's formal British leanings, whatever his birth—that leaning which Mr. Dowell seems to think so important, which will not let him loosen up and sing. The whole book is indeed fairly representative of that encrusting formalism which, barnacle-wise, is apparently overtaking and destroying all that is best in English life. The arts will surely die unless formalism is destroyed. And when you find a great theme marred by a sniffy reverence for conventionalism and the glories of a fixed condition it is a thing for tears. I would almost commend Mr. Hueffer to the futurists,[1] or to anyone that has the strength to scorn the moldy past, in the hope that he might develop a method entirely different from that which is here employed, if I did not know that at bottom the great artist is never to be commended. Rather

---

1. Avante-garde artistic movement (1909 [date of Marinetti's first *Manifesto* explaining principles]–14). Its works glorified danger, war, and the machine age. The Paris exhibition of 1912 revealed links with Cubism (see p. 4, n. 4 above). Unknown to Dreiser, Ford had already supported Futurism (see p. xiii), and by Christmas 1914 had questioned it: "there was once a time when I occupied these columns with praise of writers of vers libre and disquisitions upon Futurism. Futurism!—I ask myself sometimes whether it was the ebulliant and progressive spirit of Futurism that caused this war, or whether the ground-swell that came before this war had for one of its symptoms just Futurism? Or whether it was just larks that we shall never have again? Or whether Cubism, with its turning from the representation of material phenomena, heralded a new religious age in which truly we shall not make to ourselves the graven images of houses in Park Lane, motor-cars, and all the outward signs of the works of Mammon?" ("Annus Mirabilis," *Outlook* 35 [2 January 1915]: 15; see also p. xiv above).

from his brain, as Athena from that of Zeus, spring flawless and shining all those art forms which the world adores and preserves.

Saturday Review (Supplement) [U.K.] †

In the beginning of this novel Dowell writes: "This is the saddest story I have ever heard". For seven years he has sacrificed himself to a wife whom he has believed to have a weak heart. When she dies he finds that nothing was wrong with her except her character. For seven years he has been her patient, stupid slave, and all the while she and the man he thought his friend have been deceiving him. Certainly the story is depressing, and it amounts in the end to no more than a chronicle of sordid treachery and vice. Mr. Hueffer sees plainly that the whole thing is too unpleasant to form the subject of a direct narrative, so we are asked to become listeners whilst Dowell gives his reminiscences in broken and spasmodic gusts. Gradually the accusations and confessions take shape, and all the while we are made to feel the frightful misery of the man who is supposed to be talking. Yet, perhaps, it may ease Dowell's mind in some way to tell his wretched story with its maundering regrets and passionate outbursts. It is all very cleverly done, and it is clever of the author to contrive that we shall actually picture the miserable widower taking us into his confidence; but it is gloomy company for us to keep, and we draw from it neither pleasure nor profit. Many novelists, we fancy, would like to have the skill which went to writing *The Good Soldier*, and most, we believe, would make better use of it.

Bookman [U.K.] ‡

We should like to be able to regard this book as a satire, because it is so difficult to think that the author could otherwise have considered his characters worth describing. But the gusto and literary skill which he has brought to the task both seem to make that hypothesis untenable. We are somehow driven to conclude that the author, like his Mrs. Ashburnham, "saw life as a perpetual sex-battle between husbands who desire to be unfaithful to their wives, and wives who desire to recapture their husbands in the end. That was her sad and modest view of matrimony." One other short quotation from the volume will throw more light upon it than any words of ours, and it is a quotation we heartily endorse. "There was a great deal of imbecility about the closing scenes of the Ashburnham tragedy. Neither of those two women knew what

† 119 (19 June 1915): iv.
‡ 47 (July 1915): 117.

they wanted. It was only Edward who took a perfectly clear line, and he was drunk most of the time." When we remark that this Edward who took this clear line and all this drink is the "good soldier" of the title, ex-captain of the 14th Hussars, it will generally be agreed that Mr. Hueffer has not been very fortunate in the moment of his book's appearance. The story, indeed, has little bearing on the joys and sorrows of normal human life, but we can well imagine that the work will prove of some value to the specialist in pathology.

LITERARY
IMPRESSIONISM

JULIA VAN GUNSTEREN

[The Aesthetics of Literary Impressionism]†

* * *

At the centre of Literary Impressionist aesthetics is the act of perceiving the outside world and the manner in which it is perceived. The Literary Impressionists not only reacted against the cumbersome paraphernalia of ordinary realistic investigation, they also objected to conventional Realism because it was mechanical, clumsy and superficial, creating a merely orderly catalogue of externals, but most of all because they thought it was unreal. Whereas traditional writers started from a definable subject, i.e. experience previously organised and interpreted by the observing mind, Literary Impressionists started from perception. For them the surrounding world is not well ordered but constitutes an indistinct and obscure picture made up of an irresistible flood of confused and ever changing sense impressions. Through sensory experience they discover a new relationship with the everyday world. As André Gide puts it in *Les Nourritures Terrestres:* 'I see, I feel, I hear, I smell; therefore I am'.[1] This sensory experience is a synthetic, intuitive feeling of oneness with reality, which becomes a subjective experience.

For the Impressionist the perceived world is neither the sum of its objects, the solid reality of matter, the brute reality of an inhuman world divorced from the subject as in the Realist or Naturalist tradition, nor the symbol of a hidden reality, a representation of both the idea and the unseen, or the embodiment and revelation of the infinite, as in the Symbolist philosophy.[2] According to the Literary Impressionist, reality cannot be analysed, but can only be intuitively perceived; it is a synthesis of pure sensations, modulated by consciousness and changed into impressions. * * *

One of Joseph Conrad's aims in his writing was: 'to make you hear, to make you feel . . . before all, to make you *see!*'[3] He presented his intuitive perceptions of objects, people, events. * * *

The aim is to create an atmosphere, in subtle evocation, with discontinuous, retrospective or unfinished actions, in streams of consciousness channeled by emotion, corresponding to the way in which we experience life. No analysis or inventory of set pictures or comments on the characters is given nor is there a chronological report with a definite

---

† From *Katherine Mansfield and Literary Impressionism* (Amsterdam and Atlanta: Editions Rodopi, 1990) 51–53, 55–56. Reprinted with the permission of the publishers. The author's notes have been edited for publication here.
1. As cited from M. E. Kronegger, *Literary Impressionism* (New Haven, 1973), p. 35.
2. Cf. Kronegger, p. 36.
3. See Preface to *The Nigger of the "Narcissus,"* p. 255 below [*Editor*].

beginning, middle and end. In its effect on the reader, it is highly suggestive. The subjective aspect of Literary Impressionism and its rhetoric was noted as early as 1894 when H. Garland pointed out: 'It must never be forgotten, that they (the Impressionist painters) are not delineating a scene; they are painting a personal impression of a scene, which is vastly different'.[4]

The Literary Impressionist believes that reality is illusory. An impression of the surrounding world is often determined by circumstances. Any mental condition at any given moment must be taken into consideration. These factors are beyond any power of influence. The Impressionist's only responsibility is to render a character's reactions to the external stimuli as truthfully as he can. Here we are back again with Naturalism and its view of man at the mercy of natural forces. The Literary Impressionist presents an illusory reality rather passively, but as truthfully as possible. This passive attitude is basic to the entire 'Weltanschauung'.[5] In the end, the Literary Impressionist technique, with its assumed and apparent objectivity, creates a fictional illusion: the suggestive illusion that the reader is participating in the events, scenes or actions described.[6]

The emphasis on the act of perception leads us to the perceiver, who regards the process of perceiving impressions as reality itself. At any given moment of time, one impression is as valid as any other. The Literary Impressionist sees everything anew, through fresh and 'innocent' eyes.[7] Impressionism does not simply record the impact of raw and unadulterated sensations on a (passive) receptor. If that were so, Literary Impressionism would be little more than a compendium of impressions. But Literary Impressionism is the process by which impressions are absorbed by a perceiver.[8]

Passivity is often considered to be a most fundamental element in Literary Impressionist fiction.[9] It has been argued, correctly, that characters are the passive receptors of sensory stimuli and that the 'reduction of the artistic representation to the mood of the moment is, at the same time, the expression of a fundamentally passive outlook on life, an acquiescence in the role of the spectator'.[1] But it is too much to claim that all Impressionist characters are passive.[2] They may, in fact, have an active, restless consciousness. * * * Impressionist characters, including

---

4. Cf. Orm Overland, 'The Impressionism of Stephen Crane: A Study in Style and Technique', *Americana-Norwegica* (1966), ed. Sigmund Skard and Henry Wasser, pp. 239–285; p. 242.
5. Overland, p. 241. ["Weltarnschauung": philosophy of life (German)—*Editor.*]
6. Overland, p. 242.
7. Herbert J. Muller, 'Impressionism in Fiction: Prism vs. Mirror', *The American Scholar*, VII (Summer 1938), 355–367; p. 356.
8. Peter Stowell, *Literary Impressionism: James and Chekov* (1980), p. 25.
9. M. E. Kronegger, 'Impressionist Tendencies in Lyrical Prose', *Revue de Littérature Comparée*, 172 (1969), pp. 528–544; p. 531; Stowell, p. 43.
1. Stowell, p. 43.
2. Cf. Kronegger, 1973, p. 60.

[Katherine] Mansfield's characters, often find a 'creative synthesis' in passive perception and final 'active conception'.[3] The rendering of events and objects is a combination of carefully selected, yet seemingly random, details in a vision of fragmented reality in which all contours are blurred. But at the same time the perceiving characters often attempt to find some unifying configuration, some 'merging of subject and object' in Stowell's terminology, some 'centrifugal' (Müller) unification of the perceiver and the perceived in the Impressionist's sensory world.[4] The Impressionist's characters seem to be caught in the moment of transition between a passionate desire for a transcendental glimpse of the 'Truth' of human consciousness, and their realisation that there is no 'Truth', but only perceived fragments of highly ambiguous sensory stimuli. Between the irresolution of these two paradoxes, a major theme of Literary Impressionism, is the struggle for identity in a constantly shifting balance of perception and knowledge: the disparity between subjective and objective 'truth' and 'reality'. * * *

In Literary Impressionism the act of perception is more important than either the perceived or the perceiver.[5] No longer is there the narrator and/or character on the one hand and the perceived on the other. There is no separation between subject and object. There is only seeing and retaining.[6] With many Literary Impressionists, the act of perceiving and the act of remembering are homologous and sense impressions become an impression in the reflecting consciousness, receding into the past and invoking other impressions. The Literary Impressionist[7] stresses the fragmentary discontinuity of remembered experience, reflecting the discontinuity of human perception itself.[8]

Critics such as Gustave Geffroy in 1894, Bally in 1936 and Albères in 1966 and 1970 have associated Literary Impressionism with phenomenology. Geffroy defines an Impressionist painting as a kind of painting that tends to represent the appearance and meaning of objects in space, and attempts to synthesise these aspects in the semblance of the moment.[9] As Kronegger writes:

> With the Impressionists' perceptive experience, the reality of the novel changes; the traditional frozen forms of description (Balzac) set themselves into motion spatially. The protagonist sees reality from several angles of vision at once and the objects are released without losing sight of their earlier positions.

3. Cf. Stowell's analysis of Chekhov's and James's characters, p. 44.
4. Cf. Stowell, pp. 33–35.
5. Kronegger (1973), p. 40.
6. Kronegger (1973), p. 41.
7. Kronegger (1973) mentions Proust and Cl. Simon, p. 41.
8. Kronegger (1973; p. 41) mentions Proust, Joyce, V. Woolf, N. Sarraute, and Cl. Simon.
9. From Gustave Geffroy, La Vie Artistique, Salon de 1894, 1895.

In this indecisive universe where subjectivism mingles with objectivity, the novel is no longer a story but a confused colliding of sensations, impressions and experiences. It is not 'ready-made', shown in advance, shaped and packaged by a trained writer-narrator. It is proffered to the reader like some fluid, poetic, enigmatic substance, and instead of following the plot line we wander around as if in a daydream. The 'real' world exists only insofar as it is reflected in a character's consciousness.

The parallel with science also seems valid, as the art critic René Huyghe has observed:

> Science divides matter into billions of atoms which make the universe an immense magma of swirling, infinitesimal particles where the haphazardness and the logic of associations create bodies, shapes and objects, like so many provisional phantasms. The Impressionist for his part practises a similar divisionism: no more contours, no more shapes, no more distinct objects; a powdery haze of coloured dots whose convergence and grouping generate an illusion of things.[1]

Impressionism means a new attitude towards reality in life. The Literary Impressionist wants to express what the eye actually sees. What it often sees is a vibration of light on an object in dissolution. As Jules Laforgue says: 'a natural eye . . . reaches a point where it can see reality in the living atmosphere of forms, decomposed, refracted by beings and things, in incessant vibration. Such is the first characteristic of the Impressionistic eye'.[2]

IAN WATT

[Impressionism and Symbolism in Ford, Conrad, and Crane]†

* * * For Monet, the fog in a painting, like the narrator's haze, is not an accidental interference which stands between the public and a clear view of the artist's "real" subject: the conditions under which the viewing is done are an essential part of what the pictorial—or the literary—artist sees and therefore tries to convey.

A similar idea, expressed in a similar metaphor, occurs twenty years later in Virginia Woolf's classic characterization of "Modern Fiction"

---

1. Cf. Rene Huyghe, 'L'Impressionisme et la Pensée de son Temps', *Promothée*, Nouvelle Série, 1, 1939.
2. Laforgue, 1966 edition, pp. 176–177.
† From *Conrad in the Nineteenth Century* (Berkeley and Los Angeles: U of California P, 1979) 170–73, 196–97. Copyright © 1979 by Ian Watt. Reprinted with the permission of University of California Press.

(1919). There she exempts Conrad, together with Hardy, from her objections to traditional novels and those of her Edwardian contemporaries, H. G. Wells, Arnold Bennett, and John Galsworthy.[1] Her basic objection is that if we "look within" ourselves we see "a myriad impressions" quite unrelated to anything that goes on in such fiction; and if we could express "this unknown and uncircumscribed spirit" of life freely, "there would be no plot, no comedy, no tragedy, no love interest or catastrophe in the accepted style, and perhaps not a single button sewn on as the Bond Street tailors would have it." For, Virginia Woolf finally affirms, "Life is not a series of gig lamps symmetrically arranged; life is a luminous halo, a semi-transparent envelope surrounding us from the beginning of consciousness to the end."

The implications of these images of haze and halo for the essential nature of modern fiction are made somewhat clearer by the analogy of French Impressionist painting, and by the history of the word impressionism.

As a specifically aesthetic term, "Impressionism" was apparently put into circulation in 1874 by a journalist, Louis Leroy, to ridicule the affronting formlessness of the pictures exhibited at the Salon des Indépendants, and particularly of Claude Monet's painting entitled "Impression: Sunrise." In one way or another all the main Impressionists made it their aim to give a pictorial equivalent of the visual sensations of a particular individual at a particular time and place. One early critic suggested that "l'école des yeux" would be a more appropriate designation for them than "Impressionists";[2] what was new was not that earlier painters had been blind to the external world, but that painters were now attempting to give their own personal visual perceptions a more complete expressive autonomy; in the words of Jean Leymarie, what distinguished the French Impressionists was an intuitive "response to visual sensations, devoid of any theoretical principle."[3] It was this aim which, as E. H. Gombrich has said, allots the Impressionist movement a decisive role in the process of art's long transition from trying to portray what all men know to trying to portray what the individual actually sees.[4]

The history of the words "impression" and "impressionism" in English embodies a more general aspect of the long process whereby in every domain of human concerns the priority passed from public systems of belief—what all men know—to private views of reality—what the individual sees. Beginning with the root meaning of "impression"—from *premere*, to "press" in a primarily physical sense, as in the "impression" of a printed book—the *Oxford Dictionary* documents a semantic flow

1. *The Common Reader* (London, 1938), pp. 148–149.
2. Jacques Lethève, *Impressionnistes et Symbolistes Devant la Presse* (Paris, 1959), p. 63.
3. Jean Leymarie, *Impressionism*, trans. J. Emmons, 2 vols. (Lausanne, 1955), vol. 2, p. 28.
4. E. H. Gombrich, *The Story of Art*, 12th ed. (London, 1972), p. 406.

towards meanings whose status is primarily psychological. The meaning of impression as "the effect produced by external force or influence on the senses or mind" was apparently established as early as 1632; and afterwards it proceeded to reflect the process whereby, from Descartes onwards, the concentration of philosophical thought upon epistemological problems gradually focussed attention on individual sensation as the only reliable source of ascertainable truth. The most notable single name connected with the process is probably that of David Hume, who opened A *Treatise of Human Nature* (1739–1740) with the ringing assertion, "All the perceptions of the human mind resolve themselves into two distinct kinds, which I shall call IMPRESSIONS and IDEAS." He had then attributed greater "force and violence" to impressions, as opposed to ideas, which he defined as merely the "less lively perceptions" which occur when we reflect on our original sense-impressions.[5] It was in protest against this empirical tradition in philosophy that the first English usage of "impressionism" occurred. In 1839 John Rogers, an eccentric word-coiner who entitled his attack on popery *Antipopopriestian*, wrote an ironical panegyric of the two main English prophets of "universal doubt": "All hail to Berkeley who would have no matter, and to Hume who would have no mind; to the Idealism of the former, and to the *Impressionism* of the latter!"[6]

It is appropriate that the word "impressionism" should be connected with Hume, since he played an important part in making the psychology of individual sensation supplant traditional philosophy as the main avenue to truth and value. One incidental result of this in the romantic and post-romantic period was that the religious, imaginative, emotional and aesthetic orders of being became increasingly private, a trend which in the course of the nineteenth century led both to the Aesthetic movement and to Impressionism. The most influential figure here is Walter Pater. In the famous "Conclusion" to *The Renaissance* (1868–1873), for instance, he speaks of how every person enclosed in "the narrow chamber of the individual mind" can directly experience only "the passage and dissolution of impressions, images, sensations"; these are "unstable, flickering, inconsistent," and the individual mind is therefore condemned to keep "as a solitary prisoner its own dream of a world."

This epistemological solipsism became an important part of the cultural atmosphere of the nineties; but by then the main English usage of the term "impressionism" was in reference to the French school of painters, and to their English counterparts who came to the fore with the foundation of the New English Art Club in 1886.[7] As in France, the term was very quickly extended to ways of writing which were thought

---

5. Bk. 1, "Of the Understanding," Pt. 1, sect. i.
6. 2nd ed. (New York, 1841), p. 188.
7. See Holbrook Jackson, "British Impressionists," in *The Eighteen-Nineties* (London, 1939), pp. 240–50.

to possess the qualities popularly attributed to the painters—to works that were spontaneous and rapidly executed, that were vivid sketches rather than detailed, finished, and premeditated compositions.[8] The literary use of the term remained even more casual and descriptive; although Stephen Crane was widely categorised as an "impressionist,"[9] and in 1898 a reviewer of Conrad's first collection of short stories, *Tales of Unrest*, described him as an "impressionistic realist,"[1] there was little talk of impressionism as a literary movement until considerably later.

It was Ford Madox Ford who gave wide currency to the view that he and Conrad, like Flaubert and Maupassant, had been writers of impressionist fiction. This view was expounded in Ford's 1914 essay "On Impressionism," which sees the distinctive trait of "the Impressionist" as giving "the fruits of his own observations alone";[2] but it is Ford's memoir of Conrad which gives his fullest account of literary impressionism. The memoir was published after Conrad's death, and so we do not know whether Ford's statement there that Conrad "avowed himself impressionist" (*F M F*, 6) would have been contradicted by Conrad if communication had been possible. Garnett immediately registered an emphatic protest,[3] but later critics such as Joseph Warren Beach[4] and Edward Crankshaw[5] applied the term to Conrad, and he is now ensconced in literary history as an impressionist.

Conrad certainly knew something about pictorial and literary impressionism, but the indications are that his reactions were predominantly unfavourable.[6] * * * Conrad probably read a mildly derogatory article on "The Philosophy of Impressionism," which appeared in *Blackwood's Magazine* in May 1898,[7] and presumably knew Garnett's view of Stephen Crane as an artist of "the surfaces of life."

Conrad's own references to Crane's impressionism suggest that he shared Garnett's unsympathetic view of it. Thus, speaking of Crane's story, "The Open Boat," Conrad writes: "He is *the only* impressionist and *only* an impressionist" (*E G*, 107). This was in 1897, and Conrad's sense of the limitations of impressionism apparently hardened later; thus in 1900 he praised the "focus" of some Cunninghame Graham sketches,

8. See *OED* and Todd K. Bender, "Literary Impressionism: General Introduction," in *Preliminary Papers for Seminar # 8*, distributed for the Modern Language Association Annual Meeting, 1975 (University of Wisconsin, Madison, 1975), 1–21.
9. By Edward Garnett, for instance, in an 1898 essay reprinted in *Friday Nights* (London, 1922).
1. Cited by Bruce E. Teets and Helmut Gerber, eds., *Joseph Conrad: An Annotated Bibliography of Writings About Him* (De Kalb, Ill., 1971), p. 16.
2. See p. 260 below [*Editor*].
3. *Nation and Athenaeum* 36 (1924), 366–68.
4. In *The Twentieth-Century Novel* (New York, 1932), Conrad and Lawrence are categorised under Impressionism; Joyce comes under Post-Impressionism, Virginia Woolf under Expressionism.
5. Crankshaw writes: "The label will do as well as any other" (*Joseph Conrad*, p. 9).
6. Conrad visited Marguerite Poradowska in the Paris apartment of her cousin, Dr. Paul Gachet, close friend of Van Gogh and Cézanne, and found his collection "nightmarish" (René Rapin, ed., *Lettres de Joseph Conrad à Marguerite Poradowska* [Geneva: Droz, 1966], p. 87).
7. By C. F. Keary, no. 991, pp. 630–36.

and added: "They are much more of course than mere Crane-like impressionism" (C G, 130). Conrad was to pay much more favourable public tributes to Crane later; but his early private comments make it clear that, much like Garnett, he thought of impressionism as primarily concerned with visual appearances. * * *

                                    *   *   *

The modern critical tendency to decompose literary works into a series of more or less cryptic references to a system of non-literal unifying meanings is in large part a misguided response to a very real problem in the interpretation of much modern literature.

Many of the characteristics of that literature can be seen as the result of the convergence of the symbolist and impressionist traditions. The two movements were largely parallel manifestations in the *avant garde* ferment which affected all the arts during the last three decades of the nineteenth century; and this fusion of the impressionist and symbolist tendencies continued into the twentieth century. The Imagist movement, for instance, is primarily a development of the impressionist tendency, as Ford's connection with it suggests, but Imagism also had strong ties with the English symbolist poets. In his 1913 Imagist Manifesto, Ezra Pound, who was in part reacting against what he considered the vagueness of both impressionist and symbolist art, nevertheless telescoped the primary emphases of both tendencies when he defined his literary objective, the image, as "that which presents an intellectual and emotional complex in an instant of time," and went on to make the ringing polemic affirmation "the natural object is always the *adequate* symbol." [8]

Pound's dual principles suggest how the impressionist and symbolist emphases combined to form the basis of the characteristic expressive idiom not only of modern poetry but of modern narrative prose. The same two emphases, for example, underlie Marvin Mudrick's almost pardonable hyperbole that "After *Heart of Darkness*, the recorded moment—the word—was irrecoverably symbol." [9] "The recorded moment," with its emphasis on immediate sensation, is primarily impressionist, and so is Mudrick's subsequent analysis of how Conrad developed "the moral resources inherent in every recorded sensation."

The need to derive moral meaning from physical sensation partly arises from the fact that both the impressionists and the symbolists, as has already been noted, proscribed any analysis, prejudgment, or conceptual commentary—the images, events, and feelings were to be left to speak for themselves. This laid a particular burden on the writer's power

8. "A Stray Document," in *Make It New: Essays* (London, 1934), pp. 336–37. On Pound's view of the relationship of imagism to impressionism, see Herbert N. Schneidau, *Ezra Pound: The Image and the Real* (Baton Rouge, La., 1969), pp. 34–35.
9. "The Originality of Conrad," *Hudson Review* 11 (1958): 553.

of expression, since his objects alone had to carry a rich burden of suggested autonomous meanings. The symbolist method therefore begins by making the same descriptive demand as that of impressionism: the writer must render the object with an idiosyncratic immediacy of vision, which is freed from any intellectual prejudgment or explanatory gloss; and the reader must be put in the posture of actively seeking to fill the gaps in a text which has provoked him to experience an absence of connecting meanings. * * * [T]he obtrusive disparity between a particular image and the significance apparently attributed to it by the writer creates an insistent semantic gap, which the reader feels called upon to fill with his own symbolic interpretation.

There has presumably always been some gap between the verbal sign and its meaning; but the gap is much more obtrusive in the literature of the twentieth century. The expressive idiom of modern writing in general is characterised by an insistent separateness between the particular items of experience presented and the reader's need to generate larger connecting meanings out of them. This semantic gap does much to explain the importance and the difficulty of the modern role of the literary critic. He is faced with the task of explaining to the public in discursive expository prose a literature whose expressive idiom was intended to be inaccessible to exposition in any conceptual terms. He confronts an incompleteness of utterance, an indeterminacy of meaning, a seemingly unconscious or random association of images, which simultaneously demand and defy exegesis. In the fiction whose primary allegiance is to the impressionist tradition, such as that of Hemingway, for instance, the idiosyncratic sequence of apparently unconnected particularities in the narrative asks to be construed and translated into the realm of public discourse; but once translated into that expository language not much is left, and its residue of general meaning is likely, in the critic's rendition of it, to seem both meagre and ambiguous.

* * *

 JOHN A. MEIXNER

[Ford's Literary Technique]†

* * *

In [Ford's] earlier fiction the method consisted principally in withholding the full situation from the reader (and often from his major character) and only gradually exposing it. As Ford has written of the

† From *Ford Madox Ford's Novels* (Minneapolis: U of Minnesota P, 1962; Oxford UP, 1962) 11, 16–24. Copyright © 1962 by the University of Minnesota. Reprinted with the permission of the University of Minnesota Press.

technique, which is essentially the method of the Henry James of *What Maisie Knew*, *The Turn of the Screw*, or *The Ambassadors*:

> Supposing that your name is John, and that you have a friend called James, and for private reasons of his own James takes you into his billiard room and tries to shoot you with a rifle.
>
> Now when that happens to you nothing in the outside world says to you, in so many words, *"That Man is going to shoot me."* What happens to you roughly is this. You are taken by your friend into a room. You perceive the greenish light thrown upwards from the billiard table. . . . Your friend talks. You answer. You are thinking of what he says; of what you are to answer. You perceive other objects; you perceive that some of the cues are not in the rack, and that the last game marked ended at 100 to 64. James says something else. You notice that his voice is rather high. You answer. You notice that you are saying to yourself, "I must keep my temper!" You also notice that the clock has stopped at 3.17. . . . So it goes on, the whole way through the incident—it is a mixture of things that appear insignificant and of real action. . . . To say that James took John into the billiard room would be statement for such a writer; to present the train of action would be art.[1]

The main dramatic tension in this example * * * rests in what is revealed as the situation unfolds through time. Characters, in their effort to find the key to unlock meaning, may recall past circumstances, but their persons and the incidents in which they take part are confined within the basic movement of an advancing present. Chronology is not broken. Later in his career, after 1914, Ford was to further complicate his story-telling by the adoption of the time-shift * * * [and his] use of the [device] varied considerably from novel to novel. In *The Good Soldier* it shifted from the focus of a disturbed and disordered narrator; in *Some Do Not*, from the point of view of the author. * * * Ford's understanding that the writer's personality will permeate his work, and draw or repel readers without regard to the craftsman's skill, can be seen * * * in [a] shrewd, self-appraising comment:

> My friend on the New York *Times* calls me a master of the time-shift. He adds that a great many people dislike my books because I use that device. But he is mistaken. It is me they dislike, not the time-shift which is a thing that delights everybody.[2]

This recognition of the importance of personality in literature undoubtedly contributed greatly toward that tolerance of other artistic methods than his own which characterized Ford. * * * Technique was extremely important to him, and he constantly emphasized it, but not as an end in itself. The significance of technique, he said, lay in its

1. Ford Madox Ford, "Joseph Conrad," *The English Review*, X (December 1911), 76–77.
2. Ford, *It Was a Nightingale* (Philadelphia: Lippincott, 1933), p. 212.

freeing power. It enabled those writers possessed of personality to discover the unique forms by which that personality, in its interaction with life, could most fully be expressed.

The other doctrine that qualified Ford's aim of an objective *constatation* was the necessity, which he often emphasized, that an author be interesting—that he please his reader. Above all, he insisted, the writer must not fail to capture and hold his reader's attention, for otherwise he will make no impression.

> You will do this by methods of surprise, of fatigue, by passages of sweetness in your language, by passages suggesting the sudden and brutal shock of suicide. You will give him passages of dulness, so that your bright effects may seem more bright; you will alternate, you will dwell for a long time upon an intimate point; you will seek to exasperate so that you may the better enchant.[3]

* * *

The theory of *progression d'effet*, with its steady rise to climax, was in itself one method of holding the interest of the reader. * * * A good—an interesting—style, Ford wrote, will consist of "a constant succession of tiny unobservable surprises." These "slight crepitations of surprise, like the successive small explosions in a motor, keep the story running and lend to it actuality and life. They make it interesting at the third or fourth reading."[4] With such a stylistic ideal, of surprise crossed * * * with simplicity, it becomes easy to understand why Ford should have called Mark Twain "one of the greatest prose-writers the English language has produced."[5]

Yet despite these significant qualifications, the need for personality and for being interesting, Ford's doctrine of *constatation* remained at the core of his intention. And from it certain narrative principles followed. One, of course, was the ban on personal intrusion by the author, a commonplace of the Flaubert tradition. * * *

Another, particularly Fordian, principle was the rejection of authorial intrusion by way of an ornate and glittering style. The charged prose of writers like Meredith, Pater, and Stevenson Ford was always critical of, and this bias largely explains his early preference for the poetry of Christina Rossetti over that of her brother. * * * Ford wanted to achieve a style so simple and so naturally cadenced that it would be unnoticed.[6] The rhetorical, the literary, the pompous, and the self-conscious were to be excluded. Marching as he did under the banner of *le mot juste*, Ford took

---

3. Ford, "On Impressionism," p. 333 ["Second Article"; see p. 273 below—*Editor*].
4. Ford, "Preface," *Stories from de Maupassant* (London: 1903), p. 13.
5. Ford, *The English Novel: From the Earliest Days to the Death of Joseph Conrad* (Philadelphia: Lippincott, 1929), p. 121.
6. Ford, *Joseph Conrad: A Personal Remembrance* (London: Duckworth, 1924), pp. 193–95. [See pp. 281–83 below—*Editor.*]

pains to point out that this ideal did not mean "every word a sparkler."[7] What it meant rather was that a passage of good style "began with a fresh, usual word, and continued with fresh, usual words to the end."[8]

* * * Ford rejected the involuted constructions of Henry James's final manner and preferred his middle period—particularly *The Spoils of Poynton*, its stylistic culmination. As for Conrad's prose, that was a matter about which Ford was almost always silent, contenting himself with urging his own views. Once, however, in *Return to Yesterday*, he did allow himself to hint an estimate. "Conrad produced with agony and you saw how it was done,"[9] he wrote, and noted casually that his collaborator's English was "literary."[1] Such an observation, in the light of Ford's ideal of language, was clearly not praise.

As an avowed register of his times, Ford was obviously in the camp of the realists, but of the group which was less scientific and more poetic. The keystone of his intention lies in his statement that "the general effect of a novel must be the general effect that life makes on mankind."[2] The business of the novelist, as he put it, is "to produce an illusion of reality,"[3] to "make each of his stories an experience."[4] (The reader should be kept entirely oblivious of the author's existence—"even of the fact that he is reading a book.")[5] And in order that a narration of events strike the hearer as an experience, the novelist must make them seem as nearly as possible as they would in nature itself. He ought not to give an annotated, rounded account of a set of circumstances—a chronicle formal and objectively corrected. Rather he should present "the record of the impression of a moment."[6] It is from this last conception that Ford's theory and practice earned from his contemporaries the name of "Impressionism."

At first dubious of such a label * * *, Ford gave up resistance in time; and after 1914, when he published a long article on the subject, he often referred to himself as an impressionist—a member, as he saw it, of the same school of writers as Joseph Conrad, Henry James, Stephen Crane, Maupassant, and Flaubert. The inclusion of such names as James, Maupassant, and Flaubert should alert us, of course, to the fact that the Impressionism practised by Ford in the ten years before 1914 is markedly different from that of novelists usually labeled Impressionists: authors writing after 1910 like D. H. Lawrence, Marcel Proust, Dorothy Richardson, Virginia Woolf.[7] It varies also, if less,

7. Ford, *Thus to Revisit* (London: Chapman & Hall, 1921), p. 52.
8. Ford, *Joseph Conrad*, p. 194. [See p. 282 below—*Editor*.]
9. Ford, *Return to Yesterday* (London: Gollancz, 1931; New York: Liveright, 1932), p. 61.
1. *Ibid.*, p. 287.
2. Ford, *Joseph Conrad*, p. 180. [See p. 275 below—*Editor*.]
3. Ford, "On Impressionism," p. 323. [See pp. 263–65 below—*Editor*.]
4. Ford, "Joseph Conrad," p. 76.
5. Ford, *Joseph Conrad*, p. 186. [See p. 278 below—*Editor*.]
6. Ford, "On Impressionism," p. 174 ["First Article"; see p. 263 below—*Editor*].
7. See Herbert Muller, "Impressionism in Fiction: Prism vs. Mirror," *The American Scholar*, VII (Summer 1938), 355–67.

from the work of such acknowledged Impressionists as Crane and Conrad, who wrote earlier.

By and large, the later writers differed from their predecessors in the importance they gave to the subjective. In an effort to render felt experience—what seemed to them the actual sensation of living—they scrapped much more of the abstracting, objective function. * * * Thus, for some, like Crane and Lawrence, the visual world tends to lack definition, its actuality distorted by imposed images which transfer our interest to the states of feeling of the protagonists. Crane's use of color splashes and startling metaphor in *The Red Badge of Courage* and *Maggie* (his description in "The Open Boat" of the waves as "barbarously abrupt" was praised endlessly by Ford), and Lawrence's passion for working through symbols are cases in point. * * * Other writers, like Dorothy Richardson, Virginia Woolf, Conrad Aiken, enter the character's mind, and limit themselves to rendering the unordered flow of mental associations that passes there, employing the technique known as stream of consciousness, or interior monologue. Proust, although he does not strictly use stream of consciousness, bases his entire method on the fact of the mind's involuntary wanderings. In most Impressionist work, conventional chronology does not count for much. Either time is considered of little real significance and is not emphasized, or it is broken, while the author shifts back and forth chronologically as the mental association determines the scene.

* * *

The Impressionism of the Ford who wrote before 1914, then, was relatively more objective. While he pursued the aim of rendering the impressions life conveys to the senses, he gave greater weight to "common-sense" objective modes of perception. In many ways, Ford's storytelling technique remained traditional. He did not employ interior monologue, partly because it was not yet developed, nor did he transfigure the external world into vibrating symbol. More important, chronology was unbroken.

The absence of the time-shift in Ford's writing prior to 1914 is on several counts surprising. For one thing, his own best work—*The Good Soldier* (1915) and the Tietjens series—employs distorted chronology brilliantly, and, indeed, the device is characteristic of all his novels, and several of his memoirs, published after 1914. Secondly, Ford, in his best-known chapter on technique, in *Joseph Conrad*, declares that the use of the time-shift had been developed by Conrad and himself:

> . . . it became very early evident to us that what was the matter with the Novel, and the British novel in particular, was that it went straight forward * * * . . . That theory at least we gradually evolved.[8]

8. Ford, *Joseph Conrad*, pp. 129–130. [See pp. 274–75 below for full text of quotation—*Editor.*]

That this assertion is true of Ford's collaborator at least, there can be no doubt: Conrad's violation of natural time-order is a contribution to the craft of the novel which has long been celebrated. * * * That Conrad's new systematic use of the time-shift was initiated not very long after the two men began their association (in October, 1898), and had launched their extensive, even endless discussions on the craft of the novel, is probably not, however, a chance.

Nevertheless, in Ford's own handling of the novel till 1914, he was much more Jamesian, time being managed as in the illustration of John, James, and the billiard room—the main dramatic tension lying in the revelation of meanings as the situation unfolds through time.

After 1914, Ford showed an increased focusing on the experience of the mind itself, with its backward and forward dartings. This new emphasis on the subjective, influenced in part at least by the literary trend of the times, can be seen in *The Good Soldier* of 1915. But it was already indicated in "On Impressionism" of the preceding year, where he presents an appeal for the rendering of superimposed emotions. It is perfectly possible, Ford wrote in that essay,

> that a piece of Impressionism should give a sense of two, of three, of as many as you will, places, persons, emotions, all going on simultaneously in the emotions of the writer. It is, I mean, perfectly possible for a sensitised person, be he poet or prose writer, to have the sense, when he is in one room, that he is in another, or when he is speaking to one person he may be so intensely haunted by the memory or desire for another person that he may be absent-minded or distraught.

"Indeed," adds Ford, in a striking image,

> I suppose that Impressionism exists to render those queer effects of real life that are like so many views seen through bright glass—through glass so bright that whilst you perceive through it a landscape or a backyard, you are aware that, on its surface, it reflects a face of a person behind you. For the whole of life is really like that; we are almost always in one place with our minds somewhere quite other.[9]

Hand in hand with this emphasis on the rendering of superimposed states of feeling went, of course, the time-shift itself. Ford experimented much with this technique after 1914 and employed it differently in various novels * * *. For the moment, however, we can gain an accurate sense of Ford's later Impressionism by looking at a 1924 critical passage written to exemplify the method of the school. In *Joseph Conrad*, he wrote:

9. Ford, "On Impressionism," pp. 173–74. [See p. 263 below—*Editor.*]

> Life does not say to you: In 1914 my next door neighbour, Mr.
> Slack * * * your love affairs that are so much more compli-
> cated. . . .[1]

The contrast of this method of Impressionism with that of the billiard-
room passage, written in 1910, illustrates the extent of change in Ford's
theory. Where the focus of the earlier example went straight forward in
space and time, this one ricochets erratically within the brain.

Although the analysis of Mr. Slack and his greenhouse is ostensibly
supposed to clarify the nature of Conrad's Impressionism and the performance that earned the work of both collaborators that label, it is clear
that the method involved—interior monologue essentially—was never
that of Conrad nor, as we have seen, of the early Ford. Actually, Ford
was explaining here his own current practice—the techniques he was
then using in the Tietjens novels. Later in his last books, he was even
to employ some of the flashing imagery that in modern writing ultimately derives from Crane.

Ford's novels after 1914 moved, therefore, much closer to pure
Impressionism than can be found in his predecessors—with the possible
exception of Crane, who worked much differently. But, in the last analysis, Ford probably should not be described as an Impressionist. What
basically excludes him as such is his steady adherence to the ideal,
learned from his Continental masters, of the tightly constructed novel.
In that adherence he remained significantly traditional in his approach
to the form.

* * *

JOSEPH CONRAD

Preface to *The Nigger of the "Narcissus"* (1897)†

A work that aspires, however humbly, to the condition of art should
carry its justification in every line. And art itself may be defined as a
single-minded attempt to render the highest kind of justice to the visible
universe, by bringing to light the truth, manifold and one, underlying
its every aspect. It is an attempt to find in its forms, in its colours, in its
light, in its shadows, in the aspects of matter and in the facts of life,
what of each is fundamental, what is enduring and essential—their one
illuminating and convincing quality—the very truth of their existence.

---

1. Ford, *Joseph Conrad*, pp. 180–82. [See p. 276 below for full text of quotation—*Editor*.]
† Although this became a "Preface," it began as an "Afterword" to the fifth and last installment
in the *New Review* 17 (December 1897): 628–31. For the complex textual history of the
Preface and its function as "the most reliable . . . single statement of Conrad's general approach to writing," see Thomas Lavoie and Ian Watt in Robert Kimbrough, ed., *The Nigger
of the "Narcissus"* (Norton Critical Edition, 1979) 148–50 and 151–67 respectively.

The artist, then, like the thinker or the scientist, seeks the truth and makes his appeal. Impressed by the aspect of the world the thinker plunges into ideas, the scientist into facts—whence, presently emerging, they make their appeal to those qualities of our being that fit us best for the hazardous enterprise of living. They speak authoritatively to our common sense, to our intelligence, to our desire of peace, or to our desire of unrest; not seldom to our prejudices, sometimes to our fears, often to our egoism—but always to our credulity. And their words are heard with reverence, for their concern is with weighty matters; with the cultivation of our minds and the proper care of our bodies; with the attainment of our ambitions; with the perfection of the means and the glorification of our precious aims.

It is otherwise with the artist.

Confronted by the same enigmatical spectacle the artist descends within himself, and in that lonely region of stress and strife, if he be deserving and fortunate, he finds the terms of his appeal. His appeal is made to our less obvious capacities; to that part of our nature which, because of the warlike conditions of existence, is necessarily kept out of sight within the more resisting and hard qualities—like the vulnerable body within a steel armour. His appeal is less loud, more profound, less distinct, more stirring—and sooner forgotten. Yet its effect endures for ever. The changing wisdom of successive generations discards ideas, questions facts, demolishes theories. But the artist appeals to that part of our being which is not dependent on wisdom; to that in us which is a gift and not an acquisition—and, therefore, more permanently enduring. He speaks to our capacity for delight and wonder, to the sense of mystery surrounding our lives; to our sense of pity, and beauty, and pain; to the latent feeling of fellowship with all creation; and to the subtle but invincible conviction of solidarity that knits together the loneliness of innumerable hearts: to that solidarity in dreams, in joy, in sorrow, in aspirations, in illusions, in hope, in fear, which binds men to each other, which binds together all humanity—the dead to the living, and the living to the unborn. * * *

Fiction—if it at all aspires to be art—appeals to temperament. And in truth it must be, like painting, like music, like all art, the appeal of one temperament to all the other innumerable temperaments whose subtle and resistless power endows passing events with their true meaning, and creates the moral, the emotional atmosphere of the place and time. Such an appeal, to be effective, must be an impression conveyed through the senses; and, in fact, it cannot be made in any other way, because temperament, whether individual or collective, is not amenable to persuasion. All art, therefore, appeals primarily to the senses, and the artistic aim when expressing itself in written words must also make its appeal through the senses, if its high desire is to reach the secret spring of responsive emotions. It must strenuously aspire to the plasticity of sculpture, to the colour of painting, and to the magic suggestiveness of music—which is the art of arts. And it is only through complete, unswerving devotion to the perfect blending of form and substance; it is only through an unremitting, never-discouraged care for the shape and ring of sentences, that an approach can be made to plasticity, to colour; and the light of magic suggestiveness may be brought to play for an evanescent instant over the commonplace surface of words: of the old, old words, worn thin, defaced by ages of careless usage.

The sincere endeavour to accomplish that creative task, to go as far on that road as his strength will carry him, to go undeterred by faltering, weariness, or reproach, is the only valid justification for the worker in prose. And if his conscience is clear, his answer to those who, in the fulness of a wisdom which looks for immediate profit, demand specifically to be edified, consoled, amused; who demand to be promptly improved, or encouraged, or frightened, or shocked, or charmed, must run thus: My task which I am trying to achieve is, by the power of the written word, to make you hear, to make you feel—it is, before all, to make you *see!* That—and no more: and it is everything! If I succeed, you shall find there according to your deserts: encouragement, consolation, fear, charm—all you demand; and, perhaps, also that glimpse of truth for which you have forgotten to ask.

To snatch in a moment of courage, from the remorseless rush of time, a passing phase of life, is only the beginning of the task. The task approached in tenderness and faith is to hold up unquestioningly, without choice and without fear, the rescued fragment before all eyes and in the light of a sincere mood. It is to show its vibration, its colour, its form; and through its movement, its form, and its colour, reveal the substance of its truth—disclose its inspiring secret: the stress and passion within the core of each convincing moment. In a single-minded attempt of that kind, if one be deserving and fortunate, one may perchance attain to such clearness of sincerity that at last the presented vision of regret or pity, of terror or mirth, shall awaken in the hearts of the beholders that feeling of unavoidable solidarity; of the solidarity in mysterious origin, in toil, in joy, in hope, in uncertain fate—which binds men to each other and all mankind to the visible world.

It is evident that he who, rightly or wrongly, holds by the convictions expressed above cannot be faithful to any one of the temporary formulas of his craft. The enduring part of them—the truth which each only imperfectly veils—should abide with him as the most precious of his possessions, but they all: Realism, Romanticism, Naturalism; even the unofficial sentimentalism (which, like the poor, is exceedingly difficult to get rid of); all these gods must, after a short period of fellowship, abandon him—even on the very threshold of the temple—to the stammerings of his conscience and to the outspoken consciousness of the difficulties of his work. In that uneasy solitude the cry of Art for Art

itself, loses the exciting ring of its apparent immorality. It sounds far
off. It has ceased to be a cry, and is heard only as a whisper, often
incomprehensible, but at times, and faintly, encouraging.

Sometimes, stretched at ease in the shade of a roadside tree, we watch
the motions of a labourer in a distant field, and, after a time, begin to
wonder languidly as to what the fellow may be at. We watch the movements of his body, the waving of his arms; we see him bend down, stand
up, hesitate, begin again. It may add to the charm of an idle hour to be
told the purpose of his exertions. If we know he is trying to lift a stone,
to dig a ditch, to uproot a stump, we look with a more real interest at
his efforts; we are disposed to condone the jar of his agitation upon the
restfulness of the landscape; and even, if in a brotherly frame of mind,
we may bring ourselves to forgive his failure. We understood his object,
and, after all, the fellow has tried, and perhaps he had not the strength—
and perhaps he had not the knowledge. We forgive, go on our way—
and forget.

    And so it is with the workman of art. Art is long and life is short, and
success is very far off. And thus, doubtful of strength to travel so far, we
talk a little about the aim—the aim of art, which, like life itself, is inspiring, difficult—obscured by mists. It is not in the clear logic of a triumphant conclusion; it is not in the unveiling of one of those heartless
secrets which are called the Laws of Nature. It is not less great, but only
more difficult!

    To arrest, for the space of a breath, the hands busy about the work of
the earth, and compel men entranced by the sight of distant goals to
glance for a moment at the surrounding vision of form and colour, of
sunshine and shadows; to make them pause for a look, for a sigh, for a
smile—such is the aim, difficult and evanescent, and reserved only for
a very few to achieve. But sometimes, by the deserving and the fortunate, even that task is accomplished. And when it is accomplished—
behold! all the truth of life is there: a moment of vision, a sigh, a smile—
and the return to an eternal rest.

HENRY JAMES

[The House of Fiction]†

* * *

    The house of fiction has in short not one window, but a million—a
number of possible windows not to be reckoned, rather; every one of

---

† From "Preface" to the New York Edition (1908) of Henry James, *Portrait of a Lady* (1881).
   Originally published in *New Review* 17 (December 1897).

which has been pierced, or is still pierceable, in its vast front, by the need of the individual vision and by the pressure of the individual vision and by the pressure of the individual will. These apertures, of dissimilar shape and size, hang so, all together, over the human scene that we might have expected of them a greater sameness of report than we find. They are but windows at the best, mere holes in a dead wall, discon- nected, perched aloft; they are not hinged doors opening straight upon life. But they have this mark of their own that at each of them stands a figure with a pair of eyes, or at least with a field-glass, which forms, again and again, for observation, a unique instrument, insuring to the person making use of it an impression distinct from every other. He and his neighbours are watching the same show, but one seeing more where the other sees less, one seeing black where the other sees white, one seeing big where the other sees small, one seeing coarse where the other sees fine. And so on, and so on; there is fortunately no saying on what, for the particular pair of eyes, the window may *not* open; "fortunately" by reason, precisely, of this incalculability of range. The spreading field, the human scene, is the "choice of subject"; the pierced aperture, either broad or balconied or slit-like and low-browed, is the "literary form"; but they are, singly or together, as nothing without the posted presence of the watcher—without, in other words, the consciousness of the artist. Tell me what the artist is, and I will tell you of what he has *been* con- scious. Thereby I shall express to you at once his boundless freedom and his "moral" reference.

* * *

FORD MADOX HUEFFER [FORD]

On Impressionism†

First Article

I.

These are merely some notes towards a working guide to Impression- ism as a literary method.

I do not know why I should have been especially asked to write about Impressionism; even as far as literary Impressionism goes I claim no Papacy in the matter. A few years ago, if anybody had called me an Impressionist I should languidly have denied that I was anything of the sort or that I knew anything about the school, if there could be said to

† From *Poetry and Drama* 2.6 (June–December 1914): 167–75 (First Article) and 323–34 (Sec- ond Article).

be any school. But one person and another in the last ten years has called me Impressionist with such persistence that I have given up resistance. I don't know; I just write books, and if someone attaches a label to me I do not much mind.

I am not claiming any great importance for my work; I daresay it is all right. At any rate, I am a perfectly self-conscious writer; I know exactly how I get my effects, as far as those effects go. Then, if I am in truth an Impressionist, it must follow that a conscientious and exact account of how I myself work will be an account, from the inside, of how Impressionism is reached, produced, or gets its effects. I can do no more.

This is called egotism; but, to tell the truth, I do not see how Impressionism can be anything else. Probably this school differs from other schools, principally, in that it recognises, frankly, that all art must be the expression of an ego, and that if Impressionism is to do anything, it must, as the phrase is, go the whole hog. The difference between the description of a grass by the agricultural correspondent of *The Times* newspaper and the description of the same grass by Mr W. H. Hudson [1] is just the difference—the measure of the difference between the egos of the two gentlemen. The difference between the description of any given book by a sound English reviewer and the description of the same book by some foreigner attempting Impressionist criticism is again merely a matter of the difference in the ego.

Mind, I am not saying that the non-Impressionist productions may not have their values—their very great values. The Impressionist gives you his own views, expecting you to draw deductions, since presumably you know the sort of chap he is. The agricultural correspondent of *The Times*, on the other hand—and a jolly good writer he is—attempts to give you, not so much his own impressions of a new grass as the factual observations of himself and of as many as possible other sound authorities. * * * He will provide you, in short, with reading that is quite interesting to the layman, since all facts are interesting to men of good will; and the agriculturist he will provide with information of real value. Mr. Hudson, on the other hand, will give you nothing but the pleasure of coming in contact with his temperament, and I doubt whether, if you read with the greatest care his description of false sea-buckthorn *(hippophae rhamnoides)* you would very willingly recognise that greenish-grey plant, with the spines and the berries like reddish amber, if you came across it.

Or again—so at least I was informed by an editor the other day—the business of a sound English reviewer is to make the readers of the paper understand exactly what sort of a book it is that the reviewer is writing about. Said the editor in question: "You have no idea how many readers

---

1. English writer and naturalist (1814–1886), much admired as a stylist by Ford and Conrad; best known for *Green Mansions* (1904). See pp. 282–83 below.

your paper will lose if you employ one of those brilliant chaps who write readable articles about books. You will get yourself deluged with letter after letter from subscribers saying they have bought a book on the strength of articles in your paper; that the book isn't in the least what they expected, and that therefore they withdraw their subscriptions." What the sound English reviewer, therefore, has to do is to identify himself with the point of view of as large a number of readers of the journal for which he may be reviewing, as he can easily do, and then to give them as many facts about the book under consideration as his allotted space will hold. To do this he must sacrifice his personality, and the greater part of his readability. But he will probably very much help his editor, since the great majority of readers do not want to read anything that any reasonable person would want to read; and they do not want to come into contact with the personality of the critic, since they have obviously never been introduced to him.

The ideal critic, on the other hand—as opposed to the so-exemplary reviewer—is a person who can so handle words that from the first three phrases any intelligent person—any foreigner, that is to say, and any one of three inhabitants of these islands—any intelligent person will know at once the sort of chap that he is dealing with. Letters of introduction will therefore be unnecessary, and the intelligent reader will know pretty well what sort of book the fellow is writing about because he will know the sort of fellow the fellow is. I don't mean to say that he would necessarily trust his purse, his wife, or his mistress to the Impressionist critic's care. But that is not absolutely necessary. The ambition, however, of my friend the editor was to let his journal give the impression of being written by those who could be trusted with the wives and purses—not, of course, the mistresses, for there would be none—of his readers.

You will, perhaps, be beginning to see now what I am aiming at—the fact that Impressionism is a frank expression of personality; the fact that non-Impressionism is an attempt to gather together the opinions of as many reputable persons as may be and to render them truthfully and without exaggeration. (The Impressionist must always exaggerate.)

II.

Let us approach this matter historically—as far as I know anything about the history of Impressionism, though I must warn you that I am a shockingly ill-read man. Here, then, are some examples: do you know, for instance, Hogarth's drawing of the watchman with the pike over his shoulder and the dog at his heels going in at a door, the whole being executed in four lines? Here it is:

Now, that is the high-watermark of Impressionism; since, if you look at those lines for long enough, you will begin to see the watchman with his slouch hat, the handle of the pike coming well down into the cobblestones, the knee-breeches, the leathern garters strapped round his stocking, and the surly expression of the dog, which is bull-hound with a touch of mastiff in it.

You may ask why, if Hogarth saw all these things, did he not put them down on paper, and all that I can answer is that he made this drawing for a bet. Moreover why, if you can see all these things for yourself, should Hogarth bother to put them down on paper? You might as well contend that Our Lord ought to have delivered a lecture on the state of primary education in the Palestine of the year 32 or thereabouts, together with the statistics of rickets and other infantile diseases caused by neglect and improper feeding—a disquisition in the manner of Mrs Sidney Webb.[2] He preferred, however, to say: "It were better that a millstone were put about his neck and he were cast into the deep sea."[3] The statement is probably quite incorrect; the statutory punishment either here or in the next world has probably nothing to do with millstones and so on, but Our Lord was, you see, an Impressionist, and knew His job pretty efficiently. It is probable that He did not have access to as many Blue Books or white papers[4] as the leaders of the Fabian Society, but, from His published utterances, one gathers that He had given a good deal of thought to the subject of children.

I am not in the least joking—and God forbid that I should be thought irreverent because I write like this. The point that I really wish to make is, once again, that—that the Impressionist gives you, as a rule, the fruits of his own observations and the fruits of his own observations alone. He should be in this as severe and as solitary as any monk. It is what he is in the world for. It is, for instance, not so much his business to quote as to state his impressions—that the Holy Scriptures are a good book, or a rotten book, or contain passages of good reading interspersed with dulness; or suggest gems in a cavern, the perfumes of aromatic woods burning in censers, or the rush of the feet of camels crossing the deep sands, or the shrill sounds of long trumpets borne by archangels—clear sounds of brass like those in that funny passage in "*Aida.*"[5]

The passage in prose, however, which I always take as a working model—and in writing this article I am doing no more than showing you the broken tools and bits of oily rag which form my brains, since

---

2. Beatrice Potter Webb (1858–1943), English sociologist and economist, married (1892) to Sidney Webb (1859–1947); both leading figures in the Fabian Society (socialist society, founded 1883) and in the emerging British Labour Party.
3. See Mark 9.42.
4. British government papers outlining proposed legislation or stating policy. "Blue books": books of sociological statistics.
5. Verdi's spectacular opera (1871), set in Egypt.

once again I must disclaim writing with any authority on Impressionism—this passage in prose occurs in a story by de Maupassant called "La Reine Hortense."[6] I spent, I suppose, a great part of ten years in grubbing up facts about Henry VIII. I worried about his parentage, his diseases, the size of his shoes, the price he gave for kitchen implements, his relation to his wives, his knowledge of music, his proficiency with the bow. I amassed, in short, a great deal of information about Henry VIII. I wanted to write a long book about him, but Mr. Pollard, of the British Museum, got the commission and wrote the book probably much more soundly. I then wrote three long novels all about that Defender of the Faith.[7] But I really know—so delusive are reported facts—nothing whatever. Not one single thing! Should I have found him affable, or terrifying, or seductive, or royal, or courageous? There are so many contradictory facts; there are so many reported interviews, each contradicting the other, so that really all that I *know* about this king could be reported in the words of Maupassant, which, as I say, I always consider as a working model. Maupassant is introducing one of his characters, who is possibly gross, commercial, overbearing, insolent; who eats, possibly, too much greasy food; who wears commonplace clothes—a gentleman about whom you might write volumes if you wanted to give the facts of his existence. But all that de Maupassant finds it necessary to say is: "C'était un monsieur à favoris rouges qui entrait toujours le premier."

And that is all that I *know* about Henry VIII.—that he was a gentleman with red whiskers who always went first through a door.

III.

Let us now see how these things work out in practice. I have a certain number of maxims, gained mostly in conversation with Mr Conrad, which form my working stock-in-trade. I stick to them pretty generally; sometimes I throw them out of the window and just write whatever comes. But the effect is usually pretty much the same. I guess I must be fairly well drilled by this time and function automatically, as the Americans say. The first two of my maxims are these:

Always consider the impressions that you are making upon the mind of the reader, and always consider that the first impression with which you present him will be so strong that it will be all that you can ever do to efface it, to alter it or even quite slightly to modify it. Maupassant's gentleman with red whiskers, who always pushed in front of people when it was a matter of going through a doorway, will remain, for the mind of the reader, that man and no other. The impression is as hard

6. For de Maupassant see p. 5, n. 2 above and pp. 267, n. 3, 275, n. 3 below.
7. *The Fifth Queen* (1906), *Privy Seal* (1907), and *The Fifth Queen Crowned* (1908), Ford's Katherine Howard trilogy.

and as definite as a tin-tack. And I rather doubt whether, supposing Maupassant represented him afterwards as kneeling on the ground to wipe the tears away from a small child who had lost a penny down a drain—I doubt whether such a definite statement of fact would ever efface the first impression from the reader's mind. They would think that the gentleman with the red whiskers was perpetrating that act of benevolence with ulterior motives—to impress the bystanders, perhaps.

Maupassant, however, uses physical details more usually as a method of introduction of his characters than I myself do. I am inclined myself, when engaged in the seductive occupation, rather to strike the keynote with a speech than with a description of personality, or even with an action. And, for that purpose, I should set it down, as a rule, that the first speech of a character you are introducing should always be a gener-alisation—since generalisations are the really strong indications of char-acter. Putting the matter exaggeratedly, you might say that, if a gentleman sitting opposite you in the train remarked to you: "I see the Tories have won Leith Boroughs," you would have practically no guide to that gentleman's character. But, if he said: "Them bloody Unionists have crept into Leith because the Labourites, damn them, have taken away 1,100 votes from us," you would know that the gentleman belonged to a certain political party, had a certain social status, a certain degree of education and a certain amount of impatience.

It is possible that such disquisitions on Impressionism in prose fiction may seem out of place in a journal styled *Poetry and Drama*. But I do not think they are. For Impressionism, differing from other schools of art, is founded so entirely on observation of the psychology of the patron—and the psychology of the patron remains constant. Let me, to make things plainer, present you with a quotation. Sings Tennyson:

> And bats went round in fragrant skies,
>   And wheeled or lit the filmy shapes
>   That haunt the dusk, with ermine capes
> And woolly breasts and beady eyes.[8]

Now that is no doubt very good natural history, but it is certainly not Impressionism, since no one watching a bat at dusk could see the ermine, the wool or the beadiness of the eyes. These things you might read about in books, or observe in the museum or at the Zoological Gardens. Or you might pick up a dead bat upon the road. But to import into the record of observations of one moment the observations of a moment altogether different is not Impressionism. For Impressionism is a thing altogether momentary.

I do not wish to be misunderstood. It is perfectly possible that the remembrance of a former observation may colour your impression of the moment, so that if Tennyson had said:

8. *In Memoriam*, XCV, 9–12.

> And we remembered they have ermine capes,

he would have remained within the canons of Impressionism. But that was not his purpose, which, whatever it was, was no doubt praiseworthy in the extreme, because his heart was pure. It is, however, perfectly possible that a piece of Impressionism should give a sense of two, of three, of as many as you will, places, persons, emotions, all going on simultaneously in the emotions of the writer. It is, I mean, perfectly possible for a sensitised person, be he poet or prose writer, to have the sense, when he is in one room, that he is in another, or when he is speaking to one person he may be so intensely haunted by the memory or desire for another person that he may be absent-minded or distraught. And there is nothing in the canons of Impressionism, as I know it, to stop the attempt to render those superimposed emotions. Indeed, I suppose that Impressionism exists to render those queer effects of real life that are like so many views seen through bright glass—through glass so bright that whilst you perceive through it a landscape or a backyard, you are aware that, on its surface, it reflects a face of a person behind you. For the whole of life is really like that; we are almost always in one place with our minds somewhere quite other.

And it is, I think, only Impressionism that can render that peculiar effect; I know, at any rate, of no other method. It has, this school, in consequence, certain quite strong canons, certain quite rigid unities that must be observed. The point is that any piece of Impressionism, whether it be prose, or verse, or painting, or sculpture, is the record of the impression of a moment; it is not a sort of rounded, annotated record of a set of circumstances—it is the record of the recollection in your mind of a set of circumstances that happened ten years ago—or ten minutes. It might even be the impression of the moment—but it is the impression, not the corrected chronicle. I can make what I mean most clear by a concrete instance.

Thus an Impressionist in a novel, or in a poem, will never render a long speech of one of his characters verbatim, because the mind of the reader would at once lose some of the illusion of the good faith of the narrator. The mind of the reader will say: "Hullo, this fellow is faking this. He cannot possibly remember such a long speech word for word." The Impressionist, therefore, will only record his impression of a long speech. If you will try to remember what remains in your mind of long speeches you heard yesterday, this afternoon or five years ago, you will see what I mean. If to-day, at lunch at your club, you heard an irascible member making a long speech about the fish, what you remember will not be his exact words. However much his proceedings will have amused you, you will not remember his exact words. What you will remember is that he said that the sole was not a sole, but a blank, blank, blank plaice; that the cook ought to be shot, by God he ought to be shot.

The plaice had been out of the water two years, and it had been caught in a drain: all that there was of Dieppe about this Sole Dieppoise was something that you cannot remember. You will remember this gentleman's starting eyes, his grunts between words, that he was fond of saying "damnable, damnable, damnable." You will also remember that the man at the same table with you was talking about morals, and that your boots were too tight, whilst you were trying, in your under mind, to arrange a meeting with some lady. . . .

So that, if you had to render that scene or those speeches for purposes of fiction, you would not give a word for word re-invention of sustained sentences from the gentleman who was dissatisfied; or if you were going to invent that scene, you would not so invent those speeches and set them down with all the panoply of inverted commas, notes of exclamation. No, you would give an impression of the whole thing, of the snorts, of the characteristic exclamation, of your friend's disquisition on morals, a few phrases of which you would intersperse into the monologue of the gentleman dissatisfied with his sole. And you would give a sense that your feet were burning, and that the lady you wanted to meet had very clear and candid eyes. You would give a little description of her hair. . . .

In that way you would attain to the sort of odd vibration that scenes in real life really have; you would give your reader the impression that he was witnessing something real, that he was passing through an experience. . . . You will observe also that you will have produced something that is very like a Futurist picture—not a Cubist picture,[9] but one of those canvases that show you in one corner a pair of stays, in another a bit of the foyer of a music hall, in another a fragment of early morning landscape, and in the middle a pair of eyes, the whole bearing the title of "A Night Out." And, indeed, those Futurists are only trying to render on canvas what Impressionists *tel que moi* have been trying to render for many years. (You may remember Emma's love scene at the cattle show in *Madame Bovary*).[1]

Do not, I beg you, be led away by the English reviewer's cant phrase to the effect that the Futurists are trying to be literary and the plastic arts can never be literary. Les Jeunes[2] of to-day are trying all sorts of experiments, in all sorts of media. And they are perfectly right to be trying them.

Second Article

I *have* been trying to think what are the objections to Impressionism as I understand it—or rather what alternative method could be found. It

9. See p. 4, n. 4 above.
1. Novel by Gustave Flaubert (1821–1880), French realist writer. "Futurists": see p. 233, n. 1 above. "Tel que moi": like me (French).
2. See p. 4, n. 5 above.

seems to me that one is an Impressionist because one tries to produce an illusion of reality—or rather the business of Impressionism is to produce that illusion. The subject is one enormously complicated and is full of negatives. Thus the Impressionist author is sedulous to avoid letting his personality appear in the course of his book. On the other hand, his whole book, his whole poem is merely an expression of his personality. Let me illustrate exactly what I mean. You set out to write a story, or you set out to write a poem, and immediately your attempt becomes one creating an illusion, You attempt to involve the reader amongst the personages of the story or in the atmosphere of the poem. You do this by presentation and by presentation and again by presentation. The moment you depart from presentation, the moment you allow yourself, as a poet, to introduce the ejaculation:

O Muse Pindarian, aid me to my theme;

or the moment that, as a story-teller, you permit yourself the luxury of saying:

Now, gentle reader, is my heroine not a very sweet and oppressed lady?—

at that very moment your reader's illusion that he is present at an affair in real life or that he has been transported by your poem into an atmosphere entirely other than that of his arm-chair or his chimney-corner—at that very moment that illusion will depart. Now the point is this:

The other day I was discussing these matters with a young man whose avowed intention is to sweep away Impressionism. And, after I had energetically put before him the views that I have here expressed, he simply remarked: "Why try to produce an illusion?' To which I could only reply: "Why then write?"

I have asked myself frequently since then why one should try to produce an illusion of reality in the mind of one's reader. Is it just an occupation like any other—like postage-stamp collecting, let us say—or is it the sole end and aim of art? I have spent the greater portion of my working life in preaching that particular doctrine: is it possible, then, that I have been entirely wrong?

Of course it is possible for any man to be entirely wrong; but I confess myself to being as yet unconverted. The chief argument of my futurist friend was that producing an illusion causes the writer so much trouble as not to be worth while. That does not seem to me to be an argument worth very much because—and again I must say it seems to me—the business of an artist is surely to take trouble, but this is probably doing my friend's position, if not his actual argument, an injustice. I am aware that there are quite definite aesthetic objections to the business of producing an illusion. In order to produce an illusion you must justify; in order to justify you must introduce a certain amount of matter that may not appear germane to your story or to your poem. Sometimes, that is to say, it would appear as if for the purpose of proper bringing out of a very slight Impressionist sketch the artist would need an altogether disproportionately enormous frame; a frame absolutely monstrous. Let me again illustrate exactly what I mean. It is not sufficient to say: "Mr Jones was a gentleman who had a strong aversion to rabbit-pie." It is not sufficient, that is to say, if Mr Jones's dislike for rabbit-pie is an integral part of your story. And it is quite possible that a dislike for one form or other of food might form the integral part of a story. Mr Jones might be a hard-worked coal-miner with a well-meaning wife, whom he disliked because he was developing a passion for a frivolous girl. And it might be quite possible that one evening the well-meaning wife, not knowing her husband's peculiarities, but desiring to give him a special and extra treat, should purchase from a stall a couple of rabbits and spend many hours in preparing for him a pie of great succulence, which should be a solace to him when he returns, tired with his labours and rendered nervous by his growing passion for the other lady. The rabbit-pie would then become a symbol—a symbol of the whole tragedy of life. It would symbolize for Mr Jones the whole of his wife's want of sympathy for him and the whole of his distaste for her; his reception of it would symbolize for Mrs Jones the whole hopelessness of her life, since she had expended upon it inventiveness, sedulous care, sentiment, and a good will. From that position, with the rabbit-pie always in the centre of the discussion, you might work up to the murder of Mrs Jones, to Mr Jones's elopement with the other lady—to any tragedy that you liked. For indeed the position contains, as you will perceive, the whole tragedy of life.

And the point is this, that if your tragedy is to be absolutely convincing, it is not sufficient to introduce the fact of Mr Jones's dislike for rabbit-pie by the bare statement. According to your temperament you must sufficiently account for that dislike. You might do it by giving Mr Jones a German grandmother, since all Germans have a peculiar loathing for the rabbit and regard its flesh as unclean. You might then find it necessary to account for the dislike the Germans have for these little creatures; you might have to state that this dislike is a self-preservative race instinct, since in Germany the rabbit is apt to eat certain poisonous fungi, so that one out of every ten will cause the death of its consumer, or you might proceed with your justification of Mr Jones's dislike for rabbit-pie along different lines. You might say that it was a nervous aversion caused by having been violently thrashed when a boy by his father at a time when a rabbit-pie was upon the table. You might then have to go on to justify the nervous temperament of Mr Jones by saying that his mother drank or that his father was a man too studious for his position. You might have to pursue almost endless studies in the genealogy of Mr Jones; because, of course, you might want to account for the studiousness of Mr Jones's father by making him the bastard son of a clergyman, and then you might want to account for the libidinous habits of the clergyman in question. That will be simply a matter of your artistic conscience.

You have to make Mr Jones's dislike for rabbits convincing. You have to make it in the first place convincing to your reader alone; but the odds are that you will try to make it convincing also to yourself, since you yourself in this solitary world of ours will be the only reader that you really and truly know. Now all these attempts at justification, all these details of parentage and the like, may very well prove uninteresting to your reader. They are, however, necessary if your final effect of murder is to be a convincing impression.

But again, if the final province of art is to convince, its first province is to interest. So that, to the extent that your justification is uninteresting, it is an artistic defect. It may sound paradoxical, but the truth is that your Impressionist can only get his strongest effects by using beforehand a great deal of what one may call non-Impressionism. He will make, that is to say, an enormous impression on his reader's mind by the use of three words. But very likely each one of those three words will be prepared for by ten thousand other words. Now are we to regard those other words as being entirely unnecessary, as being, that is to say, so many artistic defects? That I take to be my futurist friend's ultimate assertion.

Says he: "All these elaborate conventions of Conrad or of Maupassant give the reader the impression that a story is being told—all these meetings of bankers and master-mariners in places like the Ship Inn at Greenwich, and all Maupassant's dinner-parties, always in the politest circles, where a countess or a fashionable doctor or someone relates a passionate or a pathetic or a tragic or a merely grotesque incident—as you have it, for instance, in the *Contes de la Bécasse* [1883][3]—all this machinery for getting a story told is so much waste of time. A story is a story; why not just tell it anyhow? You can never tell what sort of an impression you will produce upon a reader. Then why bother about Impressionism? Why not just chance your luck?"

There is a good deal to be said for this point of view. Writing up to my own standards is such an intolerable labour and such a thankless job, since it can't give me the one thing in the world that I desire—that for my part I am determined to drop creative writing for good and all. But I, like all writers of my generation, have been so handicapped that there is small wonder that one should be tired out. On the one hand the difficulty of getting hold of any critical guidance was, when I was a boy, insuperable. There was nothing. Criticism was non-existent; self-conscious art was decried; you were supposed to write by inspiration; you were the young generation with the vine-leaves in your hair, knocking

---

3. For de Maupassant, see p. 5, n. 2 above, and p. 261, n. 6 above, p. 275, n. 3 below.

furiously at the door. On the other hand, one writes for money, for fame, to excite the passion of love, to make an impression upon one's time. Well, God knows what one writes for. But it is certain that one gains neither fame nor money; certainly one does not excite the passion of love, and one's time continues to be singularly unimpressed.

But young writers to-day have a much better chance, on the aesthetic side at least. Here and there, in nooks and corners, they can find someone to discuss their work, not from the point of view of goodness or badness or of niceness or of nastiness, but from the simple point of view of expediency. The moment you can say: "Is it expedient to print *vers libre* in long or short lines, or in the form of prose, or not to print it at all, but to recite it?"—the moment you can find someone to discuss these expediences calmly, or the moment that you can find someone with whom to discuss the relative values of justifying your character or of abandoning the attempt to produce an illusion of reality—at that moment you are very considerably helped; whereas an admirer of your work might fall down and kiss your feet and it would not be of the very least use to you.

II.

This adieu, like Herrick's, to poesy, may seem to be a digression. Indeed it is; and indeed it isn't. It is, that is to say, a digression in the sense that it is a statement not immediately germane to the argument that I am carrying on. But it is none the less an insertion fully in accord with the canons of Impressionism as I understand it. For the first business of Impressionism is to produce an impression, and the only way in literature to produce an impression is to awaken interest. And, in a sustained argument, you can only keep interest awakened by keeping alive, by whatever means you may have at your disposal, the surprise of your reader. You must state your argument; you must illustrate it, and then you must stick in something that appears to have nothing whatever to do with either subject or illustration, so that the reader will exclaim: "What the devil is the fellow driving at?" And then you must go on in the same way—arguing, illustrating and startling and arguing, startling and illustrating—until at the very end your contentions will appear like a ravelled skein. And then, in the last few lines, you will draw towards you the master-string of that seeming confusion, and the whole pattern of the carpet, the whole design of the net-work will be apparent.

This method, you will observe, founds itself upon analysis of the human mind. For no human being likes listening to long and sustained arguments. Such listening is an effort, and no artist has the right to call for any effort from his audience. A picture should come out of its frame and seize the spectator.

Let us now consider the audience to which the artist should address himself. Theoretically a writer should be like the Protestant angel, a messenger of peace and goodwill towards all men. But, inasmuch as the Wingless Victory appears monstrously hideous to a Hottentot,[4] and a beauty of Tunis detestable to the inhabitants of these fortunate islands, it is obvious that each artist must adopt a frame of mind, less Catholic possibly, but certainly more Papist, and address himself, like the angel of the Vulgate, only *hominibus bonæ voluntatis.* He must address himself to such men as be of goodwill; that is to say, he must typify for himself a human soul in sympathy with his own; a silent listener who will be attentive to him, and whose mind acts very much as his acts.[5] According to the measure of this artist's identity with his species, so will be the measure of his temporal greatness. That is why a book, to be really popular, must be either extremely good or extremely bad. For Mr Hall Caine[6] has millions of readers; but then Guy de Maupassant and Flaubert have tens of millions.

I suppose the proposition might be put in another way. Since the great majority of mankind are, on the surface, vulgar and trivial—the stuff to fill graveyards—the great majority of mankind will be easily and quickly affected by art which is vulgar and trivial. But, inasmuch as this world is a very miserable purgatory for most of us sons of men—who remain stuff with which graveyards are filled—inasmuch as horror, despair and incessant strivings are the lot of the most trivial of humanity, who endure them as a rule with commonsense and cheerfulness—so, if a really great master strike the note of horror, of despair, of striving, and so on, he will stir chords in the hearts of a larger number of people than those who are moved by the merely vulgar and the merely trivial. This is probably why *Madame Bovary* has sold more copies than any book ever published, except, of course, books purely religious. But the appeal of religious books is exactly similar.

It may be said that the appeal of *Madame Bovary* is largely sexual. So it is, but it is only in countries like England and the United States that the abominable tortures of sex—or, if you will, the abominable interests of sex—are not supposed to take rank alongside of the horrors of lost honour, commercial ruin, or death itself. For all these things are the components of life, and each is of equal importance.

So, since Flaubert is read in Russia, in Germany, in France, in the United States, amongst the non-Anglo-Saxon population, and by the

---

4. Hottentots were a tribe of South Africa, the first to encounter Dutch settlers; hence here: a noble savage unacquainted with Western culture. "Winged Victory," or "Nike," was the daughter of Pallas and Styx in Greek mythology. "The Winged Victory of Samothrace" is a statue discovered in fragments in 1863, restored in 1875, and now in the Louvre. Ford may be attempting a cultural joke about this headless and armless piece. If so, the joke fails: one of the statue's best-preserved features is its wings.

5. Dowell imagines his "listener" in just these terms. See pp. 15 and 119–20 above.

6. Sir Hall Caine (1853–1931), enormously popular English novelist; author of *The Shadow of a Crime* (1885), *The Deemster* (1887), *The Prodigal Son* (1904), among others.

immense populations of South America, he may be said to have taken
for his audience the whole of the world that could possibly be expected
to listen to a man of his race. (I except, of course, the Anglo-Saxons
who cannot be confidently expected to listen to anything other than the
words produced by Mr George Edwardes,[7] and musical comedy in
general.)

My futurist friend again visited me yesterday, and we discussed this
very question of audiences. Here again he said that I was entirely wrong.
He said that an artist should not address himself to *l'homme moyen sensuel*, but to intellectuals, to people who live at Hampstead[8] and wear no
hats. (He withdrew his contention later.)

I maintain on my own side that one should address oneself to the
cabmen round the corner, but this also is perhaps an exaggeration. My
friend's contention on behalf of the intellectuals was not so much due
to his respect for their intellects. He said that they knew the A B C of an
art, and that it is better to address yourself to an audience that knows the
A B C of an art than to an audience entirely untrammelled by such
knowledge. In this I think he was wrong, for the intellectuals are persons
of very conventional mind, and they acquire as a rule simultaneously
with the A B C of any art the knowledge of so many conventions that it
is almost impossible to make any impression upon their minds. Hampstead and the hatless generally offer an impervious front to futurisms,
simply because they have imbibed from Whistler and the Impressionists
the convention that painting should not be literary.[9] Now every futurist
picture tells a story; so that rules out futurism. Similarly with the cubists.
Hampstead has imbibed, from God knows where, the dogma that all art
should be based on life, or should at least draw its inspiration and its
strength from the representation of nature, So there goes cubism, since
cubism is non-representational, has nothing to do with life, and has a
quite proper contempt of nature.

When I produced my argument that one should address oneself to the
cabmen at the corner, my futurist friend at once flung to me the jeer
about Tolstoi and the peasant. Now the one sensible thing in the long
drivel of nonsense with which Tolstoi misled this dull world[1] was the
remark that art should be addressed to the peasant. My futurist friend

---

7. Probably the most successful Edwardian theatre manager (1852–1915); introduced musical
   comedy to London.
8. Suburb of northwest London heavily colonized then and now by intellectuals, writers, painters, publishers, and the like. "*L'homme moyen sensuel*": the average sensual man.
9. James Abbot McNeill Whistler (1834–1903), American painter, etcher, wit, and eccentric
   who used abstract titles for his pictures (e.g., "Arrangement in Grey and Black" for the famous
   portrait of his mother). By "literary" here Ford seems to mean "containing referential narrative"
   of the sort found typically in Victorian genre painting. Whistler insisted that the harmonious
   arrangement of light, form, and color was the most important element in his work.
1. Although Ford published Tolstoy in *The English Review*, he seems later to have objected to
   his socialism as a betrayal of the feudal ideal. In Ford's overview of world literature, *The March
   of Literature* (1938), he ignores Tolstoy's work.

said that that was sensible for an artist living in Russia or Roumania, but it was an absurd remark to be let fall by a critic living on Campden Hill.[2] His view was that you cannot address yourself to the peasant unless that peasant have evoked folk-song or folk-lores. I don't know why that was his view, but that was his view.

It seems to me to be nonsensical, even if the inner meaning of his dictum was that art should be addressed to a community of practising artists. Art, in fact, should be addressed to those who are not preoccupied. It is senseless to address a Sirventes[3] to a man who is going mad with love, and an Imagiste[4] poem will produce little effect upon another man who is going through the bankruptcy court.

It is probable that Tolstoi thought that in Russia the non-preoccupied mind was to be found solely amongst the peasant class, and that is why he said that works of art should be addressed to the peasant. I don't know how it may be in Russia, but certainly in Occidental Europe the non-preoccupied mind—which is the same thing as the peasant intelligence—is to be found scattered throughout every grade of society. When I used just now the instances of a man made for love, or distracted by the prospect of personal ruin, I was purposely misleading. For a man mad as a hatter for love of a worthless creature, or a man maddened by the tortures of bankruptcy, by dishonour or by failure, may yet have, by the sheer necessity of his nature, a mind more receptive than most other minds. The mere craving for relief from his personal thoughts may make him take quite unusual interest in a work of art. So that is not preoccupation in my intended sense, but for a moment the false statement crystallised quite clearly what I was aiming at.

The really impassible mind is not the mind quickened by passion, but the mind rendered slothful by preoccupation purely trivial. The "English gentleman" is, for instance, an absolutely hopeless being from this point of view. His mind is so taken up by considerations of what is good form, of what is good feeling, of what is even good fellowship; he is so concerned to pass unnoticed in the crowd; he is so set upon having his room like everyone else's room, that he will find it impossible to listen to any plea for art which is exceptional, vivid, or startling. The cabman, on the other hand, does not mind being thought a vulgar sort of bloke; in consequence he will form a more possible sort of audience. On the other hand, amongst the purely idler classes it is perfectly possible to find individuals who are so firmly and titularly gentle folk that they don't have to care a damn what they do. These again are possible audiences for the artist. The point is really, I take it, that the preoccupation that is fatal to art is the moral or the social preoccupation. Actual

2. Ford's London address before and during World War I.
3. "A form of [Provençal] poem or lay, usually satirical, employed by the troubadours of the Middle Ages" [SOED]. For "troubadours," see p. 18, n. 8 above.
4. See p. 4, n. 4 above.

preoccupations matter very little. Your cabman may drive his taxi through exceedingly difficult streets; he may have half-a-dozen close shaves in a quarter of an hour. But when those things are over they are over, and he has not the necessity of a cabman. His point of view as to what is art, good form, or, let us say, the proper relation of the sexes, is unaffected. He may be a hungry man, a thirsty man, or even a tired man, but he will not necessarily have his finger upon his moral pulse, and he will not hold as æsthetic dogma the idea that no painting must tell a story, or the moral dogma that passion only becomes respectable when you have killed it.

It is these accursed dicta that render an audience hopeless to the artist, that render art a useless pursuit and the artist himself a despised individual.

So that those are the best individuals for an artist's audience who have least listened to accepted ideas—who are acquainted with deaths at street corners, with the marital infidelities of crowded courts, with the goodness of heart of the criminal, with the meanness of the undetected or the sinless, who know the queer odd jumble of negatives that forms our miserable and hopeless life. If I had to choose as reader I would rather have one who had never read anything before but the *Newgate Calendar*,[5] or the records of crime, starvation and divorce in the Sunday paper—I would rather have him for a reader than the man who had discovered the song that the sirens sang, or had by heart the whole of the *Times Literary Supplement*, from its inception to the present day. Such a peasant intelligence will know that this is such a queer world that anything may be possible. And that is the type of intelligence that we need.

Of course, it is more difficult to find these intelligences in the town than in the rural districts. A man thatching all day long has time for many queer thoughts; so has a man who from sunrise to sunset is trimming a hedge into shape with a bagging hook. I have, I suppose, myself thought more queer thoughts when digging potatoes than at any other time during my existence. It is, for instance, very queer if you are digging potatoes in the late evening, when it has grown cool after a very hot day, to thrust your hand into the earth after a potato and to find that the earth is quite warm—is about flesh-heat. Of course, the clods would be warm because the sun would have been shining on them all day, and the air gives up its heat much quicker than the earth. But it is none the less a queer sensation.

Now, if the person experiencing that sensation have what I call a peasant intelligence, he will just say that it is a queer thing and will store it away in his mind along with his other experiences. It will go along

5. The sensational *Newgate Calendar and the Divorce Court Chronicle* (1872) contained biographies of the more notorious criminals confined in Newgate Prison; popular Victorian reading.

with the remembrance of hard frost, of fantastic icicles, the death of rabbits pursued by stoats, the singularly quick ripening of corn in a certain year, the fact that such and such a man was overlooked by a wise woman and so died because, his wife, being tired of him, had paid the wise woman five sixpences which she had laid upon the table in the form of a crown; or along with the other fact that a certain man murdered his wife by the use of a packet of sheep dip which he had stolen from a field where the farmer was employed at lamb washing. All these remembrances he will have in his mind, not classified under any headings of social reformers, or generalized so as to fulfil any fancied moral law.

But the really dangerous person for the artist will be the gentleman who, chancing to put his hand into the ground and to find it about as warm as the breast of a woman, if you could thrust your hand between her chest and her stays, will not accept the experience as an experience, but will start talking about the breast of mother-nature. This last man is the man whom the artist should avoid, since he will regard phenomena not as phenomena, but as happenings, with which he may back up preconceived dogmas—as, in fact, so many sticks with which to beat a dog.

No, what the artist needs is the man with the quite virgin mind—the man who will not insist that grass must always be painted green, because all the poets, from Chaucer till the present day, had insisted on talking about the green grass, or the green leaves, or the green straw.

Such a man, if he comes to your picture and sees you have painted a haycock bright purple will say:

"Well, I have never myself observed a haycock to be purple, but I can understand that if the sky is very blue and the sun is setting very red, the shady side of the haycock might well appear to be purple." That is the kind of peasant intelligence that the artist needs for his audience.

And the whole of Impressionism comes to this: having realized that the audience to which you will address yourself must have this particular peasant intelligence, or, if you prefer it, this particular and virgin openness of mind, you will then figure to yourself an individual, a silent listener, who shall be to yourself the *homo bonæ voluntatis*—man of goodwill. To him, then, you will address your picture, your poem, your prose story, or your argument. You will seek to capture his interest; you will seek to hold his interest. You will do this by methods of surprise, of fatigue, by passages of sweetness in your language, by passages suggesting the sudden and brutal shock of suicide. You will give him passages of dulness, so that your bright effects may seem more bright; you will alternate, you will dwell for a long time upon an intimate point; you will seek to exasperate so that you may the better enchant. You will, in short, employ all the devices of the prostitute. If you are too proud for this you may be the better gentleman or the better lady, but you will be the worse artist. For the artist must always be humble and humble and again humble, since before the greatness of his task he himself is nothing. He must again be outrageous, since the greatness of his task calls for enormous excesses by means of which he may recoup his energies. That is why the artist is, quite rightly, regarded with suspicion by people who desire to live in tranquil and ordered society.

But one point is very important. The artist can never write to satisfy himself—to get, as the saying is, something off the chest. He must not write propaganda which it is his desire to write; he must not write rolling periods, the production of which gives him a soothing feeling in his digestive organs or wherever it is. He must write always so as to satisfy that other fellow—that other fellow who has too clear an intelligence to let his attention be captured or his mind deceived by special pleadings in favour of any given dogma. You must not write so as to improve him, since he is a much better fellow than yourself, and you must not write so as to influence him, since he is a granite rock, a peasant intelligence, the gnarled bole of a sempiternal oak, against which you will dash yourself in vain. It is in short no pleasant kind of job to be a conscious artist. You won't have any vine-leaves in your poor old hair; you won't just dash your quill into an inexhaustible ink-well and pour out fine frenzies. No, you will be just the skilled workman doing his job with drill or chisel or mallet. And you will get precious little out of it. Only, just at times, when you come to look again at some work of yours that you have quite forgotten, you will say, "Why, that is rather well done." That is all.

FORD MADOX FORD

[Developing the Theory of Impressionism with Conrad] †

* * *This is a novel [1] exactly on the lines of the formula that Conrad and the writer evolved. For it became very early evident to us that what was the matter with the Novel, and the British novel in particular, was that it went straight forward, whereas in your gradual making acquaintanceship with your fellows you never do go straight forward. You meet an English gentleman at your golf club. He is beefy, full of health, the

† From *Joseph Conrad: A Personal Remembrance* (London: Gerald Duckworth, 1924) 129–30, 179–84, 185–95, 197, 198–99, 200–201, 202, 204–5, 206–8, 210. The articles which constitute the book first appeared in *Transatlantic Review* (edited by Ford). Copyright 1924 by Ford Madox Ford. Reprinted with the permission of Gerald Duckworth & Co. Ltd., London. Notes are by the editor of this Norton Critical Edition.
1. Ford interestingly blurs generic boundaries here by describing his memoir as a "novel."

moral of the boy from an English Public School of the finest type. You discover, gradually, that he is hopelessly neurasthenic, dishonest in matters of small change, but unexpectedly self-sacrificing, a dreadful liar but a most painfully careful student of lepidoptera and, finally, from the public prints, a bigamist who was once, under another name, hammered on the Stock Exchange. . . . Still, there he is, the beefy, full-fed fellow, moral of an English Public School product. To get such a man in fiction you could not begin at his beginning and work his life chronologically to the end. You must first get him in with a strong impression, and then work backwards and forwards over his past. . . . That theory at least we gradually evolved.

*   *   *

It might be as well here to put down under separate headings, such as *Construction, Development* and the like, what were the formulæ for the writing of the novel at which Conrad and the writer had arrived, say in 1902 or so, before we finally took up and finished *Romance* [1903]. The reader will say that that is to depart from the form of the novel in which form this book pretends to be written. But that is not the case. The novel more or less gradually, more or less deviously lets you into the secrets of the characters of the men with whom it deals. Then, having got them in, it sets them finally to work. Some novels, and still more short stories, will get a character in with a stroke or two as does Maupassant in the celebrated sentence in the "Reine Hortense" which Conrad and the writer were never tired of—quite intentionally—misquoting: "C'était un monsieur à favoris rouges qui entrait toujours le premier. . . ."[2] He was a gentleman with red whiskers who always went first through a doorway. . . . *That* gentleman is so sufficiently got in that you need know no more of him to understand how he will act. He has been 'got in' and can get to work at once. That is called by the official British critics the static method and is, for some reason or other, contemned in England.

Other novels, however, will take much, much longer to develop their characters. Some—and this one is an example—will take almost a whole book to really get their characters in and will then dispose of the 'action' with a chapter, a line, or even a word—or two. The most wonderful instance of all of that is the ending of the most wonderful of all Maupassant's stories, 'Champs d'Oliviers'[3]. *   *   *

General Effect

We agreed that the general effect of a novel must be the general effect that life makes on mankind. A novel must therefore not be a narration,

2. See "On Impressionism," p. 261 above.
3. For de Maupassant, see p. 5, n. 2 of text and pp. 261, n. 6, and 267, n. 3 above.

a report. Life does not say to you: In 1914 my next door neighbour, Mr. Slack, erected a greenhouse and painted it with Cox's green aluminum paint. . . . If you think about the matter you will remember, in various unordered pictures, how one day Mr. Slack appeared in his garden and contemplated the wall of his house. You will then try to remember the year of that occurrence and you will fix it as August 1914 because having had the foresight to bear the municipal stock of the city of Liège you were able to afford a first-class season ticket for the first time in your life. You will remember Mr. Slack—then much thinner because it was before he found out where to buy that cheap Burgundy of which he has since drunk an inordinate quantity though whisky you think would be much better for him! Mr. Slack again came into his garden, this time with a pale, weaselly-faced fellow, who touched his cap from time to time. Mr. Slack will point to his housewall several times at different points, the weaselly fellow touching his cap at each pointing. Some days after, coming back from business you will have observed against Mr. Slack's wall. . . . At this point you will remember that you were then the manager of the fresh-fish branch of Messrs. Catlin and Clovis in Fenchurch Street. . . . What a change since then! Millicent had not yet put her hair up. . . . You will remember how Millicent's hair looked, rather pale and burnished in plaits. You will remember how it now looks, henna'd: and you will see in one corner of your mind's eye a little picture of Mr. Mills the vicar talking—oh, very kindly—to Millicent after she has come back from Brighton. . . . But perhaps you had better not risk that. You remember some of the things said by means of which Millicent has made you cringe—and her expression! . . . Cox's Aluminium Paint! . . . You remember the half empty tin that Mr. Slack showed you—he had a most undignified cold—with the name in a horse-shoe over a blue circle that contained a red lion asleep in front of a real-gold sun. . . .

And, if that is how the building of your neighbour's greenhouse comes back to you, just imagine how it will be with your love-affairs that are so much more complicated. . . .

Impressionism

We accepted without much protest the stigma: "Impressionists" that was thrown at us. In those days Impressionists were still considered to be bad people: Atheists, Reds, wearing red ties with which to frighten householders. But we accepted the name because Life appearing to us much as the building of Mr. Slack's greenhouse comes back to you, we saw that Life did not narrate, but made impressions on our brains. We in turn, if we wished to produce on you an effect of life, must not narrate but render . . . impressions.

Selection

We agreed that the whole of Art consists in selection. To render your remembrance of your career as a fish-salesman might enhance the story of Mr. Slack's greenhouse, or it might *not*. A little image of iridescent, blue-striped, black-striped, white fish on a white marble slab with water trickling down to them round a huge mass of orange salmon-roe; a vivid description of a horrible smell caused by a cat having stolen and hidden in the thick of your pelargoniums a cod's head that you had brought back as a perquisite, you having subsequently killed the cat with a hammer, but long, long before you had rediscovered her fishy booty. . . . Such little impressions might be useful as contributing to illustrate your character—one should not kill a cat with a hammer! They might illustrate your sense of the beautiful—or your fortitude under affliction—or the disagreeableness of Mr. Slack, who had a delicate sense of smell—or the point of view of your only daughter Millicent.

We should then have to consider whether your sense of the beautiful or your fortitude could in our rendering carry the story forward or interest the reader. If it did we should include it; if in our opinion it was not likely to, we should leave it out. Or the story of the cat might in itself seem sufficiently amusing to be inserted as a purposed *longueur*, so as to give the idea of the passage of time. . . . It may be more amusing to read the story of a cat with your missing dinner than to read: "A fortnight elapsed. . . ." Or it might be better after all to write boldly: "Mr. Slack, after a fortnight had elapsed, remarked one day very querulously: 'That smell seems to get worse instead of better.' "

Selection (Speeches)

That last would be compromise, for it would be narration instead of rendering: it would be far *better* to give an idea of the passage of time by picturing a cat with a cod's head, but the length of the story must be considered. Sometimes to render anything at all in a given space will take up too much room—even to render the effect and delivery of a speech. Then just boldly and remorselessly you must relate and *risk* the introduction of yourself as author, with the danger that you may destroy all the illusion of the story.

* * *

The rendering in fact of speeches gave Conrad and the writer more trouble than any other department of the novel whatever. It introduced at once the whole immense subject of under what convention the novel is to be written. For whether you tell it direct and as author—which is the more difficult way—or whether you put it into the mouth of a character—which is easier by far but much more cumbersome—the question of reporting or rendering speeches has to be faced. To pretend that any character or any author writing directly can remember whole speeches with all their words for a matter of twenty-four hours, let alone twenty-four years, is absurd. The most that the normal person carries away of a conversation after even a couple of hours is just a salient or characteristic phrase or two, and a mannerism of the speaker. Yet, if the reader stops to think at all, or has any acuteness whatever, to render Mr. Slack's speech directly: "Thet there odour is enough to do all the porters in Common Gorden in. Lorst week it wouldn' no more 'n 'v sent a ole squad of tinwiskets barmy on the crumpet . . ." and so on through an entire monologue of a page and a half, must set the reader at some point or other wondering, how the author or the narrator can possibly, even if they were present, have remembered every word of Mr. Slack's long speech. Yet the object of the novelist is to keep the reader entirely oblivious of the fact that the author exists—even of the fact that he is reading a book. This is of course not possible to the bitter end, but a reader *can* be rendered very engrossed, and the nearer you can come to making him entirely insensitive to his surroundings, the more you will have succeeded.

Then again, directly reported speeches in a book do move very slowly; by the use of indirect locutions, together with the rendering of the effects of other portions of speech, you can get a great deal more into a given space. There is a type of reader that likes what is called conversations—but that type is rather the reader in an undeveloped state than the reader who has read much. * * * But quite often we compromised and gave passages of direct enough speech.

This was one of the matters as to which the writer was more uncompromising than was Conrad. In the novel which he did at last begin on his forty-first birthday there will be found to be hardly any direct speech at all, and probably none that is more than a couple of lines in length. Conrad indeed later arrived at the conclusion that, a novel being in the end a matter of convention—and in the beginning too for the matter of that, since what are type, paper, bindings and all the rest, but matters of agreement and convenience—you might as well stretch convention a little farther, and postulate that your author or your narrator is a person of a prodigious memory for the spoken. He had one minute passion with regard to conversations: he could not bear the repetition of 'he said's and 'she said's, and would spend agitated hours in chasing those locutions out of his or our pages and substituting: 'he replied,' 'she ejaculated,' 'answered Mr. Verloc'[4] and the like. The writer was less moved by this

---

4. According to Ford earlier in this text (p. 170), the novel Conrad began on his forty-first birth-day was *The Rescue*, the plot of which Conrad sketched to William Heinemann in 1898 after the publication of *The Nigger*. Adolf Verloc is the central male protagonist of *The Secret Agent* (1907).

consideration: it seemed to him that you could employ the words 'he said' as often as you like, accepting them as being unnoticeable, like 'a,' 'the' 'his' 'her,' or 'very.'

Conversations

One unalterable rule that we had for the rendering of conversations—for genuine conversations that are an exchange of thought, not interrogatories or statements of fact—was that no speech of one character should ever answer the speech that goes before it. This is almost invariably the case in real life where few people listen, because they are always preparing their own next speeches. When, of a Saturday evening, you are conversing over the fence with your friend Mr. Slack, you hardly notice that he tells you he has seen an incredibly coloured petunia at a market-gardener's, because you are dying to tell him that you have determined to turn author to the extent of writing a letter on local politics to the newspaper of which, against his advice, you have become a large shareholder.

He says: "Right down extraordinary that petunia was——"

You say: "What would you think now of my. . . ."

He says: "Diamond-shaped stripes it had, blue-black and salmon. . . ."

You say: "I've always thought I had a bit of a gift. . . ."

Your daughter Millicent interrupts: "Julia Gower has got a pair of snake-skin shoes. She bought them at Wiston and Willocks's."

You miss Mr. Slack's next two speeches in wondering where Millicent got that bangle on her wrist. You will have to tell her more carefully than ever that she must *not* accept presents from Tom, Dick and Harry. By the time you have come out of that reverie Mr. Slack is remarking:

"I said to him use turpentine and sweet oil, three parts to two. What do you think?"

Surprise

We agreed that the one quality that gave interest to Art was the quality of surprise. That is very well illustrated in the snatch of conversation just given. If you reported a long speech of Mr. Slack's to the effect that he was going to enter some of his petunias for the local flower show and those, with his hydrangeas and ornamental sugar-beet, might well give him the Howard Cup for the third time, in which case it would become his property out and out. He would then buy two silver and cut-glass epergnes[5] one to stand on each side of the Cup on his sideboard. He always did think that a touch of silver and cut glass. . . . If, after that

5. A branched center-dish or ornament for a dinner table, usually to hold dessert, flowers, or pickles.

you gave a long speech of your own: after, naturally, you had added a few commonplaces as a politeness to Mr. Slack: if you gave a long speech in which with modesty you dwelt on the powers of observation and of the pen that you had always considered yourself to possess, and in which you announced that you certainly meant to write a letter to the paper in which you had shares—on the statuary in the façade of the new town hall which was an offence to public decency. . . . And if in addition to that you added a soliloquy from your daughter Millicent to the effect that she intended to obtain on credit from your bootmakers, charging them to your account, a pair of scarlet morocco shoes with two-inch heels with which to go joy-riding on the Sunday with a young actor who played under the name of Hildebrand Hare and who had had his portrait in your paper. . . . If you gave all these long speeches one after the other you might be aware of a certain dullness when you re-read that *compte rendu*.[6] . . . But if you carefully broke up petunias, statuary, and flower-show motives and put them down in little shreds one contrasting with the other, you would arrive at something much more coloured, animated, life-like and interesting and you would convey a profoundly significant lesson as to the self-engrossment of humanity. Into that live scene you could then drop the piece of news that you wanted to convey and so you would carry the chapter a good many stages forward.

Here, again, compromise must necessarily come in: there must come a point in the dramatic working up of every scene in which the characters do directly answer each other, for a speech or for two or three speeches. It was in this department, as has already been pointed out, that Conrad was matchless and the writer very deficient. Or, again, a point may come in which it is necessary—in which at least it is to take the line of least resistance—to report directly a whole tremendous effort of eloquence as ebullient as an oration by Mr. Lloyd George[7] on the hymns of the Welsh nation. For there are times when the paraphernalia of indirect speech, interruptions and the rest retard your action too much. Then they must go: the sense of reality must stand down before the necessity to get on.

But, on the whole, the indirect, interrupted method of handling interviews is invaluable for giving a sense of the complexity, the tantalisation, the shimmering, the haze, that life is. In the pre-war period the English novel began at the beginning of a hero's life and went straight on to his marriage without pausing to look aside. This was all very well in its way, but the very great objection could be offered against it that such a story was too confined to its characters and, too self-centredly,

6. [Literary] review (French).
7. David Lloyd George (1863–1945), Welsh radical Liberal Chancellor of the Exchequer. Ford was suspicious of him as a leading assailant of the feudal system.

went on, *in vacuo*. If you are so set on the affair of your daughter Millicent with the young actor that you forget that there *are* flower shows and town halls with nude statuary your intellect will appear a thing much more circumscribed than it should be. Or, to take a larger matter. A great many novelists have treated of the late war in terms solely of the war: in terms of pip-squeaks, trench-coats, wire-aprons,[8] shells, mud, dust, and sending the bayonet home with a grunt. For that reason interest in the late war is said to have died. But, had you taken part actually in those hostilities, you would know how infinitely little part the actual fighting itself took in your mentality. You would be lying on your stomach, in a beast of a funk, with an immense, horrid German barrage going on all over and round you and with hell and all let loose. But, apart from the occasional, petulant question: "When the deuce will our fellows get going and shut 'em up?" your thoughts were really concentrated on something quite distant: on your daughter Millicent's hair, on the fall of the Asquith[9] Ministry, on your financial predicament, on why your regimental ferrets kept on dying, on whether Latin is really necessary to an education, or in what way really *ought* the Authorities to deal with certain diseases. . . . You were there, but great shafts of thought from the outside, distant and unattainable world infinitely for the greater part occupied your mind.

It was that effect then, that Conrad and the writer sought to get into their work, that being Impressionism.

But these two writers were not unaware that there are other methods: they were not rigid in their own methods: they were sensible to the fact that compromise is at all times necessary in the execution of every work of art.

Let us come, then, to the eternally vexed seas of the Literary Ocean.

Style

We agreed on this axiom:

The first business of Style is to make work interesting: the second business of Style is to make work interesting: the third business of Style is to make work interesting: the fourth business of Style is to make work interesting: the fifth business of Style. . . .

Style, then, has no other business.

A style interests when it carries the reader along: it is then a good style. A style ceases to interest when by reason of disjointed sentences, over-used words, monotonous or jog-trot cadences, it fatigues the reader's mind. *Too* startling words, however apt, *too* just images, too great displays of cleverness are apt in the long run to be as fatiguing as

8. Strips of barbed wire-entanglements. "Pip-squeaks": small-caliber high-velocity shells.
9. Herbert Henry Asquith (1852–1928), Liberal prime minister from 1908 to 1916; ousted by Lloyd George.

the most over-used words or the most jog-trot cadences. That a face resembles a Dutch clock has been too often said; to say that it resembles a ham is inexact and conveys nothing; to say that it has the mournfulness of an old, squashed-in meat tin, cast away on a waste building lot, would be smart—but too much of that sort of thing would become a nuisance. To say that a face was cramoisy is undesirable: few people nowadays know what the word means. Its employment will make the reader marvel at the user's erudition: in thus marvelling he ceases to consider the story and an impression of vagueness or length is produced on his mind. A succession of impressions of vagueness and length render a book in the end unbearable.

There are, of course, pieces of writing intended to convey the sense of the author's cleverness, knowledge of obsolete words or power of inventing similes: with such exercises Conrad and the writer never concerned themselves.

We used to say: the first lesson that an author has to learn is that of humility. Blessed are the humble because they do not get between the reader's legs. Before everything the author must learn to suppress himself: he must learn that the first thing he has to consider is his story and the last thing that he has to consider is his story, and in between that he will consider his story.

We used to say that a passage of good style began with a fresh, usual word, and continued with fresh, usual words to the end: there was nothing more to it. When we felt that we had really got hold of the reader, with a great deal of caution we would introduce a word not common to a very limited vernacular, but that only very occasionally. Very occasionally indeed: practically never. Yet it is in that way that a language grows and keeps alive. People get tired of hearing the same words over and over again. . . . It is again a matter for compromise.

Our chief masters in style were Flaubert and Maupassant: Flaubert in the greater degree, Maupassant in the less. In about the proportion of a sensible man's whisky and soda. We stood as it were on those hills and thence regarded the world. We remembered long passages of Flaubert: elaborated long passages in his spirit and with his cadences and then translated them into passages of English as simple as the subject under treatment would bear. We remembered short, staccato passages of Maupassant: invented short staccato passages in his spirit and then translated them into English as simple as the subject would bear. Differing subjects bear differing degrees of simplicity. * * *

So we talked and wrote a Middle-High-English of as unaffected a sort as would express our thoughts. And that was all that there really was to our 'style'. Our greatest admiration for a stylist in any language was given to W. H. Hudson [1] of whom Conrad said that his writing was like the

---

1. See p. 258, n. 1 above.

grass that the good God made to grow and when it was there you could not tell how it came.

Carefully examined a good—an interesting—style will be found to consist in a constant succession of tiny, unobservable surprises. * * *

* * * The catalogue of an ironmonger's store is uninteresting as literature because things in it are all classified and thus obvious: the catalogue of a farm sale is more interesting because things in it are contrasted. No one would for long read: "Nails, drawn wire, ½ inch, per lb. . . . ; nails do., ¾ inch, per lb. . . . ; nails, do., inch, per lb. . . ." But it is often not disagreeable to read desultorily "*Lot* 267. Pair rabbit gins. *Lot* 268, Antique powder flask. *Lot* 269, Malay Kris. *Lot* 270, Set of six sporting prints by Herring. *Lot* 271, Silver caudle cup . . ." for that, as far as it goes, has the quality of surprise.

That is, perhaps, enough about Style. This is not a technical manual, and at about this point we arrive at a region in which the writer's memory is not absolutely clear as to the points on which he and Conrad were agreed. We made in addition an infinite number of experiments, together and separately in points of style and cadence. The writer * * * wrote one immense book entirely in sentences of not more than ten syllables. He read the book over. He found it read immensely long. He went through it all again. He joined short sentences: he introduced relative clauses: he wrote in long sentences that had a gentle sonority and ended with a dying fall. The book read less long. Much less long.

* * *

Cadence

This was the one subject upon which we never came to any agreement. It was the writer's view that everyone has a natural cadence of his own from which in the end he cannot escape. Conrad held that a habit of good cadence could be acquired by the study of models. His own he held came to him from constant reading of Flaubert. He did himself probably an injustice.

But questions of cadence and accentuation as of prosody in general we were chary of discussing. They were matters as to which Conrad was very touchy. His ear was singularly faulty for one who was a great writer of elaborated prose so that at times the writer used to wonder how the deuce he *did* produce his effects of polyphonic closings to paragraphs. In speaking English he had practically no idea of accentuation whatever, and indeed no particular habits. * * *

The curious thing was that when he read his prose aloud his accentuation was absolutely faultless. So that it always seemed to the writer that Conrad's marvellous gift of language was, in the end, dramatic. * * *

Conrad * * * never wrote a true short story, a matter of two or three pages of minutely considered words, ending with a smack . . . with what the French call a *coup de canon*. His stories were always what for lack of a better phrase one has to call 'long-short' stories. For these the form is practically the same as that of the novel. Or, to avoid the implication of saying that there is only one form for the novel, it would be better to put it that the form of long-short stories may vary as much as may the form for novels. The short story of Maupassant, of Tchekhov or even of the late O. Henry[2] is practically stereotyped—the introduction of a character in a word or two, a word or two for atmosphere, a few paragraphs for story, and then, click! a sharp sentence that flashes the illumination of the idea over the whole.

This Conrad—and for the matter of that, the writer—never so much as attempted, either apart or in collaboration. The reason for this lies in all that is behind the mystic word 'justification.' Before everything a story must convey a sense of inevitability: that which happens in it must seem to be the only thing that could have happened. Of course a character may cry: "If I had then acted differently how different everything would now be." The problem of the author is to make his then action the only action that character could have taken. It must be inevitable, because of his character, because of his ancestry, because of past illness or on account of the gradual coming together of the thousand small circumstances by which Destiny, who is inscrutable and august, will push us into one certain predicament. * * *

* * * Conrad—and for the matter of that the writer—was never satisfied that he had really and sufficiently got his characters in: he was never convinced that he had convinced the reader, this accounting for the great lengths of some of his books. He never introduced a character, however subsidiary, without providing that character with ancestry and hereditary characteristics, or at least with home surroundings—always supposing that character had any influence on the inevitability of the story. Any policeman who arrested any character must be 'justified' because the manner in which he effected the arrest, his mannerisms, his vocabulary and his voice, might have a permanent effect on the psychology of the prisoner. * * *

And of course the introducing of the biography of a character may have the great use of giving contrast to the tone of the rest of the book. . . . Supposing that in your history of your affair with Mr. Slack you think that the note of your orderly middle-class home is growing a little monotonous, it would be very handy if you could discover that Mr. Slack had a secret, dipsomaniacal wife, confined in a country cottage under the care of a rather criminal old couple: with a few pages of biography of that old couple you could give a very pleasant relief to the sameness of your narrative. In that way the sense of reality is procured.

---

2. Pseudonym of William Sydney Porter (1862–1910), American short-story writer.

Philosophy, Etc.

We agreed that the novel is absolutely the only vehicle for the thought of our day. With the novel you can do anything: you can inquire into every department of life, you can explore every department of the world of thought. The one thing that you can not do is to propagandise, as author, for any cause. You must not, as author, utter any views: above all you must not fake any events. You must not, however humanitarian you may be, over-elaborate the fear felt by a coursed rabbit.

It is obviously best if you can contrive to be without views at all: your business with the world is rendering, not alteration. * * *

Progression d'Effet

There is just one other point. In writing a novel we agreed that every word set on paper—*every* word set on paper—must carry the story forward and, that as the story progressed, the story must be carried forward faster and faster and with more and more intensity. That is called *progression d'effet*, words for which there is no English equivalent.

* * *

FORD MADOX FORD

Techniques †

Technique is perhaps the most odious word in the English language. I hope that by adding the above "s" some of the odium may be dispelled. It is necessary from time to time to emphasize the fact that writing in general and imaginative writing in particular are the products of craftsmanship. In the middle ages a craft was called a mystery. It is a good word, for it is a mystery why we write and a mystery how great writers do it.

They do it by observing certain rules—or after having observed certain rules for a long time, by jumping off from them. You may if you like say that great literatures have only arisen when technical rules have been jumped off from—Shakespeare and the Elizabethans having jumped off from the classicisms of *Ferrex and Porrex*; the Cockney School of Poetry[1] from the classical stultifications of an Eighteenth Century in

---

† From *Southern Review* 1 (July 1935): 20–35. Notes are by the editor of this Norton Critical Edition.

1. Term of abuse used in attacks (begun October 1817) on Leigh Hunt, Hazlitt, and Keats by John Gibson Lockhart and friends in *Blackwood's Magazine*. "*Gorboduc, or Ferrex and Porrex*": earliest known English blank verse tragedy (modeled on Seneca's work); performed 1561, pub. 1565; 1st edition attributes first three acts to Thomas Norton (1532–1584) and last two to Thomas Sackville (1536–1608).

decay; or Flaubert and the French, English, and American Impressionists, whose methods I propose here to analyse for you, from the classical
slipshodnesses that preceded them. The case of the Impressionists differs
from that of the others, however, in that they practised, and, when they
had the time, enjoined, a tightening rather than any slackening of the
rules.

Sang Mr. Kipling:

> There are five and forty ways
> Of inditing tribal lays
> And every single one of them is right![2]

That is to say that Mr. Kipling, having proved himself an extraordinarily great master of the most difficult of all crafts—that of the short
and short-long story writer—had to hasten to excuse himself by proving
that at heart he was, and always meant to be, an English gentleman.
For the English gentleman may write . . . but before all things he must
not be a writer. He may, that is to say, at odd moments sit down and
toss off something, but he must not do it earnestly or according to any
rules. Or, if he does observe any rules, he must hasten, hasten, hasten
to assert that he does not. Otherwise he would not be received in really
good drawing-rooms.

I do not mean to assert that occasionally a masterpiece may not be
tossed off or that the roll of Royal and Noble Authors does not number
a master or two. You have Clarendon who wrote the *History of the
Rebellion*, Beckford who wrote the *Letters from Portugal*. . . . But how
much more Clarendon might we not have had, had he not been father
to a queen, or how much more Beckford, had he not found it necessary
to be the nabob-builder of Fonthill? And above all, how much more
Cunninghame Graham if Mr. Robert Bontine Cunninghame Graham[3]
had not happened to be, in addition to the 'incomparable writer of
English,' Earl of Monteith, King of Scotland if he had his rights, and
the very spit and image of his connection, Henri IV of France.

That indeed is the real tragedy of English literature . . . is why
England has in fact no literature but only some great, isolated peaks.
For, to possess a Literature, a country must have a whole cloud—or
better still, a whole populace—of writers instinct with a certain skill in,

---

2. From "In the Neolithic Age" (1895), a satire on literary infighting: "But my totem saw the
shame; from his ridgepole-shrine he came, / And he told me in a vision of the night:- / 'There
are nine and sixty ways of constructing tribal lays, / And every single one of them is right!' "
3. British politician and writer (1852–1936), much admired as stylist by Ford and Conrad (introduced latter's *Tales of Hearsay*, 1925); author of over thirty books. Edward Hyde, 1st Earl of
Clarendon (1609–1674), English statesman, historian, and grandfather of two queens, Mary
II and Anne; author of *The History of the Rebellion and Civil Wars in England* (pub. posthu-
mously, 3 vols., 1704). William Beckford (1760–1844), English writer, politician, and wealthy
dilettante who, c. 1796, built Fonthill Abbey, an extravagant Gothic castle ("nabob" = rich
and luxurious person); author of famous Gothic novel *Vathek* (1786) and several travel books
including *Italy; with Sketches of Spain and Portugal, in a Series of Letters . . .*
(1834).

a certain respect for, a certain productivity of, writing. You must in that country be able to go, say to a railway bookstall, and by merely stretching out a random hand, take the first book that comes and find it to be, for certain, well written, well constructed, instinct with a certain knowledge of the values of life—such a work in short, as a proper man may let himself be seen reading without loss of self-respect. You can do that in France, you could do it in Germany before Mr. Hitler began his burnings; you are beginning to be able to do it in the United States. But in the home and cradle of the writings of our race you have not been able to do it since the XVIIth Century—when of course there were no railway bookstalls. It is only a respect for a technique that can ensure this form of civilization for a country because the writing of books is a difficult matter—the writing of any kind of book.

I am going to write particularly about the writing of works of the imagination—and specifically about the writing of novels. But the factual book is susceptible of, and gains as much by, care in construction, and the poem gains as much by attention to lucidity or verbiage and progression of effect, as does any novel. The convention of the narrative is as important to the historian of the battle of Minden as it is to the novelist trembling lest any slip in his construction should make his reader slacken or altogether lose his interest.

And the real difference between the writers of the Impressionist group, who since the days of Flaubert have dominated the public mind, and their predecessors is that the post-Flaubertians have studied, primarily, to hold just that public mind, whilst their predecessors, though wishing obviously to be read, never gave a thought to how interest may be inevitably—and almost scientifically—aroused. The novelist from, say, Richardson to Meredith[4] thought that he had done his job when he had set down a simple tale beginning with the birth of his hero or his heroine and ending when the ring of marriage bells completed the simple convention. But the curious thing was that he never gave a thought to how stories are actually told or even to how the biographies of one's friends come gradually before one.

The main difference between a novel by the forgotten James Payn[5]— who in his day was a much respected and not too popular novelist—and a work of the unforgettable author of *The Turn of the Screw* [1898], who also, you will observe was a much respected and certainly not too popular novelist, is that the one recounts whilst the other presents. The one makes statements; the other builds suggestions of happenings on suggestions of happenings.

4. George Meredith (1828–1909), British novelist and poet; author of *The Ordeal of Richard Feverel* (1859), *Modern Love* (1862), *The Egoist* (1879), among others. Samuel Richardson (1689–1761), author of *Pamela* (2 vols. 1740, 2 vols. 1741), *Clarissa Harlowe* (7 vols. 1747–48), and *The History of Sir Charles Grandison* (7 vols. 1753–54).
5. Editor of *Chambers's Journal* (1859–74) and of *Cornhill Magazine* (1882–96); author of *Not Wooed But Won* (1871) and *The Canon's Ward* (1884), among others. Ford prints "Payne."

On the face of it you would say that the way to tell a story is to begin at the beginning and go soberly through to the end, making here and there a reflection that shall show that you, the author who is to be forever present in the reader's mind, are a person of orthodox morals and what the French call *bien pensant*.

But already by the age of Flaubert, the novelist had become uneasily aware that if the author is perpetually, with his reflections, distracting his reader's attention from the story, the story must lose interest. Some one noticed that in *Vanity Fair* [1848] when Mr. Thackeray had gradually built up a state of breathless interest and Becky Sharp on the eve of Waterloo had seemed almost audibly to breathe and palpitate before your eyes, suddenly the whole illusion went to pieces. You were back in your study before the fire reading a book of made-up stuff though the moment before, you would have sworn you were in Brussels amongst the revellers. . . . And that disillusionment was occasioned by Mr. Thackeray, broken nose and all, thrusting his moral reflections upon you, in the desperate determination to impress you with the conviction that he was a proper man to be a member of the *Athenaeum Club*. . . .[6] He had, with immense but untrained and unreflecting genius, built up a whole phantasmagoria of realities in which his reader really felt himself walking amongst the actors in the real life of the desperate day that preceded Waterloo. . . . And then the whole illusion went.

It would be idle to say that it was Flaubert who first observed that the intrusion of the author destroyed the illusion of the reader.

*   *   *

Flaubert more than any of his associates clamored unceasingly and passionately that the author must be impersonal, must, like a creating deity, stand neither for nor against any of his characters, must project and never report and must, above all, forever keep himself out of his books. He must write his books as if he were rendering the impressions of a person present at a scene; he must remember that a person present at a scene does not see everything and is above all not able to remember immensely long passages of dialogue.

These dicta were unceasingly discussed by the members of Flaubert's set who included the Goncourts, Turgenev, Gautier, Maupassant and, in a lesser degree, Zola and the young James[7]—this last as disciple of

---

6. Ford extends this disparaging assessment of *Vanity Fair* in *The March of Literature* (New York: Dial Press, 1938; London: Allen & Unwin, 1939 and 1947), pp. 767–69.

7. Henry James (1843–1916), American novelist and critic whose early fiction includes *Roderick Hudson* (1876), *Daisy Miller* (1879), and *Portrait of a Lady* (1881). Edmund and Jules de Goncourt (1822–1896 and 1830–1870), French novelists who wrote together (e.g., *Soeur Philomène* [1861]) and edited the popular *Journal des Goncourts* (9 vols., 1887–96), an intimate account of Parisian society; their style paved the way for naturalism and impressionism. Ivan Sergeyvich Turgenev (1818–1883), Russian novelist, dramatist and short-story writer who lived in France; author of *A Sportsman's Sketches* (1852), *A Nest of Gentlefolk* (1859), *Fathers and Sons* (1861), *A Month in the Country* (1850), etc. Théophile Gautier (1811–1872), French

the gentle Russian genius. They met in different cafés and restaurants from the Café Procope which still exists, if fallen from its high estate, to Brébant's which has now disappeared. And their discussions were frenetic and violent. They discussed the *minutiae* of words and their economical employment; the *charpente*,[8] the architecture, of the novel; the handling of dialogue; the renderings of impressions; the impersonality of the author. They discussed these things with the passion of politicians inciting to rebellion. And in those *coenaculae*[9] the modern novel—the immensely powerful engine of our civilization—was born.

You get an admirable idea of the violence of these discussions from the several accounts that exist of the desperate encounter that took place between the young James and the giant of Croisset [Flaubert] over a point of the style of Merimée. The assembly, it would seem, had been almost unanimous in its contempt for the style of Merimée[1] and the young James, sitting, a *jeune homme modeste*, as he afterwards used to style me, in the shadow of Turgenev, had ventured to join in the chorus. But that an American should dare to open his mouth in those discussions proved too much for the equanimity of Flaubert. He said so. He said with violence. . . . To think that an American should dare to have views as to the French of one of the greatest of France's stylists! Only to think it, was enough to make Villon, Ronsard, Racine, Corneille, Chateaubriand—not of course that their style were anything to write home about—turn in their graves. . . .

The pale young James was, it is recorded, led away by the beautiful Russian genius [Turgenev] who, nevertheless, induced that brave young trans-Atlantic to call with him next day upon the giant who had inflicted that flagellation. And Flaubert, as I have elsewhere recorded, received Turgenev and his young American friend in his dressing-gown, opening his front door himself, a thing that, till the end of his life, Mr. James regarded as supremely shocking.

I don't mind repeating myself in the effort to emphasize how absolutely international a thing literature is. For Henry James, retiring to an England that appeared to him to be all one large deer park across which the sunlight fell upon ubiquitous haunts of ancient peace—the young James then, like those birds who, carrying the viscous seeds of the mistletoe on their bills and claws, establish always new colonies of the plant

---

painter, poet, novelist and critic, leading exponent of art-for-art's-sake theory, who preceded the Parnassians and Symbolists in their reaction against Romanticism. Émile Zola (1840–1902), French naturalist novelist and socialist, author of over twenty novels, including *Nana* (1880) and *Germinal* (1885); post-1893 abandoned naturalism for form of Tolstoyan Christian socialism (e.g., trilogy *Les Trois Villes* [1894, 1896, 1898]) and wrote open letter 'J'Accuse' (1898) defending Dreyfus.

8. Framework (French).
9. Dining rooms (Latin).
1. Prosper Merimée (1803–1870), French dramatist, novelist, critic, translator, and statesman; as author in reaction against Romanticism.

of the Druids, planted for a little while in the country of my birth the seeds of the novel as it at present exists.

It is said that James directly influenced Conrad in his incessant search for a new form for the novel. Nothing could be more literally false but nothing could be more impressionistically true. London was at that date—the earlier nineties—a veritable bacteriologist's soup for the culture of modern germs, and the author of *Daisy Miller*, *Roderick Hudson*, and *The Princess Casamassima*, being enthusiastically received in a city that was weary to death of the novels of James Payn, William Black,[2] and the rest of the more or less respected, sowed around him, like the mistletoe-spreading birds, an infinite number of literary Impressionist germs. And if Conrad, as is literally true, learned nothing directly of James, yet he found prepared for him a medium in which, slowly at first but with an always increasing impetus, his works could spread. It was the London of the *Yellow Book*, of R. L. Stevenson, that sedulous ape, of W. E. Henley,[3] that harsh-mouthed but very beneficent spreader of French influences.

It was a city of infinite curiosity as to new literary methods and of an infinite readiness to assimilate new ideas, whether they came from Paris by way of Ernest Dowson, from Poland by way of Conrad, or from New York or New England by way of Henry James, Stephen Crane, Harold Frederic, or Whistler, Abbey, Sargent, and George Boughton.[4] London had in fact been visited by one of its transitory phases in which nothing seemed good but what came from abroad. We were to see another such phase in '13 and '14 in the flowering days of Ezra Pound, John Gould Fletcher, Robert Frost, Marinetti, the Cubists, the Vorticists,[5] and how many other foreign movements that were to be crushed in the bud by the iron shards of war. We may see another tomorrow. At any rate it is overdue.

2. Author (1841–1898) of *In Silk Attire* (3 vols., 1869) and *Stand Fast, Craig Royston!* (3 vols., 1890), among others.
3. English poet, playwright, critic, and editor (1849–1903); introduced Kipling, Wells, and Yeats to public as editor of reviews. *Yellow Book*: magazine that fostered English "decadents" like Wilde and Beardsley; see p. 5, n. 4 of text and p. 292, n. 8 below. Robert Louis Stevenson (1850–1894), Scottish novelist, poet, playwright, essayist and travel-writer; author of *Treasure Island* (1883), *Kidnapped* (1886) *The Black Arrow* (1888) among others.
4. Edwin Austin Abbey (1852–1905), John Singer Sargent (1856–1925), George Henry Boughton (1833–1905), American-born painters who secured fame in Britain as portraitists of social celebrities. Stephen Crane (1871–1900), American novelist and short-story writer; author of *Maggie, A Girl of the Streets* (1893) and *The Red Badge of Courage* (1895), among others; friend of Ford and Conrad, and fellow experimenter with literary impressionism. Harold Frederic (1856–1898), American journalist and novelist, pioneer of realism best known for *Illumination* (US title: *The Damnation of Theron Ware*) (1896); Ford prints "Frederick." Whistler: see p. 270, n. 9 above.
5. For "Marinetti . . . Vorticists," see p. 233, n. 1, and p. 4, n. 8 above. Pound: see p. 4, n. 8 above. John Gould Fletcher (1886–1950), American poet who lived in England; friend of Amy Lowell and T. S. Eliot; associated with Imagists. Robert Frost (1874–1963), American poet whose work is rooted in New England landscape; came to England in 1912, where he found a publisher for his first collection, *A Boy's Will* (1913); Ford was one of the first to acclaim Frost's genius.

II

Into that hothouse came Conrad who had drunk of exactly the same springs as the laureate of Washington Square and the Common at Boston [James]. He had not had the advantage of being personally flagellated by Flaubert but, unlike Mr. James who, if he may be taken as having forgiven the flagellation, never, never, never, could forget the *robe de chambre*, Conrad had for Flaubert, years before he ever saw London city, an infinite veneration—an almost incredible passion for his writings, his power over phrases, his ideas of how books should be written, his berserker's literary personality. And ideas possessed Conrad with a passion that was almost an agony. It was painful sometimes to hear him read passages from Flaubert aloud, so immensely would he be impressed—and depressed—by the idea of that writer's impeccable unapproachableness. He was possessed by that divine form of jealousy of his fellow writers: when he came upon great passages in their works he would cry despairingly: "Why should Destiny have given to that fellow all those powers and to me a mere pedestrianism? Why? Why?"

James, on the other hand, appeared to regard his fellows with an aloof and extremely deferential irony which rose to the stage of humorous self-deprecation when their personal successes seemed to put them beyond the reach of material anxieties. Flaubert was for him always: "Poor, dear old Flaubert," largely, I am convinced, because towards the end of his life the Sage of Croisset, like Sir Walter Scott, suffered severe pecuniary losses. But Mr. Kipling and Sir Arthur Quiller-Couch[6] were "writers who unite in their singular personalities, as I am told, considerable literary talents, to an altogether enviable gift of popularity such as you, my modest young friend or I—*moi qui vous parle*," laying his right hand over his heart and slightly inclining himself, "could never hope to attain to."

How often, how often, how often, haven't I heard those words issue from his lips as applying not merely to Messrs. Kipling and Couch, but to poor Steevie [Crane], to Mrs. Humphry Ward,[7] and to a dozen others whose enviable gifts of popularity were infinitely superior to their literary talents.

Crane, on the other hand, was possessed by a passion, almost as vivid as that of Conrad himself, for elisions—for cutting his phrases down to an almost infinite economy of words. He was never tired of exasperatedly declaring that it was his unattainable ambition to make every one

6. Critic, novelist, and poet known as "Q" (1863–1944); a monumental presence in the Edwardian literary world but a figure of fun, like Kipling, to Ford and his young cronies.
7. Popular novelist (1851–1920) who flirted with Catholicism and founded the Women's National Anti-Suffrage League; like Ford, propaganda writer during World War I but, as Matthew Arnold's niece, also one of the mafia of Great Victorians which Ford saw as overshadowing his youth; her novels deal with religious doubt and problems of poverty, e.g., *Robert Elsmere* (1883) and *Helbeck of Bannisdale* (1898).

damned word do the work of six. So, for him, as it remains for me, his one ewe lamb amongst his books, was *The Third Violet* [1897]—a novel that appears to be almost irreclaimably forgotten even by those who have *The Red Badge of Courage* [1895] and *Maggie* [1893] by heart. I have been preaching the claims of that book for years and have never, so far as I know, made a single convert.

Those three then were, almost equally, the protagonists of literary Impressionism in Anglo-Saxondom, lesser lights like Henry Harland, Ernest Dowson, Miss Ethel Mayne,[8] and others whom it is unjust to forget but whom my treacherous memory won't recall—many others, then, in a little cloud of witnesses, having aided in that Renaissance.

It advanced, that alien cloud, across the sunlit landscape of the English nuvvle[9] with its quiet homesteads, cathedral closes, deans, bishops, county families, and hygienically clean milkmaids. And, when it had passed over, forever gone was the simple story that accompanied the Ruling Class young hero from his birth to his bell-haloed union with the pink-frocked daughter of the manor, forever gathering roses in the sunken garden that had been there since the day of Shakespeare. . . . Gone at least forever from the awakened literary consciousness. For Meredith—who, if he was anything, was the poet of "Love in a Valley" [1851] and "The Sage Enamoured and the Honest Lady" [1892] or of "The Woods of Westermain" [1883][1] and the dear, great gnarled, Greek poet, Thomas Hardy—who also wrote some novels—endured on the earth for a few years more. And, heaven knows, there remain till today whole broods of nuvvelists who have never, even yet, got the Squire, the Dean, the peer's daughter, the rose-garden, the manor, and the home farm out of their heads. And they enjoy enviable gifts of popularity and chortle somnolently along through lands where it is always summer afternoons . . . and God bless them. For I would far rather see a thousand ham novelists gaining comfortable competences and enjoying blissful post-prandial slumbers after the ingurgitation of x glasses of admirable port than one layman who has made his millions by the invention of electrically piloted warplanes or the canning of mountains of usually putrid salmon. . . . Nevertheless, for the literarily awake they have no more existence or perdurability than the thin reflections of sunken gardens seen on the glass windows of rushing automobiles.

8. Ethel Colburn Mayne (1870?–1941), novelist, short-short writer, and critic; friend of Ford and Violet Hunt. Ford prints 'Maine.' Henry Harland (1861–1905), American novelist who in England became the first editor of *The Yellow Book*, see p. 290, n. 3 above. Ernest Dowson (1867–1900), prominent Nineties English poet, friend of Beardsley, Wilde, Le Gallienne (*Yellow Book* crowd), member of Rhymers' Club.
9. Ford's word for the comfortable, undemanding popular novel.
1. All these poems (1851, 1892, and 1883 respectively) celebrate love in the face of Nature's apparent indifference.

I began by writing the word 'techniques' rather than 'technique,' so as to soften the impact on the ear of that harsh dissyllable. For there is not one only Technique, a chill enemy of mankind known only to and arbitrarily prescribed by a pedantic circle of the highbrow *intelligentsia*. Not one only, but just as many as there are writers, each one differing by a shade, the one from the other, until the difference between the leader of the advancing line and the boy at its end is as great as that that lies between the limpidities of Merimée and the clouds of virtuosities of [Proust's] *Du Côté de Chez Swann* [1913] or of *Ulysses* [1922]. Yet we are all going to Heaven and Turgenev shall be of the company.

Mr. Kipling was perfectly right when he wrote that there are five and forty ways for the writer. There are probably five hundred thousand, every single one of them being right. But to tell the whole truth, he must have added that there is only one best way for the treatment of every given subject and only one method best suited for every given writer. And such advocates of the study of technique as Conrad or Dowson or James or Crane or Flaubert are far more interested in the writer's finding himself than in establishing any one rule that shall cover every tribal lay. The young writer, for whom I am principally writing, or the old man setting up as writer, will inevitably—and very properly—go through the stage of expressing himself. He will inevitably desire to get out of his system his reactions to sex, wine, music, homosexuality, parents, puritanism, death, life, immortality, technocracy, communism and existence amongst the infinite flatnesses beneath the suns and tornadoes of the Middle West or the Mississippi Delta. But once all that *Sturm und Drang*—once that milk fever[2]—is inscribed on fair paper, the joys of autobiography are past. The aspirant finds himself faced, if he is to continue writer, with the drear necessity of rendering one human affair or another. It is then that he will have to go in search of a technique that will suit him as well as the one fishing-cane that will be indispensable to him if he is to cast his fly exactly upstream before the jaws of the waiting trout. For there are innumerable techniques but only one best one for each writer.

What then is a technique? It is a device by which a writer may appeal to his fellows—to so many of his fellows that, in the end, he may claim to have appealed to all humanity from China to the Tierra del Fuego. Nothing less will satisfy the ardent writer—the really ardent and agonisingly passionate renderer of affairs like Flaubert or James. And there are some who attain to that stupendous reward. At any rate I have been informed by a German firm of world-book distributors that the one book

---

2. A feverish attack in women shortly after childbirth. "*Sturm und Drang*": storm and stress.

that they export all over the world—to Rio de Janeiro as to the Straits
Settlements, to Prague as to Berkeley, Cal., and Pekin is—*Madame
Bovary*.

This does not mean that I am asking the neophyte to pass his life
writing *pastiches* of the affair in which poor Emma was involved. But it
does mean that, if he is a prudent man, he will read that book and
L'Éducation Sentimentale [1870] and *Bouvard et Pécuchet* [1881] a great
many times, over and over again, with minute scrutiny, to discover what
in Flaubert's methods is eternal and universal in appeal. And having
discovered what he thinks that to be, he must experiment for a long time
to see whether he can work in that method as easily as he can live in an
old and utterly comfortable coat . . . or dressing gown. And so he must
go on to other writers. For the history of Emma Bovary is not alone
amongst world-and-all-time best sellers. Next to that, and circling the
globe in flights almost as numerous, come the *Pilgrim's Progress* and the
Pickwick Papers . . . And long before them stands *The Imitation of
Christ* [3] and a little after that the *Holy Bible*. To each of these works, not
excluding the religious masterpieces, the neophyte may well apply his
microscopes and his diminishing glasses. At the last he shall come into
his own.

He will come into his own when, reading those works a final time in
a spirit of forgetfulness, for pleasure and with critical faculties put to
sleep, he shall say: "Such and such a passage pleases me," and casting
back into his subconsciousness shall add: "This fellow gets that effect by
a cadenced paragraph of long, complicated sentences, interspersed with
shorter statements, ending with a long, dying fall of words and the final
taptaptap of a three monosyllabled phrase. . . ." Just like that.

That was the quite conscious practice of Conrad when seeking to be
dramatic as it was the only less conscious practice of Flaubert. And, if
you will read again my last paragraph, you will see how dramatic—how
even a thought vulgar—such a cadence may be.

Or it may be that the devices of Conrad and Flaubert, as you take
them to be, do not suit your book after your painful studies. Or you may
say that Flaubert in France and Conrad in America lying under temporary clouds of oblivion, you will never attain to the enviable gift of
extended popularity if you let them in the slightest degree exercise an
influence on you. Try then Hudson.

Hudson, or his Latin-American running mate, Mr. Cunninghame
Graham, the most exquisite living of *prosateurs* in English, though of
right King of Scotland. Or *The Third Violet* of Stephen Crane who for
his own purposes professed to have been born and bred in the Bowery [4]
but was actually the son of some one of episcopal standing. You will

---

3. Attributed to Thomas à Kempis (c. 1379–1471).
4. See p. 82, n. 4 above.

discover that Hudson gets his effects by an almost infinite and meticulous toning down of language. If you should be fortunate enough to get hold of some of his proofsheets, you will see that he simplifies to the utmost and then beyond. I remember observing—for I went once or twice through his proofs for him—that he had once written: "The buds developed into leaves." He substituted "grew," for "developed." And, finally the passage ran: "They became leaves." . . . But of course, behind Huddie's prose there was that infinitely patient temperament of the naturalist, that infinite conscientiousness of observation, that have given the world White's *Natural History of Selborne* [1789], the few writings of Thomas Edward, the Scottish naturalist[5]—who taught *me* all I know of cadences; as well as the *Sportsman's Sketches* [1852] of Turgenev with its matchless "Bielshin Prairie" and, only yesterday, Miss Gordon's *Aleck Maury*,[6] which has a singular spiritual kinship to the *Recits d'un Chasseur*. But that quality is the product of a temperament. You may have it or you may not. If you have it you will write beautifully—but you can never acquire it. The longest study of Hudson or Turgenev will do no more for you than turn you into a writer of *pastiches*. Galsworthy would have been a real major writer if Mr. Edward Garnett had not forced him to read Mrs. Garnett's wonderful translation of *Fathers and Children*.[7]

But by all means read them for the exquisite pleasure they will give you.

Mr. Graham you may read as self-consciously as you will. His prose is always aristocratically unbuttoned; he approaches his subjects with the contemptuous negligence of the Highland Scottish noble or the Southern plantation owner. But that very contempt gives him a power of keying down drama till the result is an economy of resource such as only Stephen Crane, himself aristocratically contemptuous, has otherwise attained. There is a short—a very short—story of Mr. Graham's called "Beattock for Moffatt"—the railway porter's cry meaning: 'Beattock, change for Moffatt'—which is one of the great tragedies. It projects nothing more than the railway journey of a dying, homesick Scot of no importance, going home, with a vulgar and uncomprehending but not unkindly Cockney wife, to die of tuberculosis in Moffatt. His whole mind is given to seeing Moffatt again after a long obscuration in London. . . . And in the keen air after the stuffy railway carriage on Beattock

---

5. Ford was greatly impressed by the recorded conversations of Edward in Samuel Smiles's biography of him, *Life of a Scottish Naturalist* (1876), in which Ford heard 'my intimate cadence, the typical sentence that I try all my life to create, that I hear all the while in my ear and only once in a blue moon am aided to write . . . a dying fall, a cadence of resignation' [quoted Mixener, p. 280, n. 46 from *Transatlantic Review*, 504].

6. Caroline Gordon, American novelist and short-story writer, married to the poet and novelist Allen Tate (a friend of Ford).

7. Constance Garnett, the most important translator from Russian of her day, brought Chekhov, Dostoevsky, Gogol, Tolstoy, and Turgenev to the British reading public.

platform he dies, being fated never again to see Moffatt, that Carcassonne[8] of the North . . . dies whilst the porters are still calling 'Beattock for Moffatt'. . . . It is told almost as summarily as I have told it . . . but with just those differences of touch that make the passing of that obscure Scot as lamentable—nay, more lamentable!, than the death of Hector.

The secret of poor Steevie is very much akin to that of Mr. Graham, be his method of approach to his subject never so different. Mr. Graham—the Don Roberto of a hundred drawing-rooms—with contemptuous negligence does not record; Crane with nervous meticulousness excises and excises. Both having an unerring sense of the essential, the temperamental results arrived at are extraordinarily similar. A Crane drama will end:

The Girl said:

"You say. . . ."

He answered:

"Observe that I have never ventured to say. . . ."

She threw the third violet at his feet. . . .

Something like that—for I have no copy of *The Third Violet* from which to quote—but you can observe that, a situation of poignance having been established, such an end may be of an extreme drama.

If you compare it with the famous last sentence of *The Turn of the Screw*, you will see how two writers of the same school and training, using very similar methods in all the essentials of rendering an affair, may give an entirely different temperamental turn to their endings.

"We were alone with the quiet day," wrote Mr. James confidently and beautifully, "and his little heart . . ." he continues confidently still. But then you hear him mutter to himself. "This is too direct. This will give the effect of the *coup de canon* at the end of a Maupassant story. . . . We must delay. . . . We must give the effect of lingering. . . . We must let the reader down gently." . . . And into the direct statement that was to be completed he inserts the qualificative word "dispossessed." "We were alone with the quiet day and his little heart had stopped," would have been reporting of a high order. But: "We were alone with the quiet day and his little heart, dispossessed, had stopped," is the supreme poetry of a great genius. And yet of an amazing economy.

But it was perhaps Crane of all that school or gang—and not excepting Maupassant—who most observed that canon of Impressionism: "You must render: never report." You must never, that is to say, write: "He saw a man aim a gat at him"; you must put it: "He saw a steel ring directed at him." Later you must get in that, in his subconsciousness, he recognized that the steel ring was the polished muzzle of a revolver.

8. See p. 16, n. 8 above.

So Crane rendered it in "Three White Mice" which is one of the major short stories of the world. That is Impressionism!

IV

But the great truth that must never be forgotten by you, by me, or by the neophyte at the gate, is that the purpose of a technique is to help the writer to please, and that neither writing nor the technique behind it has any other purpose. In evolving the technique that shall fit your fishing-pole you have to think of nothing but how to please your reader. By pleasing him, you hold his attention, and once you have accomplished that, you may inject into him what you please: for you need not forget, when you write a novel, the gravity of your role as educator: only you must remember that in vain does the fowler set his net in the sight of the bird. The reader wants to be filled with the feeling that you are a clever magician; he never wants to have you intruding and remarking what a good man you are.

I will try to inculcate this most important of all lessons by presenting some instances from the writers best known to myself. With all the others I have mentioned—with the exception of Flaubert who was dead, and of Maupassant who had retired from active life before I entered the bull-ring that is the literary life—with all the others I discussed literary problems and their personal techniques, debating rather strenuously with Crane and Hudson and listening with deference to Henry James, Henry Harland, Henley, Miss Ethel Mayne, and others of the *Yellow Book* and the English-American Impressionist group.

With Conrad I descended into the arena and beside him wrestled, rain or shine, through the greater part of a decade. I will therefore now take two or three instances of details of technique and show how we approached them. Conrad, I may say, was more interested in finding a new form for the novel; I, in training myself to write *just* words that would not stick out of a sentence and so distract the reader's attention by their very justness. But we worked ceaselessly, together, on those problems, turning from the problem of the new form to that of the just word as soon as we were mentally exhausted by the one or the other.

That we did succeed eventually in finding a new form I think I may permit myself to claim, Conrad first evolving the convention of a Marlow who should narrate, in presentation, the whole story of a novel just as, without much sequence or pursued chronology, a story will come up into the mind of a narrator, and I eventually dispensing with a narrator but making the story come up in the mind of the unseen author with a similar want of chronological sequence. I must apologize for referring to my own work but, if I did not, this story would become rather incomprehensible and would lack an end, since after Conrad's death I pursued those investigations with a never-ceasing industry and belief in the use-fulness of my task—if not to myself, then at least to others. For it is almost as useful to set up an awful example that can be avoided as to erect signposts along a road that should be taken.

We evolved then a convention for the novel and one that I think still stands. The novel must be put into the mouth of a narrator—who must be limited by probability as to what he can know of the affair that he is adumbrating. Or it must be left to the official Author and he, being almost omnipotent, may, so long as he limits himself to presenting with-out comment or moralization, allow himself to be considered to know almost everything that there is to know. The narration is thus a little more limited in possibilities; the 'author's book' is a little more difficult to handle. A narrator, that is to say, being already a fictional character, may indulge in any prejudices or wrong-headednesses and any likings or dislikes for the other characters of the book, for he is just a living being like anybody else. But an author-creator, presenting his narration with-out passion, may not indulge in the expression of any prejudices or like any one of his characters more than any other; for, if he displays either of those weaknesses, he will to that extent weaken the illusion that he has attempted to build up. Marlow, the narrator of *Lord Jim* [1900], may idolize his hero or anathematize his villains with the sole result that we say: "How real Marlow is!" Conrad, however, in *Nostromo* [1904] must not let any word or preference for Nostromo or Mrs. Gould or the daughters of the Garibaldino pierce through the surface of his novel or at once we should say: "Here is this tiresome person intruding again," and at once lose the thread of the tale.

You perceive, I trust, how our eyes were forever on the reader—and if, during our fifteenth perusal of *Madame Bovary* we discerned that—as Flaubert himself somewhere confesses—the sage of Croisset was actu-ally in love with poor Emma Bovary, his creation, we hastened to observe the one to the other that *we* must never let ourselves indulge in such mental-carnal weaknesses. A giant like Flaubert might get away with it: but we must avoid temptations. . . . So you perceive how con-stantly we considered the interests of You, my Lord, in case You should one day want to glance, for diversion, through the pages we were evolving.

We were, in short, producers who thought forever of the consumer. If Conrad laid it down as a law that, in introducing a character, we must always, after a few vivid words of personal description, apportion to him a speech that *must* be a characteristic generalization, it was because we were thinking of You. We knew that if we said: "Mr. X was a foul-mouthed reactionary," you would know very little about him. But if his first words, after his introduction were: "God damn it, put all filthy Lib-erals up against a wall, say I, and shoot out their beastly livers . . ." that gentleman will make on you an impression that many following pages shall scarcely efface. Whomever else you may not quite grasp, you won't forget *him*—because that is the way people present themselves in real life. You may converse with a lady for ten minutes about the fineness of the day or the number of lumps of sugar you like in your tea and you will know little about her; but let her hazard any personal and general opinion as to the major topics of life and at once you will have her labeled, docketed and put away on the collector's shelf of your curious mind.

Similarly, in evolving a technique for the presenting of conversation, I—and in this it was rather I than Conrad, just as in the evolution of the New Form it was rather Conrad than I, though each countersigned the opinion of the other and thenceforth adopted the device so evolved—I then considered for a long time how conversations presented themselves to the mind. I would find myself in a room with a gentleman who pursued an almost uninterrupted monologue. A week after, I would find that of it I retained, verbally, only his more characteristic expletives—his 'God bless my soul's,' or his 'You don't mean to say so's' and one or two short direct speeches: "If the Government goes to the country, I will bet a hundred-weight of China tea to a Maltese orange that they will have a fifty-eight to forty-two majority of the voters against them." But I remembered the whole gist of his remarks.

And so, considering that an author-narrator, being supposed to have about the mnemonic powers of a man with a fair memory, will after the elapse of a certain period, be supposed to retain about that much of a conversation that the Reader may suppose him to have heard, I shall, when inventing conversations, give about just that proportion of direct and indirect speech, in which latter I shall present the gist of my character's argument. . . . For, if I give more direct speech than that, the reader will say: "Confound it, how does this plaguy fellow remember an oration like that, word for word? It's impossible. So I don't believe a word he says about anything else," and he will pitch my book into the wastepaper basket. . . . Of course I shall lard the indirect speeches with plenty of 'God bless my soul's' and 'Mr. X paused for a moment before continuing,' just to keep my character all the while well in the picture. . . .

These of course are only two of the technical *trouvailles* that we made in labors that cannot have been exceeded by any two slaves that worked for ten years on the building of the Tower of Babel. We made an infinite number of others, covering an infinite field of human activities and reflections. You may find them valid as representing how life comes back to you and in that case they may help you, as writer, a little way along the long road that winds up hill all the way. . . . All the way! For, so long as you remain a live writer, you will forever be questioning and re-questioning and testing and re-testing the devices that you will have evolved. Or they may not at all fill your bill: in which case you must go forward alone and may a gentle breeze forever temper for you the ardor of the sun's rays!

But you must—there is no other method—pursue your investigation in that spirit of ours. You must have your eyes forever on your Reader. That alone constitutes . . . Technique!

BIOGRAPHICAL AND
CRITICAL COMMENTARY

RICHARD ALDINGTON

[Homage to Ford Madox Ford]†

I was introduced to Ford Madox Ford by Mr. Ezra Pound in 1913. Ford Madox Hueffer, as he then called himself, had made a great reputation by his brilliant editorship of *The English Review*, which had introduced a whole generation of new writers to the reading public. Any memorial to Ford should begin with a complete set of *The English Review* under his editorship. It was not only the best English literary monthly of its time, but the best that has been issued in the 20th century. Its only rivals were the pre-War weekly, *The New Age*, under the editorship of Orage, and the post-War American *Dial* under Thayer and Seldes.

Unluckily for me I was just too young to meet Ford during the time of his editorship, so I missed the honour of being published by him. When I did get some poems into *The English Review* the editor was Austin Harrison—not at all the same thing.

At that time Ford was living on Camden Hill, Kensington. Pound, H. D. and I lived in small apartments in Church Street about three hundred yards away. We saw a good deal of Ford in those days. There were at least three distinct groups who visited Ford. There were the social people who interested me very little, but I vaguely remember the names of Lady Byron, Lady St. Helier, and a Cabinet Minister called Masterman. There were the respectably established writers, more or less of Ford's generation, such as H. G. Wells and Walter de la Mare. And there were the wild youth, impressed into the gang by Ezra. Wyndham Lewis, Gaudier Brzeska and Rebecca West are those I best remember. Oddly enough I never met D. H. Lawrence there, although Ford was the first editor to publish his work.

Ford entertained us with amusing but not necessarily literally accurate stories of the Pre-Raphaelites, Conrad, Henry James, [W. H.] Hudson and the Victorians; and smiled tolerantly at our literary and artistic heresies. For the first *Imagist Anthology* I wrote a parody of one of Ford's poems and he wrote a parody of me. I still remember how he chuckled when Ezra and I showed him my parody and how quickly and wittily he hit back. We chaffed him a lot in those days, and he never stood on his dignity, although he was 20 years our senior and an established author. Of course he realized that by treating him as one of ourselves we were unconsciously paying him the greatest compliment.

† From *New Directions* 7 (1942): 456–58. Reprinted with the permission of Alister Kershaw. Other contributors to this *New Directions* volume included John Gould Fletcher, Caroline Gordon, Ezra Pound, Allen Tate, and William Carlos Williams.

When the war came Ford began doing propaganda work for the British, and roped me in as his secretary. We worked every morning. I took down from his dictation in long hand. Ford claimed that writer's cramp made it impossible for him to write himself, and he certainly wrote a detestable hand. But I think he enjoyed dictation. He was a great worker. He did a long literary article every week and at the same time was engaged on a novel, *The Good Soldier*, and his propaganda book, *Between St. Denis and St. George*. During the months I worked with him I believe he turned out 6000 to 8000 words a week. Which didn't prevent his writing poetry. I well remember his reading us the first draft of his best poem, *On Heaven*, and later on, the poem about Antwerp and some shorter poems inspired by the delicate intense work of H. D.

I left before the propaganda book was finished, and my place was taken by an old London University classmate, Mr. A. W. G. Randall, who is now a distinguished Foreign Office official. Ford joined the Welsh Regiment; Wyndham Lewis went into the Artillery; I got into the Devons and was transferred to the Leicesters when I got to France. Our little Round Table was broken up. After 1915 I saw Ford very seldom, except occasionally in Paris. The last time I saw him was in the Players' Club in New York about four years ago. I was shocked to see how he had aged. His death set me thinking about the old days in London, and it was sad to think that Ford was gone. For all its ups and downs, I believe he enjoyed his life.

His work has been shamefully under-estimated, until quite recently. The British reviewers behaved abominably to him during the height of his creative life, and then tried to make up for it twenty years later by almost fulsome adulation. They know their job, those birds. The disparagement did him immense harm with the reading public. The later flattery did him no good. What is needed now is a thorough, documented study of Ford's immense output as poet, novelist, essayist and miscellaneous writer. At the same time I should like to see a Collected Edition of all his work, including the best of his literary journalism. This seems to me the best memorial to a writer, the only one he would really care about. More than once I have heard Ford say that what he most hoped for was that his books would be read after his death.

MARK SCHORER

[*The Good Soldier* as Comedy]†

Learning to read novels, we slowly learn to read ourselves. A few years ago, writing of Ford Madox Ford, Herbert Gorman said: 'If he enlarged upon himself he was quite justified in doing so and it seems to me that the time has come now for somebody to enlarge upon him.' I translate this remark to mean that the good novelist sees himself as the source of a subject that, when it has taken its form in his work, we may profitably examine because our analysis will bring it back to ourselves, perhaps to kiss us, more likely to slap us in the face—either way, to tell us where *we* are. These are the fruits of criticism.

The time had indeed come, and today we are hearing again about Ford Madox Ford in a way that we have not heard of him for twenty years—for until recently he has had to survive as best he could in the person of Conrad's collaborator and of that brilliant editor who said to the young D. H. Lawrence that his first novel had 'every fault that the English novel can have' and that his second was 'a rotten work of genius'. The always present friend of all the great, the abettor of all the promising young, Ford was great in his own right, and now Time indeed seems ready at last, as Herbert Gorman predicted that it would, to 'weed out his own accomplishments'.

He began work on *The Good Soldier* on his fortieth birthday—the 17th of December in 1913—and he himself thought that it was his first really serious effort in the novel. 'I had never really tried to put into any novel of mine *all* that I knew about writing. I had written rather desultorily a number of books—a great number—but they had all been in the nature of *pastiches*, of pieces of rather precious writing, or of *tours de force*' [3]. This was to be the real thing, and it was; many years later he remarked of it that it was his 'best book technically, unless you read the Tietjens books as one novel, in which case the whole design appears. But I think the Tietjens books will probably "date" a good deal, whereas the other may—and indeed need—not.' It need not have; it did not.

As in most great works of comic irony, the mechanical structure of *The Good Soldier* is controlled to a degree nothing less than taut, while the structure of meaning is almost blandly open, capable of limitless refractions. One may go further, perhaps, and say that the novel renews

† First printed in "Ford Madox Ford Symposium" as "The Good Novelist in *The Good Soldier*," *Princeton University Library Chronicle* 9 (April 1948): 128–33; revised in *Horizon* (August 1949): 132–38; revised again as "Introduction," for 3rd U.S. ed. (Knopf, 1951); reprinted as "An Interpretation" for 4th U.S. ed. (Vintage, 1957); then as "The Good Soldier: An Interpretation" in Richard A. Cassell, *Ford Madox Ford: Modern Judgments* (Macmillan, 1972) 63–69. Reprinted here with the permission of the Princeton University Libraries. Page numbers in brackets refer to this Norton Critical Edition.

a major lesson of all classic art: from the very delimitation of form arises
the exfoliation of theme. This, at any rate, is the fact about *The Good
Soldier* that gives point to John Rodker's quip that 'it is the finest French
novel in the English language', which is to say that it has perfect clarity
of surface and nearly mathematical poise, and—as an admirer would
wish to extend the remark—a substance at once exact and richly enigmatic. As a novel, *The Good Soldier* is like a hall of mirrors, so constructed that, while one is always looking straight ahead at a perfectly
solid surface, one is made to contemplate not the bright surface itself,
but the bewildering maze of past circumstances and future consequence
that—somewhat falsely—it contains. Or it is like some structure all of
glass and brilliantly illuminated, from which one looks out upon a sable
jungle and ragged darkness.

   The Good Soldier carries the subtitle 'A Tale of Passion', and the
book's controlling irony lies in the fact that passionate situations are
related by a narrator who is himself incapable of passion, sexual and
moral alike. His is the true *accidia*, and so, from his opening absurdity:
'This is the saddest story I have ever heard', on to the end and at every
point, we are forced to ask: 'How can we believe *him*? His must be
exactly the *wrong* view.' The fracture between the character of the event
as we feel it to be and the character of the narrator as he reports the
event to us is the essential irony, yet it is not in any way a simple one;
for the narrator's view as we soon discover, is not so much the wrong
view as merely *a* view, although a special one. No simple inversion of
statement can yield up the truth, for the truth is the maze, and, as we
learn from what is perhaps the major theme of the book, appearances
have their reality.

   First of all, this novel is about the difference between convention and
fact. The story consists of the narrator's attempt to adjust his reason to
the shattering discovery that, in his most intimate relationships, he has,
for nine years, mistaken the conventions of social behavior for the actual
human fact. That he did not want it otherwise, that the deception was
in effect self-induced, that he could not have lived at all with the actuality, is, for the moment, beside our point, although ultimately, for the
attitude and the architecture of the novel, it is the whole point.

   The narrator and his wife, Florence, are wealthy Americans; the
friends with whom they are intimately concerned, Edward and Leonora
Ashburnham, are wealthy English people. Together, these four seem to
be the very bloom of international society; they are all, as the narrator
repeatedly tells us, 'good people', and the Ashburnhams are even that
special kind of good people, 'good county people'. Florence is a little
pathetic, because she suffers from heart trouble and must be protected
against every shock and exposure. Leonora is perhaps a little strong-
willed in the management of her domestic affairs, but these have been
very trying and in their cause she has been altogether splendid and self-

sacrificing, a noblewoman. Edward is nearly flawless: 'the fine soldier, the excellent landlord, the extraordinarily kind, careful, and industrious magistrate, the upright, honest, fair-dealing, fair-thinking, public character . . . the model of humanity, the hero, the athlete, the father of his county, the law-giver' [66; 78]. For nine years these four have enjoyed an apparently placid and civilized friendship, visiting back and forth, meeting annually at Nauheim, where they take the seasonal hypochondriac baths, sharing in one another's interests and affairs. Then comes the tremendous, the stunning reversal: when illness proves to be a lusterless debauchery; domestic competence the maniacal will of the tigress, the egoistic composure of the serpent; heroic masculinity the most sentimental libertinism. And the narrator, charged at the end with the responsibility of caring for a little mad girl, Edward's last love, is left to relate his new knowledge of an exposed reality to his long untroubled faith in its appearance. Which he is not able to do, of course; as which of us could?

But are not these 'realities', in effect, 'appearances'? Are not the 'facts' that the narrator discovers in themselves 'conventions' of a sort? We are forced, at every point, to look back at this narrator, to scan his beguiling surprise, to measure the angle of refraction at which that veiled glance penetrates experience. He himself suggests that we are looking at events here as one looks at the image of a mirror in a mirror, at the box within the box, the arch beyond the arch beyond the arch. All on one page we find these reversals: 'Upon my word, yes, our intimacy was like a minuet. . . . No, by God, it is false! It wasn't a minuet that we stepped; it was a prison—a prison full of screaming hysterics. . . . And yet I swear by the sacred name of my creator that it was true. It was true sunshine; the true music; the true plash of the fountains from the mouths of stone dolphins. For, if for me we were four people with the same tastes, with the same desires, acting—or, no, not acting—sitting here and there unanimously, isn't that the truth?' [11–12]. The appearance had its reality. How, then, does the 'reality' suggest that it is something less—or more?

Why is Florence always 'poor Florence' or 'that poor wretch' or 'that poor cuckoo'? Why the persistent denigration of tone? Why can Florence not be charged with something less trivial and vulgar than 'making eyes at Edward'? The narrator has something to gain in Florence's loss, and that is a fragment of self-esteem. If Florence is a harlot, she is so, in part, because of her husband's fantastic failure, but if we can be persuaded of her calculated vice and of her nearly monstrous malice, her husband appears before us as the pathetic victim of life's ironic circumstance. What, again, is the meaning of the narrator's nearly phobic concern with Catholicism, or of the way in which his slurs at Leonora are justified by her attachment to that persuasion? This is a mind not quite in balance. And again, Leonora's loss is Edward's gain, and Edward's gain at last is the narrator's gain. For why are Florence's indiscretions crimes, and Edward's, with Florence, follies at worst, and at best true goodnesses of heart? Why, after his degradation, is Edward still 'a fine fellow'? In every case, the 'fact' is somewhere between the mere social convention and that different order of convention which the distorted understanding of the narrator imposes upon them.

Yet the good novelist does not let us rest here. These distortions are further revelations. Mirror illuminates mirror, each arch marks farther distances. Ford tells us that he suggested the title, *The Good Soldier*, 'in hasty irony', when the publisher's objections to *The Saddest Story* became imperative; and while, under the circumstances of 1915, the new title must have seemed, for this novel and for this real soldier, Ford, peculiarly inappropriate, certainly uncongenial enough to cause the author understandable 'horror', it is nevertheless very useful to readers today, so accustomed to war that the word 'soldier' no longer carries its special force. The novel designates Edward as the good soldier, as Edward has seen Imperial service in India. For Edward the narrator has the strongest affection and his only forgiveness. Of him, he says: 'I guess that I myself, in my fainter way, come into the category of the passion-ate, of the headstrong, and the too-truthful. [This is his weirdest absur-dity, the final, total blindness of infatuation, and self-infatuation.] For I can't conceal from myself the fact that I loved Edward Ashburnham— and that I love him because he was just myself. If I had had the courage and the virility and possibly also the physique of Edward Ashburnham I should, I fancy, have done much what he did. He seems to me like a large elder brother who took me out on several excursions and did many dashing things whilst I just watched him robbing the orchards, from a distance. And, you see, I am just as much of a sentimentalist as he was. . . .' [161]. Niggardly, niggardly half-truth!—for observe the impossible exceptions: courage, virility, physique! What sane man could expect them? The narrator aspires to be 'the good soldier', the conven-tionally fine fellow, yet has no expectation of ever being in the least like him in any but his most passive features, and these working not at the level of sexuality, as with Edward, but of malformed friendship. To understand the exact significance here, we must turn, perhaps, to another book.

In his dedicatory epistle in the 1927 edition Ford says that he hoped *The Good Soldier* would do in English something of the sort that Mau-passant's *Fort comme la Mort* did in French. The remark is suggestive in the structural terms that Ford must have had in mind; I wish, how-ever, to call attention to what may be the most accidental connection of theme. Of one of his characters Maupassant says: 'He was an old intel-lectual who might have been, perhaps, a good soldier, and who could never console himself for what he had not been.'

The vicious consolations of failure form our narrator. 'Men,' said

D. H. Lawrence, 'men can suck the heady juice of exalted self-impor-
tance from the bitter weed of failure—failures are usually the most con-
ceited of men.' Thus at the end of the novel we have forgotten the
named good soldier, and we look instead at the nominated one, the
narrator himself. His consolations are small: attendance upon the ill,
'seeing them through'—for twelve years his wife, for the rest of his life
the mad girl whom he fancies he might have loved; yet they give him a
function, at least. This is the bitter, paltry destiny that, he thinks, life
has forced upon him; thus he need never see himself as bitter or as
paltry—or, indeed, as even telling a story.

And thus we come to the final circles of meaning, and these, like
ripples round a stone tossed into a pool, never stop. For, finally, *The
Good Soldier* describes a world that is without moral point, a narrator
who suffers from the madness of moral inertia. 'You ask how it feels to
be a deceived husband. Just heavens, I do not know. It feels just nothing
at all. It is not hell, certainly it is not necessarily heaven. So I suppose
it is the intermediate stage. What do they call it? Limbo' [53]. *Accidia!*
It is the dull hysteria of sloth that besets him, the sluggish insanity of
defective love. 'And, yes, from that day forward she always treated me
and not Florence as if I were the invalid' [29]. 'Why, even to me she
had the air of being submissive—to me that not the youngest child will
ever pay heed to. Yes, this is the saddest story. . .' [41]. The saddest
story? One may say this another way, and say the same thing. *The Good
Soldier* is a comedy of humor, and the humor is phlegm.

It is in the comedy that Ford displays his great art. Irony, which makes
no absolute commitments and can thus enjoy the advantage of many
ambiguities of meaning and endless complexities of situation, is at the
same time an evaluative mood, and, in a master, a sharp one. Perhaps
the most astonishing achievement in this astonishing novel is the manner in which the author, while speaking through his simple, infatuated
character, lets us know how to take his simplicity and his infatuation.
This is comic genius. It shows, for example, in the characteristic figures,
the rather simple-minded and, at the same time, grotesquely comic metaphors: a girl in a white dress in the dark is 'like a phosphorescent fish
in a cupboard' [76]; Leonora glances at the narrator, and he feels 'as if
for a moment a lighthouse had looked at me' [29]; Leonora, boxing the
ears of one of Edward's little mistresses, 'was just striking the face of
an intolerable universe' [43]. Figures such as these, and they occur in
abundance, are the main ingredient in Ford's tone, and they are the
subtle supports of such broader statements as this: 'I should marry Nancy
if her reason were ever sufficiently restored to let her appreciate the
meaning of the Anglican marriage service. But it is probable that her
reason will never be sufficiently restored to let her appreciate the meaning of the Anglican marriage service. Therefore I cannot marry her,
according to the law of the land' [150–51]. This is a mode of comic

revelation and evaluation less difficult, perhaps, than that which is evident in Ford's figures of speech, but to sustain it as he does, with never a rupture of intent, is the highest art.

Then there are the wonderfully comic events—little Mrs Maidan dead in a trunk with her feet sticking out, as though a crocodile had caught her in its giant jaws, or the poor little mad girl saying to the narrator after weeks of silence: 'Shuttlecocks!' [160] There are the frequent moments when the author leads his characters to the most absurd anti-climaxes (as when, at the end of the fourth chapter, Leonora, in a frenzy of self-important drama, demands: 'Don't you know that I'm an Irish Catholic?' [38]), and then, with superb composure, Ford leads his *work* away from the pit of bathos into which his people have fallen. There is the incessant wit, of style and statement, the wittier for its deceptive clothing of pathos. And, most important in this catalogue of comic devices, there is the covering symbolism of illness: characters who fancy that they suffer from 'hearts', who do suffer defective hearts not, as they would have us believe, in the physiological but in the moral sense, and who are told about by a character who has no heart at all, and hence no mind. 'I never', he tells us with his habitually comic solemnity, 'I never was a patient anywhere' [21]. To which we may add: only always, in the madhouse of the world.

Is *The Good Soldier*, perhaps, a novelist's novel? Ford thought that it was his best work, and his judgment was always the judgment of the craftsman. Certainly it can tell us more about the nature of the novel than most novels or books about them: the material under perfect control, the control resulting in the maximum meaning, the style precisely evaluating that meaning. But if it is a kind of archetype of the processes of fiction, if, that is to say, it can demonstrate his craft to the craftsman, then it can also help all of us to read. And is it not true that, once we learn how to read, even if then we do not live more wisely, we can at least begin to be aware of why we have not? *The Good Soldier*, like all great works, has the gift and power of remorse.

SAMUEL HYNES

The Epistemology of *The Good Soldier*†

The problems involved in the interpretation of *The Good Soldier* all stem from one question: What are we to make of the novel's narrator? Or, to put it a bit more formally, what authority should we allow to the

† *Sewanee Review* 69.2 (Spring 1961): 225–35; reprinted in Cassell (see Schorer, above). Reprinted here with the permission of the author. Page numbers in brackets refer to this Norton Critical Edition.

version of events which he narrates? The question is not, of course, particular to this novel; it raises a point of critical theory touching every novel which employs a limited mode of narration.

The point is really an epistemological one; for a novel is a version of the ways in which a man can know reality, as well as a version of reality itself. The techniques by which a novelist controls our contact with his fictional world, and particularly his choice of point of view and his treatment of time, combine to create a model of a theory of knowledge. Thus the narrative technique of Fielding, with the author omniscient and all consciousness equally open to him, implies eighteenth-century ideas of Reason, Order, and General Nature, while the modern inclination toward a restricted and subjective narrative mode implies a more limited and tentative conception of the way man knows.

When we speak of a limited-point-of-view novel, then, we are talking about a novel which implies a limited theory of knowledge. In this kind of novel, the reality that a man can know is two-fold; the external world exists as discrete, observed phenomena, and the individual consciousness exists. That is, a man is given what his senses tell him, and what he thinks. 'The central intelligence' is a narrow room, from which we the readers look out at the disorderly phenomena of experience. We do not *know* (as we know in Fielding) that what we see has meaning; if it has, it is an order which the narrator imposes upon phenomena, not one which is inherent there. And we can know only one consciousness—the one we are in. Other human beings are simply other events outside.

This seems to be equally true of first- and third-person narration in this mode; it is difficult to see an epistemological difference between, say, *The Ambassadors* [1903] and *The Aspern Papers* [1888]. James, however, favored the third-person method, and used it in all his major novels. He did so, I think, because it enabled him to take for granted, 'by the general law of nature', as he put it, 'a primary author'; it allowed him, that is to say, to retain a vestige of authority, even though that authority 'works upon us most in fact by making us forget him'. In fact, though the 'primary author' of James's novels is a rather retiring figure, we do not forget him, and from time to time he comes forward to realign us with the truth, to tell us what we know.

In the first-person novel, on the other hand, it is at least possible to eliminate authority altogether, and to devise a narrative which raises uncertainty about the nature of truth and reality to the level of a structural principle. A classic example is the one before us, and it is in these terms that I will examine Ford's narrative techniques.

The Good Soldier is 'A Tale of Passion', a story of seduction, adultery, and suicide told by a deceived husband. These are melodramatic materials; yet the novel is not a melodrama, because the action of which it is an imitation is not the sequence of passionate gestures which in another novel we would call the plot, but rather the action of the narrator's mind as it gropes for the meaning, the reality of what has occurred. It is an interior action, taking its order from the processes of a puzzled mind rather than from the external forms of chronology and causation. This point is clear enough if one considers the way in which Ford treats the violent events which would, in a true melodrama, be climactic—the deaths of Maisie Maidan, Florence, and Ashburnham. All these climaxes are, dramatically speaking, 'thrown away', anticipated in casual remarks so as to deprive them of melodramatic force, and treated, when they do occur, almost as afterthoughts. (Ashburnham's death is literally an afterthought: Dowell says on the last page but one, 'It suddenly occurs to me that I have forgotten to say how Edward met his death', and even then he does not give us an account of the actual suicide.)

The narrative technique of *The Good Soldier* is a formal model of this interior action. We are entirely restricted to what Dowell perceives, and the order in which we receive his perceptions is the order of his thought; we never know more than he knows about his 'saddest story', and we must accept his contradictions and uncertainties as stages in our own progress toward knowledge. At first glance, Dowell seems peculiarly ill-equipped to tell this story, because he is ill-equipped to *know* a tale of passion. He is a kind of eunuch, a married virgin, a cuckold. He has apparently never felt passion—certainly he has never acted passionately. He is a stranger to human affairs; he tells his wife's aunts that he does nothing because he has never seen any call to. And he is an American, a stranger to the society in which his story takes place.

But more than all this, Dowell would seem to be disqualified as the narrator of *any* story by the doubt and uncertainty which are the defining characteristics of his mind. One phrase runs through his narrative, from the first pages to the last: 'I don't know'; and again and again he raises questions of knowledge, only to leave them unanswered: 'What does one know and why is one here?' 'Who in this world knows anything of any other heart—or of his own?' [104].

The patent inadequacies of Dowell as a narrator have led critics of the novel to dismiss his version of the meaning of the events, and to look elsewhere for authority. Mark Schorer speaks of Dowell's 'distorted understanding', and James Hafley of his 'incoherent vision',[1] and both look outside the narrator himself for objective truths to justify their judgments. But the point of technique here is simply that the factors which seem to disqualify Dowell—his ignorance, his inability to act, his profound doubt—are not seen in relation to any norm; there is neither a 'primary author' nor a 'knower' (of the kind of James's Fanny Assingham or Conrad's Marlow) in terms of which we can get a true perspective of either Dowell or the events of the novel. There is only Dowell, sitting down 'to puzzle out what I know'. The world of the novel is his world,

---

1. For Schorer, see pp. 305–10 above; James Hafley, "The Moral Structure of *The Good Soldier*," *Modern Fiction Studies* 5 (1959–60): 121–28 [*Editor*].

in which 'it is all a darkness'; there is no knowledge offered, or even implied, which is superior to his own.

In a novel which postulates such severe limits to human knowledge—a novel of doubt, that is, in which the narrator's fallibility *is* the norm—the problem of authority cannot be settled directly, because the question which authority answers: 'How can we know what is true?' is itself what the novel is about. There are, however, two indirect ways in which a sense of the truth can be introduced into such a novel without violating its formal (which is to say epistemological) limitations: either through ironic tone, which will act to discredit the narrator's version of events and to imply the correctness of some alternative version, or through the development of the narrator toward some partial knowledge, if only of his own fallibility (and indeed in an extreme case this may be the only kind of knowledge possible for him). Glenway Wescott's *The Pilgrim Hawk* [1940] and Eudora Welty's 'Why I Live at the P.O.' are examples of the first device; each offers a sequence of events which are in themselves clear enough to the reader, and the irony lies in the disparity which we feel between the way the narrator understands these events and the way we understand them. The point made is thus a point of character, the revelation of a personal failure of perception.

The Great Gatsby [1925] is a fair example of the other sort. Fitzgerald's Nick Carraway learns as the action moves, and though he misunderstands and is surrounded by misunderstanding, in the end he knows something about himself, and about Gatsby, and about the world. The point made is a point of knowledge.

It has generally been assumed by Ford's commentators that *The Good Soldier* belongs to the class of *The Pilgrim Hawk*; but in fact it is closer to *Gatsby*. Ford's novel is, to be sure, as ironic as Wescott's, but with this difference; that Ford's narrator is conscious of the irony, and consciously turns it upon himself. When he describes his own inactions, or ventures an analysis of his own character—when he says 'I appeared to be like a woman or a solicitor' [158], and describes himself as 'just as much of a sentimentalist' [161] as Ashburnham—he is consciously self-deprecating, and thus blocks, as any conscious ironist does, the possibility of being charged with self-delusion. Schorer errs on this crucial point when he says that 'the author, while speaking through his simple, infatuated character, lets us know how to take his simplicity and his infatuation'. For the author does not speak—the novel has no 'primary author'; it is Dowell himself who says, in effect, 'I am simple and infatuated' (though there is irony in this, too; he is not all *that* simple).

The case for reading the novel as Schorer does, as a comedy of humor, is based on the enormity of Dowell's inadequacies. There are two arguments to be raised against this reading. First, Dowell's failures—his failure to act, his failure to understand the people around him, his failure to 'connect'—are shared by all the other characters in the novel, and thus would seem to constitute a generalization about the human condition rather than a moral state peculiar to him. Alienation, silence, loneliness, repression—these describe Ashburnham and Leonora and Nancy, and even 'poor Florence' as well as they describe Dowell. Each character confronts his destiny alone.

Second, Dowell does have certain positive qualities which perhaps, in the light of recent criticism of the novel, require some rehabilitation. For instance, if his moral doubt prevents positive action, it also restrains him from passing judgment, even on those who have most wronged him. 'But what were they?' he asks. 'The just? The unjust? God knows! I think that the pair of them were only poor wretches creeping over this earth in the shadow of an eternal wrath. It is very terrible' [53]. And though he doubts judgment—doubts, that is, the existence of moral absolutes—he is filled with a desire to know, a compelling need for the truth to sustain him in the ruin of his life. In the action of the novel, the doubt and the need to know are equally real, though they deny each other.

Dowell has one other quality, and it is his finest and most saving attribute—his capacity for love; for ironically, it is he, the eunuch, who is the Lover. Florence and Ashburnham and Maisie Maidan suffer from 'hearts', but Dowell is sound, and able, after his fashion, to love—to love Ashburnham and Nancy, and even Leonora. It is he who performs the two acts of wholly unselfish love in the book—he crosses the Atlantic in answer to Ashburnham's plea for help, and he travels to Ceylon to bring back the mad Nancy, when Leonora will not. And he can forgive, as no other character can.

This is the character, then, through whom Ford chooses to tell this 'saddest story'. He is a limited, fallible man, but the novel is not a study of his particular limitations; it is rather a study of the difficulties which man's nature and the world's put in the way of his will to know. Absolute truth and objective judgment are not possible; experience is a darkness, and other hearts are closed to us. If man nevertheless desires to know, and he does, then he will have to do the best he can with the shabby equipment which life offers him, and to be content with small and tentative achievements.

Dowell's account of this affair is told, as all first-person narratives must be, in retrospect, but the technique is in some ways unusual. We know the physical, melodramatic world only at one remove, so that the real events of the novel are Dowell's thoughts about what has happened, and not the happenings themselves. We are never thrown back into the stream of events, as we are, for example, in the narratives of Conrad's Marlow; dramatic scenes are rare, and tend to be told in scattered fragments, as Dowell reverts to them in his thoughts. We are always with Dowell, after the event.

Yet though we are constantly reminded that all the events are over and done, we are also reminded that time passes during the telling (two years in all). The point of this device is the clear distinction that the novel makes between events and meaning, between what we have witnessed and what we know. All the returns are in, but their meaning can only be discovered (if at all) in time, by re-examination of the data, by reflection, and ultimately by love. And so Dowell tells his story as a puzzled man thinks—not in chronological order, but compulsively, going over the ground in circles, returning to crucial points, like someone looking for a lost object in a dim light. What he is looking for is the meaning of his experience.

Since the action of the novel is Dowell's struggle to understand, the events are ordered in relation to his developing knowledge, and are given importance in relation to what he learns from them. Thus we know in the first chapter that Dowell's wife, Florence, is dead, hear in the second chapter of Part II Dowell's account of that death (which he believes to be a heart attack), and only in Part III learn, through Dowell's account of Leonora's version of the event, that it was in fact suicide. We move among the events of the affair, to stand with Dowell for a moment behind Ashburnham, then to Leonora, to Nancy, and back to Ashburnham, getting in each case an account, colored always by Dowell's compassionate doubt, of the individual's version of events. The effect of this ordering is not that we finally see one version as right and another as wrong, but that we recognize an irresolvable pluralism of truths, in a world that remains essentially dark.

There are, as I have said, certain crucial points in the narrative to which Dowell returns, or around which the narrative hovers. These are the points at which the two conflicting principles of the novel—Convention and Passion—intersect. The most important of these is the 'Protest' scene, in which Florence shows Ashburnham the Protestant document, signed by Luther, Bucer and Zwingli, which has made him what he is—'honest, sober, industrious, provident, and clean-lived'. Leonora's reaction to this typical tourist scene strikes Dowell as a bit extravagant:

> 'Don't you see,' she said, with a really horrible bitterness, with a really horrible lamentation in her voice, 'Don't you see that that's the cause of the whole miserable affair; of the whole sorrow of the world? And of the eternal damnation of you and me and them. . . .' [38]

He is relieved when she tells him that she is a Roman Catholic because it seems to provide an explanation of her outburst; and later his discovery that Florence was Ashburnham's mistress offers another, and more credible explanation. But neither explanation is really adequate. For Leonora is not simply reacting either to Protestantism or to adultery; she is reacting, in the name of a rigid conventionalism, to the destructive power of passion, which may equally well take the form of religious protest or of sexual license.

Ford once described himself as 'a sentimental Tory and a Roman Catholic', and it is in these two forms that convention functions in *The Good Soldier* (and in a number of his other novels as well). Society, as Dowell recognizes, depends on the arbitrary and unquestioning acceptance of 'the whole collection of rules'. Dowell is, at the beginning of his action, entirely conventional in this sense; conventions provide him with a way of existing in the world—they are the alternatives to the true reality which man cannot know, or which he cannot bear to know. From conventions he gets a spurious sense of permanence and stability and human intimacy, and the illusion of knowledge. When they collapse, he is left with nothing.

Leonora's conventions are her 'English Catholic conscience, her rigid principles, her coldness, even her very patience' [47], conventions which are, Dowell thinks, 'all wrong in this special case' [47] (it is characteristic of him that he refuses to generalize beyond the special case). Ashburnham's are those of a sentimental Tory—'what was demanded by convention and [by] the traditions of his house' [151]. (A first draft of Ashburnham appears in *The Spirit of the People* [1907], Ford's study of the English mind; there the scene between Ashburnham and Nancy at the railway station is offered as an example of the Englishman's characteristic reticence and fear of emotion.) It is by these conventions that the husband and wife act at crucial moments; but it is not conventions alone which bring about their tragedy. It is, rather, the interaction of Convention and Passion.

Passion is the necessary antagonist of Convention, the protest of the individual against the rules. It is anarchic and destructive; it reveals the secrets of the heart which convention exists to conceal and repress; it knows no rules except its own necessity. Passion is, of course, an ambiguous term. To the secular mind it is likely to suggest simply sexual desire. But it also means suffering, and specifically Christ's sacrificial suffering. I don't mean to suggest that Ashburnham is what it has become fashionable to call a 'Christ-figure'—I dislike the critical method which consists in re-writing novels as Passion Plays—but simply that the passionate sufferings of Ashburnham (and even of Leonora) are acts of love, and as such have their positive aspects. Convention, as Dowell learns, provides no medium for the expression of such love. In conventional terms it is true, as Dowell says, that Edward and Nancy are the villains, and Leonora the heroine, but the expense of her conventional heroism is the defilement of what is best in her, and the destruction of what she loves, while the 'villains' are, in their suffering, blessed; the epigraph of the novel is their epitaph: *Beati Immaculati*, blessed are the pure.

Between the conflicting demands of Convention and Passion, the characters are, as Nancy says, shuttlecocks. 'Convention and traditions I suppose,' Dowell reflects near the end of the book, 'work blindly but surely for the preservation of the normal type; for the extinction of proud, resolute, and unusual individuals [152].' Passion works for the reverse.

In the action of Dowell's knowing, he learns the reality of Passion, but he also acknowledges that Convention will triumph, because it must. 'Society must go on, I suppose, and society can only exist if the normal, if the virtuous, and the slightly deceitful flourish, and if the passionate, the headstrong, and the too-truthful are condemned to suicide and to madness' [160–61]. Yet in the end he identifies himself unconditionally with Passion: 'I loved Edward Ashburnham,' he says, 'because he was just myself' [161]. This seems a bizarre assertion, that Dowell, the Philadelphia eunuch, should identify himself with Ashburnham, the English country squire and lover ('this is his weirdest absurdity,' Schorer remarks of this passage, 'the final, total blindness of infatuation, and self-infatuation'). But in the action of the novel the identification is understandable enough. The problem that the novel sets is the problem of knowledge, and specifically knowledge of the human heart: 'Who in this world knows anything of any other heart— or of his own?' [104]. Dowell, in the end, *does* know another human heart—Ashburnham's, and knowing that heart, he knows his own. By entering selflessly into another man's suffering, he has identified himself with him, and identity is knowledge. He is, to be sure, ill-equipped for this knowledge; he lacks, as he says, Ashburnham's courage and virility and physique—everything, one would think, that goes to make an Ashburnham. But by an act of perfect sympathy he has known what Ashburnham was, and he can therefore place himself honestly in the category of 'the passionate, of the headstrong, and the too-truthful'.

With this confession, the affair is over. The action in Dowell's mind is complete, or as complete as it can be in a novel built on doubt. The repeated questions, which Ford uses as Shakespeare uses questions in the tragedies, almost as symbols of the difficulty of knowing, disappear from the last chapter; but they are replaced, not by an emergent certainty, but by resigned admissions of the limits of human knowledge: 'I don't know. I know nothing. I am very tired' [156] and 'I can't make out which of them was right. I leave it to you' [156]. To know what you can't know is nevertheless a kind of knowledge, and a kind that Dowell did not have at the beginning of the affair. Of positive knowledge, he has this: he knows something of another human heart, and something also of the necessary and irreconcilable conflict which Passion and Convention, and which he accepts as in things. Beyond that, it is all a darkness, as it was.

318

JOHN A. MEIXNER

[*The Good Soldier* as Tragedy] †

* * *

Robie Macauley * * * writing in *The Kenyon Review*, for all his high praise and perceptive comments, classifies *[The Good Soldier]* as a 'miniature' performance and suggests that, were it not for the fact of the Tietjens books, it might be thought of as 'the lucky try of a gifted and fortunate minor novelist'. Misreading the relationship between Ashburnham and his wife, Mr Macauley formulates a partial, even mistaken meaning for the novel, and so misses the great scope of the work asserted by its original title *[The Saddest Story]*. It is not surprising, therefore, that he should dismiss that title by saying that Ford 'was always bad at naming his books'.[1]

Mr Macauley, however, is far closer to the spirit of the novel than Mark Schorer, whose critique strategically appears at the head of the 1951 and 1957 reissues of the book.[2] Unlike Mr Macauley, Mr. Schorer sympathizes with Ford's 'understandable' horror at the change. Yet his argument is not that the original was more truly expressive, but that the present title, apparently because of the 'libertine' character of Edward Ashburnham, is 'peculiarly inappropriate, certainly uncongenial enough'. Unfortunately, these same words are far more applicable to Mr Schorer's analysis. For despite his high estimation of *The Good Soldier* (he in fact deems it a great work), the book in his hands loses much of its real importance and becomes little more than a clever *tour de force*. By focusing on only one dimension, Mr Schorer has unhappily described and treated a novel of deep, intensely tragic power as a comedy and, more unhappily still, as a 'comedy of humor'.

The culminating achievement of Ford's 'cat's cradle' vision, *The Good Soldier* is, at its core, a tragedy. It tells a lacerating tale of groping human beings, caught implacably by training, character, and circumstance, who cruelly and blindly inflict on each other terrible misery and pain: 'poor wretches', as the narrator says, 'creeping over this earth in the shadow of an eternal wrath' [53]. Yet around this awful core, and without diminishing its power, Ford * * * has placed a context of comic irony. This context—which Mr Schorer has made the center of the

---

† From "Ford's Literary Technique" in *Ford Madox Ford's Novels. A Critical Study* (Minneapolis and London: U of Minnesota P and Oxford UP, 1962) 152–54, 158–60, 184–86. Copyright © 1962 by the University of Minnesota. Reprinted with the permission of the University of Minnesota Press. Reprinted Cassell (see Schorer, above). Page numbers in brackets refer to this Norton Critical Edition.

1. Robie Macauley, 'The Good Ford', *The Kenyon Review*, XI (Spring 1949), 277.
2. For Schorer, see pp. 305–10 above [*Editor*].

book—Ford uses, as we shall see, to provide the novel's ultimate commentary on the nature of human life in the twentieth century world. Indeed, in its juxtaposition of these two modes, *The Good Soldier* epitomizes in a classic way the altered tragic vision of our modern sensibility.

* * * At the heart of *The Good Soldier* is a tormented love triangle bridging two generations. Ford tells us that in writing the work he sought 'to do for the English novel what in *Forte comme la Mort* Maupassant has done for the French' [5]. And the triangle he establishes is essentially Maupassant's in that book. An older man, hopelessly in love with a younger woman, agonizingly stumbles to his doom—caught in a passion as strong as death. In Ford's hands, however, the basic triangle has undergone a fascinating, original transplantation. The older pair become husband and wife, not lover and mistress, and the girl is herself swept away by the action. The cultural situation is thoroughly anglicized, and the drama made enormously more taut, integrated, and powerful. A further change is the adding of two other characters, a wealthy, somewhat bizarre American couple, Florence and John Dowell. For many pages, in fact, the reader is led to believe that the novel is about a four-sided relationship among the Dowells and the Ashburnhams—or, more precisely, about a different triangle, for the American wife, it is soon disclosed, has been Ashburnham's mistress. Only gradually, as the novel moves through a series of bewildering turns in which the 'truth' of what unfolds continually shifts * * * does the reader finally confront the central trio.

* * *

Before examining Dowell's artistic function, however, we first must try to understand his character. For certainly, superficially considered, it is baffling. Although Ford provides various facts about him—his Philadelphia origin and wealth, for example—these are minimal and tell us little about his motivation. Where Edward, Leonora, and Nancy are 'justified'[3] with great detail and care, Dowell's background is scarcely explained at all. We learn nothing, for example, of his immediate family, nor are we given any cause, psychological or otherwise, for his lack of masculine vitality. He has no occupation. * * * What he originally saw in Florence is unclear. * * * That he should never in twelve years of marriage have suspected either her unfaithfulness or her fraudulent invention of a bad heart, which had kept him from any conjugal claims, seems almost fantastic. In Dowell something of the common state of humanity is missing, a lack reflected in the responses of other characters. Edward, he tells us twice, thought of him as not so much a man as a woman or a solicitor. In behavior, he is often peevish, even fatuous.

---

3. For Ford's theory of "justification," see "On Impressionism," pp. 265–67 above [*Editor*].

Ford's characterization of Dowell undeniably seems shaped under the comic spirit.

But that is only part of the story. For our sense of the objectively ludicrous in Dowell is very much qualified by the fact that we perceive his emotional life from within. He himself tells the story. And it is also qualified by our knowledge, which gradually becomes firmer and firmer, that this emotional life is that of an individual who is a psychic cripple.

In Dowell, Ford has created one of the most remarkable, certainly one of the most subtle, characterizations in modern literature. Almost completely from within he has caught and rendered the sensibility of a severely neurotic personality. Dowell is Prufrock before Prufrock, and not a mere sketch as in Eliot but a full-scale portrait. He is a man who, incapable of acting, is almost entirely feeling—a creature of pure pathos. Lonely and unrooted, Dowell is an alienated being, as he himself with fascinating indirection indicates in the opening chapters. With 'no attachments, no accumulations', 'a wanderer on the face of public resorts', always 'too polished up', he felt 'a sense almost of nakedness—the nakedness that one feels on the sea-shore or in any great open space' [21]. That was why the Ashburnhams had meant so much to him. They had, he implies, filled a frightening void. Dowell's absurdity does not induce laughter, but rather a grave sadness.[4]

The narrator's spiritual invalidism is manifest in many ways—his atypical behavior, his almost painful self-deprecation, his peculiar images, and on occasion, certain incongruously repetitive and overly precise observations which Ford superbly uses to reassert this knowledge. (For example, his reference to the marriage rites of the Anglican Church and the use of the word 'trotted' in the penultimate sentence of the book.) The plainest reference to his psychological state is brought out when he describes Leonora's reaction at their initial meeting. For at first, she was cautious and probing; but then into her eyes came a warm tenderness and friendly recognition. 'It implied trust; it implied the want of any necessity for barriers.' 'By God, she looked at me as if I were an invalid—as any kind woman may look at a poor chap in a bath chair. And, yes, from that day forward she always treated me and not Florence as if I were the invalid' [29]. 'I suppose, therefore,' he continues wryly, 'that her eyes had made a favourable answer. Or, perhaps, it wasn't a favourable answer' [29]. The same motif of himself as the patient is reinforced a few pages later. * * *

* * *

The appropriateness of Dowell as the medium through which the careers of the Ashburnhams and their ward is told should by now be

---

4. This deeper, more human and sympathetic side of Dowell, Mr. Schorer ignores; in his reading, Ford's narrator is merely a mindless, self-deluded fool, worthy of a passionate scorn.

clear. Either in actual life—as students of mental disorders well know—or in *The Good Soldier*, the neurotic sensibility, turned in on itself, is apt to be heightened above the normal in its perception of emotional pain. His consciousness will be peculiarly receptive to the ache in the universe.

*   *   *

Those elements which make for the tragedy of the action are classically Aristotelian: its sense of inevitability, its reversals of situation and meaning, its high poetry. Its protagonist, Edward Ashburnham, is a man much above the ordinary. He lives according to the high values of generosity, kindness, duty, and responsibility to those who depend upon him, and he can act for the right with will and determination. 'The unfortunate Edward,' Dowell writes. 'Or, perhaps, he was not so unfortunate; because he had done what he knew to be the right thing, he may be deemed happy' [136]. If Edward at his introduction seems, like Dowell, essentially a creation of comedy—an indulgent libertine, athletically handsome but basically stupid and vacuous—his dignity and stature steadily grow during the book until at its close he is an extremely impressive, noble figure. By no means a perfect man—the tragic protagonist never is—he is a good man who has never been guided by base motives. As Dowell makes clear, he was not a promiscuous libertine, but a sentimentalist.[5] * * * Sentimentality in fact is Edward's basic human weakness, his fatal flaw—even, as, ironically, it is the source of much of his virtues. Most importantly, *The Good Soldier* arouses in the reader the cathartic emotions of pity and awe at the spectacle of its admirable, greatly suffering protagonist. * * *

*   *   *

The religious framework of the world, with its vision of harmony between God, man, and nature, has been shattered. This catastrophe and its consequences Ford crystallizes through brilliant juxtaposition in at least two key places in the novel. The first is the somewhat bathetic contrast (in the concluding chapter of Part One) between the powerful, compelling image of the palm of God and the comic, half-mocking and (half-weeping) image of the death and doll-like religious funeral of Maisie Maidan. More striking still, and more obvious in its meaning, is the conjunction of the only comments which are spoken by Nancy after she goes insane. 'Credo in unum Deum Omnipotentem' is the first, and about it Dowell sadly, wearily comments: 'Those are the only reasonable words she uttered; those are the only words, it appears, that she ever will utter. I suppose that they are reasonable words; it must be extraordinarily

---

5. In Mr. Schorer's analysis, Edward is simply a libertine, having neither dignity nor depth and subject to the same distressingly hard scorn which marks the approach to Dowell. The reader would not even discern that Edward, not the narrator, is the central figure of the novel.

reasonable for her, if she can say that she believes in an Omnipotent Deity'. Almost at the end of the book Nancy speaks the other: a single word, repeated three times, 'Shuttlecocks' [160]. That is how she felt between Leonora and Edward, and that was the way Edward had felt between the women. And that is the word, Ford is saying, for man's buffeted, purposeless existence in the world that has come into being.

We can now understand also the full ambiguity and subtlety of the scene in which, when Florence had disclosed a copy of Luther's Protest, Leonora cried out: 'Don't you see that that's the cause of the whole miserable affair; of the whole sorrow of the world? And of the eternal damnation of you and me and them. . . .' [38] Her words, of course, are addressed essentially to the quietly meaningful touching by Florence of Edward's wrist. Although a staunch Roman Catholic, Leonora in reality is not a religious woman at all, operating rather according to the rigid code of the Church, to its letter rather than its spirit. Yet the reader does not yet know this fact and the words make their significant effect in his mind. By them Ford is saying that the rise of Protestantism, which symbolizes the entire modern, skeptical, fragmenting impulse, is the source of the destruction of the old consoling religious framework and the whole present sorrow of the world.

*   *   *

ARTHUR MIZENER

[Ford, Dowell, and the Sex Instinct] †

The Good Soldier has been the subject of a great deal of controversy that depends ultimately on the ambiguity of fictions narrated in the first person by a participant. In such fictions there is no way for the author to provide us with a reliable judgment of the narrator so that we can determine how to take what he tells us. We can know how to take a dramatized narrator only if we share the author's values. The author cannot tell the reader what these are; each reader must guess; and what each reader usually guesses is that the author has the same values he has.

As a result critics have seen John Dowell * * * as everything from a man "incapable of passion, sexual and moral alike," who suffered from "the dull hysteria of sloth . . . the sluggish insanity of defective love" (as Mark Schorer says) to a "narrator [who] fits the [Conrad-Ford] ideal bet-

† From *The Saddest Story: A Biography of Ford Madox Ford* (London: The Bodley Head, 1971), 258–61, 263, 265. Copyright © 1971 by Arthur Mizener. Reprinted with the permission of HarperCollins Publishers, Inc. and Lawrence Pollinger Ltd. Page numbers in brackets refer to this Norton Critical Edition.

ter than Conrad's Marlow, being even less of an idiosyncratic observer"
(as Robie Macauley says). The first kind of critic takes what Dowell tells
us as a systematically "distorted understanding" of what really happened,
dictated by the narrator's need to defend his own sexual inadequacy. For
him *The Good Soldier* is—like Edmund Wilson's version of "The Turn
of the Screw"—an ironic portrait of its narrator, "a comedy of humor."
The second sort of critic sees *The Good Soldier* as a tragic story of mis-
matched lives in which—"his preservation com[ing] from having understood more of the story than any of the other people in it"—the narrator
alone survives intact. The only recourse for criticism confronted by dis-
agreement so radical as this is to such evidence of the author's intention
as can be discovered outside the novel.[1]

Critics who share Professor Schorer's Lawrentian conception of
human nature may well be right that in real life men who demonstrate
the "fantastic [sexual] failure" of Dowell's life with Florence inevitably
have "mind[s] not quite in balance," that the judgments of such men
are the "weirdest absurdity, the final, total blindness of infatuation, and
self-infatuation." For better or for worse, however, Ford did not hold
this view. From his marriage to Elsie Martindale to his final union with
Janice Biala * * * everything he did in his life and everything he said
shows that what Dowell says about passion is not intended as ironic
exposure of Dowell's neurotic personality but is what Ford thought true.

> Of the question of the sex instinct I know very little [Dowell says,
> not meaning he understands less than most men about it but that
> no man of intelligence pontificates on the subject] and I do not
> think that it counts for very much in a really great passion. . . . I
> don't mean to say that any great passion can exist without a desire
> for consummation . . . that must be taken for granted, as, in a
> novel, or a biography, you take it for granted that the characters
> have their meals with some regularity. But the real fierceness of
> desire, the real heat of a passion long continued and withering up
> the soul of a man, is the craving for identity with the woman that
> he loves. . . . There is no man who loves a woman that does not
> desire to come to her for the renewal of his courage, for the cutting
> asunder of his difficulties. And that will be the mainspring of his
> desire for her. We are all so afraid, we are all so alone, we all so

---

1. Mark Schorer [see pp. 305–10]; Carol Ohmann supports this view in her *Ford Madox Ford*
   [: *From Apprentice to Craftsman* (Middletown: Weslyan University Press, 1964]. Robie
   Macauley [see p. 318, n. 1 above]; with some modification this view is supported by Elliott B.
   Gose in his important article, "The Strange Irregular Rhythm: An Analysis of *The Good Sol-
   dier*," *PMLA* 72 (June 1957): 404–509. A middle view of Dowell is taken by Paul L. Wiley in
   Novelist of Three Worlds [: *Ford Madox Ford* (Syracuse: Syracuse UP, 1962)], Richard A.
   Cassell in *Ford Madox Ford* [: *A Study of His Novels* (Baltimore: Johns Hopkins UP, 1961)],
   and John A. Meixner's *Ford Madox Ford's Novels* [see pp. 318–22 above]. * * * The only
   quite satisfactory discussion of Dowell * * * is in Samuel Hynes's brilliant article, "The Epistemology of *The Good Soldier*" [see pp. 310–17 above].

need from the outside the assurance of our own worthiness to exist[2] [79–80].

The belittlement in Dowell's comparison of the sexual act with eating is a considered expression of Ford's own judgment in the matter. He thought the romantic deification of the sex act was nonsense. This was also Edward Ashburnham's view. For his declaration of love to Nancy Rufford, he "was very careful to assure [Dowell] that at that time there was no physical motive. . . . No, it was simply [a matter] of her effect on the moral side of his life. . . " [77]. In his blunter way Christopher Tietjens takes the same view of the sex act. "You seduced a young woman in order to be able to finish your talks with her. You could not do that without living with her. You could not live with her without seducing her; but that was the by-product. The point is that you can't otherwise talk . . . [can't have] the intimate conversation that means the final communion of your souls." "[Ford] made Dowell proper, extremely proper," Harold Loeb says. "And Ford was like that."[3]

* * *

* * * Ford believed with some reason that he was making this dramatic detail [the "white marriage" of Dowell and Florence] more plausible by making Dowell an American. In any event, it is absurdly unhistorical—like a rigid Marxist's interpretation of *Pride and Prejudice*—to assume that Ford believed conduct like Dowell's showed a man was blindly neurotic.

* * *

The Good Soldier depends for its "heart" on the fact that Edward Ashburnham is the "hallucinated" Ford's passionately sympathetic, idealized conception of himself, of the simplicity of his motives, the goodness of his intentions, the "seriousness" of his conduct. Many of the things Edward does Ford only dreamed of doing or imagined he had done. But there is nothing in Edward's nature that Ford did not believe part of his own. There are occasional traces in the novel of the actual circumstances of his life that he is translating into the terms of its story, notably in the case of Florence. Much of the time, however, as in so many of Ford's anecdotes, the facts of Edward's situation have been changed, but the conception of Edward's self is an exact representation of Ford's conception of himself.

* * *

2. "To put the matter exaggeratedly for the sake of clearness," Ford says of Dante in *The March of Literature*, "the serious Italian writer considered that spiritual love alone could be dignified by the name of that passion, the sexual act having no more to do with it than eating or drinking."

3. *Parade's End*, II, p. 132; Harold Loeb, "Ford Madox Ford's 'The Good Soldier,' " *London Magazine*, III (December 1963), 65–73.

As a participant in the events of *The Good Soldier*, Dowell has his limitations and blindnesses, just as the rest of the characters do. But the Dowell who is telling the story knows everything that Ford does and thinks all the things that Ford did about human affairs. The ironic wit of *The Good Soldier's* style depends, not on a discrepancy between the narrator's attitude and Ford's, but on a discrepancy between Dowell's attitude as a participant in the events and Dowell's attitude as a narrator of them. All the perception, the tolerance, the humility that recognizes the limitations of its own understanding; all the poetic wit of the book's figures of speech; all the powerful ironies of the narration; all these things are Dowell's.

*   *   *

GROVER SMITH

[Dowell as Untrustworthy Narrator]†

*   *   *

Dowell, the first-person narrator of *The Good Soldier* functions on several levels. Only two of these are public: first the level on which he confesses that he is no perceiver, that he has understood nothing about his wife Florence, his friend Edward Ashburnham, Edward's wife Leonora, the ingénue Nancy Rufford, or himself; and secondly the level on which he actually sets up as a commentator on the wretched imbroglio, in effect as an artist, and reports what "must have been" the truth of it all. Such indeed is his nature: duped by his wife, his friend, and his friend's wife, he takes a ca' canny view when interpreting what has happened behind his back; but half-enlightened by his wife's and his friend's suicide, he assumes that he can now know all that is important—his various disclaimers notwithstanding. The dupe Dowell is untrustworthy because his impressions have so been; the mystagogue (the term is hardly too strong) is untrustworthy because, like the "liar" in James's story, though nothing like such a dab-hand, he has a passion for *telling*. It follows that *The Good Soldier* incorporates three histories finally: the one which Dowell has ignorantly lived through, the one which Dowell impressionistically constructs, and the one which really happened. The first two are visible, not separately but as twined together, and they are remarkably alike in feeling. For they are both rather cheap and crude. The *ignorant* Dowell's is farcical: the story of a dullard who marries a

† From *Ford Madox Ford* in Columbia Essays on Modern Writers series, no. 63 (New York: Columbia UP, 1972) 26–34. Reprinted with the permission of the publisher. Page numbers in brackets refer to this Norton Critical Edition.

slut and is cuckolded by a cad, the cad's own wife being a middle-class prude. The *impressionistic* Dowell's is literary, in fact melodramatic: the story of a decent but cold man whose wife and best friend, the one outwardly respectable and the other a passionate idealist, become lovers but are divided when the idealist falls tenderly in love with an innocent young girl; the guilty wife kills herself when her sins find her out; the idealist, frustrated by his censorious wife's intervention, kills himself with a *penknife*; the young girl goes mad; she is tended by the compassionate, decent, but cold man.

And the hidden history—the meaning which might raise these events to a tragedy commensurate with the suffering intrinsic to them? This, alas, is not told—not by Dowell, who does not know it. Meixner points out that at the core of *The Good Soldier* is a potential tragedy of enormous intensity and broad implications, whereas the story-telling apparatus surrounding it is ironically comic.[1] The apparatus suits the scale of Dowell's affective values, namely, from farce to sentimental melodrama. It is to the credit of Dowell's *unconscious* sensibility (if such a thing can be) that the reader picks up the vibrations of tragedy. * * *

Dowell, failing to grasp the principle that if truth is unknowable the ignorant man is wise, insists on contriving a dramatic image, a character, for himself as revealer. *What* he is, we cannot be certain; the image he chooses to employ is that of a leisure-class American from Philadelphia, which he calls "Philadelphia, Pa." [10]. Surely many readers have noticed that his account of his background does not hold up well: he calls his country the "United States of North America" [47]; says that he carries about with him the title deeds to his ancestral farm, "which once covered several blocks between Chestnut and Walnut Streets. These title deeds are of wampum" [10] (not anachronistic for such a purpose?); boasts that he came of a family originally English, the first Dowell having "left Farnham in Surrey in company with William Penn" [10] (there are no Penn associations at Farnham; *Ford* once lived near Limpsfield); most astonishing, reports that he learned "Pennsylvania Duitsch" (*sic*) [36] in childhood. In general, American probabilities are so foreign to him that, if we met him on a Cook's Tour, we might suspect him to be bogus. American politics, for example, he considers enigmatic: his "sort of second-nephew," Carter, "was what they called a sort of Vermont Democrat. . . . But I don't know what it means" [104]. This same Carter was "a good cricketer" [103]; it is not impossible. Florence's uncle, a manufacturer in Waterbury, was "a violent Democrat" [19] (could it have been because of the tariff on foreign clocks?). Dowell's America, in short, is essentially Ford's America; but Ford must have known much more about it—Dowell's "Pennsylvania Duitsch" makes it certain: Ford could not have been guilty of this howler, for he of all people would

1. See p. 318 above [*Editor*].

have known that Pennsylvania *Deutsch* is not Holland *Dutch*. Dowell is marked as ignorant and pretentious—and, in some sense which, even so, is not quite the literal one, as an impostor. He has touched up and tinted his own photograph.

Since this is what Ford did, too, in his memoirs, and since *The Good Soldier* is a memoir of Dowell as well as a novel of Ford, there are excellent reasons why Dowell should behave like Ford. (The Philadelphia land grant is amusingly analogous to the baronial estates in Germany for which Ford hankered in the first flush of his romance with Violet Hunt.) Does it follow that Dowell, from start to finish, is simply telling a tall tale? This question can be rephrased to come better to the point: does it follow that Dowell is inside, as well as outside, the tale Ford tells through him? Inside it *twice*, that is?—for he is certainly in it once, since it is partly about himself. Clearly it does follow, if a dupe can dupe himself. (Dowell need not be *dishonest*: that is not in question.) At the same time, it does not much matter to the tale if its frame, as well as itself, is untrustworthy. But it was essential to Ford that the untrustworthiness of the frame, the narrator, should point to the untrustworthiness of the tale. For most readers Ford's clues have proved too subtle: they have rushed in and hailed the romance of Edward Ashburnham as something ideal and noble, paying Dowell the compliment, if it is not an insult to his art, of believing in his dime-novel version of life—the version which has ousted what might have been a tragic masterpiece. Whatever we conclude about all this—and probably we had better conclude nothing—one thing may be meditated on: the indication that Dowell is not merely an untrustworthy narrator but an untrustworthy impressionist.

Before *The Good Soldier*, Ford never handled first-person narration quite successfully. There may have been two handles to his prejudice against this. On the one hand, the technique seems to involve a limitation in point of view, an absolute limitation; on the other hand, it seems absolutely committed to narration—and "we . . . must not narrate but render . . . impressions."[2] Both criticisms, in fact, concern the impressionistic method. Any narrowed point of view, even if not of the first person, substitutes something else for impressionism, or pushes something else into the foreground, namely, the nature of the single character thus favored. Ford valued the rich variety of impressionistic effects he was able to produce without point of view, and presumably saw no reason to pursue a conflicting enterprise. If point of view was to be of the first person, then narration posed a forbidding alternative to impressionism. In the event, however, the difficulties were met by inventing a narrator who could not narrate but could only "render impressions" of a life, his own, with the time-shift as a token of his ineptitude. The

2. See p. 276 above [*Editor*].

impressions became, as before, the tale. An untrustworthy narrator came into being as a result of the mistrust of narration. The new creation to be recognized in *The Good Soldier* is not time-shift, for Conrad's Marlow used that; it is the untrustworthy narrator as chief and clinching evidence of the essential untrustworthiness of narration.

No need, here, for the mysteriousness which, in James's *The Turn of the Screw*, leaves it to the reader to guess whether the narrator (the governess) is neurotic or clairvoyant or simply romantic; or which, in *The Sacred Fount*, invites suspicions that the narrator is mad or that the stylist, the old Master, is parodying himself. Here the untrustworthy narrator practically denounces himself. Moreover he is the norm for narrators, all of them painfully inept at sizing up life as it is; all obliged to back and fill, to contradict themselves and admit it. The truth, finally, can only be what convincingly *seems*.

The purposes of the time-shift are various. In the Tietjens tetralogy, which has no consistent first-person narrator, it works above all to advance the story thematically. Ford said in *It Was the Nightingale* (1933) that the novelist must never digress but always seem to digress, on the (rather odd) theory that the reader likes to be distracted and that his attention can be kept moving in a straight line only by being beguiled with the sensation of diversionary movement. (Presumably a line if crooked *enough* appears straight.) More important, the time-shift establishes a symbolic architecture of events. In *The Good Soldier* it also characterizes Dowell, largely by defining his distance from and attitude toward the incidents he relates. It is fundamentally a rhythmic, cinematographic device and belongs to the films. With the first-person narrator on hand, it recalls, though usually it does not much resemble, stream-of-consciousness monologue. One big difference is that Dowell's rendering, with the time-shift (how well named! it is as consciously controlled as the gear-shift of a racing car, or a heavy truck), keeps him separate from his tale, his vehicle. One is aware of him *here* and of his tale *there*. And the *progression d'effet* takes place in the present he fills with past events. The past is layered, not fluid like the stream of consciousness; its contents are as if arranged in trays in a cabinet, able to be drawn out of dated slots. Or to return to a metaphor already used, events in time are bulletlike, not all mixed up together like the water in a fish tank. Stream-of-consciousness techniques are constantly violating chronology. Dowell never violates chronology: he shuffles it. So he is at a distance from his past and treats it as a series. Yet he still manages to treat it as a series of appearances rather than facts, even while he acclaims as facts the impressions his memory pulls out. Lastly, his undertaking seems far more logical than stream-of-consciousness reverie, where free association becomes a lord of misrule. Time-shift effects were to recur in Ford's novels. Ford's first novel of the war, *The Marsden*

Case (1923), contains an even more complex array of them than *The Good Soldier.*

It is impossible to read *The Good Soldier* without being moved, indeed almost rocked, by the emotional force of Dowell's plea for idealism and self-sacrifice on the one hand and for the legitimacy of intense physical passion on the other. It is this intensity that has won Dowell the allegiance of so many readers, most of whom are likely to remain deaf to a criticism calling into question the way he imputes both moral idealism and passion to Ashburnham's relations with women. Yet surely he is mistaken in his estimate of Ashburnham's character: the blend of these virtues, one passive and the other active, is conceivable; but Ashburnham's tactics belie the claim Dowell makes for him. Ashburnham's relations with women are anything but morally idealistic; in the case of his supposed Dulcinea, Nancy, Ashburnham is only baffled of his prey. If the reader can believe Dowell's report of Ashburnham's flirtations and seductions, they would appear to be carried on independently of the moral virtues which make Ashburnham a good landlord—or is not this what is expected of the feudal seigneur? The conceit of Dowell that Ashburnham mirrors *him* is what explains Dowell's romantic misjudgment of the other man; in Dowell, too, a celibate ideal is yoked with a baffled and inhibited passion. Certainly this conceit accords with Dowell's habitual misjudgment of his wife Florence, whom in a sense he has encouraged in her compulsive promiscuity by his unquestioning chivalric deference to her "bad heart," and of Leonora as well, who, cold though she is in her marriage to Ashburnham, is not only a wronged woman but a good one.

To Florence's nymphomania (or whatever it is), to Ashburnham's lecherousness, and to Leonora's justice Dowell is insensitive to the extent of condemning or praising without reckoning with them. These are mainsprings of the characters' actions; it is not surprising that, failing to understand, he substitutes for the several inner agonies, the heartbreaks in solitude, a romantic melodrama stage-managed by a splendid mock-up of himself. Is uncommunicated tragedy really tragedy? The novel is there for the reading.

The device of mirroring turns up in Ford repeatedly. Ashburnham is the kinetic to Dowell's damped potential; he fulfills what Dowell only dreams of, even the "heroic" death for love—the Tristan grand stroke—with a penknife. Also he is pragmatic where Dowell is theoretical, realistic where Dowell is idealistic. He is opposite—but so is a mirror image, or what Yeats called a mask. Conrad used the romantic device of the double in "The Secret Sharer" (1912) by providing a ship's captain with an alter ego in the person of a fugitive, a murderer, who looks like him. This double externalizes the protagonist's weakness; but in the course of the tale he represents also the resourcefulness summoned up to cope with himself, and having been the secret self, he imperceptibly becomes the not-self of the protagonist. The paradoxes are confusing; perhaps Conrad was not clear about them. In *The Good Soldier* the same contradiction occurs, but it is a mistake of Dowell's, not a paradox: Dowell thinks Ashburnham is, but Ashburnham is not, his secret self. * * *

FRANK KERMODE

[Recognition and Deception] †

This is a shot at expressing a few of the problems that arise when you try to understand how novels are read. * * * Some of the problems I can best open up by talking about the way novels begin. You may remember Ian Watt's brilliant exercise on the opening of *The Ambassadors*—the demonstration by grammatical and stylistic analysis of the multidimensional quality of that "fairly ordinary" paragraph (Watt 1960). Watt shows how far it is from "straightforward" telling, getting the story moving; how very different it is from the first words of *Roderick Hudson*. * * * I suppose that if we were asked to name the first modern critical treatment of such problems we should all think of Henry James. Of course he is more directly concerned with the delightful difficulties of the 'doing' than with those of the reader's share—though he does admit, like Sterne, that it should be "quite half." But he was, notoriously, engrossed by the problem of narrative authority, and the need for authors to keep clear. There is a late essay in which he laments the low standard of criticism as the chief obstacle to the proper doing of fiction—accusing Bennett of a sort of *possession* in which mere "affirmation of energy" did duty for "treatment." "Is this *all?*" he asks. "These are the circumstances of the interest—we see, we see; but where is the interest itself?"[1] A book such as *Clayhanger*, he says, is not a monument *to* anything, but *of* "the quarried and gathered material it happens to contain." He is arguing for the *dispossession* of the author by his own technical means; he makes an elaborate plea for novels of which the technical disposition is such that they *must* be read twice. So he applauds, among contemporary novels, Conrad's *Chance*—not his favourite Conrad, but at least a book which by the elaborateness of its method makes a gap between producer and product, a gap, as he puts it, to "glory in." The existence of that gap ensures another, between the text and its reader, whose expectations are no longer subject to the usual kind of authorita-

† From "Novels: Recognition and Deception," *Critical Inquiry* 1.1 (September 1974): 103–21. Copyright © 1974 by Frank Kermode. Reprinted with the permission of the author. Page numbers in brackets refer to this Norton Critical Edition.
1. Henry James, "The New Novel," *Notes on Novelists* (New York, 1914), p. 331.

tive correction. This gap, which may be called the hermeneutic gap, is of great importance to the late James, and some of his work might be said to exist primarily in order to characterise it: *The Sacred Fount, The Turn of the Screw,* "The Figure in the Carpet" have in common that they create gaps that cannot be closed, only gloried in; they solicit mutually contradictory types of attention and close only on a problem of closure. The confounding of simple expectation—the *not* telling us what it was that Maisie knew—is a way of stimulating the reader to a fuller exercise of his imagination: to make him *read* in a more exalted sense (*not* "devour"). Consequently the *affair* will not be grasped, even in its ambiguity, without many readings, and those readings will find senses which remain inexplicit. James is an historian of civilisation of quite a different kind from his admired Balzac; if Balzac is a secretary James is an oracle.

Ford's novel, *The Good Soldier,* though begun earlier, was written finally in 1914–15, and it was certainly an attempt to comply with the prescriptions of "Notes on Novelists," by a writer who particularly admired *What Maisie Knew.* He knew that "life does not narrate"[2] and believed that to write novels as if it were otherwise was to tell lies. He wanted to be the historian of a civilisation, but in the Jamesian way. The dream of Flaubert—a shift of emphasis from story to treatment—is now at least half-realised; story is transformed into "affair," telling into "treatment." Nothing in the text is to be classifiable as formal or inert, merely consumable; everything is capable of production. Fielding, master of the feast, quickly asserts a right to digress to make piquant delays in the provision of consumables; Ford is a master of oracular digression ("of course you must *appear* to digress") but for him it is expressly a way of setting problems to the *interpreter,* who is as remote from Fielding's "consumer" as he could well be. Ford once complained that James talked too much in his last novels because he was dismayed at the discovery that he had made stories "capable of suggesting" what he had not intended; "he was aiming at explicitness, never at obscurities"; as for him, he thought it right that his "scenes" should "suggest—of course with precision—far more than they actually express or project." This is, theoretically, a step on from James, who thought he should keep more moral and technical authority over the reader than Ford wants; even "precision" here means a precision of *means,* without implications as to the control of the reader's suggestibility. He accepts as right the surrender of a larger, less controllable, share to the reader. To get the full measure of the purpose of *The Good Soldier* one had better compare Ford with a writer of very similar *intentions* but wholly inferior technical resources, such as Galsworthy. * * * My purpose now is to ask about the kinds of suggestion and *deception* practised in the opening page of

2. See p. 276 above [*Editor*].

The Good Soldier * * *; and to ask what they imply about "second readings" and the activity required of the reader.

> This is the saddest story I have ever heard. We had known the Ashburnhams for nine seasons of the town of Nauheim with an extreme intimacy—or, rather, with an acquaintanceship as loose and easy and yet as close as a good glove's with your hand. My wife and I knew Captain and Mrs. Ashburnham as well as it was possible to know anybody, and yet, in another sense, we knew nothing at all about them. This is, I believe, a state of things only possible with English people of whom, till to-day, when I sit down to puzzle out what I know of this sad affair, I knew nothing whatever. Six months ago I had never been to England, and, certainly, I had never sounded the depths of an English heart. I had known the shallows.
>
> I don't mean to say that we were not acquainted with many English people. Living, as we perforce lived, in Europe, and being, as we perforce were, leisured Americans, which is as much as to say that we were un-American, we were thrown very much into the society of the nicer English. Paris, you see, was our home. Somewhere between Nice and Bordighera provided yearly winter quarters for us, and Nauheim always received us from July to September. You will gather from this statement that one of us had, as the saying is, a "heart," and, from the statement that my wife is dead, that she was the sufferer.
>
> Captain Ashburnham also had a heart. But, whereas a yearly month or so at Nauheim tuned him up to exactly the right pitch for the rest of the twelvemonth, the two months or so were only just enough to keep poor Florence alive from year to year. The reason for his heart was, approximately, polo, or too much hard sportsmanship in his youth. The reason for poor Florence's broken years was a storm at sea upon our first crossing to Europe, and the immediate reasons for our imprisonment in that continent were doctors' orders. They said that even the short Channel crossing might well kill the poor thing.
>
> When we all first met, Captain Ashburnham, home on sick leave from an India to which he was never to return, was thirty-three; Mrs. Ashburnham—Leonora—was thirty-one. I was thirty-six and poor Florence thirty. Thus to-day Florence would have been thirty-nine and Captain Ashburnham forty-two; whereas I am forty-five and Leonora forty. You will perceive, therefore, that our friendship has been a young-middle-aged affair, since we were all of us of quite quiet dispositions, the Ashburnhams being more particularly what in England it is the custom to call "quite good people." [9–10]

On a first reading the opening sentence of Ford's novel seems to tell you that what is to follow is a story, that it is very sad, and that it is going to be told by a narrator who was privileged to hear it. Later we discover that the story involves the suicide of two of the four main personages, the sudden death of another, and the hopeless insanity of a young girl, so *saddest* is a bit lame, perhaps, and certainly misleading. We also discover that the narrator is the deceived husband of one of the suicides and the keeper of the mad girl. It is not exactly some *anecdote* he's been told, and so *heard* is strikingly peculiar. Without going any further one can, I think, say that the opening sentence of the book is *deceptive*. You ask why. Perhaps you say, ah, we're not being told directly about the story because it's more important to know what sort of a chap this is; a bit dim, obviously. There he is, at the centre of the web of adulteries and deaths, talking about *hearing a story*. And as Character is a great thing, you may say that this book is obliquely announcing that it is really going to be about this evidently odd character. However, at this stage I think you would be wiser to make a more modest guess that the opening sentence is an indication that this narrative won't have the same preten-sion to authority as Trollope's, or the same steadiness of reference to types, whether narrative or ethical, as Fielding's. The speaker is a drop-out from his own story. Later on he has a sort of apocalyptic vision of the principal characters, and there are only three of them. He will describe himself as an ignorant fool married to a cold sensualist, and repeat over and over again that what he is ignorant of is the human heart. In trying to find out he is as it were reading the story, as you are.

But it will not do to stick on the label "unreliable narrator" and leave it there. He is certainly that; at one place he is simply wrong about his own story, speaking of the mad girl as dead, though she is in the same house as the writer, alive and babbling about the omnipotence of God. It is interesting that the book, so intently organised, should contain this and other slips; they are indications that it is safer *not* to tidy it up prema-turely with such slogans, but to work at the deceptive surface, the words which so often seem, perhaps often are, formal and inert, but which, in a text which abjures authoritative direction of the reader from the outset, may not be. Consider the second sentence, as an instance of what James thought the new novel ought to have, namely a "baffled relation between the subject-matter and its emergence," and also as an instance of what Ford himself called the process of getting into the opening "the note that suggests the whole book." The word *know* in different forms occurs in this second sentence, three times in the third, twice in the fourth. In the second it is intensified—"with an extreme intimacy"—but that qualification is at once withdrawn: "or rather, with an acquain-tanceship. . . ." This withdrawal is intensified by the simile of the glove, which professes closeness and warmth but betrays itself as the index of a trivial relationship dependent on a peculiar social usage of the word "good." That this is the first of a great deal of textual whispering about *know* is familiar ground; hence articles on the "epistemology of

The Good Soldier," and the like.[3] But I don't think that is quite the point, either. *You,* like the narrator, have to decide about the word, and you can't do it yet. In the end you have to consider the ambiguities of knowing. There is the social sense: how are people known anyway? Are the English, and especially of this strongly marked period, the years before 1914, and especially the "good" English, particularly hard to *know?* And the social merges into the sexual. Both marriages are *mariages blancs,* for reasons of ignorance, timidity, and, later, adultery. How does Florence, the narrator's wife, whom he has never slept with, *know* so much: "But how can she have known what she knew? How could she have got to know it? To know it so fully. Heavens! There doesn't seem to have been the actual time. It must have been when I was taking my baths, and my Sweedish *[sic]* exercises, being manicured" [12]. So Dowell, in a complicated joke (conscious or not?) about the only kinds of exercise *he* ever took. When he says this, later in the first chapter, he is apparently talking about Florence's conversations with a wise friend, and not about her love affairs. But his not knowing Florence (who always locks her bedroom door, though capable of extremely coquettish behaviour in the bathing hut) is a complement of her knowing Jimmie and Edward all too well. His ignorance of her knowledge makes the text a sort of eunuch's report on passion, necessarily inaccurate, partial, fantasised. He knows *something,* of course; but the novel might have been called *What Dowell Knew.* The title Ford wanted really has the same force: *The Saddest Story.*

To finish with the second sentence let us not neglect "We," expanded in the third as "My wife and I." We will find that the degree of intimacy between Florence and each of the Ashburnhams was so much deeper than her husband's that this has to be read as another *deception;* and the immediate withdrawal a qualification of the term "extreme intimacy," correct for him but not at all for her, is another. So in the third sentence the first statement is true for Florence but not for Dowell; the further characteristic qualification that follows is true, but in a quite different sense for each of them, so that the effect is again deceptive.

The fourth sentence suggests, and in doing so sounds another "note that suggests the whole book," that the "state of things" represented by all this semantic confusion can be generalised: the English, the people Dowell chooses to know, are especially unknowable; this particular affair, in its sadness, may be held to suggest the state of a nation, the condition of a culture that in all senses doesn't *know.* And later the text will allow us, if we wish, to see it as a figuration of the world tragedy of 1914, as "the death of a mouse from cancer is the whole sack of Rome by the Goths" [12]. But of course when Dowell *claims* that his subject is "the falling to pieces of a people" [11], and develops this in a very pas-

---

3. See Samuel Hynes's "The Epistemology of *The Good Soldier,"* pp. 310–17 above [*Editor*].

sionate rhetorical way, a new voice enters which we may not want to accredit any more unequivocally than the others.

In the fifth sentence we discover, not only more evidence of the peculiar lack of qualifications in Dowell that make for deception, but the first use of another difficult and deceptive word, *heart*. Hearts are what Dowell finds it hard to know. In the second and third paragraphs we find that his wife had a "heart condition." This condition imposes certain constraints upon them—"perforce . . . perforce . . . we were thrown . . ." and later their condition is called "imprisonment." In the final sentence of that paragraph the reader is invited to draw a conclusion, namely that Florence had a "heart." This happens to be untrue in the proffered sense. Her fake heart condition was merely a way of keeping herself from her husband (not letting him *know* her). The death he supposes to have resulted from a heart attack was suicide; she knew her husband was about to find out that she had lovers. The phial contained not a drug prescribed for her condition, but prussic acid, to be taken if he should ever come to *know*. When we get to the end we reflect that if either of them had a heart it was Dowell himself, that he was the sufferer, or would have been had he *known*. The French title Ford gave the book was *Quelque chose au coeur*. It indicates the importance of this further semantic confusion.

This is confounded by the fact that having a heart also implies having a sexual life; only Florence and Ashburnham have this; the sport that gave him a heart was not polo (a second sense of "approximately" and another joke about exercise), the storm at sea broke Dowell's years, not Florence's; if anybody was *poor* it was he. Yet of course they *are* sick, and their sicknesses are specified later; and they die of their heart conditions, as the bumbling meditation of the fourth paragraph lets us know. The word *affair* is another medley of whispers, and so is *quiet*, related not only to "*good*" but to the secrecies of an adulterous affair continued over many years amid the meaningless decencies of a spa.

More might be said, and said differently, but I hope you'll agree that this text exploits characteristics of narrative that people tended, and still tend, to push out of their minds because of their long—but not necessarily perpetual—complicity in what is after all the rather special notion that narrative texts authoritatively establish a single standard of veracity, that deviations which amend this contract are obvious and may be simply identified. Terms such as *point of view* and its kin, and, much older, *irony*, may seem to come in handy here. But this book shows how inadequate they are. Authors can be dispossessed, as James thought they should be; he meant that a story can possess one demonically, make one dance to its tune. He thought the author should call the tune, contemplate the "affair" and *do* it. Hence the gap; hence the *deceptions*, the *multiple* voices, the absence of a simple complicity, of a truth vouched-for and certainly known. The same things could be shown in the book as a whole. Nobody has yet discovered in *The Good Soldier* a hermeneutic series that ends in a discovered truth; to this, at any rate, the scholarly journals testify.

You see how many assumptions are here called into question. Vague talk of irony, or of unreliable narrators won't do; the latter, as Wayne Booth's impressive but moralistic book demonstrates, introduces ethics at the wrong moment. We are in a world of which it needs to be said *not* that plural readings are possible (for this is true of all narrative) but that the *illusion of the single right reading is possible no longer*. It is interesting that Ford himself seems to relate this state of narrative more or less directly to the state of the world, to the ignorance and narrowness of a leisured class, a nation in subtle decline. The point of calling something a novel, as Clara Reeve remarked, is that it has something new in it [4]; the need for some degree of contemporaneity is clear to Fielding also, but the requirement grows more exigent and also more obscure with time. Novels must always create gaps between their texts and narrative types, for otherwise they could not be new; all stories are banal and the redemption from banality must be, as Baudelaire remarked of *Madame Bovary*, and James in a different way of *The Golden Bowl*, a technical wager, a matter that is of treatment, a glorying in the gap between types and text; and this gap grows larger as it intrudes more and more on writer and reader.

This point, which can be made in various ways, is familiar enough. For myths that are in a narrow sense culture-specific, the narrative types have an authority agreed between teller and listener, and the telling is attended by a kind of communal affirmation rather than by questionings. Such stories are often difficult of access to anyone who does not belong to the culture; he may think them unfinished, for example, or he may have to look only for universal but latent meanings in them. They belong to societies which change their social arrangements little, so that the passage of time creates no gap; the presentness inescapable from all views of the past is here virtually identical with the pastness inescapable from all views of the present. But the universality of allegorical reading in *literate* societies—the Stoics on Homer, the Alexandrian exegetes on the Bible—proves a need for updating which in its turn inescapably implies plurality of interpretation; and it is the next step to make texts which actually provide for such exegesis, as for example in the Gospels. In a sense the whole movement towards "secretarial" realism—with its care for authenticating detail, its transparency, its passion for credibility and intelligibility—represents a nostalgia for the types, an anachronistic myth of common understanding and shared universes of

4. Clara Reeve, *The Progress of Romance through Times, Countries, and Manners*, 2 vols. (London, 1785), vol. 1, p. 110.

meaning. At this level it is easy enough to see why the novel—the new—should try to cope with the fact that the new is puzzling, that we mortals stand alone, that to make sense of reality the mind must work with all its powers. In the lifetime of Ford there occurred the collapse of conventional narrative chronology, the attacks on "the old stable ego of character" and on conventionalised notions of "form"—on the whole concept, indeed, of a good read. Not surprisingly, some modern critics find the new kind of reading so difficult and so different from the old that they call it *writing*.

*   *   *

CAROL JACOBS

[The Passion for Talk] †

*   *   *

And in speaking to her [Nancy] on that night, he [Edward] wasn't, I am convinced, committing a baseness. It was as if his passion for her hadn't existed; as if the very words that he spoke, without knowing that he spoke them, created the passion as they went along. Before he spoke, there was nothing; afterwards, it was the integral fact of his life. [80]

Language, the talk of desire, does not mediate an already existing passion but rather generates it. And it's not simply that language generates passion: the fatal driving passion of the tale becomes this desire for talk, the "desire for communicativeness" [125]. However Dowell may condemn it in Leonora, it is certainly his single passion, determined as he is to create the text as a space for a fortnight of intimate conversation. Isn't it Edward's talk that drives Maisie to her death and Florence to suicide, and isn't it the talk at Branshaw Teleragh that ultimately brings Edward to suicide and drives Nancy to madness? Before we reach this point, let us make a detour by way of Marburg to retrace the path of this lapse into talk.

This journey, you understand, turns the relationship of the four completely on its end. The upheaval is not merely the result of Leonora's outburst (her displaced announcement that she is Irish Catholic). Dowell writes of this entire day: "I was aware of something treacherous, something frightful, something evil in the day. I can't define it and can't

† From "The (too) Good Soldier, 'a real story,' " in *Telling Time* (Baltimore: Johns Hopkins UP, 1992) 75–94; originally in *Glyph*, 3 (1978): 39–45 and 49–51. Reprinted with the permission of the author and The Johns Hopkins University Press. Page numbers in brackets refer to this Norton Critical Edition.

find a simile for it" [37]. What is it on this journey that is treacherous and indefinable, treacherous perhaps because it is that for which no simile can be found? If we can offer no definitive answer to this question, we might begin by noting that the entire journey rides on Florence's seemingly insignificant chatter. And not only Florence's, for Dowell, in turn, chooses this moment of his story to ramble on rather aimlessly, to interject the single gay, descriptive, and apparently irrelevant interlude of the novel. It is here when we are most thrown off guard that Dowell's narrative operates as an inexorably precise, almost mechanical, if ultimately problematic, allegory.

> Why, I remember on that afternoon I saw a brown cow hitch its horns under the stomach of a black and white animal and the black and white one was thrown right into the middle of a narrow stream. I burst out laughing. But Florence was imparting information so hard and Leonora was listening so intently that no one noticed me. As for me, I was pleased to be off duty; I was pleased to think that Florence for the moment was indubitably out of mischief—because she was talking about Ludwig the Courageous (I think it was Ludwig the Courageous but I am not an historian), about Ludwig the Courageous of Hessen who wanted to have three wives at once and patronized Luther—something like that!—I was so relieved to be off duty, because she couldn't possibly be doing anything to excite herself or set her poor heart a-fluttering—that the incident of the cow was a real joy to me. . . . [I]t does look very funny, you know, to see a black and white cow land on its back in the middle of a stream. It is so just exactly what one doesn't expect of a cow. [35]

This is exactly what one doesn't expect of a text; and yet it is there for us in black and white.[1] Three times, we are told, it is the "black and white" that is turned on its end. This passage that talks of Florence imparting information and history, that itself appears an informative if pointless moment of personal history, has a certain hitch. It is just about this time, while the narrator is "off duty," that Maisie Maidan is thrown into the middle of a portmanteau, with her feet in the air, like the black and white cow. It is the same moment in which Florence is maneuvering to toss Leonora aside:

> And we went up winding corkscrew staircases and through the Rittersaal, the great painted hall where the Reformer and his friends met for the first time under the protection of the gentleman that had three wives at once and formed an alliance with the gentleman that had six wives, one after the other (I'm not really interested in these facts but they have a bearing on my story). [36]

1. This interpretation is less scandalous than it seems. Elsewhere in the novel the "black and white" specifically refers to a written text. As Nancy reads of the Brand divorce case we read: "That was incredible. Yet there it was—in black and white."

These facts *are* Dowell's story. For who is the "gentleman that had six wives, one after another" if not Edward Ashburnham whose love affairs and flirtations (you have the facts for the trouble of finding them) are just about to number six at this point in the tale: Leonora, the servant girl of the Kilsyte case, the Grand Duke's mistress, Mrs. Basil, Maisie, and Florence. And who is "the gentleman that had three wives at once," under whose protection the Reformer and the man with six wives meet, if not the protective Dowell who in the course of the novel admits to having loved Leonora, Maisie Maidan, and Nancy Rufford at one and the same time.[2] And who is the Reformer, if not Florence, who, we have just been told, "was at that time engaged in educating Captain Ashburnham" [33].

Her method of education is by way of a certain text: "You see, in the archives of the Schloss in that city there was a document which Florence thought would finally give her the chance to educate the whole lot of us together" [34]. This text which holds such promise of enlightenment documents the entire problematic of the trip to Marburg—Florence's coded monologue, Dowell's narration of that monologue, and the lapse into talk in general. It does this less by way of what it says than by way of its unlikely appearance. "She was pointing at a piece of paper, like the half-sheet of a letter with some faint pencil scrawls that might have been a jotting of the amounts we were spending during the day. . . . 'There it is—the Protest'. . . . 'Don't you know that is why we were all called Protestants? That is the pencil draft of the Protest they drew up' " [36–37]. Florence points the finger at a scrap of paper, the original draft of the Protest, the point of rupture between Catholics and Protestants, and between Leonora and Edward of course. She never bothers to elaborate on its content. It resembles the "half-sheet of a letter with some faint pencil scrawls" and thereby claims the same insignificant innocence as the chatter of Florence and the conversational recordings of Dowell. Unlike the all too clear letter Maisie presently writes, the Protest is a study in illegibility. It forewarns us that the shift into talk will not fulfill a promise of revelation but will produce a text all the more demanding of interpretation.

All the more demanding of interpretation because Protestantism functions in *The Good Soldier* as the destruction of an established code, the moral code of the marriage sacrament. This is the maddening lesson that Nancy will learn at Branshaw Teleragh:

> "I thought," Nancy said, "I never imagined. . . . Aren't marriages sacraments? Aren't they indissoluble? I thought you were married . . . and . . ." She was sobbing. "I thought you were married as you are alive or dead."

2. "I suppose that I should really like to be a polygamist; with Nancy, and with Leonora, and with Maisie Maidan, and possibly even with Florence" [151].

"That," Leonora said, "is the law of the church. It is not the law of the land. . . ."

"Oh, yes," Nancy said, "the Brands are Protestants."

She felt a sudden safeness descend upon her, and for an hour or so her mind was at rest. It seemed to her idiotic not to have remembered Henry VIII and the basis upon which Protestantism rests. [141]

The Protest makes possible polygamy and divorce, having three wives at once or six wives one after another. It challenges the law of the church which insists on the indissoluble one-to-one relationship between man and wife and implicitly between sacramental text and meaning.[3]

It is this challenge that takes place as they enter the "large old chamber full of presses" in which that document is to be found. Florence

told the tired, bored custodian what shutters to open; so that the bright sunlight streamed in palpable shafts into the dim old chamber. She explained that this was Luther's bedroom and that just where the sunlight fell had stood his bed. As a matter of fact, I believe that she was wrong and that Luther only stopped, as it were, for lunch, in order to evade pursuit. But, no doubt, it would have been his bedroom if he could have been persuaded to stop the night. [36]

It is the sunlight of course that is palpable, and not the bed of Luther that Florence passionately strives to evoke. Unlike her reformer counterpart, Florence has no desire to "evade pursuit." She could well—this is her point—she could well be "persuaded to stop the night." "And then," the passage continues, "in spite of the protest of the custodian, she threw open another shutter and came tripping back to a large glass case" [36]. The custodian, who was tired and bored only a few lines back, seems to recognize the potency of those "palpable shafts" of sunlight that create beds where only printing presses stood before. He raises a "protest" as a reminder of the significance of the term, for Florence is about to illuminate *the* Protest, which is to say, as we have seen, that Florence is out to re-form it.

She continued, looking up into Captain Ashburnham's eyes: "It's because of that piece of paper that you're honest, sober, industrious, provident, and clean-lived. If it weren't for that piece of paper you'd be like the Irish or the Italians or the Poles, but particularly the Irish. . . ."

And she laid one finger upon Captain Ashburnham's wrist. [37]

---

3. It is the comprehension of this relationship between the sacramental text of the marriage service and its meaning that defines reason. [Quotes: "I should marry Nancy if her reason . . . according to the law of the land" (150–51)—*Editor.*]

It is indeed hard to put one's finger on what is happening here. As Dowell puts it two lines later, "I can't define it and can't find a simile for it," and it is now, you remember, that Leonora is driven to her "desire for communicativeness." The indefinability and the lapse into communication both revolve around Florence's reading of "the Protest" by means of a certain mode of discourse in which literal and figural language prove mutually exclusive. It is because of that piece of paper, she insists, that Edward is sober, industrious, provident, and clean-lived. Edward, of course, is none of these: he nearly drinks himself to death, is indolent, cannot control his excessive expenditures, and is heading rapidly for his sixth affair. If Florence inverts each of his characteristics, she does so, it would seem, out of ignorance. What she means by saying that Edward is clean-lived is that she wishes he weren't,[4] for the reformer wishes to go to bed with the "gentleman that had six wives one after another." She lays her hand on Edward's wrist then by way of saying—"This is my body."

What does it mean to say "This is my body" in the Castle of Marburg while pointing at a manuscript signed, we are told, by Martin Luther, Martin Bucer, and Zwingli [37]? Dowell and Florence have been "imparting information so hard" [35] that one is tempted to remain "off duty" [35]. In rejecting a literal reading of their narrations one is tempted, that is, simply to fix upon the limited mechanical allegory of Dowell's black and white cow as Maisie Maidan or Leonora[5] and of Florence's Reformer, Henry VIII, and Ludwig the Courageous as figures for Florence, Edward and Dowell. But let us shuttle back from the figurative to the historical as the document in question demands in order to restore to it its proper name. It is thus, paradoxically enough, that the black and white is turned truly on its end.

The fact of the matter is that the "piece of paper" Florence insists on calling "the Protest" can be none other than the Articles of Marburg signed in the Castle of Marburg, October 1529, by Luther, Bucer, Zwingli, and seven others.[6] "I don't really deal in facts;—[you under-

---

4. Thus Florence's mode of discourse in interpreting the significance of the "Protest" renders literal and figural language mutually exclusive. She uses a figural language of inversion whereby she claims Edward to be clean-lived in order to say she wishes he weren't. Yet the literal truth of the matter (the fact that Edward is not clean-lived) renders Florence's attempt at figural inversion senseless. The historical facts behind the scene will explain the significance of this mutual exclusion.

5. This scene of the cows has often been mentioned as a hint of the action to come, but the brief readings always remain at the level of limited allegory. See e.g. Jo-Ann Baernstein, "Image, Identity and Insight in *The Good Soldier*," in *Ford Madox Ford, Modern Judgments*, ed. Richard A. Cassell (London: Macmillan, 1972), p. 129; Meixner, p. 168; Cassell, p. 187; and R. W. Lid, *Ford Madox Ford, The Essence of His Art* (Berkeley: U of California P, 1964), p. 57.

6. The good literary historian might well protest at this point. As Violet Hunt relates * * * (in *The Desirable Alien*, 1913), it was none other than Ford himself who called the piece of paper "The Protest." * * * If I have rejected this bit of literary history in favor of actual history, it is partly because of the decade Ford spent preparing a biography of Henry VIII. He knew his Protestant history, then, better than he here lets on. * * *

stand. Along with Ford Madox Ford] I have for facts a most profound contempt."[7] It's not that "I'm . . . really interested in these facts but they have a bearing on my story." Those articles, history tells us, are the result of several days of vertiginous argument between Luther and Zwingli[8] as to the reading of the phrase "This is my body." Throughout the talks on the interpretation of these words, Luther insists that he "cannot understand them in any other way than according to their literal meaning."[9] For him, the proper interpretation of the sacrament means "The body is present in the bread" (LW 30). Zwingli and Oecolampadius, however, regard the bread of the sacrament only as a spiritual remembrance of the body of Christ. They read the phrase "This is my body" as figurative speech: "In such cases [Oecolampadius explains], words have a different meaning from what they say" (LW 37). It is precisely this difference that Luther will not accept. "A metaphor," he says, "abolishes the content altogether: e.g., as when you understand 'body' as 'the figure of a body.' . . . Your figure of speech does away with the kernel and leaves the shell" (LW 30–31).

In this shell and kernel game of the colloquy one wonders indeed where the kernel is to be found. The critical problem at hand, it would seem, continually shifts from the question of the phrase "This is my body" to the status of the sacramental bread as either literally or figuratively the body of Christ, as equivalent to the body or merely a sign for it. The shift permits a repeated repression of the role of the phrase itself in the context of the argument.[1] Significantly enough, none of the interlocutors at Marburg pronounces the phrase, presupposing it to function *either* literally *or* figuratively *in that context*. When Luther writes "Hoc est corpus meum" on the table top, he does not expect "the body [to be] present bodily in the word" (LW 25) nor does the Swiss contingent read here a figural representation. "This is my body" is rather the verbal contrivance that fabricates the discord between the literal and the figurative: it is the locus of rupture and operates altogether differently from the linguistic machines that Luther and Zwingli attempt to construct. These

7. Ford Madox Hueffer, *Memories and Impressions* (New York and London: Harper and Brothers, 1911), p. xviii.
8. This took place, incidentally, "under the protection of" Philip of Hesse (not Ludwig the Courageous) who (much later) wished to have two (not three) wives at once.
9. Martin Luther, *Luther's Works* (Philadelphia: Fortune Press, 1971), p. 37. [Cited hereafter as LW—*Editor*.]
1. This is not to say that the status of the words "This is my body" is not repeatedly questioned (LW, 19, 22, 24, 27, 41, 56). But the question is always immediately shifted beyond the confines of the colloquy: their role as language in the text of the argument is all but forgotten. Nevertheless, the discussion of the phrase puts the defender of a literal reading into something of a predicament. Once Luther insists on the bodily presence of Christ in the bread, he is forced to depend on a series of backup mechanisms to guarantee that presence. The words "This is my body" must be added to bring the body into the bread, and the words are in turn meaningless unless guaranteed by the authority of God. The problematic of literal versus figurative language thus becomes far more complex than we are able to indicate clearly in the body of the text.

latter would guarantee the presence of Christ's body, the one literally or immediately, the other figuratively or mediately. Their complicity, you will perceive, is all but manifest. The phrase "This is my body," however, is the kernel that cracks the shell: it generates days (and even years) of unending talk in which neither language as literal nor as figurative expression can gain the upper hand. "This is my body" generates the disparity between the two and their ultimate indecidability: "And talk!" [130], the passion for talk.

*   *   *

We begin at least to have some sense of why this scene takes place coincident with the shift into talk and why it is precisely this for which Dowell can find no definition and no simile. The talk in which Florence, Leonora, Edward, and later Nancy are about to indulge themselves is language denying the operations both of literal and figural adequation. It is not the answer to the camouflage of silence. It does not release those once repressed passions in a violent wave of ex-pression. The violence is not on the side of that which is expressed but is the force of language itself, language as the force of refusal:

> What had happened was just Hell. Leonora had spoken to Nancy; Nancy had spoken to Edward; Edward had spoken to Leonora— and they had talked and talked. And talked. . . . You have to imagine my beautiful Nancy appearing suddenly to Edward, rising up at the foot of his bed. . . . You have to imagine her, a silent, a no doubt agonized figure, like a spectre, suddenly offering herself to him—to save his reason! And you have to imagine his refusal— and talk. And talk! [130]

The more they talk the worse it gets. As the orgiastic exchanges become increasingly exaggerated, Dowell's narrative searches more and more desperately for the appropriate simile, for the key that will enable him to ground this violence in a "real world" counterpart:

> Those two women pursued that poor devil and flayed the skin off him *as if* they had done it with whips. I tell you his mind bled almost visibly. I seem to see him stand, naked to the waist, his forearms shielding his eyes, and flesh hanging from him in rags. I tell you that is *no exaggeration* of what I feel. It was *as if* Leonora and Nancy banded themselves together to do execution, for the sake of humanity, upon the body of a man who was at their disposal. They were *like* a couple of Sioux who had got hold of an Apache and had him well tied to a stake. I tell you there was no end to the tortures they inflicted upon him.
> Night after night he would hear them talking; talking; maddened, sweating, seeking oblivion in drink, he would lie there and hear the voices going on and on. (italics mine) [152]

But what if "the situation" excludes the possibility of tying it down? What if the flaying, whipping, bleeding, and execution are inadequate to fix that which takes place—in a figure that is "as if," that is "like," that is "no exaggeration"? What if there is indeed "no end," if the voices will insist on "going on and on"? Isn't that what Dowell must finally concede? Isn't this the unimaginable hell of a narrator who can no longer say what he wishes except through the oblique admission that it exceeds his powers of definition and simile, except by a comparative that renounces finding an equivalent violent enough to express the state of affairs? "It was a most amazing business, and I think it would have been *better* in the eyes of God if they had all attempted to gouge out each other's eyes with carving knives. But they were 'good people' " (italics mine). [158]

* * *

DAVID EGGENSCHWILER

[Comical-Tragical Illusions] †

For a quarter of a century *The Good Soldier* has caused dissention among the critical ranks. Ever since Mark Schorer's famous essay[1] divided readers as neatly as a debater's topic, we have argued whether John Dowell, the narrator, is a fool and a eunuch or a good fellow much like Ford himself, whether Edward Ashburnham, the central actor, is a hypocritical cad or a tragic (at least, melodramatic) hero, whether the author mocks or eulogizes the few, late vestiges of chivalry. * * *

To appreciate what Ford is doing in *The Good Soldier* we must first appreciate what is often slighted in interpretations: this is a very funny book, partly because the narrator is witty and quick to see incongruities, partly because the first half of the novel is essentially a comedy. As we read of the Dowells and Ashburnhams in Parts One and Two, we accept and enjoy a sexual farce with conventional character types and conventional relationships—all of which is heightened by the narrator, the cuckolded husband, who emphasizes the ludicrousness of all roles. Later we will understand that these relationships have some nasty consequences, but we should not therefore try to convince ourselves that this farce has really been a tragedy that an incompetent narrator has failed

---

† From "Very Like a Whale: The Comical-Tragical Illusions of *The Good Soldier*," *Genre* 12.3 (Fall 1979): 401–3, 405–14. Copyright © 1979 by The University of Oklahoma. Reprinted with the permission of *Genre*. Page numbers in brackets refer to this Norton Critical Edition.
1. See pp. 305–10 above [*Editor*].

to understand. Whatever their consequences, the relationships in the foursquare coterie are basically funny.

Consider the cast of characters. Edward seems a perfect replica of a nineteenth-century fictional type: the attractive and not overly bright career officer (and cavalry, at that). He would have been quite at home in *Vanity Fair*. He is handsome in a conventionally manly way (fair hair, sunburnt complexion, blue eyes, bristling mustache); he dresses elegantly but not foppishly (the pigskin cases—for guns and collars and helmets and hats—strike the right balance); to men he talks of clothes, horses, and artillery; to women he "gurgles" the ideals about love's redemption which he has picked up from popular novels; he is common-sensical about common-sensical things and sentimental about "all children, puppies, and the feeble generally" [25]; above all, with his physique, his composure, his perfectly stupid blue eyes, he is decidedly attractive to women. And such a man is married to such a woman as Leonora; only the god of farce could have united this couple and only for ribald purposes. Leonora is cold and very proper: clean-run, splendid in the saddle, tall and fair, with chilly white shoulders and a little gold key with which to lock up her heart. Knowing the moral economy of farce, we know that proud, chilly Leonora is going to take her lumps.

And, if we consider only Parts One and Two, who could be better to attract this Edward and vex this Leonora than Florrie Hurlbird Dowell, the satiric version of the American innocent abroad. On the surface she is little and fair, as radiant as a track of sunlight as she dances over the floors of castles and over the seas, trying to leave the world a little brighter for her passage through it. Below that radiant surface she is a cruel little hypocrite, a silly social climber, and a cold sensualist. Acting the playful retriever to Leonora's lean greyhound, she seems perfect to arouse Edward's manhood, Leonora's scorn, and her own husband's perplexity. Dowell completes the foursquare group by playing the cuckolded husband to an extreme that makes him a triumph of the type. Twelve years a cuckold in an unconsummated marriage, and cuckolded by an expatriated painter in Paris and a British officer in Germany—this is remarkably absurd for both duration and symmetry. Yet Dowell, as narrator, is unsparingly amusing about his own past role, as he is about the roles that the other characters assume with such gusto and such taste for conventional parts. He presents himself, well-brushed and meticulous, as a Philadelphia gentleman, performing the most unromantically slapstick elopement, guarding his wife's bedroom with an axe while she dallies with her fat painter, trying in a frenzy to keep the little tart's mind off thoughts that might set it fatally aflutter while the other three characters treat him like an emotional invalid, preserving the illusion of the innocent minuet that he dances alone.

*　*　*

At the end of Part Two the novel begins quietly to change, for Dowell has finished his introductory farce and is beginning to get on to other subjects. As long as he concentrates on himself and Florence and their relationships with others (the Ashburnhams, Jimmy, the Hurlbirds) the story will be essentially comic, for they are essentially a flat, comic couple. But by the middle of the novel Florence is packed away like poor little Maisie; she even gets a public dismissal ("You have no idea how quite extraordinarily for me that was the end of Florence" [83]), and Dowell considers the Ashburnhams in the different contexts into which his own marital tale has flowed. Near the end of Part Two, Chapter One, the change is signalled with a pointed transition. Dowell has just described his marital history from his meeting Florence through the *menage à trois* with Jimmy, and he pauses for a moment to sum up that part of the novel as a way of having done with it and preparing to get on with other things:

> Well, there you have the position, as clear as I can make it—the husband an ignorant fool, the wife a cold sensualist with imbecile fears . . . and the blackmailing lover. And then the other lover came along. . . .
>
> Well, Edward Ashburnham was worth having. Have I conveyed to you the splendid fellow that he was—the fine soldier, the excellent landlord, the extraordinarily kind, careful and industrious magistrate, the upright, honest, fair-dealing, fair-thinking public character? I suppose I have not conveyed it to you. The truth is that I never knew it until the poor girl came along—the poor girl who was just as straight, as splendid, and as upright as he. [66–67]

A fine change of direction—not particularly subtle, but precise, economical, and apparently straightforward. Dowell, Florence, and Jimmy get their brutal epithets as a way of fixing them and dismissing them from central importance in the novel. Then Edward re-enters as Florence's virile and gentlemanly lover, a contrast to pallid Dowell and vulgar Jimmy; but no sooner is he before us than he is metamorphosed from the stupid, sentimental ladies' man and cavalry officer into a paragon of public virtue. Of course Dowell has mentioned before that Edward was a fine magistrate and all, but those brief comments suggested a hypocritical split between apparent honor and secret adultery. Here is an Edward we have not seen before; and Ford, sly author, allows Dowell to accept the blame for not having represented Edward adequately. * * *

As Ford transposes his novel he repeats themes, characterizations, incidents, and situations from the first two parts, but he transforms them to create different impressions. Dowell begins Part Three by telling that, immediately after his wife's death, he surprised himself by saying that now he could marry the girl. Because he had not previously thought of caring for her, this strange outburst makes him talk about dual personalities and the difficulties of knowing one's unconscious feelings. This theme reflects the main theme of Parts One and Two—the contrast between man's social appearance and his secret desires—but with such a difference: moral and social hypocrisy has become psychological mystery. The ambiguity of man's nature has deepened from its conventional form in sexual farce—proper gentleman and lustful stallion—to more general, more disturbing forms that include all of the main characters. So Edward, too, discovers suddenly, surprisingly, and tormentingly that he loves the girl; had he been conscious of it, he assures Dowell, "he would have fled from it as from a thing accursed" [77]. And we are no longer concerned with secret lust, the adulterous itch of farce, but with inexplicable love, with passion. * * *

* * * Despite his frequent claims that people are unknowable and that he is befuddled, Dowell is an exact and extensive interpreter of what has happened, and *The Good Soldier* is extraordinarily * * * explicit about motives. If commentators have thought that the novel is about the impossibility of knowing truth, they have too readily believed Dowell's sad sighs and paid too little attention to the many truths—social, religious, and psychological—that Dowell tells us about the characters. Most of Dowell's claims of confusion and ignorance as narrator are means of creating a useful narrative tone and of allowing Ford to move convincingly through the various transformations of his tale. If Dowell pleads, and perhaps even feels, some confusion, I do not see why we should, for he guides us very well. He does cheat at times, though, only to apologize later for having given false or incomplete impressions, which he then corrects; but that deviousness is part of the teller's art in manipulating the reader and achieving his *progression d'effet*. It won't do as grounds for an epistemology.[2]

Dowell most obviously changes the impressions of incidents when he gives new versions of Edward's romantic affairs from the Kilsyte case to Maisie Maidan. The first time around, the affairs—a servant girl, a courtesan, two fellow officers' wives—seem but the amusing stages of a sentimental adulterer's progress. But they seem different when Edward is no longer the flat farcical character, when we know more of his boyhood, his marriage, his difficulties with his estate, and especially his ideals of feudal responsibility and chivalric love, which dominate his character in the second half of the novel although they were of little

2. Henry James says much the same thing about his manner of presenting Chad Newsome in *The Ambassadors:* "The true inwardness of this may be at bottom but that one of the suffered treacheries has consisted precisely, for Chad's whole figure and presence, of a direct presentability diminished and compromised—despoiled, that is, of its *proportional* advantage; so that, in a word, the whole economy of his author's relation to him has at important points to be redetermined. The book, however, critically viewed, is touchingly full of these disguised and repaired losses, these insidious recoveries, these intensely redemptive consistencies"; *The Art of the Novel*, ed. R. P. Blackmur (New York: Charles Scribner's Sons, 1934, 1962), pp. 325–26. So, too, Dowell and Ford disguise and repair, lose and recover, and are touchingly treacherous.

concern in the first half. These are not changes of fact, but of emphasis, associations, and tone. Instead of hearing that Edward reads syrupy love stories, we hear that as a boy he read Scott and Froissart, which may be just as disastrous for an impressionable romantic but which are more culturally complex in their sentimentality. Instead of hearing briefly of a "perfectly commonsplace affair at Monte Carlo" in which Edward smashes his fortune to enjoy the overpriced favors of a "cosmopolitan harpy" (an account in Part One that seems as well suited to Rawdon Crawley and his like), we are given a high comedy closer to *Don Quixote* in which Edward plays the courtly lover and fool, confusing sex and devotion, talking feudalism and eternal love while La Dolciquita talks cash and a month's rental. Mrs. Basil, scarcely more than the black-mailer's wife in Part One, is Edward's imagined "soulmate," who admires his ideals of landlordship and sympathizes with him as Leonora inhumanely reorganizes Branshaw along modern, efficient lines. Even Maisie is less the pretty little simpleton at Nauheim than she is the girl to whom Edward can carry cups of bouillon when he can no longer serve his tenants as the good landlord and the father of his people. In all these incidents Edward is still wonderfully comic—lovesick at the gambling tables in Monte Carlo or among the sheafs of severed vegeta-tion in Burma—but he is comic in a lovable, touching way. His charac-ter, in the abstract, is not very different than it was in the first two parts, but it makes different impressions. Edward was not particularly touch-ing before.

Furthermore, as Edward's role as chivalric lover develops, it becomes more romantic and less carnal. As Dowell says, the sex instinct does not count for much in a really great passion, and we are subtly preparing for Edward's passion for Nancy in which he renounces all sexual desire. So from La Dolciquita's bedroom he moves into the Burmese garden with Mrs. Basil, where "long passages of affection" overshadow occasional "falls," and then to the side of poor little Maisie, whose heart trouble insures the chastity of the relationship. The one exception to this devel-opment is the affair with Florence, which interrupts the sequence between Maisie and Nancy and which certainly is carnal. But the excep-tion not only proves and justifies the pattern, it also demonstrates how artfully Ford manipulates his narrative to create the right illusions at the right times. The affair with Florence is the only one in Parts Three and Four that is not described from Edward's point of view. Dowell tells us openly that he cannot give us Edward's point of view on Florence because Edward, of course, never spoke to him about it, and this con-cern with narrative logistics, about which Ford is not always so scrupu-lous, is a reasonable excuse to keep the relationship between Edward and Florence out of the second half of the novel where it would have ruined the image of Edward that Dowell is creating. A colleague once asked me what Edward saw in Florence, and I was puzzled, not only because I did not know but also because it had not occurred to me to wonder. That was Ford's doing. The coarse, nasty, pedantic, coldly sensual Florence in Parts One and Two does not seem out of place as the mistress of the vapid Edward we see there; *that* Edward would likely be attracted to that "personality of paper" [83]. When we have come to appreciate Edward more, to have seen him fully and to have gotten the drift of his character and his fate, Ford has shuffled Florence out of the circle of Edward's passions and made Edward's relations with her the vaguest abstraction, something we have taken for granted so long that it does not perplex. In retrospect, if we rearrange the tale into chronological order and think objectively about motivations, we are bound to be puzzled; but if we stay with the tale in the order and manner of its telling, we shall ask only those questions that the form of the tale suggests to us at various times. * * *

When Florence is pulled back into the story for a dozen pages at the beginning of Part Four, she does not come to clarify her relations with Edward but to show how she "deteriorated" Leonora with her ill-timed adultery, her coarseness, and her cruel, vain talk about the Ashburnhams' estrangement. This role contributes well to the deepening of Leonora's character that occurs steadily throughout Parts Three and Four. From the chilly, proper wife of the farce she has become for us the financially insecure Irish girl, the unappreciated manager of her husband's estate, the proudly threadbare martyr, the fanatical Catholic wife, the patient and disappointed woman who waits for her husband's return. Although she does not gain much of our sympathy, she does gain our understanding, and we are prepared for her eventual deterioration into the wicked mad woman that Dowell claims her to be in her final assaults on Edward.

The last stages of the Ashburnhams' story is, indeed, as Dowell says, the saddest part. * * * The chivalric ideals of women and love that caused Edward ridiculously to kiss the servant girl and swear undying fidelity to La Dolciquita are now literally killing him in his relations with Nancy. The role of adulterous hypocrite that Edward played in Parts One and Two is passed on to Rodney Bayham, Leonora's leporine second husband with his separate establishment in Portsmouth and his trips to Paris and Buda-Pesth. And Leonora will be perfectly happy with this normal, virtuous, slightly deceitful husband, for the life of underdone roast beef and discreet adultery turns out to be the normal life of society and the proper setting for a woman who is splendid in the saddle. Edward, who once seemed to us the epitome of that life (to Leonora's vexation), turns out instead to be one of "the passionate, the headstrong, and the too-truthful [who] are condemned to suicide and to madness"

[161], to be one of the fatally splendid personalities that a romantic tragedy cannot allow to survive among the rabbits like Rodney. Could anyone, after having read the first ninety pages of the novel have predicted Dowell's final assessment of Edward or Dowell's claim that, because he can respond imaginatively to this ideal, he too is one of the passionate, the headstrong, and the too-truthful? Yet step by step, illusion by illusion, Ford has turned his novel about, and only those who refuse to yield to the illusions, who step back for a clear-headed appraisal, will call Dowell a liar or a fool at this point.

In Part Four Dowell also plays a tragic variation on this theme of social decorum versus private passion, the theme with which we began the farce at the other end of the tale. Now we have the Ashburnhams preserving the apparent charm of a pleasant country-house-party at Branshaw while they are enduring agony and performing monstrous cruelties on each other. Now we have the secret "prison full of screaming hysterics" [12] that Dowell had perplexingly referred to in connection with Nauheim. And now we find that the social decorum is not merely a cover for inadmissable feelings; it is also one of the causes of the tragedy, of the "monstrously, . . . cruelly . . . correct" [156] actions of Leonora, Edward, and Nancy in their fated triangle. The horror of this "conventional line" is later imaged by Nancy after she has returned from Ceylon: well-dressed, quiet, beautiful, and "utterly well behaved as far as her knife and fork go," she sits at the luncheon table, utterly mad, a "picture without a meaning" [161]. As Dowell says in one of his most painful and precise witticisms, "even when she was mad Nancy could behave herself" [150].

If we were to forget that this novel is read in time and that the order of its telling is not the order of the events it purports to describe, if we were to pick and sort and rearrange details from our notes in order to try for the "right" point of view toward the characters and incidents, in order to find clues to the truth, why, we should be as confused as poor Dowell claims to be. Is Edward the normal hypocrite that he seems at first or the abnormal, too-truthful romantic that he seems at last? Is Dowell a eunuch or a headstrong, passionate man, both of which he suggests at different times? Are social conventions the form of a beautiful minuet, hiding horrible passions that threaten to destroy it, or is society the breeding ground of rabbits, the destroyer of splendid personalities? The answer to all of the questions is "Yes," but that hardly satisfies a desire to know God's truth about these characters and issues. * * *

I * * * do not see why, because we cannot produce decisive, comprehensive statements about themes or characters, we should conclude somewhat defensively that *The Good Soldier* is about the impossibility of knowing truth. As I have said, we learn many solid truths from our intelligent, interpretative narrator, and his frequent claims of ignorance and mystery seem less the subject of the book than a rhetorical device to help us suspend our disbelief as we accept his supposedly tentative, changing opinions. The relativity of knowledge was already a platitude when Ford wrote, and authors who have tried too conscientiously to demonstrate it have, like Pirandello at times, produced some quickly dated, theory-ridden works. Better, like Ford, to take the theory as a given and use it as a technique to manipulate the reader.

Finally, I do not see why we should conclude that, because Dowell's opinions change, the novel is about the teller's process of discovery, about Dowell's coming to deeper truths as he writes. This device has been used so well in modern fiction that we are too ready to let it explain problems that it will not quite solve. At the beginning of Part Four Dowell does tell us that he has been writing away for six months and "reflecting longer and longer upon these affairs" [120]; so he explains his harshness toward Florence in his subsequent account. Again Ford is using a familiar theme to ease us over a transition, to gain consent by pointing to a narrative convention. If we tried to make this convention the essence of the novel, we would create more problems than we would solve. If we are to assume that the final view of Edward is the truest one, how are we going to imagine that "splendid personality" having a nine-year affair with Florence? And are we to imagine a passionate, head-strong Dowell counting his footsteps as he waits for poor Florence to finish her medicinal baths? And are we to reread Parts One and Two to find hidden clues to these passionate natures that are finally understood in Part Four? Surely not. We must let the novel itself show us how much we are to demand from its conventions. The impressions that Dowell gives us of the foursquare coterie are quite adequate to that subject; there is no reason to believe that they distort an objective truth to which we finally win through, either with or without the narrator's insight. It is enough that we *feel* an increasing penetration, for that is essential to the *progression d'effet*.

In sum, if we are not too eager to possess this novel through moral, psychological, or epistemological themes, we can more easily enjoy—and eventually understand—its changing illusions. In transforming *The Good Soldier* from a sexual farce to a romantic tragedy, Ford may well have written an impressionistic novel, using multiple points of view by a single narrator; but it seems best not to consider this book a demonstration of impressionism, any more than a study of sexual repression or social hypocrisy. It is better to stop looking for the key to a hidden coherence than to bruise the skillful illusions in our search.

352

THOMAS C. MOSER

[The Narrative Stance of Marlow and Dowell] †

* * *

Dowell is as close to [Conrad's] Marlow as Ford could ever get; he partakes of all four versions of Marlow. Dowell's years with his wife and the Ashburnhams prove ultimately as devastatingly enlightening to him as Marlow's trip to the Congo to him. Before Marlow embarked on his voyage of discovery, he was like "a silly little bird."[1] Dowell says that he himself was simply a fool. * * * In the recurrent juxtaposition of an older, wiser Dowell with a young, naive one, we can see a trace of the relationship between old and young Marlow in "Youth" [1902]. * * * Dowell's choice of a hero is Marlovian as well. Like Jim, Edward is a big, blond, handsome, likeable, inarticulate Englishman with considerable skill in the service-profession he espouses, and with a subtle unsoundness not at all apparent to strangers. But whereas Jim's plague spot relates, tragically, to his professional performance, Edward's does not. On the other hand, Edward's overwhelming need to comfort a mournful female recalls Marlow's last subject, Captain Anthony of *Chance* [1913] and his Flora.

It surely goes without saying that Dowell especially resembles Marlow as a master (for the first time in Ford's career) of what Ford considered Conrad's greatest literary forte, the "architectonics" of the impressionistic novel.[2] * * *

Dowell recalls Marlow in his propensity to talk about how difficult it is to fulfill their common purpose to make the reader see, and about how hard the impressionistic method really is. "I am, at any rate, trying to get you to see what sort of life it was I led with Florence," he says early in the novel [17]. He admits elsewhere that he doesn't know the best way to put the story down [15]. Like Marlow in *Chance*, he acknowledges that his rambling method may make it difficult for someone to find his way "through what may be a sort of maze" [119]. Nevertheless, Dowell, like Marlow, insists upon the unquestionable, literal truth of his tale: "I console myself with thinking that this is a real story and that, after all, real stories are probably told best in the way a person telling a story would tell them" [120]. When he unintentionally gives a misleading impression, he endeavors to correct it. He is scrupulous when he is not sure: "I said to her something like—". And he refuses to

---

† From *The Life in the Fiction of Ford Madox Ford* (Princeton: Princeton UP, 1980) 156–65. Copyright © 1980 by Princeton University Press. Reprinted with the permission of the publisher. Page numbers in brackets refer to this Norton Critical Edition.

1. Joseph Conrad, *Youth and Two Other Stories* (London: Blackwood, 1902), p. 60.
2. Ford Madox Ford, *Joseph Conrad: A Personal Remembrance* (London: Duckworth, 1924), p. 169.

go beyond the strict confines of his own evidence: Leonora "probably said a good deal more to Edward than I have been able to report; but that is all that she has told me and I am not going to make up speeches" [136].

One fundamental, technical difference between Dowell's tale and the tales told by Marlow forcibly reminds us how Fordian a narrator Dowell is. Although Dowell tells the reader to pretend that they are spending a fortnight together in a cottage by the sea and that he is talking, in a low voice, to his sympathetic auditor, all this is emphatically pretense. Dowell is not talking: he is "really" writing down this sad story, and over a period of two years. The closest Marlow comes to written narration is the account of Jim's last days that he mails to his privileged listener. The difference is crucial because it allows Ford to give full rein to his solipsistic beliefs (Dowell is really writing only to himself) and to his devastating tendency to change his mind. Although Marlow's attitude always includes bewilderment, although "Heart of Darkness" and *Chance* are unique narratives inspired by special circumstances rather than frequently told yarns, and although Marlow's narratives are characteristically "inconclusive," one never has the sense that Marlow would change events or his attitude. But as Dowell writes, he comes to dislike Leonora, for whom he earlier would have given his life. Again, as Dowell writes, he suddenly sees events very differently from his earlier recollection of them. His impression at one time is that during their married years Florence was never out of his sight. The method is congenial to Ford and provides excuses for apparent errors and inconsistencies. On the other hand, it is a common experience suddenly to remember correctly something one has misremembered; it is not unknown to change one's attitude toward a friend and to harden one's heart even more against an enemy.

Marlow's auditors in "Heart of Darkness" exist as real presences who may, if they wish, talk back; Dowell's auditor is imaginary and therefore mute: "listener . . . you are so silent" [17]. Interestingly enough, whereas Marlow can recount long, complicated conversations, Dowell sticks to Ford's dictum that since one cannot, in reality, precisely remember long speeches, one should never quote more than a couple of lines.[3] Most significantly, Dowell gives us virtually nothing from his all-night-long conversation with Edward. Yet, since Dowell supposedly loves Edward more than anyone in the world, that night must have been a great event in his life.

Dowell differs from Marlow in one last, important way. Ford said that it was all right for a novelist to "create himself" if, in so doing, he would present himself as imperfect, "as benevolent but meddlesome, fine yet malicious, generous but naturally unsound."[4] Clearly Ford has in mind

3. *Ibid.*, p. 186.
4. Ford Madox Hueffer, *The Critical Attitude* (London: Duckworth, 1911), p. 34.

a character very different from Marlow, who is not only Conrad (albeit Anglicized) but also, despite his many claims to self-doubt, as perfect, in Conrad's terms, as anyone could hope to be. Dowell would seem to fit Ford's prescription of the author's self with many imperfections. In choosing Dowell to be his eyes and voice, Ford chose a man who would try to tell what he saw but who, like Ford, saw badly; who admired passionate creatures as Ford admired Conrad's passion[5] and yet himself feared intense feeling; who nevertheless was human and thus inevitably involved in suffering. To the extent that he can, Dowell suffers, his mind circling "in a weary, baffled space of pain" [149]. Blind as he has been and perhaps still is, he has seen agony great enough to drive people he loves to madness and suicide. Dowell's conviction of the meaninglessness of existence is even more desperate than Marlow's. For the latter, Jim's dilemma has fascinating ethical and metaphysical implications for all men that make his story worth telling again and again. But characteristically of Ford, Dowell is unsure whether other people's lives are at all like the lives of those good people the Ashburnhams and the Dowells. His ostensible purpose in telling the tale is not to understand it but to get it out of his head.

Such a notion has more to do, of course, with Ford the human being than with Ford the craftsman. Let us then turn from Dowell in his strictly technical function to Dowell as a profoundly human character in the novel. As the sole source of knowledge, Dowell is only too Fordian in his carelessness and inconsistency; as a painter of scenes, he is predominantly Pre-Raphaelite, with more than a touch of nocturnal terror and agonized agoraphobia. Embracing, overriding all aspects, remains Dowell the Fordian impressionist, desperate solipsist, hopeless epistemologist.

In talking of Dowell as an effective, humanly moving Fordian figure, we might as well grant at the outset that he contains (how could he escape it?) a measure of "the bad Ford." By this I mean the Ford with a godlike power over dates, a megalomanic disregard for facts, a self-destructive contempt for his own works of art. Dowell's most notorious carelessness is with the most important date in the novel (and maybe in Ford's life), August 4, 1904. This date obviously gave Ford trouble during the writing. In the manuscript he used instead July 1906.[6] Both dates were the occasions for Ford of traumatic trips to Germany: in 1904, he was shipped off in a state of despair and near-madness to seek mental health in German spas; in 1906, after some five months of separation from Elsie, when his "domestic affairs" in Jessie's words "were not

5. *Joseph Conrad, op. cit.*, p. 20.
6. Charles G. Hoffman, "Ford's Manuscript Revisions of *The Good Soldier*," *English Literature in Transition*, 9, no. 4 (1966), 151. Problems with dates in *The Good Soldier* are discussed at length by Patricia McFate and Bruce Golden, *"The Good Soldier:* A Tragedy of Self-Deception," *Modern Fiction Studies*, 9, no. 1 (Spring 1963), 50–60. See also [Richard Wald] Lid [see p. 341, n. 5], pp. 63–64. [See also Cheng, pp. 384–88 below—*Editor*.]

exactly to his liking,"[7] he took their daughters to Elsie [his wife] in Germany for their reception into the Roman Church, after which he and Elsie went to America. But also, that later date, the one Ford first lit on for his saddest story, is the time, as we know, of Ford's first recorded connection with the Marwoods,[8] the time also of his collaboration with Conrad on that strange prefiguration of *The Good Soldier, The Nature of a Crime* [1924], and the time finally, according to Jessie [Conrad's wife], when he introduced Marwood to the Conrads. Clearly, his two dearest male friends and his terrible breakdown were in the forefront of his mind as he wrote *The Good Soldier.* In the novel, August 4, 1904 is the date both of the two couples' trip to M—— and of Maisie Maidan's death [51, 57]. It is also, and impossibly, the day when the Ashburnhams arrive in Nauheim with Maisie and first meet the Dowells— impossible because the couples meet at the evening meal whereas the trip to M—— occurs in the afternoon [35] and Florence planned it "some days before" [34]. Indeed, the Dowells knew the Ashburnhams and Maisie for a month before their trip and her death [122–23]. Similar chronological confusion attends Edward's death. The fatal night when Leonora comes into Nancy's bedroom is that of November 12 [142]; the following morning Edward cables Dowell to come to them from America [148]. A fortnight passes between his arrival and Nancy's departure for India [154]. Sufficient time passes after that for Edward to get the gardener's daughter off for murdering her baby, to hunt twice, and to give two political addresses [159–60]. Then Nancy's fatal telegram arrives from Brindisi and precipitates Edward's suicide. Ten days later, that is, mid-December at the earliest, Dowell begins to learn the truth from Leonora "of a windy November evening" [73]. And yet, earlier in the novel, Ford has Dowell be present the night that Leonora goes into Nancy's bedroom [130].

Other inconsistencies are also associated with the idea of death. After Dowell sees Florence run by and hears from Bagshawe of her affair with Jimmie, how long does he sit in the hotel lounge chair before going up to find her dead? Sometimes, he thinks he went up "immediately afterwards" [75] and thus "do[es]n't know how Florence had time to write to her aunt" [128]. Yet, in his first account, he went up "a long time afterwards" [72]. If he had "run up sooner," he "might have prevented her" [83]. Dowell's references to Nancy are almost as myst— In Part I, his vision of judgment shows Edward and Na— embrace, with Florence dangling alone [53]. The— that all three are dead. Not until the second—

7. Jessie Conrad, *Joseph Conrad and His Circle* (New ... rolds, 1935), p. 112.
8. Ford became friends with Arthur and Caroline Marwo... wood, Yorkshire-born, represented to Ford an ideal of En... raised the capital for Ford's *English Review.* He also is o... the *Parade's End* tetralogy, and sometimes for Ashburnham...

9. Joseph
1. Ibid., p.

realize that Nancy would be much better off "if she were dead" [133]. The precise circumstances of Edward's last minutes are mysterious too. On page 156, Dowell implies that he and Edward discussed Nancy's awful telegram. Yet [six] pages later, Dowell reports that Edward merely "whispered something that [characteristically] I did not catch," took out the penknife, told Dowell to take the wire to Leonora, and said he needed "a bit of a rest" [162].

What sort of artist, what sort of fanatic for *le mot juste*, would permit these distracting contradictions? Perhaps, for biographical reasons, these deaths caused Ford extreme anxiety. Perhaps, in his megalomania, he thought that his reader, the man of good will with the perpetually virginal mind, would swallow anything. Perhaps, in his self-doubts and despite the many verbal changes in the manuscript, he could not bear to recheck with meticulous care the facts of this affair. A remark in his early *Pre-Raphaelite Brotherhood* [1907] on the artist's difficulty in evolving and sticking to the rules of his art may help to explain Ford's characteristic revulsion from thinking about a completed novel:

> It is as if one should with infinite care in the placing of each card build up a tall card-house, and then cry out that the only way to build a house of cards is to shake the table and begin in quite another way—because one is sick and tired of the house once it is built. (31)

Still another reason suggests itself, especially in the instance of Edward's death. Since Ford has earlier had Dowell mention Edward's comments about Nancy's wire, perhaps Ford assumes the reader will recall these comments even though Dowell omits them on the last page. "Sometimes," Ford says in the Conrad book, "to render anything at all in a given space will take up too much room—even to render the effect and delivery of a speech."[9] The problem with justification, Ford says, is that the writer must handle it so carefully that it does not delay the action of a story.[1] Sensible as is Ford's conviction that any rule can be overthrown in order either to achieve a necessary effect or to get on with the tale, it has, I suspect, a deeply personal aspect. Central to Ford's creativity is the need to get rid of or to suppress an emotion. Sometimes, in his anxiety, he probably needs to fill in as quickly as possible those chinks in the wattle-wall of his imagination so as to block out for a while the perpetual assaults of a threatening reality.

We would do well, however, not to pounce too greedily upon Ford's carelessness. Mizener has shown that Dowell's apparent inconsistency in discussing Edward's pigskin cases dramatizes the important differ-
ces between Dowell's original sense of Edward and his sense of him

Conrad, *op. cit.*, p. 207.
207.

after his death, which deepens even as Dowell writes.[2] Another, far more disconcerting instance of apparent inconsistency appears in Dowell's two presentations of Nancy offering herself to Edward, at night, by his bed. The first implies that Nancy's motive is sympathy: "You have to imagine her . . . suddenly offering herself to him—to save his reason!" [130]. Presumably at the time of writing this, Dowell has known, for six months, from Edward and Leonora, that Nancy "desired to see Edward suffer" [152]. Yet Dowell does not explicitly say this for over forty pages. Four pages after that he offers his second version:

> I have told you that the girl came one night to his room. And that was the real hell for him. . . . she looked at him with her straight eyes of an unflinching cruelty and she said: "I am ready to belong to you—to save your life." [154]

Ford's purpose is, of course, *progression d'effet*, a climax of horrors ending with Edward's quite small penknife. Yet our inconsistency has genuine meaning. Eighteen months have passed. Dowell now sees Nancy totally mad, and Leonora estranged from her past with Edward and from Nancy and Dowell. The appalling intensity of the two women's feelings is now fully evident to Dowell, as it was not quite at the time of the first telling.

If Dowell is, for better as well as for worse, a Fordian teller of tales, he is also very much a Fordian viewer of scenes and maker of images. Dowell contains a large measure of the Pre-Raphaelite: he longs for the unattainable; he sees things in bright, intense colors; his vision includes the grotesque, at once comic and terrifying. These qualities derive, no doubt, both from Ford's artistic heritage and from his tortured psyche. Dowell's hopeless Pre-Raphaelite longing for the ideal, for the "terrestrial paradise" [275], hardly needs documentation. His most extended and serene description, the famous view from the train window on the trip to M——, is explicitly Pre-Raphaelite. The moment is propitious for such a vision because he is "off duty" and "out for enjoyment" [35]. The scene recalls Ford's memory in the Conrad book of their early years together "as a time of great tranquillity" like "the surface of an old bright painting."[3] It recalls Ford's summary of the Pre-Raphaelites as succeeding "very miraculously in rendering a very charming, a very tranquil, and a very secure England." The German countryside, with its greens and reds and emeralds and purples, and with its peasant women in native dress, specifically recalls what Ford is seeing from a German train in *Ancient Lights* [1911] when he learns of the death of Holman Hunt: "It was—and the words came to my lips at the very moment—too

2. Arthur Mizener, *The Saddest Story. A Biography of Ford Madox Ford* (London: The Bodley Head, 1971), p. 265.
3. *Joseph Conrad, op. cit.*, p. 52.

brave, too Pre-Raphaelite!" Of course, Dowell's "little mounds of hay that will be grey-green on the sunny side and purple in the shadows" [35] go much farther back, to the note Madox Brown wrote about painting *The Hayfield*.[4]

✻   ✻   ✻

ROBERT GREEN

The Politics of Agnosticism †

When he wrote *The Good Soldier* Ford was still using the name of his German father, Hueffer, and nothing is so revealing of these German roots as the novelist's sustained fascination with the dynamics of illusion and reality among the English bourgeoisie at the turn of the century. As an alien, Ford could not command that innate familiarity with the minute tremors of upper-class behaviour ascribed to Tietjens or to Ashburnham. Yet, like Dowell, the American millionaire, Ford was uneasily attracted by a foreign code. Indeed the theatricality of the English upper class had been a source of wonder to Ford for some fifteen years: *The Benefactor* [1905], *The Inheritors* [1901], *A Call* [1910], and *The Spirit of the People* [1907] were all attempts to come to terms with what John Berger, in his novel G, calls the 'spectacle' or the 'theatre' of the English ruling class. Members of this class at the beginning of the century, Berger wrote, 'no longer claimed . . . justification by reference to a natural order: instead they performed a play upon a stage with its own laws and conventions.[1] Ford's inability to grasp these rules stemmed partially from an outsider's failure to decode a complex rhetoric of speech and gesture, to demarcate the boundary between play and life; but the importance Ford assigned to the behaviour of his chosen minority must be linked to factors wider than the accident of his own Anglo-German pedigree. The anecdotal germ of *The Good Soldier*—Dowell's drive to a railway-station with a couple who chat calmly despite their inner turmoil—had made its first appearance in *England and the English* eight years earlier.[2] Ford's return to, and the full fictional development of, this incident indicate that he was still fascinated with the

---

4. Ford Madox Hueffer, *Ford Madox Brown* (London: Longmans, Green & Co., 1893), p. 102.

† From *Ford Madox Ford: Prose and Politics* (Cambridge: Cambridge UP, 1981) 80–85. Copyright © 1981 by Cambridge University Press. Reprinted with the permission of the author and publisher. Page numbers in brackets refer to this Norton Critical Edition.

1. John Berger, G (Harmondsworth: Penguin Books, 1973), p. 40.

2. Ford Madox Hueffer, *England and the English* (New York: McClure Phillips and Co.); 1-volume ed. of essays in *The Soul of London* (1905), *The Heart of the Country* (1906), and *The Spirit of the People* (1907) [*Editor*].

questions it raised for him about the relationship between inner crisis and external calm among the English bourgeoisie. Ford was entranced by the power of the 'stiff upper lip' somehow to restrain and hide a man's acutest emotional conflicts. After germinating for a decade, an episode from an essay was transformed into a novel's Joycean 'epiphany'.

The Good Soldier was, then, a climactic novel in terms of Ford's own career, the most assured rendering of the theme which had absorbed him for so long. Yet it didn't offer any kind of exorcism, since the problems treated in the novel could only be resolved either by Ford's complete endorsement of a code from which he was alienated by birth and by class, or, alternatively, through his abandonment of the conventions of Edward Ashburnham, a decisive step for which he was still unprepared. The growing maturity of Ford's art was, rather, a result of the new clarity with which he was able to portray credibly the tensions between belief and social agnosticism. *The Good Soldier* doesn't present us with the agonies that result from conversion, the painful resolution of social tensions that we find in *Parade's End* in the twenties. Instead from its opening pages *The Good Soldier* records the pull and counter-pull within Dowell, as he tries to persuade himself that the 'long, tranquil life' he has enjoyed for nine years, the stately 'minuet' of his existence with Florence, Leonora and Edward—the 'good people'—is extant, has survived immortalised in some distant heaven. Working against this idealisation of the past is the narrator's certainty that in fact their foursome was 'a prison full of screaming hysterics' [12]. Which of these two incompatible views, Dowell vainly wonders, is the truth: the 'theatre', elegantly directed and costumed, of their public, visible lives; or the 'sub-text', barbarous and anarchic, of their private acts?

Even the terms in which Dowell formulates this question confirm the relevance of the theatrical imagery to the problem with which he's wrestling. He enquires:

> if for me we were four people with the same tastes, with the same desires, *acting*—or, no, *not acting*—sitting here and there unanimously, isn't that the truth? (italics added) [12]

'Acting—or . . . not acting'—the problematic and provisional nature of 'sincerity' in Dowell's circle—is, of course, a crucial question in a novel with such a high incidence of feigned heart-conditions. Notoriously *The Good Soldier* provides no answers to Dowell's constant self-interrogation. Indeed the form of the novel, so totally unconcerned with the arousal of any suspense in the reader—the suicide of Ashburnham at the end must be one of English fiction's least surprising deaths—militates against the novel's utility as a problem-solving device. What it offers instead is a consummate portrayal of the nescience and frustration of the English bourgeoisie just before the war, in which Ford now capitalises, positively and for the first time, on his own bewilderment. *Mr Fleight* [1913], a pencil sketch for *The Good Soldier*, had been marred by its hero's stunned disengagement from human society. Dowell understands little more than Blood, but, at least until the last two chapters, is prepared to question everything and to ruminate extensively. Ford's 'discovery' of Dowell allows him to treat in fictional terms what he had previously only explored successfully in his non-fiction, in *The Critical Attitude* [1911] and *Henry James* [1913]: the evanescence and transcience he found characteristic of his age.

On its publication in 1915 *The Good Soldier* was widely accused of undermining the values necessary in time of war. Sixty years later we can now see that it did in fact imply an allegiance to orthodox militarist beliefs, since out of the pervasive chaos and scepticism of which Dowell was a focal-point, Ford constructed a text that proclaimed the potential of order and discipline. The *form* of *The Good Soldier*, so engineered and modernist, indeed endorsed the promises inherent in the title—of orderliness and self-control. The crude reader in 1915 judged that a novel by Hueffer set, in part, in Nauheim and Marburg and ending with the suicide of a 'good soldier' was deeply subversive and pro-German. (Ian Hay's best-seller of the same year, *The First Hundred Thousand*, indicates what was required of a novel in 1915.) Yet, despite its superficial lack of tact, never Ford's strong point, *The Good Soldier* was fundamentally a 'soldierly' book, the work of a master fictional strategist.

Ford's creation of such a spare, pruned and efficient novel did not, however, indicate that he had finally cast in his lot with the social engineers, the 'Inheritors' of the earlier novel, the Social Imperialists. Ford's portrait of Leonora in *The Good Soldier*, that tough unromantic 'fixer,' suggests that he maintained his hostility to the materialist ambitions of the political modernists. Now, though, on the eve of war, with the Conservative Party being led by a businessman, Bonar Law, and the Liberal government increasingly dominated by Lloyd George, Ford felt deeply unsure of the prospects for survival of the 'individualism' he cherished. H. G. Wells, an opponent of Fordian individualism, had chosen a markedly 'individualistic' form—the fictional memoir, subjective, reminiscential, private—to narrate the career of the collectivist Remington, the epitome of Ford's hated 'Inheritors', in *The New Machiavelli* [1910]. Equally striking was Ford's recourse to an authoritarian form as a means of transforming into fiction his own frustrated individualism.

The Good Soldier, then, provides another illustration from this period of the familiar conjunction, noted by Shannon, of political elitism with artistic impulses that were modernist, innovative but equally elitist:

> The modern consciousness, concerned to insist on the lofty 'seriousness' of art's purposes and the need for formalistic structure and technical innovation, was fully attuned to an elitist social stance.

The idea of resistance to the pressures of a mass or 'bourgeois' reading public became in itself one of the primary tenets of the new consciousness.

The Good Soldier belongs with the work of Hulme, Eliot and Pound as an index of the collapse of the Victorian faith in 'the homogeneity of society and intellect', the end of the 'synthesis of progressive politics and moral art'[3] that *The New Machiavelli*, say, still enshrined. Equally indicative of this collapse, though less often noted, is the absence from the pages of [Beatrice] Webb's *Our Partnership* [1948] of any affiliation between her 'progressive politics' and a modernist culture. Her account of the year 1911, when she was busy publicising the Poor Law Commission's 'Minority Report', fails to recognise the cultural revolution then under her nose in London, the radical, scandalous developments in ballet, painting, sculpture, poetry and fiction. The modernity of the Webbs' dissenting 'Report', which anticipated the growth of Britain's Welfare State after 1945, and the innovations of *The Good Soldier*, which anticipated the later fictions of Joyce, Woolf and Richardson, were formally similar in that both valued discipline and centralisation, both opposed sentimentality. At the same time, however, they were politically and ideologically antagonistic, one harking back to the discredited conservatism of Salisbury, the other heralding the social democracy of Attlee and Beveridge.

The Good Soldier was as factitious as any complex Fabian or military stratagem, the most ordered of Ford's novels. He was aware, too, of the potential difficulties in such a structured, deliberate novel, writing in January 1914, while dictating *The Good Soldier*, 'that there is the danger of becoming too flawless, arid, soulless, and so on.[4] He saw that 'the cold, clear flame' that was his high objective, an austere fashioning of perplexity, could become too arctic and rarefied in a genre as committed to contingency and the unforeseen as the novel. Ford's later comments on the novel seem designed to convince us that it was the first on which he had lavished any considerable attention, though it's clear that a great deal of research underpinned the achievement of the 'Tudor trilogy'.[5] In these novels, however, Ford had tried to bring to life a vanished milieu and, despite his hard work on their 'locations' and costumes, the trilogy's relaxed and conventional form, inherited from Scott, scarcely exemplified the rigorous poetics of the novel formulated with Conrad at the turn of the century. In 1915 Ford crossed the line between conventional and innovative, between 'traditional' and 'modern'. In the terms recently adopted by David Lodge, he moved from the 'metonymy' of the historical trilogy to a text that was 'metaphorical', readerly and non-

---

3. Richard Shannon, *The Crisis of Imperialism 1865–1915* (London, 1974), pp. 269, 276–77.
4. "Literary Portraits—XX," Harvey, p. 183.
5. *The Fifth Queen* (1906), *Privy Seal* (1907), *The Fifth Queen Crowned* (1908) [*Editor*].

linear.[6] In *The Good Soldier,* that is to say, he concentrated powerfully upon the conceptual and the ahistorical, upon the deployment of his scenes to bring out clearly a patterned design that was neither chronological nor linear. Thus his nineteenth novel was the first—and arguably the last—sustained attempt to illustrate the demanding and monolithic theories Ford had long been advancing. Never again was he so driven by, above all, the search for a novel of perfect facticity.

*   *   *

◯MICHAEL LEVENSON

Character in *The Good Soldier* †

The Good Soldier repeatedly asks, What is a character?, and to that question it gives more answers than may be tactful. Ford Madox Ford was a revolutionary with a bad conscience. He was reluctant to discard those traditions which he professed to scorn, and faced with competing alternatives, he habitually preferred both. This makes him a frustration to the theorist but a delight to the literary historian, who can uncover in his work the strata of earlier methods beneath the radical experiments for which he is known. * * *

Ford upheld the extreme realist proposition that the success of prose fiction depends on its power to create "an illusion of reality," and he placed special emphasis on what he called "justification," by which he meant the task of granting motives and grounds to behavior that might otherwise appear obscure.[1] To justify is thus not to defend or to excuse. It is to submit action to a pattern that will make it, if not familiar, at least intelligible. For Ford this task involved devising a wide context, typically a personal past or a cultural disposition, which would invest a character with reasons and causes. It is not enough, he insists, to write that "Mr. Jones was a gentleman who had a strong aversion to rabbit-pie." One must "sufficiently *account* for that dislike": "You might do it by giving Mr. Jones a German grandmother, since all Germans have a peculiar loathing for the rabbit and regard its flesh as unclean. You might then find it necessary to account for the dislike the Germans have

---

6. David Lodge, *The Modes of Modern Writing* (London, 1977), pp. 75–77, 81, 84–85, and 91–93.

† From *Twentieth Century Literature* 30.1 (1984): 373–77, 379–86. Reprinted with the permission of *Twentieth Century Literature.* Page numbers in brackets refer to this Norton Critical Edition.

1. Ford Madox Ford, "Impressionism and Fiction" in *Critical Writings of Ford Madox Ford,* ed. Frank MacShane (Lincoln: Univ. of Nebraska Press, 1964), p. 43. [For an earlier discussion of "justification," see Meixner, p. 319, n. 3 above—*Editor.*]

for these little creatures; you might have to state that his dislike is a self-preservative race instinct. . . .[2] In his insistence upon justification, Ford locates himself in continuity with those Victorian realists whom he so often attacked. As dutifully as George Eliot, he demands rational explanations for surprising actions and requires general laws to assimilate individual cases. * * *

Although one remembers Dowell's narrative for its insistent formal dislocations—its inversions, postponements, repetitions, reversals—it relies in significant measure on certain, highly traditional methods of characterization. At the center of the novel appears a patient and detailed exposition of the early upbringing of Leonora and Edward, which traces the unhappily contrasting effects of Irish Catholicism and English Protestantism on the course of their married life. Dowell employs social estimates of great generality; the emphasis on the typical aspect of the Catholic or Protestant personality might have appeared with scarcely any modification in a novel of Thackeray or Trollope. In brief, he provides background of the sort that Ford sketched for Mr. Jones, a set of circumstances that might "account" for Edward and Leonora. This method of characterization tends to what one might call the "justified self" which emanates from context and embodies the social will. * * *

The justified self is the donnée of *The Good Soldier*. It is accepted as both a standard of behavior and a norm of intelligibility, with the result that figures in the novel make justification one of their chief activities. They continually invoke general laws and abstract categories in order to understand the behavior of others and to explain themselves. Dowell, of course, is the capital instance. In line with good Fordian principles, he explains individual character by situating it within a wider class, on the assumption that the best way to know a particular is to know its kind. The preeminent example is the rubric "good people," which appears frequently in the opening pages of the novel and furnishes a shorthand characterization for the four principals. * * * Conspicuously, the description "good people" fails to account for the characters it describes. It does not explain; it conceals; and the obvious incongruity between concept and character initiates far more subtle difficulties in the novel. For it becomes clear that the plot turns on this incongruity which characters exploit for their own ends.

Characters persistently engage in characterization, but more often to disguise, than to reveal, the secrets of personality. Notably, Florence confirms her seduction of Ashburnham by misdescribing his character. During the visit to the museum at M—, she descants on Luther and Ludwig the Courageous, and then, gesturing at the "pencil draft of the Protest," tells Ashburnham that "'It's because of that piece of paper that

---

2. "Impressionism and Fiction," pp. 44–45, my emphasis. [See p. 266 above—*Editor.*]

you're honest, sober, industrious, provident, and clean-lived. If it weren't for that piece of paper you'd be like the Irish or the Italians or the Poles, but particularly the Irish" [37]. * * * Florence calls Ashburnham "honest" and "clean-lived," while her eyes invite him to adultery. Leonora labors to preserve her status as a type, an "Irish Catholic," when what is at issue is not a general kind, but a particular passion.

Much of the drama of *The Good Soldier*, as Samuel Hynes has pointed out, turns on a struggle between convention and passion which presents the characters with conflicting and irreconcilable demands; as Hynes puts it, passion "reveals the secrets of the heart which convention exists to conceal and repress."[3] One can extend the point. For, it is not only a question of competing values or a struggle between expression and repression, it becomes a matter of the stability of *character as such* and our capacity to understand one another at all. In *The Good Soldier* passion is not one mode of experience among others; it is an affront to intelligibility; it not only violates the 'rules' which convention lays down; it challenges the very possibilities of rules that might govern human behavior; it is not simply that characters must choose between passion and convention; it is that character begins to lose integrity as a concept:

> For who in this world can give anyone a character? Who in this world knows anything of any other heart—or of his own? I don't mean to say that one cannot form an average estimate of the way a person will behave. But one cannot be certain of the way any man will behave in every case—and until one can do that a "character" is of no use to anyone. [104]

The notion of justification, as Ford develops it in his criticism, depends on the possibility of establishing "average estimates": Mr. Jones as a German, Germans as averse to rabbits, and so on. *The Good Soldier*, however, relies on the procedure only to press it to its limit where justifications can no longer justify, where average estimates must hesitate before singular passions. * * *

Dowell's disillusionment follows the arc of modernism. He begins with presuppositions typical of much Victorian characterization: the individual conditioned by circumstance, composed of intelligible motives, susceptible to moral analysis—the justified self. Then, confronted with the singularity of desire, his "generalizations" totter and fall. He moves to a conception of character that will become predominant in modernist narrative: the self estranged from circumstance and no

---

3. Samuel Hynes, "The Epistemology of *The Good Soldier*" [see pp. 310–317 above]. Robert Green, on the other hand, argues that the novel "mediates a conflict between received conventions and urgent passional drives." Robert Green, *Ford Madox Ford: Prose and Politics* (Cambridge: Cambridge University Press, 1981), p.98. [For an extract from Green's book, see pp. 358–62 above—*Editor*.]

longer comprehensible in its own terms, confounding familiar motives, beyond the reach of social explanation: When Leonora, that "perfectly normal woman," finds herself in a "perfectly abnormal situation" [153], then "for the first time in her life, she acted along the lines of her instinctive desires" [131]. But Dowell immediately adds that he does not know whether to think that in acting instinctively "she was no longer herself; or that, having let loose the bonds of her standards, her conventions, and her traditions, she was being, for the first time, her own natural self." How should he know? His confusion is that of one caught in the midst of an epochal transition, when it is unclear whether convention and tradition or instinctive desire is the ground of human behavior—well might he repeat, "I don't know." The passionate instant has overturned an entire history of familiarity. It defies standards of intelligibility, resists the generalities of social explanation, and rests its claim to our attention on one incontrovertible fact: it exists.

And yet, as Dowell's narrative proceeds, there emerges a surprising implication, which might be put this way. Passion, which has frustrated the attempt to justify human character, becomes finally its own justification. The first time that Ashburnham "falls" into marital infidelity, unsanctioned sexuality can still appear as anomalous, a "short attack of madness" [114], a radical and unintelligible departure from the life of principle which he has been trained to lead. But by the fifth and sixth times, the erotic surge has ceased to be surprising. Ashburnham falls at regular intervals. Indeed, he deviates as consistently as he conforms. In removing the anomalous aspect of passion, Ford recognized what Freud had begun to stress: not the singularity of the sexual impulse but its repetitions, compulsions, and obsessions. Passion, that enemy of norms and conventions, lays down its own norms, even its own conventions: "poor Edward's passions were quite logical in their progression upwards" [45]. The "discovery" of sexuality in the modern period amounts finally to the recognition that what seemed to be the anarchy of desire was in fact a civil state.

The first, the simple, irony of *The Good Soldier* depends on the incongruity between inherited categories and the behavior that they are meant to describe. Social and moral conceptions fail to explain passion; personality eludes the justifications set in motion to account for it. The private individual remains, as it were, hidden beneath the cloak of social categories. But a second, and more distressing, irony, at which we have just arrived, reveals that when the deceptive vestments of traditional characterization are removed, one may uncover not a new freedom but a new constraint. Edward violates the duties of his station only to place himself at the mercy of his loins. What is more confining than social norms?—only, perhaps, private desires.

* * *

No matter how generous our standards of behavior, as long as they are standards, they will not contain Dowell, who defies familiar notions of consistency and purpose, who credits the most implausible lies, whose moral valuations shift from sentence to sentence, whose memory leaks like an old man's, and whose attention wanders like a child's. He fails to experience emotion appropriate to the circumstance and fails to distinguish the essential from the trivial.[4] As Schorer delicately puts it, his is a "mind not quite in balance."[5] John Meixner, less delicate, calls him a "psychic cripple," "a severely neurotic personality."[6] Still, Dowell would be less puzzling if he were only more so. If he passed thoroughly beyond the bounds of reason and ethics, then we could assign him to that comfortable rubric, 'Madness in Literature'. The difficulty is that, although Dowell continually violates our expectations of rational behavior, he performs no act that would place him beyond the moral pale. He commits no physical violence, yields to no repugnant impulses, violates no taboos, causes no suffering. On the contrary, as Hynes has stressed, he seems the one character capable of selflessness.[7] He also manages to write a novel. In short, if he does not obey familiar norms, neither does he conform to our notions of lunacy. He occupies a strangely lit zone between tact and catatonia, and is no more intelligible as a madman than as a gentleman.

As a way of approaching Dowell, it will be useful to recall some well-known aspects of Fordian Impressionism. According to Ford, that reality whose illusion he sought to create was to be found in the instantaneous apprehension of experience—not in the "rounded, annotated record" but in the "impression of the moment," "the impression, not the corrected chronicle."[8] Since the world appears to us only in "various unordered pictures," the first obligation of the literary artist is a meticulous attention to that variety and disorder, to "the sort of odd vibration that scenes in real life really have."[9] Ford never denied that we ascend from perception to knowledge and from sensation to understanding but he regarded these as distinctly secondary activities. The world of solid objects and coherent events is subsequent and often spurious and is never to be mistaken for the patches of color, the fields of light, the noise, dust, and confusion out of which it arose. Not knowledge, but impression, sensation, and emotion constitute the foundation of experience. What is more, they constitute its essence. This, indeed, is a fundamental Fordian assumption with far-reaching consequences for the

---

4. Moser [see p. 352 above] calls Dowell's tone "an almost indescribable combination of irony, sentimentality, cynicism and bafflement" (p. 155).
5. See p. 307 above [Editor].
6. See p. 320 above [Editor].
7. Hynes doesn't actually state this but possibly implies it; see p. 304 above [Editor].
8. "Impressionism and Fiction," op. cit., p. 41. [See p. 314 above—Editor.]
9. Ford Madox Hueffer, "Joseph Conrad," rpt. in Critical Writings, op. cit., p. 72; "Impressionism and Fiction," p. 42. [See pp. 276 and 264 above—Editor.]

representation of character: that in the beginning of experience lies its essence.

"[T]he whole world for me," writes Dowell, "is like spots of colour in an immense canvas" [17]. This statement should do two things. It should connect Dowell himself to the Impressionist sensibility, and it should remind us of his insufficiencies as a knowing intelligence. Furthermore, it should suggest a relationship between these two features of his position. Dowell, it is plain, is more than a character and more than a narrator in *The Good Soldier*; he is an instance, and to an extent a theorist, of literary Impressionist doctrine. He not only conforms to Ford's principles of narrative; he defends those principles in Fordian terms, offering the familiar argument that, because neither life nor "real stories" follow an orderly sequence, a narrator who wants his stories to "seem most real" must proceed in "a very rambling way" [119]. Dowell meets the terms of his covenant. He disregards fact in favor of impression, follows the wanderings of memory, ignores chronology, allows unlikely juxtapositions, digresses freely. These formal dislocations have been well remarked, not least by Ford himself. What has been less well remarked is that these aspects of form become aspects of personality. Dowell's narrative method is one with his psychological provocation. The refusal to provide structure, the passive acquiescence in confusion, the divigations of memory—these are not merely technical commitments, they are distinctive and disturbing aspects of character. Having described the world as spots of color in a canvas—a remark that might seem merely a pictorial observation in the vein of Pissarro—Dowell passes immediately to a confession of weakness: "Perhaps if it weren't so I should have something to catch hold of now" [17]. The Impressionist's "various unordered pictures" become a measure of Dowell's own disorder. To the question, What ails Dowell?, it is tempting to answer: he is suffering from Impressionism.

In response to his early critics, Monet made the celebrated rejoinder, "Poor blind idiots. They want to see everything clearly, even through the fog."[1] It is a forceful reply, but it should not divert us from a blunt question: Why do fog and dusk, twilight and movement, appear so prominently in work of the Impressionist school? These paintings frequently involve difficult perceptual circumstances. * * * Indeed, this is the paradox of Impressionism. In order to reach the foundation of normal experience, it must dismantle the normal structures on which we rely. It employs distorting contexts in order to disclose the truth of immediate experience. One might also speak of the pathology of Impressionism, for what begins as the perceiving self in unusual circumstances can quickly become a perception of the unusual self, and surely it is a

---

1. As reported by Jean Renoir in *Renoir, My Father*, trans. Randolph and Dorothy Weaver (Boston: Little, Brown, 1958), p. 174.

telling fact that the Impressionist method in literature (one thinks of Conrad and Faulkner as well as Ford) serves so frequently to render emotional and moral aberration.

*   *   *

Here, a point which has been submerged must be raised into plain view. For, it should already begin to be evident that the demand for "justification" rests awkwardly alongside the enshrinement of the "momentary impression." The call for an explanatory context sounds in no simple harmony with the cry for instantaneity. In effect, two realisms meet in *The Good Soldier*. On the one hand, as we have seen, Ford follows Victorian antecedents in identifying the real and the rational. The insistence upon justification is thus first of all a demand for intelligibility, guided by the conviction that literature can account for the apparent mysteries of character. * * * Ford, however, displays a second, more characteristically "Impressionist," emphasis in which the real is identified, not with the known and understood, but with the perceived and lived. The insistence on the "impression of the moment," the "odd vibration," the "queer effect" belongs to the attempt to reproduce experience as it first strikes the perceiving consciousness, before it assumes the shape of intelligibility. Within this emphasis, attention falls not on the rational pattern but on the immediate sensation.

In his criticism Ford suggested that these two realisms were complementary: "Your Impressionist can only get his strongest effects by using beforehand a great deal of what one may call non-Impressionism. He will make, that is to say, an enormous impression on his reader's mind by the use of three words. But very likely each one of those three words will be prepared for by ten thousand other words."[2] He thus implies that the known past leads naturally to the lived present and that an intelligible history can "justify" a momentary impression. But Ford, like many others, imagines more finely than he methodizes. *The Good Soldier* reveals an incommensurability between life as known and life as experienced, and perhaps the most compelling aspect of its characterization is the flight of personality from the rational categories adduced to explain it.

Which is passion—known or lived? Certainly it would seem to be the decisive instance of lived experience refusing the canons of rationality. Indeed, it first appears that way in *The Good Soldier*. But in the further course of the novel, as I have argued, desire becomes routine and predictable—as much a matter of knowledge as sensation. Far from an exuberant denial of all restriction, it becomes finally a constraint as severe as the moral conventions which oppose it. Passion comes to indi-

2. "Impressionism and Fiction," *op. cit.*, p. 46. [See p. 267 above—*Editor*.]

cate, not so much originally lived, as obsessively reenacted experience. And yet, part of the trenchancy of *The Good Soldier* is that it imagines experience more immediate than passion. It imagines a region of character, not only before knowledge but before desire, and it does so, of course, through the figure of Dowell. Schorer sees the book's "controlling irony" in the fact that "passionate situations are related by a narrator who is himself incapable of passion."[3] But the irony runs even deeper than Schorer indicates, because Dowell's lack of passion appears not simply as a deprivation but as an opportunity. Much as his great wealth frees him from material need, so his *accidia*, to use Schorer's term, frees him from the constraints of desire. He is divested of all want. And if one should argue that this makes Dowell a mere nullity, I readily concur, disputing only the qualifier "mere."

Dowell describes himself as having "no occupation," "no business affairs" [57], "no attachments, no accumulations" [21] and "nothing in the world to do" [22]: "I suppose I ought to have done something, but I didn't see any call to do it. Why does one do things?" [17]. Doing nothing, he feels nothing, and feeling nothing, he knows nothing: "You ask how it feels to be a deceived husband. Just heavens, I do not know. It feels just nothing at all" [53]. In important respects, let us recognize, Dowell *is* nothing. No "paradigm of traits" can describe him, because there is nothing substantial to describe: no determining past, no consistency of opinion, no deep belief, no stable memory. He cannot be "justified." There is no accounting for Dowell.

* * * For, Dowell's "nullity" is simply the final consequence of the Impressionist pursuit of immediate experience, the attempt to render an aboriginal stratum of personality that exists before doing, feeling, and knowing take shape. At the instant of experience, one is neither humble, nor kind, nor greedy, nor wise. The notion of a trait, as a persistent attribute of character, cannot yet apply. Character exists only after the fact, and it is Ford's boldest stroke to imagine a personality virtually without attributes—subjectivity before it has assumed the articulations of character. In Dowell, Ford gestures at a nothing that precedes something in human personality, a formless, contentless, traitless self which does nothing, feels nothing, knows nothing, and which exists as a pure consciousness behind every one of its manifestations. Such a state, of course, must remain a bare ideal. Even if it can exist (which one has reason to doubt) it certainly cannot persist. Dowell collides painfully into the world, not once but continually. The novel begins with his fall into consciousness, and falling into consciousness becomes his vocation. At every moment, he confronts experience as though for the first time, and to the last he remains *rudimentary*. * * *

3. See p. 306 above [*Editor*].

In his most provocative remark, Dowell writes at the end of the novel that

> I guess that I myself, in my fainter way, come into the category of the passionate, of the headstrong, and the too-truthful. For I can't conceal from myself the fact that I loved Edward Ashburnham—and that I love him because he was just myself. If I had had the courage and the virility and possibly also the physique of Edward Ashburnham I should, I fancy, have done much what he did. He seems to me like a large elder brother who took me out on several excursions and did many dashing things whilst I just watched him robbing the orchards, from a distance. [161]

Wiley calls this "the ultimate in self-deception," and Schorer "his weirdest absurdity, the final, total blindness of infatuation, and self-infatuation . . . for observe the impossible exceptions: courage, virility, physique! What sane man could expect them?"[4] But is it a question of sanity? Or is it perhaps that still more difficult issue, the question of character as such? Dowell refuses here, refuses with a supreme negligence, to define himself in terms of traits. He regards courage, virility, and physique as secondary qualities, mere contingencies which scarcely bear on the problem of identity. He speaks of watching Ashburnham "from a distance," but it is himself that he sees from a distance, examining his endowments as though they had only accidental relation to the being that possessed them.

* * *

As a man, Dowell is weak and led by the nose, but as an author he is a free agent who can utter any opinion, no matter how unlikely, without fear of constraint. All else about Dowell may be doubtful, but one thing is certain: he writes, and part of the force of Fordian Impressionism lies in its recognition that character in narrative may be a late and clumsy reconstruction but narrating voice is prior and ineliminable. The passivity of the cuckold gives way to the restless activity of the writer, who asserts and retracts, confesses and denies, soliloquizes and apostrophizes, changes his story, changes his mind, and arrives finally at the point of exhaustion: "It is so difficult to keep all these people going" [142]. Within a novel that so frequently refers to the power of convention and circumstance, the act of writing becomes a way to recover autonomy. This is not the freedom of a heroic agent gloriously ascendant, who tramples conventions in pursuit of noble ends. Dowell's is free action in its most primitive aspect, an unformed self taking its first steps toward articulation and expressing only partly what it knows and mostly what it wants.

4. Paul L. Wiley [see p. 323, n. 1 above], p. 200; Schorer [see p. 308 above], p. xi.

The moral agony of *The Good Soldier*, and its difficulty, depend in large measure on the way that this single fiction contains incommensurable principles of characterization. The novel which asks, What is a character?, makes drama out of its competing answers. The justified self, which personifies the cultural context and embodies its values, struggles against the 'passionate' self which personifies and justifies only itself. This contrast would seem sufficiently grave, but *The Good Soldier*, as I have been suggesting, imagines a further refinement and a new provocation in Dowell, who appears less as a character than a voice, only faintly and incidentally attached to a body, a culture, a religion, and a history. Ford looks past the exigencies of circumstance and the urgencies of desire, past convention, past consistency, past justification, to character in its most irreducible aspect. The movement toward Dowell is like the movement toward the Cartesian *cogito*, but once Ford arrives at this spare foundation, he, too, begins the task of reconstruction. Dowell's freedom, tenuous though it may be, offers an escape from conventions that had burdened the novel as they had burdened English society, and it offers Ford an opportunity to confront character at its inception: *The Good Soldier* opens by dramatizing the collapse of those moral and psychological categories by which we habitually live, but it continues by dramatizing those awkward and tentative acts by which morality and character are renewed. Out of "nothing" Dowell begins to choose a world. He thus reanimates the ethical sense that had languished in Edward, petrified in Leonora, and died in Florence. Morality, degraded by convention and thwarted by passion, hesitantly reappears in the simple judgments of a mind struggling to weigh its preferences. After the endless repetitions of "I don't know," Dowell says nay to Florence and Leonora and yea to Nancy and Edward. He may not yet know, but he *decides*, and in so deciding, he gives a picture of morality in its nascent state, founded not on inherited norms but on original judgments of value.

The temptation is great to see Dowell in a state of final disintegration, the coherence of the self lost in a shower of impressions. But what appears as the disintegration of character might better be regarded as a condition that oddly resembles it, namely the formation of character. * * * Dowell comes confusedly into being. Each new utterance is a fresh collision between the mind and its environs. Assuredly, this is not a familiar condition, but neither is it madness. It is rather an imaginary posture of human consciousness that Impressionism is particularly suited to render: a radical innocence that perpetually rediscovers the world and posits itself in startled speech.

ANN BARR SNITOW

[The Tragedy of Desire] †

To understand the tone of *The Good Soldier*, we must remember the world into which it came in 1914. Ford described Ashburnham's milieu: "Edward was sunk in his chair; there were in the room two candles, hidden by green glass shades. The green shades were reflected in the glasses of the bookcases that contained not books but guns with gleaming brown barrels and fishing-rods in green baize over-covers. There was dimly to be seen, above a mantlepiece encumbered with spurs, hooves and bronze models of horses, a dark-brown picture of a white horse" [136]. Edward Ashburnham, his walls lined with guns and rods instead of books, was one very important element in this world. *Blast*, Wyndam Lewis' revolutionary little magazine where the first installment of *The Good Soldier* appeared, was another. * * * The good soldier, Edward Ashburnham, the man with lands, the man who can lead other men, is a man with no ideas, no sense of what is happening in the world now that the feudal heritage he values has been completely undermined. And his story appears in *Blast*, a periodical that could never have appeared on the tables of Edward's * * * Branshaw Teleragh. The purposelessness, the blindness that are the themes of *The Good Soldier* come in part from this split in Edward Ashburnham's culture between power and meaning.

* * * Ashburnham did not read things like *Blast* not only because his world had lost all touch with cultural vitality but also because *Blast* could not conceivably have helped him to understand his condition. The vorticists were too wrapped up in their own romance, the romance of new worlds for old. *Blast* praised the machine-age sensibility, the industrial state—"this bareness and hardness"—and said that the English, as the inventors of this hardness, "should be the great enemies of Romance."[1]

* * *

The Good Soldier is about a society whose internal order and meaning has dried up leaving nothing but a shell, an empty structure of social forms by which its people can live. Ford uses irony as the most sensitive probe to feel out this distance between passional life and empty forms. * * * [It] is about people who lie. Some lie to protect society while others lie to undermine it, but they are all so confused about what is

† From *Ford Madox Ford and the Voice of Uncertainty* (Baton Rouge and London: Louisiana State UP, 1984) 161–64, 166, 168–70, 183. Copyright © 1984 by Louisiana State University Press. Reprinted with the permission of the publishers. Page numbers in brackets refer to this Norton Critical Edition.
1. Unsigned editorial matter, *Blast*, 41.

true that every perception is bifurcated and can only be expressed by irony. Hence Dowell speaks ironically, but in a world of liars irony goes wild and rival meanings undercut each other infinitely.

If irony is a fitting voice with which to describe a world of liars, it is also fitting for describing a world in which few people experience things directly. The characters in the novel who feel strongly are defeated by this world of exhausted repression. Their pain comes to us filtered through the sensibility of that most passive of voyeurs, John Dowell. He is an ironist because irony is an effective way to record contradictions without resolving them. Dowell and the other characters fear resolution; from their advanced condition of passivity or doubt or fear, irony is a small refuge.

* * *

* * * Because Dowell's position in the novel is intentionally ambiguous, as one is reading the novel and, if possible, even in remembering, it is best to think of him in the way the gestalt psychologists think of a simple design on a solid background. If one concentrates on the ground, it becomes the design and the design recedes in the mind and becomes the ground. One reverses this process again and again, figure-ground, figure-ground, until something the psychologists call flipping takes place. Perception of the design as first the background and then as the design again alternates very quickly so that one *almost* sees both qualities at once.

That is exactly what happens in looking at Dowell as narrator: first he is reliable judge, then execrable fool, then properly self-deprecating ironist, then condescending failure. All these partially true images of him must constantly be vying with each other in the reader's mind, a different one coming uppermost with each twist of the narrative. Only then can the many perspectives that interested Ford emerge from the mouth of a single narrator.

* * *

One need only look at specific passages in *The Good Soldier* to see the problems which arise if one takes too strict a view of Dowell. Take, for example, Dowell's tantalizing description of his courtship of Florence. One becomes increasingly interested in knowing about Florence as more and more grotesque hints are given about her. Florence's aunts mysteriously beg Dowell not to marry her: "Don't do it, John. Don't do it. You're a good young man" [60]. Ford contrives that our knowledge of Florence and her first lover Jimmy's extraordinary plan for continuing their liaison under Dowell's roof comes as slowly as possible. Ford justifies this elaborate withholding of vital information about Florence by establishing a dual nature in his narrator. At the same time that Dowell is telling us about his odd courtship in the light of what he has learned since, he is also intent on reexperiencing events as they were to him when they occurred. Critics who have found Dowell exasperating and idiotically limited are ignoring his often-stated desire to reenter events like a *halluciné*, miraculously shorn of hindsight and able to recapture the very shape and taste of his original mistakes.

This double perspective is further complicated by the reader's degree of initiation. For example, one who reads *The Good Soldier* for the first time can only take the following passage about Florence's early travels in Europe at face value as an unironic description of unexceptionable events:

> They [Florence and her Uncle Hurlbird] were to have spent two months more in that tranquil bosom, but inopportune events, apparently in her uncle's business, had caused their rather hurried return to Stamford. The young man called Jimmy remained in Europe to perfect his knowledge of that continent. He certainly did: he was most useful to us afterwards. [58]

But one who has read *The Good Soldier* before knows that this "tranquil bosom" is the home of a blackguard and the "inopportune events" that force Florence and her uncle to depart are that she has been discovered coming out of that "most useful" Jimmy's bedroom at five o'clock in the morning. Jimmy's knowledge of the continent, we later learn, has been gained at Uncle Hurlbird's expense: he has paid Jimmy to remain behind, away from his all too corruptible niece. Finally, during those years when Jimmy was "most useful" to Dowell and Florence in their travels, he was actually Florence's lover, the one who first helped her lay the ground rules of her elaborate and lifelong deception of Dowell. All this perfidy, melodrama and surprise is decorously hidden behind what must appear to the uninitiated first reader as a straightforward piece of narration.

If these are the facts, how are we to take Dowell's way of alluding to them? The new reader of the novel takes Dowell's flat description at face value and is only slowly, deliciously undeceived. No novel of Ford's offers so many kinds of excitement at the level of plot surprise. But if one has read the novel before, Dowell's voice is perceived as more complex. Is he being dry? ("He was most useful to us afterwards.") Is he being bitter, almost sarcastic? (The "tranquil bosom.") Or is he merely so preoccupied by the demands of re-creating the past that for the moment he has become inattentive to what he now knows and is instead concentrating on the act of narration itself?

*   *   *

In one sense, then, *The Good Soldier* remains a social novel to its end. But in spite of Ford's claim that he was interested above all in anatomizing his times, the conclusion of the novel is a social novelist's swan song. The novel begins with social analysis, as a comedy of manners, but finds the tools of this analysis inadequate to express modern experience. The stable ironies of traditional social comedy fall apart under the pressure of modern circumstances. They become circular, disturbing, irresolvable. Finally, the social theme itself is eclipsed by a new emphasis on private desperation, and that wandering probe, irony, is laid aside in exhaustion. Dowell's subjective experience, earlier put through so many forms of scrutiny, dissection, reevaluation, is finally accepted for the limited but irreducible thing it is. At least no external social observation is offered to ironically undercut it.

Ford thought he should be a social novelist, and yet he felt an estrangement from what was happening in England during the Edwardian years that sometimes bordered on the pathological and that probably contributed to his nervous breakdowns, retreats, and private, asocial nightmares like those he described in *The Young Lovell* written in the same year as *The Good Soldier*.

Perhaps this collapse of specifically social comedy is one of the things Ford had in mind when he called *The Good Soldier* his "great auk's egg," "something of a race that will have no successors."[2] Indeed, the end of *The Good Soldier* is in some respects a dead end. "So life peters out" [161], says Dowell and so ends a number of his trains of thought. Dowell and Ford are together in recognizing that an old way of life has become impossible; they are together, too, in remaining emotionally committed to a culture that has lost its vitality.

*　　*　　*

EUGENE GOODHEART

What Dowell Knew †

The Good Soldier remains one of the most puzzling works of modern fiction, because it has none of the anchoring affirmations or negations that control the works of the classic modernists, early and late: James, Conrad, Joyce and Lawrence. If the classic modernists had a vision of the abyss, they also knew the compensations of aesthetic consciousness or moral commitment or spiritual transcendence. A moral fecklessness provides *The Good Soldier* with a paradoxical energy that makes the novel seem well in advance of its time: postmodern rather than modern. The fecklessness determines the character of the narration.

2. Ford's "Dedicatory Letter"; see p. 4 of text [*Editor*].
  † From "What Dowell Knew: A Reading of *The Good Soldier*," *Antaeus* 56, special Ford issue (Spring 1986): 70–80. Reprinted with the permission of the author. Page numbers in brackets refer to this Norton Critical Edition.

At the beginning of *The Good Soldier*, the narrator John Dowell establishes the equivocal, if not contradictory, mode of his narration. He knew the Ashburnhams "with an extreme intimacy" and yet he "knew nothing at all about them." The narration does not mark a progress from ignorance to knowledge. "When I sit down to puzzle out what I know of this sad affair I knew nothing whatever." (A somewhat confusing shift in tense from "know" to "knew," for there is no real difference between what he knew about the Ashburnhams nine seasons earlier when he and his wife first met them and what he knows now.) The saddest truth in this the saddest story is that he "know[s] nothing—nothing in the world—of the hearts of men" [12]. Yet the story he tells is about "hearts" diseased and passionate, too frail to survive the shocks of their own passions.

One is tempted to ascribe Dowell's ignorance to his utter failure as a man—that is, as a sexual being. What could this "eunuch" be expected to know of characters like Edward, Leonora and his own wife Florence, since unlike them, he had never been touched by passion? I think Ford means us to take the opposite view: Dowell's freedom from passion gives him a more or less disinterested eye, a capacity to contemplate the spectacle of the passions of others without being unduly unsettled by them. He is the Negatively Capable narrator, whose personality is the vehicle for others to manifest their own personalities. Dowell is not the venal unreliable narrator, whose moral and sexual deficiencies are the subject of the novel.[1] He is rather a Device who makes possible the exploration of the passionate lives of others. Since Dowell is a participant in the drama, one of the four that "danced the minuet" and a cuckold, the victim of an awful deception, Ford must assure his objectivity by neutralizing his passions. "You ask how it feels to be a deceived husband. Just heavens, I do not know. It feels just nothing . . ." [53]. Whatever we may think of a man incapable of feeling the humiliation of having been cuckolded is irrelevant to the narrative necessity of guaranteeing Dowell's cold eye. Dowell shows how secure he is from the deformations of passion when he characterizes his apparently genuine attachment to Nancy in an astonishing simile: "I [just] want[ed] to marry [Nancy] as some people go to Carcassonne" [84].

I don't mean to deprive Dowell of his status as a character by speaking of him as a device. His lack of sexual passion or susceptibility to sexual humiliation may indeed be read as *accidia*, "the dull hysteria of sloth . . . the sluggish insanity of defective love," as Mark Schorer characterizes it.[2] And for all his apparent indifference to the humiliation that he

---

1. Eight years later, Hemingway was to publish *The Sun Also Rises*, a novel about an impotent hero, whose impotence was a mark of his integrity in a world gone dissolute. I don't mean to suggest that Dowell is a comparable figure of integrity ° ° °, only that a post-Freudian moralizing about the sexual deficiencies of a character may be irrelevant to the theme of the novel, as it would be to the theme of *The Sun Also Rises*.

2. See p. 309 above [*Editor*].

has suffered at the hands of his wife, he is on more than one occasion venomously unforgiving of her. When she dies, he speaks of her as having had no more reality than a piece of paper. Dowell's feelings and responses are ambivalent and inconsistent. But he is nevertheless a device in that his character permits Ford to achieve the effect of cold clarity about a situation marked by inconsistency and bewildering shifts of attitude and feeling within the other characters. Dowell is the perfect reflection of Edward Ashburnham, for instance, who is at once a womanizer and an idealizer of female virtue, or of Leonora, whose strict Irish-Catholic morality (English style) does not prevent her from effectively pimping for her husband. The contradictions and anomalies in the presented world require at once a moral slothfulness and a defective emotional life in the narrator, so that there will be no interference with his powers of observation. (After Florence's death, Dowell falls into a cataleptic state, a condition that doesn't prevent him from having impressions, nor from comparing Edward's talk to that of a novelist, whose business is "to make you see things clearly.") Dowell has the "aloof" view that Ford says in his little book *The English Novel* [1930] is the ideal towards which the novel aspires.

Dowell's narration confounds the distinction on which knowledge is based—the distinction between illusion and reality. Thus the four together danced a minuet and behaved as a unanimity for nine long seasons. Was this a lie, a mere deception? Dowell equivocates: "it wasn't a minuet . . . it was a prison, a prison full of screaming hysterics." But immediately afterward, almost in the same breath, Dowell swears by his creator that "it was true sunshine; the true music" [12]. And isn't it true that the reader of the novel hears both the screaming hysterics and the music? The narration does not demystify the minuet, for demystification is based on a hierarchy of illusion and reality, and the hierarchy no longer exists.

The vexed question about Dowell's reliability is a misleading question, because the narration subverts the distinction between reliable and unreliable narration. Reliable narration assumes an identity or continuity between novelist and narrator, unreliable narration assumes a discrepancy between them. If Dowell is unreliable, he is not to be distinguished from the novelist's consciousness. However inconsistent we may find Dowell, there is no truth beyond the truth that he sees— no standards beyond those which Dowell himself provides to judge shifts in consciousness, attitude, etc. The narrator's consciousness is coterminous with the author novelist's consciousness. Ford knows no more about his characters than does Dowell. The sudden bewildering shifts in tone, the oscillating judgments or feelings have no transcendent resolution in the author's consciousness. The narrative perspective is a virtual parody of the Negative Capability. Dowell sees with an empathetic selflessness that leaves him at the mercy of events. His uncertainty, bewilderment, skepticism and solipsism represent a view that only the reader can transcend, if indeed he can transcend it. Narrator and author are equally helpless before the scene they survey.

The identity between narrator and author is an invitation to a biographical reading of the novel. Thomas Moser's recent interpretation reveals the sources of the novel in the life. Florence and Leonora not only correspond to Violet Hunt and his first wife Elsie Hueffer, respectively, the curious and distorted ways they are seen by Dowell correspond to Ford's self-serving views of Violet and Elsie.[3] But reduction of the novel to biography threatens the integrity of the novel. The distinction of *The Good Soldier* is in its objectification of the quandaries of character and sexuality that Ford as well as many of his contemporaries found themselves in during the crucial period before World War I. For all the appreciative criticism of *The Good Soldier*, readers have not, in my view, sufficiently appreciated Ford's contribution to the deauthorizing tendency in modern fiction. Ford exercises his extraordinary technical skill in *The Good Soldier* not so much in the interest of form as in the interest of making us see with maximum vividness and uncertainty our sexual and moral lives. Since he cannot bring his characters forward in action and dialogue in an unmediated way, for that would imply the accessible knowledge that the epistemology of the novel denies, he entrusts the narration to a highly conscious, highly articulate character whose main concern is to allow the other characters to be formed through his narration. It is a remarkable anomaly that the characters speak so little in the novel (there is, for instance, very little direct evidence that Edward Ashburnham is the great talker Dowell says he is) and yet are so vividly present. All that is possible in the way of knowledge of others are the impressions we have of them, and so the novelist is obliged to create the most vivid register of impressions, a role that Dowell performs perfectly.[4]

What is the reason for the radical unknowability of this world to even a clear-eyed observer? If he is the cold disinterested eye, or obversely the non-personality capable of entering empathetically the lives of others, why should he be so ignorant of the hearts of others? Dowell offers a reason in the first paragraph, but it is a reason that does not finally illuminate and satisfy. He attributes his ignorance to English character. Does he mean that English character is more concealed or repressed than American character? On the evidence of Dowell's character and that of his wife, both Americans, that would hardly seem the case. Compared with Dowell and Florence, Edward and even Leonora Ashburnham wear their hearts on their sleeves. Or is it an American obtuseness

3. The distortions consist (in Moser's view) in the fact that Violet was not the empty chatterbox, the piece of paper Dowell reduces her to, nor was Elsie the cruel, frigid creature that Leonora is meant to be. [For Moser's book, see p. 352 above—*Editor*.]
4. This puts Ford's doctrine of impressionism in a nutshell.

in the presence of the English, Dowell never having learned to read the signs of English character accurately? There is, of course, considerable evidence of Dowell's obtuseness: most notably, his failure to perceive that his wife had been deceiving him from the very beginning of their relationship. But the obtuseness does not depend on cultural difference. I want to argue that Dowell's ignorance is a mimesis of the darkness that shrouds all motive, that character, as the novel understands it, is beyond knowing, and not simply because it is radically unknowable, but because its very existence is in doubt. Dowell's ignorance is not an aspect of his unreliability as a narrator, because reliability of perception and knowledge is no longer a possibility in this world. Without reliability, there can be no unreliability.

Dowell understands his own ignorance as an expression of universal ignorance. "Who in this world knows anything of any other heart—or of his own?" And the reason is that "one cannot be certain of the way any man will behave in any case." Lacking that certainty, the very idea of " 'character' is of no use to anyone" [104]. Dowell illustrates the difficulty in his speculation about the Kilsyte case, in which Edward Ashburnham gives a weeping young girl a kiss to comfort her for the loss of her lover. At the moment, Edward's thoughts were purely paternal and consoling. But during the trial in which he was accused of a darker motive, "it came suddenly into his head whilst he was in the witness box . . . the recollection of the softness of the girl's body as he had pressed her to him. And from that moment, that girl appeared desirable to him—and Leonora completely unattractive" [104]. Character disappears when behavior is at the mercy of the unsuspected motive, the stray impulse, the sudden access of passion. And since character is the intelligibility of the self, how can anyone know another person if character has dissolved into a welter of motive, impulse and passion? (Even Leonora, whose normality and conventional virtue is stressed throughout the novel, is, in time of crisis, "incapable of taking any line whatever."[5]) The extraordinary shifts in point of view, often bewildering and contradictory, are not signs of obtuseness or stupidity in Dowell. On the contrary, they correspond to the shifting nature of the "characters" themselves.[6]

The stray impulse, the unsuspected motive has always informed human behavior: why should it now present such a puzzling aspect? In the past, civilization had erected conventions and traditions as more or

5. When Dowell dismisses Florence's death—"She just went completely out of existence, like yesterday's paper"—he is distinguishing her moral nullity from the moral character of the others. But one wonders whether all the characters are not little more than paper, texts composed of vacuous talk.

6. If Dowell were a character in a D. H. Lawrence novel, his ignorance would be seen as a reflection of his bodiless character. Not to live in the body is not to truly know. Lawrence repudiates mind consciousness because it is a false consciousness—and it is false consciousness because it is unembodied. *Blood* was his metaphor for embodied consciousness. No character in a Lawrence novel surpasses Dowell as an example of mind consciousness.

less successful bulwarks against the unexpected threat from within. The conventions and traditions become internalized in the virtues that compose a character. *The Good Soldier* is a story of the breakdown of standards and the confusion of civilized values. And the focus of the breakdown and confusion is the most difficult of all moralities, sexual morality. Close to the beginning of the novel Leonora, the continually betrayed and "virtuous" wife of Ashburnham, confesses that she once tried and failed to take a lover. "And I burst out crying and I cried and I cried for the whole eleven miles. Just imagine me crying. And just imagine me making a fool of the poor dear chap like that. It certainly wasn't playing the game, was it now?" [13]. Dowell wonders whether the last remark is that "of a harlot," or of what every decent woman "thinks at the bottom of her heart?" [13]. Characteristically, he can't answer the question; nor does he believe that anyone can answer the question. And then he formulates the paradox of civilization in the grand manner of the cultural critic and moralist:

> Yet, if one doesn't know at this hour and day, at this pitch of civilization to which we have attained, after all the preachings of all the moralists . . . And if one doesn't know as much as that about the first thing in the world, what does one know and why is one here? [13–14]

The convention that regulates extramarital chastity cannot be automatically invoked, because it is often purchased at the price of genuine feeling. (Edward, the man of strong sexual feeling, cannot find satisfaction in a wife whom he admires—or hates—but cannot love.) This unresolvable conflict, this insoluble problem has become a banality of our sexual existence.

Ford began writing the book on December 17, 1913, and the most important date in the book is August 4, the day Florence was born, began her affair with Jimmy, married Dowell, began her affair with Edward and committed suicide. It is also the day (August 4, 1914) that England entered World War I, the day that modern life began for England. Without a commitment to a particular point of view, the novel, in modernist fashion, subverts the conventional understandings of Victorian and Edwardian England. Ford questions the verbal foundations of the conventions. "And that was quite in the early days of her discovery of his infidelities—if you like to call them infidelities." If they are not infidelities, what are they, acts that imply a new kind of fidelity to the promptings of one's heart? But the novel does not mean to sentimentalize "infidelity," since it offers a dubious picture of Edward's "sliding" heart as in the instance of the Kilsyte case.[7]

When Dowell suggests that his story has a happy ending ("the vil-

---

7. The Chaucerian word is appropriate here.

lains—for obviously Edward and the girl were villains—have been punished by suicide and madness. The heroine—the perfectly normal,
virtuous, and slightly deceitful heroine—has become the happy wife
. . ." [160]), he is exercising an unstable irony, which permits us to hear
a possible grain of truth in the statement. Edward's character, like every
other issue in the novel, is undecidable.

Sondra Stang makes an extremely suggestive connection between *The
Good Soldier* and the two late great essays of Freud, *Beyond the Pleasure
Principle* and *Civilization and its Discontents*, published respectively
five and fifteen years after *The Good Soldier*. In Stang's reading, the
novel explores the repressions of spirit and passion inflicted by civilization on characters who have lived at the pitch of civilization. Though
she does not hold Dowell in high esteem as a character (she speaks of
him as a faux-naif, a narrator in bad faith), she credits him with raising
the fundamental Freudian questions:

> Why do men find it impossible to be happy? How can they live if
> they are not to deny their instincts? What, in that case, are they to
> do with their instincts? What are they to do with the demands that
> civilization makes of them and the ways it codifies those demands
> and regulates human relationships? Given the nature of their
> natures, how can men work out ways of dealing with the world
> outside them—and the world they make? How much do men gain
> from civilization, and what in turn must they give up for it? What
> is civilization worth—how much suffering?
>
> In short, how can men find a workable relationship between
> their instincts and civilized life?[8]

Edward's tragedy is the "extinction of a splendid personality, like the fall
of a great civilization."[9] He betrays himself in "the atrophy of sexual
power through disuse and paralysis. Edward has compartmented his sexual life."[1] And Leonora, "the normal type" with little passionate energy
to repress, survives through her commitment to convention and tradition.

Stang's reading, which is much richer than these remarks convey, is,
as I say, extremely suggestive[2] but it places the novel in a moral framework that does not quite suit even the essays of Freud. Stang is fully
alive to the extraordinary inconsistency of statement and overstatement,
of tones and attitudes in Dowell's narration, but she is apparently
unwilling to accept the inconsistency and contradiction as ultimate data.

8. Sondra J. Stang, *Ford Madox Ford* (New York: The Ungar Publishing Co., Inc., 1977), pp.
   71–72.
9. *Ibid.*, p. 89.
1. *Ibid.*, p. 82.
2. The essay is one of the best we have on *The Good Soldier*, for it grasps what few essays on the
   novel seem to comprehend: the sexual and moral quandaries of men and women at a critical
   moment in the history of civilization. It refuses to be diverted by an excessive (and often sterile)
   preoccupation with the problematics of point of view.

She tries to resolve the irreducible ambiguities of the novel. Edward's passions after all are themselves the product of a civilization based on traditions and conventions of honor, which account for the split within him between the idealization of women and sexual promiscuity. The split is the source of guilt, which produces a recoil from sexuality (in his passionate love of Nancy). Does this represent the atrophy of sexual power and paralysis? I think that to formulate the question in this way is to misrepresent Edward's predicament.

In *The Good Soldier*, sexuality is a force that not only generates disorder, it creates new forms of deception. There are the deceptions of a society that denies the existence of sexuality, but there are also the deceptions of sexuality itself (for instance, in the behavior of Edward as well as of Florence). Unlike Lawrence, Ford (in *The Good Soldier*) is no advocate of free sexual expression. He understands (through his narrator) the price paid for its expression as well as for its repression.

In an extended excursus, Dowell evokes with a moving eloquence peculiar to him the nature of passion (of Edward's passion) as a desire that includes but transcends sex, a desire for identity with the beloved, a desire for courage, for support:

> . . . if such a passion comes to fruition, the man will get what he wants. He will get the moral support, the encouragement, the relief from the sense of loneliness, the assurance of his own worth. But these things pass away as the shadows pass across sun-dials. It is sad, but it is so. The pages of the book will become familiar; the beautiful corner of the road will have [been] turned too many times. Well, this is the saddest story. [80]

The tragedy of desire then is in the ephemeral character of the rare moments of satisfaction. The pathos of desire is that people rarely, if ever, have "what they want." Paradisal longings only intensify the overwhelming sense of life as "broken, tumultuous, agonized . . . periods punctuated by screams, by imbecilities, by deaths, by agonies" [151]. It is not the repression of passion that makes for unhappiness, but the expression of passion that makes for the most intense happiness for the moment and for the deepest sadness, for it too must pass. Dowell here sounds the note not of Freud, but of Ecclesiastes.[3]

The world of *The Good Soldier* is filled with talk about religion, and it is god-forsaken. Religion is seen as a cultural characteristic and as a source of neurosis. Irish-Catholics in England and America lead lives quite different from the untidy lives of Mediterranean Catholics. It is impossible to disentangle Leonora's Irish-Catholicism from her sexual

---

3. *The Sun Also Rises* once again comes to mind with its poignant sense of the fleeting quality of all happiness. If *The Sun Also Rises* is not the saddest story, it is because an idea of value (incarnated in the grace and integrity of Jake Barnes) survives the devastations of the novel. It is difficult to say what is redeemable in *The Good Soldier*.

frigidity. On the other hand, in Edward the religious sentiment has a power rarely found in the English novel. In one of the most moving scenes in the novel, Dowell discovers Edward in a tormented state before an image of the Virgin Mary, praying for strength to resist the temptations of Nancy Rufford. For Edward, she is not simply an object of sexual love: she has come to be identified in his mind with the image of the Virgin herself. Edward's death at the end seems like a martyrdom, though it is difficult to say precisely what the terms of the martyrdom are. What one senses however is that the novel expresses a yearning for the religious life and a regret at its passing, because religion is the medium for soul-making. Perhaps that is what Dowell means when he responds to Leonora's declaration that she is "an Irish Catholic" after she had been offended by Florence: "Those words gave me the greatest relief that I have ever had in my life. They told me, I think, almost more than I have ever gathered at any one moment—about myself" [38].

The principal conceit of the novel is the diseased heart which must be protected from the shocks of experience. Florence's heart, however, is not literally or medically diseased: the disease is a ruse by which she manages to keep her infidelities from her husband. Rather than suffering from heart disease, she is heartless. Leonora too for all her virtues lacks the full-hearted passion of love, as does Dowell. Only Edward and perhaps Nancy seem capable of genuine passion, but Edward's heart is too unruly to achieve grace. The images of paradise, hell and limbo that permeate the novel suggest a vision of a failed Divine Comedy.

The Good Soldier is a story whose vividness and intensity are in excess of its meaning—or lack of meaning. Ford's famous commitment to impressionism is a statement that we have nothing but impressions. Yet the impressions bespeak not an emptiness but a felt absence. There are no longer any substantial invisibilities, only insubstantial visibilities. All permanent, meaningful structures (God, character, the virtues) have disappeared, but not the desire for them. The poignant paradox of the novel is that the aloof narrator, faithful to the surfaces of life, is a mute witness to what he cannot see and cannot know: the God that has abandoned men to their self-destructive devices. Dowell's refrain that he knows nothing expresses a humility that has an almost evangelical conviction. "I don't know what anyone has to be proud of" [42]. Dowell silently chastises the pride of Leonora's Powys connection, as the narrative itself chastises the pride of every character in it.

The Good Soldier is not Ford's final word. The tetralogy *Parade's End* has as its hero a character whose moral passion and integrity approach saintliness. Like Edward Ashburnham, Christopher Tietjens is a type of eighteenth-century aristocrat for whom honor is deeper than life, but unlike Edward he is not prone to inconsistency. He is a man of integrity whose actions are a series of refusals. He refuses to divorce his wife, though she has been unfaithful to him, because she is the mother of his child. Whether the child is his or his wife's lover's is uncertain, but it does not alter the case. He refuses to take money from his brother Mark (and his father), because his father committed suicide, believing that Tietjens had sold his wife. He refuses to turn in his friend Macmaster, who has plagiarized his research in order to gain advancement. And finally, he refuses to have an affair with Valentine Wannop out of respect for her chastity.

Tietjens is a reinvention of Edward Ashburnham, an integrity secure against every temptation, whereas Edward was an integrity susceptible to every temptation. Tietjens is an appearance, who never betrays his reality. But he is no more effectual than Edward. "A fabulous monster," his resentful wife justly characterizes him. His refusals are a rejection of the world in which he lives, a negative desire to live the life of Christ, in which every gift and power he possesses is mortified. ("It was a condemnation of a civilization that he, Tietjens, possessed of enormous physical strength, should never have needed it before.")

The narrative (there is no authorial narrator) fully acknowledges the futility of Tietjens' character through its various perspectives, but it also cherishes his idealism. It is as if Ford wishes to secure himself against the emerging nihilist "truth" that he or his narrator Dowell had discovered in *The Good Soldier:* that every "value" is a lie or, if not a lie, susceptible to betrayal by some energy that contradicts it. (Edward Ashburnham, the aristocratic man of honor, lives a life of lechery, which is aborted by a self-destructive Dantean passion for a Beatrice-like girl.) In Tietjens, Ford invents a fabulous monster out of his own ineffectual moral yearning, against the evidence of his novelistic clear-sightedness. In *Parade's End* he rewrote (perhaps without really knowing it) the saddest story.

VINCENT J. CHENG

A Chronology of *The Good Soldier* †

What kind of a book is *The Good Soldier?* What genre of novel? Readers and critics alike, while enchanted by Ford's tale, have long puzzled over how to approach this novel. Samuel Hynes claims that the action of this novel "is not the sequence of passionate gestures which in another novel we would call the plot, but rather the action of the narrator's mind as it gropes for the meaning. . . . the real events of the novel are Dow-

† From "A Chronology of *The Good Soldier*," *English Language Notes* 24 (September 1986): 91–97. Reprinted with the permission of the author and *English Language Notes*. Page numbers in brackets refer to this Norton Critical Edition.

ell's thoughts about what has happened, and not the happenings themselves. . . . The point . . . is the clear distinction that the novel makes
between events and meaning. . . ."[1] Such an epistemological approach
to the novel has certainly proven to be revealing; yet I would suggest that
the "plot" *does* matter: for how we are meaningfully to interpret Dowell's
impressions of the tale must ultimately depend on what the tale actually
is, on what happened (or may have happened). And determining *that*,
in a book so impressionistically narrated, is no simple matter—especially
on a first reading.[2]

* * *

[W]e find that, in the year 1913, at the very same time that he was
writing *The Good Soldier*, Ford was saying, in his essay "On Impressionism":

> But one point is very important. The artist can never write to
> satisfy himself—to get, as the saying is, something off the chest. He
> must not write propaganda which it is his desire to write. . . . No,
> you will be just the skilled workman doing his job with drill or
> chisel or mallet. And you will get precious little out of it. Only,
> just at times, when you come to look again at some work of yours
> that you have quite forgotten, you will say, "Why, that is rather
> well done." That is all.[3]

Which is exactly what Ford then does in 1927, writing the "Dedicatory
Letter" to a new edition of *The Good Soldier*, taking retrospective pride
in the workmanship of his novel: "Great heavens, did I write as well as
that. . . . I will permit myself to say that I was astounded at the work I
must have put into the construction of the book, at the intricate tangle
of references and cross-references" [4–5]. His satisfaction lies in the
craftsmanship, in the plotting. * * *

Ford wrote in his study of Henry James that in reading James the
reader's mind passes "between the great outlines and the petty details."[4]
So also [in] *The Good Soldier*. Much has been written and made of the
"great outlines" and the social or epistemological significances of *The
Good Soldier*. But how * * * accessible are the petty details in this book?
Is this novel one in which we can pinpoint facts and events and "the
intricate tangle of references and cross-references" in which Ford took
such professional pride?

We should at least try. Ford went to great pains to concoct not only a

---

1. See pp. 311–12, 314, 315 above [*Editor*].
2. David Eggenschwiler emphasizes artfully the effects of a first reading * * *, in which the
   reader is most likely taken in by the narration of "the magician and artist." See pp. 344–51
   above—*Editor*.]
3. See p. 274 above [*Editor*].
4. Ford Madox Hueffer, *Henry James: A Critical Study* (London, 1914; reprinted New York,
   1964), p. 155.

social commentary or a narrative epistemology, but a novel in the French mode of *vraisemblance*—a tale realistically told by a narrator, a 'real' story with real details. * * * What *exactly* are the natures of these relationships? And what actually happens? * * *

We can start by providing ourselves with a clear chronology (or as clear as possible) of the events in the story, to do for *The Good Soldier* what Faulkner did in his appendices to *The Sound and the Fury* and *Absalom, Absalom!*[5] Perhaps it is Philistine vulgarity to rearrange an impressionistic work of art into a chronology of events. But I mean here, like Mr. Jimmy, to make myself "useful" [58], not beautiful—to perform a useful task of reconstruction.

Dowell born 1868; Edward born 1870 or 1871; Leonora born 1873; Florence born 1874. (See page [10] where everyone's ages are given at their 1904 meeting in Nauheim.)

1892?: Edward Ashburnham marries Leonora Powys (see page [91]: he didn't marry before the age of 22); Edward is prepared to become a Roman Catholic, but insists that any male offspring be raised Anglican. They live at Branshaw Teleragh happily for a few years (exactly how many seems unclear; Dowell says that Leonora "could not have been a happier girl for five or six years. For it was only at the end of that time that clouds began, as the saying is, to arise"—page [95]. The 1895 date, however, for the La Dolciquita affair, and the even earlier Kilsyte case, argue that this period of relative connubial bliss was, in fact, shorter. Dowell states on page [41] that the Kilsyte case "came at the very beginning of [Edward's] finding Leonora cold and unsympathetic.").

Sometime before 1895, the Kilsyte case: Edward is tried and acquitted for kissing a servant girl on a train.

1895 (this date according to Dowell, page [44], though for some reason Elliot B. Gose[6] claims that this event occurred in 1897): Edward meets La Dolciquita, mistress of a Russian Grand Duke, at Monte Carlo, and has a brief fling with her at Antibes; he goes badly into debt. Shortly thereafter, Leonora takes over the management of the estate.

1896: The Ashburnhams lease out Branshaw, and go to India. (I compute this date from the fact that, according to Dowell on page [111] they spent "eight years in India," returning in 1904.) Sometime during those eight years, Edward has a love affair with Mrs. Basil; toward the end of this period, the Ashburnhams meet the Maidans.

August 4, 1899: on her birthday, Florence Hurlbird sets out with her uncle and Jimmy on a tour around the world—"a birthday present to celebrate her coming of age." [57]

August 4, 1900: Dowell later conjectures that on this date Florence begins a love affair with Jimmy in Paris ("She yielded to an action that certainly

---

5. Theodore Dreiser, in an early book review, felt the need for the same. [See p. 231 above—*Editor.*]
6. See p. 323, n. 1 above [*Editor*].

coloured her whole life. [. . .] She was probably offering herself a birth-day present that morning"—page [57]) and is discovered coming out of Jimmy's bedroom at five in the morning by Bagshawe. [71–72]

August 4, 1901: Despite the Hurlbirds' hints that Florence is not chaste, John Dowell marries Florence; they set sail for Europe from America; Florence begins her deception of Dowell, pretending to have a "heart."

1901–1903: Florence conducts her sexual affair with Jimmy in Europe under Dowell's unsuspecting nose; in 1903 she tires of Jimmy. [65]

1904: Edward and Leonora return from India with Maisie Maidan. At Nauheim that summer, Florence witnesses Leonora boxing Maisie's ears; the Ashburnhams become acquainted with the Dowells. Thomas C. Moser and R. W. Lid[7] both discuss Ford's confusion about the exact date of this first meeting.

August 4, 1904: The "Protest" scene. On a trip to the town of M——, Florence dramatically guides Edward, Leonora, and Dowell to Luther's "protest," hinting that she and Edward are having an affair.

The four return to Nauheim that evening. Maisie, having overheard a conversation between Edward and Florence, writes Leonora a letter, then dies of a heart attack.

1904–1913: Unbeknownst to Dowell, Edward and Florence have an affair for nine years. For example: in September 4–21, 1904, Edward accompanies Florence and Dowell to Paris; in December 1904 Edward visits them again, and "knocked Mr. Jimmy's teeth down his throat"; in 1905, Edward visits them in Paris three times, once with Leonora; and so on. [69–70]

August 4, 1913: At Nauheim, Florence overhears Edward declare his love to his ward, Nancy Rufford, then sees Bagshawe talking to Dowell; Florence commits suicide. Dowell assumes that she died of a heart attack. He expresses his intention to marry Nancy.

Soon thereafter, Edward, Nancy, and Leonora return to Branshaw Teleragh (on September 1, 1913, according to page [142]), and Dowell returns to America to settle the financial problems of the Hurlbird estate. At Branshaw, Edward, Leonora, and Nancy live a hellish life together for some time. Edward decides that Nancy is to go to her father in India. He cables Dowell to come and help ease things; Dowell goes to Branshaw and lives pleasantly with Edward, Leonora and Nancy for "ten peaceful days" (or perhaps a "fortnight." On the day of Nancy's departure, Edward and Dowell drive her to the train station.

The above events at Branshaw occur during November and December, though the exact dates are unclear (see Moser and Arthur Mizener on Ford's inconsistencies here[8]).

One afternoon, some days later, a telegram arrives from Nancy, saying that she is having a "rattling good time" [162]. Edward commits suicide.

---

7. Moser [p. 352 above], Lid [see p. 341, n. 5 above], p. 63.
8. Moser p. 162; Mizener [see p. 322 above], p. 567.

One week after Edward's funeral [73], Leonora begins a long conversation with Dowell, in which she "let me into her full confidence" [74]. Dowell learns for the first time of Florence's affair with Edward [73]; he also learns for the first time that Florence committed suicide [74]. The reader is to assume that much of the details of the "Ashburnham tragedy" must, of necessity, have been revealed to Dowell during this conversation.

Shortly thereafter, Dowell begins to compose *The Good Soldier*, and works at it for six months [120], composing all but the last two chapters. Then, Leonora and Dowell receive a letter from Colonel Rufford with the information that Nancy, having learned in Aden of Edward's suicide, has gone mad; he requests Leonora to come and see Nancy. Dowell agrees to go instead. This would be sometime in mid-1914.

Eighteen months elapse, during which time Dowell has traveled through Europe, Africa and Asia; has found Nancy and has brought her back to Branshaw Teleragh. Meanwhile Leonora has married Rodney Bayham, and is pregnant. Dowell buys Branshaw, and lives there with a witless Nancy.

Dowell now finishes writing *The Good Soldier*. This would be now late 1915 or early 1916—a curious computation, since Ford's *The Good Soldier* itself had already been published on March 17, 1915!

 PAUL B. ARMSTRONG

[Dowell as Trustworthy Narrator] †

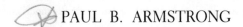

* * *

My reading of *The Good Soldier* results from my own decision to regard Dowell as a narrator who struggles, with mixed but increasing success, to give a trustworthy account of his history. * * * If Dowell grows in understanding, he does so by writing. His narration employs language not only as a means of communication but also as a tool for reflection—an instrument that makes possible the objectification and analysis of unreflected thoughts and feelings. Dowell repeatedly calls attention to his activity as the author of his text: "you must remember that I have been writing away at this story now for six months and reflecting longer and longer upon these affairs" [120]. We must remember the actual act of expression as a crucial dramatic element in Dowell's story because to write—or, even more vividly, to speak as he imagines he does "in a country cottage with a silent listener" [119–20]—is to make

† From *The Challenge of Bewilderment: Understanding and Representation in James, Conrad and Ford* (Ithaca and London: Cornell UP, 1987) 195–99. Copyright © 1987 by Cornell University. Reprinted with the permission of Cornell University Press. Page numbers in brackets refer to this Norton Critical Edition.

the self present to itself by presenting it to others. * * * "This is the saddest story I have ever heard" [9], Dowell claims as he begins his tale. As we learn later, Dowell has indeed "heard" much of the story he tells from informants like Leonora and Edward. Even more, though, Dowell "hears" his story for the first time as he tells it. Dowell only discovers what he thinks and what his history means by offering his experience to himself in language. His unreflective experience already had meaning— but tacit meaning that awaits explication in words so that it can be examined. The act of writing puts Dowell at a remove from his unreflective engagement with the world. By taking up his pen, he takes his first step from the obscurity and confusion of primordial experience toward the clarity and coherence of retrospective interpretation.[1]

As he educates himself by writing, Dowell also advances his ability to express his new awareness of himself and his world. In the first few pages of the novel, Dowell shifts ground often—offering an assessment only to withdraw or reverse it, moving unpredictably from topic to topic, interrupting lines of development just as they get going, jumping unexpectedly from one level of discourse to another (from reporting past events, to judging himself and others, to philosophizing about the human condition). The jolts, contradictions, and incongruities at the start of the novel constitute a switch point where the reader must decide about the narrator's reliability: Are these disruptions an indication of incompetence and evasiveness, or are they an honest expression of confusion and pain? Is this a devious, defensive narrator, or one who is unusually sincere about his anguish and uncertainty? The epistemological issue Ford plays with here is the dilemma of choosing between unmasking and faith—of deciding whether to suspect or trust the surface presented to us. *The Good Soldier* is an ambiguous novel because neither choice can be conclusive. Both are guesses about the hidden or as yet undisclosed. They are wagers about what the future is likely to reveal, but they also influence those disclosures by setting up expectations that may to a considerable degree be self-confirming (once one starts seeing lies everywhere, where does one stop? when, similarly, does trust prove blinding?). Ford calls attention to this dilemma by forcing his readers to make a decision about his narrator which, however they choose, they cannot perfectly justify.

Toward the end of the novel, Dowell shows himself much more able to focus his attention and organize events than he was at the start. For a trusting interpreter, this can be seen as evidence that his reflections have increased his understanding (although a suspicious reader may of course

---

1. Jacobs's deconstructionist interpretation misses this aspect of the novel because she regards writing as autonomous and disembodied, detached from any originating subjectivity: "As the narrative rolls along in this manner, we begin to suspect that *the text itself* is a kind of adulterer, continually turning from the straight line of narration in which *it* might remain true to what *it* said before" (35). [See pp. 337–44 above—*Editor.*]

reply that his deceptions have just become more skillful). For example, Dowell's gripping account of the impassioned and maddeningly labyrinthine entanglement of Leonora, Edward, and Nancy during their last days at Branshaw Teleragh has much more concentration, penetration, and narrative control than he could muster when he began his story. "Is all this digression or isn't it digression?" Dowell asks near the beginning; "again I don't know" [17]. But after much reflecting on the unreflected, Dowell gains enough sophistication about meaning and expression to evaluate his narrative strategy self-consciously. Acknowledging that he has not kept the time line of his story strictly chronological, Dowell explains: "I cannot help it. It is so difficult to keep all these people going. I tell you about Leonora and bring her up to date; then about Edward, who has fallen behind. And then the girl gets hopelessly left behind. I wish I could put it down in diary form" [142]. And then he reorients the reader by providing a brief chronology.

Dowell's bewilderment earlier about whether or not he was digressing differs from his resigned if disappointed awareness here about what he loses by choosing one way of organizing his story rather than another. His ability to orient the reader chronologically differs from his disorienting shifts at the outset. His grasp of alternative modes of narration differs from his frantic grasping about in the early pages for a way to tell his story. All of these changes ask us to reevaluate the doubts the novel's beginning raises about Dowell's competence. Suspicious readers may find his new coherence as devious as his earlier disjunctions. Others—like myself—may grant his narration increasing credence on the grounds that his growth in mastery as a writer is an index of what he has discovered by writing.

By trying to make life narrate, Dowell learns about the difficulties of narration and, to a large extent, how to resolve them. He therefore departs somewhat from the Jamesian type of writer-narrator who rehearses the past without changing his or her mind or style (as, for example, in "The Aspern Papers," *The Turn of the Screw*, or *The Sacred Fount*). Writing is not for Jamesian narrators an act of reflection whereby they increase their understanding and control over their story. This difference is attributable to the difference between Ford's fascination with the gap between reflection and the unreflected (with writing as a means of closing it) and James's interest in interpretation as an act of composition (with writing as a means for his narrators to present the assumptions and procedures by which they made coherent if not always reliable sense of their worlds). Dowell also differs from Conrad's Marlow whose narrative competence does not change significantly as he tells Jim's story.[2] Because the meaning of Jim's experience [in *Lord Jim* (1900)] is ultimately indeterminate, Marlow can only circle around it

2. For a further comparison of Marlow and Dowell, see Moser, pp. 156–61. [See pp. 352–58 above—*Editor*.]

without ever reaching it. Greater narrative skill would not change his epistemological dilemma, and his development as a storyteller is consequently not an issue. Although Dowell can never close completely the gap between reflection and the unreflected, he can narrow it by improving his abilities as an interpreter and a teller of tales—and one source of the drama of his novel is the question of whether he will rise to this challenge.

Although Dowell contemplates the alternative of re-creating a diary, a rigidly chronological narrative would not dramatize the temporality of self-consciousness with the hermeneutic verisimilitude that distinguishes *The Good Soldier*. The relation between present and past in Dowell's way of telling his story re-creates in narrative form the temporal dynamics of reflection as a process of remembering.[3] At one point Dowell pauses to remark: "looking over what I have written, I see that I have unintentionally misled you when I said that Florence was never out of my sight. Yet that was the impression that I really had until just now. When I come to think of it she was out of my sight most of the time" [63–64]. This passage contains in miniature the temporal structure of the novel. In recounting his original "impression" and then correcting it retrospectively, Dowell gives the past as he understood it and the present in which he reconsiders this unreflected understanding. Dowell's discovery about Florence here invokes not only the distant past of their relation but also the more immediate past of his writing. From the perspective of the narrative present, Dowell looks back to his original experience across the horizon of what he has just written. His previous reflections have given him a better situation for understanding, just as his new knowledge of Florence projects the possibility of future enlightenment as his narrative proceeds.

* * *

DAVID H. LYNN

[Dowell as Unromantic Hero] †

And if everything is so nebulous about a matter so elementary as the morals of sex, what is there to guide us in the more subtle

---

3. This is one of the epistemological foundations of the much-discussed time-shifts * * *—what Arthur Mizener calls "the double perspective of the novel, the simultaneous awareness of what the experience was like for a participant as it was actually occurring and of what the full knowledge of hindsight shows it to have been" (268). What Mizener describes as a static, relatively straightforward juxtaposition is actually a dynamic, developing process that covers, as Robie Macauley [see p. 318, n. 1 above] notes, "all the tenses of memory" (272).

† From *The Hero's Tale: Narrators in the Early Modern Novel* (New York: St. Martin's Press, 1989) 49–53, 55–56, 59–61, 65–68, 70–71. Copyright © 1989 by David H. Lynn. Reprinted

morality of all other personal contacts, associations, and activities?
[15]

John Dowell is an unlikely hero. * * * A cuckold of extraordinary blindness, by all indications a virgin though twelve years married, his personal history begins and ends with the role of nursemaid for women
unwilling or unable to return his affection. A catalogue of critics decry-
ing his supposed spiritual as well as physical impotence would be substantial; Mark Schorer, for example, claims that in *The Good Soldier*
'passionate situations are related by a narrator who is himself incapable
of passion, sexual and moral alike'.[1] And John G. Hessler in a more
recent article dismisses the possibility of Dowell's moral growth: 'His
narrative does not represent any progress of the heart, any coming to
insight.'[2] Yet albeit lame and isolated, Dowell is very much what my
first sentence posits—a hero—both in the context of * * * Ford's other
novels and as a narrator who undergoes a moral education, tells his tale
as a means of imposing order on chaos, and makes a final heroic gesture
of human responsibility and love.

The structure of Dowell's frame narrative is neither static nor a completed circle as in *Heart of Darkness* [1899; 1902], *The Great Gatsby*
[1925], and *The Sun Also Rises* [1926]. The narrators of those works
possess relatively stable points of view in time and space. The experiences they recount are securely behind them. As in *Lord Jim*, however,
the narration of *The Good Soldier* takes place over an extended period,
while events of the central tale continue to unfold, modifying perspectives on all that has come before. The narrative *evolves*. Characters,
events, and judgments are revealed and juxtaposed, then sorted anew.
This form, this evolution, is a correlative to Dowell's own growth. His
transformation of Ashburnham from a slightly stupid hypocrite into a
romantic hero represents a new moral sensibility for Dowell himself.
* * * By the end he has discovered in himself a deep, formerly unsuspected, capacity for love. He pairs it with a new radical scepticism—a
perspective of general irony, which again marks the fulfillment of a narrator's education. The Marlow of *Heart of Darkness* and *Lord Jim* [1900]
establishes his frame on that same vision and begins to speak; with his
moral growth complete, Dowell falls silent.

*   *   *

In wandering with Dowell back and forth across the territory of his
memory, we are more intimately caught up in the slow momentum

with the permission of St. Martin's Press, Inc. and Macmillan Publishers (UK) Ltd. Page
numbers in brackets refer to this Norton Critical Edition.

1. See p. 306 above [*Editor*].
2. John G. Hessler, 'Dowell and *The Good Soldier*: The Narrator Re-Examined', *The Journal of
   Narrative Technique*, 9 (Spring 1979), 115.

through which he generates a new character and moral perspective for himself. Testimony and events continue after the tale has begun: Dowell's conversations off-stage with Leonora Ashburnham, her eventual marriage to Rodney Bayham, and Dowell's trip to Ceylon to retrieve Nancy Rufford are examples. Yet none of these points of contact between the central story and the narrative alters those events that led Dowell to speak in the first place: his discovery of nine years of betrayal in his relations with the Ashburnhams and the suicide of Edward Ashburnham. Rather, the two years it takes him to finish the tale, the events that occur during these years and, most important, the act of narration and the necessity of imposing pattern, all enable Dowell to come to terms with those first undeniable facts. He has changed, not they. * * * Until the moment he sits down to write he knew nothing. But with nearly his first written words he has claimed an initial insight, that with the English one can have long-standing relations and yet know only their public roles, nothing of the depths of their hearts.

* * * Samuel Hynes, in perhaps the most important essay on the novel, claims that the narrative 'raises uncertainty about the nature of truth and reality to the level of a structural principle.'[3] The strategy [of spatial or thematic structuring] takes three distinct aspects in the narrative. The first is the repetition of a scene or event, each time with a greater sense of context or background in the reader's, as well as Dowell's, mind. * * * A second * * * is the simple juxtaposition of events, scenes, or characters without apparent causal relation: 'setting side by side details which do not naturally connect, and thus compelling in the reader an imaginative leap and resolution between them'.[4] On the train from Nauheim to M——, Dowell sees in a field 'a brown cow hitch its horns under the stomach of a black and white animal and the black and white one [is] thrown right into the middle of a narrow stream' [35]. No explicit link is necessary with the events to come.

The third method * * * most clearly establishes a parallel between Dowell's continuing search and re-creation of his memory, and the reader's own memory and reinterpretation of events that appeared early in the novel in light of later knowledge. Our interpretive struggle mirrors his. Dowell's nightmare image of divine judgment on Ashburnham and Florence includes a mysterious third figure. Our initial sense is that this must be Maisie Maiden; only much later do we finally realise that the 'poor girl' is Nancy Rufford.

> But upon an immense plain, suspended in mid-air, I seem to see three figures, two of them clasped close in an intense embrace, and one intolerably solitary. . . . And the immense plain is the hand

3. See p. 311 above [Editor].
4. John A. Meixner [see p. 318 above], p. 168.

of God, stretching out for miles and miles, with great spaces above
it and below it. And they are in the sight of God, and it is Florence
that is alone. . . . * * * [53]

The continuing interplay of Dowell's self-conscious memory with
what it remembers—immediate, unreflective experience—is discussed
from a phenomenological perspective by Paul Armstrong.[5] What we
know as 'personal identity' or character, a mature sense of self, is gener-
ated largely, Armstrong argues, by this same process of reflection on past
experience. In a real sense, Dowell, before he brings himself to speak,
has lacked some necessary element of individualized character. He
seems to have been incapable of an interpretive detachment from either
his on-going daily routine as an expatriate nursemaid or from the significant events in his own past. Yet with the manifold discoveries succeeding Edward Ashburnham's suicide such a detachment quickly
develops as Dowell strives to understand. Armstrong suggests that 'Dowell's narration brings together both his unreflective experience and his
self-conscious reflections. The action of his novel is the interaction of
these two levels of intentionality.'[6] But Dowell's 'new awareness could
not develop until his blind engagement with the world collapsed'.[7]

                              *   *   *

The damning aspect of Dowell's innocence before Ashburnham's suicide lies in another radical split within his character: between the conscious habits and values of his daily regimen and the unconscious desires
he has so thoroughly repressed as to castrate himself. * * *

Dowell conceals from himself his own latent desires. He is, in other
words, the agent of his own regulation and spiritual maiming. And as a
husband he plays a similar role of censor, or attempts to, trying to keep
Florence isolated from dangerous excitement:

> [M]y whole attentions, my whole endeavors were to keep poor dear
> Florence on to topics like the finds at Gnossos and the mental spiri-
> tuality of Walter Pater. I had to keep her at it, you understand, or
> she might die. [18]

Through Dowell we see Ford's enmity, present in much of his pre-
war fiction, towards Pater and the great 'men of ideas' of a generation
earlier who 'were marked by their blindness to the real problems around
them'.[8] The fragmentation of Dowell's character is a manifestation of
what Ford saw as a broader cultural malaise. * * * Spiritually lamed

5. Paul B. Armstrong, 'The Epistemology of *The Good Soldier*: A Phenomenological Reconsideration', *Criticism*, 22.3 (Summer 1980), 230–251. [See also pp. 388–91 above—*Editor*.]
6. *Ibid.*, 232.
7. *Ibid.*, 237.
8. Norman Leer, *The Limited Hero in the Novels of Ford Madox Ford* (East Lansing: Michigan
   State University Press, 1966), p. 5.

though he may be, Dowell does have passions and desires, though they are unconscious, nearly irretrievable. They become apparent to him only after the fact, when the safe, secure world he has known has already begun to fragment. * * * [But] Dowell's realisation that the conventions which have governed his life are both arbitrary and illusory carries with it a more severe reaction against society itself than does Marlow's. For although Marlow finds that the social world is rife with corruption and that the codes which bind men together are artifices, the struggle for renewed community remains the source of human values. The ideals that are the sinews of solidarity may be illusions, but they are in some sense necessary.

* * *

As with Marlow and Jim, we have a narrator initially addressing a character who seems to stand for the most profound breach between appearance and reality, between the expectation of virtue and the reality of ignominy. Dowell wrestles with Ashburnham's 'failure' (this verdict is later significantly muted, while for Jim it is not), as a first, immediate step in regaining his equilibrium. If he can find secure ground on which to *judge* Ashburnham, some sort of moral order may yet be salvaged. * * * The Ashburnham who cuts his throat with a pen knife at the end is not the same character who has just killed himself before Dowell begins to tell that story. And this dynamic portrait, in turn, represents Dowell's own growth. * * *

The starting point * * * is also the beginning of his attempt to puzzle out what he knows of the affair with the Ashburnhams. * * * The beginning, for Dowell, is the word. He tentatively reaches out from the isolation, strives to * * * impose form on the chaos about him by speaking and making a story. Besides transforming private experience into history—a series of events in meaningful relation—his impulse is for purgation as well, to get the sight out of his head. Yet Dowell lacks Marlow's audience, even another solitary soul who has expressed concern. Without someone to acknowledge him, language and story seem meaningless, unshared, little more than a garbled shout. Thus Dowell projects a comfortable illusion *for himself*, an imaginary stage-set that will allow him to continue with the game.

* * *

One characteristic trait that survives in Ashburnham throughout * * * is his sense of responsibility. This is the feature that Dowell finds most admirable, at the last truly heroic, and Dowell will adopt it as central to his own new character. * * * The same impulse, however, when combined with Ashburnham's quest for an ideal love, renders him both vulnerable to women and absurd. * * * When Ashburnham has been driven furthest from himself, enduring the shrill insistencies * * * of Florence for nine years, having no real communication with his wife, the two surviving noble traits of his character—his sense of personal responsibility and his yearning for an ideal, fulfilling love—come directly into conflict. He falls in love with Nancy Rufford.

*   *   *

As with Dowell's continuing use of the narrative to understand himself and * * * his experience, speech reveals to Ashburnham his own passion for the girl. He swears to Dowell that until he first declared his love in the Casino of Nauheim, he had 'regarded her exactly as he would have regarded a daughter' [77]. It is not simply that in speaking Ashburnham stumbles on his own hidden emotions; as Dowell interprets the event, those emotions are partly created by the words that express them.

> It was as if his passion for her hadn't existed; as if the very words that he spoke, without knowing that he spoke them, created the passion as they went along. Before he spoke, there was nothing; afterwards, it was the integral fact of his life. [80]

Ashburnham's night-long confession to Dowell anticipates what the other will do in turn—make a story of his experience and tell his tale to a silent audience, 'a woman or a solicitor' [26], as if to make it real, to have it exist independently of his own thoughts. * * * The love for Nancy that Ashburnham unearths in his own words immediately comes into conflict with his code of personal responsibilities. The words have escaped an unconscious source. Otherwise 'he would have fled from it as from a thing accursed' [77]. * * *

* * * The radical irony that marked [Ford's] tone at the start, undercutting all meaning and values, [thus] slowly evolves on the same course as his moral education, to embrace both a scepticism towards society at large and the redemptive significance of love and responsibility. When Dowell acts to fulfil these ideals, though in a small and circumscribed way, he will merit the status of hero.

At almost the exact centre of the narrative, Dowell discloses his love for Nancy Rufford, first declared to Leonora the same night as his wife's death and only hours after Ashburnham has spoken to the girl of his own passion. What follows, however, is no paean to Dowell's love, but his attempt to fathom and articulate Ashburnham's behaviour, and a discourse on the nature of man's love for woman. This section represents the first significant clue to Dowell's gradual moral development. The change is manifest in his perception of paradox in Ashburnham's nature; no longer is the issue simply one of appearance and reality—of the superficial behaviour of a gentleman and the appetites of a raging stallion—indeed, the coin has been reversed. Ashburnham's apparent guilt as a seducer and hypocrite, which Dowell was brought to see by Leonora, conceals or coexists with an undeniable nobility of spirit. While his sudden confession of passion to the girl may be the 'most monstrously wicked thing Edward Ashburnham ever did in his life' [78], Dowell nevertheless can no longer think of him 'as anything but straight, upright, and honourable' [78]. No irony undercuts this statement as it had earlier. Rather, Dowell's appraisal of Ashburnham's character represents his own changing view of the world: that such paradox is unavoidable, that honourable action and love do achieve meaning in the face of a corrupt society, though they may finally be destroyed by it.

Only in passing does Dowell mention his own love for Nancy Rufford; this is not his story, he contends, and his feelings bear so little on what 'happens'. Yet in trying to explain Ashburnham's love for the girl, and then moving to a general discourse on the subject, Dowell demonstrates that he too is learning to love. Never has he claimed that he once loved Florence—merely that he was determined to marry her. Whatever physical passion he may have felt for her or Leonora or other women has been repressed to the point of extinction. Even after discovering his love for Nancy, Dowell seems baffled by the fact. In telling the story, in wrestling with Ashburnham and the others, however, he has learned enough to speak of love with confidence and intimacy.

* * *

The measure of change in Dowell's judgment of Ashburnham can also be seen in the full turn of his ironic tone. Rather than the repeated assertion that Ashburnham was a 'good soldier', undercut by the brittle irony of disabused bitterness, by the end Dowell is ready to claim that the 'villains—for obviously Edward and the girl were villains—have been punished by suicide and madness' [160]. Here the irony simultaneously mocks social standards of judgment (which Dowell had earlier shared) and establishes Ashburnham and Nancy as something quite other than villains. Indeed, the absolute and clearly ironical term *villain* guides the reader's reconstruction of an alternative meaning to an opposite extreme. In Dowell's eyes, therefore, the essential truth of Ashburnham's character lies in this single absolute contradiction to society's comfortable verdict. The earlier apparent paradoxes of appearance and reality, of simultaneous virtue and vice, have disappeared. Ashburnham has become an integrated character, a romantic hero brutalized by a hostile environment.

Dowell's allegiance with villains who have threatened the equanimity of society reveals the significant change in his own character as well. His embracing of Ashburnham represents a rejection of the social world and its codes—all that had formerly given his life structure. Instead, his new moral identity is founded on those elements of his own nature he has discovered while telling the tale—principally his capacity for love—on the romantic ideals he has adopted from Ashburnham, and on a radical scepticism towards modern society.

> Society must go on, I suppose, and society can only exist if the normal, if the virtuous, and the slightly deceitful flourish, and if the passionate, the headstrong, and the too-truthful are condemned to suicide and madness. But I guess that I myself, in my fainter way, come into the category of the passionate, of the headstrong, of the too-truthful. [160–161]

Dowell's moral growth and his emergence as a heroic figure are predicated on this paradoxical awareness. Yet this perspective of general irony isolates Dowell at the end of *The Good Soldier* to much the same degree he had earlier been isolated by his own blindness, self-deception, and impotence. Once again he is charged with the care of a woman, Nancy Rufford, who cannot love him. In accepting this responsibility he affirms a final tie with Ashburnham, who also insisted on assuming responsibility for the women he loved. And they have both loved this woman. More than that, Dowell has *chosen*. Having judged the rabbit-like world of Leonora and Rodney Bayham, of normality and intolerance, he has rejected it and chosen to retreat to Branshaw Teleragh and be nursemaid to Nancy. The situation is grotesque—not yet in Ford's fiction can the retreat be, as in *Parade's End*, both a rejection of the modern world and a positive alternative to it. Nevertheless, Dowell has acted, heroically, according to imperatives of responsibility and of love, for Nancy Rufford as well as for Edward Ashburnham.

Yet despite identifying with the Ashburnham he has created, Dowell is no romantic hero. Like Marlow * * * he lacks a vital immediacy, an ability to plunge impulsively into his dream and to act in the world. His irony now, rather than his blindness, distances him from his past and from the social world. He must imagine watching his romantic hero robbing orchards in the distance. Yet it is also this ironic awareness that lets him *see*. And that, for Ford, is a heroic achievement: to learn to see by telling the tale—and to have told that tale.

Selected Bibliography

Items are generally recorded in chronological order rather than in the alphabetical order of the authors' or editors' surnames. (Alphabetical order is only used when items appearing in the same year are chronologically indistinguishable.) This is to allow the reader to see the development of the history of Ford studies. Authors' surnames are highlighted for rapid scanning of the lists, and those quoted in the Biographical and Critical Commentary section are also marked with an asterisk.

BIBLIOGRAPHIES

The single most useful source is David Dow **Harvey**'s exhaustive *Ford Madox Ford: 1873–1939. A Bibliography of Works and Criticism* (Princeton UP, 1962; New York: Gordian Press, 1972). This is a descriptive bibliography in six main sections: Books (including Collaborations and Pamphlets), Contributions to Books by Other Writers (including Translations by Ford); Manuscripts, Letters, Miscellanea; Contributions to Periodicals; Periodical Articles about Ford; Books Significantly Mentioning Ford. So extensive are the quotations that it acts as a book to be read rather than merely as a work of reference. In the absence of a volume of Ford's collected journalism, for instance, Harvey offers a substantial sample of it. To supplement this with later material there is Linda **Tamkin**'s "A Secondary Source Bibliography on Ford Madox Ford, 1962–1979," *The Bulletin of Bibliography* 38. 1 (January–March 1981); reprinted special Ford issue *Ford Madox Ford*, guest ed. Sondra **Stang**, *Antaeus* 56 (Spring 1986): 219–230, and Rita **Malenczyk**, "A Secondary Source Bibliography on Ford Madox Ford, 1979–1985" in the same number of *Antaeus*, 231–44. For a bibliography of more recent items, see special Ford issue *Ford Madox Ford and the Arts*, ed. Joseph **Wiesenfarth**, *Contemporary Literature* [University of Wisconsin Press] 30. 2 (Summer 1989).

BIOGRAPHIES

Douglas **Goldring**, *The Last Pre-Raphaelite. A Record of the Life and Writings of Ford Madox Ford* (London: Macdonald & Co., 1948); U.S. ed. *Trained For Genius* (New York: Dutton, 1949). Frank **MacShane**, *The Life Work of Ford Madox Ford* (New York: Horizon, 1965; London: Routledge, 1965). Arthur **Mizener**,* *The Saddest Story. A Biography of Ford Madox Ford* (New York: World, 1971; London: The Bodley Head, 1971). Alan **Judd**, *Ford Madox Ford* (London: Collins, 1990; reprinted Flamingo paperback, 1991).

OTHER BIOGRAPHICAL MATERIAL

Violet **Hunt**, *The Flurried Years* (London: Hurst and Blackett, 1926); U.S. ed. *I Have This to Say* (New York: Boni and Liveright, 1926). Stella **Bowen**, *Drawn from Life: Reminiscences* (London: Collins, 1941; reprinted Virago paperback, 1984). "Homage to Ford Madox Ford: 1875–1939," *New Directions*, 7 (1942): 441–94 (whole issue: contributors include Richard **Aldington**,* Sherwood **Anderson**, John Gould **Fletcher**, Caroline **Gordon**, Katherine Anne **Porter**, Ezra **Pound**, Allen **Tate**, and William Carlos **Williams**). Douglas **Goldring**, *South Lodge: Reminiscences of Violet Hunt, Ford Madox Ford and the English Review Circle* (London: Constable, 1943). David **Garnett**, *Great Friends: Portraits of Seventeen Writers* (London: Macmillan, 1979). Thomas C. **Moser**,* *The Life in the Fiction of Ford Madox Ford* (Princeton: Princeton UP, 1980). Nicholas **Delbanco**, *Group Portrait: Joseph Conrad, Stephen Crane, Henry James, and H. G. Wells* (New York: Morrow, 1982). Barry C. **Johnson**, ed., *Tea and Anarchy! The Bloomsbury*

Diary of Olive Garnett, 1890–1893 (London: Bartletts Press, 1989) (unusual glimpse of Ford's young manhood in anarchist circles). Joan **Hardwick**, *Immodest Violet: The Life of Violet Hunt* (London: Andre Deutsch, 1990).

AUTOBIOGRAPHY

As Ford Madox **Hueffer**: *Ancient Lights and Certain New Reflections, Being the Memories of a Young Man* (London: Chapman and Hall, 1911). As Ford Madox **Ford**: *Thus to Revisit: Some Reminiscences* (London: Chapman and Hall, 1921); *Joseph Conrad: A Personal Remembrance* (London: Duckworth, 1924); *Return to Yesterday* (London: Gollancz, 1931; New York: Horace Liveright, 1932); *It Was the Nightingale* (Philadelphia: J. B. Lippincott Co., 1933; London: William Heinemann Ltd., 1934).

LETTERS

Richard M. **Ludwig**, ed., *Letters of Ford Madox Ford* (Princeton: Princeton UP, 1965). Brita **Lindberg-Seyersted**, ed., *Pound/Ford, the Story of a Literary Friendship: The Correspondence between Ezra Pound and Ford Madox Ford and Their Writings about Each Other* (New York: New Directions, 1982). Sondra J. **Stang**, ed., Chapter VIII: "Sixty Unpublished Letters" in *The Ford Madox Ford Reader* (Manchester: Carcanet, 1986) 465–512. Sondra J. **Stang** and Karen **Cochran**, eds., *The Correspondence of Ford Madox Ford and Stella Bowen* (Indiana UP, 1993).

LITERARY CRITICISM ON *THE GOOD SOLDIER*

Books

Richard A. **Cassell**, *Ford Madox Ford: A Study of His Novels* (Baltimore: Johns Hopkins UP, 1961). John A. **Meixner**,* *Ford Madox Ford's Novels: A Critical Study* (Minneapolis and London: U of Minnesota P and Oxford UP, 1962). Paul L. **Wiley**, *Novelist of Three Worlds: Ford Madox Ford* (Syracuse: Syracuse UP, 1962). Caroline **Gordon**, *A Good Soldier: A Key to the Novels of Ford Madox Ford* (Davis: University of California Library, 1963). Richard Wald **Lid**, *Ford Madox Ford: The Essence of His Art* (Berkeley and Los Angeles: U of California P, 1964). Carol **Ohmann**, *Ford Madox Ford: From Apprentice to Craftsman* (Middletown: Wesleyan UP, 1964). Norman **Leer**, *The Limited Hero in the Novels of Ford Madox Ford* (East Lansing: Michigan State UP, 1966). Hugh **Kenner**, *The Pound Era* (Berkeley and Los Angeles: U of California P, 1971). Grover **Smith**,* *Ford Madox Ford*, Columbia Essays on Modern Writers, 63, (New York and London: Columbia UP, 1972). Sondra J. **Stang**, *Ford Madox Ford* (New York: Frederick Ungar, 1977). Thomas C. **Moser**,* *The Life in the Fiction of Ford Madox Ford* (1980, see Biography above). Robert **Green**,* *Ford Madox Ford: Prose and Politics* (Cambridge: Cambridge UP, 1981). John **Batchelor**, *The Edwardian Novelists* (London: Duckworth, 1982). Ann Barr **Snitow**,* *Ford Madox Ford and the Voice of Uncertainty* (Baton Rouge: Louisiana State UP, 1984). Paul B. **Armstrong**,* *The Challenge of Bewilderment,: Understanding and Representation in James, Conrad and Ford* (Ithaca and London: Cornell UP, 1987). David H. **Lynn**,* *The Hero's Tale: Narrators in the Early Modern Novel* (New York: St. Martin's Press, 1989).

Articles

Mark **Schorer**,* "The Good Novelist in *The Good Soldier*," *Princeton University Library Chronicle*, 9 (April 1948): 128–33 and *Horizon* (August 1949): 132–38. Robie **Macauley**, "The Good Ford," *The Kenyon Review* 11 (Spring 1949): 277. Elliott B. **Gose**, "The Strange Irregular Rhythm: An Analysis of *The Good Soldier*," 72 *PMLA* (June 1957): 404–509). James **Hafley**, "The Moral Structure of *The Good Soldier*," *Modern Fiction Studies* 5 (1959–60): 121–28. Samuel **Hynes**,* "The Epistemology of *The Good Soldier*," *Sewanee Review* 69 (Spring 1961): 225–35. Ambrose **Gordon**, Jr., "At The Edge of Silence: *The Good Soldier* As 'War Novel,' " *Modern Fiction Studies* 9. 1 (1963): 67–68. Patricia **McFate** and Bruce **Golden**, "*The Good Soldier*: A Tragedy of Self-Deception," *Modern Fiction Studies* 9. 1 (Spring 1963): 50–60. Harold **Loeb**, "Ford Madox Ford's 'The Good Soldier,' " *London Magazine* 3 (December 1963): 65–73. T. J. **Henighan**, "The Desirable Alien: A Source for Ford Madox Ford's *The Good Soldier*," *Twentieth Century Literature* 11. 1 (1965): 25–29. Charles G. **Hoffman**, "Ford's Manuscript Revisions of *The Good Soldier*," *English Literature in Transition* 9. 4 (1966): 145–52. Jo-Ann **Baernstein**, "Image, Identity and Insight in *The Good Soldier*," *Critique* 9. 1 (1967): 19–42. Daniel R. **Barnes**, "Ford and the 'Slaughtered Saints': A New Reading of *The Good Soldier*," *Modern Fiction Studies* 14. 2 (1968): 157–70. Sondra J. **Stang**, "A Reading of Ford's *The Good Soldier*," *Modern Language Quarterly* 30. 4 (1969): 545–63. Reynold **Siemens**, "The Juxtaposition of Composed Renderings in Ford's *The Good Soldier*," *Humanities Association Bulletin* (Canada) 23. 3 (1972): 44–49. Frank **Kermode**,* "Novels: Recognition and Deception," *Critical Inquiry* 1. 1 (September 1974): 103–21. Denis **Donaghue**, "A Reply to Frank Kermode," *Critical Inquiry* 1. 2 (December 1974): 447–52. Zohreh T. **Sullivan**, "Civilization and Its Darkness: Conrad's *Heart of Darkness* and Ford's *The Good Soldier*," *Conradiana* 8 (1976): 110–20. Carol **Jacobs**,* "The (too) Good Soldier: 'A Real Story' " in *Glyph 3: Johns Hopkins Textual Studies* (Baltimore: Johns Hopkins UP, 1978): 32–51. Hilda D. **Spear**, "The Accuracy of Impressions: Kaleidoscopic Viewpoints in *The Good Soldier*," *Durham University Journal* 70. 2 (June 1978): 149–53. Robert **Green**, "*The Good Soldier:* Ford's Cubist Novel," *Modernist Studies* 3 (1979): 49–59. Stuart Y. **McDougal**, " 'Where Even the Saddest Stories Are Gay': Provence and *The Good Soldier*," *Journal of Modern Literature* 7. 3 (September 1979): 552–54. John G. **Hessler**, "Dowell and *The Good Soldier:* The Narrator Re-Examined," *The Journal of Narrative Technique* 9. 1 (Winter 1979): 53–60 [reprinted *JNT* 9. 2 (Spring 1979): 109–16]. David **Eggenschwiler**,* "Very Like a Whale: The Comical-Tragical Illusions of The Good Soldier," *Genre* 12.3 (Fall 1979): 401–14. Avrom **Fleishman**, "The Genre of *The Good Soldier:* Ford's Comic Mastery," *Studies in the Literary Imagination* 13. 1 (Spring 1980): 31–42. Paul B. **Armstrong**, "The Epistemology of *The Good Soldier:* A Phenomenological Reconsideration," *Criticism* 22. 3 (Summer 1980): 230–51. Denis **Donoghue**, "Listening to the Saddest Story," *Sewanee Review* 88. 4 (Fall 1980): 557–71 [reprinted **Stang**, ed., *The Presence of Ford Madox Ford* (see "Other" below)]. Paul B. **Armstrong**, "The Hermeneutics of Literary Impressionism: Interpretation and Reality in James, Conrad, and Ford," *Centennial Review* 27. 4 (Fall 1983): 244–69. Michael **Levenson**,* "Character in *The Good Soldier*," *Twentieth Century Literature* 30. 1 (1984): 373–87. Eugene **Goodheart**,* "What Dowell Knew: A Reading of *The Good Soldier*," *Antaeus* 56 (Spring 1986): 70–80. Vincent J. **Cheng**,* "A Chronology of *The Good Soldier*," *English Language Notes* 24. 1 (September 1986): 91–97.

Other

Frank **MacShane**, ed., *The Critical Writings of Ford Madox Ford* (Lincoln: U of Nebraska P, 1964). Richard A. **Cassell**, ed., *Ford Madox Ford: Modern Judgements* (London: Macmillan, 1972) [collection of essays and extracts, including **Schorer**, **Meixner**, and **Hynes**]. Frank **Mac Shane**, ed., *Ford Madox Ford: The Critical Heritage* (London: Routledge, 1972) [contemporary reviews]. C. Ruth **Sabol** and Todd K. **Bender**, *A Concordance to Ford Madox Ford's "The Good Soldier"* (New York and London: Garland Publishing, Inc., 1981) [pagination unfortunately does not correspond with U.K. or U.S. first editions]. Sondra J. **Stang**, ed., *The Presence of Ford Madox Ford* (Philadelphia: U of Pennsylvania P, 1981) [collection of essays and reminiscences], and *The Ford Madox Ford Reader* (Manchester: Carcanet, 1986) [selections from Ford's writings, including letters]. William **Cookson** and Peter **Dale**, eds., *Agenda. Ford Madox Ford* 27.4/28.1 (Winter 1989/Spring 1990) [Special double issue including two hitherto unpublished pieces by Ford—"Pure Literature" and "In the Sick Room"—and essays by Howard Erskine-Hill, Carol Jacobs, Alan Judd, Max Saunders, Derek Stanford, Sondra Stang and Carl Smith, and Donald Davie]. Raffaella **Baccolini** and Vita **Fortunati**, eds., *Scrittura e Sperimentazione in Ford Madox Ford* (Florence: Alinea Editrice, 1994), Saggi e Documenti/113 [collection of essays by, among others, the editors, Malcolm Bradbury, Max Saunders, Mario Domenichelli, Alan Judd and Edward Naumburg, Jr., proceedings of the conference "Writing and Experimentation in Ford Madox Ford" held at the University of Bologna, December 1989].